Americas, Africa, Asia, & the Pacific 2001

HOSTELLING INTERNATIONAL

D1740519

Welcome
Bienvenue
Willkommen
Bienvenido

The information in this Guide has been supplied by the Youth Hostel Associations of each country represented. Hostels are listed alphabetically by country and city, and symbols indicate hostel opening times, prices, facilities etc. - these are explained in the fold-out section at the front of this Guide. For further information about hostels worldwide either contact your local Youth Hostel Association (YHA) or visit our Internet home page at www.iyhf.org.

Every effort has been made to ensure that the information contained in this Guide is correct, and Hostelling International can accept no responsibility for any inaccuracies or for changes subsequent to publication.

How to use this Guide

Queensberry Hill Youth Hostel - Melbourne, Australia

This guide is organized in two parts - the Introduction and the Hostel Directory. See Contents (inside front cover) for full details.

In the **Introduction** you will find general information such as: how to make advance bookings using the International Booking Network (IBN), international emergency telephone numbers, member discounts, and Hostelling International Assured Standards.

The **Hostel Directory** is an alphabetical listing, by country and town, of hostels belonging to full members of the International Youth Hostel Federation. At the end of the directory you will find an alphabetical listing, by country, of supplementary accommodation provided by affiliate organizations.

Comment se servir de ce guide

Ce guide se présente en deux parties - l'introduction et le répertoire des auberges. Voir l'Index (verso de la couverture du devant) pour en savoir plus.

Santiago Youth Hostel - Chile

Dans **l'Introduction**, vous trouverez des renseignements généraux sur, par exemple, les réservations par l'intermédiaire du système informatisé de réservation, IBN (International Booking Network), les numéros d'urgence internationaux, les remises auxquelles vous avez droit en tant que membre, et ce que veulent dire les Normes Garanties Hostelling International.

Le **Répertoire des Auberges** est une liste alphabétique, par pays et par ville, des auberges affiliées aux associations membres (à part entière) de la Fédération Internationale des Auberges de Jeunesse (IYHF). A la fin du répertoire, vous trouverez une autre liste alphabétique, par pays, contenant la liste des hébergements secondaires proposés par des organisations affiliées.

English

Français

Deutsch

Español

2

Wie Sie diesen Führer benutzen

Dubai Youth Hostel - UAE

Der Führer besteht aus zwei Teilen - die Einführung und das internationale Herbergsverzeichnis. Siehe Inhaltsverzeichnis (innere Titelseite) für Einzelheiten.

In der **Einführung** finden Sie allgemeine Informationen, z.B. wie man über das "International Booking Network" (IBN) Betten im Voraus buchen kann, internationale Notrufnummern, Mitgliederrabatte und "Hostelling International Assured Standards".

Das **Herbergsverzeichnis** ist eine alphabetisch, nach Ländern und Orten eingeteilte Übersicht aller Herbergen von Vollmitgliedern der Internationalen Jugendherbergsföderation (IYHF). Am Ende des Verzeichnis befindet sich eine Liste mit zusätzlichen Übernachtungsangeboten von angegliederten Organisationen.

Cómo utilizar esta Guía

Esta guía ha sido elaborada en dos partes: la introducción y las listas de albergues. En el Indice (ver el reverso de la portada) se especifican las diferentes secciones.

En la **Introducción** usted encontrará información general, por ejemplo: cómo realizar reservas con antelación a través de nuestra red internacional de reservas IBN (International Booking Network), los números de teléfono de emergencia internacionales, los descuentos

Manila International Youth Hostel - Philippines

que usted, en su calidad de miembro, puede conseguir y la definición de las Normas Garantizadas de Hostelling International.

En las **Listas de Albergues** están catalogados alfabéticamente por país y por ciudad los albergues afiliados a las Asociaciones miembros de pleno derecho de la Federación Internacional de Albergues Juveniles (IYHF). Al final de dichas listas, en una sección aparte, se relacionan alfabéticamente por país alojamientos suplementarios administrados por otras organizaciones afiliadas.

Introduction to Hostelling International

Welcome to the world of Hostelling International - a unique network of accommodation centres where you can enjoy a good night's sleep in friendly surroundings at an affordable price.

Hostelling International is the brand name of the International Youth Hostel Federation, the organization representing Youth Hostel Associations, worldwide. Hostelling International is the largest, most experienced network dedicated to travellers of all ages, young and old. Only in Bavaria, Germany is access limited to guests aged under 27. You can find out more by visiting our website www.iyhf.org. **For budget accommodation you can trust, look for the blue triangle symbol.**

Sydney Beachouse Youth Hostel - Australia

Benefits of Membership

To stay at a Youth Hostel, you must become a member of your national Youth Hostel Association. If there is no national YHA in your country, you can purchase a Hostelling International Card or a Welcome Stamp on arrival at your chosen hostel.

Membership offers a wide range of benefits - including:

- 4,200 **accommodation** centres in more than 60 countries worldwide - open to people of **all ages**, and offering a choice of single, double and dormitory rooms.

- Participation in all Hostelling International **activities**, programmes and events.

- Thousands of **discounts** worldwide - from travel and sports activities, to restaurants, museums and entertainment! A selection of discounts is listed at the back of this Guide. For the full story, check out www.iyhf.org.

- Advance **reservations** up to 6 months ahead using the International Booking Network (IBN) system - **see page 8** for further information.

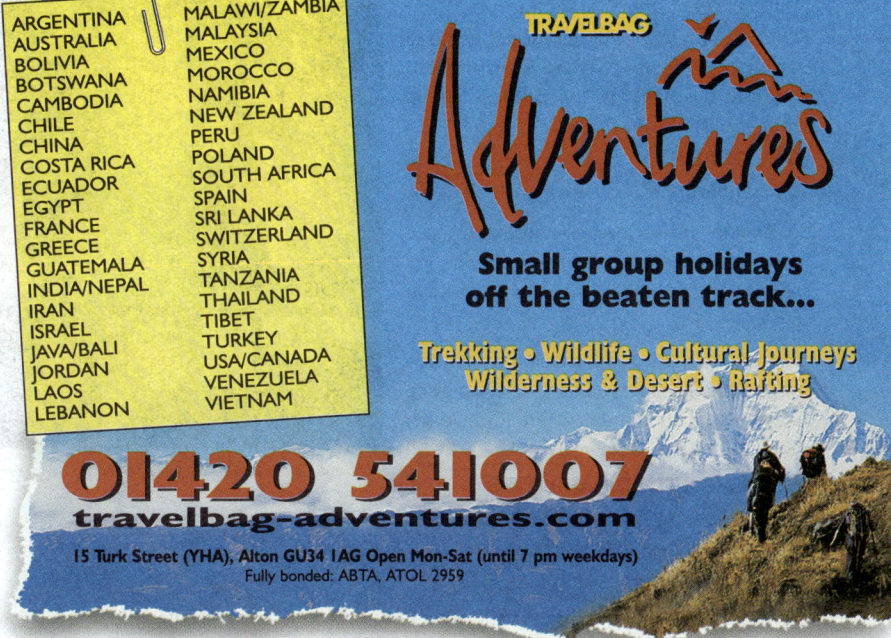

Quality Standards You Can Count On

Hostelling International's Assured Standards Scheme means you can rely on a consistent level of services and facilities wherever you stay.

- **Welcome** - hostels are open to all. You can join if you are not already a member, and you can make advance reservations. Plus you will have access to essential facilities if the hostel closes for a period during the day.

- **Comfort** - a good night's sleep (including the hire of freshly-laundered linen if it is not included in the overnight charge), and sufficient washing/shower facilities. Meals are generally available, along with self-catering facilities and a food store close by.

- **Cleanliness** - the highest standards of hygiene wherever you travel.

- **Security** - for you and your possessions, including lockers for luggage and valuables.

- **Privacy** - in showers, washing areas and toilets. Most hostels provide single sex dormitories - although if requested, a mixed sex dormitory may be offered to people travelling together.

Standards are monitored by Hostelling International and by you, the user. **There are Comment Cards at the back of this Guide - tell us what you think!**

HOSTEL GRADES

▲ **Standard:** applies to the majority of hostels.

△ **Simple:** applies to smaller hostels, or those in remote locations with simple facilities - you may find limited staffing and shorter opening hours.

Some hostels listed in this Guide are outside the Assured Standards Scheme - these provide accommodation in areas where it would not otherwise be available.

Auckland City Youth Hostel - New Zealand

TRAVELLERS WITH DISABILITIES &

Hostelling International welcomes travellers with disabilities - hostels suitable for wheelchair access display the & symbol in this Guide.

ENVIRONMENTAL CHARTER

Hostels adhere to the IYHF Environmental Charter. This lays down criteria for the consumption and conservation of resources, waste disposal and recycling, nature conservation and the provision of environmental education.

Bookings & Reservations

BOOK AHEAD THROUGH [IBN]

Our computerized booking system offers simple, low-cost booking up to 6 months in advance for nearly 300 key hostels in 40 countries worldwide. In this Guide, hostels accepting advance bookings display the [IBN] symbol and are highlighted in blue.

IBN is unique in the budget accommodation sector - benefits include:

- Pay when you book, using local currency.
- Make reservations during your travels - **see pages 41 - 51 for [IBN] global booking centres.**
- You can often pay by credit card - see opposite.
- In many countries, one call to the Central Reservations Office reserves a series of overnight stays in several hostels.

OTHER BOOKING INFORMATION

- Advance booking isn't essential during low season, but at busy times or in key cities, it is advisable to avoid disappointment - family rooms are soon occupied, and groups should book ahead of time.
- Book by fax or letter to your chosen hostel - if booking by letter, enclose an international postal reply coupon and a self-addressed envelope.
- If you make an advance booking without paying a deposit you will usually be required to arrive at the hostel by 1800 hours, unless a different time is agreed.

We know you will enjoy the hostel experience. You will certainly be able to afford it. We look forward to meeting you.

Yusung Youth Hostel - Daejon, South Korea

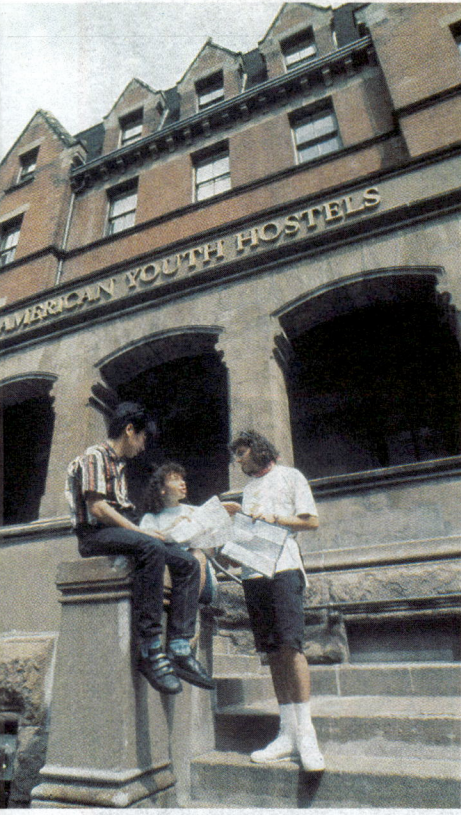

New York International Youth Hostel - USA

BOOKINGS & RESERVATIONS

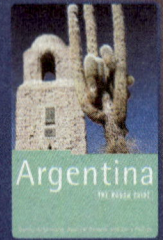
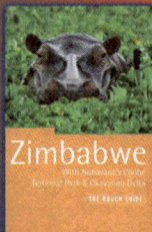

Bienvenue à Hostelling International

Bienvenue au monde d'Hostelling International - un réseau unique d'hébergement où vous pouvez passer une bonne nuit de sommeil dans un milieu accueillant et à des prix abordables.

Hostelling International est la marque de la Fédération Internationale des Auberges de Jeunesse (International Youth Hostel Federation), l'organisation qui représente les Associations d'Auberges de Jeunesse à travers le monde. Hostelling International est le plus grand réseau d'hébergement et celui qui a la plus longue expérience du service des voyageurs de tous les âges, qu'ils soient jeunes ou moins jeunes. La seule exception concerne en Bavière, en Allemagne, où seuls les usagers de moins de 27 ans sont admis dans les auberges. Pour en savoir plus, consultez notre site Internet à www.iyhf.org. **Pour un hébergement économique auquel vous pouvez vous fier, suivez le triangle bleu.**

Schirrman-Münker Youth Hostel - Montevideo, Uruguay

11

Les Avantages que vous apporte l'Adhésion

Afin d'être admis à séjourner dans une auberge de jeunesse, il vous faudra devenir membre de l'Association d'Auberges de Jeunesse de votre pays. S'il n'existe pas d'Association nationale dans votre pays, vous pouvez acheter une carte ou un Timbre de Bienvenue (*Welcome Stamp*) à votre arrivée à l'auberge.

La qualité d'adhérent HI vous permet de bénéficier d'un grand nombre de privilèges, parmi lesquels citons:

- 4200 **établissements** dans plus de 60 pays du monde - ils sont ouverts aux jeunes de **tous les âges** et proposent un choix d'hébergements de capacité variable: des chambres individuelles ou pour deux personnes ou bien encore des dortoirs.

- La possibilité de participer aux **activités** et manifestations en tout genre organisées par Hostelling International.

- Des milliers de **réductions** à travers le monde, sur tout: voyages, activités sportives, restaurants, musées, divertissements! Nous vous en donnons un avant-goût **à la fin de ce guide** mais pour la liste complète, faites un tour sur www.iyhf.org.

- La possibilité de **réserver** jusqu'à six mois à l'avance par IBN - **voir page 16** pour plus de détails.

Banff International Youth Hostel - Canada

Travelex

Commission free
foreign currency and foreign travellers cheques. From over 300 locations **worldwide.**

Also take advantage of our 'spend or return' **Buy Back Plus.** You can return any unspent currency to us not only at the original purchase rate, but also commission free.

To qualify for this offer, just present your Hostelling International membership card at any of our worldwide locations.

Offers not available for the exchange of one Euro legacy currency into another (e.g. the offer is not available for the exchange of Belgium Francs into Deutsche Marks or Italian Lira).
Local terms and conditions apply.   **www.travelex.com**

Des Normes de Qualité qui vous sont garanties

Le Plan pour la Garantie des Normes en Auberges a été mis en place par Hostelling International pour vous assurer une qualité constante dans nos prestations et nos installations, quelle que soit l'auberge où vous séjournez.

- **Accueil** - les auberges sont ouvertes à tous. Vous pourrez y acquérir une adhésion si vous n'êtes pas encore membre et y effectuer des réservations. De plus, l'accès à certaines parties de l'auberge vous est garanti, lorsque celle-ci ferme dans la journée.

- **Confort** - une bonne nuit de sommeil (ainsi que la possibilité de louer des draps propres, s'ils ne sont pas déjà compris dans le prix de la nuitée) et des douches/lavabos en nombre suffisant. Une forme ou une autre de restauration est généralement disponible, ainsi qu'une cuisine équipée pour préparer ses propres repas et un magasin d'alimentation à l'auberge ou à proximité.

- **Propreté** - un haut degré d'hygiène et de propreté où que vous vous rendiez.

- **Sécurité** - de votre personne et de vos biens (consignes pour bagages et objets de valeur).

- **Intimité** - dans les douches, les blocs sanitaires et les toilettes. La plupart des auberges proposent un hébergement dans des dortoirs non-mixtes, bien que certains établissements pourront offrir, sur demande, des chambres ou dortoirs mixtes à des groupes voyageant ensemble.

La présence de ces normes dans les auberges sera contrôlée par Hostelling International et par vous, les usagers. **Il y a des fiches-commentaires à la fin de ce guide - Dites-nous ce que vous en pensez!**

Ashanti Lodge Youth Hostel - Cape Town, South Africa

Maracaia Youth Hostel - Porto Seguro, Brazil

CATEGORIES D'AUBERGES

▲ **Standard:** s'applique à la majorité des auberges.

△ **Simple:** s'applique aux établissements plus petits ou à ceux qui sont situés dans des lieux reculés et qui proposent donc des prestations plus simples: entre autre, le personnel y sera limité ainsi que les heures d'ouverture.

Quelques-unes des auberges listées dans ce guide ne font pas partie du Plan de Garantie des Normes en Auberge. Celles-ci ont toutefois été inclues dans le guide parce qu'elles permettent de fournir un hébergement là où il y aurait eu une absence totale de structures économiques d'accueil.

VOYAGEURS HANDICAPPES &

Hostelling International accueille les voyageurs handicappés - les auberges qui disposent d'installations facilitant l'accès aux fauteuils roulants sont indiquées par le symbole &.

CHARTE SUR L'ENVIRONNEMENT

Les auberges s'engagent à adhérer à la Charte sur l'Environnement de l'IYHF. Celle-ci dicte les critères de consommation et de préservation des ressources, d'élimination des déchets et de recyclage, de défense de l'environnement et prévoit également que les auberges devront jouer un rôle dans l'éducation écologique.

Réservations

RESERVEZ A L'AVANCE GRACE A [IBN]

Notre réseau international de réservation (IBN) vous offre une solution simple et économique pour réserver à l'avance, dans plus de 300 sites-clés, répartis dans 40 pays à travers le monde. Dans notre listing, les auberges proposant ce service de réservation apparaissent sur fond bleu et sont indiquées par le symbole [IBN].

IBN est unique dans le secteur de l'hébergement économique - les avantages sont nombreux:

- Réglez à la réservation, dans la devise de votre pays ou du pays dans lequel vous vous trouvez.

- Réservez tout au long de votre voyage - **voir pages 41 - 51 pour les centres de réservation** [IBN].

- Vous pourrez souvent régler par carte de crédit - voir ci-contre.

- Dans de nombreux pays, un seul coup de téléphone à une centrale de réservation vous permettra de réserver une série de nuitées dans plusieurs auberges.

AUTRES POINTS A NOTER SUR LES RESERVATIONS

- Hors saison, il n'est pas toujours nécessaire de réserver à l'avance, mais pendant les périodes de forte demande ou dans les grandes villes touristiques, nous vous conseillons vivement de le faire pour vous éviter une déception. Il est à noter que les chambres familiales sont très demandées et que les groupes doivent toujours réserver avant de se présenter.

- Il est possible de réserver par fax ou par courrier - si vous le faites par courrier, n'oubliez pas de joindre un coupon-réponse international, ainsi qu'une enveloppe à vos nom et adresse.

- Si vous réservez sans verser d'arrhes, vous devrez normalement arriver à l'auberge avant 18h, à moins d'avoir convenu avec l'auberge d'une heure différente pour votre arrivée.

Nous sommes sûrs que votre expérience des auberges sera agréable. Elle sera de toutes façons abordable. Nous sommes impatients de faire votre connaissance.

Jockey Club Mt Davis Youth Hostel - Hong Kong

EXPLICATION DES SYMBOLES

Auberges participant au Plan pour la Garantie des Normes en Auberge

Catégorie Normale
Catégorie Simple
Numéro de téléphone
Numéro de facsimilé
Adresse e-mail
Open Dates: Dates d'ouverture de l'auberge
Auberge ouverte toute l'année
Open Hours: Heures d'ouverture de l'auberge
Auberge ouverte 24 heures
Reservations: Renseignements sur les réservations
Réservation recommandée
IBN Réservations IBN disponibles (voir introduction principale à ce sujet)
CC Les cartes de crédit sont acceptées
Beds: Nombre de lits
Nombre de chambres au nombre indiqué de lits
Lits de style japonais
Price (range): Tarif pour une nuitée
BB inc Petit déjeuner compris dans le prix de la nuitée
Draps compris
Location de draps

Facilities: Prestations offertes par l'auberge
Convient aux ajistes en fauteuil roulant
Accueil des Groupes
Chambres familiales disponibles
Réservé aux femmes
Réservé aux hommes
Tous les repas sont disponibles (sauf indication contraire):
B Petit déjeuner
L Déjeuner
D Dîner (repas du soir)
Cuisine à la disposition des membres
Café/Bar disponibles
Abri vélo à l'auberge
Remises disponibles
Salles communes à l'auberge
TV Salle de télévision à l'auberge
Bibliothèque pour adhérents
Accès à l'Internet à l'auberge
Salles de réunion
Il est possible de laver son linge à ou près de l'auberge
Dépôt de Bagages pour adhérents
Petit magasin à votre service à ou près de l'auberge
Casiers individuels à l'auberge
Climatisation
Ascenseur à l'auberge
P Possibilités de parking à ou près de l'auberge

Informations touristiques
Bureau de Change à ou près de l'auberge
Jardin à l'auberge
Terrain de jeu à l'auberge
Disco à l'auberge
Sauna à l'auberge
Tennis de Table à l'auberge
Volley-Ball à l'auberge
Auberge écologique
L'auberge est située dans un bâtiment historique

Directions: Moyens de transport et indications pour se rendre à l'auberge
2 NE Direction et distance approximative en km en ligne droite du centre-ville à l'auberge
Aéroport principal le plus proche
A Autobus pour l'aéroport
Port: Nom et distance à partir du centre-ville
Train: gare la plus proche et distance jusqu'à l'auberge
Bus (à partir du centre-ville): No/Nos, point d'arrivée et distance jusqu'à l'auberge
Trams ou trolleys (à partir du centre-ville): No/Nos, point d'arrivée et distance jusqu'à l'auberge
U Métro: Nom de la ligne, nom de la station et distance jusqu'à l'auberge
Arrêt de bus
Arrêt de tram
ap point d'arrivée

Attractions: Attraits touristiques de l'auberge et de la région
Région boisée ou forestière
Région de montagnes ou de collines
Plage à ou près de l'auberge
Location de vélos à ou près de l'auberge
Région de ski alpin
Région de ski de fond
Région de randonnée pédestre
Équitation à ou près de l'auberge
Tennis à ou près de l'auberge
Natation à ou près de l'auberge
Mon Tue Lundi Mardi
Wed Thur Mercredi Jeudi
Fri Sat Vendredi Samedi
Sun Dimanche
Ave Hwy Avenue Autoroute
Rd St Route Rue
Su Wi Eté Hiver

ZEICHENERKLÄRUNG

Herbergen im Rahmen des zugesicherten Standardprogrammes

Normaler Standard
Einfacher Standard
Telefonnummer
Telefaxnummer
E mail-Adresse
Open Dates: Herberge geöffnet (Tage)
Herberge ganzjährlich geöffnet
Open Hours: Herberge geöffnet (Zeiten)
Herberge 24 Stunden geöffnet
Reservations: Reservierungsinformationen
Reservierung empfohlen
IBN IBN Reservierungen verfügbar (siehe: Einleitung für Einzelheiten)
CC Kreditkarten werden akzeptiert
Beds: Bettenzahl
Anzahl der Räume mit entsprechender Bettenausstattung
Betten im japanischen Stil
Price (range): Übernachtungspreis
BB inc Frühstück ist im Übernachtungspreis enthalten
Bettwäsche im Preis enthalten
Bettwäsche kann ausgeliehen werden

Facilities: Ausstattung in oder in der Nähe der Herberge
Für Rollstuhlbenutzer geeignet
Aufnahme von Gruppen
Familienräume vorhanden
Nur für Frauen
Nur für Männer
Mahlzeiten erhältlich (sofern nicht anders angegeben):
B Frühstück
L Mittagessen
D Abendessen
Küche für Mitglieder
Café/Bar vorhanden
Fahrradschuppen vorhanden
Rabatte & Konzessionen erhältlich
Gemeinschaftsraum vorhanden
TV Fernsehraum in der Herberge
ruhiger Leseraum vorhanden
Internet-Zugang in der Herberge
Tagungsräume
Einrichtungen zur Wäschepflege in (oder in der Nähe) der Herberge
Gepäckaufbewahrung für Mitglieder
Kleines Geschäft in (oder in der Nähe) der Herberge
Schließfächer vorhanden
Klimaanlage
Personenaufzug in der Herberge
P Parkmöglichkeiten in (oder in der Nähe) der Herberge

Touristeninformation
Geldwechsel in oder in der Nähe der Herberge möglich
Garten vorhanden
Spielplatz vorhanden
Disco in der Herberge
Sauna in der Herberge
Tischtennis in der Herberge
Volleyball in der Herberge
"Grüne Herberge"
Herberge in einem historischen Gebäude

Directions: Verkehrsanbindung zu und von der Herberge
2 NE Richtung und ungefähre Entfernung in km vom Stadtzentrum bis zur Herberge (Luftlinie)
Nächster größerer Flughafen
A Flughafenbus
Hafen: Name und Entfernung vom Stadtzentrum
Eisenbahn: nächster Bahnhof und Entfernung bis zur Herberge
Bus (vom Stadtzentrum): Nummer(n), günstigste Haltestelle und Entfernung bis zur Herberge
Straßenbahn oder O-Bus (vom Stadtzentrum): Nummer(n), günstigste Haltestelle und Entfernung bis zur Herberge
U U-Bahn: Name der Linie, Name der Haltestelle und Entfernung bis zur Herberge
Bus-Haltestelle
Straßenbahn-Haltestelle
ap günstigste Haltestelle

Attractions: Attraktionen in der Herberge oder in der Umgebung
Waldgebiet vorhanden
Gebirge vorhanden
Strand in der Nähe der Herberge
Fahrradverleih in (oder in der Nähe) der Herberge
Ski-Aplin-Gebiet
Skilanglaufgebiet
Gebiet zum Wandern
Reiten in oder in der Nähe der Herberge
Tennis in oder in der Nähe der Herberge
Schwimmbad in oder in der Nähe der Herberge
Mon Tue Montag Dienstag
Wed Thur Mittwoch Donnerstag
Fri Sat Sun Freitag Samstag Sonntag
Ave Hwy Allee Landstraße
Rd St Straße
Su Wi Sommer Winter

EXPLICACION DE LOS SIMBOLOS

Albergues que participan en el Plan de Normas Garantizadas

Categoría Normal
Categoría Sencilla
Número de teléfono
Número de fax
Dirección de correo electrónico
Open Dates: Fechas de apertura
Albergue abierto todo el año
Open Hours: Horas de apertura
Albergue abierto las 24 horas del día
Reservations: Información sobre reservas
Es recomendable reservar
IBN Se pueden hacer reservas a través de IBN (véase la introducción general para más información)
CC Se aceptan tarjetas de crédito
Beds: Número total de camas
Número de habitaciones con número de camas indicado
Camas de estilo japonés
Price (range): Precio por noche
BB inc Desayuno incluido en el precio por noche
Sábanas incluidas en el precio por noche
Alquiler de sábanas

Facilities: Instalaciones y prestaciones que ofrece el albergue
Preparado para uso de disminuidos físicos
Se aceptan grupos
Habitaciones familiares
Sólo para mujeres
Sólo para hombres
Se sirven todas las comidas (a menos que se indique lo contrario):
B Desayuno
L Comida
D Cena
Cocina para huéspedes
Bar-Cafetería
Cobertizo para bicicletas en el albergue
Se pueden obtener descuentos a través del albergue
Salas comunes en el albergue
TV Salón de TV en el albergue
Biblioteca para socios
Acceso a Internet en el albergue
Sala(s) de conferencias
Posibilidad de lavar la ropa/Lavandería en el albergue o cerca de él
Lugar donde guardar el equipaje/consigna para socios
Pequeña tienda en el albergue o cerca de él
Casillas/armarios con cerradura en el albergue

Aire acondicionado
P Ascensor en el albergue
Aparcamiento en el albergue o cerca de él
Información turística
Cambio de divisas en el albergue o cerca de él
Jardín en el albergue
Parque infantil en el albergue
Discoteca en el albergue
Sauna en el albergue
Ping-pong en el albergue
Vóleibol en el albergue
Albergue ecológico
Albergue en edificio histórico

Directions: Cómo llegar al albergue: Medios de transporte
2 NE Dirección y distancia aproximada en km. en línea recta desde el centro de la ciudad hasta el albergue.
Aeropuerto más cercano
A Autobús al aeropuerto
Puerto: Nombre y distancia desde el centro de la ciudad
Tren: Estación más cercana y distancia hasta el albergue
Autobús (desde del centro de la ciudad): Nº, parada y distancia hasta el albergue
Tranvía o trolebús (desde el centro de la ciudad): Nº, parada y distancia hasta el albergue
U Metro: Nombre de la línea, nombre de la estación y distancia hasta el albergue
Parada de autobús
Parada de tranvía
ap Apeadero

Attractions: Actividades que ofrecen el albergue y sus alrededores
Zona forestal/bosques
Zona montañosa/montes
Playa en el albergue o cerca de él
Alquiler de bicicletas en el albergue o cerca de él
Zona de esquí alpino
Zona de esquí de fondo
Zona de marcha/senderismo
Equitación en el albergue o cerca de él
Tenis en el albergue o cerca de él
Natación en el albergue o cerca de él
Mon Tue Lunes Martes
Wed Thur Miércoles Jueves
Fri Sat Viernes Sábado
Sun Domingo
Ave Hwy Avenida Autopista
Rd St Carretera Calle
Su Wi Verano Invierno

HOW TO USE THE SIGNS

❶ OPEN THIS FLAP

❷ TURN TO THE COUNTRY IN WHICH YOU ARE AT STAY

❸ COMPARE THE SIGNS FOR EXPLANATION

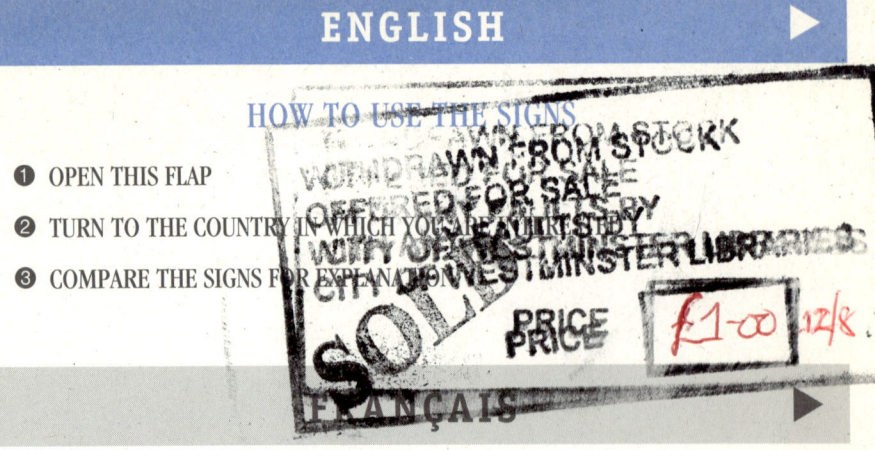
COMMENT INTERPRETER LES SYMBOLES

① OUVRIR CE VOLET

② REPORTEZ-VOUS AU PAYS QUI VOUS INTERESSE

③ COMPAREZ LES SIGNES POUR EN AVOIR L'EXPLICATION

ANLEITUNG ZUR BENUTZUNG DER ZEICHEN

❶ ÖFFNEN SIE DIESES FALTBLATT

❷ SUCHEN SIE DAS LAND ÜBER WELCHES SIE AUSKÜNFTE HABEN MÖCHTEN

❸ VERGLEICHEN SIE DIE ZEICHEN AUF DER KLAPPE MIT DENEN DES LANDES

COMO UTILIZAR LOS SIMBOLOS

① ABRA ESTA SOLAPA

② BUSQUE EL PAIS QUE LE INTERESA

③ COMPARE LOS SIMBOLOS PARA OBTENER SU EXPLICACION

Cover Design and Hostelling International advertisements by Big Design, London.
Inside Front Cover, pages 1-32 & "We want to hear from you" pages by Elanders (UK) Limited.

IYHF acknowledges the help of Member Associations in providing photographs for pages 1-32.

In pursuance of the Environmental Charter adopted by IYHF's 39th International Conference, this book has been produced using only paper from environment-friendly sources. The Nordic Council of Ministers decided in November 1989 to introduce common Nordic environmental labelling of products. Today, the 'Swan' is the only existing environmental label for printed matter in Europe. The criteria is set with this main target area:

The effect on the environment is minimised within the production process.

The product itself:

This product is 100% recyclable.

The ink, varnish and glue does not contain chemicals classified as environmentally hazardous according to EU directives.

The paper used is produced with low environmental impact (emissions) not with chemicals classified as environmentally hazardous according to EU directives.

Published in 2000 by
International Youth Hostel Federation
Secretariat, 1st Floor, Fountain House, Parkway, Welwyn Garden City,
Hertfordshire, AL8 6JH, England

Registered under the Charity Act in England.

Distributed in the United Kingdom by World Leisure Marketing
… and through Hostelling International outlets worldwide.
"Hostelling International" is the brand name of Youth Hostelling Worldwide

HOSTELLING INTERNATIONAL

NORDIC ENVIRONMENTAL LABEL

EXPLANATION OF SIGNS

Hostels within the Assured Standards Scheme

▲	Standard Grade
△	Simple Grade
☎	Telephone number
✆	Facsimile number
✉	E-mail address
Open Dates:	Dates hostel Open
	Hostel open all year
Open Hours:	Times hostel Open
	Hostel open 24 hours
Reservations:	Reservation Information
Ⓡ	Reservation recommended
IBN	IBN reservations available (see main introduction for details)
CC	Credit cards accepted
Beds:	Total number of beds
	Number of rooms containing indicated number of beds
	Japanese style beds
Price (range):	Overnight fee
BBinc	Breakfast included in Overnight Fee
	Linen included in fee
	Linen can be hired
Facilities:	Facilities available at the hostel
♿	Suitable for wheelchair users
	Groups welcome
	Family rooms available
	Female only
	Male only
⚭	All meals available (unless otherwise specified):
B	Breakfast
L	Lunch
D	Dinner (evening meal)
	Self catering facilities provided
	Café/Bar available
	Cycle Store at hostel
	Discounts & Concessions available
	Common room(s) in hostel
TV	TV room in hostel
	Library for members' use
	Internet Access at hostel
	Conference room(s)
	Laundry facilities available at or near the hostel
	Luggage storage for members
	Basic store available at or near the hostel
8	Lockers available at hostel
	Air Conditioning
	Lift in hostel
P	Parking facilities available at or near the hostel
i	Tourist Information
	Currency Exchange at or near hostel
	Garden at hostel

	Playground at hostel
	Disco in hostel
	Sauna in hostel
	Table Tennis at hostel
	Volleyball at hostel
	Green hostel
	Hostel is in a historical building
Directions:	Transport for getting to & from the hostel
2NE	Direction and approximate distance in km in straight line from city centre to hostel
✈	Nearest major Airport
	Airport bus
	Harbour/Port: Name and distance from City Centre
	Train: nearest Station and distance to hostel
	Bus (from City Centre): No/Nos, alighting point and distance to hostel
	Tram or trolley bus (from City Centre): No/Nos, alighting point and distance to hostel
U	Underground: Line name, Station name and distance to hostel
	Bus Stop
	Tram Stop
ap	alighting point
Attractions:	Attractions at the hostel or in the surrounding area
	Forested/Wooded area
	Mountainous/Hilly area
	Beach at or near hostel
	Cycle rental available at or near the hostel
	Alpine Skiing area
	Cross Country Skiing area
	Hiking area
U	Horseriding at or near hostel
	Tennis at or near hostel
	Swimming at or near hostel
Mon Tue	Monday Tuesday
Wed Thur	Wednesday Thursday
Fri Sat Sun	Friday Saturday Sunday
Ave Hwy	Avenue Highway
Rd St	Road Street
Su Wi	Summer Winter

RESERVEZ PAR CARTE DE CREDIT AUPRES DES CENTRES SUIVANTS

Angleterre & Pays de Galles	☎	(1629) 581 418
Australie	☎	(2) 9261 1111
Canada	☎	(1) 800 663 5777
Ecosse	☎	(8701) 553 255
Etats-Unis	☎	(202) 783 6161
France	☎	(1) 44 89 87 27
Irlande du Nord	☎	(28) 9032 4733
Nouvelle Zélande	☎	(3) 379 9808
République d'Irlande	☎	(1) 830 1766
Suisse	☎	(1) 360 1414

Kitayuzawa Youth Hostel - Hokkaido, Japan

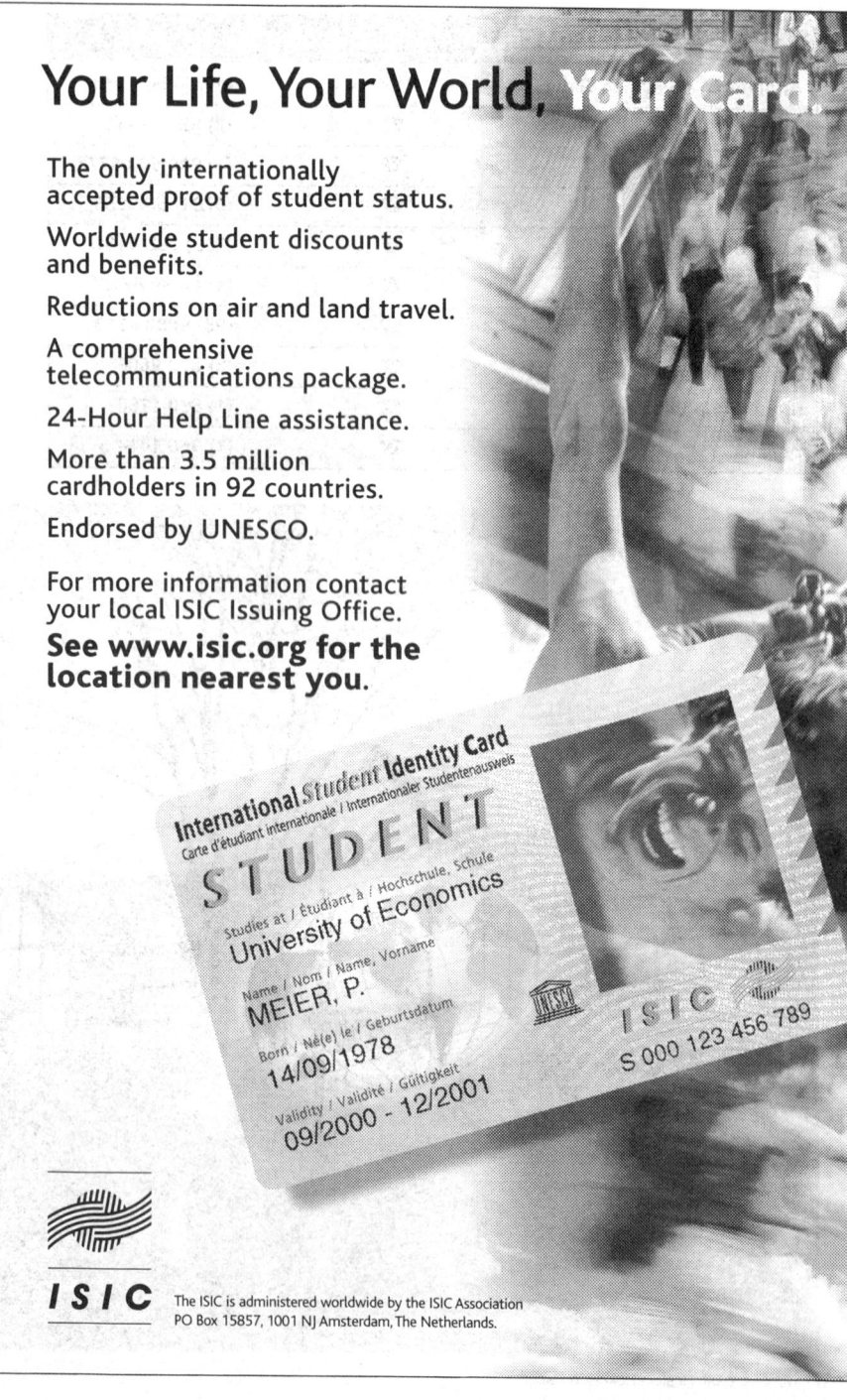

Einführung zu Hostelling International

Willkommen in der Welt von Hostelling International - ein unvergleichliches Netz von Unterkünften, wo Sie in einem gastfreundlichen Umfeld gut und preiswert übernachten können.

Hostelling International ist der Markenname der Internationalen Jugendherbergsföderation (IYHF), eine Organisation, die Jugendherbergen weltweit vertritt. Hostelling International ist das größte und erfahrenste Netzwerk, das sich für Reisende jeden Alters - jung und alt - engagiert. Nur in Bayern, Deutschland, liegt die Altersgrenze für Gäste unter 27 Jahre. Mehr darüber erfahren Sie auf unserer Website www.iyhf.org. **Für preisgünstige und bewährte Unterkünfte, schauen Sie nach dem blauen Dreieck-Symbol.**

Chicago Youth Hostel - USA

Vorteile der Mitgliedschaft

Um in einer Jugendherberge zu übernachten, müssen Sie Mitglied Ihres nationalen Jugendherbergsverbands (JHV) werden. Sollte Ihr Land keinen JHV haben, können Sie bei Ankunft in der Herberge eine "Hostelling International Card" oder "Welcome Stamps" erwerben.

Die Mitgliedschaft bietet eine breite Palette an Leistungen - inklusive:

- 4,200 **Unterkünfte** weltweit in über 60 Ländern - für **alle Altersgruppen** - mit einer Auswahl an Einzel-, Doppel- und Mehrbettzimmern.

- Teilnahme an allen Hostelling International **Aktivitäten**, Programmen und Veranstaltungen.

- Tausende von **Rabatten** weltweit - für Reise- und Sportaktivitäten bis zu Restaurants, Museen und Unterhaltung! Eine Auswahl an Rabatten finden Sie **im hinteren Teil dieses Führers.** Für einen ausführlichen Bericht checken Sie unter www.iyhf.org.

- Mit dem "International Booking Network" (IBN) können **Reservierungen** bis zu 6 Monate im Voraus gebucht werden - **siehe Seite 24** für weitere Informationen.

Stafford Gables Youth Hostel - Dunedin, New Zealand

Gesicherte Qualitätsstandards

"Hostelling International Assured Standards Scheme " heißt, Sie können sich in unseren Herbergen auf einen gleichbleibenden Service- und Ausstattungsstandard verlassen - wo immer Sie auch übernachten.

- **Empfang** - Herbergen sind für alle Altersgruppen geöffnet. Sie können, wenn Sie es noch nicht sind, Mitglied werden und Reservierungen im Voraus buchen. Wenn die Herberge für einen Teil des Tages geschlossen ist, haben Sie trotzdem Zugang zu allen notwendigen Einrichtungen.

- **Komfort** - eine gute Nachtruhe (inklusive Verleih frischer Bettwäsche, falls nicht im Übernachtungspreis enthalten) und genügend Wasch-/Dusch-Einrichtungen. Mahlzeiten sowie Selbstversorgungsausstattungen werden generell angeboten. Nahrungsmittelgeschäfte befinden sich meistens in Herbergsnähe.

- **Sauberkeit** - die höchsten Hygienestandards wo immer Sie reisen.

- **Sicherheit** - für Sie und Ihr Eigentum, inklusive Schließfächer für Gepäck und Wertsachen.

- **Privatsphäre** - in Duschen, Waschräumen und Toiletten. In unseren Herbergen gibt es überwiegend nach Geschlecht getrennte Schlafräume - aber auf Anfrage können auch gemeinsame Schlafräume für Gruppenreisende gebucht werden.

Standards werden von Hostelling International und von Ihnen überwacht. **Im hinteren Teil dieses Führers finden Sie Kommentarkarten - sagen Sie uns Ihre Meinung!**

Hurghada International Youth Hostel - Egypt

HERBERGSKATEGORIEN

▲ **Standard:** Gilt für den größten Teil der Herbergen.

△ **Einfach:** Gilt für kleinere oder sich in abgelegenen Gegenden befindende Herbergen, in denen Sie einfache Einrichtungen, wenig Personal und beschränkte Öffnungszeiten vorfinden könnten.

Einige Herbergen in diesem Führer entsprechen nicht den Richtlinien des "Assured Standards Scheme" - dies sind Unterkünfte in Gebieten, wo es sonst keine geben würde.

REISENDE MIT BEHINDERUNGEN ♿

Hostelling International heißt Reisende mit Behinderungen willkommen - Jugendherbergen für Rollstuhlfahrer sind im Verzeichnis mit ♿ gekennzeichnet.

UMWELTCHARTA

Herbergen befolgen die Richtlinien der IYHF Umweltcharta. Diese schreibt die Kriterien für Verbrauch und Sparen von Ressourcen, Abfallbeseitigung und Recycling, Umweltschutz und Förderung der Umweltschutzerziehung vor.

Pu Jiang Youth Hostel - Shanghai, China

Buchungen & Reservierungen

BUCHEN IM VORAUS DURCH [IBN]

Unser computergestütztes Reservierungssystem bietet einfache und preisgünstige Reservierungen bis zu 6 Monaten im Voraus für fast 300 Schlüsselherbergen in 40 Ländern weltweit. Alle angeschlossenen Herbergen, die Vorausreservierungen akzeptieren, sind in diesem Führer mit dem [IBN] Symbol gekennzeichnet und in blau hervorgehoben.

IBN ist im preisbewussten Unterkunftssektor einzigartig - Leistungen umfassen:

- Zahlen Sie in der Landeswährung wenn Sie buchen.

- Reservierungen während Ihrer Reise - **siehe Seiten 41 - 51 für** [IBN] **Internationale Buchungszentren.**

- Sie können oft auch mit Kreditkarten zahlen - siehe gegenüber.

- In vielen Ländern reicht ein Anruf beim Zentralen Reservierungsbüro, um mehrere Übernachtungen in verschiedenen Herbergen zu buchen.

Nairobi Youth Hostel - Kenya

WEITERE BUCHUNGSINFORMATIONEN

- Vorausbuchungen sind in der Nebensaison nicht unbedingt notwendig, aber in Hauptreisezeiten oder in beliebten Städten sind sie zu empfehlen, damit Enttäuschungen vermieden werden. Familienzimmer sind schnell vergeben, und Gruppen sollten immer im Voraus buchen.

- Buchen Sie per Fax oder Brief bei der ausgewählten Herberge. Bei schriftlicher Buchung bitte einen internationalen Antwortschein plus selbst adressierten und frankierten Briefumschlag beilegen.

- Bei Vorausbuchungen ohne Anzahlung sollten Sie vor 18.00 Uhr in der Herberge eintreffen, sofern keine andere Zeit vereinbart wurde.

Wir sind sicher, ein Herbergsaufenthalt wird Ihnen viel Freude machen. Auf jeden Fall können Sie sich diesen leisten. Wir freuen uns auf Ihren Besuch.

KREDITKARTEN-RESERVIERUNGEN BEI DIESEN ZENTREN		
Australien	☎	(2) 9261 1111
England & Wales	☎	(1629) 581 418
Frankreich	☎	(1) 44 89 87 27
Kanada	☎	(1) 800 663 5777
Neuseeland	☎	(3) 379 9808
Nordirland	☎	(28) 9032 4733
Republik Irland	☎	(1) 830 1766
Schottland	☎	(8701) 553 255
Schweiz	☎	(1) 360 1414
USA	☎	(202) 783 6161

Riyadh Youth Hostel - Saudi Arabia

Hostelling International - Introducción

Bienvenido al mundo de Hostelling International - una red de alojamientos sin igual, en los que usted pasará una buena noche, en un ambiente acogedor y a precios asequibles.

Hostelling International es la marca de la Federación Internacional de Albergues Juveniles (IYHF), la organización que representa a las Asociaciones de Albergues Juveniles de todo el mundo. Hostelling International es la red más extensa y con más experiencia del servicio a los viajeros de todas las edades, tanto los jóvenes como los menos jóvenes (sólo en Bavaria, Alemania, se aplica un límite máximo de edad de 26 años en los albergues). Para más información, visite nuestra página Internet www.iyhf.org. **Si desea alojamiento económico de confianza, busque el triángulo azul.**

Fes Youth Hostel - Morocco

Ventajas de la Afiliación

Para alojarse en un albergue juvenil, es necesario hacerse miembro de la Asociación de Albergues Juveniles del país en que uno viva. Si no existe una Asociación de Albergues Juveniles en su país, usted tendrá la oportunidad de adquirir una tarjeta Hostelling International o un "sello de bienvenida" (*Welcome Stamp*) a su llegada al albergue elegido.

Su afiliación a Hostelling International le brinda toda una serie de ventajas, a saber:

- 4.200 **establecimientos** repartidos por más de 60 países del mundo - abiertos a personas **de todas las edades** y ofreciendo alojamiento en habitaciones individuales, dobles y múltiples.

- La posibilidad de participar en las **actividades**, los programas y los acontecimientos de todo tipo organizados por Hostelling International.

- Miles de **descuentos**, a nivel mundial y en todo: viajes, deportes, restaurantes, museos, diversiones, etc. Al final de esta Guía encontrará una selección de descuentos - pero, para verlos todos, consulte nuestra página *web* www.iyhf.org.

- La oportunidad de realizar **reservas** con un máximo de 6 meses de antelación a través de nuestra red internacional de reservas (IBN) - **ver pág. 30** para más información.

Sapporo House Youth Hostel - Japan

Normas de Calidad Garantizadas

El Plan de las Normas Garantizadas ha sido instituido por Hostelling International para asegurarle un nivel de calidad uniforme en nuestras instalaciones y prestaciones, sea cual sea el albergue en el que usted se aloje.

- **Recibimiento** - Los albergues están abiertos a todos. Usted podrá hacerse miembro en el albergue mismo si no lo es aún y realizar reservas con antelación en otros albergues. Además, aunque el establecimiento cierre durante parte del día, usted tendrá acceso a las zonas más imprescindibles del mismo.

- **Comodidad** - Una buena noche (así como la posibilidad de alquilar sábanas recién lavadas si no se incluyen en el precio de la pernoctación) y suficientes lavabos/duchas. Normalmente se sirven comidas en los albergues y suele haber, además, una cocina para uso de los huéspedes. Asimismo, hay generalmente una tienda de comestibles cerca del albergue.

- **Limpieza** - Las más rigurosas normas de higiene dondequiera que usted se aloje.

- **Seguridad** - Personal y de sus pertenencias, que incluye la disponibilidad de consignas de equipaje y casillas con llave para los objetos de valor.

- **Intimidad** - En las duchas, los lavabos y los aseos. En la mayoría de los albergues, el alojamiento consiste en dormitorios múltiples separados para hombres y mujeres, aunque es posible que algunos de ellos dispongan de habitaciones mixtas para quienes viajen juntos y las soliciten.

La aplicación de estas normas en los albergues es objeto de un seguimiento por parte de Hostelling International, pero también por parte de usted, el usuario. **Al final de la guía encontrará unos impresos en los que puede enviarnos sus comentarios - ¡díganos lo que opina!**

Bangkok International Youth Hostel - Thailand

CLASIFICACIÓN DE LOS ALBERGUES

▲ **Categoría Normal:** se aplica a la mayoría de los albergues.

△ **Categoría Sencilla:** se aplica a los albergues más pequeños y a los situados en lugares remotos, cuyas instalaciones y prestaciones son sólo básicas - por ejemplo, es posible que el personal y el horario de apertura sean limitados.

Algunos de los albergues relacionados en esta Guía no pertenecen al Plan de las Normas Garantizadas - han sido incluidos en ella porque están situados en lugares en los que no nos es posible ofrecer otro tipo de alojamiento.

VIAJEROS MINUSVÁLIDOS ♿

Los disminuidos físicos son bienvenidos en los albergues de Hostelling International - los establecimientos que disponen de acceso para sillas de ruedas llevan el símbolo ♿ en la Guía.

NORMAS MEDIOAMBIENTALES

Los albergues deben cumplir con las Normas Medioambientales de IYHF. Estas establecen los criterios relativos al consumo y conservación de recursos, a la eliminación de residuos y su reciclaje, a la protección de la naturaleza y a la provisión de educación medioambiental.

City Youth Hostel - Guangzhou, China

Reservas

RESERVE CON ANTELACIÓN A TRAVÉS DE [IBN]

Nuestro sistema informatizado de reservas constituye una forma sencilla y económica de reservar con un máximo de 6 meses de antelación, en casi 300 albergues claves repartidos por 40 países del mundo. En nuestra Guía, los establecimientos que disponen de este servicio llevan el símbolo [IBN] y se destacan de los demás por su fondo azul.

IBN es único en el sector del alojamiento económico - las ventajas que presenta son numerosas:

- Pague al reservar en la moneda del país en el que se encuentre.
- Haga reservas a lo largo de todo su viaje - **ver pág. 41 - 51: Centros de Reservas [IBN] del mundo.**
- Podrá generalmente pagar con tarjeta de crédito - ver el recuadro en la página contigua.
- En muchos países, una sola llamada a la Central de Reservas le permitirá reservar varias pernoctaciones en diferentes albergues.

RESERVAS - OTROS PUNTOS IMPORTANTES

- No es imprescindible reservar con antelación durante la temporada baja, pero en temporada alta y en las grandes ciudades es recomendable hacerlo para no llevarse desilusiones - las habitaciones familiares, en particular, se ocupan con rapidez y los grupos también deben reservar con tiempo.
- Reserve por fax o por carta dirigiéndose directamente al albergue deseado - si reserva por correo, adjunte un cupón internacional de respuesta pagada y un sobre con su nombre y dirección.
- Si reserva con antelación pero sin abonar un depósito, normalmente deberá llegar al albergue antes de las 18 h., a menos que haya concertado previamente otra hora de llegada.

Estamos seguros de que disfrutará de su estancia en nuestros albergues y de que no le saldrá cara la experiencia. Esperamos tener el agrado de su visita.

Praia do Forte Youth Hostel - Brazil

RESERVE CON TARJETA DE CRÉDITO EN LAS SIGUIENTES CENTRALES:		
Australia	☎	(2) 9261 1111
Canadá	☎	(1) 800 663 5777
Escocia	☎	(8701) 553 255
Estados Unidos	☎	(202) 783 6161
Francia	☎	(1) 44 89 87 27
Inglaterra y Gales	☎	(1629) 581 418
Irlanda del Norte	☎	(28) 9032 4733
Nueva Zelanda	☎	(3) 379 9808
República de Irlanda	☎	(1) 830 1766
Suiza	☎	(1) 360 1414

J's Bay Youth Hostel - Byron Bay, Australia

Español

RESERVAS

HOSTELLING INTERNATIONAL

eKit
Communication Card

Travel Safety Net - it is new!

HI-eKit offers travel, medical and legal advice and assistance 24hrs a day, via the HI-eKit phone service or the website. Another reason why HI-eKit is the essential travel accessory.

Remember to use the Travel Vault

You can secure details about all your important travel documents such as passport and credit cards, in the on-line Travel Vault.

The easy part is joining

You can join for FREE almost anywhere in the world.

Join on-line

Just visit our web-site at:

www.hi.ekit.com

or

Join over the phone

Simply dial the access number for the country you are in (listed on the tear-out card) and then press **0**

US$5 JOINING BONUS!

You will recieve a $5 joining bonus when you pre-pay your card. To claim your bonus, just quote this reference code; **HIAD56**.

Rechargeable

Add more money to your card anytime over the phone or via the web.

This card is yours for life.
So tear out one of the cards attached, join, then record
your HI-eKit number and PIN in the space provided.
Start making your life easier while you are traveling!

Join Now
Get US$5
Free Bonus!

Low Cost Calls

Travel Safety Net

Voicemail

Free Email

Access Numbers

We update and add access numbers regularly.
Visit the ekit website for the most current access numbers.

Country	Access No.
Australia	1800-11-44-78
- Adelaide economy✱	08-8468-4888
- Brisbane economy✱	07-3318-3102
- Melbourne economy✱	03-9909-0888
- Perth economy✱	08-9281-6942
- Sydney economy✱	02-8208-3000
Bahamas	1800-3890-209
Brazil	0008 156 203 0287
Canada	1877-635-3575
China	10800-140-0208
Colombia	980-916-4730
Costa Rica	0800-015-0158
Denmark	8088-2823
Dominican Republic	1888-1563-164
Fiji	00800-7126
France	0800-914-999
Germany	0800-100-7239
Greece	00800-125-282
Hong Kong	800-906-017
Ireland	1800-557-980
	1800-555-081
Israel	1800-945-0287
Italy	800-875-801
Japan	0053-116-0057
Luxembourg	8002-9240
	8002-9148
Malaysia	813-803-8813
Mexico	0018-005-140-287
Monaco	0800-914-823
Netherlands	0800-024-9931

Country	Access No.
New Zealand	0800-11-44-78
- Auckland economy✱	09-912-8211
Norway	800-16607
Peru	0800-50631
Poland	00800-111-4353
Puerto Rico	1800-531-9684
Singapore	800-101-1217
South Africa	0800-992-921
South Korea	00798-14-800-4442
Spain	900-931-951
	900-971-537
Sweden	0200-214-883
Switzerland	0800-111-444
	0800-897-306
Thailand	001-800-12-066-3330 ▼
United Kingdom	0800-169-8646
	0800-376-2366 ▼
- Nationwide economy✱	0845-085-0855
- London economy✱	0207-943-2772
United States	1800-706-1333
- 48 States	1800-318-7039
- Alaska	1800-527-6786
- Hawaii	213-927-0100
- Los Angeles economy✱	1877-5030-287
Virgin Islands	800-874-896
Vatican City	

✱ Use the economy number, where available for cheaper calls.
▲ Unavailable from pay-phones in some cases.
Additional access numbers are provided in some countries for use in busy periods.

eKit
visit: www.hi.ekit.com

Using the eKit Phone Service

1 Call the access number of the country you're in. (See User Guide for access numbers)
2 Enter your eKit number:

 then press **#**

3 Enter your PIN:

 then press **#**

4 To make a call, press **2**, then enter the country code, area code *(without the 0)* and phone number.

 To **listen to voicemail**, press **1**
Use any touch tone phone worldwide
Do not insert into telephone

Other eKit Features

Recharge
Via the phone or website with your credit card.

Voicemail
Others can leave you a message by dialing (US) +1 213 927 0102, (UK) +44 207 943 2757, or (AUST) +61 02 8208 3030

Free email
Set up yourname@ekit.com on the website.

Travel Vault
Securely store important travel details in eKit's online travel vault.

eKit
www.hi.ekit.com

$5 bonus

This card is rechargeable

Free Email
Voicemail
Travel Safety Net
Low Cost Calls

Communication Card

Hostelling International Saves You $$ And it is so EASY!

HI-eKit ...The essential travel accessory

travel the world, *keep in touch* and *save money!*

Join Now Get US$5 Free Bonus!

How Can You Save Money on Calls?

HI-eKit offers low rates on international calls from pay-phones and hotel phones. Use HI-eKit from over 55 countries, more coming soon!

Unlike some phone cards, HI-eKit provides:

- no monthly charges or connection fees
- charges are in 15 second increments
- same rates 24 hours a day, 7 days a week

Saving you money!

Voicemail - over the phone or web

Your HI-eKit comes with its own voicemail box, so family and friends can leave you messages any time. Listen to them over the phone or web.

FREE email

More than just an ordinary email service - you can even listen to your email over the phone. Get **yourname@ekit.com** for FREE today.

Bonus offer when you charge your card - US$5 FREE calls!

www.hi.ekit.com

$5 bonus

This card is rechargeable

 **Low Cost Calls**

 **Travel Safety Net**

 Voicemail

 **Free Email**

Access Numbers

We update and add access numbers regularly.
Visit the eKit website for the most current access numbers.

Country	Access No.	Country	Access No.
Australia	1800-11-44-78	New Zealand	0800-11-44-78
- Adelaide economy✱	08-8468-4888	- Auckland economy✱	09-912-8211
- Brisbane economy✱	07-3318-3102	Norway	800-16607
- Melbourne economy✱	03-9909-0888	Peru	0800-50631
- Perth economy✱	08-9281-6942	Poland	00800-111-4353
- Sydney economy✱	02-8208-3000	Puerto Rico	1800-531-9684
Bahamas	1800-3890-209	Singapore	800-101-1217
Brazil	0008-156-203-0287	South Africa	0800-992-921
Canada	1877-635-3575	South Korea	00798-14-800-4442
	1800-808-5773	Spain	900-931-951
China	10800-140-0208		900-971-537
Colombia	980-915-4730	Sweden	0200-214-883
Costa Rica	0800-015-0158	Switzerland	0800-111-444
Denmark	8088-2823		0800-897-306
Dominican Republic	1888-1563-164	Thailand	001-800-12-066-3330 ▲
Fiji	00800-7126	United Kingdom	0800-169-8646
France	0800-914-999		0800-376-2366 ▲
Germany	0800-100-7239	- Nationwide economy✱	0845-085-0855
Greece	00800-125-282	- London economy✱	0207-943-2772
Hong Kong	800-900-017	United States	
Ireland	1800-557-980	- 48 States	1800-706-1333
	1800-555-180	- Alaska	1800-318-7039
Israel	1800-945-0287	- Hawaii	1800-527-6786
Italy	800-875-801	- Los Angeles economy✱	213-927-0100
Japan	0053-116-0057	- Virgin Islands	1877-5030-287
Luxembourg	8002-9240	Vatican City	800-874-896
	8002-9148		
Malaysia	1800-803-813		
Mexico	0018-005-140-287		
Monaco	0800-914-823		
Netherlands	0800-024-9931		

Additional access numbers are provided in some countries for use in busy periods.
▲ Unavailable from pay-phones in some cases.
✱ Use the economy number, where available, for cheaper calls.

EUROPE

Youth Hostels within Europe are listed in the Hostelling International Guide - Europe. The addresses of the full member Associations are given below:

Les AJ de l'Europe sont cataloguées dans le guide Hostelling International Guide - Europe. Les adresses des associations membres à part entière sont indiquées ci-dessous:

Die europäischen Jugendherbergen sind im Hostelling International Guide - Europa aufgeführt. Die Adressen der vollberechtigten Mitgliedsverbände sind unten angegeben:

Los albergues juveniles de los países europeos figuran en Guía de Europa. A continuación se encuentran las direcciones de las Asociaciones miembros de pleno derecho de Hostelling International de dichos países:

AUSTRIA:

Österreichischer Jugendherbergsverband,
Hauptverband, 1010 Vienna, Schottenring 28.
☎ (1) 5335353, 5335354 ✆ (1) 5350861
✉ oejhv@chello.at, oejhvzentrale@oejhv.at, backpackeraustria@at
🖥 www.oejhv.or.at

Österreichisches Jugendherbergswerk,
Helferstorferstrasse 4, A-1010 Vienna.
☎/✆ (1) 5331833
✉ oejhw@oejhw.or.at
🖥 www.oejhw.or.at

BELGIUM:

Les Auberges de Jeunesse,
Rue de la Sablonnière 28, B1000 Brussels.
☎ (2) 2195676 ✆ (2) 2191451
✉ info@laj.be
🖥 www.laj.be

Vlaamse Jeugdherbergcentrale,
Van Stralenstraat 40, B-2060 Antwerp.
☎ (3) 2327218 ✆ (3) 2318126
✉ info@vjh.be
🖥 www.vjh.be

CROATIA:

Hrvatski Ferijalni i Hostelski Savez (Croatian Youth Hostel Association),
Savska cesta 5/1, 10000 Zagreb.
☎ (1) 4829294, 4829297 ✆ (1) 4829296
✉ hfhs@zg.tel.hr
🖥 www.nncomp.com/hfhs

CZECH REPUBLIC:

KMC-Club of Young Travellers,
Karolíny Světlé 30, 11000 Prague 1.
☎/✆ (2) 22220347, 22221328
✉ kmc@kmc.cz
🖥 www.kmc.cz

DENMARK:

DANHOSTEL,
Vesterbrogade 39, DK 1620 Copenhagen V.
☎ 33313612 ✆ 33313626
✉ ldv@danhostel.dk
🖥 www.danhostel.dk

ENGLAND & WALES:

Youth Hostels Association (England & Wales),
Trevelyan House, 8 St Stephens Hill, St Albans, Hertfordshire, AL1 2DY.
☎ (870) 8708808 ✆ (1727) 844126
✉ customerservices@yha.org.uk
🖥 www.yha.org.uk

FINLAND:

Suomen Retkeilymajajärjestö-SRM,
Yrjönkatu 38 B 15, 00100 Helsinki.
📞 (9) 565 7150 📠 (9) 565 71510
✉ info@srm.inet.fi
🖳 www.srmnet.org

FRANCE:

Fédération Unie des Auberges de Jeunesse,
27 rue Pajol, 75018 Paris.
📞 (0) 1 44898727 📠 (0) 1 44898710
✉ fuaj@fuaj.org

GERMANY:

Deutsches Jugendherbergswerk,
Bad Meinberger Str. 1, D-32760 Detmold.
📞 (5231) 9936-0 📠 (5231) 993666
✉ info@djh.org
🖳 www.djh.de

HUNGARY:

Magyarországi Ifjúsági Szállások Szövetsége,
H-1077 Budapest V11, Almássy tér 6.
📞/📠 (1) 3435167
✉ travel@hostels.hu

ICELAND:

Bandalag Íslenskra Farfugla (Icelandic Youth Hostel Association),
Sundlaugavegur 34, 105 Reykjavík.
📞 5538110 📠 5889201
✉ info@hostel.is
🖳 www.hostel.is

IRELAND (NORTHERN):

Hostelling International - Northern Ireland,
22 Donegall Rd, Belfast BT12 5JN.
📞 (2890) 315435 📠 (2890) 439699
✉ info@hini.org.uk
🖳 www.hini.org.uk

IRELAND (REPUBLIC OF):

An Óige, Irish Youth Hostel Association,
61 Mountjoy St, Dublin 7.
📞 (1) 8304555 📠 (1) 8305808
✉ mailbox@anoige.ie
🖳 www.irelandyha.org

ISRAEL:

Israel Youth Hostels Association,
Binyanei Hauma, 1 Shazar Street, P O Box 6001, Jerusalem 91060.
📞 (2) 6558400 📠 (2) 6558430
✉ iyha@iyha.org
🖳 www.youth-hostels.org.il

ITALY:

Associazione Italiana Alberghi per la Gioventù,
Via Cavour 44, 00184 Rome.
📞 064871152 📠 064880492
✉ aig@uni.net
🖳 www.hostels-aig.org

LUXEMBOURG:

Centrale des Auberges de Jeunesse Luxembourgeoises,
24-26 Place de la Gare, L-1616 Luxembourg.
📞 26293-500 📠 26293-503
✉ information@youthhostels.lu
🖳 www.youthhostels.lu

MALTA:

NSTS, 220 St. Paul St, Valletta, VLT 07.
📞 244983 📠 230330
✉ nsts@nsts.org
🖳 www.nsts.org

NETHERLANDS:

Stichting Nederlandse Jeugdherberg Centrale,
P.O. Box 191, 1006 AD Amsterdam.
📞 (10) 264 6064 📠 (10) 264 6061
✉ info@njhc.org
🖳 www.njhc.org

NORWAY:

Norske Vandrerhjem,
Dronningensgate 26, N-0154 Oslo.
☎ 23139300 ✆ 23139350
✉ hostels@online.no
🖥 www.vandrerhjem.no

POLAND:

*Polskie Towarzystwo Schronisk Mlodzieżowych
(Polish Youth Hostel Association),*
ul Chocimska 28, 00-791 Warsaw.
☎ (22) 8498128, 8498354 ✆ (22) 8498354
✉ hostellingpol.ptsm@pro.onet.pl
🖥 www.hostelling.com.pl

PORTUGAL:

MOVIJOVEM,
Av. Duque d'Avila 137, 1069-017 Lisbon.
☎ (21) 3596000 ✆ (21) 3596001
✉ movijovem@movijovem.pt
🖥 www.sej.pt

SCOTLAND:

Scottish Youth Hostels Association,
7 Glebe Crescent, Stirling FK8 2JA.
☎ (1786) 891400 ✆ (1786) 891333
✉ info@syha.org.uk
🖥 www.syha.org.uk

SLOVENIA:

PZS - Hostelling International Slovenia,
Gosposvetska 84, 2000 Maribor.
☎ (2) 2342137 ✆ (2) 2342136
✉ pzs@psdsi.com
🖥 www.psdsi.com/pzs

SPAIN:

Red Española de Albergues Juveniles,
c/.José Ortega y Gasset 71, Madrid 28006.
☎ (91) 3477700 ✆ (91) 4018160
✉ streaj@mtas.es
🖥 www.mtas.es/injuve/intercambios/
albergues/reaj.html

SWEDEN:

Svenska Turistföreningen,
Amiralitetshuset Skeppsholmen, PO Box 25,
101 20 Stockholm.
☎ (8) 4632100 ✆ (8) 6781958
✉ info@stfturist.se
🖥 www.meravsverige.nu

SWITZERLAND:

Schweizer Jugendherbergen,
Schaffhauserstr 14, PO Box 161, CH 8042 Zürich.
☎ (1) 3601414 ✆ (1) 3601460
✉ bookingoffice@youthhostel.ch
🖥 www.youthhostel.ch

YUGOSLAVIA (FEDERAL REPUBLIC OF):

Ferijalni savez Jugoslavije,
Belgrade 11000, Makedonska 22/2.
☎ (11) 622956, 622584 ✆ (11) 3220762

INTERNATIONAL TELEPHONE CODES AND EMERGENCY CONTACT NUMBERS
INDICATIFS TÉLÉPHONIQUES INTERNATIONAUX ET NUMÉROS D'URGENCE

Country	GMT	Int Code	Country Code	Medical	Police	Fire
Algeria	+1	00	+213		17	14
Argentina	-4	00	+5411	107	101	100
Australia	+8/+10	0011	+61	000	000	000
Austria	+1	00	+43	144	133	122
Bahrain	+3	0	+973	999	999	999
Bangladesh	+6	00	+880	500121-5, 5050525-29	8322501-8	9556666-7 9555555-7
Belgium	+1	00	+32	100	101	100
Brazil	-2/-5	00	+55	192	190	193
Bulgaria	+2	00	+359	150	166	160.
Canada	-3/-11	00	+1	911	911	911
Chile	-6	00	+56	131	133	132
China	+8	00	+86	120	110	119
China - Hong Kong	+8	00	+852	999	999	999
Colombia	-5	009/007/005	+57	132	112	119
Costa Rica	-6	00	+506	911	117	118
Croatia	+1	00	+385	94	92	93
Czech Republic	+1	00	+420	155	158	150
Denmark	+1	00	+45	112	112	112
Egypt	+2	00	+20	123	122	125
Estonia	+2	800	+372	112	112/110	112
Faeroe Islands	GMT	00	+298	000	000	000
Finland	+2	999	+358	112	10022	112
France	+1	00	+33	15	17	18
Germany	+1	00	+49	112	110	112
Greece	+2	00	+30	166	100	199
Guatemala	-6	00	+502	125/128	120/110	123/122
Hungary	+1	00	+36	104	107	105
Iceland	GMT	00	+354	112	112	112
India	+5.5	00	+91	102	100	101
Indonesia	+7/+9	001 or 008	+62	118	110	113
Ireland - Republic	GMT	00	+353	999	999	999
Israel	+2	00	+972	101	100	102
Italy	+1	00	+39	118	112	115
Japan	+9	001	+81	119	110	119
Kenya	+3	0196	+254	999	999	999
Latvia	+1	00	371	03	02	01
Lebanon	+2	00	961	140	112	175
Libya	+2	00	+218	191	193	190
Lithuania	+1	8-10	+370	03	02	01
Luxembourg	+1	00	+352	112	113	112

Country	GMT	Int Code	Country Code	Medical	Police	Fire
Macedonia	+1	99	+389	94	92	93
Malaysia	+8	00	+60	999	999	994
Malta	+1	00	+356	196	191	191
Mexico	-6/8	00	+52	080	080	080
Morocco	GMT	00	+212	15	19	15
Nepal	+5.45	00	+977	102	100	101
Netherlands	+1	00	+31	112	112	112
New Caledonia	+10	00	+687	15	17	18
New Zealand	+12	00	+64	111	111	111
Nicaragua	+6	001	+505	128	118	115
Norway	+1	00	+47	113	112	110
Pakistan	+5	00	+92	15	15	16
Peru	-5	00	+51	105	105	116
Philippines	+8	00	+63	00632-8319 731	117	00632-8269 131
Poland	+1	0	+48	999	997	998
Portugal	+1	00	+351	112	112	112
Qatar	+3	0	+974	999	999	999
Romania	+2	00	40	961	955	981
Russia	+2/+12	8-10	+7	02	01	03
Saudi Arabia	+3	00	+966	977	999	998
Singapore	+8	001	+65	995	999	995
Slovakia	+1	00	+421	155	158	150
Slovenia	+1	00	+386	112	113	112
South Africa	+2	01	+27	10177	10111	10111
South Korea	+9	001/002	+82	119	112	119
Spain	+1	00	+34	061	091	
Sudan	+3	00	+249	779500	780751	774444
Sweden	+1	00	+46	112	112	112
Switzerland	+1	00	+41	144	117	118
Taiwan	+8	00	+886	119	110	119
Thailand	+7	001	+66	1155	191	199
Tunisia	+1	00	+216	190	197	198
Turkey	+2	00	+90	112	155	110
UAE	+4	00	+971	999	292222	669999
United Kingdom	GMT	00	+44	999	999	999
Uruguay	-3	00	+598	105	109	104
USA	-6/9	011	+1	911	911	911
Venezuela	-4	00	+58	171	171	171
Yugoslavia	+1	99	+381	94	92	93

HOSTELLING INTERNATIONAL

Make your credit card bookings at these centres
Réservez par cartes de crédit aux centres suivants
Reservieren Sie per Kreditkarte bei diesen Zentren
Reserve con tarjeta de crédito en los siguientes centros

English

Australia	☎ (2) 9261 1111
Canada	☎ (800) 663 5777
England & Wales	☎ (1629) 581 418
France	☎ (1) 44 89 87 27
Northern Ireland	☎ (28) 9032 4733
Republic of Ireland	☎ (1) 830 1766
New Zealand	☎ (3) 379 9808
Scotland	☎ (8701) 553 255
Switzerland	☎ (1) 360 1414
USA	☎ (202) 783 6161

Français

Angleterre & Pays de Galles	☎ (1692) 581 418
Australie	☎ (2) 9261 1111
Canada	☎ (800) 663 5777
Écosse	☎ (8701) 553 255
États-Unis	☎ (202) 783 6161
France	☎ (1) 44 89 87 27
Irlande du Nord	☎ (28) 9032 4733
Nouvelle-Zélande	☎ (3) 379 9808
République d'Irlande	☎ (1) 830 1766
Suisse	☎ (1) 360 1414

Deutsch

Australien	☎ (2) 9261 1111
England & Wales	☎ (1629) 581 418
Frankreich	☎ (1) 44 89 87 27
Irland	☎ (1) 830 1766
Kanada	☎ (800) 663 5777
Neuseeland	☎ (3) 379 9808
Nordirland	☎ (28) 9032 4733
Schottland	☎ (8701) 553 255
Schweiz	☎ (1) 360 1414
USA	☎ (202) 783 6161

Español

Australia	☎ (2) 9261 1111
Canadá	☎ (800) 663 5777
Escocia	☎ (8701) 553 255
Estados Unidos	☎ (202) 783 6161
Francia	☎ (1) 44 89 87 27
Inglaterra y Gales	☎ (1629) 581 418
Irlanda del Norte	☎ (28) 9032 4733
Nueva Zelanda	☎ (3) 379 9808
República de Irlanda	☎ (1) 830 1766
Suiza	☎ (1) 360 1414

IBN INTERNATIONAL BOOKING NETWORK

INTERNATIONAL BOOKING NETWORK [IBN] BOOKING CENTRES

The International Booking Network (IBN) enables you to book a bed up to 6 months in advance of your stay (depending on availability) at nearly 300 key hostels around the world. The locations listed below all offer outward bookings by IBN. The hostels in the network are listed within each of the country sections and highlighted in blue. They are also indicated with the symbol [IBN].

CENTRES DE RESERVATION [IBN] (INTERNATIONAL BOOKING NETWORK)

Le réseau international de réservation (International Booking Network - IBN) vous permet de réserver un lit jusqu'à six mois à l'avance (selon les disponibilités), dans près de 300 auberges à travers le monde. Les sites listés ci-dessous vous offrent tous la possibilité d'effectuer des réservations par le biais d'IBN. Les auberges appartenant au réseau IBN sont indiquées en bleu dans le listing des auberges de chaque pays et également par le symbole [IBN].

INTERNATIONAL BOOKING NETWORK [IBN] BUCHUNGSZENTREN

International Booking Network (IBN) ermöglicht Ihnen das Buchen einer Unterkunft bis zu 6 Monaten im voraus (je nach Verfügbarkeit) in ca. 300 der wichtigsten Jugendherbergen rund um den Globus. In den unten aufgelisteten Buchungszentren können internationale Buchungen durch IBN vorgenommen werden. Die im Netzwerk zusammengeschlossenen Jugendherbergen sind innerhalb jeder Ländersektion aufgeführt und blau hervorgehoben. Sie sind auch mit dem Symbol [IBN] gekennzeichnet.

INTERNATIONAL BOOKING NETWORK [IBN] CENTROS DE RESERVAS

La Red Internacional de Reservas IBN le permite reservar una cama hasta 6 meses antes de su estancia (siempre y cuando haya camas disponibles) en casi 300 albergues claves del mundo. Los centros relacionados a continuación ofrecen todos ellos la posibilidad de realizar reservas a través de IBN. Los albergues que pertenecen a la red IBN aparecen impresos en color azul en las listas de albergues de cada país y llevan, además, el símbolo [IBN].

IBN

ARGENTINA

Red Argentina de Alojamiento para Jóvenes
Buenos Aires – National Office
Florida 835, 3rd Floor Of.319, C1005AAQ
Buenos Aires
☎ (54) (11) 4511-8712
✆ (54) (11) 4312-0089
✉ raaj@hostels.org.ar

AUSTRALIA

Australian Youth Hostels Association
Adelaide – YHA South Australia
38 Sturt Street, Adelaide, South Australia 5000
☎ (61) (8) 8231-5583
✆ (61) (8) 8231-4219
✉ yhasa@ozemail.com.au

Brisbane – YHA Queensland
154 Roma Street, Brisbane, Queensland 4000
☎ (61) (7) 3236-1680
✆ (61) (7) 3236-1702
✉ membership@yhaqld.org

Cairns – YHA Queensland
20-24 McLeod Street, Cairns, Queensland 4870
☎ (61) (7) 4051-0772
✆ (61) (7) 4031-3158
✉ cnsyha@yhaqld.org

Canberra – YHA New South Wales
191 Dryandra Street, O'Connor, Canberra, ACT 2602
☎ (61) (2) 6248-9155
✆ (61) (2) 6249-1731
✉ canberra@yhansw.org.au

Darwin - YHA Northern Territory
69 Mitchell Street, Darwin, NT 0801
☎ (61) (8) 8981-6344
✆ (61) (8) 8981-6674
✉ yhant@yhant.org.au

Melbourne – YHA Victoria
Level 1, 377 Little Lonsdale Street,
Melbourne, Victoria 3000
☎ (61) (3) 9670-7991
✆ (61) (3) 9670-9840
✉ yha@yhavic.org.au

Perth – YHA Western Australia
236 William Street, Northbridge, Perth,
Western Australia 6003
☎ (61) (8) 9227-5122
✆ (61) (8) 9227-5123
✉ enquiries@yhawa.com.au

Sydney – YHA New South Wales
GPO Box 5276, 422 Kent St, Sydney,
New South Wales 2001
☎ (61) (2) 9261-1111
✆ (61) (2) 9261-1969
✉ yha@yhansw.org.au

Sydney - travel.com.au
80 Clarence Street, Sydney 2000
☎ (61) (2) 9290-1500
✆ (61) (2) 9262-2774
✉ ibn@travel.com.au

AUSTRIA

Österreichischer Jugendherbergsverband
Graz – ÖJHV YGH
Idlhofgasse 74, A-8020 Graz
☎ (43) (316) 7083
✆ (43) (316) 7083-88
✉ jgh-graz@jgh.at

Graz –Logo Youth Information Service
Karmeliterplatz1, A-8010 Graz
☎ (43) (316) 1799
✆ (43) (316) 877 4900
✉ info@logo.at

Klagenfurt – ÖJHV Regional Office
Neckheimgasse 6, 9020 Klagenfurt
☎ (43) (463) 230019
✆ (43) (463) 230022
✉ oejhv-kaernten@oejhv.or.at

Salzburg –
Kaigasse 24, A5020 Salzburg
☎ (43) (662) 841165
☏ (43) (662) 840164
🌐 jhw.sbg@aon.at

Vienna – ÖJHV National Office
1010 Wien, Gonzagag.22
☎ (43) (1) 5335353
☏ (43) (1) 5350861
🌐 oejhv-wien-travel-service@oejhv.or.at,
oejhv@chello.at

Österreichisches Jugendherbergswerk
Vienna – ÖJHW National Office
1010 Wien, Helferstorferstrasse 4
☎ (43) (1) 5331833
☏ (43) (1) 533183385
🌐 oejhw@oejhw.or.at, travel@supertramp.co.at

BELGIUM

Belgium - Les Auberges de Jeunesse
Brussels – Les AJ National Office
Rue de la Sablonnière 28, B-1000 Bruxelles
☎ (32) (2) 219 5676
☏ (32) (2) 219 1451
🌐 info@laj.be

Belgium - Vlaamse Jeugdherbergcentrale
Antwerp – VJH National Office
Van Stralenstraat 40, B-2060 Antwerpen
☎ (32) (3) 232 7218
☏ (32) (3) 231 8126
🌐 vjh@vjh.be

BRAZIL

Federaçao Brasiliera dos Albergues da Juventude
Curitiba – Regional Office
Rua Padre Agostinho 645, Mercês, Curitiba,
Paraná CEP - 80430-050
☎ (55) (21) 233-2746
☏ (55) (21) 233-2834
🌐 ajcwb@uol.com.br

Porto Alegre – Regional Office
Rua Dos Andradas, 1137 S. 214,
Centro - Porto Alegre, RS CEP: 90020-008
☎ (55) (51) 226-5380
☏ (55) (51) 226-5380
🌐 turjovem@zaz.com.br

Rio de Janeiro – Regional Office
Rua da Assembleia No 10, Sala 1616,
Centro-CEP:20011-000, Rio de Janeiro
☎ (55) (21) 5312234
☏ (55) (21) 5312234
🌐 albergue@microlink.com.br

São Paulo – Regional Office
Rua Sete de Abril, 386 Cj. 22, CEP 01044-908,
Sao Paulo - SP
☎ (55) (11) 2580388
☏ (55) (11) 2580388
🌐 info@alberguesp.com.br

CANADA

Canadian Hostelling Association
Edmonton – Travel Shop
10926 - 88 Avenue, Edmonton, Alberta T6G 0Z1
☎ (1) (780) 439-3089
☏ (1) (780) 433-7781
🌐 travelshop@hostellingintl.ca

Montréal – Boutique Tourisme Jeunesse
4008 Rue St Denis, Montréal, Québec H2W 2M4
☎ (1) (514) 844-0287
☏ (1) (514) 844-5246
🌐 boutiquetjmtl@videotron.net

Montréal – Tourisme Jeunesse
4545 Pierre de Coubertin, C P 1000,
Succursale M, Montréal, Québec H1V 3R2
☎ (1) (514) 252-3117
☏ (1) (514) 252-3119
🌐 info-tj@tourismejeunesse.org

Ottawa – National Office
400-205 Catherine Street, Ottawa, Ontario, K2P 1C3
☎ (1) (613) 237-7884
☏ (1) (613) 237-7868
🌐 info@hostellingintl.ca

IBN

Québec City – Boutique Tourisme Jeunesse
94 Boulevard René-Lévesque Ouest, Québec City,
Québec G1R 2A4
☏ (1) (418) 522-2552
✆ (1) (418) 522-2455
✉ boutiquetjqc@vidoetron.net

Toronto – International Travel
56 Church Street, Toronto, Ontario M5C 2G1
☏ (1) (416) 363-0697 ext.15
✆ (1) (416) 368-6499
✉ ressale@hostellingint-gl.on.ca

Vancouver – Regional Office
134 Abbott Street, Suite 402, Vancouver,
British Colombia, V6B 2K4
☏ (1) (604) 684-7101
✆ (1) (604) 684-7181
✉ info@hihostels.bc.ca

CHILE

*Asociación Chilena de Albergues Turísticos
Juveniles*
Santiago – National Office
Hernando de Aguirre 201,OF 602, Providencia
☏ (56) (2) 2333220
✆ (56) (2) 2333220
✉ hostelling@hostelling.cl

CHINA

*Beijing, Shanghai and Guangdong Youth
Hostel Associations of China*
Guangzhou – c/o National Office
185 Huanshi Xi Road, Guangzhou,
Guangdong Province.
☏ (86) (20) 86677422
✆ (86) (20) 86665039
✉ gdyhac@public.guangzhou.gd.cn

Hong Kong Youth Hostels Association
Hong Kong – National Office
Room 225, Block 19, Shek Kip Mei Estate,
Shamshuipo, Kowloon, Hong Kong
☏ (852) 27881638
✆ (852) 27883105
✉ hkyha@datainternet.com

CROATIA

Croatian Youth Hostel Association
Zagreb – National Office
Dezmanova 9, 10000 Zagreb
☏ (385) (1) 484-7474
✆ (385) (1) 484-7472
✉ hfhs-cms@zg.tel.hr

CZECH REPUBLIC

KMC Club of Young Travellers
Prague – National Office
KMC - Travel Service Booking Centre, Praha 1,
Karolíny Svetlé 30, 110 00 Prague
☏ (420) (2) 22220347
✆ (420) (2) 22220347
✉ kmc@kmc.cz

DENMARK

Danhostel
Copenhagen – National Office
Hostelling International Denmark,
Vesterbrogade 39, DK1620, Copenhagen V
☏ (45) 33313612
✆ (45) 33313626
✉ ldv@danhostel.dk

ECUADOR

Idiomas s.a.
Guayaquil –
Junin 203 y Panama, Floor 2, Office 4, Guayaquil.
☏ (593) (4) 56-4488
✆ (593) (4) 56-6939
✉ idiomas@idiomas.com.ec

ENGLAND & WALES

Youth Hostels Association (England & Wales)
Credit/Debit Card Reservations only –
PO Box 67, Matlock, Derbyshire DE4 3YX
☏ (44) (1629) 581418
📠 (44) (1629) 581062
✉ ibnreservations@yha.org.uk

1st Western Air Travel
Totnes –
1st Western Air Travel, Bickham, Totnes,
Devon, TQ9 7NJ
☏ (44) (870) 3301100
📠 (44) (870) 3301133
✉ info@westernair.co.uk

London - Overseas Visitors Club
OVC House, 41 Longridge Road, Earls Court,
London SW5 9SD
☏ (44) 20 7244 8055
📠 (44) 20 7259 2323
✉ ovclondon@excite.co.uk

ESTONIA

Estonian Youth Hostels Association
Tallin – National Office
Tatari 39-310, EE0001 Tallinn
☏ (372) 6461455
📠 (372) 6461595
✉ eyha@online.ee

FINLAND

Suomen Retkeilymajajärjestö-SRM
Helsinki – National Office
Yrjönkatu 38 B 15, 00100 Helsinki
☏ (358) (9) 565 7150
📠 (358) (9) 565 7150
✉ info@srm.inet.fi

FRANCE

Fédération Unie des Auberges de Jeunesse
Paris – National Office
27 Rue Pajol, 75018 Paris
☏ (33) (1) 44898727
📠 (33) (1) 44898710
✉ fuaj@fuaj.org

Paris – FUAJ Beaubourg
9 Rue Brantome, 75003 Paris
☏ (33) (1) 48047040
📠 (33) (1) 42770329
✉ fuajbeau@caramail.com

GERMANY

Deutsches Jugendherbergswerk
Berlin – Brandenburg Regional Office
Tempelhofer Ufer 32, D-10963 Berlin
☏ (49) (30) 2649520
📠 (49) (30) 2620437
✉ djh-berlin-brandenburg@jugendherberge.de

Detmold – National Office
Deutsches Jugendherbergswerk, Service GmbH,
32754 Detmold
☏ (49) (5231) 7401-1
📠 (49) (5231) 740149
✉ ibn@djh.de

Dresden - Sachsen Regional Office
Maternistrasse 22, 01067 Dresden
☏ (49) (351) 4942211
📠 (49) (351) 4942213
✉ servicecenter@djh-sachsen.de

Düsseldorf – Rheinland Regional Office
Postfach 110301, 40503 Düsseldorf
☏ (49) (211) 5770321
📠 (49) (211) 5770350
✉ service-center@djh-rheinland.de

Hamburg – Nordmark Regional Office
Rennbahnstrasse 100, 22111 Hamburg
☏ (49) (40) 65599529
📠 (49) (40) 65599552
✉ loewel@djh-nordmark.de

IBN

Munich – YH München Booking Center
Wendl-Dietrich-Strasse 20, 80634 München
☎ (49) (89) 131156
✆ (49) (89) 1678745
✉ jhmuenchen@djh-bayern.de

HUNGARY

Magyarországi Ifjusági Szállások
Budapest – Mellow Mood
1134 Budapest, Dorzsa Gyorgy ut 152
☎ (36) (1) 3408585
✆ (36) (1) 3208425
✉ travel@hostels.hu

INDIA

Youth Hostels Association of India
New Delhi - International Hostel
5 Nyaya Marg, Chanakyapuri, New Delhi 110021.
☎ (91) (11) 6116285
✆ (91) (11) 4676349
✉ yhostel@del2.vsnl.net.in

IRELAND - NORTHERN

Hostelling International - Northern Ireland
Belfast – National Office
22 Donegall Road, Belfast, BT12 5JN
☎ (44) (28) 32315435
✆ (44) (28) 32439699
✉ info@hini.org.uk

IRELAND - REPUBLIC

An Oige
Dublin – Booking Centre
61 Mountjoy Street, Dublin 7
☎ (353) (1) 830 4555
✆ (353) (1) 830 5808
✉ mailbox@anoige.ie

ISRAEL

Israel Youth Hostels Association
Jerusalem – National Office
Jerusalem 1 Shazar St, International Convention
Center, PO Box 6001, Jerusalem 91060
☎ (972) (2) 655-8406, 8442
✆ (972) (2) 655-8432
✉ iyhytb@iyha.org.il

ITALY

Assoc Italiana Alberghi per la Gioventu
Bologna – Regional Office
Via dell' Unione n.6/a, 40126 Bologna
☎ (39) (051) 224913
✆ (39) (051) 224913
✉ aig_bo@iperbole.bologna.it

Catania – Local Office
Via Andrea Costa 34/B, 95127 Catania, Sicily
☎ (39) (095) 539853
✆ (39) (095) 539853
✉ aigcatania@iol.it

Florence – Regional Office
Viale Augusto Righi 2/4, 50137 Florence
☎ (39) (055) 600315
✆ (39) (055) 610300

Genoa – Regional Office
Salita Salvatore Viale n 1, Genova
☎ (39) (010) 586407
✆ (39) (010) 586407

Naples – Regional Office
Salita della Grotta a Piedigrotta 23, 80122 Naples
☎ (39) (081) 7612346, 7611215
✆ (39) (081) 7612391

Palermo – Regional Office
Via Houel 5, 90138 Palermo, Sicily
☎ (39) (091) 336595
✆ (39) (091) 336595

Rome – National Office
Via Cavour 44, 00184 Rome
☎ (39) (06) 4871152
✆ (39) (06) 4880492
✉ aig@uni.net

Venice – Regional Office
Calle Castelforte S. Rocco, 3101 San Polo,
30125 Venezia
☎ (39) (041) 5204414
✆ (39) (041) 5204034
✉ hostel@libero.it

JAPAN

Japan Youth Hostels Inc
Kyoto – Kyoto Youth Hostel Association
29 Uzumasa-Nakayama-cho, Ukyo-ku,
Kyoto 616-8191
☎ (81) (75) 462-9185
✆ (81) (75) 462-2289
✉ utano-yh@mbox.kyoto-inet.or.jp

Nagoya-Aichi – Aichi Youth Hostel Association
Aichiken Seinen Kaikan, 18-8 Sakae 1 chome,
Naka-ku, Nagoya 460-0008
☎ (81) (52) 221-6080
✆ (81) (52) 221-6057

Osaka – Osaka Youth Hostel Association
Nankai-Nipponbashi Building 2F, 1-3-19,
Nipponbashi-nishi, Naniwa ku,
Osaka 556-0004
☎ (81) (6) 6633-8621
✆ (81) (6) 6634-0751
✉ yhaosaka@osk3.3web.ne.jp

Tokyo – National Office (JYH)
Suidobashi Nishiguchi Kaikan, 2-20-7,
Misaki-cho, Chiyoda-ku, Tokyo 101-0061
☎ (81) (3) 3288-1417
✆ (81) (3) 3288-1248
✉ info@jyh.or.jp

Tokyo – Tokyo Youth Hostels Association
Saiwai Building, 4 Goban-cho, Chiyoda-Ku,
Tokyo 102-0076
☎ (81) (3) 3261-0191
✆ (81) (3) 3261-0190
✉ tyh@aggre.co.jp

Tokyo-Yoyogi – Tokyo-Yoyogi Youth Hostel
3-1 Yoyogi-Kamizono-cho, Shibuya-ku,
Tokyo 151-0052
☎ (81) (3) 3467-9163
✆ (81) (3) 3467-9417
✉ yoyogi@jyh.gr.jp

KOREA - SOUTH

Korea Youth Hostels Association
Seoul – National Office
Rm 408, Juksun Hyundai Bldg 80, Juksun-Dong,
Jongro-Ku, Seoul 110-052
☎ (82) (2) 725-3031
✆ (82) (2) 725-3113
✉ inform@kyha.or.kr

LITHUANIA

Lithuanian Youth Hostels
Vilnius – National Office
Filaretai Youth Hostel
Filaretu Street 17, 2007 Vilnius
☎ (370) (2) 254627 / 262660
✆ (370) (2) 220149
✉ filaretai@post.omnitel.net

MALAYSIA

Malaysian Youth Hostels Association
Kuala Lumpur – MSL Travel Centre
66, Jalan Putra, 50350 Kuala Lumpur
☎ (60) (3) 4424722
✆ (60) (3) 4433707
✉ msl@po.jaring.my

IBN

MALTA

NSTS Student & Youth Travel
Valletta –
220 St Paul Street, Valletta VLT07
📞 (356) 244983
📠 (356) 230330
📧 nsts@nsts.org

MEXICO

Guadalajara – Mundo Joven Travel Shop
Av. Patria 600 local 13-E, Plaza Amistad,
Guadalajara, Jalisco 45110
📞 (52) (36) 730936
📠 (52) (36) 733656

Mexico City – Mundo Joven Travel Shop
Insurgentes sur 1510-D, Mexico City DF 03920
📞 (52) (5) 6613233
📠 (52) (5) 6631556
📧 hostellingmexico@remaj.com,
productos@mundojoven.com.mx

Mexico City – Viajes Educativos
Insurgentes sur 421 Loc. B-10, Col. H Condesa
c.p. 06170 Mexico DF.
📞 (52) (5) 5740899 / 5740896
📠 (52) (5) 5743521
📧 ve@ve.com.mx

NEW ZEALAND

Auckland – USIT Beyond Travel Centre
18 Shortland Street, Auckland
📞 (64) (9) 379-4224
📠 (64) (9) 366-6275
📧 enquiries@usitbeyond.co.nz

Youth Hostels Association of New Zealand
Christchurch - National Office
P O Box 436, Level 3, Union House,
193 Cashel Street, Christchurch
📞 (64) (3) 379-9970
📠 (64) (3) 365-4476
📧 info@yha.org.nz

NORWAY

Norske Vandrerhjem
Oslo – National Office
Dronningensgate 26, PB 364 Sentrum, N-0102 Oslo
📞 (47) (23) 139300
📠 (47) (23) 139350
📧 hostels@online.no

PERU

Asociación Peruana de Albergues Turísticos Juveniles
Lima – National Office
AJ Turistico Internacional,
Av Casimiro Ulloa 328, Lima 18
📞 (51) (1) 2423068
📠 (51) (1) 4448187
📧 hostell@terra.com.pe

PORTUGAL

Movijovem
Lisbon – National Office
Av Duque de Avila 137, 1069-017 Lisbon
📞 (351) 213596000
📠 (351) 213596001
📧 movijovem@movijovem.pt,
reservas@movijovem.pt

RUSSIA

St Petersburg – Russian Youth Hostels,
Sindbad Travel
3rd Sovetskaya Ulitsa 28, St Petersburg
📞 (7) (812) 327-8384
📠 (7) (812) 329-8019
📧 ryh@ryh.ru

Moscow – Blue Chip Travel
Chistoprudny Blvd. 12A, Suite 628, 101000 Moscow
📞 (7) (095) 916-9364
📠 (7) (095) 924-4968
📧 info@world4u.ru

Moscow – STAR Travel
Leningradskypr. 80/21, 3rd Floor,
125178 Moscow
☏ (7) (095) 797-9555
📠 (7) (095) 797-9554
✉ star@glasnet.ru

SCOTLAND

Scottish Youth Hostels Association
Stirling – National Office
7 Glebe Crescent, Stirling, FK8 2JA
☏ (44) (541) 553255
📠 (44) (1786) 891350
✉ reservations@syha.org.uk

SINGAPORE

Singapore – STA Travel Pte Ltd
33A Cuppage Road, Cuppage Terrace,
Singapore 229458
☏ (65) 7377188
📠 (65) 7372591
✉ osu@statravel.com.sg

SLOVAKIA

CKM SYTS
Bratislava – CKM 2000 Travel
Vysoka 32, 814 45 Bratislava
☏ (421) (7) 52731024
📠 (421) (7) 52731025
✉ ckm2000@ckm.sk

SOUTH AFRICA

Hostels Association of South Africa
Cape Town – National Office
3rd Floor, St Georges House, 73 St Georges Mall,
Cape Town, 8001
☏ (27) (21) 242511
📠 (27) (21) 244119
✉ info@hisa.org.za

Durban – Africa Wonderland Tours
19 Smith Street, Durban 4001, Natal
☏ (27) (31) 3324944
📠 (27) (31) 3324551
✉ wonderland.durban@pixie.co.za

Johannesburg – Africa Wonderland Tours
Inchanga Ranch, Inchanga Road, Witkoppen,
4 Ways, Johannesburg
☏ (27) (11) 708-1459
📠 (27) (11) 708-1464
✉ wonderland@pixie.co.za

SPAIN

Red Española de Albergues Juveniles
Alicante – IVAJ
Pl. San Cristobal, 8-10, 03002 Alicante
☏ (34) (965) 144789
📠 (34) (965) 144789
✉ turivaj@ivaj.gva.es

Barcelona – ICSJ Youth Tourism
Passeig De Mare De Deu Del Coll 41-51, 08023
Barcelona, Catalunya
☏ (34) (93) 2105151
📠 (34) (93) 2100798
✉ tujcom@usa.net

Barcelona/TUJUCA
c/Rocafort 116-122, 08015 Barcelona
☏ (34) (93) 4838363
📠 (34) (93) 4838347
✉ atencio_@tujuca.com

Madrid – TIVE Office
C/Fernando el Catolico 88, 28015 Madrid
☏ (34) (91) 5437412
📠 (34) (91) 5440062
✉ tive.juventud@comadrid.es

Valencia – Turivaj
c/ Del Hospital, 11, 46001 Valencia
☏ (34) (96) 3869952
📠 (34) (96) 3869903
✉ turivaj@ivaj.gva.es

IBN

SWEDEN

Swedish Touring Club
Stockholm – National Office
Box 25, 101 20 Stockholm
☎ (46) (8) 4632100
✆ (46) (8) 6781958
✉ info@stfturist.se

SWITZERLAND

Schweizer Jugendherbergen
Zurich – National Office
Schaffhauserstrasse 14, Postfach, CH-8042 Zurich
☎ (41) (1) 360-1414
✆ (41) (1) 360-1460
✉ bookingoffice@youthhostel.ch

TAIWAN

Kaohsiung City –
Kaohsiung International Youth Hostel
120 Wen wu First Street, Kaohsiung
☎ (886) (7) 2012477
✆ (886) (7) 2156322
✉ kokiyh@ms57.hinet.net

Taipei – Chinese Taipei Youth Hostel Association
12F-2, 50 Chung Hsiao West Road, Sec 1, Taipei
☎ (886) (2) 23317272
✆ (886) (2) 23317272
✉ aabc@ms8.hinet.net

Taipei – Federal Vacation
7F, 41 Tung-Hsin Rd, Taipei 110
☎ (886) (2) 87681133
✆ (886) (2) 87681515
✉ tci@tptsl.seed.net.tw

Taipei –
Kang Wen Culture & Education Foundation
1208A/12F, 142, Chung-Hsiao E Rd, Sec 4, Taipei
☎ (886) (2) 27751138
✆ (886) (2) 27212784
✉ gftours@tptsl.seed.net.tw

THAILAND

Thai Youth Hostels Association
Bangkok – National Office
25/14 Phitsanulok Road, Se-Sao Thewet, Dusit,
BKK 10300
☎ (66) (2) 628-7413, 7414, 7415
✆ (66) (2) 628-7416
✉ bangkok@tyha.org

TURKEY

Instanbul – Gençtur Tourism & Travel
Istiklai Cad. Zambak Sok. 15/5,
Taksim 80080, Istanbul
☎ (90) (212) 2492515
✆ (90) (212) 2492554
✉ ibn@genctur.com

UNITED STATES

Hostelling International – American Youth Hostels
Boston –
Eastern New England Council Travel Centre
1105 Commonwealth Avenue, Boston, MA 02215
☎ (1) (617) 719-0900 ext. 10
✆ (1) (617) 719-0904
✉ travelctr_hienec@juno.com

Boulder –
Rocky Mountain Council Travel Centre
1310 College Avenue, Suite 315, Boulder,
Colorado 80302
☎ (1) (303) 442-1166
✆ (1) (303) 442-4453
✉ hi-rocky@indra.com

Los Angeles – Los Angeles Council Travel Centre
1434 Second Street, Santa Monica, CA 90401
☎ (1) (310) 393-3413
✆ (1) (310) 393-1769
✉ hiayhla@aol.com

New York – HI-New York Hostel Shop
891 Amsterdam Avenue, New York, NY 10025
☎ (1) (212) 932-2300
🖷 (1) (212) 932-2574
📧 reserve@hinewyork.org

Philadelphia –
Delaware Valley Council Travel Centre
624 South 3rd Street, Philadelphia, PA 19147
☎ (1) (215) 925-6004
🖷 (1) (215) 925-4874
📧 hidvc@hi-dvc.org

San Francisco –
Golden Gate Council Travel Centre
425 Divisadero Street, Suite 307, San Francisco,
CA 94117-2242
☎ (1) (415) 701-1320
🖷 (1) (415) 863-3865
📧 travelsf@norcalhostels.org

St Louis – Gateway Council Travel Centre
7187 Manchester Road, St Louis, MO 63143-2450
☎ (1) (314) 644-4660
🖷 (1) (314) 644-6192
📧 info@gatewayhiayh.org

Washington DC – HI-AYH National Office
☎ (1) (202) 783-6161
🖷 (1) (202) 783-6171
📧 hiayhserv@hiayh.org

URUGUAY

Asociacion de Alberguistas del Uruguay
Montevideo – National Office
Pablo del Maria 1583/008, 11200 Montevideo
☎ (598) (2) 400-4245
🖷 (598) (2) 400-1326
📧 aau@adinet.com.uy

"Own only what you can carry with you; know language, know countries, know people. Let your memory be your travel bag."

"Ne possède que ce que tu peux emporter avec toi; connais les langues, connais les pays, connais les gens. Que ta mémoire te serve de sac de voyage."

„Besitze nur, was du mitnehmen kannst; lerne Sprache, Länder, Leute kennen. Lass deine Erinnerung deine Reisetasche sein."

"Posee solamente lo que puedas llevar contigo; conoce los idiomas, conoce los países, conoce a la gente. Deja que tu memoria sea tu bolso de viaje."

Alexander Solzhenitsyn

International Booking Network

The advantages are clear

www.iyhf.org

HOSTELLING INTERNATIONAL ®

IBN INTERNATIONAL BOOKING NETWORK

Algeria

ALGERIE

ALGERIEN

ARGELIA

**Fédération Algérienne des Auberges de Jeunesse,
Camp de Jeunes Analj
Zeralda.**

☎ (213) (2) 329011
🖷 (213) (2) 329024

A copy of the Hostel Directory for this Country can be obtained from:
The National Office.

Capital:	Algiers	**Population:**	30,000,000
Language:	Arabic	**Size:**	2,381,741 sq km
Currency:	DA (dinar)	**Telephone Country Code:**	213

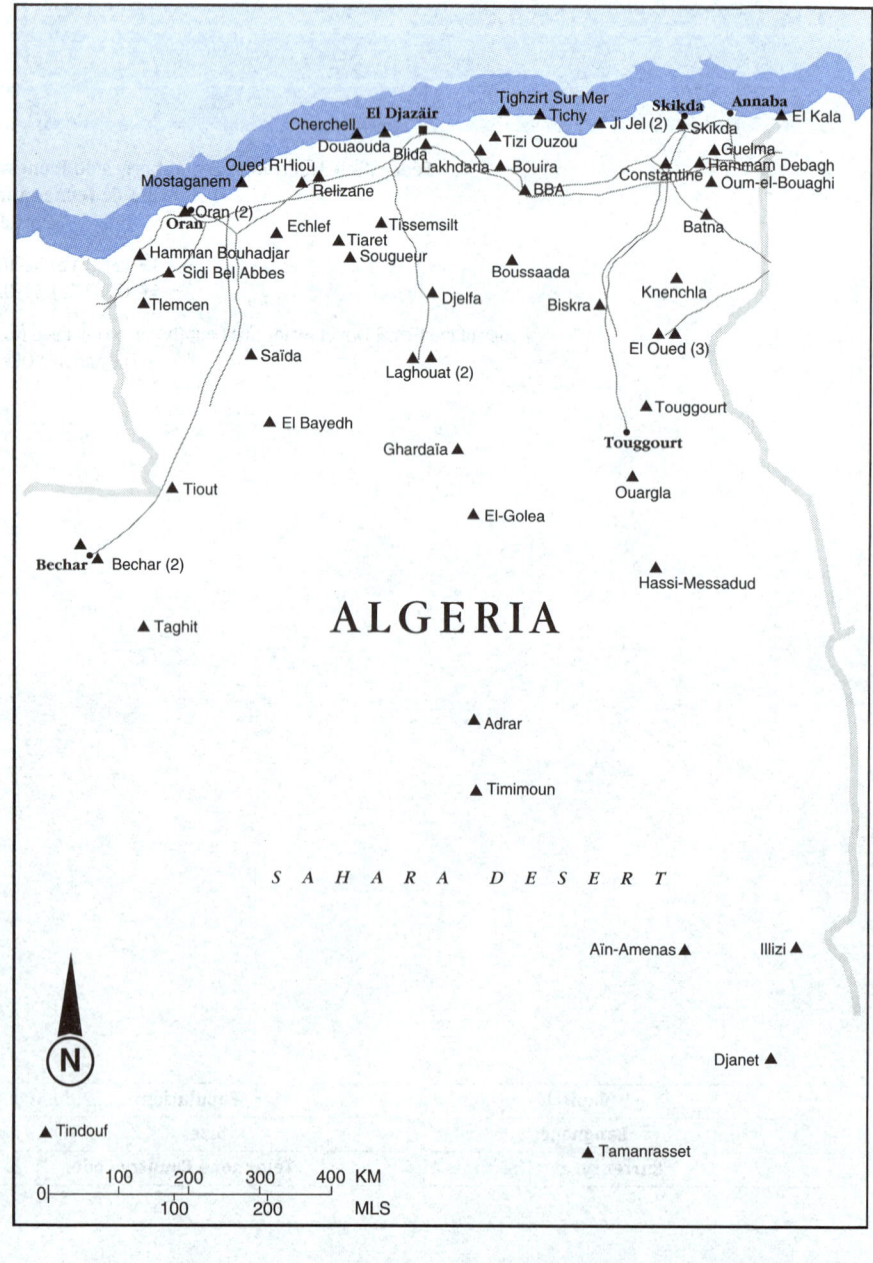

Cherchell
El Djazäir
Douaouda
Blida
Lakhdaria
Oued R'Hiou
Relizane
Mostaganem
Oran (2)
Oran
Echlef
Tiaret
Tissemsilt
Sougueur
Hamman Bouhadjar
Sidi Bel Abbes
Tlemcen
Saïda
Djelfa
El Bayedh
Laghouat (2)
Ghardaïa
Tiout
El-Golea
Bechar
Bechar (2)
Taghit

Tighzirt Sur Mer
Tichy
Tizi Ouzou
Bouira
BBA
Boussaada

Ji Jel (2)
Skikda
Annaba
El Kala
Skikda
Guelma
Hammam Debagh
Constantine
Oum-el-Bouaghi
Batna
Knenchla
Biskra
El Oued (3)
Touggourt
Touggourt
Ouargla
Hassi-Messadud

ALGERIA

Adrar

Timimoun

S A H A R A   D E S E R T

Aïn-Amenas
Illizi

Djanet

N

Tindouf

Tamanrasset

| | 100 | 200 | 300 | 400 | KM |
0 | | 100 | | 200 | | MLS |

English

Hostels are located in cities, in the countryside, on the coast and on hills/mountains.

Price range

Price range DA 100. 🖵.

Rooms and Reservations

R during Jan-Apr, Jul, Aug, Oct-Dec. (👪). Reservations via Hostel by ❶ ❻. Hostels are single sex only. Smoking rooms are available.

Guests

Membership Card and Passport/Photo ID are required. The maximum stay is 7 days. 👪 welcome. Group bookings via Hostel or National Office by ❶ ❻.

Open times

Main hostels: open 🖭, 08:00-22:00hrs. Reception open: 08:00-22:00hrs. Resident manager. **Other hostels:** open 🖭, 08:00-22:00hrs. Reception open: 08:00-22:00hrs. Resident manager.

Meals

🍽 BLD **R** For individuals & for 👪. 🚬.

Travelling around

For ease of travel use ✈ 🚌 Self-Drive.

Travel/Activity Packages

Tours/sightseeing, cycling/mountain biking and walking/trekking packages available. Package bookings via Hostel or National Office by ❶ ❻.

Passports and Visas

Passport and Visa required.

Health

All medical treatment is free.

Français

Les auberges sont situées dans les villes, à la campagne, sur le littoral et à la montagne.

Tarifs des nuitées

Tarifs des nuitées 100 DA. 🖵.

Chambres et réservations

R jan-avril, juil, août, oct-déc. (👪). Réservations via l'auberge par ❶ ❻. Les auberges sont uniquement non-mixtes. Des chambres pour fumeurs sont disponibles.

Usagers

La carte d'adhérent ainsi que le passeport/pièce d'identité avec photo sont à présenter. La durée maximale du séjour est de 7 jours. Accueil des 👪. Réservations pour groupes via l'auberge ou le Bureau National par ❶ ❻.

Horaires d'ouverture

Grandes auberges: ouvertes 🖭, entre 8h-22h. Accueil ouvert entre 8h-22h. Gérant réside sur place. **Autres auberges:** ouvertes 🖭, entre 8h-22h. Accueil ouvert entre 8h-22h. Gérant réside sur place.

Repas

🍽 BLD **R** Pour individuels & pour 👪. 🚬.

Déplacements

Modes de transport recommandés ✈ 🚌 Voiture.

Forfaits Voyages/Activités

Forfaits circuits touristiques, cyclotourisme/VTT et randonnées pédestres disponibles. Réservations des forfaits via l'auberge ou le Bureau National par ❶ ❻.

Passeports et visas

Passeport et visa obligatoires.

Santé

Tous les soins médicaux sont gratuits.

Deutsch

Herbergen befinden sich in Städten, auf dem Land, an der Küste und in Bergen/Gebirgen.

Preisspanne

Preisspanne 100 DA. 🖳.

Zimmer und Reservierungen

🄡 während Jan-Apr, Jul, Aug, Okt-Dez. (👪). Reservierungen über Herberge per ❶ ❻. Herbergen sind nur Single Sex. Es gibt Zimmer für Raucher.

Gäste

Mitgliedsausweis und Reisepass/ Personalausweis sind erforderlich. Der maximale Aufenthalt beträgt 7 Tage. 👪 willkommen. Gruppenbuchungen über Herberge oder Landesverband per ❶ ❻.

Öffnungszeiten

Hauptherbergen: Zugang 🖳, 08:00-22:00Uhr. Rezeption zwischen 08:00-22:00Uhr. Herbergsmanager wohnt im Haus. **Andere Herbergen:** Zugang 🖳, 08:00-22:00Uhr. Rezeption zwischen 08:00-22:00Uhr. Herbergsmanager wohnt im Haus.

Mahlzeiten

🍽 BLD 🄡 Für Einzelreisende & für 👪. ☂.

Reisen im Land

Reisen ist einfach mit ✈ 🚐 Selbstfahrer.

Reise-/Aktivitäten-Packages

Touren/sightseeing, Fahrrad/Mountainbiking und wandern/trekking-Packages erhältlich.

Package-Buchungen über Herberge oder Landesverband per ❶ ❻.

Reisepässe und Visa

Reisepass/Einreisevisum erforderlich.

Gesundheit

Alle medizinischen Behandlungen sind kostenlos.

Español

Los albergues están situados en las ciudades, el campo, la costa y la montaña.

Tarifas mínima y máxima

Tarifas mínima y máxima 100 DA. 🖳.

Habitaciones y Reservas

🄡 en ene-abr, jul, ago, oct-dic. (👪). Reservas a través del albergue por ❶ ❻. Los albergues son sólo para hombres o mujeres. Los albergues disponen de habitaciones para fumadores.

Huéspedes

Los huéspedes deben presentar su Carnet de Alberguista y su pasaporte o carnet de identidad. La estancia máxima es de 7 días. Se admiten 👪. Reservas de grupo a través del albergue o la Asociación Nacional por ❶ ❻.

Horarios y fechas de apertura

Albergues principales - abiertos 🖳, 08:00-22:00h. Horario de recepción: 08:00-22:00h. Gerente residente. **Otros albergues** - abiertos 🖳, 08:00-22:00h. Horario de recepción: 08:00-22:00h. Gerente residente.

Comidas

🍽 BLD 🄡 Para individuales y para 👪. ☂.

Desplazamientos

Transportes recomendados: ✈ 🚌
Automóvil.

Viajes Combinados con Actividades

Viajes combinados con visitas turísticas,
cicloturismo/bicicleta de montaña y
senderismo. Reserva de viajes combinados a
través del albergue o la Asociación Nacional por
❶ ❶.

Pasaportes y Visados

Pasaporte y visado obligatorios.

Información Sanitaria

Asistencia médica gratuita.

"He who would travel happily must travel light."

"Celui qui veut voyager joyeusement doit voyager légèrement."

„Wer glücklich reisen will, sollte nur wenig Gepäck mitnehmen."

"El que quiera viajar feliz debe viajar ligero de equipaje."

Antoine de Saint-Exupéry

Location/Address	Telephone No. Fax No.	Beds	Opening Dates	Facilities
▲ **Adrar** - Centre-Ville Adrar-Centre-Ville, 01000 Adrar.	☏ (7) 960899	50	🗓12	⬭ P ▣
▲ **Aïn-Amenas** - Aïn-Amenas BP140, Aïn-Amenas, Wilaya Illizi.	☏ (9) 438159 🖷 (9) 438159	50	🗓12	ᵻᵻᵻ 🍽 (R) ♿ P ☕
▲ **Annaba** - Centre-Ville Sidi Brahim Annaba, 23000 Wilaya d'Annaba.	☏ (8) 844983	50	🗓12	⬭ P
▲ **Batna** - Centre-Ville Hai-Enasr-Cite Du S Juillet, Batna.	☏ (4) 869600 🖷 (4) 869600	50	🗓12	(R) ⬭
▲ **Béchar** ex Cantine Scolaire, Cité Riadi, 08000 Béchar.	☏ (7) 810844	50	🗓12	⬭ P ▣
▲ **Béchar** - Centre Ville Hai Essalem.	☏ (7) 819386	50	🗓12	ᵻᵻᵻ 🍽 ⬭ P
▲ **Biskra** - Centre-Ville Cité des Moudjahidines, Biskra.	☏ (4) 745841	50	🗓12	ᵻᵻᵻ 🍽 ⬭ P ▣
▲ **Blida** Route du Nouveau Stade, Blida.	☏ (3) 416098 🖷 (3) 416098	50	🗓12	ᵻᵻᵻ 🍽 (R) 0.4N P ☕
△ *Bordj-Bou-Arreridj* - *Parc Attraction* *Ave du 24 Avril, Route de Setif,* *Bordj-Bou-Arreridj.*	☏ (5) 685687	30	🗓12	ᵻᵻᵻ 🍽 0.5E ⬭ P
△ *Boussaada* - *Centre-Ville* *Route de Biskra, BP 23, Wilaya de M'Sila.*	☏ (5) 522258	50	🗓12	⬭ P
▲ **Cherchell** - Centre-Ville Route de Tenes, Wilaya de Tipasa.	☏ (1) 439752 🖷 (1) 439752	50	🗓12	ᵻᵻᵻ 🍽 (R) ⬭ P ▣
▲ **Constantine** - Centre-Ville MJ Cité Filali, Constantine.	☏ (4) 926186	60	🗓12	ᵻᵻᵻ 🍽 ⬭
▲ **Djanet** - Aj du Tassili Auberge de Jeunesse, Djanet, Wilaya D'illizi.		50	🗓12	ᵻᵻᵻ 🍽 0.2NE P ▣ ☕
▲ **Djelfa** - Centre-Ville Cite du 5 Juillet, Centre Parc Omnisport.	☏ (3) 873205	50	🗓12	ᵻᵻᵻ 🍽 (R) P ▣ ☕
△ *Douaouda-Marine* - *La Sauge* *23 Rue Bouzar Boulem, BP10,* *42445 Wilaya de Tipaza.*	☏ (1) 409268	40	🗓12	⬭ ▣
△ *Elbayedh* - *Centre-Ville* *Elbayedh Centreville.*	☏ (7) 718825	50	🗓12	ᵻᵻᵻ 🍽 ⬭ P
▲ **Echlef Centre Ville** - Gare Ferroviaire Echlef (Gare Ferroviaire).	☏ (3) 777279	50	🗓12	ᵻᵻᵻ 🍽 ⬭ P
△ *El-Golea* *Auberge de Jeunesse, El-Golea,* *Wilaya de Ghardaïa.*	☏ (9) 815781	50	🗓12	ᵻᵻᵻ 🍽 ⬭ P ▣ ☕
△ *El-Kala* - *Centre-Ville* *Cité du 19 Juin, Wilaya de Tarf 36100.*	☏ (8) 661237	40	🗓12	⬭
▲ **El-Oued** - Houari Boumediene AJ El-Oued, BP 151 - Zone Industrielle, Route de Tebessa, El-Oued.	☏ (4) 228196	50	🗓12	ᵻᵻᵻ 🍽 ♿ ⬭ P ▣
▲ **El-Oued** - AJ Taleb el Arabi El-Oued.	☏ (4) 229521	50	🗓12	ᵻᵻᵻ 🍽 ♿ ⬭ P

Location/Address	Telephone No. Fax No.	Beds	Opening Dates	Facilities
▲ Ghardaïa - Daïa-Ben-Dahoua BP74 Daïa-Ben-Dahoua, RP 85CTR.	☎ (9) 871884 📠 (9) 871884	50	🗓	[10 S]
▲ Guelma - Centre-Ville Rue Gahdour Tahar BP195.	☎ (8) 205953	42	🗓	
△ *Hammam Boubadjar - Centre-Ville* *Wilaya de Aïn-Temouchent.*	☎ (7) 636706 📠 (7) 635406	100	🗓	
△ *Hamam Debagh - Haman Debagh* *Hamam Debagh.*	☎ (8) 228765	50	🗓	[25 NE]
▲ Hassi Messaoud - Centre-Ville Hassi - Messaoud Centre.		50	🗓	
△ *Jijel - AJ Taher* *Rue du 1er Novembre, Taher, Wilaya de Jijel, BP 106.*	☎ (5) 449192	70	🗓	
▲ Laghouat - Centre-Ville Rue Emir Khaled, Wilaya de Laghouat.	☎ (9) 922302 📠 (9) 931264	48	🗓	
△ *Laghouat - Aj du Stade* *Route de Ghardaia, Laghouat.*	☎ (9) 934512	60	🗓	
△ *Khenchela - Ai Silane-Khenchla* *Auberge de Jeunesse Aïn Silane.*	☎ (4) 322803	80	🗓	
▲ Mostaganem - Salamandre Plage Salamandre, Mostaganem.	☎ (6) 265263 📠 (6) 265263	50	🗓	
△ *Nakhla - Les Dunes* *APC Nakhla, Wilaya El-Oued 39180.*	☎ (4) 205822 📠 (4) 205154	50	🗓	
△ *Oran - Seddikia* *AJ Oran, 3 rue Benadjila Labouari, Seddikia, Wilaya d'Oran.*	☎ (6) 533125	40	🗓	
△ *Oran - Centre-Ville* *AJ Oran, 19 rue Maoued Ahmed, Oran.*	☎ (6) 408026 📠 (6) 408299	40	🗓	
▲ Ouargla - Centre-Ville AJ Rose des Sables, Ave de la Palestine, Route de Ghardaïa, Ouargla.	☎ (9) 713301 📠 (9) 715680	40	🗓	
▲ Relizane - Oued Rhiou.R. Zeghloul.	☎ (6) 976122 📠 (6) 976996	50	🗓	
▲ Sidi Belabes - Centre-Ville Rue du 17 Octobre.	☎ (7) 565858	80	🗓	
▲ Skikda - Centre-Ville Cite Freres Saker.	☎ (8) 755418 📠 (8) 755418	50	🗓	[0.3 N]
▲ Taghit - L'Erg Wilaya de Bechar.		50	🗓	
△ *Tamanrasset - Centre-Ville-Tabagart* *Ex centre culturel, Quartier Tabagart, BP458.*	☎ (9) 332004	50	🗓	
▲ Tiaret - Centre-Ville Auberge de Jeunesse, Centre Ville, Tiaret.	☎ (7) 429762	50	🗓	[1 NE]
▲ Tichy - AJ Du Rivage AJ Tichy, Wilaya de Bejaïa.	☎ (5) 235460 📠 (5) 235460	40	🗓	[1 S]

Location/Address	Telephone No. Fax No.	Beds	Opening Dates	Facilities
▲ **Timimoun** - Timimoun Centre-Ville, Timimoun, Wilaya Adrar.	☏ (7) 904394 📠 (7) 904394	50	📇	⚇ 🍽 🄁 0.1 S ♿ 🅿 🔲
▲ **Tindouf** - Centre-Ville Tindouf Centre.	☏ (7) 932562, (7) 932510, (7) 921466 📠 (7) 921466	50	📇	⚇ 🍽 🗝 🅿
▲ **Tiout** - AJ De La Palmerais Wilaya de Naama.	☏ (7) 771330	50	📇	⚇ 🍽 ♿ 🗝 🅿
▲ **Tissemsilt** - Centre-Ville Arib-Djillali, Tissemsilt.	☏ (7) 479131 📠 (7) 499592	50	📇	⚇ 🍽 🄁 0.7 S ♿ 🅿 ☕
▲ **Tlemcen** - Centre-Ville Quartier Kebbasse Tlemcen.	☏ (7) 207860 📠 (7) 207845	50	📇	⚇ 🍽 🄁 ♿ 🅿 🔲 ☕
▲ **Touggourt** - Kheir-Eddine BP54-Touggourt 30200, W Ouargla.	☏ (9) 682129 📠 (9) 674709	80	📇	🍽 🗝 🅿 🔲

YOUTH HOSTEL ACCOMMODATION
OUTSIDE THE ASSURED STANDARDS SCHEME

Location/Address	Telephone No. Fax No.	Beds	Opening Dates	Facilities
Illizi - Centre-Ville AJ Tassili, Illizi 33000.	☏ (9) 421235	50	📇	⚇ 🍽 🗝
Tiaret - Sougueur AJ Machou Ahmed, Sougueur, 14000 W Tiaret.	☏ (7) 288133	100	📇	🗝 🅿 🔲

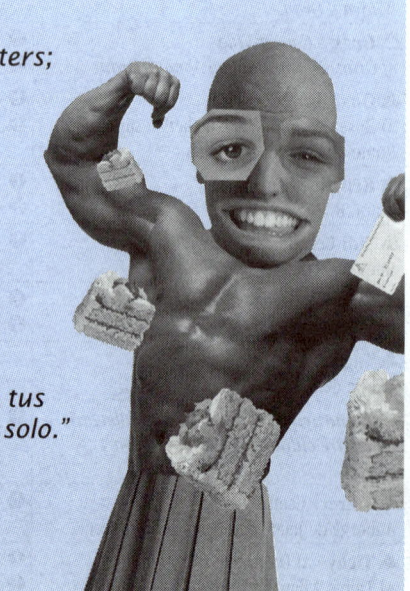

*"Travel only with thy equals or thy betters;
if there are none, travel alone."*

*"Ne voyage qu'avec tes égaux ou tes
supérieurs; si tu n'en as pas, voyage
tout seul."*

*„Reise nur mit deinesgleichen oder
Höherstehenden; wenn es keine gibt,
reise allein."*

*"Viaja solamente con tus iguales o con tus
superiores; si no tienes ninguno, viaja solo."*

The Dhammapada

Australia

AUSTRALIE
AUSTRALIEN
AUSTRALIA

YHA Australia
PO Box 314,
Camperdown 1450,
New South Wales,
Australia.

☎ (61) (2) 9565-1699
🖷 (61) (2) 9565-1325
🄴 yha@yha.org.au
🖳 www.yha.com.au

A copy of the Hostel Directory for this Country can be obtained from:
The National Office

Capital:	Canberra	**Population:**	18,600,000
Language:	English	**Size:**	7,686,848 sq km
Currency:	Australian dollar	**Telephone Country Code:**	61

TASMANIA

Stanley▲
George Town
Devonport▲ ▲Bridport
▲Wingaleah
Launceston ▲ St Helens
Deloraine ●
Great Lake
Cradle Mountain▲ ▲Bicheno
Queenstown● ▲Coles Bay
Strahan▲ Oatlands▲ Swansea
Mt Field National Park▲ ▲Triabunna
Hobart▲ ●**Hobart**
Huon Valley▲▲
Lune River▲ ▲Port Arthur
▲Bruny Island

Darwin●
Darwin
▲Mary River
Adelaide River▲ ▲Kakadu
Pine Creek▲

▲Kununurra

Broome▲

Port Hedland●

▲Exmouth

L. Mackay

Monkey Mia/Shark Bay▲
▲Denham

GIBSON DESERT

WESTERN AUSTRALIA

Ayers Rock
●▲

●Geraldton
Dongara▲

Lancelin▲
Rottnest Island▲ ▲**Perth**
Fremantle▲ Perth
Bunbury▲

Kalgoorlie
●

▲Northam

G R E A T   V I C T O R I A   D E S E R T

▲Dunsborough
Porongurup▲
Augusta▲ ▲Esperance
Pemberton▲ ▲Walpole ▲Albany

| 200 | 400 | 600 | 800 | 1000 | KM |
0
| 200 | 400 | 600 | MLS |

N

Kakadu

Katherine

Cooktown
Cape Tribulation
Port Douglas

Cairns
Cairns

NORTHERN TERRITORY

Mt Surprise
Mission Beach
Cardwell

Magnetic Island
Townsville

Tennant Creek

Airlie Beach
Mackay

Alice Springs
Alice Springs
Kings Canyon

QUEENSLAND

Rockhampton
Great Keppel Island

Kroombit
Bundaberg
Hervey Bay
Fraser Island
Rainbow Beach
Noosa
Maroochydore

Charleville

Brisbane
Brisbane
Springbrook
Surfers
Paradise
Gold Coast

Mt Warning/Murwillumbah
Tenterfield
Byron Bay
Byron Bay
Lennox Head

L. Eyre

SOUTH AUSTRALIA

Ballina

L. Torrens

NEW SOUTH WALES

Armidale
Bellingen
Coffs Harbour
Port Macquarite

Tamworth

Broken Hill
Broken Hill

Scone
Forster

Quorn/Flinders Ranges

Girvan
Terrigal
Newcastle
Shoal Bay

Port Pirie

Dubbo

Sydney (4)
Sydney - Pittwater
Sydney Collaroy

Blue Mountains/Katoomba
Sydney

Mildura
Murray
Adelaide
Adelaide
Murray Bridge
Victor Harbor
Port Elliot
Kangaroo Island

Bundanoon
Garie Beach
Gerringong

Canberra
Canberra
Batemans Bay

Albury

VICTORIA
Echuca
Thredbo
Narooma
Bega
Merimbula
Mallacoota
Lakes Entrance

Bendigo
Ballarat
Daylesford
Taggerty
Mount Buller
Gelantipy

Robe
Halls Gap
Bonnie Doon

Melbourne
Melbourne

Port Fairy
Queenscliff
Lorne
Sorrento
Phillip Island
Port Campbell
Apollo Bay

English

YHA Australia offers you 150 of the best places to stay in Australia, from the beach to the bush to the cities. Advance booking is generally recommended all year, but especially from Nov-Feb along the east coast and Tasmania, and from Jun-Sept in the Northern Territory and North Queensland. Hostels are located in cities, in the countryside, on the coast and on hills/mountains.

Price range

Price range A$ 15-20.

Rooms and Reservations

Ⓡ during Jan, Feb, Jun-Aug, Nov, Dec. (All Rooms). Reservations via ⒤ⒷⓃ ☖ or Hostel by ❶ ❻ ❸. All hostels are non-smoking.

Guests

Membership Card is required. The maximum stay is 14 days. Age limits may apply for children - check with hostel. ♦♦♦ welcome. Group bookings via ⒤ⒷⓃ ☖ or Hostel by ❶ ❻ ❸.

Open times

Main hostels: open 🗓, 🕐. Reception open: 🕐. Resident manager. **Other hostels:** open 🗓, 🕐. Reception open: 08:00-22:00hrs. Resident manager.

Meals

🍴 B For individuals & for ♦♦♦. ♂.

Discounts

HI Member Discounts available - see discounts section and www.iyhf.org or www.yha.com.au.

Travelling around

Limitations exist in some areas due to large distances. However the large number of travel options make covering these distances easy. For ease of travel use ✈ 🚌 ⛴ 🚍 Self-Drive. International Driving Licence may be required - check with the nearest embassy or consulate.

Travel/Activity Packages

Tours/sightseeing and accommodation/transport packages available. Package bookings via ☖.

Passports and Visas

Passport, Photo ID and Visa required.

Health

Vaccination certificates required. Medical insurance is recommended.

Français

La YHA Australia vous propose 150 des meilleurs lieux de séjour en Australie, de la plage à la brousse en passant par ses plus belles villes. Il est généralement conseillé de réserver a l'avance toute l'année, mais surtout entre novembre et février, sur la côte est et la Tasmanie, et de juin à septembre dans le Territoire du Nord et le North Queensland. Les auberges sont situées dans les villes, à la campagne, sur le littoral et à la montagne.

Tarifs des nuitées

Tarifs des nuitées 15-20 A$.

Chambres et réservations

Ⓡ jan, fév, juin-août, nov, déc. (Toutes chambres). Réservations via ⒤ⒷⓃ ☖ ou l'auberge par ❶ ❻ ❸. Toutes les auberges sont non-fumeurs.

Usagers

La carte d'adhérent est à présenter. La durée maximale du séjour est de 14 jours. Il est possible que des limites d'âge soient en vigueur pour les enfants - vérifiez auprès de l'auberge. Accueil des 👪. Réservations pour groupes via ⟨IBN⟩ 🖥 ou l'auberge par ❶ ❷ ❸.

Horaires d'ouverture

Grandes auberges: ouvertes 🔲, 🕐. Accueil ouvert 🕐. Gérant réside sur place. **Autres auberges:** ouvertes 🔲, 🕐. Accueil ouvert entre 8h-22h. Gérant réside sur place.

Repas

🍽 B Pour individuels & pour 👪. 🍳.

Remises

Remises pour les adhérents HI - voir la section "Remises" et notre site: www.iyhf.org ou www.yha.com.au.

Déplacements

Il existe des limitations dans certaines zones à cause des grandes distances. Néanmoins, grâce au vaste choix de transports à votre disposition, franchir ces distances est chose facile. Modes de transport recommandés ✈ 🚌 ⛴ 🚐 Voiture. Un permis de conduire international pourra vous être exigé. Vérifiez auprès de l'ambassade ou du consulat le plus proche.

Forfaits Voyages/Activités

Forfaits circuits touristiques et hébergement/ transport disponibles. Réservations des forfaits via 🖥.

Passeports et visas

Passeport, pièce d'identité avec photo et visa obligatoires.

Santé

Les certificats de vaccination sont obligatoires. Une assurance médicale de voyage est conseillée.

Deutsch

YHA Australia bietet Ihnen 150 der besten Aufenthaltsplätze in Australien, vom Strand zum Busch bis zu den Städten. Es wird allgemein empfohlen, während des ganzen Jahres im Voraus zu buchen, aber besonders von Nov. -Feb. entlang der Ostküste und Tasmanien, und von Juni-Sept im Nord Territorium und Nord-Queens-Land. Herbergen befinden sich in Städten, auf dem Land, an der Küste und in Bergen/Gebirgen.

Preisspanne

Preisspanne 15-20 A$.

Zimmer und Reservierungen

Ⓡ während Jan, Feb, Jun-Aug, Nov, Dez. (Alle Zimmer). Reservierungen über ⟨IBN⟩ 🖥 oder die Herberge per ❶ ❷ ❸. Rauchen ist in allen Herbergen NICHT gestattet.

Gäste

Mitgliedsausweis ist erforderlich. Der maximale Aufenthalt beträgt 14 Tage. Altersbegrenzungen für Kinder möglich - in der Herberge nachfragen. 👪 willkommen. Gruppenbuchungen über ⟨IBN⟩ 🖥 oder Herberge per ❶ ❷ ❸.

Öffnungszeiten

Hauptherbergen: Zugang 🔲, 🕐. Rezeption 🕐. Herbergsmanager wohnt im Haus. **Andere Herbergen:** Zugang 🔲, 🕐. Rezeption zwischen 08:00-22:00Uhr. Herbergsmanager wohnt im Haus.

Mahlzeiten

🍽 B Für Einzelreisende & für 👪. 🍳.

Ermäßigungen

HI-Mitgliedsrabatt ist erhältlich – siehe Teil für Rabatte und Ermäßigungen und www.iyhf.org oder www.yha.com.au.

Reisen im Land

Aufgrund großer Entfernungen bestehen in einigen Gebieten Beschränkungen. Jedoch macht eine große Anzahl von Reiseoptionen das Überbrücken dieser Entfernungen leicht. Reisen ist einfach mit ✈ 🚆 ⛴ 🚌 Selbstfahrer. Internationaler Führerschein ist u. U. erforderlich - mit nächstgelegener Botschaft oder Konsulat klären.

Reise-/Aktivitäten-Packages

Touren/sightseeing und Unterkunft/Transport-Packages erhältlich. Package-Buchungen über 🖰.

Reisepässe und Visa

Reisepass, Personalausweis und Einreisevisum erforderlich.

Gesundheit

Schutzimpfungsbescheinigungen sind erforderlich. Unfall-/Krankenversicherung wird empfohlen.

Español

La Asociación de Albergues Juveniles Australianos (YHA Australia) le ofrece 150 de los mejores lugares en los que pasar una temporada de Australia ya sea en la playa, el despoblado o las ciudades. Normalmente, es recomendable reservar con antelación todo el año, pero sobre todo de noviembre a febrero en la costa oriental y Tasmania, y de junio a septiembre en el Territorio del Norte y en Queenslandia del Norte. Los albergues están situados en las ciudades, el campo, la costa y la montaña.

Tarifas mínima y máxima

Tarifas mínima y máxima 15-20 A$.

Habitaciones y Reservas

R en ene, feb, jun-ago, nov, dic. (Todas las habitaciones). Reservas por (IBN) 🖰 o a través del albergue por ❶ ❶ ❸. Está prohibido fumar en todos los albergues.

Huéspedes

Los huéspedes deben presentar su Carnet de Alberguista. La estancia máxima es de 14 días. Es posible que exista un límite de edad para los niños - consulte con el albergue. Se admiten 👪. Reservas de grupo por (IBN) 🖰 o a través del albergue por ❶ ❶ ❸.

Horarios y fechas de apertura

Albergues principales - abiertos 🗓, ⏰. Horario de recepción: ⏰. Gerente residente. **Otros albergues** - abiertos 🗓, ⏰. Horario de recepción: 08:00-22:00h. Gerente residente.

Comidas

🍽 B Para individuales y para 👪. ♂.

Descuentos

Se conceden descuentos a los miembros de Hostelling International – véase la sección sobre descuentos y las páginas Internet www.iyhf.org y www.yha.com.au.

Desplazamientos

Existen restricciones en ciertas regiones debido a las grandes distancias. Pero gracias a la gran variedad de transportes a su disposicion, resulta facil recorrer estas distancias. Transportes recomendados: ✈ 🚆 ⛴ 🚌 Automóvil. Puede ser necesario un permiso de conducir internacional – infórmese en la embajada o consulado más cercanos.

Viajes Combinados con Actividades

Viajes combinados con visitas turísticas y alojamiento/transporte. Reserva de viajes combinados por 🖰.

Pasaportes y Visados

Pasaporte o carnet de identidad y visado obligatorios.

Información Sanitaria

Certificados de vacunación obligatorios. Seguro médico recomendado.

Adelaide -
Adelaide Central YHA

135 Waymouth St,
Adelaide SA 5000.
☎ (8) 82236007
🖷 (8) 82232888
✉ adelyha@chariot.net.au

Open Dates:	🗓
Open Hours:	🕐 access
Reservations:	**R** ⸱CC⸱
Price Range:	$17.00-48.00
Beds:	210 - 15x² 🛏 15x⁴ 🛏 15x⁶ 🛏
Facilities:	♿ 👫 🔌 ☕ 🚲 🏨 📺 📋 🖥 1x🍽 🗄 📷 🏧 🔼 🅿 ⓘ

Directions:

✈	5km
🚂	Central Railway Station 1km
🚌	Coach Terminal 200m

Attractions: 🚴

Airlie Beach -
Airlie Beach YHA

394 Shute Harbour Rd,
Airlie Beach,
Queensland 4802.
☎ (7) 49466312, (Freecall 1800 247251)
🖷 (7) 49467053
✉ airliebeach@yhaqld.org

Open Dates:	🗓
Open Hours:	07.00-19.00hrs (🕐 access-rooms)
Reservations:	**R** ⸱CC⸱
Price Range:	$16.50-$22.00 📱
Beds:	80 - 4x² 🛏 8x⁶ 🛏
Facilities:	👫 4x 👫 🔌 🏨 📺 🖵 🗄 📷 🅿 ⓘ 🔼

Directions:

✈	Proserpine 45km
🚂	Proserpine 30km
🚌	200m

Attractions: 🔍30m ⋃ 🏊

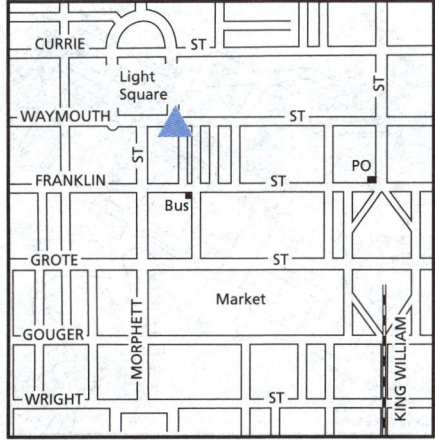

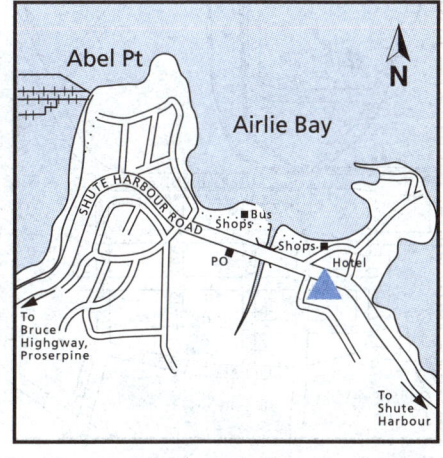

0   1.5km

Alice Springs -
Pioneer YHA

**Corner of Parsons St and Leichhardt Terrace,
Alice Springs,
 Northern Territory 0870.**
- **(8) 89528855**
- **(8) 89524144**
- **alicepioneer@yhant.org.au**

Open Dates:	🗓
Open Hours:	06.30-21.30hrs (Please ring if arriving after hours)
Reservations:	CC
Price Range:	$18.00 (Dorm Rate)
Beds:	62 - 14x⁴ 1x⁶
Facilities:	♿ 🚻 🚿 📺 🍴 🔲 🧳 🏧 🔒 ♨ ℹ ✂ ⛲

Directions:

✈	Alice Springs Airport 15km
A🚌	Airport Shuttle bus available ($9.00 one-way, $15.00 return)
🚂	Regular Services, "Ghan" Alice - Adelaide 2km
🚌	500m

Attractions: 🚴 🏊

Blue Mountains -
Blue Mountains YHA

**66 Waratah St,
Katoomba,
New South Wales 2780.**
- **(2) 47821416**
- **(2) 47826203**
- **bluemountains@yhansw.org.au**

Open Dates:	🗓
Open Hours:	07.00-22.00hrs
Reservations:	R CC
Price Range:	$16.00-20.00
Beds:	184 - 27x² 16x⁴ 12x⁶ 2x⁶
Facilities:	🚻 2x 🚻 🚿 📺 🍴 🔲 🔒 Ⓟ ℹ ✂

Directions:

🚂	Katoomba 1km

Attractions: 🌳 ⛰ 🚴 🏃 ⛎ 🔍3km 🏊1km

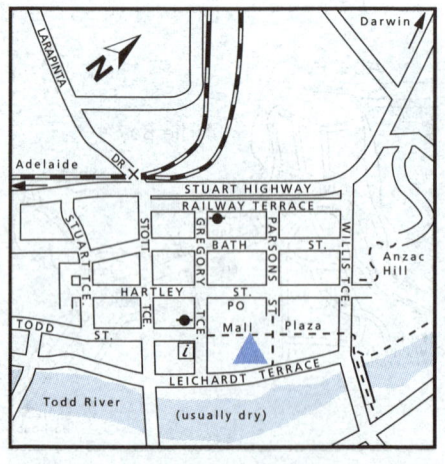

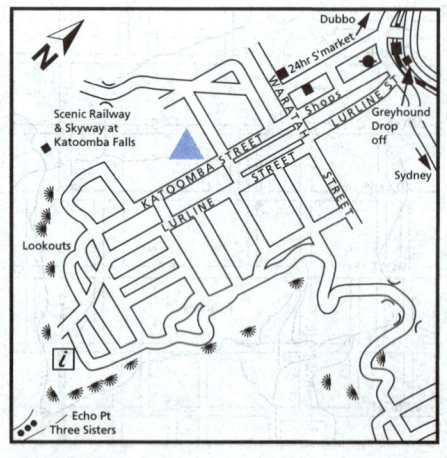

Brisbane -
Brisbane City YHA

392 Upper Roma St,
Brisbane,
Queensland 4000.
t (7) 32361004
f (7) 32361947
e brisbanecity@yhaqld.org

Open Dates:	
Open Hours:	
Reservations:	R IBN CC
Price Range:	$17.50-31.00
Beds:	143 - 32x^2 20x

Facilities:

Directions:

✈	Brisbane International 25km
A	Direct to YH
🚂	Roma Street 600m
🚌	Brisbane Transit Centre 600m ap Brisbane Transit Centre

Byron Bay -
Cape Byron YHA

Cnr Byron & Middleton St,
Byron Bay,
New South Wales 2481.
t (2) 66858788, (Freecall 1800 652627)
f (2) 66858814
e byronyha@nrg.com.au

Open Dates:	
Open Hours:	07.00-22.00hrs
Reservations:	R CC
Price Range:	$17.00-37.00
Beds:	124 - 8x^2 22x^5 1x^6

Facilities:

Directions:

🚂	from Sydney 300m
🚌	from Sydney/Brisbane 200m

Attractions: 100m

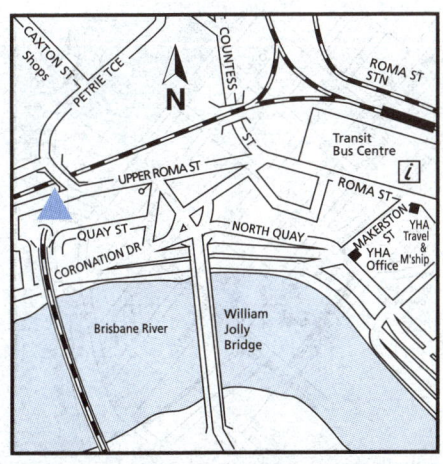

Byron Bay -
J's Bay YHA

7 Carlyle St,
Byron Bay,
New South Wales 2481.
t (2) 66858853, (Freecall 1800 678195)
f (2) 66856766
e jbay@nor.com.au

Open Dates: ⬚₁₂
Open Hours: 08.00-14.00hrs; 16.00-21.00hrs
Reservations: **R** **CC**
Price Range: $18.00-35.00 ⬚
Beds: 94 - 8x² 5x 10x⁵
Facilities: 2x ♦♦♦ 🛏 ⬚ 📺 ⬚ ⬚ **P**
Directions:
🚂 daily to/from Sydney/Brisbane 500m
🚌 regular to/from Sydney & Brisbane 500m
Attractions: ⬚ ⬚200m ⬚ ⬚

Cairns -
Cairns Central YHA

20-24 McLeod St,
Cairns,
Queensland 4870.
t (7) 40510772
f (7) 40313158
e cairnscentral@yhaqld.org

Open Dates: ⬚₁₂
Open Hours: 06.30-23.00hrs (⬚ access-rooms)
Reservations: **R** **IBN** **CC**
Price Range: $18.00-22.00 ⬚
Beds: 170 - 20x² 11x⁶ 4x⁶
Facilities: ♦♦♦ 3x ♦♦♦ 🛏 ⬚ 📺 ⬚ ⬚ ⬚ ⬚
⬚ **P** ⬚ ⬚
Directions:
✈ Cairns International 12km
A🚌 Direct to YH
🚂 Bunda Street 200m
🚌 500m
Attractions: ⬚ ⬚10km ⬚

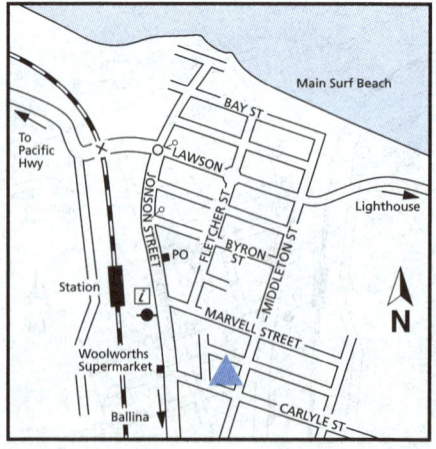

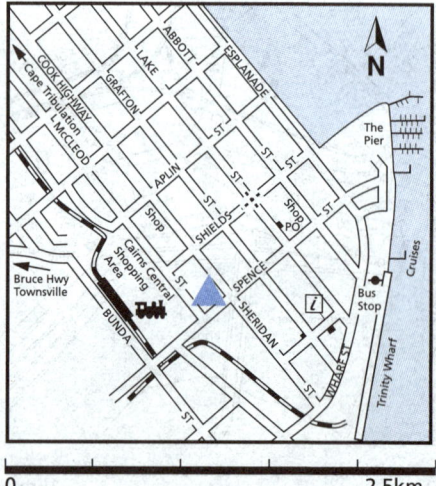

Cairns -
YHA on the Esplanade

93 The Esplanade,
Cairns,
Queensland 4870.
📞 (7) 40311919
📠 (7) 40314381
📧 cairnsesplanade@yhaqld.org

Open Dates:	🗓
Open Hours:	07.00-20.00hrs (🕐 access-rooms)
Reservations:	R CC
Price Range:	$18.50-22.00 💷
Beds:	68 - 10x² 8x⁶
Facilities:	� ⛴ 🛏 📺 📖 ☕ ▢ 🖼 🚲 ⊜ 🛈 💬

Directions:

✈	Cairns International 8km
A 🚌	Direct to YH
🚃	800m
🚌	800m
Attractions:	🔍 ∪10km 🏊

Canberra -
Canberra YHA

191 Dryandra St,
O'Connor,
Australian Capital Territory 2602.
📞 (2) 62489155
📠 (2) 62491731
📧 canberra@yhansw.org.au

Open Dates:	🗓
Open Hours:	07.00-22.00hrs
Reservations:	R IBN CC
Price Range:	$18.00-26.00 💷
Beds:	124 - 6x² 18x⁴ 4x⁵
Facilities:	♘iii 🍴 ⛴ 🛏 📺 ▢ 🚲 P 🛈 ❄ 🎿

Directions:

✈	Canberra 14km
🚃	Kingston 10km
🚌	Jolimont Centre 5km
Attractions:	🎣 ⛰ 🏃 🏊2km

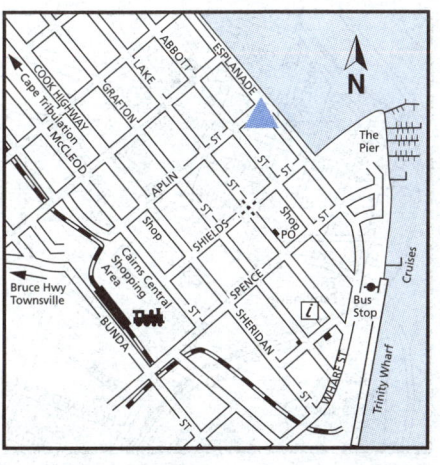

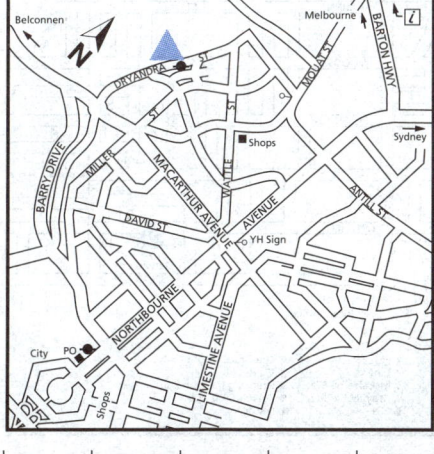

0	2.5km
0	6km

Darwin -
Darwin City YHA

69 Mitchell St,
Darwin,
Northern Territory 0801.
t (8) 89813995
f (8) 89816674
e darwinyha@yhant.org.au

Open Dates:	🗓️
Open Hours:	🕐 Reception(🕐)
Reservations:	**R** (IBN) (CC)
Price Range:	$18.00-27.00 🛏️
Beds:	324 - 21x² 🛏️ 6x³ 🛏️ 53x⁴ 🛏️ 2x⁶ 🛏️
Facilities:	♿ 🚻 🚿 🛄 📺 🎮 📷 🖼️ 🎱 ⊜ ℹ️ 📶 ♻️

Directions:

✈️	Darwin International 15km
A🚌	Free airport shuttle if reservation is made before arrival
🚌	Local Bus Depot, Greyhound Pioneer, McCafferty's 200m

Attractions: 🔍 2km 🚴 🏊

Fremantle -
Backpackers Inn Freo YHA

11 Pakenham St,
Fremantle,
Western Australia 6160.
t (8) 94317065
f (8) 93367106
e bpinn_freo@hotmail.com

Open Dates:	🗓️
Reservations:	**R** (CC)
Price Range:	$16.00
Beds:	140
Facilities:	🍴 🚿 🖼️

Directions:

A🚌	Bus ap hostel
🚢	Rottnest ferry - 4 mins walk
🚂	2 mins walk
🚌	2 mins walk

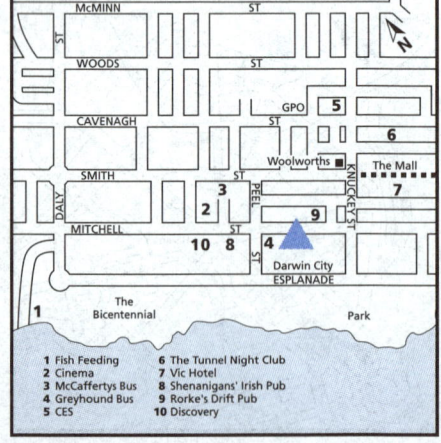

1 Fish Feeding
2 Cinema
3 McCaffertys Bus
4 Greyhound Bus
5 CES
6 The Tunnel Night Club
7 Vic Hotel
8 Shenanigans' Irish Pub
9 Rorke's Drift Pub
10 Discovery

0   1.5km

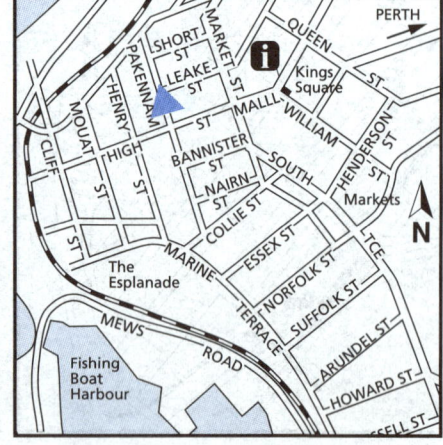

Hobart -
Adelphi Court YHA

17 Stoke St,
New Town, Hobart,
Tasmania 7008.
📞 (3) 62284829
📠 (3) 62782047
📧 yhatas@yhatas.org.au

Open Dates:	🗓
Open Hours:	07.30-22.30hrs (16.12-15.03); 08.00-10.30; 16.00-19.00hrs (16.03-15.12)
Reservations:	R CC
Price Range:	$20.00-26.00
Beds:	109 - 13x² 6x³ 16x⁴ 4x⁵ 1x⁶
Facilities:	♟ 4x ♟ 🍴 (B) 🚿 ♨ 📺 📖 2 x 🍷 🗄 🧳 ♿ 🅿 ℹ 😊 ♣ 🔍 🏕 🏛
Directions:	2N from city centre
✈	Hobart 18km
A🚌	Airporter ap hostel
⛴	Devonport 300km
🚌	25-42, 100, 105-128 stop 13; 15-16 stop 8A
Attractions:	🚴 ⛏1km ⚓1km

Melbourne -
Queensberry Hill YHA

78 Howard St,
North Melbourne,
Victoria 3051.
📞 (3) 93298599
📠 (3) 93268427
📧 queensberryhill@yhavic.org.au

Open Dates:	🗓
Open Hours:	🕐
Reservations:	IBN CC
Price Range:	$20.00-21.00
Beds:	348 - 10x¹ 20x² 50x⁴ 2x⁶ 4x⁶
Facilities:	♿ ♟ 18x ♟ 🍴 (BD) 🚿 ♨ 📺 🍳 🗄 🧳 ♿ 🔄 🅿 ℹ 😊
Directions:	1.4N from city centre
✈	Melbourne 26km
A🚌	Skybus 100m
⛴	Station Pier 3.2km
🚆	Spencer St 1.4km
🚌	ap Franklin St
🚊	Tram 55 from William St 200m ap Queensberry St, stop 11
U	Melbourne Central 1km
Attractions:	🚴 ⚓1km

Melbourne -
Chapman Gardens YHA

76 Chapman St,
North Melbourne,
Victoria 3051.
📞 (3) 93283595
📠 (3) 93297863
📧 chapman@yhavic.org.au

Open Dates:	🗓
Open Hours:	🕐
Reservations:	⊂CC⊃
Price Range:	$20.00 💷
Beds:	120 - 46x^2🛏 2x^3🛏 4x^4🛏
Facilities:	👬 🚿 🛏 📺 🧺 🗄 💼 8 🅿 ℹ ♒

Directions:

✈	Melbourne 26km
A🚐	Skybus 50m
🚢	Station Pier 4.2km
🚂	Spencer 2.5km
🚌	Franklin St 1.5Km; Spencer 2.5km
🚎	#57 from Elizabeth St, travel N ap Stop 18, Abbotsford St
Ⓤ	Melbourne Central 1.2km

Attractions: 🚴 🏊 2km

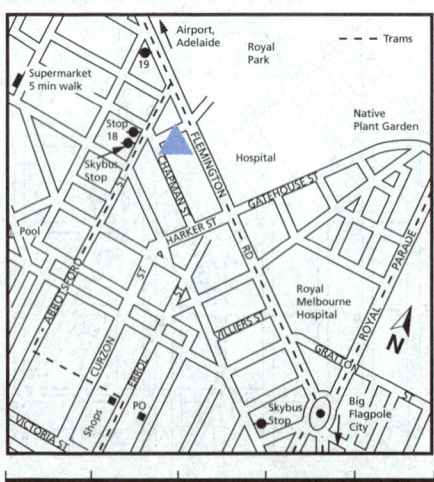

Perth - Northbridge
YHA Backpackers

42-48 Francis St,
Northbridge,
Western Australia 6003.
📞 (8) 93287794
📠 (8) 93287794
📧 yhanb@hotmail.com

Open Dates:	🗓
Open Hours:	08.00-22.00hrs (may close 12.00-15.00hrs Winter only) 🕐 check-in for advance bookings
Reservations:	Ⓡ ⊂CC⊃
Price Range:	$15.00-18.00 (Free linen with weekly accommodation) 💷
Beds:	108 - 4x^2🛏 1x^5🛏 9x^6🛏 5x^6🛏
Facilities:	🚿 🛏 📺 🧺 🗄 🏧 ℹ

Directions: 0.5S from city centre

A🚐	Free Airport Shuttle if reservation made before arrival
🚂	5 mins walk 200m
🚌	5 mins walk 200m

Attractions: 🚴

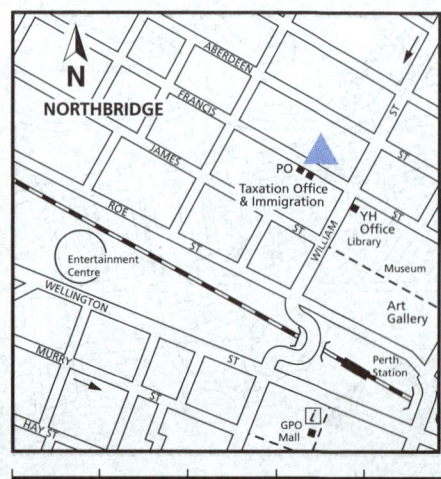

Perth - Britannia International YHA

253 William St,
Northbridge,
Western Australia 6003.
- ☎ (8) 93286121
- ✆ (8) 92279784
- ✉ britannia@yhawa.com.au

Open Dates:	🗓12
Open Hours:	⏲
Reservations:	**R** (IBN) (CC)
Price Range:	$16.00-19.00 🔆
Beds:	134 - 28x¹🛏 26x²🛏 1x³🛏 3x⁴🛏 3x⁶🛏 2x⁶🛏
Facilities:	♿ 👪 1x 👪 🚿 🏢 📺 🧺 🗄 🖼 🏧 💱 ℹ️ 🎴
Directions:	[0.5S] from city centre
A🚌	ap hostel
🚂	5 mins walk
🚌	5 mins walk from City bus station
Attractions:	🚲

Rockhampton - Rockhampton YHA

60 MacFarlane St,
North Rockhampton,
Queensland 4701.
- ☎ (7) 49275288
- ✆ (7) 49226040
- ✉ rockhampton@yhaqld.org

Open Dates:	🗓12
Open Hours:	reception. 07.00-12.00, 17.00-22.00 (⏲ access-rooms)
Reservations:	**R** (CC)
Price Range:	$16.50-20.00
Beds:	52
Facilities:	👪 🚿 🗄 🅿
Directions:	
🚂	4km
🚌	Brisbane + N daily 1km McCaffertys, 3km Greyhound, pickup during office hours.

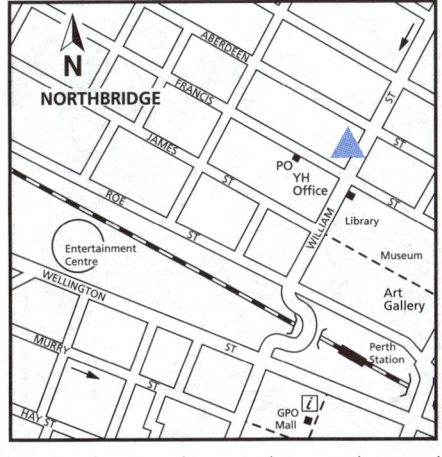

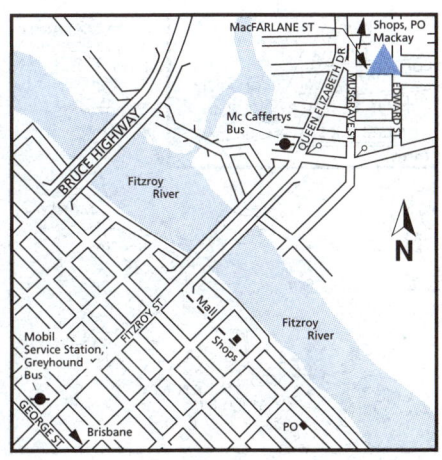

0   2.5km

Sydney -
Sydney Beachouse YHA

Sydney Beachouse,
4 Collaroy St,
Collaroy Beach,
New South Wales 2097.
t (2) 99811177
f (2) 99811114
e mail@sydneybeachouse.com.au

Open Dates:	🗓
Reservations:	**R** **CC**
Price Range:	$22.00-30.00
Beds:	228 - 7x² 30x⁴ 10x⁶
Facilities:	♿ ♟ ⑩ 🍴 🚿 🛏 📺 🗄 🅿 ⑦

Directions:

✈	Sydney 30km
A🚌	20km
🚆	Sydney Central 20km
🚌	ap hostel 50m

Attractions:

There are 6 hostels in Sydney.
See following pages.

Sydney -
Sydney Central YHA

Sydney Central YHA,
11 Rawson Place. (cnr Pitt St and Rawson)
opposite Central Station.
t (2) 92819111
f (2) 92819199
e sydcentral@yhansw.org.au

Open Dates:	🗓
Open Hours:	🕐
Reservations:	**IBN** **CC**
Price Range:	$22.00-30.00 📋
Beds:	532 - 54x² 82x⁴ 12x⁶ 3x⁶
Facilities:	♟ ⑩ 🍴 🚿 🛏 📺 📺 🗄 💼 ⛲ 🔒 ☕ ⬍ ⑦ 🚿 🅾 🛁 🎱

Directions:

✈	Sydney 10km
A🚌	Airport Express 100m
🚆	Central 100m
🚌	All buses stop at Central Station 100m ap Central Station
Ⓤ	Central Station 100m

Attractions: 🔍 ⚡500m ⚓

There are 6 hostels in Sydney.
See following pages.

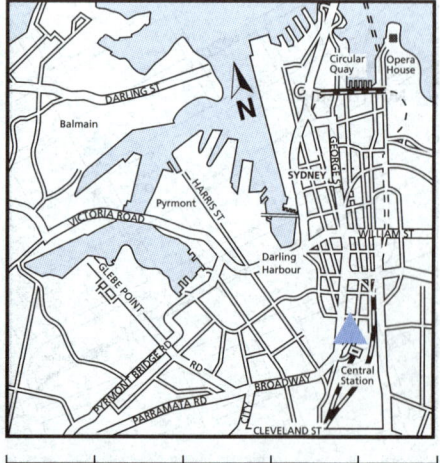

Sydney -
Glebe Point YHA

262 Glebe Point Rd,
Glebe,
New South Wales 2037.
📞 (2) 96928418
📠 (2) 96600431
📧 glebe@yhansw.org.au

Open Dates:	🗓12
Open Hours:	07.00-19.30hrs; 20.00-23.00hrs
Reservations:	IBN CC
Price Range:	$22.00-31.00 🛏
Beds:	151 - 21x²🛏 6x³🛏 19x⁴🛏 3x⁵🛏
Facilities:	🛏 🍴 📺 🧺 ▣ 📷 🔲 ℹ ♿

Directions:

✈	Sydney 16km
A🚌	Airport Express 352 16km
🚃	Central 2.5km
🚌	431 or 434 2.5km ap hostel 10m
U	Central Station 2.5km

Attractions: ⚓2km

There are 6 hostels in Sydney.
See following pages.

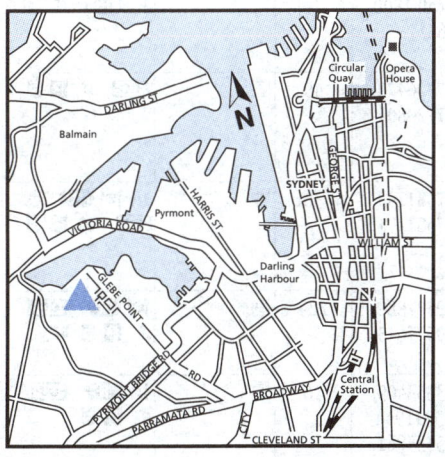

Location/Address	Telephone No. Fax No.	Beds	Opening Dates	Facilities
▲ **Adelaide** - Adelaide Central YHA **135 Waymouth St, Adelaide SA 5000.** e adelyha@chariot.net.au	☎ (8) 82236007 📠 (8) 82232888	210	🗓	R 👤♿ CC 👕 P 📦 ☕ 🏍
▲ **Adelaide** - Adelaide Gilles St YHA [IBN] 290 Gilles St, Adelaide, South Australia 5000. e adelyha@chariot.net.au	☎ (8) 82236007 📠 (8) 82232888	52	🗓	👫 R 2S ♿ CC 👕 P 📦
▲ **Adelaide River** - Mount Bundy YHA Haynes Rd, Adelaide River NT 0846. e mt.bundy@octa4.net.au	☎ (8) 89767009 📠 (8) 89767113	21	🗓	👫 R CC 👕 P
▲ **Airlie Beach** - Club Habitat YHA **394 Shute Harbour Rd, Airlie Beach, Queensland 4802.** e airliebeach@yhaqld.org	☎ (7) 49466312, (Freecall 1800 247251) 📠 (7) 49467053	80	🗓	👫 R CC 👕 P 📦
▲ **Albany** - Bayview YHA 49 Duke St, Albany, Western Australia 6330. e yhaalbany@hotmail.com	☎ (8) 98423388 📠 (8) 98423388	63	🗓	👫 🍴 CC 👕 P 📦
▲ **Albury-Wodonga** - Albury Motor Village YHA 372 Wagga Rd (Hume Hwy), Lavington NSW 2641. e albury@yhavic.org.au	☎ (2) 60402999 📠 (2) 60403160	24	🗓	👫 4.6N CC 👕 P 📦
▲ **Alice Springs** - Ossie's YHA Cnr Lindsay Ave & Warburton St, Alice Springs NT 0870. e ossies@ossies.com.au	☎ (8) 89522308 📠 (8) 89522211	37	🗓	👫 R 2NE CC 👕 P 📦
▲ **Alice Springs** - Pioneer YHA **Corner of Parsons St and Leichhardt Terrace, Alice Springs, Northern Territory 0870.** e alicepioneer@yhant.org.au	☎ (8) 89528855 📠 (8) 89524144	62	🗓	♿ CC 👕 📦
▲ **Apollo Bay** - Surfside Backpackers YHA Corner Great Ocean Rd & Gambier St, Apollo Bay, Victoria 3233. e apollobay@yhavic.org.au	☎ (3) 52377263, (Freecall 1800 357263)	22	🗓	👫 R 0.2S ♿ CC 👕 P 📦
▲ **Armidale** - Pembroke Leisure Park YHA 39 Waterfall Way, Armidale, New South Wales 2350. e pembroke@mail.northnet.com.au	☎ (2) 67726470 📠 (2) 67729804	40	🗓	CC 👕 P 📦
▲ **Augusta** - Baywatch Manor YHA 88 Blackwood Ave, Augusta, WA 6290. (320km S of Perth). e baywatch@netserv.net.au	☎ (8) 97581290 📠 (8) 97581291	36	🗓	👫 🍴 R ♿ CC 👕 P 📦
▲ **Ayers Rock** - Outback Pioneer YHA Ayers Rock Resort, Ayers Rock, NT 0872. e reservations@ayersrockresort.com	☎ (8) 89577888 📠 (8) 89577615	224	🗓	🍴 R CC 👕 P 📦 ☕
▲ **Ballarat** - Sovereign Hill Lodge YHA Magpie St, Sovereign Hill, Ballarat, Victoria 3350. e ballarat@yhavic.org.au	☎ (3) 53333409, (3) 53311944 📠 (3) 53335861	16	🗓	👫 R CC 👕 P 📦

Location/Address	Telephone No. Fax No.	Beds	Opening Dates	Facilities
▲ **Ballina** - Travellers Lodge YHA 36 Tamar St, Ballina, New South Wales 2478. @ scarboro@nor.com.au	☎ (2) 66866737 📠 (2) 66866342, (2) 66866737	18	🗓	††† ⦿ ㏄ ⚲ Ⓟ ⬛
▲ **Batemans Bay** - Batemans Bay Tourist Park YHA Old Princes Hwy, Batemans Bay, New South Wales 2536. @ info@shadywillows.com.au	☎ (2) 44724972 📠 (2) 44724045	38	🗓	††† 1 SE ㏄ Ⓟ ⬛
▲ **Bega** - Bega Valley YHA 3 Kirkland Crescent, Bega, New South Wales 2550. @ ronmead@telstra.easymail.com.au	☎ (2) 64923103 📠 (2) 64922335	20	🗓	⚲ Ⓟ
▲ **Bellingen** - Bellingen YHA Backpackers 2 Short St, Bellingen NSW 2454. @ belloyha@midcoast.com.au	☎ (2) 66551116 📠 (2) 66551358	38	🗓	††† 0.1 SE ⚲ Ⓟ ⬛
▲ **Bendigo** - Bendigo YHA 33 Creek St South, Bendigo Vic 3550. @ bendigo@yhavic.org.au	☎ (3) 54437680 📠 (3) 54437680	26	🗓	Ⓡ 0.4 SW ♿ ㏄ ⚲ Ⓟ ⬛ 🚲 ☼
△ *Bicheno* *Tasman Hwy, Tasmania 7215.* *(3km N of Bicheno township).* @ *yhatas@yhatas.org.au*	☎ *(3) 63751293*	*18*	🗓	⚲ Ⓟ ⬛
▲ **Blue Mountains** - Blue Mountains YHA **66 Waratah St, Katoomba, New South Wales 2780.** @ bluemountains@yhansw.org.au	☎ (2) 47821416 📠 (2) 47826203	184	🗓	††† Ⓡ ㏄ ⚲ Ⓟ ⬛
▲ **Blue Mountains** - Hawkesbury Heights YHA Hawkesbury Rd, Hawkesbury Heights, New South Wales, 2777.	☎ (2) 47545621 📠 (2) 47545621	12	🗓	Ⓟ
▲ **Bonnie Doon** - Lakeside Leisure Resort YHA Hutchinsons Rd, Bonnie Doon, Victoria 3720. @ bonniedoon@yhavic.org.au	☎ (3) 57787252 📠 (3) 57787569	32	🗓	㏄ ⚲ Ⓟ ⬛
△ *Bridport* - *Bridport Seaside Lodge YHA* *47 Main St, Bridport TAS 7262.* @ *seasidelodge@bigpond.com.au*	☎ *(3) 63561585* 📠 *(3) 63561585*	*26*	🗓	††† Ⓡ ㏄ ⚲ Ⓟ ⬛ 🚲
▲ **Brisbane** - Brisbane City YHA IBN **392 Upper Roma St, Brisbane, Queensland 4000.** @ brisbanecity@yhaqld.org	☎ (7) 32361004 📠 (7) 32361947	143	🗓	††† ⦿ Ⓡ ♿ ㏄ ⚲ Ⓟ ⬛ ☕
▲ **Broken Hill** - Tourist Lodge YHA 100 Argent St, Broken Hill, New South Wales 2880. @ mcrae@pcpro.net.au	☎ (8) 80882086 📠 (8) 80879511	77	🗓	††† Ⓡ ㏄ ⚲ Ⓟ ⬛
▲ **Broome** - The Last Resort YHA 2 Bagot St, Broome, Western Australia 6725. @ lastresort@smartchat.com.au	☎ (8) 91935000 📠 (8) 62931119	100	🗓	††† ⦿ Ⓡ ㏄ ⚲ Ⓟ ⬛

Location/Address	Telephone No. Fax No.	Beds	Opening Dates	Facilities
▲ **Bruny Island** - Lumeah YHA 5 Lumeah Rd, Adventure Bay, Tasmania 7150 (38km from 🚢; for transport to & from ☎ YH 1 day in advance). ✉ lumeah@tassie.net.au	☎ (3) 62931265 📠 (3) 62931119	18	🔲	� R P
▲ **Bunbury** - Backpackers Residency YHA Corner of Stirling & Moore Sts, Bunbury, Western Australia 6230. ✉ yhabunbury@hotmail.com	☎ (8) 97912621 📠 (8) 97914742	45	🔲	♦♦ CC ✂ P ▯
▲ **Bundaberg** - Kellys Beach Resort YHA 6 Trevors Rd, Bargara (Bundaberg) QLD. ✉ perfectholiday@kellysbeachresort.com.au	☎ (7) 41547200 📠 (7) 41547300	86	🔲	♦♦ 🍴 ♿ CC ✂ P ▯ ☀
▲ **Bundanoon** - Bundanoon YHA Railway Ave, Bundanoon, New South Wales 2578.	☎ (2) 48836010 📠 (2) 48837470	37	🔲	♦♦ 🍴 R CC ✂ P ▯
▲ **Byron Bay** - Cape Byron YHA **Cnr Byron & Middleton St, Byron Bay,** **New South Wales 2481.** ✉ byronyha@nrg.com.au	☎ (2) 66858788, (Freecall 1800 652627) 📠 (2) 66858814	124	🔲	R CC ✂ P ▯ ☕
▲ **Byron Bay** - J's Bay YHA **7 Carlyle St, Byron Bay,** **New South Wales 2481.** ✉ jbay@nor.com.au	☎ (2) 66858853, (Freecall 1800 678195) 📠 (2) 66856766	94	🔲	♦♦ R CC ✂ P ▯
▲ **Cairns** - Cairns Central YHA IBN **20-24 McLeod St, Cairns,** **Queensland 4870.** ✉ cairnscentral@yhaqld.org	☎ (7) 40510772 📠 (7) 40313158	170	🔲	♦♦ R CC ✂ P ▯
▲ **Cairns** - YHA on the Esplanade **93 The Esplanade, Cairns,** **Queensland 4870.** ✉ cairnsesplanade@yhaqld.org	☎ (7) 40311919 📠 (7) 40314381	68	🔲	♦♦ R CC ✂ ▯
▲ **Canberra** - Canberra YHA IBN **191 Dryandra St, O'Connor,** **Australian Capital Territory 2602.** ✉ canberra@yhansw.org.au	☎ (2) 62489155 📠 (2) 62491731	124	🔲	🍴 R CC ✂ P ▯
▲ **Cape Tribulation** - Crocodylus Village YHA Lot 5, Buchanan Creek Rd, Cow Bay, North Queensland 4873. ✉ crocodylus@internetnorth.com.au	☎ (7) 40989166 📠 (7) 40989131	110	🔲	♦♦ 🍴 R CC ✂ P ▯ ☕
▲ **Cardwell** - Hinchinbrook Hostel YHA 175 Bruce Hwy, Cardwell, Queensland 4849. ✉ kookaburra@znet.net.au	☎ (7) 40668648 📠 (7) 40668910	72	🔲	♦♦ CC ✂ P ▯
▲ **Coffs Harbour** - Coffs Harbour YHA 110 Albany St, Coffs Harbour, New South Wales 2450. ✉ coffsyha@key.net.au	☎ (2) 66526462 📠 (2) 66526462	52	🔲	♦♦ R CC ✂ P ▯
▲ **Coles Bay** - "Iluka Backpackers" YHA Esplanade, Coles Bay, Tasmania 7215. ✉ iluka@trump.net.au	☎ (3) 62570115 📠 (3) 62570384	32	🔲	♦♦ 🍴 CC ✂ P ▯

Location/Address	Telephone No. Fax No.	Beds	Opening Dates	Facilities
▲ **Cooktown** - Pam's Place YHA Cnr Boundary & Charlotte Streets, Cooktown 4871. 📧 pamplace@tpg.com.au	☎ (7) 40695166 🖷 (7) 40695964	66	🕮	�11 ⊂CC⊃ ☞ P 🗗
△ *Cradle Mountain -* *Cradle Mountain Backpackers YHA* *Cradle Mountain Rd,* *Cradle Mountain TAS 7306.* 📧 *cradle@cosycabins.com*	☎ *(3) 64921395* 🖷 *(3) 64921438*	*46*	🕮	♟1 ⓡ ⊂CC⊃ ☞ P 🗗 ♿
▲ **Darwin** - Darwin City YHA ⬚IBN⬚ **69 Mitchell St, Darwin,** **Northern Territory 0801.** 📧 darwinyha@yhant.org.au	☎ (8) 89813995 🖷 (8) 89816674	324	🕮	ⓡ ♿ ⊂CC⊃ ☞ 🗗
▲ **Daylesford** - Wildwood YHA 42 Main Rd, Hepburn Springs VIC 3461. 📧 daylesford@yhavic.org.au	☎ (3) 53484435 🖷 (3) 53483555	15	🕮	♟1 ⦿ ⓡ 3N ♿ ⊂CC⊃ ☞ P 🗗 🚲
▲ **Deloraine** - "Highview Lodge" YHA 8 Blake St, Deloraine, Tasmania 7304. 📧 bodach@microtech.com.au	☎ (3) 63622996	30	🕮	♟1 ☞ P 🗗
▲ **Denham** - Bay Lodge YHA 95 Knight Terrace, Denham, Western Australia 6537. 📧 baylodge@wn.com.au	☎ (8) 99481278 🖷 (8) 99481031	22	🕮	♟1 ⦿ ♿ ⊂CC⊃ P 🗗
▲ **Devonport** - Devonport YHA 'Mac Wright House', 115 Middle Rd, Devonport, Tasmania 7310. 📧 yhatas@yhatas.org.au	☎ (3) 64245696 🖷 (3) 64249952	45	🕮	♟1 2SW ☞ P 🗗
▲ **Dongara** - Dongara Backpackers YHA 32 Waldeck St, Dongara, Western Australia 6525. (350km N of Perth). 📧 enquiries@yhawa.com.au	☎ (8) 99271581 🖷 (8) 99271581	24	🕮	♟1 ⊂CC⊃ ☞ P 🗗
▲ **Dubbo** - Dubbo Backpackers YHA 87 Brisbane St, Dubbo, New South Wales 2830. 📧 yhadubbo@lisp.com.au	☎ (2) 68820922 🖷 (2) 68820922	29	🕮	♟1 ⊂CC⊃ ☞ P 🗗
▲ **Dunsborough** - Three Pines Beach Resort YHA Three Pines Resort, 285 Geographe Bay Rd, Quindalup, Western Australia 6282. (260km S of Perth). 📧 dunsboroughyha@hotmail.com	☎ (8) 97553107 🖷 (8) 97553107	74	🕮	ⓡ ⊂CC⊃ ☞ P 🗗
▲ **Echuca** - Echuca Gardens YHA 103 Mitchell St, Echuca, Victoria 3564. 📧 echuca@yhavic.org.au	☎ (3) 54806522 🖷 (3) 54826951	16	🕮	♟1 ⓡ 0.8E ⊂CC⊃ ☞ P 🗗
▲ **Esperance** - Blue Waters Lodge YHA 249 Goldfields Rd, Esperance, Western Australia 6450. (770km SE of Perth). 📧 yhaesperance@hotmail.com	☎ (8) 90711040 🖷 (8) 90711040	127	🕮	♟1 ⊂CC⊃ ☞ P 🗗

Location/Address	Telephone No. Fax No.	Beds	Opening Dates	Facilities
▲ **Exmouth** - Pete's Exmouth Backpackers YHA Cnr Murat and Truscott Cres, Exmouth, Western Australia 6707. ⓔ exmouthvillage@nwc.net.au	① (8) 99491101 ⓕ (8) 99491402	40	🔟12	⍾◎ Ⓡ ⊂CC⊃ ☞ Ⓟ 🔟
▲ **Forster** - Dolphin Lodge YHA 43 Head St, Forster, New South Wales 2428. ⓔ dolphin_lodge@hotmail.com	① (2) 65558155 ⓕ (2) 65558155	80	🔟12	⍾⍾ Ⓡ ⊂CC⊃ Ⓟ 🔟
▲ **Fremantle** - Backpackers Inn Freo YHA **11 Pakenham St, Fremantle,** **Western Australia 6160.** ⓔ bpinn_freo@hotmail.com	① (8) 94317065 ⓕ (8) 93367106	140	🔟12	⍾◎ Ⓡ ⊂CC⊃ ☞ 🔟
△ *Garie Beach* - *Garie Beach YHA* *Royal National Park,* *New South Wales. (50km S of Sydney).*	① *(2) 92611111*	*12*	🔟12	Ⓡ ☞
▲ **Gelantipy** - Karoonda Park YHA Gelantipy, Victoria 3885 (Via Buchan). ⓔ gelantipy@yhavic.org.au	① (3) 51550220 ⓕ (3) 51550308	22	🔟12	⍾⍾ ◎ ⊂CC⊃ ☞ Ⓟ 🔟
▲ **Geraldton** - Foreshore Backpackers YHA 172 Marine Terrace, Geraldton, WA 6530. ⓔ foreshorebp@hotmail.com	① (8) 99213275 ⓕ (8) 99213233	41	🔟12	⍾⍾ ⊂CC⊃ ☞ Ⓟ 🔟
▲ **George Town** - "Travellers Lodge" YHA 4 Elizabeth St, George Town, Tasmania 7253. ⓔ yhatas@yhatas.org.au	① (3) 63823261	18	🔟12	⍾⍾ ☞ Ⓟ
▲ **Gerringong** - Nestor House YHA Fern St, Gerringong, New South Wales 2534.	①/ⓕ (2) 42341249	24	🔟12	☞ Ⓟ
△ *Girvan* - *Girvan YHA* *via Stroud 2425, New South Wales.*	① *(2) 49976639*	*12*	🔟12	☞ Ⓟ
▲ **Gold Coast** - Coolangatta YHA 230 Coolangatta Rd, Bilinga, Queensland 4225. (105km S of Brisbane). ⓔ yhacool@netspace.net.au	① (7) 55367644 ⓕ (7) 55995436	80	🔟12	⍾⍾ ◎ Ⓡ ⊂CC⊃ ☞ Ⓟ 🔟
▲ **Great Keppel Island** - YHA Backpackers Village Keppel Haven, Great Keppel Island, Queensland 4700. ⓔ ktsgki@networx.com.au	① (7) 49275288 ⓕ (7) 49226040	60	🔟12	⍾⍾ ◎ Ⓡ ⊂CC⊃ ☞ 🔟 ☕
▲ **Halls Gap** - Grampians YHA Eco Hostel Grampians Rd, Halls Gap, Victoria 3381. ⓔ grampians@yhavic.org.au	① (3) 53564544 ⓕ (3) 53564543	60	🔟12	⍾⍾ Ⓡ ♿ ⊂CC⊃ ☞ Ⓟ 🔟
▲ **Hervey Bay** - Colonial Log Cabin Resort 820 Boat Harbour Drive, Hervey Bay, Queensland 4655. ⓔ herveybay@bigpond.com.au	① (7) 41251844, (Freecall 1800 818280) ⓕ (7) 41253161	115	🔟12	⍾⍾ ◎ ♿ ⊂CC⊃ ☞ Ⓟ 🔟 ☕
▲ **Hobart** - Adelphi Court YHA **17 Stoke St, New Town, Hobart,** **Tasmania 7008.** ⓔ yhatas@yhatas.org.au	① (3) 62284829 ⓕ (3) 62782047	109	🔟12	⍾⍾ ◎ Ⓡ 2N ⊂CC⊃ ☞ Ⓟ 🔟

Location/Address	Telephone No. Fax No.	Beds	Opening Dates	Facilities
▲ **Hobart** - Montgomery's YHA Backpackers 9 Argyle St, Hobart, Tasmania 7000. **e** engel@southcom.com.au	**t** (3) 62344790 **f** (3) 62344450	38	📅12	♦♦ ⵕ◻ 🅡 -CC- ⸖ ◻ ☕ 🚲
▲ **Huon Valley** - "Balfes Hill" YHA "Balfes Hill", Cradoc Rd, Cradoc, Tasmania 7109. (11km S of Huonville). **e** arjlewis@hotmail.com	**t** (3) 62951551 **f** (3) 62950875	60	📅12	♦♦ ♿ ⸖ 🅿 ◻
▲ **Kakadu National Park** - Gagudju Lodge YHA off Kakadu Hwy, NT 0886 PO Box 696 Jabiru NT 0886. **e** cooinda1@bigpond.com	**t** (8) 89790145 **f** (8) 89790148	69	📅12	0.2W -CC- 🅿 ◻
▲ **Kalgoorlie** - Goldfields Backpackers YHA 166 Hay St, Kalgoorlie, Western Australia 6430. **e** goldbpak@gold.net.au	**t** (8) 90911482 **f** (8) 90911484	36	📅12	♿ -CC- ⸖ 🅿 ◻
▲ **Kangaroo Island** - Penguin Walk YHA 33 Middle Tce, Penneshaw, Kangaroo Island, SA 5022. **e** yha@ki-ferryconnections.com	**t** (8) 85531233 **f** (8) 85531190	51	📅12	♦♦ ⵕ◻ 🅡 110S -CC- ⸖ 🅿 ◻ ☕
▲ **Katherine** - Palm Court Backpackers YHA Corner Third and Giles, Katherine, NT 0850. **e** palm_court@hotmail.com	**t** (8) 89722722 **f** (8) 89711443	87	📅12	♦♦ ♿ -CC- ⸖ 🅿 ◻
Katoomba ☞**Blue Mountains**				
▲ **Kings Canyon** - Kings Canyon YHA Ernest Giles Rd, Watarrka National Park, Kings Canyon NT 0872. **e** reservations@ayersrockresort.com.au	**t** (8) 89567992 **f** (8) 89567410	120	📅12	♦♦ ⵕ◻ 🅡 -CC- ⸖ 🅿 ◻ ☕
▲ **Kroombit** - Kroombit Tourist Park YHA "Lochenbar", PO Box 135, Biloela, QLD 4715. **e** lochenbar@kroombit.com.au	**t** (7) 49922186 **f** (7) 49924186	142	📅12	♦♦ ⵕ◻ 35E -CC- ⸖ 🅿 ◻
▲ **Kununurra** - Desert Inn YHA Cnr Konkerberry Drive & Tristania St, Kununurra, Western Australia 6743. **e** advertur@comswest.net.au	**t** (8) 91682702 **f** (8) 91682271	28	📅12	-CC- ⸖ 🅿 ◻
▲ **Lakes Entrance** - Riviera Backpackers YHA 5 Clarkes Rd, Lakes Entrance, Victoria 3909. **e** lakesentrance@yhavic.org.au	**t** (3) 51552444 **f** (3) 51554558	56	📅12	♦♦ 1NE -CC- ⸖ 🅿 ◻
▲ **Lancelin** - Lancelin Lodge YHA 10 Hopkins St, Lancelin, Western Australia 6044. **e** lanlodge@windspeed.net.au	**t** (8) 96552020 **f** (8) 96552021	40	📅12	♦♦ ♿ -CC- ⸖ 🅿 ◻
▲ **Lennox Head** - Lennox Head YHA Beachouse 3 Ross St, Lennox Head NSW 2478. **e** lennoxbacpac@hotmail.com.au	**t** (2) 66877636 **f** (2) 66877739	46	📅12	♦♦ -CC- ⸖ 🅿 ◻
▲ **Lorne** - Great Ocean Rd Backpackers YHA 10 Erskine Ave, Lorne, Victoria 3232. (142km SW from Melbourne). **e** lorne@yhavic.org.au	**t** (3) 52891809 **f** (3) 52892508	32	📅12	♦♦ -CC- ⸖ 🅿 ◻

Location/Address	Telephone No. Fax No.	Beds	Opening Dates	Facilities
▲ **Lune River** - Lune River YHA Main Rd, Lune River, Tasmania 7109. **e** luneriver@trump.net.au	☎ (3) 62983163 🖷 (3) 62983177	20		� P 🖅
▲ **Mackay** - Larrikin Lodge YHA 32 Peel St, Mackay, Queensland 4740. **e** larrikin@mackay.net.au	☎ (7) 49513728 🖷 (7) 49572978	26		♦♦ ✧ P 🖅
▲ **Magnetic Island** - Geoff's Place YHA 10 Horseshoe Bay Rd, Horseshoe Bay, Magnetic Island, North Queensland. **e** geoffsplace@beyond.net.au	☎ (7) 47785577 🖷 (7) 47785781	158		¶O¶ CC ✧ P 🖅 ☕ ✿
▲ **Mallacoota** - Mallacoota Lodge YHA 51-55 Maurice Ave, Mallacoota 3892. **e** mallacoota@yhavic.org.au	☎ (3) 51580455 🖷 (3) 51580453	12		♦♦ CC ✧ P 🖅
▲ **Maroochydore** - Maroochydore YHA Backpackers 24 Schirrmann Drive, Maroochydore, Queensland 4558. (112km N of Brisbane). **e** mail@yhabackpackers.com	☎ (7) 54433151 🖷 (7) 54793156	48		♦♦ ¶O¶ CC ✧ P 🖅
▲ **Mary River Park** - Mary River YHA Arnhem Hwy, Mary River NT. **e** general@maryriverpark.com.au	☎ (8) 89788877 🖷 (8) 89788899	11		
▲ **Melbourne** - Queensberry Hill YHA **(IBN)** **78 Howard St, North Melbourne, Victoria 3051.** **e** queensberryhill@yhavic.org.au	☎ (3) 93298599 🖷 (3) 93268427	348		♦♦ ¶O¶ 1.4N ♿ CC ✧ P 🖅
▲ **Melbourne** - Chapman Gardens YHA **76 Chapman St, North Melbourne, Victoria 3051.** **e** chapman@yhavic.org.au	☎ (3) 93283595 🖷 (3) 93297863	120		CC ✧ P 🖅
▲ **Merimbula** - Wandarrah Lodge YHA 8 Marine Parade, Merimbula, New South Wales 2548. **e** wanlodge@asitis.com.au	☎ (2) 64953503 🖷 (2) 64953163	44		♦♦ ¶O¶ R CC P 🖅
▲ **Mildura** - Rosemount Guest House YHA 154 Madden Ave, Mildura, Victoria 3500. (560Km NW of Melbourne). **e** mildura@yhavic.org.au	☎ (3) 50231535 🖷 (3) 50231535	10		¶O¶ CC ✧ P 🖅
▲ **Mission Beach** - Treehouse YHA Bingil Bay Rd, Mission Beach, North Queensland 4852. **e** treehouse.yha@znet.net.au	☎ (7) 40687137 🖷 (7) 40687028	60		¶O¶ CC ✧ P 🖅
▲ **Monkey Mia/Shark Bay** - Monkey Mia Dolphin Resort YHA Monkey Mia Rd, Monkey Mia, Shark Bay, Queensland 6537. **e** sales@monkeymia.com.au	☎ (8) 99481320 🖷 (8) 99481034	32		♦♦ ¶O¶ R CC ✧ P 🖅 ⚲

Location/Address	Telephone No. Fax No.	Beds	Opening Dates	Facilities
▲ **Mount Field National Park** - Mt Field N.P. YHA Main Rd, Mt Field National Park, Tasmania 7140. ℮ yhatas@yhatas.org.au	☎ (3) 62881369	24	🔲12	� ☞ 🅿 ⓞ
▲ **Mt Buller** - YHA Lodge The Ave, Mt Buller Alpine Village, Victoria 3723. (240km NE Melbourne). ℮ mountbuller@yhavic.org.au	☎ (3) 57776181 🖷 (3) 57776691	46	Jun–Oct	♦♦♦ Ⓡ ⌐CC┐ ☞ ⓞ
▲ **Mt Surprise** - Undara Experience YHA Swags Tent Village, Lava Lodge, Undara, Queensland 4871. (270km West of Cairns). ℮ res@undara.com.au	☎ (7) 40971411 🖷 (7) 40971450	94	🔲12	♦♦♦ ⅈⓄⅈ Ⓡ ⌐CC┐ ☞ 🅿 ⓞ ☕
▲ **Mt Warning/Murwillumbah** - Riverside YHA 1 Tumbulgum Rd, Murwillumbah, New South Wales 2484. ℮ mbahyha@norex.com.au	☎ (2) 66723763	24	🔲12	⌐CC┐ ☞ 🅿 ⓞ
▲ **Narooma** - Bluewater Lodge YHA 8 Princes Hwy, Narooma, NSW 2546. ℮ naroomayha@narooma.com	☎ (2) 44764440 🖷 (2) 44765444	48	🔲12	♦♦♦ ⅈⓄⅈ 1N ⌐CC┐ ☞ 🅿 ⓞ
▲ **Newcastle** - Newcastle Beach YHA Backpackers 30 Pacific St, Newcastle, New South Wales 2300. ℮ yhanewcastle@hunterlink.net.au	☎ (2) 49253544 🖷 (2) 49253944	100	🔲12	ⅈⓄⅈ ⌐CC┐ ☞ ⓞ
▲ **Noosa Heads** - Halse Lodge Guesthouse YHA 2 Halse Lane, Noosa Heads, Queensland 4567. ℮ backpackers@halselodge.com.au	☎ (7) 54473377, (Freecall 1800 242567) 🖷 (7) 54472929	97	🔲12	ⅈⓄⅈ ⌐CC┐ ☞ 🅿 ⓞ
▲ **Oatlands** - Oatlands YHA 9 Wellington St, Oatlands, Tasmania 7205. (80km N of Hobart). ℮ yhatas@yhatas.org.au	☎ (3) 62541320	10	🔲12	☞ 🅿 ⓞ
▲ **Pemberton** - Pimelea Chalets YHA Stirling Rd, Pemberton, Western Australia 6260. ℮ yhapemberton@hotmail.com	☎ (8) 97761153 🖷 (8) 97761819	63	🔲12	♦♦♦ ⌐CC┐ ☞ 🅿 ⓞ
▲ **Perth** - Northbridge YHA Backpackers **42-48 Francis St, Northbridge, Western Australia 6003.** ℮ yhanb@hotmail.com	☎ (8) 93287794 🖷 (8) 93287794	108	🔲12	Ⓡ 0.5S ⌐CC┐ ☞ ⓞ
▲ **Perth** - Britannia International YHA ⌐IBN┐ **253 William St, Northbridge, Western Australia 6003.** ℮ britannia@yhawa.com.au	☎ (8) 93286121 🖷 (8) 92279784	134	🔲12	♦♦♦ Ⓡ 0.5S ♿ ⌐CC┐ ☞ ⓞ

Location/Address	Telephone No. Fax No.	Beds	Opening Dates	Facilities
▲ **Perth Hills** - Djaril-Mari YHA Mundaring Weir Rd, Mundaring, Western Australia 6073. (40km E of Perth-located in midst of bushland).	☎ (8) 92951809 🖷 (8) 92950749	36	🛏	♐ ♿ ☜ P ▣
▲ **Phillip Island (Cowes)** - Amaroo Park YHA 97 Church St, Cowes, Phillip Island, Victoria 3922. ✉ phillipisland@yhavic.org.au	☎ (3) 59522548 🖷 (3) 59523620	50	🛏	♐ ⛴ CC ☜ P ▣ ☕
▲ **Pine Creek** - Pine Creek YHA Lot 242, Wilcox St, Pine Creek, Northern Territory 0847. ✉ yhapinecreek@bigpond.com.au	☎ (8) 89761078 🖷 (8) 89761078	28	🛏	R CC P
▲ **Porongurup** - Porongurup Backpackers YHA Porongurup Rd, Porongurup, Western Australia 6324. ✉ homebake@omninet.com.au	☎ (8) 98531110 🖷 (8) 98531116	15	🛏	♐ ⛴ CC ☜ P ▣ ☕
▲ **Port Arthur** - Roseview YHA Champ St, Port Arthur, Tasmania 7182. (100km S of Hobart). ✉ yhatas@yhatas.org.au	☎ (3) 62502311	44	🛏	♐ CC ☜ P ▣
▲ **Port Campbell** - Port Campbell YHA 18 Tregea St, Port Campbell 3269. ✉ portcampbell@yhavic.org.au	☎ (3) 55986305 🖷 (3) 55986305	64	🛏	⛴ 0.1 W CC ☜ P ▣
▲ **Port Douglas** - Port O'Call Lodge YHA Port St, Port Douglas, Queensland 4871. ✉ info@portocall.com.au	☎ (7) 40995422, (Freecall 1800 892800) 🖷 (7) 40995495	95	🛏	♐ ⛴ CC ☜ P ▣ ☕
▲ **Port Elliot** - Arnella By The Sea YHA 28 North Tce, Pt Elliot, South Australia 5212. ✉ narnu@bigpond.com	☎ (8) 85543611 🖷 (8) 85552633	17	🛏	♐ ⛴ R 110 SE CC ☜ P ▣ ☕
▲ **Port Fairy** - Port Fairy YHA 8 Cox St, Port Fairy, Victoria 3284. (290km SW of Melbourne). ✉ portfairy@yhavic.org.au	☎ (3) 55682468 🖷 (3) 55682302	50	🛏	♐ ⛴ CC ☜ P ▣
▲ **Port Hedland** - Dingo's Oasis B'packer and Bunkhouse YHA 59 Kingsmill St, Port Headland, Western Australia 6721. ✉ dingososasis@hotmail.com	☎ (8) 91731000 🖷 (8) 91735159	30	🛏	⛴ ☜ P ▣
▲ **Port Macquarie** - Beachside Backpackers YHA 40 Church St, Port Macquarie, New South Wales 2444. ✉ portmacqyha@hotmail.com	☎ (2) 65835512 🖷 (2) 65835512	30	🛏	♐ CC ☜ P ▣

Location/Address	Telephone No. Fax No.	Beds	Opening Dates	Facilities
▲ **Queenscliff** - The Queenscliff Inn YHA 59 Hesse St, Queenscliff, Victoria 3225. e queenscliff@yhavic.org.au	☎ (3) 52583737 🖷 (3) 52583737	10	🛏12	♟ ⑂ R CC ♂ P ⑃ ☕
▲ **Quorn/Flinders Rangers** - Andu Lodge YHA 12 First St, Quorn, South Australia 5433. e headbush@dove.net.au	☎ (8) 86486655 🖷 (8) 86486655	50	🛏12	CC ♂ P ⑃ 🚲
▲ **Rainbow Beach** - The Rocks Backpacker Resort YHA Spectrum St, Rainbow Beach, Queensland 4581. e yhaqld@yhaqld.org	☎ 1800 646867 🖷 (7) 54863229	60	🛏12	♟ ⑂ CC ♂ P ⑃
▲ **Robe** - Robe Longbeach YHA 70-80 The Esplanade, Robe, South Australia 5276. e robelongbeachpark@bigpond.com	☎ (8) 87682237 🖷 (8) 87682730	20	🛏12	♟ ⑂ R 350SE CC ♂ P ⑃ ☕
▲ **Rockhampton** - Rockhampton YHA **60 MacFarlane St, North Rockhampton,** **Queensland 4701.** e rockhampton@yhaqld.org	☎ (7) 49275288 🖷 (7) 49226040	52	🛏12	♟ R CC ♂ P ⑃
▲ **Rottnest Island** - Kingstown Barracks YHA Kingstown, Rottnest Island. (27km W of Perth).	☎ (8) 93729780 🖷 (8) 92925141	54	🛏12	⑂ R 27W ♿ CC
▲ **Scone** - Scone YHA 1151 Segenhoe Rd, Scone, New South Wales 2337. e yhascone@hunterlink.net.au	☎ (2) 65452072 🖷 (2) 65452072	26	🛏12	♟ ⑂ ♂ P
▲ **Shoal Bay** - Shoal Bay YHA 61 Beachfront Rd, Shoal Bay, New South Wales 2315. e shoalbaymotel@bigpond.com	☎ (2) 49810982 🖷 (2) 49841052	18	🛏12	♟ CC ♂ P ⑃
▲ **Sorrento** - Sorrento YHA 3 Miranda St, Sorrento, Victoria 3943. e sorrento@yhavic.org.au	☎ (3) 59844323 🖷 (3) 59844323	30	🛏12	♟ CC ♂ P
▲ **Springbrook** - Springbrook Mountain Lodge YHA 317 Repeater Station Rd, Springbrook QLD 4213. e springbrooklodge@ion.tm	☎ (7) 55335366 🖷 (7) 55335366	20	🛏12	♟ 46W CC ♂ P ⑃
▲ **St Helens** - St Helens YHA 5 Cameron St, St Helens, Tasmania 7216. e yhatas@yhatas.org.au	☎ (3) 63761661	22	🛏12	♟ ♂ P ⑃
▲ **Stanley** - Stanley YHA Wharf Rd, c/- Caravan Park, Stanley, Tasmania 7331. e yhatas@yhatas.org.au	☎ (3) 64581266 🖷 (3) 64581266	12	🛏12	CC ♂ P ⑃
▲ **Strahan** - Strahan YHA Harvey St, Strahan, Tasmania 7468. e strahancentral@trump.net.au	☎ 1800 444442, (3) 64717255 🖷 (3) 64717513	64	🛏12	♟ CC ♂ P ⑃

Location/Address	Telephone No. Fax No.	Beds	Opening Dates	Facilities
▲ **Surfers Paradise/Gold Coast -** British Arms International B'packers Resort YHA Mariner's Cove, 70 Seaworld Drive, Surfers Paradise, Queensland 4217. ✉ info@britisharms.com.au	☎ (7) 55711776, (Freecall 1800 680269) 🖷 (7) 55711747	118	🔟	👬 🍴 4N CC ✇ P ▣
▲ **Swansea** - Swansea YHA 5 Franklin St, Swansea, Tasmania. ✉ yhatas@yhatas org.au	☎ (3) 62578367	22	🔟	👬 ✇ P ▣
▲ **Sydney** - Sydney Beachouse YHA **Sydney Beachouse, 4 Collaroy St, Collaroy Beach, New South Wales 2097.** ✉ mail@sydneybeachouse.com.au	☎ (2) 99811177 🖷 (2) 99811114	228	🔟	👬 🍴 R ♿ CC ✇ P ▣
▲ **Sydney** - Sydney Central YHA IBN **Sydney Central YHA, 11 Rawson Place. (cnr Pitt St and Rawson) opposite Central Station.** ✉ sydcentral@yhansw.org.au	☎ (2) 92819111 🖷 (2) 92819199	532	🔟	🍴 CC ✇ ▣
▲ **Sydney** - Cronulla Beach YHA Level 1, 40-42 Kingsway, Cronulla NSW 2230. ✉ enquiries@cronullabeachyha.com	☎ (2) 95277772 🖷 (2) 95270533	46	🔟	♿ CC ✇ P ▣ 🚲 ✿
▲ **Sydney** - Dulwich Hill YHA 407 Marrickville Rd, Dulwich Hill, NSW 2203. ✉ dulwichhillyha@oranalodge.com.au	☎ (2) 95500054 🖷 (2) 95500570	134	🔟	👬 R CC ✇ P ▣ 🚲 ✿
▲ **Sydney** - Glebe Point YHA IBN **262 Glebe Point Rd, Glebe, New South Wales 2037.** ✉ glebe@yhansw.org.au	☎ (2) 96928418 🖷 (2) 96600431	151	🔟	CC ✇ ▣
▲ **Sydney** - Pittwater YHA Halls Wharf, via Church Point, New South Wales 2105. (30km N of Sydney, W shore of Pittwater). ✉ pittwater@rivernet.com.au	☎ (2) 99992196 🖷 (2) 99974296	32	🔟	👬 CC ✇
△ *Taggerty -* *Australian Bush Settlement YHA* *2618 Marondah Hwy, Taggerty, Victoria.* *(104km NE of Melbourne).* ✉ *taggerty@yhavic.org.au*	☎ *(3) 57747378* 🖷 *(3) 57747442*	*25*	🔟	✇ P ▣
▲ **Tamworth** - Tamworth YHA 169 Marius St, Tamworth. ✉ tamworhyha@optusnet.com.au	☎ (2) 67612600 🖷 (2) 67612002	43	🔟	0.2N CC ✇ P ▣ 🚲 ✿
▲ **Tennant Creek** - Safari Backpackers YHA 12 Davidson St, Tennant Creek, Northern Territory, 0860. ✉ safari@swtch.com.au	☎ (8) 89622207 🖷 (8) 89623188	27	🔟	👬 🍴 CC ✇ P ▣
▲ **Tenterfield** - Tenterfield Lodge YHA 2 Manners St, Tenterfield NSW 2372. ✉ tenterfieldlodge@globalfreeway.com.au	☎ (2) 67361477 🖷 (2) 67363552	20	🔟	0.5W CC ✇ P ▣ 🚲

Location/Address	Telephone No. Fax No.	Beds	Opening Dates	Facilities
▲ **Terrigal** - Terrigal Beach Lodge YHA 12 Campbell Crescent, Terrigal, New South Wales 2260. e yha@terrigalbeachlodge.com.au	☎ (2) 43853330 ✆ (2) 43853330	36	🏠12	♦♦♦ ⓘⓞⓘ 0.1N ⊂CC⊃ ⚲ 🅿 ▣
▲ **Thredbo** - Thredbo YHA 8 Jack Adams Path, Thredbo Alpine Village, New South Wales 2625. e thredbo@yhansw.org.au	☎ (2) 64576376 ✆ (2) 64576043	52	🏠12	♦♦♦ Ⓡ ⊂CC⊃ ⚲ ▣
△ *Triabunna* - *Triabunna YHA* *Spencer St, Triabunna, Tasmania 7190.* e *yhatas@yhatas.org.au*	☎ (3) 62573439 ✆ (3) 62573439	*34*	🏠12	♦♦♦ ⚲ 🅿 ▣
▲ **Walpole** - Tingle All Over YHA 60 Nockolds St, Walpole, Western Australia 6398.	☎ (8) 98401041 ✆ (8) 98401041	23	🏠12	♦♦♦ Ⓡ ⊂CC⊃ ⚲ 🅿
▲ **Winnaleah** - Merlinkei Farm YHA 524 Racecourse Rd, Winnaleah, Tasmania 7265. e mervync@vision.net.au	☎ (3) 63542152 ✆ (3) 63541000	22	🏠12	⚲ 🅿 ▣

YOUTH HOSTEL ACCOMMODATION OUTSIDE THE ASSURED STANDARDS SCHEME

Coles Bay - Freycinet National Park Coles Bay, Tasmania 7215. e yhatas@yhatas.org.au	☎ c/o (3) 62349617	10	🏠12	Ⓡ ⚲ 🅿

"To travel hopefully is a better thing than to arrive."

"Voyager avec espoir est mieux que d'arriver."

„Mit Hoffnung zu reisen ist besser, als sein Ziel zu erreichen"

"Viajar con esperanza es mejor que llegar."

Robert Louis Stevenson

HOSTELLING
INTERNATIONAL

Take the HI way!

For HI quality accommodation at the best prices.

Visit one of our 4200 hostels in over 60 countries.

www.iyhf.org

Brazil

BRESIL
BRASILIEN
BRASIL

**Federação Brasileira dos Albergues da Juventude,
Rua General Dionísio, 63-Botafogo - Rio de Janeiro
CEP: 22271-050, Brasil.**

📞 (55) (21) 2860303
📠 (55) (21) 2865652
✉ info@hostel.org.br
🖳 www.hostel.org.br

A copy of the Hostel Directory for this Country can be obtained from:
The National Office

Capital:	Brasilia		**Population:**	182,320,000
Language:	Portuguese		**Size:**	511,965 sq km
Currency:	R$ (Real)		**Telephone Country Code:**	55

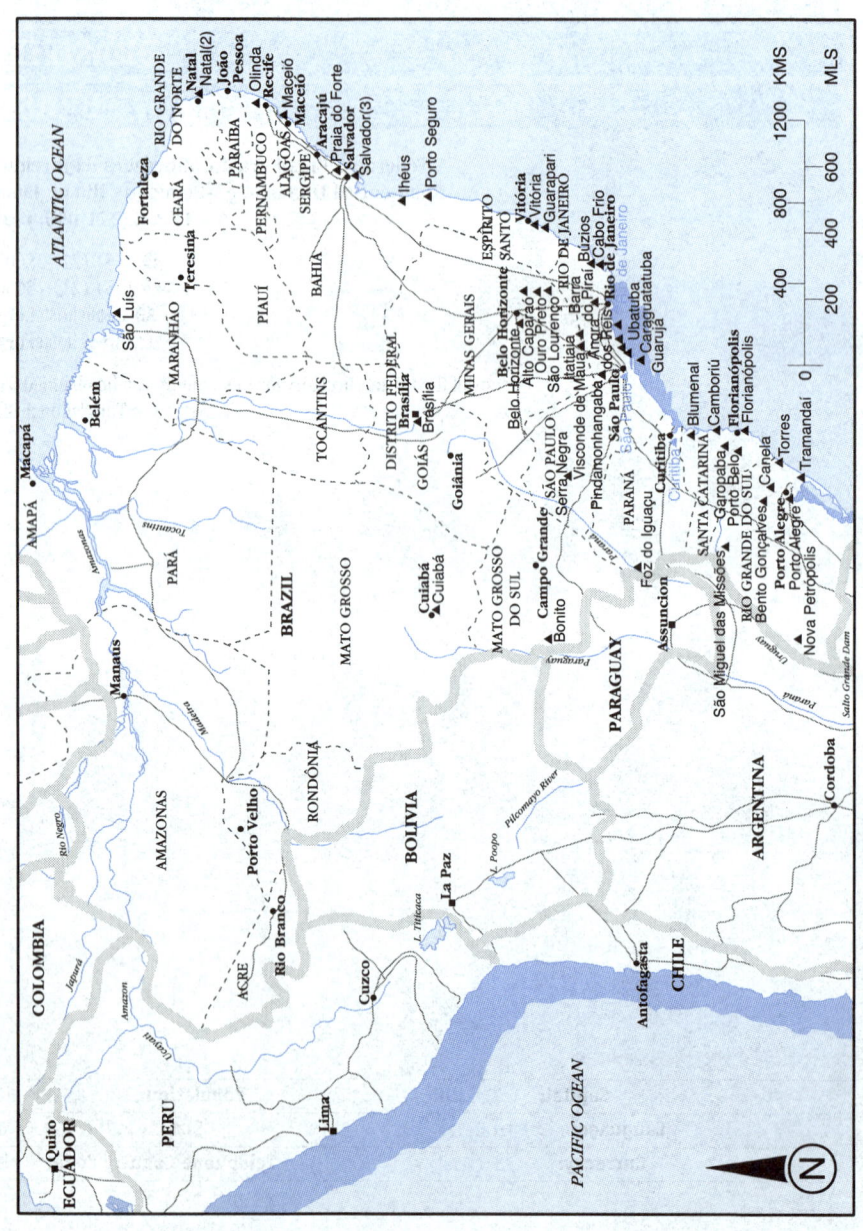

English

Hostels are located in cities, in the countryside, on the coast and on hills/mountains.

Price range

Price range US$ 7.00-11.00. BB inc SH.

Rooms and Reservations

R 🔳 (All Rooms). Reservations via IBN 🔳 or Hostel by ❶ ❷ ❸. Smoking is limited - please check.

Guests

Membership Card is required. The maximum stay is 15 days. Age limits may apply for mixed age groups - check with hostel. ♦♦♦ welcome. Group bookings via 🔳 or Hostel by ❶ ❷ ❸ (Reservation charges may apply).

Open times

Main hostels: open 🔳, 🕐. Reception open: 🕐. **Seasonal hostels** are generally open Jan, Feb, Jul.

Meals

🍽 B 🔶.

Travelling around

For ease of travel use ✈ 🚌.

Travel/Activity Packages

Tours/sightseeing and accommodation/transport packages available. Package bookings via Hostel.

Passports and Visas

Passport required.

Health

Vaccinations are required - check with your medical advisor. Emergency medical treatment is free.

Français

Les auberges sont situées dans les villes, à la campagne, sur le littoral et à la montagne.

Tarifs des nuitées

Tarifs des nuitées 7.00-11.00 US$. BB inc SH.

Chambres et réservations

R 🔳 (Toutes chambres). Réservations via IBN 🔳 ou l'auberge par ❶ ❷ ❸. Il est permis de fumer dans certaines chambres - veuillez vérifier.

Usagers

La carte d'adhérent est à présenter. La durée maximale du séjour est de 15 jours. Il est possible que des limites d'âge soient en vigueur pour les groupes d'âges mixtes - vérifiez auprès de l'auberge. Accueil des ♦♦♦. Réservations pour groupes via 🔳 ou l'auberge par ❶ ❷ ❸ (Des frais de réservation pourront vous être facturés).

Horaires d'ouverture

Grandes auberges: ouvertes 🔳, 🕐. Accueil ouvert 🕐. **Auberges saisonnières** ouvertes généralement jan, fév, juil.

Repas

🍽 B 🔶.

Déplacements

Modes de transport recommandés ✈ 🚌.

Forfaits Voyages/Activités

Forfaits circuits touristiques et hébergement/transport disponibles. Réservations des forfaits via l'auberge.

Passeports et visas

Passeport obligatoire.

Santé

Des vaccinations sont obligatoires - veuillez vérifier auprès de votre médecin. Soins d'urgence gratuits.

Deutsch

Herbergen befinden sich in Städten, auf dem Land, an der Küste und in Bergen/Gebirgen.

Preisspanne

Preisspanne 7.00-11.00 US$. BB|inc ⚏.

Zimmer und Reservierungen

R ⚏ (Alle Zimmer). Reservierungen über IBN ⚏ oder die Herberge per ❶ ❷ ❸. Rauchen ist begrenzt - bitte checken.

Gäste

Mitgliedsausweis ist erforderlich. Der maximale Aufenthalt beträgt 15 Tage. Altersbegrenzungen für Gruppen gemischten Alters möglich - in der Herberge nachfragen. ⛷ willkommen. Gruppenbuchungen über ⚏ oder die Herberge per ❶ ❷ ❸ (Reservierungskosten könnten anfallen).

Öffnungszeiten

Hauptherbergen: Zugang ⚏, ⏱. Rezeption ⏱. **Saison-Herbergen** sind normalerweise Jan, Feb, Jul geöffnet.

Mahlzeiten

⚏ B ⚏.

Reisen im Land

Reisen ist einfach mit ✈ 🚌.

Reise-/Aktivitäten-Packages

Touren/sightseeing und Unterkunft/Transport-Packages erhältlich. Package-Buchungen über Herberge.

Reisepässe und Visa

Reisepass erforderlich.

Gesundheit

Schutzimpfungen sind erforderlich - mit Ihrem Arzt checken. Nur im Notfall sind medizinische Behandlungen kostenlos.

Español

Los albergues están situados en las ciudades, el campo, la costa y la montaña.

Tarifas mínima y máxima

Tarifas mínima y máxima 7.00-11.00 US$. BB|inc ⚏.

Habitaciones y Reservas

R ⚏ (Todas las habitaciones). Reservas por IBN ⚏ o a través del albergue por ❶ ❷ ❸. Está permitido fumar sólo en algunas salas/habitaciones - infórmese.

Huéspedes

Los huéspedes deben presentar su Carnet de Alberguista. La estancia máxima es de 15 días. Es posible que exista un límite de edad para los grupos de personas de diferentes edades - consulte con el albergue. Se admiten ⛷. Reservas de grupo por ⚏ o a través del albergue por ❶ ❷ ❸ (Es posible que se aplique un suplemento en concepto de gastos de reserva).

Horarios y fechas de apertura

Albergues principales - abiertos ⚏, ⏱. Horario de recepción: ⏱. **Albergues de temporada** suelen abrir: ene, feb, jul.

Comidas

⚏ B ⚏.

Desplazamientos

Transportes recomendados: ✈ 🚌.

Viajes Combinados con Actividades

Viajes combinados con visitas turísticas y alojamiento/transporte. Reserva de viajes combinados a través del albergue.

Pasaportes y Visados

Pasaporte obligatorio.

Información Sanitaria

Vacunación obligatoria - consulte con su centro médico. Asistencia médica de urgencia gratuita.

Rio de Janeiro -
Rio Hostel

Rua General Dionísio 63,
Botafogo,
22271-050 Rio de Janeiro,
RJ.
🕻 **(21) 2860303,**
🖷 **(21) 2865652**
🕿 **riohostel@riohostel.com.br**

Open Dates:	📅
Open Hours:	🕐
Reservations:	ⓡ IBN -CC-
Price Range:	$9.50-11.00 € 19.00-22.00
Beds:	70 - 1x^2🛏 2x^4🛏 1x^5🛏 6x^6🛏 2x^6🛏
Facilities:	♿ 👬 👬 🍽 (B) 🛡 🏨 📺 📧 🧺 1 x 🍷 🔲 🖼 🎱 8 🔄 💱 🅿 ℹ 🍼
Directions:	8S from city centre
✈	Internacional 20km
⛴	Do RJ 11km
🚌	172, 176, 409 500m
U	Botafogo 1.5km
Attractions:	🔍 3km

Location/Address	Telephone No. Fax No.	Beds	Opening Dates	Facilities
△ *Alto Caparaó* - *Pousada Querencia* *Av. Pico Da Bandeira, 1061 - Centro* *Alto Caparaó-MG. CEP: 36836-000.*	☎ (32) 7472566 🖷 (32) 7472566	18	12	⊙ R CC P
▲ **Angra dos Reis** - Pousada Rio Bracuí Estrada Santa Rita 4, Bracuí, Angra dos Reis/RJ, CEP 23900-000. ✉ ajriobracui@quick.com.br	☎ (24) 3631234 🖷 (24) 3631234	40	12	R P
▲ **Bahia** - Do Porto Salvador Rua Barão do Sergy 197, Barra-Salvador, Bahia. CEP 40140-040. ✉ albergue@e-net.com.br	☎ (71) 2646600 🖷 (71) 2644006	50	12	⊙ 5N
▲ **Barra do Piraí** - Na Toca Estrada Municipal Rui Pio Davi Gomes, 1876 Dorândia, Barra do Piraí, Rio de Janeiro State. CEP 27160-000.	☎ (24) 4331171	28	12	⊙ R P
▲ **Belo Horizonte** - Chalé Mineiro Rua Santa Luzia 288, 30260-120 Belo Horizonte, MG. ✉ chale@horizontes.net	☎ (31) 4671576 🖷 (31) 4671576	54	12	⊙ 3E P
▲ **Bento Gonçalves** - Pousada Casa Mia Travessa Niterói 71, 95700-000 Bento Gonçalves, RS.	☎ (54) 4511215	54	12	R P
△ *Blumenau* - *Pousada Grun Garten* *Rua São Paulo, 2457-Itoupara* *Seca-Blumenau-SC. CEP: 89030-000.* ✉ *gruuengarten@hotmail.com.br*	☎ (47) 3234332 🖷 (47) 3234332	56	12	⊙ R P
▲ **Bonito** - Bonito Rua Lucio Borralho, 716 - Villa Donária - Bonito - MS, CEP 79290-000. ✉ ajbonito@zaz.com.br	☎ (67) 2551462 🖷 (67) 2551462	56	12	⊙ P
▲ **Brasilia** - Brasilia Setor De Areas Isoladas Norte, Sain Camping-Plano Piloto. CEP: 70800-200.	☎ (61) 3236538; (61) 2231440 🖷 (61) 3255740	80	12	⊙ R ♿ CC P
△ *Búzios* - *Praia dos Amores* *Av Bento Ribeiro Dantas,* *92 - Praia da Tartaruga - Búzios - RJ.* *CEP 28905-000.*	☎ (24) 6232422	50	12	R 1N
△ *Cabo Frio* - *São Lucas* *Rua Goiás 266, Jardim Excelsior,* *28915-170 Cabo Frio, RJ.*	☎ (24) 6453037	36	12	R P
△ *Camboriú* - *Alpino* *Rua Estados Unidos,* *180-Nações. CEP: 83330-000.*	☎ (47) 3673332 🖷 (47) 3673332	40	12	
▲ **Canela** - Pousada do Viajante Rua Ernesto Urbani 132, 95680-000 Canela, RS.	☎ (54) 2822017	40	12	R 0.2S P
△ *Caraguatatuba* - *Recanto das Andorinhas* *Rua Engº João Fonseca 112. 11660-200* *Caraguatatuba, SP.*	☎ (12) 4221862; (12) 4226181	35	12	R P

Location/Address	Telephone No. Fax No.	Beds	Opening Dates	Facilities
△ *Cuiabá* - *Portal Do Pantanal* *Av. Isaac Póvoas, 655-Centro* *Cuiabá-MT. CEP: 78000-000.* ⓔ *albergue@dinet.com.br*	❶ *(65) 6248999* ❺ *(65) 6248999*	*38*	🛏️	ⅲ ⌶⊙ Ⓡ ⊞CC⊟ ♂ Ⓟ ⊡ ☕
△ *Curitiba* - *Curitiba* *Rua Padre Agostinho 645, Mercês 80430-050,* *Curitiba, PR.* ⓔ *ajcwb@uol.com.br*	❶ *(41) 2332746* ❺ *(41) 2332834*	*50*	🛏️	ⅲ 3W ♂ Ⓟ ⊡
▲ **Florianópolis** - Canasvieiras R.Dr.João de Oliveira, 100, Florianópolis / SC-CEP:88054-970.	❶ (48) 2251692 ❺ (48) 2251692	140	🛏️	ⅲ Ⓡ Ⓟ
▲ **Florianópolis** - Ilha de Santa Catarina Rua Duarte Schutel 227. 88015-640 Florianópolis, SC.	❶ (48) 2253781 ❺ (48) 2251692	70	🛏️	ⅲ Ⓡ 4N ♂ Ⓟ ⊡
▲ **Foz do Iguaçú** - Paudimar Rodovia das Cataratas, KM 12,5, Remanso Grande, Foz do Iguaçú, PR 85863-000. ⓔ paudimar@foznet.com.br	❶ (45) 5722430 ❺ (45) 5722430	100	🛏️	ⅲ ⌶⊙ ♂ Ⓟ ⊡
▲ **Foz do Iguaçú** - Paudimar Centro Rua Rui Barbosa, 634-Centro- Foz do Iguaçú-PR. CEP: 85863-000. ⓔ paudimar@foz.net.com.br	❶ (45) 5745503 ❺ (45) 5745503	68	🛏️	ⅲ ⌶⊙ Ⓡ ⊞CC⊟ ♂ Ⓟ ⊡ ☕ ✿
△ *Garopaba* - *Praia Do Ferrugeu* *Estrada Geral Do Capão,* *S/No Garopaba-SC. CEP: 88495-000.*	❶ *(48) 2540035*	*40*	*01.01–31.03*	⌶⊙ Ⓡ ♂ Ⓟ ⊡
△ *Guarapari* - *Guaralbergue* *Avenida F, Quadra 40, Itapebussu,* *29200-000 Guarapari, ES.*	❶ *(27) 2610475* ❺ *(27) 2610475*	*100*	🛏️	ⅲ Ⓡ 0.8S ♂ Ⓟ ⊡
△ *Guarujá* - *Guarujá* *Rua das Camélias, 10 - Praia da Enseada -* *Guarujá, SP-CEP: 11441-110.*	❶ *(13) 3517779*	*51*	🛏️	ⅲ Ⓡ 2NE Ⓟ ⊡
▲ **Ilhéus** - Fazenda Tororomba Rua Luiz Eduardo Magalhães S/N - Centro - Olivença - Ilhéus - BA, CEP: 45650-000. ⓔ tororomba@uol.com.br	❶ (73) 2691139 ❺ (73) 2691150	100	🛏️	ⅲ ⌶⊙ Ⓡ 5S Ⓟ ⊡
△ *Itatiaia* - *Ipê Amarelo* *Rua João Mauricio de Macedo Costa 352,* *27580-000 Itatiaia, RJ.*	❶ *(243) 521232*	*45*	🛏️	ⅲ Ⓡ 1E Ⓟ ⊡
△ *Maceió* - *Nossa Casa* *Rua Prefeito Abdon Arroxelas, 327,* *Ponta Verde, 57035-380 Maceió, AL.*	❶ *(82) 2312246*	*75*	🛏️	ⅲ Ⓡ 6S ♂ Ⓟ ⊡
▲ **Natal** - Lua Cheia Rua Dr Manoel Augusto Bezerra de Araújo, 500 Ponta Negra, Natal, R/N, CP 59090-430. ⓔ luacheia@digi.com.br	❶ (84) 2363696 ❺ (84) 2364747	80	🛏️	ⅲ ⌶⊙ Ⓡ Ⓟ ⊡
▲ **Natal** - Verdes Mares Rua Das Algas, 2166-Praia De Ponta Negra, CEP 59090-410.	❶ (84) 2362872 ❺ (84) 2362872	30	🛏️	ⅲ Ⓟ ⊡

Location/Address	Telephone No. Fax No.	Beds	Opening Dates	Facilities
△ *Nova Petrópolis* - *Bou Pastor* *Estrada RS 235, KM 14 - Linha Brasil -* *Nova Petrópolis-RS. CEP: 95150-970.*	☎ *(54) 2988066* 🖷 *(54) 2988066*	*60*	▣12	⋔ R P ▣
△ *Olinda* - *Cheiro do Mar* *Ave Ministro Marcos Freire 95,* *53030-000 Olinda, PE.*	☎ *(81) 4290101* 🖷 *(81) 4652224*	*46*	▣12	⋔ ⍾ R 1.5S ⚲ P ▣
▲ **Olinda** - Pousada Saó Judas Tadeu Av Brasilia, 16-Jardim Brasil II, Olinda-PE. CEP: 53230-710.	☎ (81) 4264531	40	▣12	⋔ R ⊞CC⊟ ⚲ P ▣ ☕
▲ **Ouro Preto** - Ouro Preto Rua Costa Sena, 30-Largo Decoimbra Ouro Preto-MG. CEP: 35400-000. ✉ albergue@feop.com.br	☎ (31) 5516705	45	▣12	⋔ ⍾ R ⊞CC⊟ ⚲ P ▣ ☕
△ *Pindamonhangaba* - *Recanto Tropical* *Rua Dr, João Romeiro,* *92 12400-000 Pindamonhangaba, SP.*	☎ *(12) 2422737*	*24*	▣12	R P ▣
▲ **Porto Belo** - Porto Belo Rua José J. Anâncio, 246 Porto Belo - SC. CEP: 88210.000.	☎ (48) 2431057 🖷 (47) 3694483	40	01.01–31.03	⋔ ⍾ R ⚲ P ☕
▲ **Porto Seguro** - Maracaia Rodovia Port Seguro - Km 77.5 - 45820-000 Coroa Vermelha, Santa Cruz de Cabrália, BA. ✉ ajmaracaia@portonet.com.br	☎ (73) 8721155 🖷 (73) 8721156	180	▣12	⋔ ⍾ R 15N ⚲ P ▣
▲ **Porto Seguro** - Porto Seguro R. Cova da Moça, 720 - Trevo de Porto Seguro - BA, CEP 45810-000.	☎ (73) 2881742 🖷 (73) 2881742	80	▣12	⋔ ⍾ R ▣
▲ **Praia do Forte** - Praia do Forte Rua da Aurora No. 3, Praia do Forte/BA, CEP 48280-000. ✉ praiadoforte@albergue.com.br	☎ (71) 6761094 🖷 (71) 6761094	62	▣12	⋔ 0.2S ⚲ P ▣ ☕
▲ **Rio de Janeiro** - Rio Hostel (IBN) **Rua General Dionísio 63, Botafogo, 22271-050 Rio de Janeiro, RJ.** ✉ riohostel@riohostel.com.br	☎ (21) 2860303, 🖷 (21) 2865652	70	▣12	⋔ ⍾ R 8S ♿ ⊞CC⊟ ⚲ P ▣
▲ **Salvador** - Do Pelô Rua Ribeiro dos Santos 5, Salvador, BA, CEP 40030-020.	☎ (71) 2428061, 🖷 (71) 2428061	60	▣12	⋔ ⍾ R ▣
▲ **Salvador** - Laranjeiras Rua Inácio Accioli, 13-Pelourinho-Salvador-BA. CEP: 40030-020. ✉ alaranj@zaz.com.br	☎ (71) 3211366	60	▣12	⋔ R ⊞CC⊟ ⚲ ▣ ☕
▲ **Saó Lourenço** - Recanto Dos Carvalhos Rodovia MG (Dutra/ Caxambu) 158 Samambaia -Saó Lourenço-MG. CEP: 37470-000. ✉ info@recantodoscarvalhos.com.br	☎ (35) 3312098	54	▣12	⋔ ⍾ R ⊞CC⊟ ⚲ P ▣ ☕
△ *Saó Luis* - *Solar Das Pedras* *Rua Da Palma, 127-Centro-* *Saó Luiz Ma. CEP: 65010-440.* ✉ *ag.solardaspedras.ma@bol.wm.br*	☎ *(98) 2320953;* *(98) 2326694*	*40*	▣12	⋔ ⍾ R ⊞CC⊟ ⚲ P ▣ ☕

Location/Address	Telephone No. Fax No.	Beds	Opening Dates	Facilities
▲ **Saó Miguel Das Missoés** - Pousada Das Missoés Rua Saó Nicolau, 601-Saó Miguel Das Missoés-RS. CEP: 98865-000. ✉ turjovem@zaz.com.br	☎ (55) 3811202; (55) 3811297	90	📅12	�♀ 🍴 Ⓡ CC ☂ P 🔲 ☕
▲ **São Paulo** - Magdalena Tagliafero Estrada Turística do Jaraguá 651, Parque Estadual do Jaraguá, 05161-000 São Paulo, SP. ✉ info@alberguesp.com.br	☎ (11) 2580388 ☏ (11) 2580388	50	📅12	�♀ Ⓡ 18W CC ☂ P 🔲
△ *São Paulo* - *Praça Da Árvore Rua Pageú, 266 - Saúde - São Paulo - SP, CEP 04139-000.* ✉ *spalberg@internetcom.com.br*	☎ *(11) 50715148*	*44*	📅12	�♀ Ⓡ 0.5NE CC 🔲 ☕
△ *São Roque* - *Palhoça Est da Bela Vista, 154- São Roque - SP, CEP 18130-000.*	☎ *(11) 4254363*	*40*	📅12	�♀ P 🔲 ☕
▲ **Serra Negra** - Estância Clube Veranêio Rodovia Serra Negra, Águas de Lindóia, Km 156, CEP: 13970-000, SP Serra Negra.	☎ (19) 8922155	54	📅12	�♀ 🍴 Ⓡ 3E P 🔲
▲ **Torres** - São Domingos Rua Julio de Castilhos 875, CEP:95560-00 Torres, RS.	☎ (51) 6641865 ☏ (51) 6641022	180	📅12	�♀ Ⓡ ☂ P 🔲
▲ **Ubatuba** - Cora Coralina Rodovia Oswaldo Cruz, 89km, 11680-000 Ubatuba, SP. ✉ info@alberguesp.com.br	☎ (11) 2580388 ☏ (11) 2580388	26	📅12	�♀ 🍴 Ⓡ 6W CC ☂ P 🔲
△ *Visconde De Mavá* - *Do Visconde Estrada Do Vale Das Cruzes, S/No Valedascruzes-Visconde De Mavá-RJ. CEP: 27525-000.*	☎ *(24) 99796476*	*30*	📅12	�♀ 🍴 Ⓡ CC ☂ P 🔲 ☕
△ *Vitória* - *Príncipe Av. Dario Lourenço De Souza, 120 Ilha Do Príncipe CEP: 29026-080.*	☎ *(27) 3222799* ☏ *(27) 2233392*	*50*	📅12	�♀ 🍴 Ⓡ CC P 🔲 ☕

"Everywhere is nowhere. When a person spends all his time in foreign travel, he ends by having many acquaintances, but no friends."

"Partout est nulle part. Lorsque quelqu'un passe son temps à voyager à l'étranger, il finit avec beaucoup de connaissances, mais sans amis."

„Überall ist nirgendwo. Wenn jemand ständig fremde Länder bereist, hat er letztendlich viele Bekannte, aber keine Freunde."

"Todas partes es ninguna parte. Cuanda una persona dedica todo su tiempo a viajar al extranjero, acaba teniendo muchos conocidos, pero ningún amigo."

Seneca

Canada

CANADA
KANADA
CANADA

Hostelling International - Canada (National Office),
205 Catherine St, Suite 400, Ottawa,
Ontario K2P 1C3 Canada.

☎ (1) (613) 237-7884
✆ (1) (613) 237-7868
✉ info@hostellingintl.ca
🖳 www.hostellingintl.ca

A copy of the Hostel Directory for this Country can be obtained from:
The National Office

Capital:	Ottawa	**Population:**	29,955,000
Language:	English, French	**Size:**	9,976,139 sq km
Currency:	$ (dollar)	**Telephone Country Code:**	1

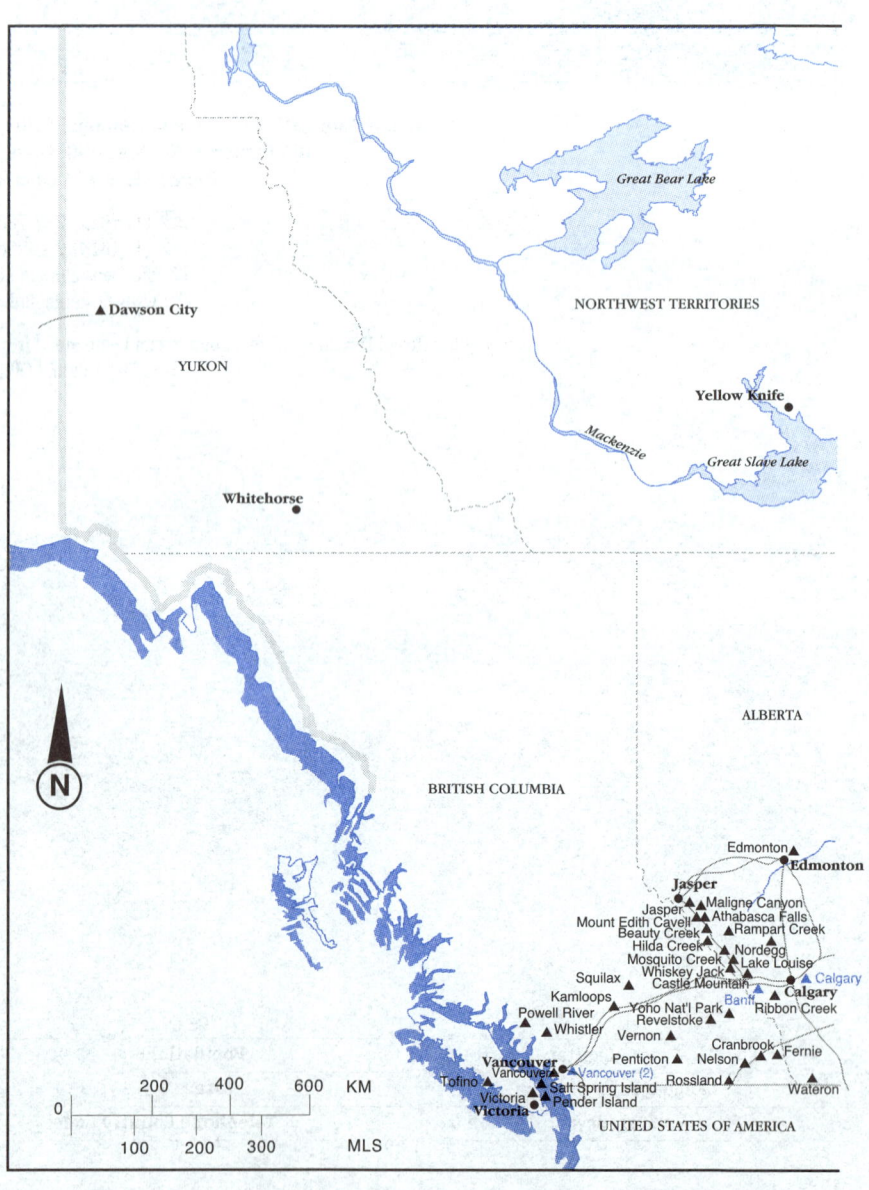

Great Bear Lake

NORTHWEST TERRITORIES

▲ Dawson City

YUKON

Yellow Knife ●

Mackenzie

Great Slave Lake

Whitehorse ●

N

ALBERTA

BRITISH COLUMBIA

Edmonton ▲
● Edmonton

Jasper
Jasper ●   Maligne Canyon ▲
Mount Edith Cavell ▲   Athabasca Falls ▲
Beauty Creek ▲   Rampart Creek ▲
Hilda Creek ▲   Nordegg ▲
Mosquito Creek ▲   Lake Louise ▲
Squilax ▲   Whiskey Jack ▲
           Castle Mountain ▲
Kamloops ●   ▲ Calgary
Powell River ●   Yoho Nat'l Park ▲   Banff ● Calgary ▲
Whistler ▲   Revelstoke ▲   Ribbon Creek ▲
           Vernon ▲
                        Cranbrook ▲
           Penticton ▲   Nelson ▲   Fernie ▲
Tofino ▲   Vancouver ▲ Vancouver (2)
Victoria ▲   Salt Spring Island   Rossland ▲
Victoria ▲   Pender Island   Wateron ▲

Vancouver

UNITED STATES OF AMERICA

200   400   600   KM
0
100   200   300   MLS

NORTHWEST TERRITORIES

CANADA

MANITOBA

SASKATCHEWAN

Nelson

Saskatchewan

Lake Winnipeg

ONTARIO

▲ Power View

Regina▲●
Regina

▲● **Winnipeg**
Winnipeg

Thunder Bay▲

UNITED STATES OF AMERICA

Lake Superior

BAFFIN ISLAND

HUDSON BAY

QUEBEC

NEWFOUNDLAND

ONTARIO

CANADA

Thunder Bay

Lake Superior

Sault Ste Marie

Marquette

Lake Huron

MICHIGAN

Lake Michigan

Calgaco

Indianapolis

Fort Coulonge

Wakefield

Orillia

Barrie

Peterborough

Toronto

Niagara

Detroit

Cleveland

PENNSYLVANIA

Pittsburgh

Ottawa

Kingston

Lake Ontario

Buffalo

Lake Eire

NEW YORK

Mont Tremblant

Val David

Montreal

Ottawa

St. Lawrent

VERMONT

NEW HAMPSHIRE

Boston

MASSACHUSETTS

CONNECTICUT

New York

Peribonka

St Jean Lake

La Tuque

Saguenay River

Trois Rivieres

Racine

Magog/Orford

MAINE

Quebec

Ile d'Orleans

RHODE ISLAND

Sept Iles

Rivière-du-Loup

GULF OF ST. LAWRENCE

Sainte-Anne-des-Monts

Cap Aux Os

Pointe-a-la-Garde

Campbellton

Nelson

NEW BRUNSWICK

Charlottetown

Fredericton

Alma

St John

Halifax

Annapolis Royal

South Milford

La Have

Wentworth

NOVA SCOTIA

NEWFOUNDLAND

St John's

0   500   1000 KM

200   400   600 MLS

English

Hostels are located in cities, in the countryside, on the coast and on hills/mountains.

Price range

Price range $14-25. 🛏 Sheet sleeping bag required.

Rooms and Reservations

R during Jan, May-Oct, Dec. (All Rooms). Reservations via **IBN** 🖥 or Hostel by ❶ ❷ ❸. All hostels are non-smoking.

Guests

Membership Card is required. The maximum stay is 7 days. ♦♦♦ welcome. Group bookings via **IBN** 🖥 or Hostel by ❶ ❷ ❸.

Open times

Main hostels: open 🗓, ◷. Reception open: ◷. **Other hostels:** open 🗓.

Meals

For individuals & for ♦♦♦. ☞.

Discounts

HI Member Discounts available - see discounts section and www.iyhf.org or www.hostellingintl.ca.

Travelling around

For ease of travel use 🚌 Self-Drive.

Travel/Activity Packages

Tours/sightseeing and accommodation/transport packages available. Package bookings via 🖥 or Hostel by ❶ ❷ ❸.

Passports and Visas

Passport required.

Health

Medical insurance is recommended.

Français

Les auberges sont situées dans les villes, à la campagne, sur le littoral et à la montagne.

Tarifs des nuitées

Tarifs des nuitées 14-25$. 🛏 Sac-drap obligatoire.

Chambres et réservations

R jan, mai-oct, déc. (Toutes chambres). Réservations via **IBN** 🖥 ou l'auberge par ❶ ❷ ❸. Toutes les auberges sont non-fumeurs.

Usagers

La carte d'adhérent est à présenter. La durée maximale du séjour est de 7 jours. Accueil des ♦♦♦. Réservations pour groupes via **IBN** 🖥 ou l'auberge par ❶ ❷ ❸.

Horaires d'ouverture

Grandes auberges: ouvertes 🗓, ◷. Accueil ouvert ◷. **Autres auberges:** ouvertes 🗓.

Repas

Pour individuels & pour ♦♦♦. ☞.

Remises

Remises pour les adhérents HI - voir la section "Remises" et notre site: www.iyhf.org ou www.hostellingintl.ca.

Déplacements

Modes de transport recommandés 🚌 Voiture.

Forfaits Voyages/Activités

Forfaits circuits touristiques et hébergement/transport disponibles. Réservations des forfaits via 🖥 ou l'auberge par ❶ ❷ ❸.

Passeports et visas

Passeport obligatoire.

Santé

Une assurance médicale de voyage est conseillée.

Deutsch

Herbergen befinden sich in Städten, auf dem Land, an der Küste und in Bergen/Gebirgen.

Preisspanne

Preisspanne 14-25 $. 🔲 Leinenschlafsack erforderlich.

Zimmer und Reservierungen

R während Jan, Mai-Okt, Dez. (Alle Zimmer). Reservierungen über **IBN** 🔲 oder die Herberge per **t** **f** **e**. Rauchen ist in allen Herbergen NICHT gestattet.

Gäste

Mitgliedsausweis ist erforderlich. Der maximale Aufenthalt beträgt 7 Tage. ♦♦♦ willkommen. Gruppenbuchungen über **IBN** 🔲 oder die Herberge per **t** **f** **e**.

Öffnungszeiten

Hauptherbergen: Zugang 🔲, 🕐. Rezeption 🕐. **Andere Herbergen:** Zugang 🔲.

Mahlzeiten

Für Einzelreisende & für ♦♦♦. 🗝.

Ermäßigungen

HI-Mitgliedsrabatt ist erhältlich – siehe Teil für Rabatte und Ermäßigungen und www.iyhf.org oder www.hostellingintl.ca

Reisen im Land

Reisen ist einfach mit 🚌 Selbstfahrer.

Reise-/Aktivitäten-Packages

Touren/sightseeing und Unterkunft/Transport-Packages erhältlich. Package-Buchungen über 🔲 oder die Herberge per **t** **f** **e**.

Reisepässe und Visa

Reisepass erforderlich.

Gesundheit

Unfall-/Krankenversicherung wird empfohlen.

Español

Los albergues están situados en las ciudades, el campo, la costa y la montaña.

Tarifas mínima y máxima

Tarifas mínima y máxima 14-25$. 🔲 Saco sábana imprescindible.

Habitaciones y Reservas

R en ene, may-oct, dic. (Todas las habitaciones). Reservas por **IBN** 🔲 o a través del albergue por **t** **f** **e**. Está prohibido fumar en todos los albergues.

Huéspedes

Los huéspedes deben presentar su Carnet de Alberguista. La estancia máxima es de 7 días. Se admiten ♦♦♦. Reservas de grupo por **IBN** 🔲 o a través del albergue por **t** **f** **e**.

Horarios y fechas de apertura

Albergues principales - abiertos 🔲, 🕐. Horario de recepción: 🕐. **Otros albergues** - abiertos 🔲.

Comidas

Para individuales y para ♦♦♦. 🗝.

Descuentos

Se conceden descuentos a los miembros de Hostelling International – véase la sección

sobre descuentos y las páginas Internet
www.iyhf.org y www.hostellingintl.ca.

Desplazamientos

Transportes recomendados: 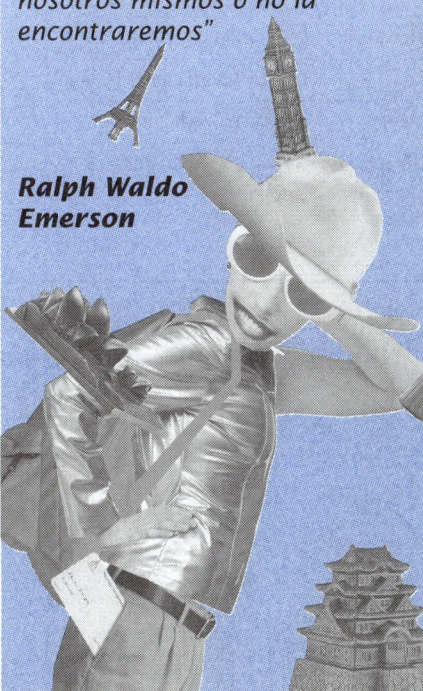 Automóvil.

Viajes Combinados con Actividades

Viajes combinados con visitas turísticas y
alojamiento/transporte. Reserva de viajes
combinados por 🖰 o a través del albergue por
t f e.

Pasaportes y Visados

Pasaporte obligatorio.

Información Sanitaria

Seguro médico recomendado.

"Though we travel the world over to find the beautiful, we must carry it with us or we find it not."

"Bien que nous parcourons le monde pour trouver ce qui est beau, nous devons le porter en nous ou nous ne le trouvons pas."

„Obwohl wir die ganze Welt bereisen, um das Schöne zu finden, müssen wir es in uns selber tragen, sonst werden wir es nicht finden."

"Aunque demos la vuelta al mundo buscando la belleza, tenemos que llevarla dentro de nosotros mismos o no la encontraremos"

Ralph Waldo Emerson

Banff -
International

PO Box 1358,
807 Coyote Rd,
Banff,
Alberta,
T0L 0C0.
❶ (403) 7624122
❶ (403) 7623441

Open Dates:	🗓
Open Hours:	🕐
Reservations:	**R** ⁻CC⁻
Price Range:	$20.00-24.00 (dorm); $52-60 (private) 🖼
Beds:	216 - 7x³ 24x⁴ 2x⁵ 12x⁶
Facilities:	7x ❘❘ 🍽 🛁 💧 ☀ 🛏 🧺 2 x 🍷 🔲 📷 🎱 🅿 🏧 🏠
Directions:	150W from city centre
✈	Calgary International 160km
A🚌	Brewster/Greyhound 3km
Attractions:	🏕 ⛰ 🚵 🏊 2640m+ ⛷ 🚶 🚡 3km

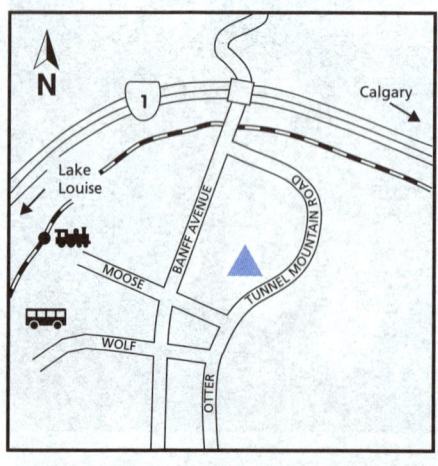

Edmonton -
International

10647-81 Ave Edmonton,
AB,
T6E 1Y1.
❶ (780) 9886836
❶ (780) 9888698
❷ eihostel@hostellingintl.ca

Open Dates:	🗓
Open Hours:	🕐
Reservations:	**R** ⁻CC⁻
Price Range:	Starting at $17.00
Beds:	88
Facilities:	❘❘❘ ❘❘❘ 🛁 🛏 📺 📄 🧺 1 x 🍷 📷 🧺 🎱 🅿
Directions:	
✈	Sky Shuttle-University 26km
A🚌	Sky Shuttle, Varscona Hotel 26km
🚌	#12 Kingsway; #9 Southgate 10km
🚌	#9 from 101St & 155Ave drops at 109St & Whyte Ave
Attractions:	🚵 ⛷ 🚶 🏊

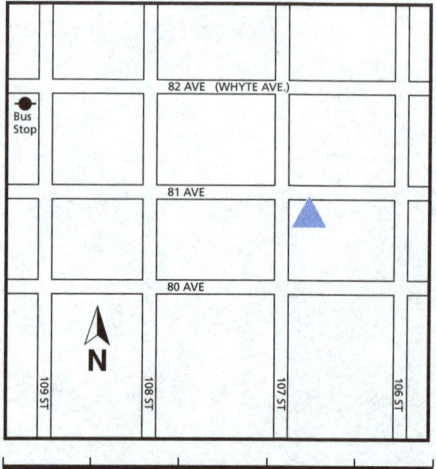

Halifax -
Heritage House

Halifax Heritage House Hostel,
1253 Barrington St,
Halifax,
Nova Scotia,
B3J 1Y3.
- **(902) 4223863**
- **(902) 422 0116**
- **hfxhostel@ns.sympatico.ca**

Open Dates:	📅
Open Hours:	08.00-23.00hrs
Reservations:	R ⌐CC⌐
Price Range:	$18.00
Beds:	73 - 2x¹ 4x⁴ 1x⁵ 3x⁶ 4x⁶⁺
Facilities:	1x ... TV ...

Directions:

✈	Halifax International
⛴	Halifax Harbour 1km
🚌	Via Rail 500m
🚌	Acadian Bus Depot 4km ap Terminal
🚋	#7, #9 100m ap South & Barrington Streets

Attractions: 🚴 🏃 🎿 🏊

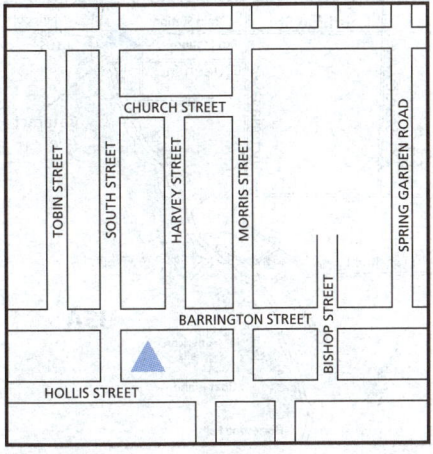

Lake Louise -
International Hostel

Village Rd,
Box 115,
Lake Louise,
Alberta,
T0L 1E0.
- **(403) 5222200**
- **(403) 5222253**

Open Dates:	📅
Open Hours:	🕐
Reservations:	R ⌐CC⌐
Price Range:	From $22.00 (dorm); $54.00-62.00 (private)
Beds:	150 - 7x¹ 5x² 4x³ 34x⁴ 6x⁵
Facilities:	40x ... 1x ... P ...

Directions: 200W from city centre

✈	Calgary International 200km
A 🚌	Airporter 500m
🚌	Greyhound 500m

Attractions: 🏕 ⛺ 🚴 🎿 1500m 🎿 🏃 ⛷ 4km 🎣 1km

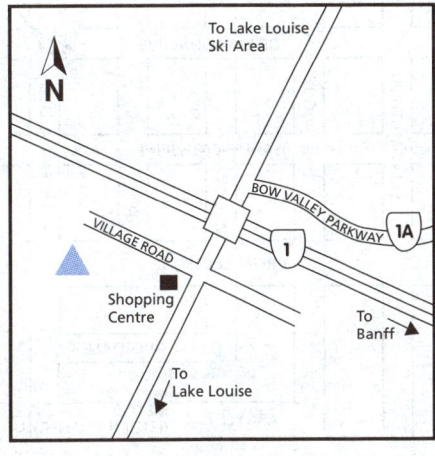

Montréal -
Auberge de Montreal

1030,
Rue Mackay,
Montréal,
Québec,
H3G 2H1.
☎ (514) 8433317
📠 (514) 9343251
✉ info@hostellingmontreal.com

Open Dates:	📅
Open Hours:	🕐
Reservations:	**R** IBN CC
Price Range:	$21.00-24.00 (dorm); $52.00-64.00 (private) 💶
Beds:	246 - 15x² 3x³ 24x⁴ 8x⁶ 6x⁶
Facilities:	♦♦♦ 39x ♦♦♦ 🍽 (B) 🛏 TV 📺 🔥 💼 🔒 ⊜ P ℹ 🔧

Directions:

✈	Dorval 12km
A🚌	Hostel door
🚂	Central 500m
U	Lucien L'Allier 200m

Niagara Falls -
International

4549 Cataract Ave,
Niagara Falls,
Ontario,
L2E 3M2.
☎ (905) 3570770, 1-888 7490058
📠 (905) 3577673
✉ nfhostel@hostellingint-gl.on.ca

Open Dates:	📅
Open Hours:	🕐
Reservations:	**R** IBN CC
Price Range:	$16.90 💶
Beds:	88 - 6x² 16x⁴ 2x⁶
Facilities:	♦♦♦ ♦♦♦ 🛏 🔥 💼 TV 📺 🔒 P ℹ 🌿

Directions:	0.1 NE from city centre
🚂	200m
🚌	200m

Ottawa -
International

75 Nicholas St,
Ottawa,
Ontario,
K1N 7B9.
☏ (613) 2352595
🖷 (613) 2359202
✉ info@hostellingintl.on.ca

Open Dates:	🗓
Open Hours:	🕓 (01.05-31.09); 07.00-02.00hrs (01.10-31.04)
Reservations:	**R** **IBN** **CC**
Price Range:	$18.00-22.00 (dorm); $47.00-51.00 (private)
Beds:	148 - 1x² 12x⁴ 3x⁵ 11x⁶ 2x⁶
Facilities:	👪 3x 👫 ♂ 🏨 📺 🧺 🗄 🍴 8 🅿 ✍ ☕ ♿ 🏤
Directions:	0.1E from city centre
✈	Ottawa International 15km
A🚌	to Novotel Hotel 50m
🚆	via Rail 3.2km
🚌	Ottawa Bus Central Station ap Rideau Center 100m
Attractions:	⛰ 🎡 2km 🚴 🎿 ⛵ 2km

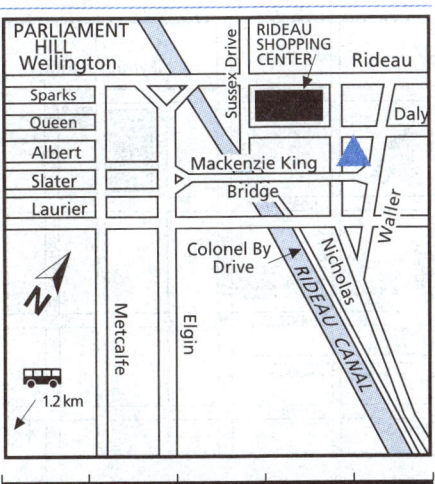

Québec -
Centre International de Séjour de Québec

19 rue Ste Ursule,
Québec, G1R 4E1.
☏ (418) 6940755
🖷 (418) 6942278
✉ cisq@mail.org

Open Dates:	🗓
Open Hours:	🕓
Reservations:	**R** **IBN** **CC**
Price Range:	$17.00-19.50 (dorm); $46.00-50.00 (private)
Beds:	233 - 6x¹ 6x² 4x³ 33x⁴ 1x⁵ 4x⁶ 4x⁶
Facilities:	👫 ♂ 🏨 📺 🧺 🧹 2 x 🍴 🗄 🖼 ☕ 8 ✍ ♿ ☕ 🏤
Directions:	
✈	Québec City International 15km
A🚌	La Quebecoise 20km
⛴	Québec - Levis Ferry 2km
🚆	Gare du Palais 1km
🚌	Bus from 🚆 and 🚌; #800 or #25 200m ap Terminus Place d'Youville, walking distance
Attractions:	🚴 🎿 🎣 2km ⛵ 2km

Toronto -
International

76 Church St,
Toronto,
Ontario,
M5C 2G1.
 (416) 9714440; 1-877 8488737
 (416) 9714088
 thostel@hostellingint-gl.on.ca

Open Dates:	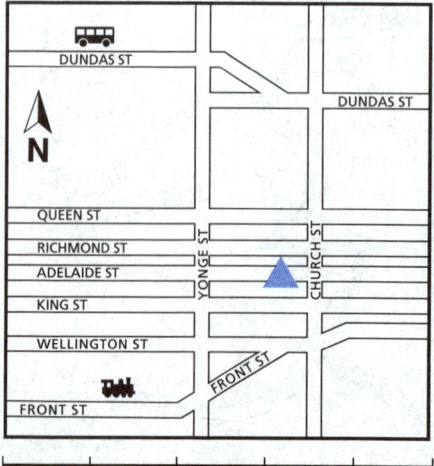
Open Hours:	
Reservations:	R IBN CC
Price Range:	$18.95-20.09
Beds:	185 - 5x² 5x³ 13x⁴ 12x⁶ 5x⁶
Facilities:	5x

Directions:

✈	Pearson International 30km
A	From all terminals
🚂	Union 500m
U	King Station
Attractions:	

Vancouver -
HI Vancouver Downtown

1114 Burnaby St,
Vancouver,
BC, V6E 1P1.
 (604) 6844565; Toll Free: 1-888-203-4302
 (604) 6844540
 van-downtown@hihostels.bc.ca

Open Dates:	
Open Hours:	
Reservations:	R IBN CC
Price Range:	$19.95-23.95 (dorm); $54.95-63.95 (private)
Beds:	223 - 7x² 16x³ 44x⁴
Facilities:	23x 1x

Directions:

✈	Vancouver International 15km
A	Parkhill Hotel 25m
⛴	Tsawwassen 32km
🚂	Pacific Central 2.5km
🚌	#6 1km ap Thurlow & Davie
U	Granville 1.5km
Attractions:	1230m 1.5km 50m

There are 2 hostels in Vancouver. See following pages.

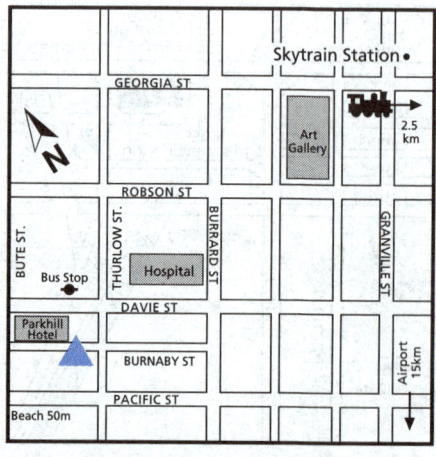

Victoria - HI Victoria

516 Yates St,
Victoria,
BC,
V8W 1K8.
☎ (250) 3854511; Toll Free: 1-888-883-0099
🖶 (250) 3853232
✉ victoria@hihostels.bc.ca

Open Dates:	🗓
Open Hours:	🕐
Reservations:	Ⓡ CC
Price Range:	$16.50 💳
Beds:	110 - 2x² 1x⁴ 1x⁶ 4x⁶
Facilities:	♿ ♦♦♦ 2x ♦♦♦ ✂ ✿ 📷 TV ♨ ⊡ 🖼 8 ℹ ♨ ♠ ⌗

Directions:

✈	Victoria 28km
A🚌	Shuttle to door
⛴	Swartz Bay 32km, Victoria 700m
🚂	E+N Via 200m
🚌	#70 280m ap Yates & Douglas

Attractions: ⚲1.5km 🚴 ☞ 🏊

Winnipeg - Ivey House International Hostel

210 Maryland St,
Winnipeg,
Manitoba,
R3G 1L6.
☎ (204) 7723022
🖶 (204) 7841133
✉ iveyhouse@hotmail.com

Open Dates:	🗓
Open Hours:	08.00-10.00hrs; 16.00-24.00hrs
Reservations:	Ⓡ CC
Price Range:	$16.00 (dorm) 💳
Beds:	41
Facilities:	♦♦♦ ♦♦♦ ✂ ✿ 📷 TV ♨ ⊡ 🖼 P ℹ

Directions:	3E	from city centre
✈		Winnipeg International 7km
🚂		Via 2km
🚌		#29 500m ap 29 Sherbrook 500m

Attractions: 🚴 🏊

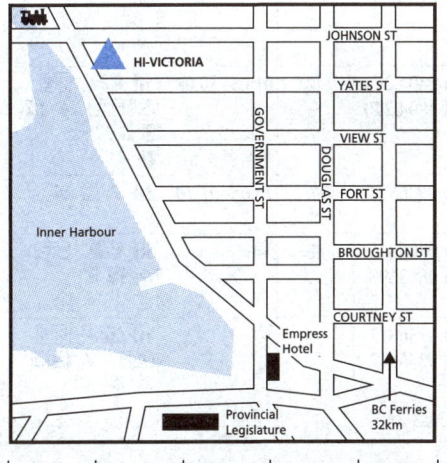

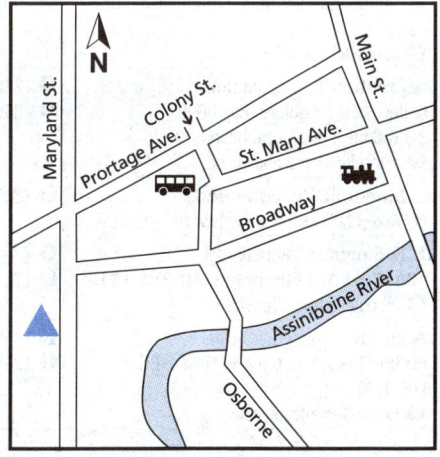

Location/Address	Telephone No. Fax No.	Beds	Opening Dates	Facilities
△*Acton* - *Blue Springs Camp* *14009 6th Line Nassagaweya, RR#1 Acton, Ontario, L7J 2L7.* e *bluesprings@ont.scouts.ca*	t (519) 853 2209 f (519) 853 1982	47	01.05–31.10	R 5W CC P
△*Alma* - *Fundy National Park Hostel* *129 Devils Half Acre, Alma, New Brunswick, E4H 4Y9 (S on Trans-Canada #2 linked by Rte 114).* e *hostellingintl@ns.sympatico.ca*	t (506) 8872216 f (506) 8872226	30	01.06–30.09	R CC P
▲**Banff** - International IBN **PO Box 1358, 807 Coyote Rd, Banff, Alberta, T0L 0C0.**	t (403) 7624122 f (403) 7623441	216	12	R 150W CC P
▲**Barrie** - Georgian Green Summer Hostel 144 Bell Farm Rd, Barrie, ON, L4M 5K5. e georgiangreen@cois.on.ca	t (705) 7350772 f (705) 7398615	48	01.05–11.08	R 5NE CC P
▲**Calgary** - International IBN 520-7th Ave, SE Calgary, Alberta, T2G 0J6.	t (403) 2698239 f (403) 2666227	120	12	R CC P
▲**Campbellton** - Campbellton Lighthouse Youth Hostel 1 Ritchie St, P.O. Box 100, Campbellton, New Brunswick, E3N 3G1. e julie.jardine@campbellton.org	t (506) 7597044 f (506) 7597403	20	17.06–25.08	R CC P
▲**Cap-Aux-Os** Auberge de Cap-Aux-Os, 2095 Boul Grande-Grève, (Québec) G4X 6L7. e aujecao@globetrotter.net	t (418) 8925153 f (418) 8925292	56	01.01–31.10	R CC P
△*Castle Mountain* - *Castle Mountain* *Box 1358, Banff, AB, T0L 0C0 (on hwy #1A, 1.5km E of the junction with hwy #1 & #93 S).*	t (403) 7624122 f (403) 7623441	36	12	R CC P
▲**Charlottetown** 153 Mount Edward Rd, Charlottetown, PEI, C1A 7N4. e peihostel@isn.net	t (902) 8949696 f (902) 6286424	60	01.06–07.09	CC P
▲**Cranbrook** - Purcell House College of the Rockies, Bag 9000, 2700 College Way, Cranbrook, BC. e purcellhouse@cotr.bc.ca	t (250) 489 8282 f (250) 489 8240	42	01.05–30.08	R 2NE CC P
△*Dawson City* - *River Hostel* *PO Box 32, Dawson City, Yukon, Y0B 1G0.*	t (867) 9936823	36	15.05–01.10	P
▲**Edmonton** - International **10647-81 Ave Edmonton, AB, T6E 1Y1.** e eihostel@hostellingintl.ca	t (780) 9886836 f (780) 9888698	88	12	R CC P
▲**Fernie** - Raging Elk Hostel PO Box 1899, 892 6th Ave, Fernie, BC, V0B 1M0. e raginelk@elkvalley.net	t (250) 4236811 f (250) 4236812	90	12	R 0.2N CC P

Location/Address	Telephone No. Fax No.	Beds	Opening Dates	Facilities
▲ **Fredericton** - International Hostel (Rosary Hall) 621 Churchill Row, Fredericton, New Brunswick, E3B 1M3.	☎ (506) 4504417 ✆ (506) 4629692	40	🗓12	♔♔ 1E ☞ 🅿 ▣
▲ **Fort Coulonge** Auberge Esprit, 3, Chemin Esprit, Davidson, Québec, J0X 1R0. ✉ esprit@iosphere.net	☎ (819) 6833241 ✆ (819) 6833641	36	01.05–30.09	♔♔ 🍽 ℝ 3W ♿ ℂℂ ☞ 🅿 ▣ ☕
▲ **Halifax** - Heritage House **Halifax Heritage House Hostel, 1253 Barrington St, Halifax, Nova Scotia, B3J 1Y3.** ✉ hfxhostel@ns.sympatico.ca	☎ (902) 4223863 ✆ (902) 422 0116	73	🗓12	♔♔ ℝ ℂℂ ☞ ▣
△ *Hilda Creek* - *Hilda Creek Box 1358, Banff, Alberta, T0L 0C0 (8km S of Columbia Icefields Centre & 120km N of Lake Louise on hwy #93).*	☎ *(403) 7624122* ✆ *(403) 7623441*	*21*	*22.12–27.10; 07.01–14.06 (Thurs–Sun)*	ℝ ℂℂ ☞ ✿
▲ **Ile D'Orléans** Auberge Le P'tit Bonheur, 183, Côte Lafleur, Ile D'Orléans, Québec, G0A 3W0.	☎ (418) 8292588 ✆ (418) 8290900	40	🗓12	♔♔ 🍽 ℝ 1W ℂℂ ☞ 🅿 ▣
△ *Jasper National Park* - *Maligne Canyon Hostel Box 387, Jasper, Alberta, T0E 1E0. (11km E of Jasper on Maligne Lake Rd, SE from Hwy #16).* ✉ *jihostel@hostellingintl.ca*	☎ *(780) 8523215* ✆ *(780) 8525560*	*24*	🗓12	ℝ ℂℂ ☞ 🅿
△ *Jasper National Park* - *Mount Edith Cavell Hostel Box 387, Jasper, Alberta, T0E 1E0. (from Jasper Townsite: 9km S on Hwy #93, turn right on Hwy 93A for 5km to Mount Edith Cavell turnoff, follow rd 13km).* ✉ *jihostel@hostellingintl.ca*	☎ *(780) 8523215* ✆ *(780) 8525560*	*32*	🗓12	ℝ ℂℂ ☞ 🅿
△ *Jasper National Park* - *Athabasca Falls Hostel Box 387, Jasper, Alberta, T0E 1E0. (32km S of Jasper on the E side, 200m past Athabasca Falls - turn off Hwy #93).* ✉ *jihostel@hostellingintl.ca*	☎ *(780) 8523215* ✆ *(780) 8525560*	*40*	🗓12	ℝ ℂℂ ☞ 🅿
△ *Jasper National Park* - *Beauty Creek Hostel Box 387, Jasper, Alberta, T0E 1E0. (87km S of Jasper & 17km N of Columbia Icefield Centre on W side of Hwy #93).* ✉ *jihostel@hostellingintl.ca*	☎ *(780) 8523215* ✆ *(780) 8525560*	*24*	🗓12	ℝ ℂℂ ☞ 🅿

Location/Address	Telephone No. Fax No.	Beds	Opening Dates	Facilities
▲ **Jasper National Park** - Jasper International Hostel Box 387, Jasper, Alberta, T0E 1E0. (3km S of Jasper on Hwy 93, right on Whistler's Mountain Rd: follow for 4km). ℮ jihostel@hostellingintl.ca	☎ (780) 8523215 ☏ (780) 8525560	80	⓵₂	♔ Ⓡ ⌐CC⌐ ☞ Ⓟ ⊡
▲ **Kamloops** - HI Kamloops 7 West Seymour St, Kamloops, BC, V2C 1E4. ℮ kamloops@hihostels.bc.ca	☎ (250) 8287991 ☏ (250) 8282442	75	⓵₂	♔ Ⓡ 0.1 E ⌐CC⌐ ☞ Ⓟ ⊡ ☀
▲ **Kingston** - Louise House Summer Hostel 329 Johnson St, Kingston, ONT, K7L 1Y6. ℮ colin.windsor@sympatico.ca	☎ (613) 3852033; when open (613) 5318237 ☏ (613) 3851707; when open (613) 5319763	60	01.05–31.08	♔ ⑂ Ⓡ 0.2 N ⌐CC⌐ ☞ Ⓟ ⊡
▲ **La Have** La Have Marine Hostel, PO Box 92, La Have, Nova Scotia, B0R 1C0.	☎ (902) 6882908 ☏ (902) 6881083	8	01.06–01.10	♔ ⌐CC⌐ ☞ Ⓟ ⊡
▲ **La Tuque** Auberge la Residence 352, Ave Brown, La Tuque, Québec, G9X 2W4. ℮ aubergelaresidence@sympatico.ca	☎ (819) 5239267 ☏ (819) 5233678	46	⓵₂	♔ ☞ Ⓟ ⊡
▲ **Lake Louise** - International Hostel **Village Rd, Box 115, Lake Louise, Alberta, T0L 1E0.**	☎ (403) 5222200 ☏ (403) 5222253	150	⓵₂	♔ ⑂ Ⓡ 200 W ♿ ⌐CC⌐ ☞ Ⓟ ⊡ ☕ ⑉ ☀
▲ **Magog-Orford** Auberge du Centre d'Arts Orford, 3165 Chemin du Parc, Orford, Québec, J1X 7A2 (located in Parc du Mont-Orford). ℮ arts.orford@sympatico.ca	☎ (819) 8438595 ☏ (819) 8437274	240	01.05–31.10	♔ ⑂ Ⓡ 5 N ⌐CC⌐ ☞ Ⓟ
▲ **Montréal** - Auberge de Montreal ⒤ⒷⓃ **1030, Rue Mackay, Montréal, Québec, H3G 2H1.** ℮ info@hostellingmontreal.com	☎ (514) 8433317 ☏ (514) 9343251	246	⓵₂	♔ ⑂ Ⓡ ⌐CC⌐ ☞ Ⓟ ⊡
▲ **Mont-Tremblant Village** Auberge Internationale du Mont-Tremblant 2213, Chemin Principal BP1001, Mont Tremblant, Québec J0T 1Z0. ℮ info@hostellingtremblant.com	☎ (819) 4256008 ☏ (819) 4253760	88	⓵₂	♔ ⑂ Ⓡ 0.5 NE ⌐CC⌐ ☞ Ⓟ ⊡ ⑉ ☍
△ *Mosquito Creek* - *Mosquito Creek Banff National Park, Alberta.* *(27 km N of Lake Louise on Hwy #93, 211km S of Jasper).*	☎ *(403) 7624122* ☏ *(403) 7623441*	*38*	*17.12–02.01; 15.11–15.05 (Wed–Sun only); 16.05–11.10*	♔ Ⓡ ⌐CC⌐ ☞ Ⓟ ☀
▲ **Nelson** - Dancing Bear Inn 171 Baker St., Nelson, BC, V1L 4H1. ℮ dbear@netidea.com	☎ (250) 3527573 ☏ (250) 3529818	43	⓵₂	♔ Ⓡ ⌐CC⌐ ☞ Ⓟ ⊡ ☀

Location/Address	Telephone No. Fax No.	Beds	Opening Dates	Facilities
▲ **Niagara Falls** - International (IBN) **4549 Cataract Ave, Niagara Falls, Ontario, L2E 3M2.** ℮ nfhostel@hostellingint-gl.on.ca	❶ (905) 3570770, 1-888 7490058 ❺ (905) 3577673	88	⌐12	♦♦♦ R 0.1 NE CC ☞ P ⊡ 🚲 ✿
▲ **Nordegg** - Shunda Creek Hostel General Delivery, Nordegg, Alberta, T0M 2H0. (located 3km N of Hwy 11 on the Shunda Creek Recreation Area Rd, 87km E of Banff National Park and 94km W of Rocky Mountain House). ℮ shunda@hostellingintl.ca	❶ (403) 7212140 ❺ (403) 7212140	48	⌐12	♦♦♦ CC ☞ P ⊡
▲ **Orillia** - Orillia Home Hostel 198 Borland St East, Orillia, Ontario, L3V 2C3.	❶ (705) 3250970 ❺ (705) 3259826	9	⌐12	♦♦♦ �🍴 R ☞ P ⊡ ✿
▲ **Ottawa** - International (IBN) **75 Nicholas St, Ottawa, Ontario, K1N 7B9.** ℮ info@hostellingintl.on.ca	❶ (613) 2352595 ❺ (613) 2359202	148	⌐12	♦♦♦ R 0.1 E CC ☞ P ⊡
▲ **Pender Island** - Coopers Landing Inc. 5734 Canal Rd, Pender Island, BC, V0N 2M1. ℮ info@cooperslanding.com	❶ (250) 629 6133; 1-888-921-3111 ❺ (250) 629 3649	18	01.02–31.10	♦♦♦ R CC ☞ P 🚲
▲ **Penticton** - HI Penticton 464 Ellis St, Penticton, BC, V2A 4M2. ℮ penticton@hihostels.bc.ca	❶ (250) 4923992 ❺ (250) 4928755	47	⌐12	♦♦♦ R 0.2 E CC ☞ P ⊡ 🚲 ✿
▲ **Péribonka** Auberge Ile-Du-Repos de Péribonka, 105 Ile-de-Repos Rd, C P 38, Ste-Monique de Honfleur, Lac Saint-Jean, Québec, G0W 2T0. ℮ ilerepos@globetrotter.net	❶ (418) 3475649 ❺ (418) 3474810	70	⌐12	♦♦♦ �🍴 R 5 E ♿ CC P ⊡ 🍺
▲ **Peterborough** - Severn Court Summer Hostel 555 Wilfred Drive, Peterborough, ON, K9K 1W1. ℮ severn.court@sympatico.ca	❶ (705) 7401150 ❺ (705) 7400944	48	01.05–18.08	♦♦♦ R 8 SW ♿ CC ☞ P ⊡
▲ **Pointe-à-la-Garde** Auberge Le Château Bahia, 152 Boul. Perron, Pointe-à-la-Garde, Québec, G0C 2M0. ℮ aubchaba@globtrotter.net	❶ (418) 7882048 ❺ (418) 7882048	48	⌐12	♦♦♦ �🍴 R 3 E CC ☞ P ⊡
△ *Powell River* - Fiddlehead Farm *PO Box 421, Powell River, BC, V8A 5C2. (Extremely remote area: make R at least one week in advance to ensure pick-up by private boat from the bus, Comox ferry or Powell Lake Marina).* ℮ *retreat@fiddleheadfarm.org*	❶ *(604) 4833018* ❺ *(604) 4853832*	*22*	*01.04–31.10*	♦♦♦ �🍴 R
△ *Powerview* - The Maskwa Project *Box 130, Powerview, Winnipeg, Manitoba, R0E 1P0.*	❶ *(204) 3674390*	*20*	⌐12	R ☞ P
▲ **Québec** - Centre International de Séjour de Québec (IBN) **19 rue Ste Ursule, Québec, G1R 4E1.** ℮ cisq@mail.org	❶ (418) 6940755 ❺ (418) 6942278	233	⌐12	R CC ☞ ⊡

Location/Address	Telephone No. Fax No.	Beds	Opening Dates	Facilities
▲ **Racine** Auberge de la Grande Ligne, 318 Ch de la Grande Ligne, Racine, Québec, J0E 1Y0.	☎ (450) 532 3177 🖷 (450) 532 4082	25	🏠12	♂♂ ⑩ Ⓡ ☞ 🅿 ⬛
△ *Rampart Creek* - *Rampart Creek Box 1358, Banff, AB, T0L 0C0. (95km N of Lake Louise & 34km S of the Columbia Icefield Centre on hwy #93.)*	☎ *(403) 7624122* 🖷 *(403) 7623441*	*30*	*15.11–08.10; 17.11–21.12 (Thurs–Mon only)*	Ⓡ ⊂CC⊃ ☞ 🅿 ❀
▲ **Regina** - Turgeon International Hostel 2310 McIntyre St, Regina, Saskatchewan, S4P 2S2. ✉ hihostels.sask@sk.sympatico.ca	☎ (306) 7918165 🖷 (306) 721 2667	30	01.02–23.12	♂♂ 1SW ⊂CC⊃ ☞ 🅿 ⬛ ☕ ❀
▲ **Revelstoke** - Revelstoke Traveller's Hostel and Guesthouse Hostel address: 400 Second St. West, Revelstoke, BC, V0E 2S0. Mailing address: P.O. Box 1739, Revelstoke, BC, V0E 2S0. ✉ info@hostels.bc.ca	☎ (250) 837 4050 Toll Free: 1-888-663-8825 🖷 (250) 837 6410	62	🏠12	♂♂ Ⓡ ⊂CC⊃ ☞ 🅿 ⬛ 🚲
▲ **Ribbon Creek** - Ribbon Creek Box 1358, Banff, AB, T0L 0C0 (70km W of Calgary on Trans Canada hwy at Kananaskis turn off (hwy #40 S) follow signs to Kananaskis village).	☎ (403) 7624122 🖷 (403) 7623441	47	15.11–08.10 (closed Tue)	♂♂ Ⓡ ♿ ⊂CC⊃ ☞ 🅿 ⬛ ❀
▲ **Rivière du Loup** Auberge Internationale de Rivière du Loup, 46 Hotel de Ville, Rivière du Loup, Québec, G5R 1L5. (200km to Québec City). ✉ aubergeriviere-du-loup@moncourrier.com	☎ (418) 8627566 🖷 (418) 8621843	65	🏠12	♂♂ ⑩ Ⓡ ♿ ⊂CC⊃ ☞ 🅿 ⬛ 🚲 ❀
▲ **Rossland** - Mountain Shadow Hostel 2125 Columbia Ave, Box 100, Rossland, BC, V0G 1Y0. ✉ mshostel@knet.kootenay.net	☎ (250) 3627160 🖷 (250) 3627150	40	🏠12	♂♂ Ⓡ ⊂CC⊃ ☞ 🅿 ⬛ ❀
▲ **Sainte-Anne-des-Monts** Auberge L'Echouerie, 295 1e Ave Sainte-Anne-des-Monts, Québec, G0E 2G0. ✉ auberge.int.echouerie@globtrotter.net	☎ (418) 7631555 🖷 (418) 7639229	89	🏠12	♂♂ ⑩ Ⓡ 2E ⊂CC⊃ ☞ 🅿 ⬛ ☕
▲ **Salt Spring Island** - The Forest Retreat 640 Cusheon Lake Rd, Salt Spring Island, BC, V8K 2C2. ✉ hostel@saltspring.com	☎ (250) 5374149	35	01.03–31.10	♂♂ Ⓡ 5SE ⊂CC⊃ ☞ 🅿 🚲 ❀
▲ **Sault Ste Marie** - The Algonquin Hotel 864 Queen St East Sault Ste Marie, Ontario, P6A 2B4. ✉ algonquinhotel@on.aibn.com	☎ (705) 2532311; Toll Free: 1-888-269-7728 🖷 (705) 9420269	30	🏠12	♂♂ ⑩ Ⓡ ⊂CC⊃ ☞ 🅿 🚲
▲ **Sept-Iles** Auberge Internationale Le Tangon, 555 Cartier, Sept-Îles, Québec, G4R 2T8. ✉ tangon@bbsi.net	☎ (418) 9628180 (Su) 🖷 (418) 9612965	42	🏠12	♂♂ ⑩ Ⓡ ⊂CC⊃ ☞ 🅿 ⬛

Location/Address	Telephone No. Fax No.	Beds	Opening Dates	Facilities
▲ **Shuswap Lake** - Squilax General Store and Hostel Hostel address: TCH Hwy 1 (10km east of Chase) Squilax, BC, Mailing address: Rural Route #2, S2-C11, V0E 1M0. 🅔 squilax@jetstream.net	☎ (250) 6752977 🖷 (250) 6752977	23	🔒12	♛♙ ℝ 🄲🄲 🛡 🄿 🗀 🚲 ✿
△ *South Milford* - *Raven Haven Hostel* *P.O. Box 100, Annapolis Royal, Nova Scotia,* *B0S 1A0.*	☎ *(902) 5327320* 🖷 *(902) 5322096*	*6*	*15.06–30.09*	♛♙ ℝ 22S ♿ 🄲🄲 🛡 🄿
▲ **Thunder Bay** - Confederation College-Sibley Hall Residence 960 William St, Thunder Bay, Ontario, P7C 4W1.	☎ (807) 4756381 🖷 (807) 625 9596	100	14.05–14.08	♛♙ 🍽 ℝ 🄲🄲 🄿 🗀
▲ **Tofino** - Whalers on the Point Guesthouse Box 296, 81 West St, Tofino BC, V0R 2Z0. 🅔 info@tofinohostel.com	☎ (250) 725 3443 🖷 (250) 725 3463	56	🔒12	♛♙ ℝ 0.2W ♿ 🄲🄲 🛡 🄿 🗀 🚲 ✿
▲ **Toronto** - International [IBN] **76 Church St, Toronto, Ontario, M5C 2G1.** 🅔 thostel@hostellingint-gl.on.ca	☎ (416) 9714440; 1-877 8488737 🖷 (416) 9714088	185	🔒12	♛♙ ℝ 🄲🄲 🛡 🗀 ✿
▲ **Trois Rivières** Auberge Internationale la Flottille, 497 Radisson, Trois Rivières, Québec, G9A 2C7. 🅔 flottille@tr.cgocable.ca	☎ (819) 3788010 🖷 (819) 3784334	49	🔒12	♛♙ 🍽 ℝ ♿ 🄲🄲 🛡 🄿 🗀 🚲
▲ **Val David** Le Chalet Beaumont, 1451 Beaumont, Val David, Québec, J0T 2N0.	☎ (819) 3221972 🖷 (819) 3223793	72	🔒12	♛♙ 🍽 ℝ 🄲🄲 🛡 🄿 🗀 🚲
▲ **Vancouver** - HI Vancouver Jericho Beach [IBN] 1515 Discovery St (Jericho Park), Vancouver, BC, V6R 4K5. 🅔 van-jericho@hihostels.bc.ca	☎ (604) 2243208 Toll Free: 1-888-203-4303 🖷 (604) 2244852	286	🔒12	♛♙ 🍽 ℝ 5SW 🄲🄲 🛡 🄿 🗀 ☕ 🚲 ✿
▲ **Vancouver** - HI Vancouver Downtown [IBN] **1114 Burnaby St, Vancouver, BC, V6E 1P1.** 🅔 van-downtown@hihostels.bc.ca	☎ (604) 6844565; Toll Free: 1-888-203-4302 🖷 (604) 6844540	223	🔒12	♛♙ ℝ ♿ 🄲🄲 🛡 🄿 🗀 🚲 ✿
▲ **Vernon** - Lodged Inn 3201 Pleasant Valley Rd, Vernon, BC, V1T 4L4. 🅔 lodgedinn@telus.net	☎ (250) 549 3742 Toll Free: 1-888-737-9427 🖷 (250) 549 3748	32	🔒12	♛♙ ℝ 0.5E 🄲🄲 🛡 🄿 🗀 🚲 ✿
▲ **Victoria** - HI Victoria **516 Yates St, Victoria, BC, V8W 1K8.** 🅔 victoria@hihostels.bc.ca	☎ (250) 3854511; Toll Free: 1-888-883-0099 🖷 (250) 3853232	110	🔒12	♛♙ ℝ ♿ 🄲🄲 🛡 🗀 ✿
▲ **Wakefield** - Gatineau Park International Hostel Sentiers Carman Trails, 66 Chemin, Carman, Chelsea, (Québec) J9B 2K3. 🅔 carman@magma.ca	☎ (819) 4593180 🖷 (819) 4592113	30	🔒12	🍽 ℝ 15W 🛡 🄿 🗀

Location/Address	Telephone No. Fax No.	Beds	Opening Dates	Facilities
▲ **Waterton Lakes National Park** - Waterton Lodge Hostel, Waterton Lakes Lodge, Corner of Cameron Falls Drive & Windflower Ave, in Waterton townsite. ✉ info@watertonlakeslodge.com	☎ (403) 8592150/ 2151 📠 (403) 8592229	22	01.02–31.10	⑂ ▯ R ♿ ⒸⒸ ⑃ P ▯ ☕ ⚙
▲ **Wentworth** RR #1, Wentworth, Nova Scotia, B0M 1Z0. (Route 4 (Trans-Canada) to Wentworth Valley; exit on Valley Rd - follow signs to YH). ✉ wentworthhostel@ns.sympatico.ca	☎ (902) 5482379 📠 (902) 5482389	25	🗓12	⑂ ♿ ⒸⒸ ⑃ P ▯
△ *Whiskey Jack - Whiskey Jack Yoho National Park, BC. (near Alberta border, 27km W of Lake Louise on Hwy #1 (Trans-Canada), 13km W along Yoho Valley Rd from Kicking Horse Camp Ground).*	☎ (403) 7624122 📠 (403) 7623441	27	25.06–08.10	R ⒸⒸ ⑃ P ⚙
▲ **Whistler** - HI Whistler PO Box 128, 5678 Alta Lake Rd, Whistler, BC, V0N 1B0. (121km N of Vancouver on Hwy 99, turn off on Alta Lake Rd, continue 5km). ✉ whistler@hihostels.bc.ca	☎ (604) 9325492 📠 (604) 9324687	32	🗓12	⑂ R ⒸⒸ ⑃ P 🚲 ⚙
▲ **Winnipeg** - Ivey House International Hostel **210 Maryland St, Winnipeg, Manitoba, R3G 1L6.** ✉ iveyhouse@hotmail.com	☎ (204) 7723022 📠 (204) 7841133	41	🗓12	⑂ R 3E ⒸⒸ ⑃ P ▯ ⚙

"Certainly, travel is more than the seeing of sights; it is a change that goes on, deep and permanent, in the ideas of living."

"Il est certain que le voyage, c'est plus que la simple visite des sites touristiques; c'est un changement en continu, profond et permanent, sur l'idée que nous nous faisons de la vie."

„Gewiss ist Reisen mehr als Sehenswürdigkeiten anschauen; es findet eine tiefe und bleibende Veränderung der Lebensansichten statt."

"No cabe duda que viajar es más que hacer turismo; es un cambio continuo, profundo y permanente, en el concepto que tenemos de la vida"

Miriam Beard

Chile

CHILI

CHILE

CHILE

**Asociación Chilena de Albergues Turísticos Juveniles,
Hernando de Aguirre 201 of 602,
Providencia,
Santiago, Chile.**

☎ (56) (2) 2333220
✆ (56) (2) 2332555
✉ histgoch@entelchile.net
hostelling@hostelling.cl
🖵 www.hostelling.cl

**Travel Section:
Student Flight Center
Hernando de Aguirre #201 of 401,
Providencia,
Santiago, Chile.**

☎ (56) (2) 3350395
✆ (56) (2) 3350394
✉ studentflightcenter@sertur.cl

A copy of the Hostel Directory for this Country can be obtained from:
The National Office

Capital:	Santiago	**Population:**	15,000,000
Language:	Spanish	**Size:**	756,945 sq km
Currency:	$ peso	**Telephone Country Code:**	56

L. Poopo BOLIVIA

N

BRAZIL

Antofagasta

PARAGUAY

São Paulo

CHILE

Asuncion

Cuitaba

Isla de Pascua
(Easter Island)

Florianápolis

PACIFIC OCEAN

Porto Alegre

Cordoba

Viña del Mar

Mendoza

URUGUAY

Santiago

Santiago

Rosario

Chillán

Buenos Aires

Montevideo

Salto del Laja

Temuco

Temuco

Pucón

ARGENTINA

Bahía Blanca

ATLANTIC OCEAN

Valdivia

Valdivia

Frutillar

Ancud

FALKLAND ISLANDS (UK)

Punta
Arenas

TIERRA DEL FUEGO

DRAKE PASSAGE

0   400   800 KM

200   400   MLS

English

Price range
Price range US$ 10-20.

Rooms and Reservations
R 🗒 (All Rooms). Reservations via **IBN** or Hostel by ❶ ❷ ❸. (Reservation charges may apply). Smoking is limited - please check.

Guests
Membership Card and Passport/Photo ID are required. The maximum stay is 5 days. ♦♦♦ welcome. Group bookings via Hostel by ❶ ❷ ❸ (Reservation charges may apply).

Open times
Main hostels: open 🗒, 🕐. Reception open: 🕐. **Other hostels:** open 🗒, 🕐. Reception open: 🕐.

Meals
🍽 B **R** For individuals & for ♦♦♦.

Discounts
HI Member Discounts available - see discounts section and www.iyhf.org.

Travelling around
For ease of travel use ✈ 🚆 🚌 Self-Drive. International Driving Licence required.

Passports and Visas
Passport/Photo ID required.

Health
Medical insurance is recommended.

Français

Tarifs des nuitées
Tarifs des nuitées 10-20 US$.

Chambres et réservations
R 🗒 (Toutes chambres). Réservations via **IBN** ou l'auberge par ❶ ❷ ❸. (Des frais de réservation pourront vous être facturés). Il est permis de fumer dans certaines chambres - veuillez vérifier.

Usagers
La carte d'adhérent ainsi que le passeport/pièce d'identité avec photo sont à présenter. La durée maximale du séjour est de 5 jours. Accueil des ♦♦♦. Réservations pour groupes via l'auberge par ❶ ❷ ❸ (Des frais de réservation pourront vous être facturés).

Horaires d'ouverture
Grandes auberges: ouvertes 🗒, 🕐. Accueil ouvert 🕐. **Autres auberges:** ouvertes 🗒, 🕐. Accueil ouvert 🕐.

Repas
🍽 B **R** Pour individuels & pour ♦♦♦.

Remises
Remises pour les adhérents HI - voir la section "Remises" et notre site: www.iyhf.org.

Déplacements
Modes de transport recommandés ✈ 🚆 🚌 Voiture. Permis de conduire international obligatoire.

Passeports et visas
Passeport/pièce d'identité avec photo obligatoires.

Santé
Une assurance médicale de voyage est conseillée.

Deutsch

Preisspanne

Preisspanne 10-20 US$.

Zimmer und Reservierungen

R 🏠 (Alle Zimmer). Reservierungen über
IBN oder die Herberge per ❶ ❷ ❸.
(Reservierungskosten könnten anfallen).
Rauchen ist begrenzt - bitte checken.

Gäste

Mitgliedsausweis und Reisepass/
Personalausweis sind erforderlich. Der
maximale Aufenthalt beträgt 5 Tage.
♦♦♦ willkommen. Gruppenbuchungen über
Herberge per ❶ ❷ ❸ (Reservierungskosten
könnten anfallen).

Öffnungszeiten

Hauptherbergen: Zugang 🏠, 🕐. Rezeption
🕐. **Andere Herbergen:** Zugang 🏠, 🕐.
Rezeption 🕐.

Mahlzeiten

🍽 B **R** Für Einzelreisende & für ♦♦♦.

Ermäßigungen

HI-Mitgliedsrabatt ist erhältlich – siehe Teil für
Rabatte und Ermäßigungen und www.iyhf.org.

Reisen im Land

Reisen ist einfach mit ✈ 🚌 🚐
Selbstfahrer. Internationaler Führerschein
erforderlich.

Reisepässe und Visa

Reisepass/Personalausweis erforderlich.

Gesundheit

Unfall-/Krankenversicherung wird empfohlen.

Español

Tarifas mínima y máxima

Tarifas mínima y máxima 10-20 US$.

Habitaciones y Reservas

R 🏠 (Todas las habitaciones). Reservas por
IBN o a través del albergue por ❶ ❷ ❸.
(Es posible que se aplique un suplemento en
concepto de gastos de reserva). Está permitido
fumar sólo en algunas salas/habitaciones -
infórmese.

Huéspedes

Los huéspedes deben presentar su Carnet de
Alberguista y su pasaporte o carnet de
identidad. La estancia máxima es de 5 días. Se
admiten ♦♦♦. Reservas de grupo a través del
albergue por ❶ ❷ ❸ (Es posible que se
aplique un suplemento en concepto de gastos
de reserva).

Horarios y fechas de apertura

Albergues principales - abiertos 🏠, 🕐.
Horario de recepción: 🕐. **Otros albergues -**
abiertos 🏠, 🕐. Horario de recepción: 🕐.

Comidas

🍽 B **R** Para individuales y para ♦♦♦.

Descuentos

Se conceden descuentos a los miembros de
Hostelling International – véase la sección
sobre descuentos y nuestra página Internet en
www.iyhf.org.

Desplazamientos

Transportes recomendados: ✈ 🚌 🚐
Automóvil. Es necesario un permiso de
conducir internacional.

Pasaportes y Visados

Pasaporte o carnet de identidad obligatorio.

Información Sanitaria

Seguro médico recomendado.

Santiago

Cienfuegos 151,
Santiago de Chile.
☎ (2) 6718532
🖷 (2) 6728880
✉ histgoch@entelchile.net

Open Dates:	🗓12
Open Hours:	🕐
Reservations:	Ⓡ IBN ⊏CC⊐
Beds:	120
Facilities:	👫 🍽 🍷 🛵 📺 🍺 🖥 💼 8 🅿 ℹ️ 🚼 🌿 🐾
Directions:	1.5NE from city centre
✈	Arturo Merino Benitez 21km
🚌	Centropuerto 500m; Tour Express 500m
⛴	Valparaiso 120km
🚂	Estacion Central 1km
🚌	2 blocks
Ⓤ	1, 2 Los Heroes 300m; Santa Ana Station, Line 2 400m
Attractions:	⛰

"The true traveler is he who goes on foot, and even then, he sits down a lot of the time."

"Le vrai voyageur est celui qui va à pied, et encore, il s'assoit une grande partie du temps."

„Der wahre Reisende ist derjenige, der zu Fuß geht, und selbst dann setzt er sich sehr häufig nieder."

"El verdadero viajero es el que va a pie, y aun así pasa mucho tiempo sentado."

Colette

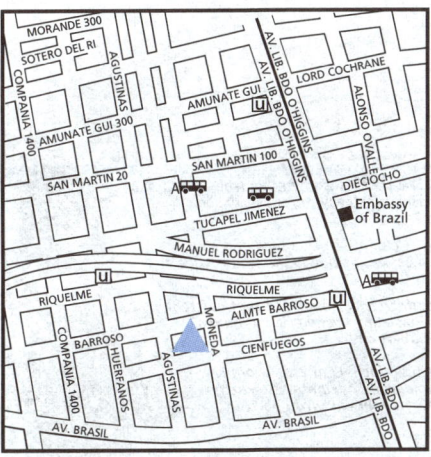

Location/Address	Telephone No. Fax No.	Beds	Opening Dates	Facilities
△ **Ancud** - *Hospedaje Vista Al Mar* *Avda Costanera 918.*	☎ *(65) 622617* ✆ *(65) 622617*	*26*	▥₁₂	♀♂ 0.5 SE ⚲ P
▲ **Chillán** - Complejo Turístico "Las Trancas" Km 73.5 Camino a las Termas de Chillán, Chillán.	☎ (42) 243211 ✆ (42) 243211	36	▥₁₂	♀♂ �"⚞ 73.3 SE P ▯ ☕
△ **Frutillar** - *Residencial Winkler* *Phillipi 1155, Frutillar.*	☎ *(65) 421388* ✆ *(65) 421388*	*28*	▥₁₂	♀♂ ⚞ ⚲ P ▯
▲ **Isla de Pascua** - Residencial "Kona Tau" Avaripua S/N. ✉ konatau@entelchile.net	☎ operator system 321	16	▥₁₂	⚞ P
▲ **Pucón** - Hosteria ¡Ècole! General Urrutia 592, Pucón. ✉ trek@ecole.cl	☎ (45) 441675 ✆ (45) 441660	47	▥₁₂	♀♂ ⚞ Ⓡ CC P ☕
▲ **Punta Arenas** - Residencial Sonia Kuscevic Pasaje Darwin 175, Punta Arenas.	☎ (61) 248543 ✆ (61) 248543	12	▥₁₂	P ▯
▲ **Salto del Laja** - Complejo Turístico Los Manantiales Panamericana Sur 485.	☎ (43) 314275 ✆ (43) 314275		▥₁₂	⚞ ⚲ P ☕
▲ **Santiago** [IBN] **Cienfuegos 151, Santiago de Chile.** ✉ histgoch@entelchile.net	☎ (2) 6718532 ✆ (2) 6728880	120	▥₁₂	⚞ Ⓡ 1.5 NE CC P ▯ ☕ ⛟
△ **Temuco** - *Residencial Temuco* *Manuel Rodríguez 1341, 2° Piso.*	☎ *(45) 233721* ✆ *(45) 233721*	*20*	▥₁₂	♀♂ Ⓡ ⚲ ▯
△ **Valdivia** - *Residencial Germania* *Picarte 873, Valdivia.*	☎ *(63) 212405*	*34*	▥₁₂	P ▯
▲ **Viña del Mar** - Hotel Asturias Av. Valparaíso 299, Viña del Mar. ✉ hotelasturi@entelchile.net	☎ (32) 711565 ✆ (32) 711565	50	▥₁₂	♀♂ ⚞ Ⓡ 0.4 E ▯ ☕

China (People's Republic of)

CHINA (PEOPLE'S REPUBLIC OF)
CHINA (PEOPLE'S REPUBLIC OF)
CHINA (PEOPLE'S REPUBLIC OF)

Beijing, Shanghai & Guangdong
c/o Guangdong YHA,
185, Huanshi Xi Road,
Guangzhou,
China.

☎ (86) 20 86677422
🖷 (86) 20 86665039

Capital:	Beijing	**Population:**	1,270,000,000
Language:	Mandarin, Cantonese	**Size:**	9,596,960 sq km
Currency:	Yuan (Renminbi)	**Telephone Country Code:**	86

Hong Kong (Special Administrative Region - SAR)
Hong Kong Youth Hostels Association,
Room 225, Block 19,
Shek Kip Mei Estate,
Sham Shui Po,
Kowloon,
Hong Kong.

☎ (852) 27881638
🖷 (852) 27883105
✉ hkyha@datainternet.com
🖳 www.yha.org.hk

A copy of the Hostel Directory for this Country can be obtained from:
The National Office

Capital:	Hong Kong	**Population:**	6,805,600
Language:	Cantonese, English, Mandarin	**Size:**	1,097 sq km
Currency:	HK$	**Telephone Country Code:**	852

English

Hostels are located in cities and in the countryside.

Price range

Price range US$ 4-11. BB inc 🛏.

Rooms and Reservations

R 🛏 (All Rooms). Reservations via IBN or Hostel by t f e. (Reservation charges may apply). Smoking is limited - please check.

Guests

Membership Card and Passport/Photo ID are required. ††† welcome. Group bookings via IBN Hostel or National Office by t f (Reservation charges may apply).

Open times

Main hostels: open 🛏, ⏰. Reception open: ⏰. Resident manager. **Other hostels:** open 🛏.

Meals

🍽 BL R For individuals & for †††. 🗸.

Travelling around

For ease of travel use ✈ 🚃 🚌.

Travel/Activity Packages

Tours/sightseeing and accommodation/transport packages available. Package bookings via Hostel by f e.

Passports and Visas

Passport and Visa required.

Health

Medical insurance is recommended.

Français

Les auberges sont situées dans les villes et à la campagne.

Tarifs des nuitées

Tarifs des nuitées 4-11 US$. BB inc 🛏.

Chambres et réservations

R 🛏 (Toutes chambres). Réservations via IBN ou l'auberge par t f e. (Des frais de réservation pourront vous être facturés). Il est permis de fumer dans certaines chambres - veuillez vérifier.

Usagers

La carte d'adhérent ainsi que le passeport/pièce d'identité avec photo sont à présenter. Accueil des †††. Réservations pour groupes via IBN l'auberge ou le Bureau National par t f (Des frais de réservation pourront vous être facturés).

Horaires d'ouverture

Grandes auberges: ouvertes 🛏, ⏰. Accueil ouvert ⏰. Gérant réside sur place. **Autres auberges:** ouvertes 🛏.

Repas

🍽 BL R Pour individuels & pour †††. 🗸.

Déplacements

Modes de transport recommandés ✈ 🚃 🚌.

Forfaits Voyages/Activités

Forfaits circuits touristiques et hébergement/transport disponibles. Réservations des forfaits via l'auberge par f e.

Passeports et visas

Passeport et visa obligatoires.

Santé

Une assurance médicale de voyage est conseillée.

Deutsch

Herbergen befinden sich in Städten und auf dem Land.

Preisspanne

Preisspanne 4-11 US$. ᵇᵇ ⁱⁿᶜ 🗔.

Zimmer und Reservierungen

Ⓡ 🔲 (Alle Zimmer). Reservierungen über ⟦IBN⟧ oder die Herberge per ❶ ❻ ❷. (Reservierungskosten könnten anfallen). Rauchen ist begrenzt - bitte checken.

Gäste

Mitgliedsausweis und Reisepass/ Personalausweis sind erforderlich. ♦♦♦ willkommen. Gruppenbuchungen über ⟦IBN⟧ Herberge oder die Landesverband per ❶ ❻ (Reservierungskosten könnten anfallen).

Öffnungszeiten

Hauptherbergen: Zugang 🔲, 🕒. Rezeption 🕒. Herbergsmanager wohnt im Haus. **Andere Herbergen:** Zugang 🔲.

Mahlzeiten.

🍴 BL Ⓡ Für Einzelreisende & für ♦♦♦. ♂.

Reisen im Land

Reisen ist einfach mit ✈ 🚟 🚌.

Reise-/Aktivitäten-Packages

Touren/sightseeing und Unterkunft/Transport-Packages erhältlich. Package-Buchungen über Herberge per ❻ ❷.

Reisepässe und Visa

Reisepass/Einreisevisum erforderlich.

Gesundheit

Unfall-/Krankenversicherung wird empfohlen.

Español

Los albergues están situados en las ciudades y el campo.

Tarifas mínima y máxima

Tarifas mínima y máxima 4-11 US$. ᵇᵇ ⁱⁿᶜ 🗔.

Habitaciones y Reservas

Ⓡ 🔲 (Todas las habitaciones). Reservas por ⟦IBN⟧ o a través del albergue por ❶ ❻ ❷. (Es posible que se aplique un suplemento en concepto de gastos de reserva). Está permitido fumar sólo en algunas salas/habitaciones - infórmese.

Huéspedes

Los huéspedes deben presentar su Carnet de Alberguista y su pasaporte o carnet de identidad. Se admiten ♦♦♦. Reservas de grupo por ⟦IBN⟧ o a través del albergue o la Asociación Nacional por ❶ ❻ (Es posible que se aplique un suplemento en concepto de gastos de reserva).

Horarios y fechas de apertura

Albergues principales - abiertos 🔲, 🕒. Horario de recepción: 🕒. Gerente residente. **Otros albergues** - abiertos 🔲.

Comidas

🍴 BL Ⓡ Para individuales y para ♦♦♦. ♂.

Desplazamientos

Transportes recomendados: ✈ 🚟 🚌.

Viajes Combinados con Actividades

Viajes combinados con visitas turísticas y alojamiento/transporte. Reserva de viajes combinados a través del albergue por ❻ ❷.

Pasaportes y Visados

Pasaporte y visado obligatorios.

Información Sanitaria

Seguro médico recomendado.

Beijing -
Beijing International Youth Hostel

No.9 Jian Guo Men Nei Da Jie,
Beijing 100005.
☎ (10) 65126688-6145, 6146
🖷 (10) 65229494
✉ BIH-YH@Sohu.com

Open Dates: 🗓12

Open Hours: 🕒

Reservations: Ⓡ (IBN) -CC-

Price Range: RMB 50 (US$6)

Beds: 148 - 2x² 18x⁶

Facilities: ♟ ▯ 🍺 TV ▮ 🧺 ▯ ☺ P

Directions: 2E from city centre

✈ 32km

A🚌 ap Beijing International Hotel

🚂 Beijing Railway Station 600m,
Beijing West Railway 10km

🚌 122 from Beijing West Railway
Station ap Beijing Railway Station

Beijing -
Beijing Zhaolong International Youth Hostel

2 Workers Stadium Rd (N),
Chaoyang District,
Beijing.
☎ (10) 65972299-6111, 6116
🖷 (10) 65972288
✉ ZLH@zhaolonghotel.com.cn

Open Dates: 🗓12

Open Hours: 🕒

Reservations: Ⓡ (IBN) -CC-

Price Range: RMB 50-60 (US$ 6-8)

Beds: 140 - 10x² 15x⁴ 6x⁶

Facilities: ♟ ▯ 🍺 TV 🧺 ▯ ☺ P

Directions: 6NE from city centre

✈ Capital Airport 23km

A🚌 ap Zhaolong Hotel

🚂 Beijing Railway Station 8km

🚌 703 ap Tuan Jie Hu Station;
403/120/113/701 ap Zhaolong Hotel

🚃 115 ap Zhaolong Hotel

Attractions: 🏊

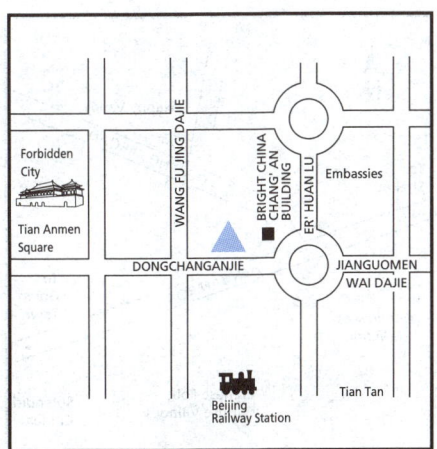

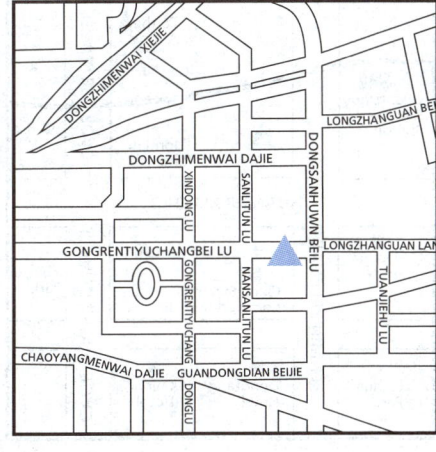

Guangzhou -
City Youth Hostel

179,
Huanshi Xi Rd,
Guangzhou.
t (20) 86666889
f (20) 86679787
e youthhostel-gd@21cn.com

Open Dates:	ⓛ
Open Hours:	⧖
Reservations:	Ⓡ ⒾⒷⓃ ⒸⒸ
Price Range:	RMB 68-168
Beds:	91x^1 48x^2 10x^3
Facilities:	(icons)
Directions:	
✈	Baiyun 4km
A🚌	Special Line 50m
⛴	Zhoutouzui 20km
🚃	Guangzhou 200m
🚌	122, 133, 30, 812, 210, 240, 218, 191 250m ap Caonuan Park
Attractions:	🏊 3km

Shenzhen -
Happy Valley Youth Hostel

Overseas Chinese Town Nanshan,
Shenzhen.
t (755) 6949443
f (755) 6949445

Open Dates:	ⓛ
Reservations:	Ⓡ ⒾⒷⓃ
Price Range:	RMB 60-90
Beds:	302
Facilities:	(icons) 1 x
Directions:	9W from city centre
✈	Huangtian International 24km
⛴	Shekou Port 13km
🚃	Luohu 17km
🚌	101, 105, 301, 204, 209, 210, 223, 113, 420, 423, 427, 434, 439, 450, 456, 465, 501, 502, 507, 511, 523 100m ap Window of the World
Attractions:	🏌 🚴 🏊400m ⛵400m

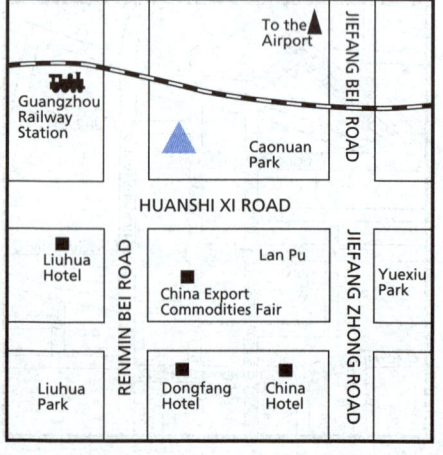

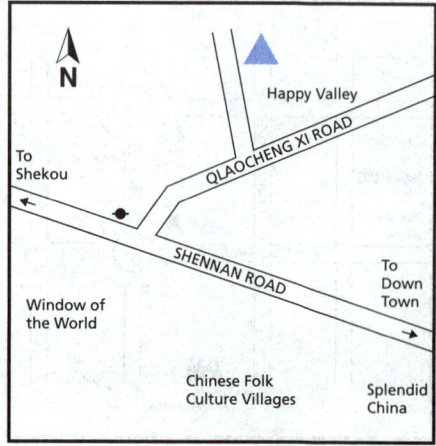

Location/Address	Telephone No. Fax No.	Beds	Opening Dates	Facilities
▲ Beijing - Beijing International Youth Hostel (IBN) No.9 Jian Guo Men Nei Da Jie, Beijing, 100005. e BIH-YH@Sohu.com	☎ (10) 65126688 -6145, 6146 ✆ (10) 65229494	148		2E CC
▲ Beijing - Beijing Zhaolong International Youth Hostel (IBN) 2 Workers Stadium Rd (N), Chaoyang District, Beijing. e ZLH@zhaolonghotel.com.cn	☎ (10) 65972299 -6111, 6116 ✆ (10) 65972288	140		6NE CC
▲ Foshan - Zhujiang Youth Hostel (IBN) No. 1, Qiren Rd, Foshan, Guangdong.	☎ (757) 2287512 ✆ (757) 2292263	48		
▲ Guangzhou - City Youth Hostel (IBN) 179, Huanshi Xi Rd, Guangzhou. e youthhostel-gd@21cn.com	☎ (20) 86666889 ✆ (20) 86679787			CC
▲ Guilin - Guilin Youth Hostel (IBN) 46 Bin Jiang Rd, Guilin, Guangxi.	☎ (773) 2819936 ✆ (773) 2827116	129		
▲ Kunming - Kunming Youth Hostel (IBN) 232 Daguan Raod, Kunming, Yuannan. e youthhostel.km@sohu.com	☎ (871) 5301395 ✆ (871) 5301395	218		
▲ Li Jiang - Li Jiang Youth Hostel (IBN) Lixing Yuan, Xianggf Lila Rd, Lijiang City, Yunnan. e youthhostel.lj@sohu.com	☎ (888) 5163579 ✆ (888) 5163579	58		
△ Nanhai - Mt. Xiqiao Youth Hostel (IBN) Xiqiao Hill, Nanhai.	☎ (757) 6886799 ✆ (757) 6889689	64		60SW CC
▲ Shanghai - Pu Jiang Youth Hostel (IBN) 15 Huang Pu Rd, Shanghai 200080. e sales@pujianghotel	☎ (21) 63246388 ✆ (21) 63243179	150		
▲ Shenzhen - Happy Valley Youth Hostel (IBN) Overseas Chinese Town Nanshan, Shenzhen.	☎ (755) 6949443 ✆ (755) 6949445	302		9W
▲ Zhaoqing - Seven Star Crags International Youth Hostel (IBN) Seven Star Crags Scenic Spot, 5260, 40 Zhaoqing, Guangdong.	☎ (758) 2226688 ✆ (758) 2224155	170		
△ Zhaoqing YH - Mt. Dinghu International Youth Hostel (IBN) Mt. Dinghu, Zhaoqing.	☎ (758) 2621668 ✆ (758) 2621665	100		18NE
△ Zhuhai - International Youth Hostel (IBN) 51 Hua Shan, Zhuhai Special Economic Zone.	☎ (756) 3332038, 3332036	120		CC

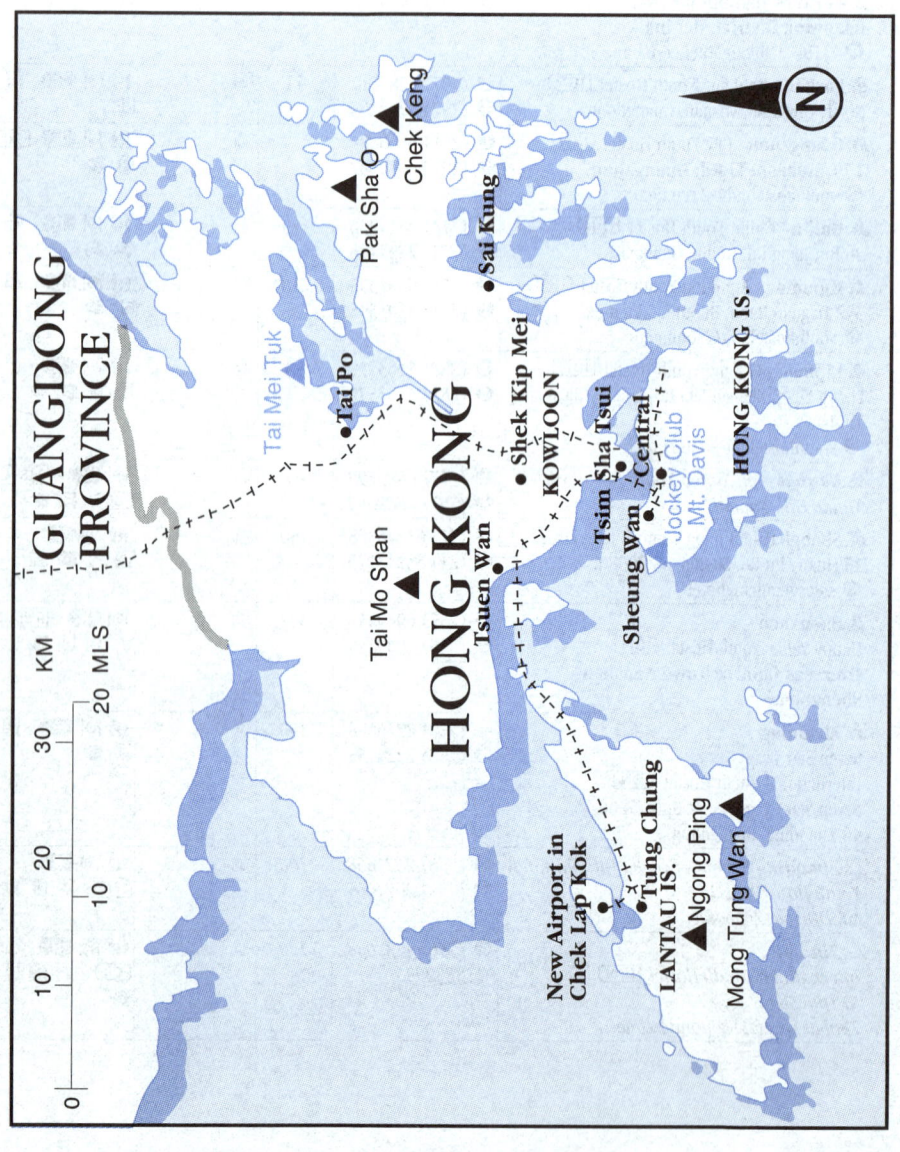

English

Hostels are located in cities and in the countryside.

Price range

Price range HK$ 35-75. .

Rooms and Reservations

R 🔲 (All Rooms). Reservations via **IBN** or National Office by ❶ ❷. (Reservation charges may apply). Smoking is limited - please check.

Guests

Membership Card is required. The maximum stay is 7 days. ♦♦♦ welcome. Group bookings via National Office by ❶ ❷ (Reservation charges may apply).

Open times

Main hostels: open 🔲, 07:00-23:00hrs. Reception open: 07:00-23:00hrs. Resident manager. **Other hostels:** open 🔲, 07:00-10:00hrs, 16:00-23:00hrs. Reception open: 07:00-10:00hrs, 16:00-23:00hrs. Resident manager.

Meals

♦.

Travelling around

For ease of travel use 🚂 🚌.

Passports and Visas

Passport and Visa required.

Health

Medical insurance is recommended.

Français

Les auberges sont situées dans les villes et à la campagne.

Tarifs des nuitées

Tarifs des nuitées 35-75 HK$. .

Chambres et réservations

R 🔲 (Toutes chambres). Réservations via **IBN** ou le Bureau National par ❶ ❷. (Des frais de réservation pourront vous être facturés). Il est permis de fumer dans certaines chambres - veuillez vérifier.

Usagers

La carte d'adhérent est à présenter. La durée maximale du séjour est de 7 jours. Accueil des ♦♦♦. Réservations pour groupes via le Bureau National par ❶ ❷ (Des frais de réservation pourront vous être facturés).

Horaires d'ouverture

Grandes auberges: ouvertes 🔲, entre 7h-23h. Accueil ouvert entre 7h-23h. Gérant réside sur place. **Autres auberges:** ouvertes 🔲, entre 7h-10h, 16h-23h. Accueil ouvert entre 7h-10h, 16h-23h. Gérant réside sur place.

Repas

♦.

Déplacements

Modes de transport recommandés 🚂 🚌.

Passeports et visas

Passeport et visa obligatoires.

Santé

Une assurance médicale de voyage est conseillée.

Deutsch

Herbergen befinden sich in Städten und auf dem Land.

Preisspanne

Preisspanne 35-75 HK$. 🔖.

Zimmer und Reservierungen

R 🈁 (Alle Zimmer). Reservierungen über (IBN) oder die Landesverband per ➊ ➋. (Reservierungskosten könnten anfallen). Rauchen ist begrenzt - bitte checken.

Gäste

Mitgliedsausweis ist erforderlich. Der maximale Aufenthalt beträgt 7 Tage. 👪 willkommen. Gruppenbuchungen über Landesverband per ➊ ➋ (Reservierungskosten könnten anfallen).

Öffnungszeiten

Hauptherbergen: Zugang 🈁, 07:00-23:00Uhr. Rezeption zwischen 07:00-23:00Uhr. Herbergsmanager wohnt im Haus. **Andere Herbergen:** Zugang 🈁, 07:00-10:00Uhr, 16:00-23:00Uhr. Rezeption zwischen 07:00-10:00Uhr, 16:00-23:00Uhr. Herbergsmanager wohnt im Haus.

Mahlzeiten.

.

Reisen im Land

Reisen ist einfach mit 🚇 🚌.

Reisepässe und Visa

Reisepass/Einreisevisum erforderlich.

Gesundheit

Unfall-/Krankenversicherung wird empfohlen.

Español

Los albergues están situados en las ciudades y el campo.

Tarifas mínima y máxima

Tarifas mínima y máxima 35-75 HK$. 🔖.

Habitaciones y Reservas

R 🈁 (Todas las habitaciones). Reservas por (IBN) o a través de la Asociación Nacional por ➊ ➋. (Es posible que se aplique un suplemento en concepto de gastos de reserva). Está permitido fumar sólo en algunas salas/habitaciones - infórmese.

Huéspedes

Los huéspedes deben presentar su Carnet de Alberguista. La estancia máxima es de 7 días. Se admiten 👪. Reservas de grupo a través de la Asociación Nacional por ➊ ➋ (Es posible que se aplique un suplemento en concepto de gastos de reserva).

Horarios y fechas de apertura

Albergues principales - abiertos 🈁, 07:00-23:00h. Horario de recepción: 07:00-23:00h. Gerente residente. **Otros albergues** - abiertos 🈁, 07:00-10:00h, 16:00-23:00h. Horario de recepción: 07:00-10:00h, 16:00-23:00h. Gerente residente.

Comidas

.

Desplazamientos

Transportes recomendados: 🚇 🚌.

Pasaportes y Visados

Pasaporte y visado obligatorios.

Información Sanitaria

Seguro médico recomendado.

Hong Kong -
Jockey Club Mt. Davis YH

(formerly Ma Wui Hall),
Top of Mt Davis Path,
off Victoria Rd,
 Kennedy Town,
Hong Kong Island.
☎ (852) 2817 5715
🖷 (852) 2788 3105
ℯ hkyha@datainternet.com

Open Dates:	🗓️12
Open Hours:	07.00-23.00 hrs
Reservations:	Ⓡ ⒾⒷⓃ
Price Range:	HK$65-75 🍽️
Beds:	169 - 2x² 1x³ 13x⁴ 1x⁶ 5x⁶
Facilities:	♿ ⅲ17x ⅲ 🚿 📺 🅿️ 🖼️ 🔒 ☰
Directions:	4W from city centre
✈	Hong Kong International
A🚌	SI to Tung Chung AR Station & MTR ap Sheung Wan & taxi or hostel shuttle bus to hostel

Tai Mei Tuk -
Bradbury Lodge

66 Tai Mei Tuk Rd,
Tai Mei Tuk,
Tai Po,
New Territories.
☎ (852) 2662 5123
🖷 (852) 2788 3105
ℯ hkyha@datainternet.com

Open Dates:	🗓️12
Open Hours:	07.00-10.00hrs; 16.00-23.00hrs
Reservations:	Ⓡ ⒾⒷⓃ
Price Range:	HK$45-55 🍽️
Beds:	96 - 4x² 2x⁴ 8x⁶
Facilities:	♿ ⅲ ⅲ 🚿 8 ☰
Directions:	16NE from city centre
✈	Hong Kong International
🚂	KCR to Tai Po Market Station then
🚌	KMB 75K (daily) or 275R (Sun & Public Holidays) ap Tai Mei Tuk terminus; walk S with sea on right towards Water Sports Centre, YH 4 mins from 🚌

Attractions: 🚴 🚶

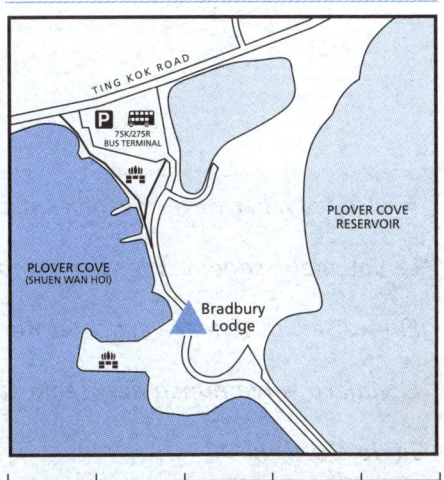

Location/Address	Telephone No. Fax No.	Beds	Opening Dates	Facilities
△ *Chek Keng* - Bradbury Hall *Chek Keng, Sai Kung, New Territories.* ✆ *hkyha@datainternet.com*	☎ *(852) 2328 2458* ✉ *(852) 2788 3105*	*94*	🗓12	Ⓡ
▲ **Hong Kong** - Jockey Club Mt. Davis YH (IBN) **(formerly Ma Wui Hall),** **Top of Mt Davis Path, off Victoria Rd,** **Kennedy Town, Hong Kong Island.** ✆ hkyha@datainternet.com	☎ *(852) 2817 5715* ✉ *(852) 2788 3105*	169	🗓12	♔ Ⓡ 4W ♿ ⛶
△ *Mong Tung Wan* - *Jockey Club Mong Tung Wan Hostel* *Mong Tung Wan, Lantau Island.* ✆ *hkyha@datainternet.com*	☎ *(852) 2984 1389* ✉ *(852) 2788 3105*	*88*	🗓12	Ⓡ
▲ **Ngong Ping** - S G Davis YH Ngong Ping, Lantau Island. ✆ hkyha@datainternet.com	☎ *(852) 2985 5610* ✉ *(852) 2788 3105*	52	🗓12	♔ Ⓡ 28SW
△ *Pak Sha O* - Pak Sha O YH *Hoi Ha Rd, Pak Sha O, Sai Kung,* *New Territories.* ✆ *hkyha@datainternet.com*	☎ *(852) 2328 2327* ✉ *(852) 2788 3105*	*112*	🗓12	Ⓡ
▲ **Tai Mei Tuk** - Bradbury Lodge (IBN) **66 Tai Mei Tuk Rd, Tai Mei Tuk, Tai Po,** **New Territories.** ✆ hkyha@datainternet.com	☎ *(852) 2662 5123* ✉ *(852) 2788 3105*	96	🗓12	♔ Ⓡ 16NE ♿
△ *Tai Mo Shan* - Sze Lok Yuen *Off Tai Mo Shan Rd, Tsuen Wan,* *New Territories.* ✆ *hkyha@datainternet.com*	☎ *(852) 2488 8188* ✉ *(852) 2788 3105*	*92*	🗓12	Ⓡ

"A wise traveller never despises his own country."

"Le voyageur sage ne méprise jamais son propre pays."

„Ein weiser Reisender verachtet nie das eigene Land."

"El viajero sabio nunca desprecia su propio país."

Carlo Goldoni

Costa Rica

COSTA RICA

COSTA RICA

COSTA RICA

**Red Costarricense de Albergues Juveniles,
PO Box 1355-1002, Paseo de los Estudiantes
Avenida Central, Calles 29 y 31
San José, Costa Rica.**

☎ (506) 2348186,
(506) 2244085,
(506)2536588
✆ (506) 2244085
✉ recajhi@sol.racsa.co.cr
🖳 www.hostelling-costarica.com

A copy of the Hostel Directory for this Country can be obtained from:
The National Office

Capital:	San José		**Population:**	3,500,000
Language:	Spanish		**Size:**	51,100 sq km
Currency:	colón		**Telephone Country Code:**	506

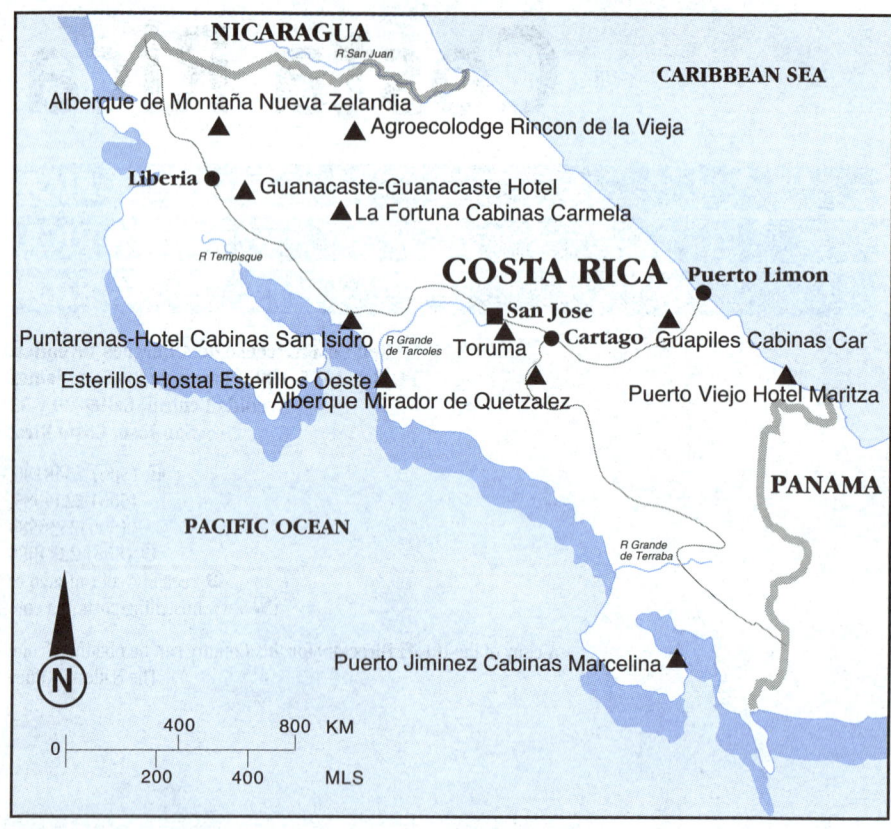

English

Hostels are located in cities, in the countryside, on the coast and on hills/mountains.

Price range

Price range US$ 11-14. 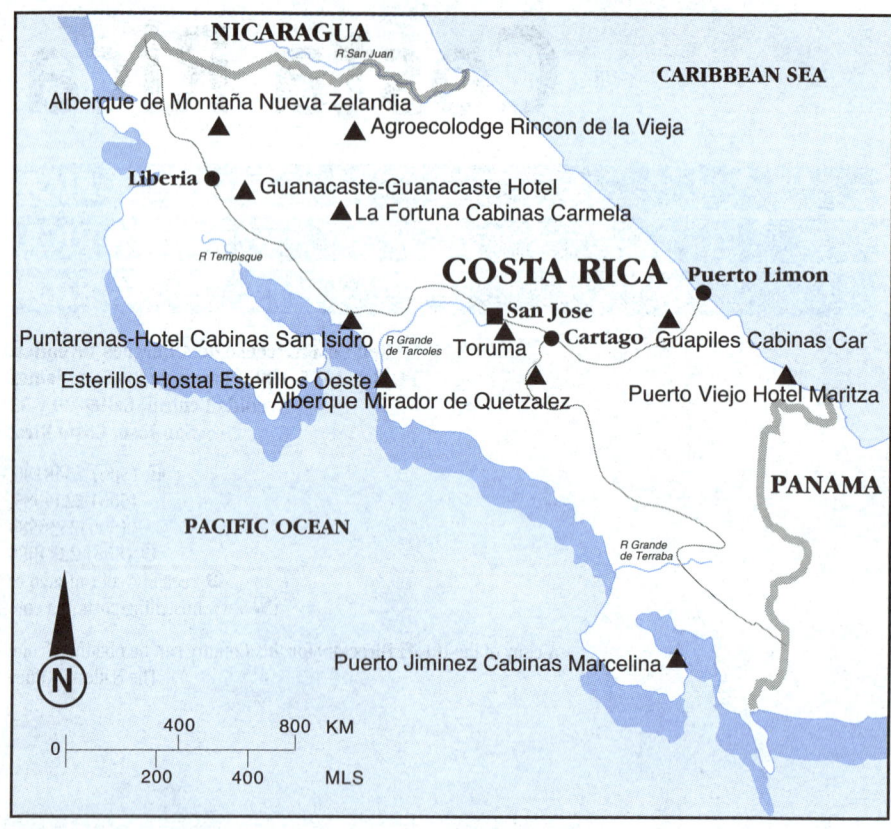.

Rooms and Reservations

R (All Rooms). Reservations via Hostel or National Office by **t f e**. Smoking is limited - please check.

Guests

iii welcome. Group bookings via Hostel or National Office by **t f e**.

Open times

Main hostels: open , . Reception open: 07:00-22:00hrs. Resident manager.

Meals

.

Discounts

HI Member Discounts available - see discounts section and www.iyhf.org.

Travelling around

For ease of travel use   Self-Drive.

Passports and Visas

Passport and Visa required.

Health

Medical insurance is recommended.

Français

Les auberges sont situées dans les villes, à la campagne, sur le littoral et à la montagne.

Tarifs des nuitées

Tarifs des nuitées 11-14 US$. 🗔.

Chambres et réservations

R 🗓 (Toutes chambres). Réservations via 🖳 l'auberge ou le Bureau National par ❶ ❻ ❺. Il est permis de fumer dans certaines chambres - veuillez vérifier.

Usagers

Accueil des ♗♗♗. Réservations pour groupes via 🖳 l'auberge ou le Bureau National par ❶ ❻ ❺.

Horaires d'ouverture

Grandes auberges: ouvertes 🗓, ⏱. Accueil ouvert entre 7h-22h. Gérant réside sur place.

Repas

☕.

Remises

Remises pour les adhérents HI - voir la section "Remises" et notre site: www.iyhf.org.

Déplacements

Modes de transport recommandés ✈ 🚌 Voiture.

Passeports et visas

Passeport et visa obligatoires.

Santé

Une assurance médicale de voyage est conseillée.

Deutsch

Herbergen befinden sich in Städten, auf dem Land, an der Küste und in Bergen/Gebirgen.

Preisspanne

Preisspanne 11-14 US$. 🗔.

Zimmer und Reservierungen

R 🗓 (Alle Zimmer). Reservierungen über 🖳 Herberge oder Landesverband per ❶ ❻ ❺. Rauchen ist begrenzt - bitte checken.

Gäste

♗♗♗ willkommen. Gruppenbuchungen über 🖳 Herberge oder Landesverband per ❶ ❻ ❺.

Öffnungszeiten

Hauptherbergen: Zugang 🗓, ⏱. Rezeption zwischen 07:00-22:00Uhr. Herbergsmanager wohnt im Haus.

Mahlzeiten

☕.

Ermäßigungen

HI-Mitgliedsrabatt ist erhältlich – siehe Teil für Rabatte und Ermäßigungen und www.iyhf.org.

Reisen im Land

Reisen ist einfach mit ✈ 🚌 Selbstfahrer.

Reisepässe und Visa

Reisepass/Einreisevisum erforderlich.

Gesundheit

Unfall-/Krankenversicherung wird empfohlen.

Español

Los albergues están situados en las ciudades, el campo, la costa y la montaña.

Tarifas mínima y máxima

Tarifas mínima y máxima 11-14 US$. .

Habitaciones y Reservas

R ▦ (Todas las habitaciones). Reservas por ☎ o a través del albergue o la Asociación Nacional por **❶ ❷ ❸**. Está permitido fumar sólo en algunas salas/habitaciones - infórmese.

Huéspedes

Se admiten **♦♦♦**. Reservas de grupo por ☎ o a través del albergue o la Asociación Nacional por **❶ ❷ ❸**.

Horarios y fechas de apertura

Albergues principales - abiertos ▦, ☺. Horario de recepción: 07:00-22:00h. Gerente residente.

Comidas

☕.

Descuentos

Se conceden descuentos a los miembros de Hostelling International – véase la sección sobre descuentos y nuestra página Internet en www.iyhf.org.

Desplazamientos

Transportes recomendados: ✈ 🚌 Automóvil.

Pasaportes y Visados

Pasaporte y visado obligatorios.

Información Sanitaria

Seguro médico recomendado.

"A person travels the world over in search of what he needs and returns home to find it."

"L'on parcourt le monde à la recherche de ce dont on a besoin et l'on revient chez soi pour le trouver."

„Der Mensch bereist die ganze Welt auf der Suche nach dem, was er braucht und kehrt heim, um es dort zu finden."

"Recorremos el mundo en busca de lo que necesitamos para al final encontrarlo en casa a nustro regreso"

George Moore

Location/Address	Telephone No. Fax No.	Beds	Opening Dates	Facilities
▲ **Alajuela** - Agroeco Lodge Rincon De La Vieja Aguas Claras de Upala. Take the Route to Buenos Aires de Aguas Claras de Upala, 6km east from Dos Rios de Upala.	☎ (506) 2811117 ✆ (506) 2244085	40	12	♦♦♦ ⊙ ⓡ 6E P 🗄 🚲
▲ **Esterrillos** - Hostal Esterillos Take the route to Quepos 22.5km east from Jaco Beach. ✉ obnerca@racsa.co.cr	☎ (506) 4465967 ✆ (506) 4465967	42	12	♦♦♦ ⓡ 0.5E ♿ CC ☞ P 🗄 🚲
▲ **Guauacaste** - Alberge de Moutaua Nueua Zelandia Quedrada Grande, Finca Nueua Zelandia. ✉ bricha@sol.racsa.co.cr	☎ (506) 6664300 ✆ (506) 6664300	18	12	♦♦♦ ⓡ CC P 🗄 ☕ 🚲
▲ **Guanacaste** - Hotel Guanacaste Liberia, Guanacaste. ✉ htlguana@sol.racsa.co.cr	☎ 6662287; 6660085 or RECAJ 2244085 ✆ 6662287	68	12	♦♦♦ ⊙ ⓡ 0.5W CC ☞ P
▲ **La Fortuna** - Cabinas Carmela Beside Catholic Church, La Fortuna.	☎ (506) 4799010 ✆ (506) 4799010	21	12	♦♦♦ ⓡ 0.1S ♿ CC P 🗄
▲ **Limon** - Cabinas Car Guapiles. 50m west from the Catholic Church. ✉ recajhi@sol.racsa.co.cr	☎ (506) 7100035 ✆ (506) 7101489	61	12	♦♦♦ ⊙ ⓡ ♿ CC P 🗄 🚲
▲ **Puerto Viejo** - Hotel Maritza 25 Mts East from Bus Stop Puerto Viejo.	☎ (506) 7500003 ✆ (506) 7500313	45	12	♦♦♦ ⓡ 0.2E CC P 🗄 ☕
▲ **Puntararenas** - Cabinas Marcelina Puerto Jimenez. North side from the Catholic Church. ✉ osanatur@sol.racsa.co.cr	☎ (506) 7355007 ✆ (506) 7355440	12	12	♦♦♦ ⓡ CC P 🗄 🚲
▲ **Puntarenas** - Hotel Cabinas San Isidro 700mts West Sanabria Hospital, El Roble (Pacific Beach), 100Kms from San José.	☎ 2805200, 6630031 or RECAJ 2348186 ✆ 2244611 or 2244085	300	12	♦♦♦ ⊙ ⓡ 10W ♿ CC ☞ P 🗄 ☕
▲ **San José** - Albergue Mirador de Quetzales Interamericana sur 70km, turn right for 1km. ✉ recajhi@sol.racsa.co.cr	☎ 3818456	30	12	♦♦♦ ⊙ ⓡ 70S P 🗄 🚲
▲ **San José** - Toruma Toruma Hostel, Avenida Central, calle 29 y 31, San José. ✉ recajhi@sol.racsa.co.cr	☎ 2348186 ✆ 2244085	87	12	♦♦♦ ⊙ 2E CC P

HOSTELLING INTERNATIONAL

Make your credit card bookings at these centres
Réservez par cartes de crédit aux centres suivants
Reservieren Sie per Kreditkarte bei diesen Zentren
Reserve con tarjeta de crédito en los siguientes centros

English

Australia	☎ (2) 9261 1111
Canada	☎ (800) 663 5777
England & Wales	☎ (1629) 581 418
France	☎ (1) 44 89 87 27
Northern Ireland	☎ (28) 9032 4733
Republic of Ireland	☎ (1) 830 1766
New Zealand	☎ (3) 379 9808
Scotland	☎ (8701) 553 255
Switzerland	☎ (1) 360 1414
USA	☎ (202) 783 6161

Français

Angleterre & Pays de Galles	☎ (1692) 581 418
Australie	☎ (2) 9261 1111
Canada	☎ (800) 663 5777
Écosse	☎ (8701) 553 255
États-Unis	☎ (202) 783 6161
France	☎ (1) 44 89 87 27
Irlande du Nord	☎ (28) 9032 4733
Nouvelle-Zélande	☎ (3) 379 9808
République d'Irlande	☎ (1) 830 1766
Suisse	☎ (1) 360 1414

Deutsch

Australien	☎ (2) 9261 1111
England & Wales	☎ (1629) 581 418
Frankreich	☎ (1) 44 89 87 27
Irland	☎ (1) 830 1766
Kanada	☎ (800) 663 5777
Neuseeland	☎ (3) 379 9808
Nordirland	☎ (28) 9032 4733
Schottland	☎ (8701) 553 255
Schweiz	☎ (1) 360 1414
USA	☎ (202) 783 6161

Español

Australia	☎ (2) 9261 1111
Canadá	☎ (800) 663 5777
Escocia	☎ (8701) 553 255
Estados Unidos	☎ (202) 783 6161
Francia	☎ (1) 44 89 87 27
Inglaterra y Gales	☎ (1629) 581 418
Irlanda del Norte	☎ (28) 9032 4733
Nueva Zelanda	☎ (3) 379 9808
República de Irlanda	☎ (1) 830 1766
Suiza	☎ (1) 360 1414

IBN INTERNATIONAL BOOKING NETWORK

Egypt

EGYPTE

ÄGYPTEN

EGIPTO

Egyptian Youth Hostels Association,
1 El-Ibrahimy Street, Garden City,
Cairo, Egypt.

☎ (20) (2) 7961448, 7940527
f (20) (2) 7950329
e eyhamo@usa.net

Office Hours: Sat-Thurs 08.30-19.30hrs

Travel Section: Egyptian Youth Travel Bureau,
7 Dr Abdel Hamid Saiid St, Maarouf,
Cairo, Egypt.

☎ (20) (2) 5779773
f (20) (2) 5758099

A copy of the Hostel Directory for this Country can be obtained from:
The National Office

Capital:	Cairo		**Population:**	65,000,000
Language:	Arabic		**Size:**	1,001,449 sq km
Currency:	LE (Egyptian £) = 100 piastres		**Telephone Country Code:**	20

As-Sallum
Matruh
Alexandria
Damanhur
Al-Qahirah Cairo
Fayoum
EGYPT
Nile
Port Said
Ismailia
Suez
ISRAEL
Al Arish
Sharm El Sheikh
Assyout Souhag
Hurghada
Luxor
Aswan Aswan
Nasir Lake
SUDAN

N

0   50   100   150   KMS
        50   MLS

English

Egypt recognises ISIC and offers discounts at museums and on trains. Electrical current is 220 volt AC. Egypt is 2 hours ahead of Greenwich Mean Time. Hostels are located in cities and on the coast.

Price range

Price range LE 14-30. BB|inc 🛏.

Rooms and Reservations

R 🖷 (2🛏 3🛏 ♦♦♦). Reservations via Hostel or National Office by ❶ ❷. (Reservation charges may apply). Smoking is limited - please check.

Guests

Membership Card and Passport/Photo ID are required. The maximum stay is 14 days. ♦♦♦ welcome. Group bookings via Hostel or National Office by ❶ ❷ (Reservation charges may apply).

Open times

Main hostels: open 🖷, 07:00-10:30hrs, 13:00-22:00hrs. Reception open: 🕓. Resident manager. **Other hostels:** open 🖷, 08:00-10:30hrs, 13:00-22:00hrs. Reception open: 08:00-23:59hrs. Resident manager.

Meals

🍽 BLD **R** For individuals & for ♦♦♦. ♂ Not all utensils provided - check with hostel.

Travelling around

For ease of travel use ✈ 🚂 ⛴ 🚌 Self-Drive. Drive on the left.

Travel/Activity Packages

Tours/sightseeing, water sports and accommodation/transport packages available. Package bookings via Hostel or National Office by ❶ ❷.

Passports and Visas

Passport and Visa required.

Health

Vaccination certificates required. Emergency medical treatment is free.

Français

La carte ISIC est valide en Egypte et des remises sont proposées dans les musées, sur les billets de train etc. Le voltage utilisé en Egypte est 220 volts. L'Egypte est en avance de 2 heures sur l'heure du méridien de Greenwich. Les auberges sont situées dans les villes ou sur le littoral.

Tarifs des nuitées

Tarifs des nuitées 14-30 LE. BB|inc 🛏.

Chambres et réservations

R 🖷 (2🛏 3🛏 ♦♦♦). Réservations via l'auberge ou le Bureau National par ❶ ❷. (Des frais de réservation pourront vous être facturés). Il est permis de fumer dans certaines chambres - veuillez vérifier.

Usagers

La carte d'adhérent ainsi que le passeport/pièce d'identité avec photo sont à présenter. La durée maximale du séjour est de 14 jours. Accueil des ♦♦♦. Réservations pour groupes via l'auberge ou le Bureau National par ❶ ❷ (Des frais de réservation pourront vous être facturés).

Horaires d'ouverture

Grandes auberges: ouvertes 🖷, entre 7h-10h30, 13h-22h. Accueil ouvert 🕓. Gérant réside sur place. **Autres auberges:** ouvertes 🖷, entre 8h-10h30, 13h-22h. Accueil ouvert entre 8h-23h59. Gérant réside sur place.

Repas

🍽 BLD **R** Pour individuels & pour ††† . ☞
Pas tous les ustensils sont fournis - à vérifier
auprès de l'auberge.

Déplacements

Modes de transport recommandés ✈ 🚄
🚢 🚌 Voiture. Conduite à gauche.

Forfaits Voyages/Activités

Forfaits circuits touristiques, sports aquatiques
et hébergement/transport disponibles.
Réservations des forfaits via l'auberge et le
Bureau National par ❶ ❷ .

Passeports et visas

Passeport et visa obligatoires.

Santé

Les certificats de vaccination sont obligatoires.
Soins d'urgence gratuits.

Deutsch

Ägypten erkennt ISIC an und bietet Rabatt bei
Museen und Zügen. Elektr. Strom ist 220 Volt
AC. Ägypten ist der WEZ 2 Stunden voraus.
Herbergen befinden sich in Städten und an der
Küste.

Preisspanne

Preisspanne 14-30 LE. [BB]inc 🍴 .

Zimmer und Reservierungen

R 🛏 (²🛏 ³🛏 †††). Reservierungen über
Herberge oder Landesverband per ❶ ❷ .
(Reservierungskosten könnten anfallen).
Rauchen ist begrenzt - bitte checken.

Gäste

Mitgliedsausweis und Reisepass/
Personalausweis sind erforderlich. Der
maximale Aufenthalt beträgt 14 Tage.

††† willkommen. Gruppenbuchungen über
Herberge oder Landesverband per ❶
❷ (Reservierungskosten könnten anfallen).

Öffnungszeiten

Hauptherbergen: Zugang 🛏 ,
07:00-10:30Uhr, 13:00-22:00Uhr. Rezeption
🕐. Herbergsmanager wohnt im Haus. **Andere
Herbergen:** Zugang 🛏 , 08:00-10:30Uhr,
13:00-22:00Uhr. Rezeption zwischen
08:00-23:59Uhr. Herbergsmanager wohnt im
Haus.

Mahlzeiten

🍽 BLD **R** Für Einzelreisende & für ††† . ☞
Nicht alle Utensilien werden bereitgestellt - in
der Herberge nachfragen.

Reisen im Land

Reisen ist einfach mit ✈ 🚄 🚢 🚌
Selbstfahrer. Links fahren.

Reise-/Aktivitäten-Packages

Touren/sightseeing, Wassersport und
Unterkunft/Transport-Packages erhältlich.
Package-Buchungen über Herberge oder
Landesverband per ❶ ❷ .

Reisepässe und Visa

Reisepass/Einreisevisum erforderlich.

Gesundheit

Schutzimpfungsbescheinigungen sind
erforderlich. Nur im Notfall sind medizinische
Behandlungen kostenlos.

Español

Se conceden descuentos en el precio de museos
y billetes de tren en Egipto a los titulares del
Carnet Internacional de Identidad para
Estudiantes (ISIC). La corriente eléctrica es de
220 v CA. Egipto lleva 2 horas de adelanto sobre

la hora media de Greenwich. Los albergues están situados en las ciudades y la costa.

Tarifas mínima y máxima

Tarifas mínima y máxima 14-30 LE. BB^inc ⛃.

Habitaciones y Reservas

R 🛏 (2🛏 3🛏 👪). Reservas a través del albergue o la Asociación Nacional por ❶ ❷. (Es posible que se aplique un suplemento en concepto de gastos de reserva). Está permitido fumar sólo en algunas salas/habitaciones - infórmese.

Huéspedes

Los huéspedes deben presentar su Carnet de Alberguista y su pasaporte o carnet de identidad. La estancia máxima es de 14 días. Se admiten 👪. Reservas de grupo a través del albergue o la Asociación Nacional por ❶ ❷ (Es posible que se aplique un suplemento en concepto de gastos de reserva).

Horarios y fechas de apertura

Albergues principales - abiertos 🛏, 07:00-10:30h, 13:00-22:00h. Horario de recepción: ⌚. Gerente residente. **Otros albergues** - abiertos 🛏, 08:00-10:30h, 13:00-22:00h. Horario de recepción: 08:00-23:59h. Gerente residente.

Comidas

🍽 BLD **R** Para individuales y para 👪. 🍴 La cocina no dispone de todos los utensilios - consulte con el albergue.

Desplazamientos

Transportes recomendados: ✈ 🚌 ⛴ 🚐 Automóvil. Se conduce por la izquierda.

Viajes Combinados con Actividades

Viajes combinados con visitas turísticas, deportes náuticos y alojamiento/transporte. Reserva de viajes combinados a través del albergue o la Asociación Nacional por ❶ ❷.

Pasaportes y Visados

Pasaporte y visado obligatorios.

Información Sanitaria

Certificados de vacunación obligatorios. Asistencia médica de urgencia gratuita.

"Travelling is like gambling: it is always connected with winning and losing, and generally where it is least expected we receive more or less what we hoped for."

"Le voyage est pareil au jeu: il est toujours question de gagner et de perdre, et en général l'on reçoit plus ou moins ce que l'on espérait, alors que l'on s'y attend le moins."

„Reisen kommt dem Glücksspiel gleich: es ist immer mit Gewinn und Verlust verbunden, und wir bekommen allgemein dort, wo wir es am wenigsten erwarten, mehr oder weniger das, was wir erhofft hatten."

"El viajar es como un juego de azar: tiene que ver siempre con ganar y perder y, generalmente, en el momento menos pensado recibimos más o menos lo que esperábamos."

Johann Wolfgang Von Goethe

Hurghada - International

Hurghada Hostel,
Beside Aquarium Museum.
☎ (65) 540411
🖷 (65) 544989

Open Dates: 🗓12

Open Hours: ⏱

Reservations: Ⓡ

Beds: 160 - 16x³🛏 28x⁴🛏

Facilities: ♿ 🚻 🚻 🍴 🛏 ☕ 🚲 ⚙ 🏨 📺 🛏 🧺 1 x 🍷 📷 💼 💈 🔢 🅿 ✏ 🛋 ⚡ ⚠ 🔍 🏓

Attractions: 🏛 🎿 ∪ ⚓ 🏊

"They change their climate,
not their soul, who rush
across the sea."

"Ils changent de climat, pas
d'âme, ceux qui se
précipitent pour traverser
les océans."

„Die, die über das Meer
eilen, wechseln zwar das
Klima, jedoch nicht ihre
Seele."

"Cambian de clima, no de
alma, quienes veloces
atraviesan mares."

Horace

Red Sea

Marine
Biological Museum

TO SUEZ

HURGHADA

TO AIRPORT

Governorate

Location/Address	Telephone No. Fax No.	Beds	Opening Dates	Facilities
▲ Alexandria - El Shatbi Y.H 32 Port Said St, Shatbi, Raml, Alexandria.	☏ (3) 5975459 🖷 (3) 5964759	200	🗓	
△ Assyout Lux Housing El Walidia, Bldg 3.	☏ (88) 324846	40	🗓	
△ Aswan 16 Abtal El Tahrir St, Aswan.	☏ (97) 302313 🖷 (97) 302313	76	🗓	
▲ Cairo 135 Abdel Aziz Al Saoud St, El Manial, Kobri El Gamaa (University Bridge), Cairo.	☏ (2) 3640729; (2) 3624593 🖷 (2) 3684107	167	🗓	
△ Damanhour 9 El Shaheed Gawad Hosni St, Damanhour.	☏ (45) 314056	30	🗓	
△ El Fayoum Lux Housing Block of Flats, Hadaka, Block 7, Flat No 7, 8 Fayoum.	☏ (84) 350005	24	🗓	
△ Hurghada New Tourist Centre, Hurghada.	☏ (65) 442432	42	🗓	
▲ Hurghada - International **Hurghada Hostel,** **Beside Aquarium Museum.**	☏ (65) 540411 🖷 (65) 544989	160	🗓	
▲ Ismailia Emara Touristic Rd, Temsah Lake.	☏ (64) 322850 🖷 (64) 331429	266	🗓	
△ Mersa Matrouh Behind 4 El Galaa St, Salloum Rd, Mersa Matrouh.	☏ (046) 4932331	52	🗓	
▲ Port Said - El-Nasr El Amin St & Kornaish (near Sport Stadium), Port Said.	☏ (66) 228702 🖷 (66) 226433	145	🗓	
▲ Sharm-El-Sheikh PO 46619: 290km SE of Suez.	☏ (69) 660317 🖷 (69) 660317	120	🗓	
△ Sohag 5 Port Said St, Sohag.	☏ (93) 324395	28	🗓	
▲ New Sohag Assyout Sohag Rd in front of Elmanzalawy Factory.	☏ (93) 311430 🖷 (93) 321323	72	🗓	
▲ Suez Sharia Tariq El Horia (near Sport Stadium), PO 171, Suez.	☏ (62) 339069	105	🗓	

YOUTH HOSTEL ACCOMMODATION
OUTSIDE THE ASSURED STANDARDS SCHEME

Location/Address	Telephone No. Fax No.	Beds	Opening Dates	Facilities
Luxor 16 Maabad El Karnak St, near the Education and Administration Centre: approach via City Gate nearest to airport.	☏ (95) 372139 🖷 (95) 370539	275	🗓	

India

INDE

INDIEN

INDIA

**Youth Hostels Association of India,
5 Nyaya Marg, Chanakyapuri,
New Delhi 110 021, India.**

☎ (91) (11) 6871969
(91) (11) 6110250
🖷 (91) (11) 6113469
Telegraphic address: 'Youthostel, New Delhi 110 021'
✉ yhostel@del2.vsnl.net.in
🖳 www.yhaindia.org

A copy of the Hostel Directory for this Country can be obtained from:
The National Office.

Capital:	New Delhi	Population:	1,004,482,970
Language:	Hindi	Size:	3,287,590 sq km
Currency:	Rs (rupees)	Telephone Country Code:	91

Patnitop

Dalhousie
Rup Nagar
Panchkula
Kurukshetra   Nainital
Delhi
Namchi
Naharlagun
Jodhpur   Jaipur   Agra   Shillong   Dimapur
Kankroli   Patna   Tura   Imphal
Gandhinagar   Aizawl
Vadodra   Bhopal

Puri
Aurangabad   Gopalpur on Sea

Secunderabad

Hassan
Panaji   Tirupati

Mysore   Chennai
Calicut   Pondicherry   Port Blair
Tiruchirapalli
Cochin
Vellanad
Trivendrum

Scale 1:25,000,000
km 100 0 100   300   500 km

English

Visitors are required to book their accommodation in advance. Hostels are located in cities, in the countryside, on the coast and on hills/mountains.

Price range

Price range Rs20 for HI members/students, others Rs40-250. BB^{inc} ☐ ☐ Sheet sleeping bag required.

Rooms and Reservations

R 🖼 (2🛏 3🛏 4🛏 6🛏 6+🛏 👪).
Reservations via **IBN** Hostel or National Office by ❶ ❷ ❸. (Reservation charges may apply). All hostels are non-smoking.

Guests

Membership Card and Passport/Photo ID are required. The maximum stay is 5 days. 👪 welcome. Group bookings via **IBN** Hostel or National Office by ❶ ❷ ❸ (Reservation charges may apply).

Open times

Main hostels: open 🖼, 10:00-17:00hrs. Reception open: 10:00-17:00hrs. Resident warden. **Other hostels:** open 🖼, 10:00-17:00hrs. Reception open: 10:00-17:00hrs. Resident warden.

Meals

🍽 BLD **R** For individuals & for 👪. 🍴.

Discounts

HI Member Discounts available - see discounts section and www.iyhf.org.

Travelling around

For ease of travel use ✈ 🚌 Discount to Indrail pass holders in possession of a valid passport. 🚐 Self-Drive.

Travel/Activity Packages

Tours/sightseeing, walking/trekking and accommodation/transport packages available. Package bookings via Hostel or National Office by ❶ ❷ ❸.

Passports and Visas

Passport, Photo ID and Visa required.

Health

Vaccinations are required - check with your medical advisor. Vaccinations are advised - check with your medical advisor. Vaccination certificates required. Medical insurance is recommended.

Français

Il est demandé aux visiteurs de réserver leur hébergement à l'avance. Les auberges sont situées dans les villes, à la campagne, sur le littoral et à la montagne.

Tarifs des nuitées

Tarifs des nuitées 20 for HI members/students, others Rs40-250Rs. BB^{inc} ☐ ☐ Sac-drap obligatoire.

Chambres et réservations

R 🖼 (2🛏 3🛏 4🛏 6🛏 6+🛏 👪).
Réservations via **IBN** l'auberge et le Bureau National par ❶ ❷ ❸. (Des frais de réservation pourront vous être facturés). Toutes les auberges sont non-fumeurs.

Usagers

La carte d'adhérent ainsi que le passeport/pièce d'identité avec photo sont à présenter. La durée maximale du séjour est de 5 jours. Accueil des 👪. Réservations pour groupes via **IBN** l'auberge et le Bureau National par ❶ ❷ ❸ (Des frais de réservation pourront vous être facturés).

Horaires d'ouverture

Grandes auberges: ouvertes 🖾, entre
10h-17h. Accueil ouvert entre 10h-17h. Gérant
réside sur place. **Autres auberges:** ouvertes
🖾, entre 10h-17h. Accueil ouvert entre
10h-17h. Gérant réside sur place.

Repas

🍽 BLD **R** Pour individuels & pour ♦♦♦. 🗺.

Remises

Remises pour les adhérents HI - voir la section
"Remises" et notre site: www.iyhf.org.

Déplacements

Modes de transport recommandés ✈ �
Remises pour les titulaires d'une carte Indrail
en possession d'un passeport valide. 🚌
Voiture.

Forfaits Voyages/Activités

Forfaits circuits touristiques, randonnées
pédestres et hébergement/transport
disponibles. Réservations des forfaits via
l'auberge et le Bureau National par ❶ ❷ ❸.

Passeports et visas

Passeport, pièce d'identité avec photo et visa
obligatoires.

Santé

Des vaccinations sont obligatoires - veuillez
vérifier auprès de votre médecin. Des
vaccinations sont conseillées - veuillez vérifier
auprès de votre médecin. Les certificats de
vaccination sont obligatoires. Une assurance
médicale de voyage est conseillée.

Deutsch

Besucher müssen Ihre Unterkunft im Voraus
buchen. Herbergen befinden sich in Städten, auf

dem Land, an der Küste und in
Bergen/Gebirgen.

Preisspanne

Preisspanne 20 for HI members/students,
others Rs40-250Rs. BB inc 🍴 🛏
Leinenschlafsack erforderlich.

Zimmer und Reservierungen

R 🖾 (2🛏 3🛏 4🛏 6🛏 6🛏 ♦♦♦).
Reservierungen über **IBN** Herberge oder
Landesverband per ❶ ❷ ❸.
(Reservierungskosten könnten anfallen).
Rauchen ist in allen Herbergen NICHT gestattet.

Gäste

Mitgliedsausweis und
Reisepass/Personalausweis sind erforderlich.
Der maximale Aufenthalt beträgt 5 Tage.
♦♦♦ willkommen. Gruppenbuchungen über
IBN Herberge oder Landesverband per ❶
❷ ❸ (Reservierungskosten könnten anfallen).

Öffnungszeiten

Hauptherbergen: Zugang 🖾,
10:00-17:00Uhr. Rezeption zwischen
10:00-17:00Uhr. Herbergsmanager wohnt im
Haus. **Andere Herbergen:** Zugang 🖾,
10:00-17:00Uhr. Rezeption zwischen
10:00-17:00Uhr. Herbergsmanager wohnt im
Haus.

Mahlzeiten

🍽 BLD **R** Für Einzelreisende & für ♦♦♦. 🗺.

Ermäßigungen

HI-Mitgliedsrabatt ist erhältlich – siehe Teil für
Rabatte und Ermäßigungen und www.iyhf.org.

Reisen im Land

Reisen ist einfach mit ✈ 🚜 Rabatt für
Indrail-Passbesitzer mit gültigem Reisepass.
🚌 Selbstfahrer.

Reise-/Aktivitäten-Packages

Touren/sightseeing, Wandern/Trekking und Unterkunft/Transport-Packages erhältlich. Package-Buchungen über Herberge oder Landesverband per ❶ ❶ ❸.

Reisepässe und Visa

Reisepass, Personalausweis und Einreisevisum erforderlich.

Gesundheit

Schutzimpfungen sind erforderlich - mit Ihrem Arzt checken. Schutzimpfungen werden empfohlen - mit Ihrem Arzt checken. Schutzimpfungsbescheinigungen sind erforderlich. Unfall-/Krankenversicherung wird empfohlen.

Español

Es imprescindible reservar con antelación. Los albergues están situados en las ciudades, el campo, la costa y la montaña.

Tarifas mínima y máxima

Tarifas mínima y máxima 20 for HI members/students, others Rs40-250Rs. ⠀BB⠀inc ⠀⠀ Saco sábana imprescindible.

Habitaciones y Reservas

❶ ⠀12⠀ (2⠀ 3⠀ 4⠀ 6⠀ 6⠀ ⠀⠀). Reservas por ⠀IBN⠀ o a través del albergue o la Asociación Nacional por ❶ ❶ ❸. (Es posible que se aplique un suplemento en concepto de gastos de reserva). Está prohibido fumar en todos los albergues.

Huéspedes

Los huéspedes deben presentar su Carnet de Alberguista y su pasaporte o carnet de identidad. La estancia máxima es de 5 días. Se admiten ⠀⠀. Reservas de grupo por ⠀IBN⠀ o a

través del albergue o la Asociación Nacional por ❶ ❶ ❸ (Es posible que se aplique un suplemento en concepto de gastos de reserva).

Horarios y fechas de apertura

Albergues principales - abiertos ⠀12⠀, 10:00-17:00h. Horario de recepción: 10:00-17:00h. Gerente residente. **Otros albergues** - abiertos ⠀12⠀, 10:00-17:00h. Horario de recepción: 10:00-17:00h. Gerente residente.

Comidas

⠀⠀ BLD ⠀R⠀ Para individuales y para ⠀⠀. ⠀⠀.

Descuentos

Se conceden descuentos a los miembros de Hostelling International – véase la sección sobre descuentos y nuestra página Internet en www.iyhf.org.

Desplazamientos

Transportes recomendados: ✈ 🚌 Se concede un descuento a los titulares de la tarjeta Indrail y de un pasaporte en regla. 🚐 Automóvil.

Viajes Combinados con Actividades

Viajes combinados con visitas turísticas, senderismo y alojamiento/transporte. Reserva de viajes combinados a través del albergue o la Asociación Nacional por ❶ ❶ ❸.

Pasaportes y Visados

Pasaporte o carnet de identidad y visado obligatorios.

Información Sanitaria

Vacunación obligatoria - consulte con su centro médico. Vacunación recomendada - consulte con su centro médico. Certificados de vacunación obligatorios. Seguro médico recomendado.

New Delhi -
International YH

5 Nyaya Marg,
Chanakyapuri,
New Delhi 110021.

☎ (11) 6116285; (11) 4101246
✆ (11) 6113469
✉ yhostel@del2.vsnl.net.in

Open Dates:	🗓
Open Hours:	🕐
Reservations:	**R** **IBN**
Price Range:	Rs 50-250 (Dormitory); Rs 300-700 (Rooms) 🛏
Beds:	162
Facilities:	♿ ♦♦♦ 4x ♦♦♦ 🍽 💻 🏢 📺 🔋 🗄 2 x🍴 🔲 📷 🚿 🔋 ⊜ 🔲 **P** 🔲 🚲 ♻ 🏠

Directions:

✈	Indira Gandhi International 16km
🚃	New Delhi 8km, Delhi Main 16km, Nizamuddin 12km
🚌	604, 620, 640, 680, 710, 720 ap Chanakyapuri Police Station, New Delhi 350m

Attractions: ⚶ ⛵3km

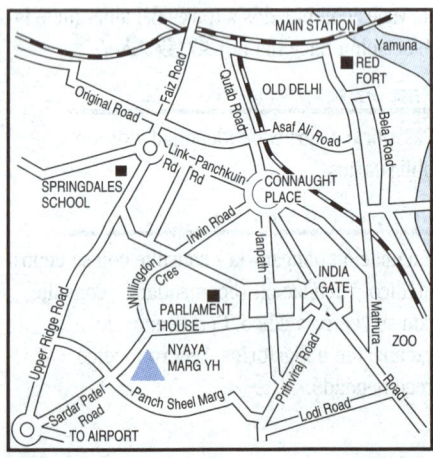

"The tourist who moves about to see
and hear and open himself to all the
influences of the places which condense
centuries of human greatness is only a
man in search of excellence."

"Le touriste qui voyage pour voir et
entendre et s'ouvrir à toutes les
influences des lieux qui condensent des
siècles de grandeur humaine est tout
simplement un homme à la recherche
de l'excellence."

„Der Tourist, der unterwegs ist, um zu
schauen und zu hören und sich den
Einflüssen der Orte zu eröffnen, die
Jahrhunderte menschlicher Größe
zusammenfassen, ist einfach ein
Mensch auf der Suche nach
Großartigem."

"El turista que se desplaza para ver y
oír y abrirse a todas las influencias de
los lugares en que se condensan siglos
de grandeza humana es simplemente
un hombre en busca de excelencia."

Max Lerner

Location/Address	Telephone No. Fax No.	Beds	Opening Dates	Facilities
△ **Agra** Sanjay Place, M G Rd, Agra 282002, Uttar Peradesh.	☎ (562) 354462	86	🗓12	♔♔ 🍽 Ⓡ ☞ 🅿 🔲 ☕
△ **Aizwal** Luangmual, Aizawal, 796009 Mizoram.	☎ (389) 832243	120	🗓12	♔♔ ☞ 🅿
△ **Aurangabad** Padampura Corner, Station Rd, Aurangabad 431005, Maharashtra.	☎ (240) 334892	60	🗓12	♔♔ 🍽 Ⓡ 🅿 🔲 ☕
▲ **Bhopal** North TT Nagar, Near Hotel Palash, Bhopal 462003, Madhya Pradesh.	☎ (755) 553670, (755) 711560	60	🗓12	♔♔ 🍽 🅿 🔲 ☕
△ **Calicut (Kozhikode)** East Hill, P.O. West Hill, Calicut - 673005, Kerala.	☎ (495) 381354	50	🗓12	♔♔ 🍽 ☞ 🅿 🔲 ☕
▲ **Chennai** Indira Nagar, Chennai - 600 020, Tamil Nadu.	☎ (44) 4420233	46	🗓12	🍽 Ⓡ 🅿 🔲 ☕
△ **Cochin** - Kochi Youth Hostel NGO Qrts Junction Thrikkakara, Kakanadu Route Distt Ernakulam, Cochin, 682021 Kerala.	☎ (484) 422808, (484) 424399	51	🗓12	♔♔ 🍽 Ⓡ ☞ 🅿 🔲 ☕
▲ **Dalhousie** Near bus-stand, Dalhousie 176304, Himachal Pradesh.	☎ (1899) 42189 📠 (1899) 40929	40	🗓12	🍽 Ⓡ ☞ 🅿 🔲 ☕
△ **Dimapur** Opposite Railway Station, Dimapur 7971112, Nagaland.	☎ (3862) 26733	44	🗓12	
△ **Gandhinagar** Opposite Government Arts & Science College, Sector -16, Gandhinagar 382016, Gujarat.	☎ (2712) 22364	42	🗓12	🍽 Ⓡ ☞ 🅿 🔲 ☕
△ **Gopalpur-on-Sea** Gopalpur-on-Sea, Distt. Ganjam 761002, Orissa.	☎ (6621) 82324	18	🗓12	♔♔ 🍽 Ⓡ ☞ 🅿 ☕
△ **Hassan** Behind Dist. Stadium, Hassan 573201, Karnataka.	☎ (8172) 46168	44	🗓12	♔♔ Ⓡ ☞ 🅿 🔲 ☕
△ **Imphal** Khuman Lampak, Imphal Sports Complex, Imphal 795001, Manipur.	☎ (3852) 320013, (3852) 220714	50	🗓12	🍽 Ⓡ ☞ 🅿 🔲 ☕
▲ **Jaipur** Bhagwan Das Rd, Near S.M.S Stadium, Jaipur 302004, Rajasthan.	☎ (141) 740515, (141) 741130	80	🗓12	♔♔ 🍽 Ⓡ ☞ 🅿 🔲 ☕
▲ **Jodhpur** Circuit House Rd, Ratanada, Jodhpur 342011, Rajasthan. 📧 youthhostel-jodhpur@bigfoot.com	☎ (291) 510160, (291) 629902 📠 (291) 619911	60	🗓12	♔♔ 🍽 ☞ 🅿 🔲 ☕
△ **Kurukshetra** G T Rd, Pipli, Kurukshetra 132118, Haryana.	☎ (1744) 30016	22	🗓12	♔♔ 🍽 Ⓡ ☞ 🅿 🔲

Location/Address	Telephone No. Fax No.	Beds	Opening Dates	Facilities
▲ **Mysore** Opp. Maruthi Temple, Gangothri Layout, Saraswatipuram, Mysore 570009, Karnataka.	☎ (821) 544704	112		
△ *Naharlagun* PO Naharlagun, 791110, Arunachal Pradesh.	☎ (3781) 4730	64		
▲ **Nainital** Ardwell, Mallital, Nainital 263001, Uttar Pradesh.	☎ (5942) 36353, (5942) 36168	44		
△ *Namchi* Namchi 737126, South Sikkim.	☎ (3595) 63774	60		
▲ **New Delhi** - International YH IBN **5 Nyaya Marg, Chanakyapuri, New Delhi 110021.** ✉ yhostel@del2.vsnl.net.in	☎ (11) 6116285; (11) 4101246 ✆ (11) 6113469	162		
▲ **Panaji** Miramar, Panaji 403001, Goa.	☎ (832) 420735	60		
△ *Panchkula* Ambala Kalka Rd, Sector 3, Near Majri Chowk, Panchkula, 133001, Haryana.	☎ (172) 566423	45		
△ *Patna* Fraser Rd, Near Maurya Hotel, Patna GPO, Patna 800 001, Bihar.	☎ (612) 211486	40		
△ *Patnitop* PO Kud 182142, Dist Udhampur, J&K.		44		
△ *Pondicherry* Neithal St, Solai Nagar, Muthialpet, 605003, Pondicherry.	☎ (413) 237495	56		
△ *Port Blair* Aberdeen Bazar, PO 744104, Andaman and Nicobar Islands.	☎ (3192) 20459, (3192) 20431	38		
△ *Puri* Chakratirtha Rd, Puri 752002, Orissa.	☎ (6752) 22424	49		
△ *Rup Nagar (Ropar)* Nr New Bus Stand, Opposite Nehru Stadium, Rup Nagar (Ropar), 140001 Punjab.	☎ (1881) 20350	48		
△ *Secunderabad* Near Sailing Club, Secunderabad, Andhra Pradesh.	☎ (40) 7114914	87		
▲ **Shillong** Opposite Central Telegraph Office, Vivekananda Marg, Shillong 793001, Meghalaya.	☎ (364) 224382, (364) 222246	56		
△ *Tiruchirapalli* Near Anna Stadium, Khaja Malai, Tiruchirapalli 620 023, Tamil Nadu.	☎ (431) 421508	46		3E

Location/Address	Telephone No. Fax No.	Beds	Opening Dates	Facilities
△ ***Tirupati*** *Near Reserve Police Quarters, M R Palle, Tirupati - 517 502, Andhra Pradesh.*	*(8574) 40300*	*46*	12	1.5S
△ ***Trivandrum (Thiruvananthapuram)*** *- Veli Youth Hostel Nr Boat Club, Veli, Trivandrum 695021, Kerala.*	*(471) 501230*	*44*	12	
△ ***Tura*** *Stadium Area, P.O. Chandmari (Lower), West Garo Hills. Tura, 794002 Meghalaya.*	*(3651) 32126*	*50*	12	
△ ***Vellanad*** *Mitra Niketan Hostel, PO Vellanad 695543, Dist Trivandrum, Kerala.*	*(47288) 451564*	*7*	12	

"Traveling is not just seeing the new; it is also leaving behind. Not just opening doors; also closing them behind you, never to return. But the place you have left forever is always there for you to see whenever you shut your eyes."

"Voyager, ce n'est pas seulement voir du nouveau; c'est aussi quitter. Non pas simplement ouvrir des portes; mais aussi en fermer derrière soi, pour ne jamais revenir. Mais le lieu que vous avez quitté pour toujours sera toujours là pour vous à chaque fois que vous fermez les yeux."

„Reisen bedeutet nicht nur, das Neue zu sehen, sondern auch Dinge zurückzulassen. Nicht nur Türen zu öffnen, sondern auch, diese hinter sich zu schließen, um niemals zurückzukehren. Aber den Ort, von dem du Abschied genommen hast, kannst du immer wieder sehen, sobald du die Augen schließt."

"Viajar no es simplemente ver cosas nuevas; es también dejar atrás. No sólo abrir puertas; sino cerralas detrás de uno, para nunca más volver; Pero el lugar que dejaste para siempre seguirá existiendo para ti y podrás verlo con sólo cerrar los ojos."

Jan Myrdal

International Booking Network

The advantages are cle[ar]

www.iyhf.org

HOSTELLING INTERNATIONAL

Japan

JAPON

JAPAN

JAPON

Japan Youth Hostels, Inc,
Suidobashi Nishiguchi Kaikan,
2-20-7, Misaki-cho, Chiyoda-ku, Tokyo 101-0061, Japan.

☎ (81) (3) 3288-1417
🖷 (81) (3) 3288-1248

Travel Section: Suidobashi-nishiguchi-kaikan, 2F
2-20-7 Misaki-cho, Chiyoda-ku,
Tokyo 101-0061, Japan.

☎ (81) (3) 3288-0260
🖷 (81) (3) 3288-1490
@ info@jyh.or.jp
🖳 www.jyh.or.jp/

A copy of the Hostel Directory for this Country can be obtained from:
The National Office

Capital:	Tokyo	**Population:**	125,864,000
Language:	Japanese	**Size:**	377,780 sq km
Currency:	¥ (yen)	**Telephone Country Code:**	81

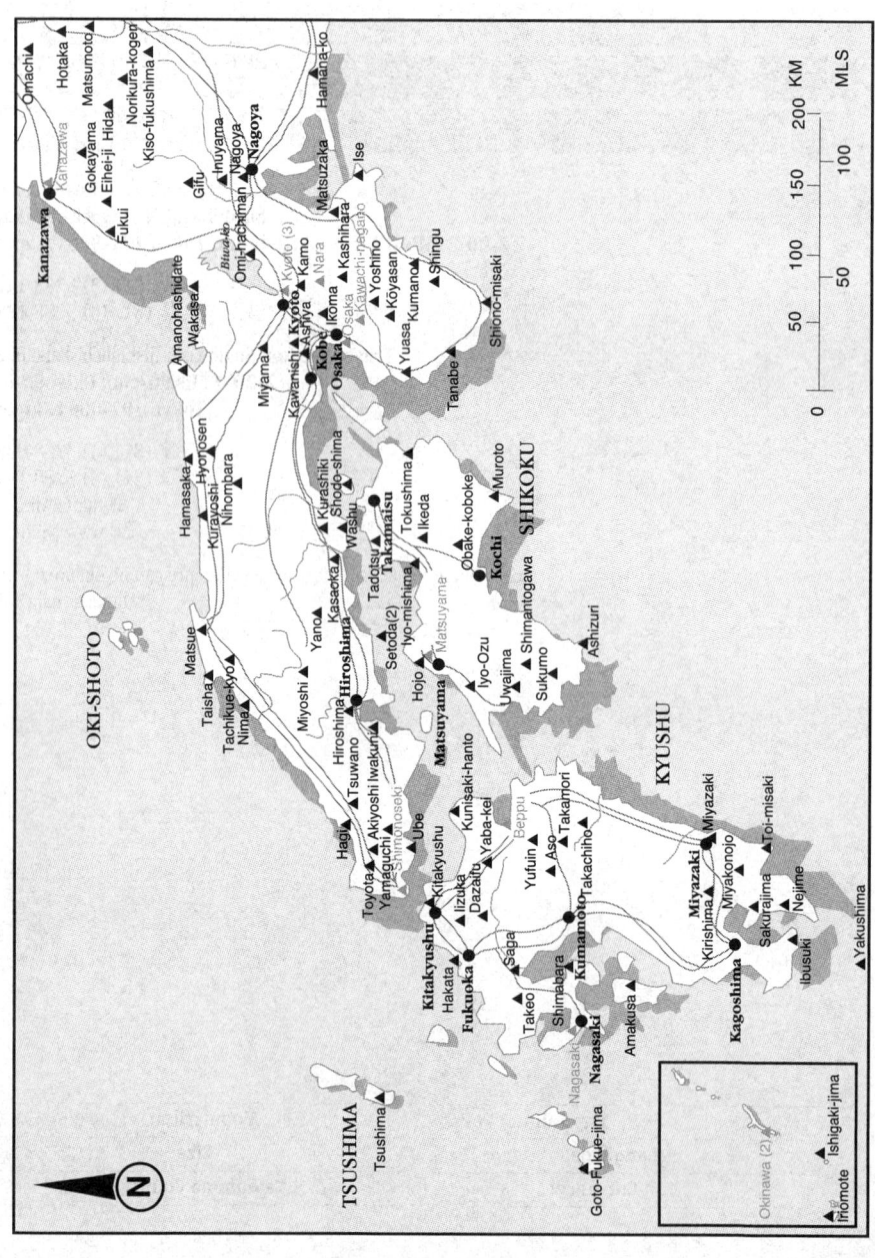

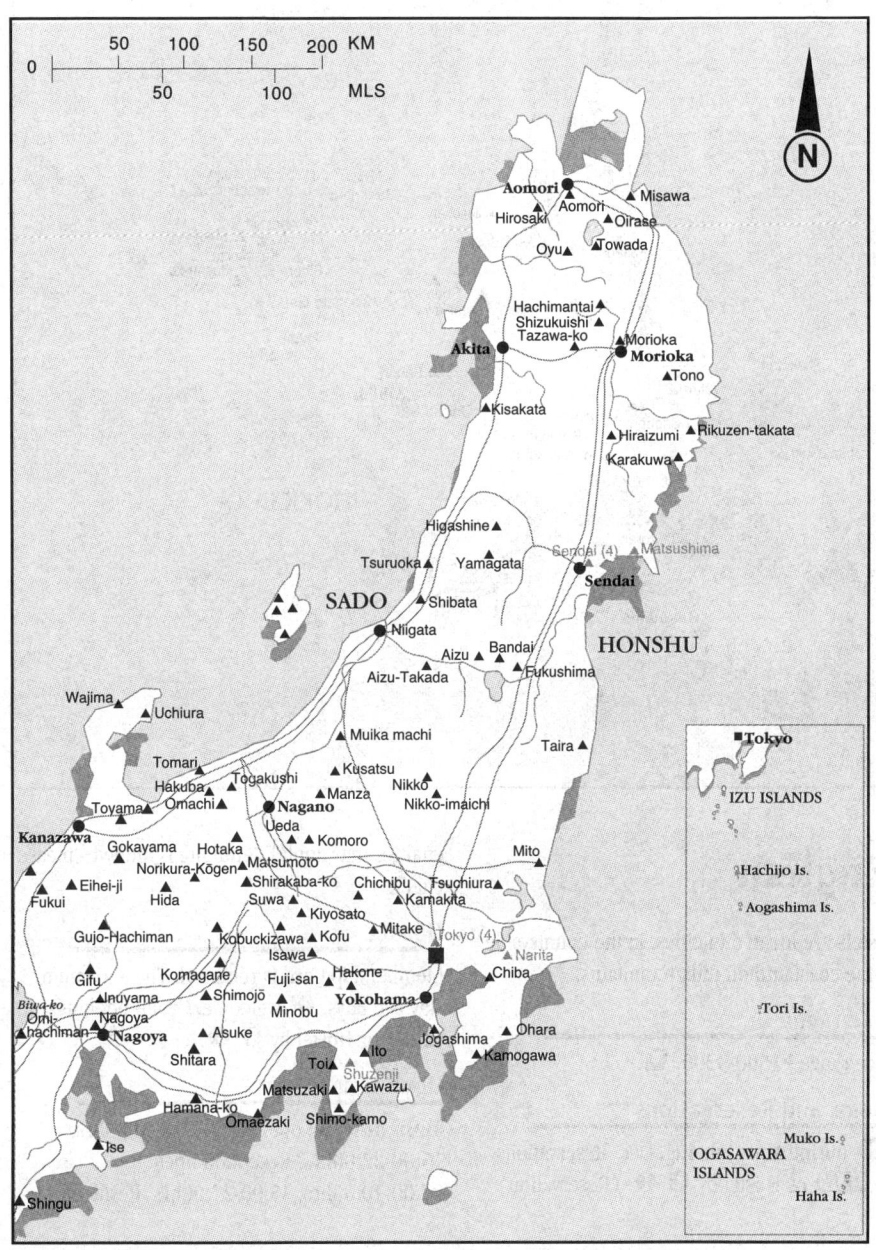

50   100   150   200 KM
0
      50   100   MLS

N

Aomori ●
Hirosaki ▲ Aomori ▲ Misawa
                    ▲ Oirase
        Oyu ▲ Towada

Hachimantai ▲
Shizukuishi ▲
        Tazawa-ko ▲ Morioka
Akita ●   ● Morioka
                     ▲ Tono

    ▲ Kisakata

        ▲ Hiraizumi ▲ Rikuzen-takata
        Karakuwa ▲

Higashine ▲

Tsuruoka ▲ Yamagata ▲   Sendai (4) ▲ Matsushima
                          ● Sendai
        ▲ SADO ▲ Shibata
        ▲
        ● Niigata
            Aizu ▲ Bandai ▲   HONSHU
        Aizu-Takada   ▲ Fukushima

Wajima ▲
        ▲ Uchiura
        ▲ Muika machi   Taira ▲   ■ Tokyo
Tomari ▲   ▲ Kusatsu
Hakuba ▲ Togakushi Nikko ▲   IZU ISLANDS
Toyama ▲ Omachi ▲ ● Nagano Manza Nikko-imaichi
Kanazawa ● Gokayama Hotaka Ueda
        ▲   Norikura-Kōgen ▲ Matsumoto ▲ Komoro   Mito   Hachijo Is.
▲ Eihei-ji   Hida   ▲ Shirakaba-ko Chichibu Tsuchiura ▲   Aogashima Is.
Fukui   Suwa ▲ ▲ Kamakita
        Gujo-Hachiman ▲ Kiyosato
        Kobuckizawa ▲ Kofu Mitake ▲ Tokyo (4)
        Isawa ▲   ▲ Narita
Gifu Komagane ▲ Fuji-san ▲ Hakone   ▲ Chiba   Tori Is.
Biwa-ko Inuyama ▲ Shimojō   ▲ Yokohama ●
Omi-   Nagoya   Minobu
hachiman ● Nagoya ▲ Asuke   Jogashima ▲ Ohara
        Shitara   Toi ▲ Ito ▲ Kamogawa
        Matsuzaki ▲ ▲ Kawazu
        Hamana-ko Omaezaki Shimo-kamo
        ▲ Ise
▲ Shingu   Muko Is.
                                     OGASAWARA
                                     ISLANDS   Haha Is.

English

Hostels are located in cities, in the countryside, on the coast and on hills/mountains.

Price range

Price range ¥1500-3200. .

Rooms and Reservations

 during Mar, Jul, Aug, Dec. Reservations via IBN or Hostel by  . (Reservation charges may apply). Smoking is limited - please check.

Guests

Membership Card is required. The maximum stay is 6 days.  welcome. Group bookings via IBN or Hostel by  .

Open times

Main hostels: open , 07:00-10:00hrs, 15:00-22:00hrs. Reception open: 07:00-10:00hrs, 15:00-22:00hrs. Resident

manager. **Other hostels:** open 🗒,
07:00-10:00hrs, 15:00-22:00hrs. Reception
open: 07:00-10:00hrs, 15:00-22:00hrs.
Resident manager. **Seasonal hostels** are
generally open Jul, Aug.

Meals

🍴 BD **R** For individuals & for 👪.

Discounts

HI Member Discounts available - see discounts
section and www.iyhf.org.

Travelling around

For ease of travel use 🚂.

Passports and Visas

Passport and Visa required.

Health

Medical insurance is recommended.

Français

Les auberges sont situées dans les villes, à la
campagne, sur le littoral et à la montagne.

Tarifs des nuitées

Tarifs des nuitées 1500-3200¥. 🛏.

Chambres et réservations

R mar, juil, août, déc. Réservations via
IBN ou l'auberge par ☎ 📠. (Des frais de
réservation pourront vous être facturés). Il est
permis de fumer dans certaines chambres -
veuillez vérifier.

Usagers

La carte d'adhérent est à présenter. La durée
maximale du séjour est de 6 jours. Accueil des
👪. Réservations pour groupes via **IBN** ou
l'auberge par ☎ 📠.

Horaires d'ouverture

Grandes auberges: ouvertes 🗒, entre
7h-10h, 15h-22h. Accueil ouvert entre 7h-10h,
15h-22h. Gérant réside sur place. **Autres
auberges:** ouvertes 🗒, entre 7h-10h,
15h-22h. Accueil ouvert entre 7h-10h, 15h-22h.
Gérant réside sur place. **Auberges
saisonnières** ouvertes généralement juil, août.

Repas

🍴 BD **R** Pour individuels & pour 👪.

Remises

Remises pour les adhérents HI - voir la section
"Remises" et notre site: www.iyhf.org.

Déplacements

Modes de transport recommandés 🚂.

Passeports et visas

Passeport et visa obligatoires.

Santé

Une assurance médicale de voyage est
conseillée.

Deutsch

Herbergen befinden sich in Städten, auf dem
Land, an der Küste und in Bergen/Gebirgen.

Preisspanne

Preisspanne 1500-3200 ¥. 🛏.

Zimmer und Reservierungen

R während Mär, Jul, Aug, Dez.
Reservierungen über **IBN** oder die Herberge
per ☎ 📠. (Reservierungskosten könnten
anfallen). Rauchen ist begrenzt - bitte checken.

Gäste

Mitgliedsausweis ist erforderlich. Der maximale
Aufenthalt beträgt 6 Tage. 👪 willkommen.

Gruppenbuchungen über (IBN) oder die
Herberge per ☎ 📠.

Öffnungszeiten

Hauptherbergen: Zugang 🖾,
07:00-10:00Uhr, 15:00-22:00Uhr. Rezeption
zwischen 07:00-10:00Uhr, 15:00-22:00Uhr.
Herbergsmanager wohnt im Haus. **Andere
Herbergen:** Zugang 🖾, 07:00-10:00Uhr,
15:00-22:00Uhr. Rezeption zwischen
07:00-10:00Uhr, 15:00-22:00Uhr.
Herbergsmanager wohnt im Haus.
Saison-Herbergen sind normalerweise Jul,
Aug geöffnet.

Mahlzeiten

🍴 BD ® Für Einzelreisende & für 👪.

Ermäßigungen

HI-Mitgliedsrabatt ist erhältlich – siehe Teil für
Rabatte und Ermäßigungen und www.iyhf.org.

Reisen im Land

Reisen ist einfach mit 🚂.

Reisepässe und Visa

Reisepass/Einreisevisum erforderlich.

Gesundheit

Unfall-/Krankenversicherung wird empfohlen.

Español

Los albergues están situados en las ciudades, el
campo, la costa y la montaña.

Tarifas mínima y máxima

Tarifas mínima y máxima 1500-3200¥. 🛏.

Habitaciones y Reservas

® en mar, jul, ago, dic. Reservas por (IBN)
o a través del albergue por ☎ 📠. (Es posible
que se aplique un suplemento en concepto de

gastos de reserva). Está permitido fumar sólo
en algunas salas/habitaciones - infórmese.

Huéspedes

Los huéspedes deben presentar su Carnet de
Alberguista. La estancia máxima es de 6 días. Se
admiten 👪. Reservas de grupo por (IBN) o a
través del albergue por ☎ 📠.

Horarios y fechas de apertura

Albergues principales - abiertos 🖾,
07:00-10:00h, 15:00-22:00h. Horario de
recepción: 07:00-10:00h, 15:00-22:00h.
Gerente residente. **Otros albergues** - abiertos
🖾, 07:00-10:00h, 15:00-22:00h. Horario de
recepción: 07:00-10:00h, 15:00-22:00h.
Gerente residente. **Albergues de temporada**
suelen abrir: jul, ago.

Comidas

🍴 BD ® Para individuales y para 👪.

Descuentos

Se conceden descuentos a los miembros de
Hostelling International – véase la sección
sobre descuentos y nuestra página Internet en
www.iyhf.org.

Desplazamientos

Transportes recomendados: 🚂.

Pasaportes y Visados

Pasaporte y visado obligatorios.

Información Sanitaria

Seguro médico recomendado.

Hiroshima -
Hiroshima YH

1-13-6 Ushita-shin-machi,
Higashi-ku Hiroshima-shi,
Hiroshima-ken 732-0068.
☎ (82) 2215343
🖷 (82) 2215377
✉ hyh@mint.ocn.ne.jp

Open Dates:	🗓12
Open Hours:	07.00-10.00hrs; 15.00-22.00hrs
Price Range:	¥1940 (¥1680 for under 18's) 🍴
Beds:	104 - 4x² 1x⁴ 11x⁶ 3x⁶
Facilities:	👫 🍽 (BD) 🛏 60 x 🚻 🔲 📷 💺 🅿 ℹ️ 🚲 🔍 🏠
Directions:	3NW from city centre
✈	Hiroshima 50km
🚌 A	No number 50km
⛴	Hiroshima Port 8km
🚆	Hiroshima 4km
🚌	Lots of buses go to Ushita ap Ushita-Shinmachi-Ichōme
🚋	No number 700m ap Ushita
Attractions:	🏊

Kyoto - Utano

29 Nakayama-cho Uzumasa,
Ukyō-ku,
Kyoto-shi,
Kyoto-fu 616-8191.
☎ (75) 4622288
🖷 (75) 4622289
✉ utano-yh@mbox.kyoto-inet.or.jp

Open Dates:	🗓12
Open Hours:	07.00-22.30hrs
Reservations:	IBN CC
Price Range:	¥2650 (01.04-30.06; 01.09-30.11); ¥2800 (01.07-31.08; 01.12-31.03) (¥2150 for under 18's) 🍴
Beds:	168 - 3x² 2x⁵ 19x⁶ 🗓
Facilities:	♿ 👫 4x 👫 🍽 (BD) 🛏 📺 💺 🧺 🔲 📷 🍴 🔳 💺 🅿 ℹ️ 🚲 🔺 🔍
Directions:	8NW from city centre
✈	Kansai International 100km
🚆	JR Hanazono 2km
🚌	#26 from Kyoto 🚆 ap Youth Hostel-mae 50m
Attractions:	🚴 🚶 ⛷

There are 3 hostels in Kyoto. See following
pages.

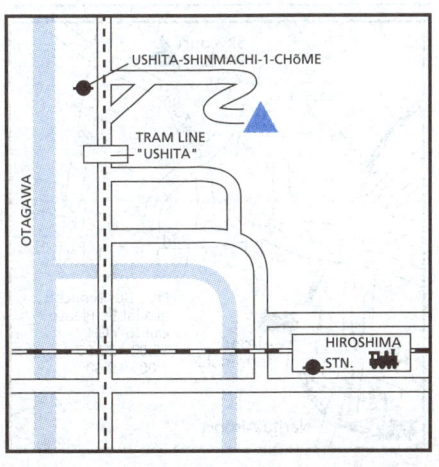

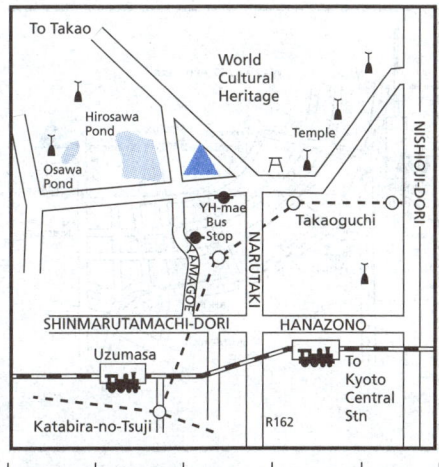

Nagasaki -
Nagasaki YH

1-1-16 Tateyama,
Nagasaki-shi,
Nagasaki-ken 850-0007.
t (95) 8235032
f (95) 8234321
e nyh60625@jeans.ocn.ne.jp

Open Dates:	04.01-28.12
Open Hours:	07.00-10.00hrs; 15.00-22.00hrs
Reservations:	IBN
Price Range:	¥3000 BB inc
Beds:	122 - 15x6
Facilities:	5x (B) TV 1 x P i
Directions:	1 NE from city centre
✈	Nagasaki 40km
A (bus)	Airport Limousine Bus 40km
(ferry)	Nagasaki 2km
(train)	Nagasaki 1km
Attractions:	3km

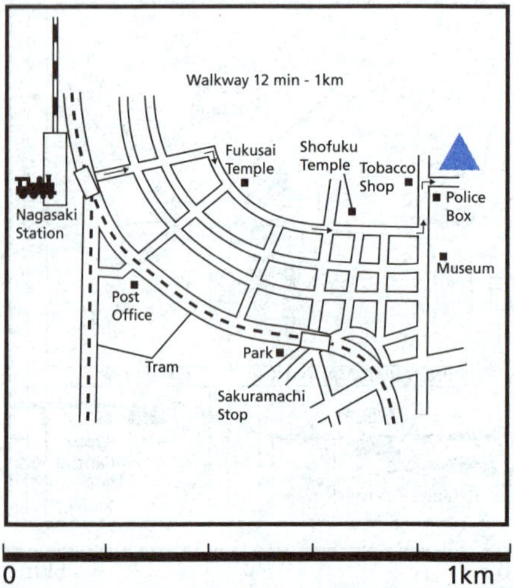

Walkway 12 min - 1km
Nagasaki Station
Fukusai Temple
Shofuku Temple
Tobacco Shop
Police Box
Museum
Post Office
Tram
Park
Sakuramachi Stop
0
1km

Narita -
Skycourt Narita YGH

161 Shinden,
Taiei-machi,
Katori-gun,
Chiba-ken 287-0224.
t (478) 736211
f (478) 736212
e hsky21@basil.ocn.ne.jp

Open Dates:	12
Open Hours:	(clock)
Reservations:	IBN CC
Price Range:	¥4000
Beds:	125 - 80x1 15x2 5x3
Facilities:	(BD) TV 1 x P i
Directions:	62 E from city centre
✈	Narita 10km
A (bus)	#14 (Terminal 1); #26 (Terminal 2) 10km
(ferry)	Kisarazu 70km
(train)	Narita-Kūkō Terminal 2 5.5km
Attractions:	

Skycourt Narita YGH
GS MOBIL
R79
R44
Free Bus service available. Please call to YGH
15:00 - 22:00
7:00 - 10:00
Airport Terminal 2
Narita Airport
0
8km

Osaka -
Osaka International YH

1-5 Hagoromo-koen,
Takaishi-shi,
Osaka 592-0002.
📞 (722) 658539
📠 (722) 673682

Open Dates:	01.01-21.05; 24.05-12.11; 15.11-31.12
Open Hours:	06.00-10.00hrs; 15.00-23.00hrs
Reservations:	IBN CC
Price Range:	¥3150
Beds:	220 - 4x² 6x⁴ 29x⁶ 1x⁶
Facilities:	7x 🚻 🍴 (BD) 👕 🖥 📺 5 x 🍷 🔟 📷 🛁 🔢 ⊜ 💵 i 📯 ♨ 🚿 🏕
Directions:	16 SW from city centre
✈	Kansai International 25km
⛴	Osaka 20km
🚂	Hagoromo 1km
Attractions:	🏔 🚶 ✎500m ⛵500m

Tokyo - *Yoyogi YH*

c/o National Olympics Memorial Youth
Center,
3-1 Yoyogi,
Kami-zono-cho,
Shibuya-ku,
Tokyo 151-0052.
📞 (3) 34679163
📠 (3) 34679417
📧 yoyogi@jyh.gr.jp

Open Dates:	🗓
Open Hours:	07.00-09.00hrs (Check-out); 17.00-20.00hrs (Check-in)
Reservations:	R IBN CC
Price Range:	¥3000
Beds:	60 - 60x¹
Facilities:	🚻 ☕ 🖥 🔟 📷 🛁 ⊜ 💵
Directions:	7 W from city centre
✈	Narita 70km
A🚌	Limousine bus to Shinjyuku 70km
🚂	Sangubashi Odakyu Line 500m
U	Yoyogi-Kōen, Chiyoda Line 800m

There are 4 hostels in Tokyo. See following
pages.

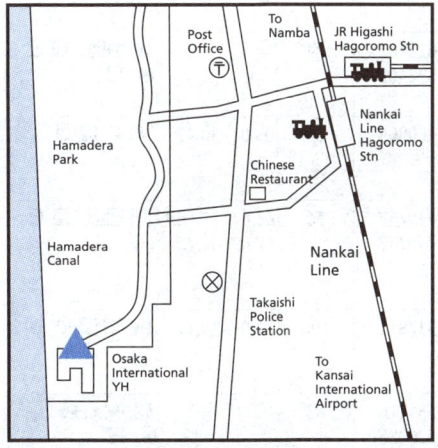

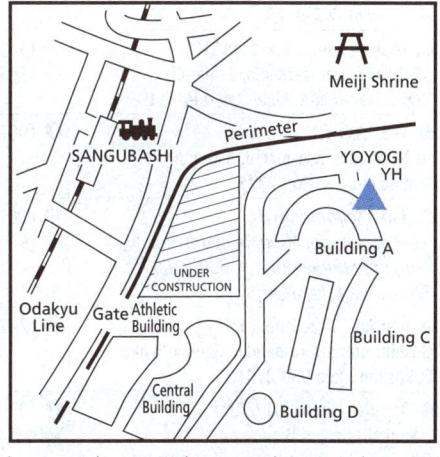

Location/Address	Telephone No. Fax No.	Beds	Opening Dates	Facilities
▲ **Abashiri** - Ryuhyo-no-oka YH 22-6 Meiji, Abashiri-shi, Hokkaido 093-0085.	☏ (152) 438558	28	🔲₁₂	�ppl ⵁ CC🔲 P 🔲 🔲
▲ **Abashiri** - Genseikaen YH 208-2 Kita-hama, Abashiri-shi, Hokkaido 099-3112.	☏ (152) 462630	44	21.01–09.04; 26.04–09.11	ⵁ P 🔲 🔲
▲ **Aizu-shiokawa** - Aizu-no-sato YH 36 Hatakeda, Kofune, Aizu-shiokawa-cho, Yama-gun, Fukushima-ken 969-3532.	☏ (241) 272054 ℻ (241) 272054	14	07.01–23.12	P 🔲
▲ **Aizu Takada** - Aizuno YH 88 Kakiyashiki, Terazaki, Aizu-Takada-machi, Onuma-gun, Fukushima-ken 969-6271. ✉ aizunoyh@anet.ne.jp	☏ (242) 551020 ℻ (242) 551020	18	🔲₁₂	ⵁ P 🔲
▲ **Akiyoshidai** - Akiyoshidai YH 4236-1, Akiyoshi, Shuho-cho, Mine-gun, Yamaguchi-ken, 754-0511.	☏ (8376) 20341	55	01–19.01; 01.02–19.06; 01.07–31.12	ⵁ 🍴 P 🔲 🔲
△ *Amakusa* - *Amakusa YH* *180 Hondo, Hondo-cho, Hondo-shi, Kumamoto-ken 863-0003.*	☏ *(969) 223085*	*28*	🔲₁₂	ⵁ 🍴 P 🔲
▲ **Amanohashidate** - Amanohashidate YH 905 Nakano, Miyazu-shi, Kyoto-fu 629-2232.	☏ (772) 270121	60	🔲₁₂	ⵁ P 🔲 🔲
△ *Aomori* - *Aomori Moyakogen YH* *9-5 Yamabuki Moya Aomori-Shi Aomori-Ken 030-0133.*	☏ *(17) 7642888* ℻ *(17) 7642889*	*14*	🔲₁₂	�ppl ⵁ 🔲
▲ **Asahikawa** - Asahikawa YH 18-chome, 7-jo, Kamui, Asahikawa-shi, Hokkaido, 070-8017.	☏ (166) 612800	49	🔲₁₂	ⵁ P 🔲
▲ **Ashiya** - Rokko-Ashiya YH 40-30 Okuike-minami-cho, Ashiya-shi, Hyogo-ken 659-0004.	☏ (797) 380109	92	11.01–20.12	�ppl ⵁ P 🔲
△ *Ashizuri* - *Ashizuri YH* *1351-3, Ashizuri-Misaki, Tosa-Shimizu-shi, Kochi-ken, 787-0315.*	☏ *(8808) 80324* ℻ *(8808) 80327*	*20*	🔲₁₂	ⵁ P 🔲 🔲
▲ **Asuke** - Asuke Satoyama YH 27-2 Saka, Tsubakidachi, Asuke-cho, Higashikamo-gun, Aichi-ken 444-2419.	☏ (565) 622462 ℻ (565) 622462	24	🔲₁₂	♩ppl ⵁ ♿ P 🔲 ☕ 🔲
▲ **Aso** - Aso YH 922-2 Bochu, Aso-machi, Aso-gun, Kumamoto-ken 869-2225.	☏ (967) 340804	60	03.01–30.12	ⵁ 🍴 P 🔲
△ *Aso* - *Senomoto YH* *6332 Senomoto, Minami-oguni-machi, Aso-gun, Kumamoto-ken 869-2400.* ✉ *senomoto@jyh.gr.jp*	☏ *(967) 440157* ℻ *(967) 440157*	*56*	*01.01–15.06; 01.07–31.12*	ⵁ CC🔲 P 🔲
▲ **Bandai** - Ura-Bandai YH Goshiki-numa, Ura-bandai, Azuma-kyoku, Fukushima-ken 969-2701.	☏ (241) 322811	100	21.04–30.11	♩ppl ⵁ P 🔲 🔲 ☕
▲ **Beppu** - Beppu YH [IBN] 2 Kankaiji-onsen, Beppu-shi, Oita-ken 874-0822.	☏ (977) 234116 ℻ (977) 220086	82	🔲₁₂	♩ppl ⵁ CC🔲 P 🔲 🔲

Location/Address	Telephone No. Fax No.	Beds	Opening Dates	Facilities
▲ **Biei** - Bibaushi Liberty YH Shigaichi, Bibaushi, Biei-cho, Kamikawa-gun, Hokkaido 071-0472.	☎ (166) 952141	20	01.01–31.03; 01.05–10.11; 21–31.12	♀♂ ⦿ CC P ⦾
▲ **Biei** - Potato no Oka YH Ōmura Murayama, Biei-cho, Kamikawa-gun, Hokkaido, 071-0218.	☎ (166) 923255	30	01.01–10.04; 21.04–30.11; 11–31.12	♀♂ ⦿ R CC P ⦾ 日
▲ **Bihoro** - Bihoro YH 31 Moto-machi, Bihoro-cho, Abashiri-gun, Hokkaido 092-0063.	☎ (1527) 32560 ℻ (1527) 32560	80	01.04–31.10	♀♂ ⦿ P ⦾
▲ **Chiba** - Chiba-shi YH 955 Yasashido-cho, Midori-ku, Chiba-shi, Chiba-ken 267-0062.	☎ (43) 2941850	60	06.01–28.12	⦿ ⚡ P ⦾
△ *Daisetsu-zan -* *Daisetsu-zan Shirakaba-so YH* *Asahidake-onsen, 1418, Higashikawa-cho,* *Kamikawa-gun, Hokkaido 071-0372.*	☎ *(166) 972246*	*46*	⟦12⟧	♀♂ ⦿ P ⦾
▲ **Dazaifu** - Dazaifu YH 1-18-1 Sanjo, Dazaifu-shi, Fukuoka-ken 818-0111.	☎ (92) 9228740 ℻ (92) 9228762	15	⟦12⟧	♀♂ ⦿ P ⦾ 日
▲ **Eihei-ji** - Monzen Yamaguchi-so YH 22-3 Shihi, Eihei-ji-machi, Yoshida-gun, Fukui-ken 910-1228.	☎ (776) 633123	28	⟦12⟧	⦿ P ⦾
△ *Erimo* - *Erimo-Misaki YH* *236-6 Erimo-misaki, Erimo-machi,* *Horo-izumi-gun, Hokkaido 058-0342.*	☎ *(1466) 31144* ℻ *(1466) 31074*	*70*	⟦12⟧	♀♂ ⦿ CC ⚡ P ⦾ ☕
△ *Fuji-san* - *Fuji-yoshida YH* *339 2-chome, Shimo-yoshida-hon-cho,* *Fuji-yoshida-shi 403-0004, Yamanashi-ken.*	☎ *(555) 220533*	*30*	*04.01–29.12*	⦿ P 日
▲ **Fuji-san** - Kawaguchi-ko YH 2128 Funazu, Kawaguchi-ko-machi, Minami-tsuru-gun 401-0301.	☎ (555) 721431 ℻ (555) 721431	50	20.03–05.11	♀♂ ⦿ P ⦾ 日
△ *Fuji-san Fujinomiya -* *Fumoto-no-ie YH* *251 Sugita, Fujinomiya-shi,* *Shizuoka-ken 418-0021.*	☎ *(544) 274314* ℻ *(544) 274445*	*8*	*01.01–31.08; 01.10–31.12*	♀♂ ⚡ ⦾
▲ **Fuji-san** - Gotemba YH 3857 Higashiyama, Gotemba-shi, Shizuoka-ken 412-0024.	☎ (550) 823045	52	⟦12⟧	⦿ P 日
▲ **Fuji-san** - Yamanaka-ko Iiz YGH Asahigaoka, Yamanakako-mura, Minami-Tsuru-gun, Yamanashi-ken, 401-0500.	☎ (555) 620020	100	⟦12⟧	⦿ P ⦾
▲ **Fukagawa** - Irumu-no-Oka YH 546-2, Otoe, Otoe-cho, Fukagawa-shi, Hokkaido, 074-1273.	☎ (164) 251000 ℻ (164) 251000	14	01.01–31.03; 11.04–30.11; 11–31.12	♀♂ ⦿ P ⦾
▲ **Fukui** - Fukuiken Seinenkan YH 3-11-17 Ōte, Fukui-shi, Fukui-ken 910-0005.	☎ (776) 225625	10	04.01–28.12	P ⦾ 日

Location/Address	Telephone No. Fax No.	Beds	Opening Dates	Facilities
▲ **Fukuoka** - Shikano-shima-sō YH 1526-2, Shikano-shima, Higashi-ku, Fukuoka-shi, Fukuoka-ken, 811-0323.	☎ (92) 6030009	50	🏠12	♙♙ ⛺ 20 NW ℗ ▣ 日
▲ **Fukushima** - Azuma-kogen Star Hunt YH Takayu-onsen, 1-49 Jin-no-mori, Machiniwasaka, Fukushima-shi, Fukushima-ken 960-2261.	☎ (24) 5911412	70	01.01–31.05; 21.06–31.12	⛺ CC ℗ ▣
▲ **Fukushima** - YGH Atoma 15-2, Funaishi, Sakuramoto, Fukushima-shi, Fukushima-ken 960-2151. ⓔ yghatoma@ma4.justnet.ne.jp	☎ (24) 5912523 ℻ (24) 5912523	29	🏠12	♙♙ ⛺ 🖉 ℗ ▣ ☕ 日
▲ **Furano** - Rokugō Furarin YH 1 Higashi-Rokugo, Furano-shi, Hokkaido, 076-0162.	☎ (167) 292172	25	🏠12	⛺ ℗ ▣ 日
▲ **Gifu** - Gifu YH 4716-17 Kamikanoyama, Gifu-shi, Gifu-ken 500-8121.	☎ (58) 2636631 ℻ (58) 2636631	55	04.01–28.12	♙♙ ⛺ ℗ ▣
▲ **Gokayama** - Ecchu Gokayama YH 24 Oze, Kamitaira-mura, Higashi- tonami-gun, Toyama-ken 939-1971.	☎ (763) 673331	20	01.07–31.10	⛺ 🖉 ℗ ▣ 日
▲ **Gujo-Hachiman** - Gujo-Tosenji YH 417 Ozaki-cho, Hachiman-cho, Gujo-gun, Gifu-ken, 501-4217.	☎ (575) 670290	38	06.01–10.08; 19.08–28.12	♙♙ ℗ 日
▲ **Goto-Fukue-jima** - Goto-Miiraku Sunset YH 493 Hamono-kurigō, Miiraku-cho, Minami-Matsuura-gun, Nagasaki-ken.	☎ (959) 843151	100	01.01–31.05; 21.06–31.12	♙♙ ⛺ ℗ ▣
▲ **Haboro** - Haboro Yuho YH 260 Sakae-machi, Haboro-cho, Tomamae-gun, Hokkaido 078-4123.	☎ (1646) 22146 ℻ (1646) 22146	23	01.01–31.10; 01–31.12	♙♙ ⛺ ℗ ▣
▲ **Hachimantai** - Hachimantai YH 5-2 Midorigaoka, Matsuo-mura, Iwate-gun, Iwate-ken 028-7304.	☎ (195) 782031	50	🏠12	⛺ 🖉 ℗ ▣
▲ **Hagi** - Hagi YH 109-22 Horinouchi, Hagi-shi, Yamaguchi-ken 758-0057.	☎ (838) 220733	68	01–15.01; 10.02–31.12	♙♙ ⛺ ℗ ▣
△ *Hakata - Skycourt Hakata YGH* *4-73 Gion-cho, Hakata-ku, Fukuoka-shi,* *Fukuoka-ken 812-0038.*	☎ *(92) 2624400* ℻ *(92) 2628111*	*24*	🏠12	♙♙ ▣
▲ **Hakodate** - Hakodate YGH IBN 17-6 Hourai-cho, Hakodate-shi, Hokkaido 040-0043.	☎ (138) 267892	42	01–09.01; 21.01–9.04; 21.04–19.11; 21–31.12	♙♙ ℗ ▣
▲ **Hakone** - Sengokuhara YH 912 Sengokuhara, Hakone-machi, Ashigara-shimo-gun, Kanagawa-ken, 250-0631. ⓔ hakone-@pop21.odn.ne.jp	☎ (460) 48966 ℻ (460) 46578	27	05.01–27.12	♙♙ CC 🖉 ℗ ▣ 日

Location/Address	Telephone No. Fax No.	Beds	Opening Dates	Facilities
▲ **Hakuba** - Hakuba-no-sato Schondorf YH Tsugaike-kogen, Otari-mura, Kita Azumi-gun Nagano-ken 399-9400.	☎ (261) 833011	37	🛏12	ⵙ P 日
▲ **Hamana-ko** - Hamana-ko YH 223-2 Uchiyama, Arai-machi, Hamana-gun, Shizuoka-ken 431-0304.	☎ (53) 5940670	80	🛏12	ⵙ P ⬜
▲ **Hamasaka** - Hamasaka YH Shiroyama-enchi, Hamasaka-cho, Mikata-gun, Hyogo-ken 669-6701. ✉ hamasaka@jyh.gr.jp	☎ (796) 821282 📠 (796) 822099	80	01–14.01; 16.02–31.12	ⵙ CC P ⬜
▲ **Hamasaka** - Moroyose-so YH 461 Moroyose, Hamasaka-cho, Mikata-gun, Hyogo-ken 669-6753.	☎ (796) 821279 📠 (796) 823614	40	03.01–30.12	ⵙ P ⬜ 日
▲ **Hida Furukawa** - Hida Furukawa YH 180 Shimpo, Furukawa-chō, Yoshiki-gun, Gifu-ken 509-4272.	☎ (577) 752979 📠 (577) 752979	22	01.01–29.03; 11.04–31.12	ⵙ P ⬜ 日
△ *Higashine - Higashine Barefoot YH 1-3-39 Kami-machi, Minami-higashine-shi, Yamagata-ken 999-3765.*	☎ *(237) 471057* 📠 *(237) 471057*	*10*	🛏12	ⵙ P
▲ **Hiraizumi** - Motsu-ji YH 58 Osawa, Hiraizumi-machi, Nishi-iwai-gun, Iwate-ken 029-4102.	☎ (191) 462331	36	🛏12	ⵙ P ⬜
▲ **Hirosaki** - Hirosaki YH 11 Mori-machi, Hirosaki-shi, Aomori-ken 036-8205.	☎ (172) 337066 📠 (172) 337066	24	04.01–29.12	ⵙ P ⬜ 日
▲ **Hiroshima** - Hiroshima YH **1-13-6 Ushita-shin-machi, Higashi-ku Hiroshima-shi, Hiroshima-ken 732-0068.** ✉ hyh@mint.ocn.ne.jp	☎ (82) 2215343 📠 (82) 2215377	104	🛏12	ⵙ 3NW P ⬜
▲ **Hiroshima** - Hiroshima Bayside Saka YH 401-8 Ueda, Kōgai-Sakamachi, Hiroshima-shi, Hiroshima-ken 731-4335.	☎ (82) 8850700	12	🛏12	ⵙ 13SE P ⬜ 日
▲ **Hiroshima** - Higashi Hiroshima YH 3148 Hara, Happonmatsu-machi, Higashi Hiroshima-shi, Hiroshima-ken 739-0151.	☎ (824) 290305	27	06.01–29.12	ⵙ 15E P ⬜ 日
▲ **Hiroshima** - Miyajima-guchi YH 1-4-14 Miyajima-guchi, Ono-machi, Saeki-gun, Hiroshima-ken 739-0411.	☎ (829) 561444 📠 (829) 561444	30	🛏12	ⵙ ⬜
△ *Hojyo - Hojyo Suigun YH 1527 Tauji, Hojo-Shi, Ehime-Ken, 799-2430.*	☎ *(89) 9924150* 📠 *(89) 9924150*	*10*	01.01–09.02; 21.02–31.12	ⵙ CC P 日
▲ **Hotaka** - Azumino Pastoraru YH Ariake-Toyosato, Hotaka-cho, Minami-azumi-gun, Nagano-ken 399-8301.	☎ (263) 836170 📠 (263) 836416	32	01–16.01; 08.02–31.12	ⵙ P ⬜

Location/Address	Telephone No. Fax No.	Beds	Opening Dates	Facilities
▲ **Hyōnosen** - Wakasa Hyonosen YH 631-10 Tsukuyone, Wakasa-cho, Yazu-gun, Tottori-ken 680-0728. ✉ hyonosen@jyh.gr.jp	☎ (858) 821700, (858) 820980	96	01.01–15.06; 01.07–31.12	⑩ 🅿 ⓞ 🗓
△ *Ibusuki - Tamaya YH 5-27-8 Yuno-hama, Ibusuki-shi, Kagoshima-ken 891-0406.*	☎ *(993) 223553*	*35*	🄸₁₂	⑩ 🅿 ⓞ 🗓
▲ **Ibusuki** - Yunosato YH 2-38-20, Omure, Ibusuki-shi, Kagoshima-ken 891-0401.	☎ (993) 225680	20	🄸₁₂	👫 ⑩ 🅿 ⓞ
▲ **Iizuka** - Yakiyama-Kōgen YH 1270-14 Yakiyama, Iizuka-shi, Fukuoka-ken 820-0047.	☎ (948) 226385 📠 (948) 227234	90	01.01–30.11; 10–31.12	⑩ 20E 🅿 ⓞ
▲ **Ikeda** - Awa-Ikeda YH 3798, Sako, Nishiyama, Ikeda-cho, Miyoshi-gun, Tokushima-ken, 778-0040.	☎ (883) 725277	22	04.01–01.04; 04.04–29.12	⑩ 🅿 🗓
▲ **Ikoma** - Senko-ji YH 188 Narukawa, Heguri-cho, Ikoma-gun, Nara-ken 636-0945. ✉ senkoji@kcn.ne.jp	☎ (745) 450652 📠 (745) 454444	30	🄸₁₂	👫 ⑩ 🅿 ⓞ 🗓
▲ **Inuyama** - Inuyama International YH 162-1, Tsugao-Himuro, Inuyama-shi, Aichi-ken, 484-0091.	☎ (568) 611111	80	04.01–27.12	⑩ Ⓡ ☞ 🅿 ⓞ 🗓
▲ **Iriomote** - Irumote-sō YH 870 Uehara, Taketomi-cho, Yaeyama-gun, Okinawa-ken 907-1541.	☎ (9808) 56255	45	01.01–10.11; 21–31.12	👫 ⑩ 🅿 ⓞ 🗓
▲ **Iriomote** - Iriomote-jima Midori-sō YH 572-5 Uehara, Taketomi-cho, Yaeyama-gun, Okinawa-ken 907-1541.	☎ (9808) 56526	32	🄸₁₂	👫 ⑩ 🅿 ⓞ 🗓
▲ **Isawa** - Isawa Onsen YH 106-2 Yamasaki, Isawa-machi, Higashi-yatsushiro-gun, Yamanashi-ken 406-0022.	☎ (55) 2622110	29	🄸₁₂	⑩ ☞ 🅿 ⓞ
▲ **Ise** - Ise-shima YH 1219-82 Anagawa, Isobe-cho, Shima-gun, Mie-ken 517-0213.	☎ (599) 550226	80	01–20.01; 01.02–20.06; 21.06–31.12	👫 ⑩ 🅿 ⓞ 🗓
▲ **Ise** - Taikō-ji YH 1659 Ei, Futami-cho, Watarai-gun, Mie-ken 519-0602.	☎ (596) 432283	28	🄸₁₂	⑩ ☞ ⓞ 🗓
▲ **Ishigaki-jima** - Trek Ishigaki-jima YH 165-12 Hoshino, Ishigaki-shi, Okinawa-ken 907-0241.	☎ (9808) 68257	12	04.01–29.12	⑩ 🅿
▲ **Itō** - Izu-Kogen Aoikaze YH 1250-34, Yawatano, Ito-shi, Shizuoka-ken, 413-0232.	☎ (557) 513785	15	🄸₁₂	⑩ 🅿 ⓞ 🗓
▲ **Iwakuni** - Iwakuni YH 1-10-46 Yokoyama-cho, Iwakuni-shi, Yama- guchi-ken 741-0081.	☎ (827) 431092 📠 (827) 430123	60	05.01–28.12	👫 ⑩ ☞ 🅿 ⓞ 🗓

Location/Address	Telephone No. Fax No.	Beds	Opening Dates	Facilities
▲ **Iyo-mishima** - Shin-hasedera YH 3214 Sangawa-cho, Iyo-mishima-shi, Ehime-ken 799-0431.	☎ (896) 250202 🖷 (896) 250333	30	06.01–09.06; 01.07–12.08; 17.08–29.12	ⅲ ⑩ ☛ 🅿 🗑 🗓
▲ **Jōgashima** - Jōgashima YH 121 Yoroshi, Jogashima, Misaki-cho, Miura-shi, Kanagawa-ken 238-0237.	☎ (468) 813893	104	🏠12	⑩ ☛ 🅿 🗑
▲ **Kamakitako** - Lake View YH 86-1 Gongen-dō, Moroyama-machi, Iruma-gun, Saitama-ken 350-0454.	☎ (492) 940219	48	🏠12	⑩ ☛ 🅿 🗑
△ *Kamogawa* - *Wat House Kamogawa YH* *1317-17 Futomi Kamogawa-shi Chiba-ken* *299-2862.*	☎ *(470) 929114* 🖷 *(470) 929114*	*8*	*01.01–19.06;* *21.07–19.11;* *21–31.12*	ⅲ ⑩
▲ **Kanazawa** - Kanazawa YH [IBN] Utatsuyama-koen, 37 Suehiro-cho, Kanazawa-shi, Ishikawa-ken 920-0833. ✉ kanazawa@jyh.gr.jp	☎ (76) 2523414 🖷 (76) 2528590	80	01–31.01; 15.02–31.12	ⅲ ⑩ ☒CC☒ ☛ 🅿 🗑 🗓
▲ **Kanazawa** - Matsui YH 1-9-3 Kata-machi, Kanazawa-shi, Ishikawa-ken 920-0981.	☎ (76) 2210275	15	03.01–29.12	⑩ 🅿 🗑 🗓
▲ **Karakuwa** - Riasu Karakuwa YH 2-8 Nakai, Karakuwa-machi, Motoyoshi-gun, Miyagi-ken 988-0563.	☎ (226) 322490	28	🏠12	⑩ ☛ 🅿 🗑 🗓
▲ **Kasaoka** - Kasaoka-ya YH 5658 Nishi-hon-machi, Kasaoka-shi, Okayama-ken 714-0081.	☎ (865) 634188	21	04.01–30.12	⑩ 🅿 🗑 🗓
△ *Kashihara* - *Asuka Road YH* *70-8 Kihara-cho, Kashihara-shi,* *Nara-ken 634-0004.*	☎ *(744) 210988* 🖷 *(744) 210988*	*16*	*01–10.01;* *01.02–31.12*	ⅲ ⑩ 🗑
▲ **Kawachi-Nagano** - Kawachi-Nagano YH [IBN] 1305-2 Amano-cho, Kawachi-nagano-shi, Osaka-fu 586-0086. ✉ kawachi@jyh.gr.jp	☎ (721) 531010	80	01–16.01; 22.01–05.06; 12.06–31.12	⑩ 🅿 🗑 🗓
△ *Kawanishi* - *Inagawa Sansō YH* *1-21-9 Yato, Kawanishi-shi,* *Hyogo-ken 666-0131.*	☎ *(727) 513565*	*20*	*06.01–26.12*	⑩ ☛ 🅿 🗑 🗓
▲ **Kawazu** - Amagi Harris Court YH 28-1 Nashimoto, Kawazu-machi, Kamo-gun, Shizuoka-ken 413-0501. ✉ harris@shizuokanet.ne.jp	☎ (558) 357253 🖷 (558) 368931	48	🏠12	ⅲ ⑩ 🅿 🗑 🗓
△ *Kirishima* - *Jingumae YH* *2459 Taguchi, Kirishima-cho, Aira-gun,* *Kagoshima-ken 889-4201.*	☎ *(995) 571188*	*25*	*04.01–30.12*	⑩ 🅿 🗑
▲ **Kisakata** - Kisakata Seinen-no-ie YH 19-2 Iriko no ma, Kisakata-machi, Yuri-gun, Akita-ken 018-0108.	☎ (184) 433154	52	04.01–28.12	⑩ 🅿 🗑

Location/Address	Telephone No. Fax No.	Beds	Opening Dates	Facilities
▲ **Kiso-Fukushima** - Kiso Ryojoan YH 634 Shinkai, Kiso-fukushima-machi, Kiso-gun, Nagano-ken 397-0002.	☎ (264) 237716 🖷 (264) 237716	47	🗓	�♏ ⛟ P ▣ 🗄
▲ **Kita-kyūshū** - Kita-kyūshū YH Hobashira-shizenkoen, 7 Hobashira, Yahata-higashi-ku, Kita-kyūshū-shi, Fukuoka-ken 805-0056. ✉ kitakyu@jyh.gr.jp	☎ (93) 6818142	56	01–20.01; 01.02–10.06; 21.06–31.12	⛟ P ▣ 🗄
▲ **Kitayuzawa** - Kitayuzawa YH 50 Kitayuzawa-onsen-cho, Otaki-mura, Usu-gun, Hokkaido 052-0316. ✉ kitayuzawa@jyh.gr.jp	☎ (142) 686552	40	01.01–20.05; 01.06–20.11; 01–31.12	⛟ CC P ▣ 🗄
▲ **Kiyosato** - Kiyosato YH 3545 Kiyosato, Takane-cho, Kita-koma-gun, Yamanashi-ken 407-0301.	☎ (551) 482125	50	🗓	⛟ P 🗄
▲ **Kobe** - Kobe Tarumi YH 5-58, Kaigan-dori, Tarumi-ku, Kobe-shi, Hyogo, 655-0036.	☎ (78) 7072133 🖷 (78) 7071575	28	🗓	⛡ P ▣
▲ **Kobuchizawa** - Yatsugatake Pony YH 3332-495, Kamisasao, Kobuchizawa-cho, Kita Koma-gun, Yamanashi-ken 408-0041.	☎ (551) 364044	15	20.03–30.11	⛟ P ▣ 🗄
▲ **Kōfu** - Kōfu Highland YH 1355 Kamiobina-machi, Kōfu-shi, Yamanashi-ken 400-1101. ✉ takumi@yin.or.jp	☎ (552) 518020	50	🗓	⛟ CC P ▣
▲ **Komagane** - Komagane YH 25-1 Akaho, Komagane-shi, Nagano-ken, 399-4117.	☎ (265) 833856	49	🗓	♟♟ ⛟ P ▣
▲ **Komoro** - Komoro YH 3876-4, Minami-ga-hara, Komoro-shi, Nagano-ken, 384-0063.	☎ (267) 235732 🖷 (267) 235732	40	🗓	⛟ CC P ▣
▲ **Koshimizu** - Ohotsuku Koshimizu YH 137-4 Hama-koshimizu, Koshimizu-machi, Shari-gun, Hokkaido 099-3452.	☎ (152) 642011	75	01.01–31.10; 15–31.12	⛟ ⛡ P ▣
▲ **Koyasan** - Koyasan YH 628, Koyasan, Koya-cho, Ito-gun, Wakayama-ken, 648-0211. ✉ skoyasan@mint.ocn.no.jp	☎ (736) 563889 🖷 (736) 563889	13	01–10.01; 20.02–31.12	♟♟ ⛟ CC P ▣ 🗄
▲ **Kumamoto** - Kumamoto-ken Seinen Kaikan YH 3-17-15 Suizenji, Kumamoto-shi, Kumamoto-ken, 862-0950.	☎ (96) 3816221 🖷 (96) 3822715	60	04.01–28.12	P ▣ ⛽ 🗄
▲ **Kumamoto** - Suizenji YH 1-2-20 Hakusan, Kumamoto-shi, Kumamoto-ken 860-0959.	☎ (96) 3719193 🖷 (96) 3719218	20	03.01–29.12	▣ 🗄
▲ **Kumano** - Kumano-shi Seinen-no-ie YH 2-13 Haichigi, Arima-cho, Kumano-shi, Mie-ken 519-4325.	☎ (5978) 90800 🖷 (5978) 91115	12	04.01–28.12	⛟ P ▣ 🗄

Location/Address	Telephone No. Fax No.	Beds	Opening Dates	Facilities
▲ **Kunisaki** - Kunisaki-hantō Kunimi YH 3750 Imi, Kunimi-cho, Higashi-kunisaki-gun, Oita-ken 872-1401.	☎ (978) 820104	60	01.01–06.11; 17.11–31.12	ⓧ ㏄ ☞ 🅿 🔲 🗓
▲ **Kurashiki** - Kurashiki YH 1537-1 Mukaiyama, Kurashiki-shi, Okayama- ken 710-0044. 🅴 kurashiki@jyh.gr.jp	☎ (86) 4227355 📠 (86) 4227364	60	01–28.01; 08.02–31.12	ⅲ ⓧ 🅿 🔲
▲ **Kurayoshi** - Kōhō-ji YH 195 Shimoasozu, Hawai-cho, Tōhaku-gun, Tottori-ken 682-07.	☎ (858) 352054	35	ⓘ₁₂	ⓧ ☞ 🅿 🔲 🗓
▲ **Kusatsu** - Kusatsu-kogen YH Tengu-yama-shita, Kusatsu, Kusatsu-machi, Agatsuma-gun, Gumma-ken 377-1711. 🅴 kusatsu@jyh.gr.jp	☎ (279) 883895 📠 (279) 886880	96	01.01–20.06; 01.07–20.11; 01–31.12	ⅲ ⓧ ㏄ 🅿 🔲 🗓
▲ **Kushiro** - Kushiro Shitsugen Toro YH 7 Toro, Shibecha-cho, Kawakami-gun, Hokkaido 088-2261.	☎ (1548) 72510	14	ⓘ₁₂	ⓧ 🅿 🔲 🗓
▲ **Kussharo** - Kussharo-Genya YGH 443-1 Kussharo-genya, Teshikaga-cho, Kawakami-gun, Hokkaido 088-3341. 🅴 genya@seagreen.ocn.ne.jp	☎ (1548) 42609	28	01.01–31.03; 29.04–31.10; 24–31.12	ⓧ ㏄ 🅿 🔲
▲ **Kyoto** - Higashiyama YH ⒤ⒷⓃ 112 Goken-cho, Shirakawa-bashi, San-jō-dōri, Higashiyama-ku, Kyotō-shi, Kyoto-fu 605-0036. 🅴 kyoto-yh@mx.biwa.ne.jp	☎ (75) 7618135 📠 (75) 7618138	150	01.01–20.06; 01.07–30.11; 11–31.12	ⅲ ⓧ 4NE 🅿 🔲 🗓
▲ **Kyoto** - Utano ⒤ⒷⓃ **29 Nakayama-cho Uzumasa, Ukyō-ku, Kyoto-shi, Kyoto-fu 616-8191.** 🅴 utano-yh@mbox.kyoto-inet.or.jp	☎ (75) 4622288 📠 (75) 4622289	168	ⓘ₁₂	ⅲ ⓧ 8NW ♿ ㏄ ☞ 🅿 🔲 🗓
▲ **Kyoto** - Kitayama YH ⒤ⒷⓃ Koetsuji-han, Takagamine, Kita-ku, Kyoto-shi, Kyoto-fu 603-8478.	☎ (75) 4925345	43	30.01–29.12	ⅲ ⓧ 8N ㏄ 🅿 🔲
▲ **Mashū-ko** - Mashū-ko YH 883 Genya, Teshikaga-machi, Kawakami-gun, Hokkaido 088-3222.	☎ (1548) 23098 📠 (1548) 24875	78	01.01–30.11; 21–31.12	ⅲ ⓧ ㏄ 🅿 🔲 🍺 🗓
▲ **Matsue** - Lakeside YH 1546 Kososhi-machi, Matsue-shi, Shimane-ken 690-0151.	☎ (852) 368620 📠 (852) 368620	50	ⓘ₁₂	ⅲ ⓧ 🅿 🔲 🗓
▲ **Matsumoto** - Asama Onsen YH 1-7-15 Asama Onsen, Matsumoto-shi, Nagano-ken 390-0303.	☎ (263) 461335	110	04.01–27.12	🅿
▲ **Matsushima** - Pila Matsushima YH ⒤ⒷⓃ 89-48 Minami-akazaki, Nobiru, Naruse-machi, Monou-gun, Miyagi-ken 981-0411. 🅴 matsushima@jyh.gr.jp	☎ (225) 882220	100	ⓘ₁₂	ⅲ ⓧ ㏄ 🅿 🔲 🗓
▲ **Matsuyama** - Matsuyama YH ⒤ⒷⓃ 22-3 Himezuka Otsu, Dogo, Matsuyama-shi, Ehime-ken 790-2502.	☎ (89) 9336366 📠 (89) 9336378	66	01–20.01; 01.02–20.06; 01.07–20.11; 01–31.12	ⅲ ⓧ ☞ 🅿 🔲 🗓

Location/Address	Telephone No. Fax No.	Beds	Opening Dates	Facilities
▲ **Matsuzaki** - Sanyo-so YH 73-1 Naka, Matsuzaki-machi, Kamo-gun, Shizuoka-ken 410-3626.	☎ (558) 420408	63	▥12	꿰ᵔ P ▣ 🗓
▲ **Minobu** - Minobu-Sanso YH 2780 Umedaira, Minobu-cho, Minami-koma-gun, Yamanashi-ken.	☎ (5566) 23034	15	▥12	ⅲ 꿰ᵔ P 🗓
▲ **Misawa** - Kawayo Green YH Kawayo-green-farm, 3331 Mukaiyama, Shimoda-machi, Kamikita-gun, Aomori-ken 039-2151.	☎ (178) 562756 ✆ (178) 564112	26	01–06.01; 06.02–31.12	ⅲ 꿰ᵔ CC P ▣ ☕
△ *Mitake* - *Mitake YH* *57 Mitake-san, Ōme-shi, Tokyo 198-0175.*	☎ *(428) 788774*	*30*	▥12	꿰ᵔ 🗓
▲ **Mito** - Kairakuen YH 1-1-18, Midori-cho, Mito-shi, Ibaraki-ken 310-0034.	☎ (29) 2261388	61	▥12	꿰ᵔ P
▲ **Miyakojima** - Miyakojima YH 1325-3, Shimozato, Hirara-shi, Okinawa-ken, 906-0013.	☎ (9807) 37700	28	▥12	꿰ᵔ P ▣ 🗓
▲ **Miyakonojō** - Miyakonojō YH 6361-1, Tohoku-cho, Miyakonojō-shi, Miyazaki-ken 885-0004.	☎ (986) 380022	13	▥12	꿰ᵔ P ▣ 🗓
▲ **Miyama** - Heimat YH 57 Nakasai, Kobuchiko, Miyama-cho, Kitakuwata-gun, Kyoto-fu 601-0775.	☎ (771) 750997 ✆ (771) 750997	13	01.01–10.06; 21.06–31.12	ⅲ 꿰ᵔ Ⓡ P ▣ 🗓
▲ **Miyazaki** - Miyazaki-ken Fujin-kaikan YH 1-3-10 Asahi, Miyazaki-shi, Miyazaki-ken 880-0803.	☎ (985) 245785	20	04.01–28.12	꿰ᵔ P 🗓
▲ **Miyazaki** - Aoshima YH 1-11 Aoshima Nishi, Miyazaki-shi, Miyazaki-ken 889-2163.	☎ (985) 651657 ✆ (985) 651657	60	▥12	ⅲ 꿰ᵔ P ▣ 🗓
▲ **Miyoshi** - Miyoshi YH Terato, Miyoshi-machi, Miyoshi-shi, Hiroshima-ken 728-0021.	☎ (824) 631759	20	04.01–12.08; 17.08–28.12	꿰ᵔ P ▣
▲ **Monbetsu** - Toyosato-Muminmura YH 115 Toyosato, Monbetsu-cho, Saru-gun, Hokkaido, 059-2126.	☎ (1456) 26388	24	▥12	꿰ᵔ P ▣
▲ **Morioka** - Morioka YH 1-9-41 Takamatsu, Morioka-shi, Iwate-ken 020-0114.	☎ (19) 6622220	70	▥12	ⅲ P ▣
▲ **Muika-machi** - Muika-machi Onsen International YH 1920-1 Oguriyama, Muika-machi, Minami-uonuma-gun, Niigata-ken 949-6636. 📧 muikamachi@jyh.gr.jp	☎ (257) 722842	180	01.01–20.06; 01.07–20.10; 01.11–31.12	꿰ᵔ CC P ▣ 🗓
▲ **Muroran** - Muroran YH 3-12-2 Miyuki-cho, Muroran-shi, Hokkaido 050-0084.	☎ (143) 443357	74	01–15.01; 27.01–31.12	꿰ᵔ P ▣

Location/Address	Telephone No. Fax No.	Beds	Opening Dates	Facilities
△ *Muroto* - *Hotsumisaki-ji YH* *4058-1 Muroto-misaki-machi, Muroto-shi, Kochi-ken 781-71.*	☎ *(887) 230024*	*60*	📷	⊗P◻🄴
▲ **Nagasaki** - Nagasaki YH IBN **1-1-16 Tateyama, Nagasaki-shi, Nagasaki-ken 850-0007.** ✉ nyh60625@jeans.ocn.ne.jp	☎ (95) 8235032 🖷 (95) 8234321	122	04.01–28.12	⋔ 1 NE ✄ P ◻
▲ **Nagoya** - Aichi-ken Seinenkaikan YH 1-18-8 Sakae, Naka-ku, Nagoya-shi, Aichi-ken 460-0008.	☎ (52) 2216001 🖷 (52) 2043508	50	05.01–27.12	1 SE P ◻ 🄴
▲ **Nagoya** - Nagoya YH 1-50 Kameiri, Tashiro-cho, Chikusa-ku, Nagoya-shi, Aichi-ken 464-0803.	☎ (52) 7819845 🖷 (52) 7819845	93	04.01–28.12	⋔ ⊗ 10 E ♿ P ◻ 🄴
▲ **Nara** - Kasugano YH 1358-1 Takabatake-cho, Nara-shi 630-8301.	☎ (742) 235667	11	📷	⋔ ⊗ P ◻ 🄴
▲ **Nara** - Nara YH IBN 1716 Hōren-cho, Nara-shi, Nara-ken 630-8113. ✉ nara@jyh.gr.jp	☎ (742) 221334	200	01–20.01; 01.02–20.06; 11.07–31.12	⊗ P ◻ 🄴
▲ **Nara** - Nara-ken Seishōnen-kaikan YH 72-7 Ikenokami, Handa-hirakicho, Nara-shi, Nara-ken 630-8111.	☎ (742) 225540	59	05.01–27.12	⋔ ⊗ P ◻ 🄴
▲ **Narita** - Skycourt Narita YGH IBN **161 Shinden, Taiei-machi, Katori-gun, Chiba-ken 287-0224.** ✉ hsky21@basil.ocn.ne.jp	☎ (478) 736211 🖷 (478) 736212	125	📷	⋔ ⊗ 62 E -CC- P ☕
▲ **Nejime** - Kinko-wan South Road YH 718-2, Kawaminami, Nejime-cho, Kimotsuki-gun, Kagoshima-ken, 893-2502.	☎ (9942) 45632 🖷 (9942) 45632	18	📷	⊗ R -CC- P ◻
▲ **Nihonbara** - Nihonbara Kogen YH 158 Ichiba, Shōboku-cho, Katsuta-gun, Okayama-ken 708-1206.	☎ (868) 362165	30	📷	⊗ ✄ P ◻
▲ **Niikappu** - Funhorse-Niikappu YH 489 Takae, Niikappu-cho, Niikappu-gun, Hokkaido, 059-2413.	☎ (1464) 72317 🖷 (1464) 74150	58	01.03–31.10	⋔ ⊗ P ◻
▲ **Nikko** - Daiyagawa YH 1075 Naka-hatsuishi-machi, Nikko-shi, Tochigi-ken 321-1402.	☎ (288) 541974 🖷 (288) 541974	26	01–24.01; 01.02–31.12	⋔ ⊗
▲ **Nikko** - Green Road Nikko Suginamiki YH 2112-7 Kiwadajima, Imaichi-shi, Tochigi-ken 321-2375.	☎ (288) 260951 🖷 (288) 261775	30	📷	⋔ ⊗ P ◻ ☕ 🄴
△ *Nima* - *Jofuku-ji YH* *1114 Nima-machi, Nima-cho, Nima-gun, Shimane-ken 699-2301.*	☎ *(8548) 83019*	*15*	📷	⊗ ✄ P ◻ 🄴
▲ **Niseko** - Niseko Annupuri YH 479-4, Niseko, Niseko-cho, Abuta-gun, Hokkaido, 048-1511.	☎ (136) 582084 🖷 (136) 582084	18	01.01–06.04; 29.04–19.10; 10–31.12	⋔ ⊗ P ◻

Location/Address	Telephone No. Fax No.	Beds	Opening Dates	Facilities
▲ **Niseko** - Niseko Kōgen YH 336 Niseko, Niseko-cho, Abuta-gun, Hokkaido, 048-1511. 📧 kogenyh@rose.ocn.ne.jp	☎ (136) 441171 🖷 (136) 441171	29	01.01–07.04; 26.04–31.10; 01–31.12	ⅲ ⑩ 🅿 ⊡ 🗎
▲ **Nishi-Tosa** - Shimanto-gawa YH 493-2 Hage, Nishi-Tosa-mura, Hata-gun, Kochi-ken, 787-1323.	☎ (880) 541352	12	01–10.01; 01.02–20.06; 21.06–20.12; 21–31.12	⑩ 🅿 ⊡
▲ **Noboribetsu** - Akashiya-só YH 6-4 Noboribetsu-onsen, Noboribetsu-shi, Hokkaido, 058-0551.	☎ (143) 842616 🖷 (143) 842616	15	📵	ⅲ 🅿 ⊡ 🗎
△ *Noboribetsu* - *Kanefuku YH* *132 Noboribetsu Onsen, Noboribetsu-shi,* *Hokkaido 059-0551.*	☎ *(143) 842565*	*26*	*08.01–24.12*	⑩ 🅿 ⊡ 🗎
▲ **Norikura** - Norikura-Kogen Onsen YH Norikura-kōgen, Azumi-mura, Minami-Azumi-gun, Nagano-ken 390-1513.	☎ (263) 932748	37	📵	⑩ 🅿 ⊡ 🗎
▲ **Noto Uchiura** - Isaribi YH Yo 51-6 Ogi, Uchiura-machi, Suzu-gun, Ishikawa-ken 927-0553.	☎ (768) 740150	20	📵	ⅲ ⑩ 🅿 ⊡
△ *Obihiro* - *Toipirka Kitaobihiro* *52-8 Kita4senhigashi Shimoshiboro,* *Otofuke-cho, Kato-gun, Hokkai do 080-0272.*	☎ *(155) 304165* 🖷 *(155) 304165*	*26*	*01.01–10.04;* *01.05–20.11;* *21–31.12*	ⅲ ⑩
▲ **Oboke-Koboke** - Jofuku-ji YH 158 Aō, Ōtoyo-machi, Nagaoka-gun, Kōchi-ken 789-0167.	☎ (887) 740301 🖷 (887) 740302	30	06.01–07.11; 19.11–29.12	⑩ 🅿 ⊡ 🗎
▲ **Ohara** - Seaside-Ohara YH 2122-27, Idoya, Iwafune, Ohara-machi, Isumi-gun, Chiba-ken 298-0011.	☎ (470) 628735	12	📵	⑩ 🅿 ⊡
▲ **Oirase** - Oirase YH Yakiyama, Towada-ko-machi, Kamikita-gun, Aomori-ken 034-0301.	☎ (176) 742031 🖷 (176) 742032	40	📵	ⅲ ⑩ 🅿 ⊡
▲ **Okinawa** - City Front Harumi YH [IBN] 2-22-10 Tomari, Naha-shi, Okinawa-ken 900-0012.	☎ (98) 8673218 🖷 (98) 8625219	42	📵	ⅲ 💳 🅿 ⊡ 🗎
▲ **Okinawa** - Okinawa International YH 51 Onoyama-cho, Naha-shi, Okinawa-ken 900-0026. 📧 okinawa@jyh.gr.jp	☎ (98) 8570073 🖷 (98) 8593567	200	01–07.01; 19.01–31.12	ⅲ ⑩ 💳 🅿 ⊡ 🗎
▲ **Okuchichibu** - Lake View YH 3755 Otaki, Otaki-mura, Chichibu-gun, Saitama-ken 369-1901.	☎ (494) 550056	38	📵	⑩ 🅿 ⊡ 🗎
▲ **Ōmachi** - Hakuba-Sanroku-Onsen YH 10594 Taira, Ōmachi-shi, Nagano-ken 398-0001.	☎ (261) 221820	48	📵	⑩ 🅿 ⊡ 🗎
▲ **Omaezaki** - Omaezaki YH 43-7 Omaezaki, Omaezaki-cho, Haibara-gun, Shizuoka-ken 421-0601.	☎ (548) 634518	35	📵	ⅲ ⑩ 🅿 ⊡ 🗎

Location/Address	Telephone No. Fax No.	Beds	Opening Dates	Facilities
▲ Ōmi - Ōmi Hachiman YH 610 Maruyama-cho, Ōmi-hachiman-shi, Shiga-ken 523-0805.	☎ (748) 322938	30	🄵12	
▲ Ōsaka - Hattori Ryokuchi YH 1-3 Hattori-ryokuchi, Toyonaka-shi, Ōsaka-fu 560-0873.	☎ (6) 68620600	92	04.01–27.12	6N
▲ Osaka - Osaka International YH (IBN) 1-5 Hagoromo-koen, Takaishi-shi, Osaka 592-0002.	☎ (722) 658539 📠 (722) 673682	220	01.01–21.05; 24.05–12.11; 15.11–31.12	16SW CC
▲ Osaka - Osaka-shiritsu Nagai YH 1-1 Nagai-koen, Higashi-Sumiyoshi-ku, Osaka-shi, 546-0034.	☎ (6) 66995631	100	05.01–27.12	
△ Otaru - Otaru Tenguyama YH 2-16-22 Mogami, Otaru-shi, Hokkaido 047-0023.	☎ (134) 341474	52	🄵12	CC
▲ Ōtsu - Saikyō-ji YH 5-13-1 Sakamoto, Ōtsu-shi, Shiga-ken 520-0113.	☎ (77) 5780013 📠 (77) 5783418	15	01.01–09.08; 17.08–24.12	
▲ Ōyu - Ōyu Onsen Kuromori YH 63 Kaminoyu, Towada-ōyu, Kazuno-shi, Akita-ken 018-5421. e kuromori@ink.or.jp	☎ (186) 372144	30	🄵12	
▲ Ozu - Ozu-kyodokan YH San-no-maru, Ozu-shi, Ehime-ken 795-0012. e fwhy3863@mb.infoweb.ne.jp	☎ (893) 242258 📠 (893) 591143	15	🄵12	
▲ Rebun - Momoiwa-sō YH Motochi, Kabuka, Rebun-cho, Rebun-gun, Hokkaido 097-1201.	☎ (1638) 61421	68	01.06–30.09	
▲ Rikuzen-takata - Rikuzen-takata YH 1000 Takata-Matsubara, Rikuzen-takata-shi, Iwate-ken 029-2204.	☎ (192) 554246 📠 (192) 554260	68	01.01–05.06; 16.06–31.12	CC
△ Sado-ga-shima - Sado-Hakusan YH Yamada, Sawada-machi, Sado-gun, Niigata-ken 952-1321.	☎ (259) 524422	15	🄵12	
▲ Sado-ga-shima - Sado Belle Mer YH 369-4 Himezu, Aikawa-machi, Sado-gun, Niigata-ken 952-2134.	☎ (259) 752011	26	🄵12	
△ Sado-ga-shima - Ogi-sakuma-so YH 1562 Ogi-cho, Sado-gun, Niigata-ken 952-0604.	☎ (259) 862565	13	01.03–30.11	
▲ Sado-ga-shima - Green Village YH 750-4 Uriuiya, Niibo-mura, Sado-gun, Niigata-ken 952-0106. e greenvyh@cocoa.ocn.ne.jp	☎ (259) 222719 📠 (259) 223302	14	01–04.01; 01.03–31.12	CC
▲ Saga - Saga-ken Seinen Kaikan YH 1-21-50 Hinode, Saga-shi, Saga-ken 849-0923.	☎ (952) 312328	56	04.01–28.12	

Location/Address	Telephone No. Fax No.	Beds	Opening Dates	Facilities
▲ **Sahoro** - Sahoro YH 26 2-chome, 4-Jō-minami, Shintokuchō, Kamikawa-gun, Hokkaido 081-0014.	☎ (1566) 46550	17	01.01–06.04; 25.04–10.11; 01–31.12	⑩ P 🖰 🗄
▲ **Sakurajima** - Sakurajima YH 189 Yokoyama, Sakurajima-cho, Kagoshima-gun, Kagoshima-ken 891-1419.	☎ (99) 2932150	100	🔟₁₂	⑩ P 🖰 🗄
△ *Sapporo* - Sapporo House YH 3-1 Nishi 6-chome, Kita 6-jō, Kita-ku, Sapporo-shi, Hokkaido 060-0806.	☎ (11) 7264235	30	02.01–30.12	♦♦♦ ⑩ 0.3W 🖰 🗄
△ *Sapporo* - *Sapporo International YH* *5-35 6-Chome 6-jo, Toyohiya Toyohira-ku,* *Sapporo-shi, Hokkaido 062-0906.*	☎ *(11) 8253120*	*120*	🔟₁₂	♦♦♦ ⑩ CC
▲ **Saroma** - Saroma-kohan YH Saroma-kohan, Hama-Saroma, Saroma-cho, Tokoro-gun, Hokkaido 093-0423.	☎ (1587) 62515	60	01–04.01; 01.02–04.04; 26.04–04.11; 28–31.12	♦♦♦ ⑩ CC 🗡 P 🖰 🗄
▲ **Sendai** - Dōchūan YH IBN 31 Kitayashiki, Ōnoda, Taihaku-ku, Sendai-shi, Miyagi-ken 982-0014.	☎ (22) 2470511 📠 (22) 2470759	40	01.01–04.06; 21.06–05.11; 21.11–31.12	♦♦♦ ⑩ P 🖰 ☕ 🗄
△ *Sendai* - *Esupora Miyagi YH* *4-5-1 Saiwai-Cho, Miyagino-ku, Sendai-shi,* *Miyagi-ken 983-0836.*	☎ *(22) 2934631* 📠 *(22) 2934634*	*24*	*04.01–28.12*	♦♦♦ ⑩ 🗄
▲ **Sendai** - Maple-Sendai-YH 1-9-35 Kashiwagi, Aoba-ku, Sendai-shi, Miyagi-ken 981-0933.	☎ (22) 2343922 📠 (22) 2343922	23	🔟₁₂	♦♦♦ ⑩ P 🖰 🗄
▲ **Sendai** - Sendai-Chitose YH 6-3-8 Odawara, Aoba-ku, Sendai-shi, Miyagi-ken 983-0003.	☎ (22) 2226329 📠 (22) 2657551	23	06.01–29.12	♦♦♦ ⑩ P 🖰 🗄
▲ **Setoda** - Setoda 668-1 Setoda-cho, Toyota-gun, Hiroshima-ken 722-2411.	☎ (8452) 70224 📠 (8452) 70282	30	🔟₁₂	♦♦♦ ⑩ P 🗄
▲ **Setoda** - Setoda Shimanami YH 58 Tarumi, Setoda-cho, Toyota-gun, Hiroshima-ken 722-2404.	☎ (8452) 73137	28	🔟₁₂	⑩ P 🖰
△ *Shakotan* - *Shakotan YH* *297 Yobetsu-cho, Shakotan-machi,* *Shakotan-gun, Hokkaido 046-0322.*	☎ *(135) 465051*	*70*	🔟₁₂	⑩ 🗡 P 🗄
▲ **Shari** - Kiyosato Ihatov YH 282 Kōyō, Kiyosato-cho, Shari-gun, Hokkaido 099-4403. 📧 balloon@vc-net.ne.jp	☎ (1522) 53995	24	🔟₁₂	⑩ 🗡 P 🖰 🗄
▲ **Shibata** - Kadoyonezawa Ryokan YH 863 Sugatani, Oaza, Shibata-shi, Niigata-ken 959-2511. 📧 k-nikaidou@inet.shibata.or.jp	☎ (254) 292008 📠 (254) 292200	12	11.01–09.08; 21.08–24.12	♦♦♦ ⑩ P 🖰
▲ **Shikotsu-ko** - Shikotsu-ko YH IBN Shikotsu-kohan, Chitose-shi, Hokkaido 066-0281.	☎ (123) 252311	108	01.01–30.11; 11–31.12	⑩ 🗡 P 🖰 🗄

Location/Address	Telephone No. Fax No.	Beds	Opening Dates	Facilities
△ *Shimabara* - Shimabara YH 7938 Shimo-kawashiri-machi, Shimabara-shi, Nagasaki-ken 855-0861.	☎ *(957) 624451*	48		
▲ **Shimamaki** - Shimamaki YH 21 Chihase, Shimamaki-mura, Shimamaki-gun, Hokkaido 048-0631.	☎ (136) 745264	23	01.03–20.11	
△ *Shimojo* - Shimojo Land YH 7852-98 Mutsusawa, Shimajo-mura, Shimoina-gun, Nagano-ken 399-2101.	☎ *(260) 272714* 📠 *(260) 271022*	12		
▲ **Shimo-kamo** - Gensu YH 289 Shimo-kamo, Minami-izu-machi, Kamo-gun, Shizuoka-ken 415-0303.	☎ (558) 620035	24		
▲ **Shimonoseki** - Hinoyama YH 3-47 Mimosusogawa-machi, Shimonoseki-shi, Yamaguchi-ken 751-0813.	☎ (832) 223753	52	01.01–20.06; 01.07–20.11; 21.11–31.12	
▲ **Shingū** - Hayatama YH 1-1-9 Kamihon-machi, Shingū-shi, Wakayama-ken 647-0003.	☎ (735) 222309	13	02.01–30.12	
▲ **Shingū** - Kajika-sō YH 1408 Kawayu, Hongū-cho, Higashi-muro-gun, Wakayama-ken.	☎ (735) 420518 📠 (735) 420518	30		
△ *Shiokari* - Shiokari Onsen YH 3 Shiokari, Wassamu-cho, Kamikawa-gun, Hokkaido 098-0125.	☎ *(16532) 2168* 📠 *(16532) 2512*	30	01.01–20.06; 01.07–20.12	
▲ **Shiono-misaki** - Misaki Lodge YH 2864-1 Shiono-misaki, Kushimoto-cho, Nishimuro-gun, Wakayama-ken 649-3502.	☎ (735) 621474	26		
▲ **Shirakaba-ko** - Shirakaba-ko YH 3418 Kitayama, Chino-shi, Nagano-ken 391-0301. @ hise1103@po.cnet-nc.ne.jp	☎ (266) 682031 📠 (266) 683378	70	01.01–07.05; 21.05–31.12	
▲ **Shirakaba-ko** - Tateshina Shirakaba-kōgen YH 1020 Megamiko-dori, Tateshina-machi, Kitasaku-gun, Nagano-ken 384-2309. @ tateshina@jyh.gr.jp	☎ (267) 556601	70		
▲ **Shirakaba-ko** - Tateshina Kleine YH 5890 Kitayama, Chino-shi, Nagano-ken 391-0301.	☎ (266) 772077	14		
▲ **Shiretoko** - Iwaobetsu YH Iwaobetsu, Shari-machi, Shari-gun, Hokkaido 099-4356.	☎ (1522) 42311	91	01.01–25.03; 29.04–27.10; 24–31.12	
▲ **Shizukuishi** - Shizukuishi YH 19-1 Hayasaka, Dai-10-Chiwari, Nagayama, Shizukuishi-cho, Iwate-gun, Iwate-ken 020-0585.	☎ (19) 6932854	17		

Location/Address	Telephone No. Fax No.	Beds	Opening Dates	Facilities
▲ **Shōdoshima** - Olive YH Olive-mura, Uchinomi-cho, Shozu-gun, Kagawa-ken 761-4434.	☏ (879) 826161 🖷 (879) 826060	123	01–20.01; 01.02–20.06; 01.07–31.12	♁ ⑩ cc⊃ P ⬛ 日
▲ **Shuzenji** - Shuzenji YH (IBN) 4279-152 Shuzenji-machi, Shuzenji, Tagata-gun, Shizuoka-ken 410-2416.	☏ (558) 721222	120	01–17.01; 23.01–29.05; 04.06–31.12	⑩ cc⊃ P ⬛
▲ **Shuzenji** - Kiya-ryokan YH 388 Warabo, Naka-izu-cho, Tagata-gun, Shizuoka-ken 410-2564.	☏ (558) 830146	15	▣12	⑩ P ⬛ 日
▲ **Sōun-kyō** - Sōun-kyō YH Sōun-kyō, Kamikawa-machi, Kamikawa-gun, Hokkaido 078-1701.	☏ (1658) 53418	75	01.06–31.10	⑩ P ⬛
▲ **Sukumo** - Sukumo YH 196 Kamiari, Hashigami-machi, Sukumo-shi, Kochi-ken 788-0044.	☏ (880) 640233	15	01–20.01; 11.02–20.06; 11.07–31.12	⑩ 🚲 P ⬛ 日
▲ **Suwa-ko** - Youpen House YH 8932-2 Takagi, Shimo-suwa-machi, Suwa-gun, Nagano-ken 393-0033.	☏ (266) 277075	28	▣12	⑩ P ⬛ 日
▲ **Tachikue-kyō** - Tachikue-kyō YH Tachikue, Ottachi-machi, Izumo-shi, Shimane-ken 693-0393.	☏ (853) 450102	30	05.01–29.12	⑩ P
△ *Tadotsu* - *Kaigan-ji YH* *997 Nishi-shirakata, Tadotsu-cho,* *Nakatado-gun, Kagawa-ken 764-0037.*	☏ *(877) 333333*	*45*	*04.01–12.08;* *16.08–30.12*	⑩ P ⬛ 日
▲ **Taira** - Taira YH 26 Kamanodai, Taira Shimokabeya, Iwaki-shi, Fukushima-ken 970-0101.	☏ (246) 347581 🖷 (246) 347581	58	06.01–27.12	♁ ⑩ 🚲 P ⬛
▲ **Taisha** - Ebisuya YH Shinmon-dōri, Taisha-machi, Hinokawa-gun, Shimane-ken 699-0711.	☏ (853) 532157	28	01.01–31.05; 21.06–31.12	⑩ P ⬛ 日
▲ **Takachiho** - Takachiho YH 5899-2 Mitai, Takachiho-cho, Nishi-Usuki-gun, Miyazaki-ken 882-1101.	☏ (982) 723021	28	▣12	⑩ P ⬛ 日
▲ **Takachiho** - Yamatoya YH 1148 Mitai, Takachiho-cho, Nishi-Usuki-gun, Miyazaki-ken 882-1101.	☏ (982) 722243	15	▣12	♁ ⑩ P 日
▲ **Takamori** - Murataya Ryokan YH 1672 Takamori, Takamori-machi, Aso-gun, Kumamoto-ken 869-1602.	☏ (9676) 20066	30	▣12	⑩ P ⬛ 日
▲ **Takayama** - Hida-Takayama-Tensho-ji YH 83 Tenshoji-cho, Takayama-shi, Gifu-ken 506-0832.	☏ (577) 326345 🖷 (577) 352986	95	▣12	♁ ⑩ P ⬛ 日
▲ **Takeo** - Takeo Onsen YH Nagashima, Takeo-machi, Takeo-shi, Saga-ken 843-0021. ✉ takeo@jyh.gr.jp	☏ (954) 222490 🖷 (954) 201208	80	01.01–26.05; 06.06–31.12	♁ ⑩ cc⊃ P ⬛

Location/Address	Telephone No. Fax No.	Beds	Opening Dates	Facilities
▲ **Tanabe** - Ohgigahama YH 35-1 Shinyashiki-cho, Tanabe-shi, Wakayama-ken 646-0033.	☎ (739) 223433	15	🗓	⚥ 🗄 🏠
▲ **Tazawa-ko** - Tazawa-ko YH 33-8 Kami-ishikami, Obonai, Tazawa-ko-machi, Senboku-gun, Akita-ken 014-1201.	☎ (187) 431281	37	🗓	¶ P 🗄 🏠
▲ **Togakushi-Kogen** - Yokokura YH 3347 Chūsha, Togakushi-mura, Kami-minochi-gun, Nagano-ken 381-4100.	☎ (26) 2542030	50	🗓	¶ P 🗄 🏠
△ *Toi - Takasagoya-ryokan YH* *790-1 Toi, Toi-machi, Tagata-gun,* *Shizuoka-ken 410-3302.*	☎ *(558) 980200*	*21*	🗓	¶ P 🗄 🏠
△ *Toi - Toi-misaki YH* *Toi-misaki, Kushima-shi,* *Miyazaki-ken 888-0222.*	☎ *(987) 761397*	*28*	🗓	¶ ⚥ P 🗄
▲ **Tokachi-Ikeda** - Kitanokotan YH 99-4 Toshibetsu-nishi-machi, Ikeda-cho, Nakagawa-gun, Hokkaido 083-0031.	☎ (1557) 23666	14	01–15.01; 28.01–04.04; 21.04–10.05; 22.05–05.11; 23–31.12	¶ P 🗄
▲ **Tokushima** - Tokushima YH 7-1 Hama, Ohara-machi, Tokushima-shi, Tokushima-ken 770-8012. ✉ tokushima@jyh.gr.jp	☎ (88) 6631505 📠 (88) 6632407	60	01–19.01; 01.02–31.12	¶ CC P 🗄
▲ **Tokyo** - Yoyogi YH [IBN] **c/o National Olympics Memorial Youth** **Center, 3-1 Yoyogi, Kami-zono-cho,** **Shibuya-ku, Tokyo 151-0052.** ✉ yoyogi@jyh.gr.jp	☎ (3) 34679163 📠 (3) 34679417	60	🗓	R 7W CC 🗄 ⬤
▲ **Tokyo** - International YH Central Plaza 18F, 1-1 Kagura-gashi, Shinjuku-ku, Tokyo 162-0823.	☎ (3) 32351107	158	04.01–28.12	⚤ ¶ 4NW ⚥ 🗄 🏠
▲ **Tokyo** - Skycourt Koiwa YGH [IBN] 6-11-4 Kita Koiwa, Edogawa-ku, Tokyo 133-0051.	☎ (3) 36724411 📠 (3) 36724400	37	🗓	⚤ CC P 🗄
▲ **Tokyo** - Skycourt Asakusa YGH 6-35-8 Asakusa, Taito-ku, Tokyo, 111-0032.	☎ (3) 38754411 📠 (3) 38754941	28	🗓	CC P
▲ **Tomakomai** - Utonai-ko YH 150-3 Uenae, Tomakomai-shi, Hokkaido 059-1365.	☎ (144) 582153	68	🗓	¶ ⚥ P
▲ **Tomari-Toyama** - Tenkyo-ji YH 913 Ōienoshō, Asahi-machi, Shimo-niikawa-gun, Toyama-ken 939-0722.	☎ (765) 833339	28	🗓	¶ ⚥ P 🏠
▲ **Tōno** - Tōno YH 13-39-5, Tsuchibuchi, Tsuchibuchi-cho, Tōno-shi, Iwate-ken 028-0555.	☎ (198) 628736 📠 (198) 628736	28	🗓	⚤ ¶ CC P 🗄 ⬤ 🏠

Location/Address	Telephone No. Fax No.	Beds	Opening Dates	Facilities
▲ Toya-ko - Shōwa-shinzan YH 103 Sōbetsu-onsen, Sōbetsu-chō, Usu-gun, Hokkaido 052-0103.	☎ (142) 752283	67	🛏12	🍴 P 🔲 日
▲ Toyama - Toyama YH 3377 Matsushita, Hamakurosaki, Toyama-shi, Toyama-ken 931-8414.	☎ (76) 4379010	41	04.01–27.12	🕍 🍴 P 🔲
▲ Tsuchiura - Masuo YH 1-7-14 Komatsu, Tsuchiura-shi, Ibaraki-ken 330-0823.	☎ (298) 214430	10	04.01–28.12	🔲
△ *Tsuruoka - Tsuruoka YH 1-1 Miyanomae, Tsuruoka-Shi, Yamagata-Ken 999-7463.* ✉ *kryoma@mail.dewa.or.jp*	☎ *(235) 733205* ✆ *(235) 733205*	*60*	🛏12	🕍 🍴 ✎ P
▲ Tsushima - Seizan-ji YH 1453 Kokubu, Izuhara-machi, Shimoagata-gun, Nagasaki-ken 817-0022.	☎ (9205) 20444	16	🛏12	🍴 ✎ P 🔲 日
▲ Tsuwano - Tsuwano YH 819-ko Washihara, Tsuwano-machi, Kanoashi-gun, Shimane-ken, 699-5613.	☎ (8567) 20373	28	🛏12	🍴 ✎ P 🔲 日
△ *Ube - Tokiwa-kohan YH Hiraki, 654 Takabata, Kami-ube, Ube-shi, Yamaguchi-ken 755-0452.*	☎ *(836) 213613*	*30*	🛏12	🍴 P 🔲
▲ Ueda - Mahoroba YH 40-1 Bessho-Onsen, Ueda-shi, Nagano-ken 386-1431.	☎ (268) 385229	19	🛏12	🍴 P 🔲 日
▲ Uwajima - Uwajima YH Atagokōen, Uwajima-shi, Ehime-ken 798-0045.	☎ (895) 227177 ✆ (895) 227177	40	01.01–10.06; 01.07–20.11; 01–31.12	🍴 P 🔲
▲ Wajima - Sosogi-kajiyama YH 4-1 Sosogi-kibe, Machino-machi, Wajima-shi, Ishikawa-ken 928-0206.	☎ (768) 321145	15	04.01–12.08; 19.08–29.12	🍴 P 🔲 日
▲ Wakasa - Mihamaso YH 19-92 Hayase, Mihama-cho, Mikata-gun, Fukui-ken 919-1124.	☎ (770) 320301	14	🛏12	🍴 ✎ P 🔲
▲ Wakkanai - Wakkanai YH 3-9-1 Komadori, Wakkanai-shi, Hokkaido 097-0003.	☎ (162) 237162	60	🛏12	🍴 ⊂CC⊃ P 🔲 日
▲ Wakkanai - Wakkanai Moshiripa YH 2-9-5 Chuo, Wakkanai-shi, Hokkaido 097-0022.	☎ (162) 240180	34	01.02–10.04; 21.04–31.10; 01–31.12	🍴 🔲
▲ Washūzan - Washūzan YH 1666-1 Obatake, Kurashiki-shi, Okayama-ken 711-0924.	☎ (86) 4799280	60	04.01–27.12	🍴 P 🔲
▲ Yabakei - Yamaguniya YH 1933-1 Ao-no-dōmon, Hon-yabakei-machi, Shimoke-gun, Oita-ken 871-0202.	☎ (979) 522008	30	03.01–30.12	🍴 P 🔲 日

Location/Address	Telephone No. Fax No.	Beds	Opening Dates	Facilities
▲ **Yakushima** - Yakushima YH 258-24 Hirauchi, Yaku-cho, Kumage-gun, Kagoshima-ken 891-4406.	☎ (9974) 73751	19	01–10.01; 01.02–10.04; 21.04–31.06; 11.07–30.11; 21–31.12	⛷ CC ✂ P ▨ ☐
▲ **Yamagata** - Yamagata YH 293-3 Kurosawa, Yamagata-shi, Yamagata-ken 990-2311.	☎ (23) 6883201	20	▥	⛷ P ▨ ☐
▲ **Yamaguchi-toyoda** - Jinjo-ji YH 624 Era, Toyota-cho, Toyoura-gun, Yamaguchi-ken 750-0452.	☎ (8376) 60286	30	▥	⛷ ✂ P ▨ ☐
▲ **Yamaguchi** - Yamaguchi YH 801 Miyano-kami, Yamaguchi-shi, Yamaguchi-ken 753-0001.	☎ (839) 280057	30	01–05.01; 27.01–19.06; 06.07–31.12	⛷ ✂ P ▨ ☐
▲ **Yano** - Shizen-no-mori M.G. YH 470-1 Yano-onsen, Jyōge-cho, Kōnu-gun, Hiroshima-ken 729-3423.	☎ (847) 623244	24	▥	⛷ P
▲ **Yoshino-Yama** - Kizo-in YH 1254 Yoshino-yama, Yoshino-machi, Yoshino-gun, Nara-ken 639-3115.	☎ (7463) 20575 ☎ (7463) 22519	90	01.03–26.12	ⅲ ⛷ P ▨
▲ **Yuasa** - Arida Orange YH 809 Suhara, Yuasa-machi, Arida-gun, Wakayama-ken 643-0005.	☎ (737) 624536	30	01–20.01; 01.02–31.12	⛷ P ▨
△ *Yubari* - *Yubari Forest YH 554 Numanosawa, Yubari-Shi, Hokkaido 068-0751.*	☎ *(1235) 72535*	*15*	*01.01–19.03; 21.04–09.11; 11–31.12*	ⅲ ⛷
▲ **Yufuin** - Yufuin YH 441-29 Kawakami, Yufuin-cho, Oita-gun, Oita-ken 879-5102.	☎ (977) 843734	21	01–20.01; 01.02–20.06; 01.07–30.11; 11–31.12	ⅲ ⛷ P ▨ ☐

"Travel is ninety percent anticipation and ten percent recollection"

"Le voyage c'est 90% de l'anticipation et 10% de souvenir"

„Reisen ist neunzig Prozent Erwartung und zehn Prozent Erinnerung."

"Viajar es un 90% de expectativa y un 10% de recuerdos."

Edward Street

Kenya

KENYA

KENYA

KENIA

**Kenya Youth Hostels Association,
PO Box 48661, Nairobi, Kenya.**

**Secretariat: Nairobi Youth Hostel,
Ralph Bunche Road, near Nairobi Hospital,
PO Box 48661, Nairobi, Kenya**

☏ (254) (2) 721765, 723012, 720353
✆ (254) (2) 724862
✉ kyha@africaonline.co.ke
🖳 www.safariweb.com/kyha

A copy of the Hostel Directory for this Country can be obtained from:
The National Office

Capital:	Nairobi		**Population:**	28,000,000
Language:	English/Swahili		**Size:**	582,646 sq km
Currency:	Ksh (shilling)		**Telephone Country Code:**	254

English

Call the national office for further information about hostels in the country. Hostels are located in cities, in the countryside and on hills/mountains.

Price range

Price range $5.50-8.00. 🗑.

Rooms and Reservations

🅡 🗓 (All Rooms) by ❶ ❶ ❷. (Reservation charges may apply). Smoking is limited - please check.

Guests

Membership Card and Passport/Photo ID are required. The maximum stay is 7 days. Age limits may apply for children - check with hostel. ♟♟♟ welcome. Group Bookings by ❶ ❶ ❷ (Reservation charges may apply).

Open times

Main hostels: open 🗓, 06:30-23:30hrs. Resident manager. **Other hostels:** open 🗓, 06:30-23:30hrs. Resident manager.

Meals

🍽 B 🅡 For individuals & for ♟♟♟. ☞ Not all utensils provided - check with hostel.

Travelling around

For ease of travel use 🚌 Self-Drive.

Travel/Activity Packages

Tours/sightseeing and cycling/mountain biking packages available. Package bookings by ❶ ❶ ❷.

Français

Veuillez contacter le bureau national de l'association pour un complément d'informations sur les auberges du pays. Les auberges sont situées dans les villes, à la campagne et à la montagne.

Tarifs des nuitées

Tarifs des nuitées 5.50-8.00$. 🗑.

Chambres et réservations

🅡 🗓 (Toutes chambres) par ❶ ❶ ❷. (Des frais de réservation pourront vous être facturés). Il est permis de fumer dans certaines chambres - veuillez vérifier.

Usagers

La carte d'adhérent ainsi que le passeport/pièce d'identité avec photo sont à présenter. La durée maximale du séjour est de 7 jours. Il est possible que des limites d'âge soient en vigueur pour les enfants - vérifiez auprès de l'auberge. Accueil des ♟♟♟. Réservations pour groupes par ❶ ❶ ❷ (Des frais de réservation pourront vous être facturés).

Horaires d'ouverture

Grandes auberges: ouvertes 🗓, entre 6h30-23h30. Gérant réside sur place. **Autres auberges:** ouvertes 🗓, entre 6h30-23h30. Gérant réside sur place.

Repas

🍽 B 🅡 Pour individuels & pour ♟♟♟. ☞ Pas tous les ustensils sont fournis - à vérifier auprès de l'auberge.

Déplacements

Modes de transport recommandés 🚌 Voiture.

Forfaits Voyages/Activités

Forfaits circuits touristiques et cyclotourisme/VTT disponibles. Réservations des forfaits par ❶ ❶ ❷.

Deutsch

Rufen Sie die Nationale Geschäftsstelle für Informationen über Herbergen im Land an. Herbergen befinden sich in Städten, auf dem Land und in Bergen/Gebirgen.

Preisspanne

Preisspanne 5.50-8.00 $. 🖵.

Zimmer und Reservierungen

R 🖾 (Alle Zimmer) per ❶ ❺ ❸. (Reservierungskosten könnten anfallen). Rauchen ist begrenzt - bitte checken.

Gäste

Mitgliedsausweis und Reisepass/ Personalausweis sind erforderlich. Der maximale Aufenthalt beträgt 7 Tage. Altersbegrenzungen für Kinder möglich - in der Herberge nachfragen. ♦♦♦ willkommen. Gruppenbuchungen per ❶ ❺ ❸ (Reservierungskosten könnten anfallen).

Öffnungszeiten

Hauptherbergen: Zugang 🖾, 06:30-23:30Uhr. Herbergsmanager wohnt im Haus. **Andere Herbergen:** Zugang 🖾, 06:30-23:30Uhr. Herbergsmanager wohnt im Haus.

Mahlzeiten.

🍽 B **R** Für Einzelreisende & für ♦♦♦. ☛ Nicht alle Utensilien werden bereitgestellt - in der Herberge nachfragen.

Reisen im Land

Reisen ist einfach mit 🚐 Selbstfahrer.

Reise-/Aktivitäten-Packages

Touren/sightseeing und Fahrrad/ Mountainbiking-Packages erhältlich. Package-Buchungen per ❶ ❺ ❸.

Español

Llame a la oficina nacional para más información acerca de los albergues del país. Los albergues están situados en las ciudades, el campo y la montaña.

Tarifas mínima y máxima

Tarifas mínima y máxima 5.50-8.00$. 🖵.

Habitaciones y Reservas

R 🖾 (Todas las habitaciones) por ❶ ❺ ❸. (Es posible que se aplique un suplemento en concepto de gastos de reserva). Está permitido fumar sólo en algunas salas/habitaciones - infórmese.

Huéspedes

Los huéspedes deben presentar su Carnet de Alberguista y su pasaporte o carnet de identidad. La estancia máxima es de 7 días. Es posible que exista un límite de edad para los niños - consulte con el albergue. Se admiten ♦♦♦. Reservas de grupo por ❶ ❺ ❸ (Es posible que se aplique un suplemento en concepto de gastos de reserva).

Horarios y fechas de apertura

Albergues principales - abiertos 🖾, 06:30-23:30h. Gerente residente. **Otros albergues** - abiertos 🖾, 06:30-23:30h. Gerente residente.

Comidas

🍽 B **R** Para individuales y para ♦♦♦. ☛ La cocina no dispone de todos los utensilios - consulte con el albergue.

Desplazamientos

Transportes recomendados: 🚐 Automóvil.

Viajes Combinados con Actividades

Viajes combinados con visitas turísticas y cicloturismo/bicicleta de montaña. Reserva de viajes combinados por ❶ ❺ ❸.

Nairobi -
Nairobi Youth Hostel

Ralph Bunche Rd,
PO Box 48661,
Nairobi. (near Nairobi hospital; GPO 2km).
📞 (2) 721765, 720353
📠 (2) 724862
✉ kyha@africaonline.co.ke

Open Dates: 🗓

Open Hours: 06.30-23.30hrs

Reservations: Ⓡ IBN

Price Range: $5.50-8.00 📖

Beds: 96 - 8x🛏 4x🛏 3x🛏 3x🛏

Facilities: 👪 2x 👪 🍽 🍴 🛏 📺 🧺 🗄 🖼
               ♿ 🔢 🅿 ℹ️ 🚲

Directions:

✈   Jomo Kenyatta International 18km

A🚌   Stage Coach #34 18km

🚌   Central 3km

🚌   111, 4, 8, 42, 40, 28 & 135 both
            Stage Coach & Matatus Mini Coach
            3km ap Traffic Police HQ

Attractions: 🏢 ⛰ ♨5km ✇500m ⚓500m

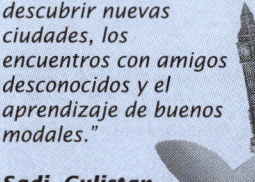

"Of journeying the benefits are many: the freshness it bringeth to the heart, the seeing and hearing of marvelous things, the delight of beholding new cities, the meeting of unknown friends, and the learning of high manners."

Le voyage apporte bien des bienfaits: la fraîcheur qu'il donne au coeur, l'occasion de voir et d'entendre bien des merveilles, le délice de découvrir de nouvelles cités, la rencontre d'amis inconnus et l'apprentissage de belles mannières."

„Wer reist, gewinnt viel: die Frische, die es dem Herzen bringt, das Sehen und Hören wunderbarer Dinge, die Freude, neue Städte zu betrachten, unbekannte Freunde zu treffen und edle Sitten zu erlernen."

"Muchas son las ventajas que deparan los viajes: el frescor que aportan al corazón, la oportunidad de ver y oír cosas maravillosas, el placer de descubrir nuevas ciudades, los encuentros con amigos desconocidos y el aprendizaje de buenos modales."

Sadi, Gulistan

[Map: Nairobi]

To Naivasha
Nairobi River
NGARA RD
University
ROAD
UNIVERSITY WAY
RIVER ROAD
State House
COMMERCIAL
UHURU
TOM MBOYA ST
STATE
Central Park
KENYATTA AV
GPO
Hilton
MOI AV
STATE HOUSE AV
City Square
Cathedral
Min of Works
Parliament
VALLEY ROAD
Uhuru Park
BISHOPS RD
SELASSIE
AV
Flora House
HAILE
Railway Museum
TWR HILL ROAD
NGONG
Traffic Police HQ
HIGHWAY
To Mombasa Airport

Location/Address	Telephone No. Fax No.	Beds	Opening Dates	Facilities
△ *Embu* - *Embu Scout* - *Kenya Scout Association* *P.O. Box 1859, Embu.*	☎ *254 0161 20823* or *254 0161 30459*	*36*	*01.12–01.12. 01*	👫 🍽 ℝ 130NE ♿ ☛ 🅿 🖨 ☼
△ *Mt Kenya* *PO Box 274, Naro Moru, Nyeri.*	☎ *(176) 62412*	*38*	🔳12	☛ 🅿
▲ **Nairobi** - Nairobi Youth Hostel ⟨IBN⟩ **Ralph Bunche Rd, PO Box 48661, Nairobi. (near Nairobi hospital; GPO 2km).** @ kyha@africaonline.co.ke	☎ (2) 721765, (2) 720353 📠 (2) 724862	96	🔳12	👫 🍽 ℝ ☛ 🅿 🖨
△ *Naivasha* - *Naivasha YMCA Hostel* *P.O. Box 1006, Naivasha.* @ *ymcacamp@maj.org*	☎ *254 0311 30396* 📠 *254 0311 30396*	*30*	*01.12–01.12. 01*	👫 🍽 ℝ 100NW ☛ 🅿 🖨 ☼
△ *Nanyuki* - *Nanyuki Riverside* *P.O. Box 101, Nanyuki.* @ *riverside@mt.kenya.org*	☎ *254 0176 32429* 📠 *254 0176 32523*	*60*	*01.12–01.12. 01*	👫 🍽 ℝ 200N ♿ ⟨CC⟩ 🅿 🖨 🅿 🚲 ☼

"In former days, women were unwelcome in Kyokans (Japanese-style inns) when they travelled alone. I learned from a newspaper article that such would never happen in youth hostels, and that stimulated me to stay at hostels. I was amazed to know that so many different people from all walks of life stayed together in one room, knowing each other, becoming friends and making pleasant company among themselves."

"Dans le temps, les femmes n'étaient pas les bienvenues dans les Kyokans (auberges japonaises), lorsqu'elles voyageaient seules. Lorsque j'ai lu dans un article de journal que cela n'arriverait jamais dans les Auberges de Jeunesse, j'ai eu envie d'y faire un séjour. J'ai été vraiment fascinée de voir que tant de gens d'horizons différents partageaient la même chambrée, apprenaient à se connaître, devenaient amis et passaient du bon temps tous ensemble."

"Früher waren Frauen in "Kyokans" (japanischen Gästehäusern) nicht willkommen wenn sie allein reisten. In einem Zeitungsartikel las ich, dass so etwas in Jugendherbergen niemals geschehen könnte, was mich dazu anregte, in Jugendherbergen zu übernachten. Ich war erstaunt, wieviele Menschen aus allen Berufen und Gesellschaftsschichten hier zusammenkommen, Zimmer miteinander teilen, neue Freundschaften schließen und gemeinsam viel Vergnügen haben."

"Antiguamente, las mujeres que viajaban solas no eran bienvenidas en los Kyokans (hostales japoneses). Cuando leí un día en el periódico que ésto no podría nunca suceder en un albergue juvenil, me entraron ganas de alojarme en uno de ellos. Quedé maravillada al comprobar que tantas personas diferentes, de todas las profesiones y condiciones sociales, compartían una misma habitación, se conocían, hacían amistad y lo pasaban bien juntas."

Sugako Hashida

South Korea

COREE DU SUD
SÜDKOREA
COREA DEL SUR

**Korea Youth Hostels Association,
Rm 408, Juksun Hyundai Building 80
Juksun-Dong, Jongro-Ku,
Seoul 110-052.
South Korea.**

☎ (82) (2) 7253031
𝟋 (82) (2) 7253113
℮ inform@kyha.or.kr
🖳 www.kyha.or.kr

A copy of the Hostel Directory for this Country can be obtained from:
The National Office

Capital:	Seoul	Population:	44,850,000
Language:	Korean	Size:	99,200 sq km
Currency:	Won	Telephone Country Code:	82

Sulaksan
Naksan

Pochun Bears Town
Ilyoung Shalom
Kwanglim   Kangchon
Kanghwa Namsan
International   Chung Pyung Academy
Kangwha
Youth Center   Daemyung Hongchun
Kyongin   Dunnae
Olympic Parktel   Yang Pyong   Hyundai Sungwoo
Anyang   Wonju Hwaseung   Yong Pyong
Seoul
Korean Folk Village   Ipo Chonwoo   Pyongchang
Yangji Pine   Everland
Chungjuho Woraksan   Sobacksan
Eumsung   Suanbo Sajo Maeul
Chonan Sangnok

Sokrisan Heungwoon

ULLUNGDO

TOKDO

EAST SEA

Kyeryongsan Kapsa
WEST SEA   Buyeo   Yusong

Chilgok Choil
Chilgok Academy
Kyongju Bomun
Moaksan   Kyongju Bulkuksa
Jun Ju   Kyongju-Shilla

SOUTH KOREA
Kochanggun Sonunsan
Kwangsan-Gu   Pusan   Dongsung

Sunchonshi

Namhae

Haenam

Cheju   Myongdoam

CHEJUDO

English

Hostels are located in cities, in the countryside, on the coast and on hills/mountains.

Price range

Price range Won 5,460-14,300. € 5-13.

Rooms and Reservations

🆁 🖥 (All Rooms). Reservations via 🖱 or Hostel by ❶ ❷. All hostels are non-smoking.

Guests

Membership Card is required. The maximum stay is 6 days. Pets are allowed - check with hostel. ♀♀♀ welcome. Group bookings via 🖱 Hostel or National Office by ❶ ❷.

Open times

Main hostels: open 🖥, 🕐. Reception open: 🕐. Resident manager. **Other hostels:** open 🖥, 16:00-23:00hrs. Reception open: 07:00-23:00hrs. Resident manager.

Meals

🍽 BD 🆁 For individuals & for ♀♀♀. ☞ (Charges may apply).

Discounts

HI Member Discounts available - see discounts section and www.iyhf.org.

Travelling around

For ease of travel use 🚢 Self-Drive.

Passports and Visas

Passport and Visa required.

Health

Medical insurance is recommended.

Français

Les auberges sont situées dans les villes, à la campagne, sur le littoral et à la montagne.

Tarifs des nuitées

Tarifs des nuitées 5,460-14,300 Won. € 5-13.

Chambres et réservations

🆁 🖥 (Toutes chambres). Réservations via 🖱 ou l'auberge par ❶ ❷. Toutes les auberges sont non-fumeurs.

Usagers

La carte d'adhérent est à présenter. La durée maximale du séjour est de 6 jours. Les animaux domestiques sont autorisés mais vérifiez lesquels auprès de l'auberge. Accueil des ♀♀♀. Réservations pour groupes via 🖱 l'auberge ou le Bureau National par ❶ ❷.

Horaires d'ouverture

Grandes auberges: ouvertes 🖥, 🕐. Accueil ouvert 🕐. Gérant réside sur place. **Autres auberges:** ouvertes 🖥, entre 16h-23h. Accueil ouvert entre 7h-23h. Gérant réside sur place.

Repas

🍽 BD 🆁 Pour individuels & pour ♀♀♀. ☞ (Une contribution pourra vous être demandée).

Remises

Remises pour les adhérents HI - voir la section "Remises" et notre site: www.iyhf.org.

Déplacements

Modes de transport recommandés 🚢 Voiture.

Passeports et visas

Passeport et visa obligatoires.

Santé

Une assurance médicale de voyage est
conseillée.

Deutsch

Herbergen befinden sich in Städten, auf dem
Land, an der Küste und in Bergen/Gebirgen.

Preisspanne

Preisspanne 5,460-14,300 Won. € 5-13.

Zimmer und Reservierungen

R 🗒 (Alle Zimmer). Reservierungen über
🖳 oder die Herberge per ❶ ❷. Rauchen ist
in allen Herbergen NICHT gestattet.

Gäste

Mitgliedsausweis ist erforderlich. Der maximale
Aufenthalt beträgt 6 Tage. Haustiere sind erlaubt
- in der Herberge nachfragen. ♦♦♦ willkommen.
Gruppenbuchungen über 🖳 Herberge oder
Landesverband per ❶ ❷.

Öffnungszeiten

Hauptherbergen: Zugang 🗒, ◷. Rezeption
◷. Herbergsmanager wohnt im Haus. **Andere
Herbergen:** Zugang 🗒, 16:00-23:00Uhr.
Rezeption zwischen 07:00-23:00Uhr.
Herbergsmanager wohnt im Haus.

Mahlzeiten

🍴 BD **R** Für Einzelreisende & für ♦♦♦. ☛
(Kosten können anfallen).

Ermäßigungen

HI-Mitgliedsrabatt ist erhältlich – siehe Teil für
Rabatte und Ermäßigungen und www.iyhf.org.

Reisen im Land

Reisen ist einfach mit 🚢 Selbstfahrer.

Reisepässe und Visa

Reisepass/Einreisevisum erforderlich.

Gesundheit

Unfall-/Krankenversicherung wird empfohlen.

Español

Los albergues están situados en las ciudades, el
campo, la costa y la montaña.

Tarifas mínima y máxima

Tarifas mínima y máxima 5,460-14,300 Won.
€ 5-13.

Habitaciones y Reservas

R 🗒 (Todas las habitaciones). Reservas
por 🖳 o a través del albergue por ❶ ❷. Está
prohibido fumar en todos los albergues.

Huéspedes

Los huéspedes deben presentar su Carnet de
Alberguista. La estancia máxima es de 6 días. Se
admiten animales - consulte con el albergue. Se
admiten ♦♦♦. Reservas de grupo por 🖳 o a
través del albergue o la Asociación Nacional por
❶ ❷.

Horarios y fechas de apertura

Albergues principales - abiertos 🗒, ◷.
Horario de recepción: ◷. Gerente residente.
Otros albergues - abiertos 🗒, 16:00-23:00h.
Horario de recepción: 07:00-23:00h. Gerente
residente.

Comidas

🍴 BD **R** Para individuales y para ♦♦♦. ☛
(Es posible que se aplique un suplemento por
el uso de la misma).

Descuentos

Se conceden descuentos a los miembros de
Hostelling International – véase la sección

sobre descuentos y nuestra página Internet en www.iyhf.org.

Desplazamientos

Transportes recomendados: 🚢 Automóvil.

Pasaportes y Visados

Pasaporte y visado obligatorios.

Información Sanitaria

Seguro médico recomendado.

Buyeo -
Samjung Buyeo YH

105-1 Kukyo-ri,
Buyeo-Eup,
Buyeo-Gun,
Choongnam-Do 323-800.
☎ (41) 8353102
❶ (41) 8353791

Open Dates:	🗓
Open Hours:	🕐
Reservations:	Ⓡ (IBN) -CC-
Price Range:	8900 🛏
Beds:	582 - 8x² 🛏 26x⁶ 🛏 11x⁶ 🛏
Facilities:	⚻16x ⚻ 🍽 ☕ 🍺 🧺 📺 2 x 🍸 🛏 ♨ 8 ☕ Ⓟ ⓘ 🧺 ♿ ⛺

Directions:

✈	Kunsan 50km
A🚌	Baekma Airport Bus 50km
🚂	Nonsan 30km
🚌	Kumnam Bus 500m ap Kumnam Bus Terminal

Attractions: ⌖ ⛰ 🔍 🚶 🏊

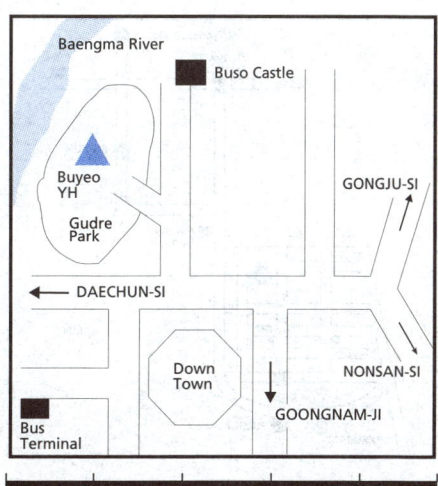

Kyungju -
Kyungju Cheil Youth Hostel

63-63 Jinhyun-Dong,
Kyungju-shi,
Kyungbuk-Do.
☎ (54) 7460086
✆ (54) 7464215

Open Dates:	📅12
Beds:	10x²🛏 5x⁴🛏 20x⁶🛏
Facilities:	👪35x 👬 🍽 🚿 🍺 🛎 📺1 x 🍴 🔒 ⚒ ☕ 🅿 🧺 ⚡
Attractions:	⛲ ⛰ 🚶

Seoul -
Olympic Parktel YH

88 Bangyi-Dong,
Songpa-Ku,
Seoul 138-050.
☎ (2) 4102114
✆ (2) 4102100

Open Dates:	📅12
Open Hours:	🕐
Reservations:	Ⓡ CC
Price Range:	14300 💶
Beds:	967 - 9x¹🛏 84x²🛏 52x³🛏 20x⁴🛏 20x⁵🛏 10x⁶🛏
Facilities:	♿ 👪180x 👬 🍽 🚿 🛎 📺 📺 20 x 🍴 🔒 🖼 ⚒ 🅱 ☕ ⬆ 🅿 ℹ 🧺 🌿 🎿 🏠 🎏
Directions:	25 SE from city centre
✈	Kimpo 40km
A🚌	600 or Kal Limousine line 4 40km
🚌	569, 568, 212, 21, 813, 16, 70 100m ap Olympic Park
Ⓤ	Sungnae 300m
Attractions:	⛲ ⛰ 🚴 🚶 ♨500m 🏊

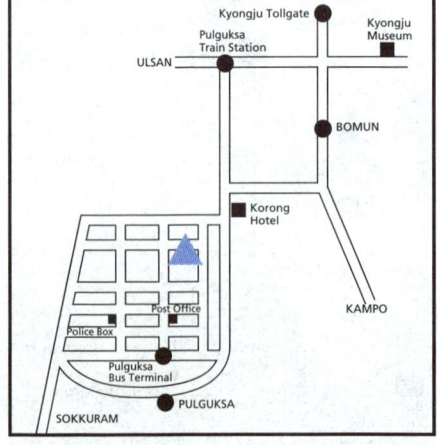

Location/Address	Telephone No. Fax No.	Beds	Opening Dates	Facilities
▲ **Anyang** - Anyang YH 241-14, Suksu-dong, Manan-gu, Kyunggi-Do.	☎ (31) 4718111 ✆ (31) 4728106	292		♀♀ ⑩ ® 4NW & ☞ P ☕
▲ **Boeun** - Sokrisan Heungwoon YH 238, Sangpan-ri, Naesokri-myun, Boeun-kun, Chungbuk-do.	☎ (43) 5425799 ✆ (43) 5433634	511		♀♀ ⑩ ® 16NE ☞ P ☕
▲ **Buyeo** - Samjung Buyeo YH (IBN) **105-1 Kukyo-ri, Buyeo-Eup, Buyeo-Gun, Choongnam-Do 323-800.**	☎ (41) 8353102 ✆ (41) 8353791	582		♀♀ ⑩ ® ⊟CC⊟ ☞ P ▣ ☕
▲ **Cheju** - Cheju YH 483, Nameup-ri, Awol-eup, Bukcheju-kun, Cheju-do.	☎ (64) 7998811 ✆ (64) 7998821	498		♀♀ ⑩ ® 15S & ⊟CC⊟ ☞ P ☕
▲ **Cheju** - Cheju Myongdoam YH 234-66, Bongae-Dong, Cheju-Shi, Cheju-Do.	☎ (64) 7218233 ✆ (64) 7218235	225		♀♀ ⑩ ® 15NE ☞ P ☕
△ *Chilgok* - *Chilgok Academy YH* *349-1, Namyul-Ri, Sukjuk-Mun, Chilgok-Kun, Kyongbuk.*	☎ *(54) 9759966* ✆ *(54) 9759967*	*121*		♀♀ ⑩ ® 10.2SE ☞ ☕ P
△ *Chilgok* - *Chilgok-Choil YH* *164, Yongsu-Ri, Gasan-Myun, Chilkok-kun, Kyoungbuk-Do.*	☎ *(54) 9710602* ✆ *(53) 3536572*	*106*		♀♀ ⑩ ® ☞ P
▲ **Chonan** - Chonan Sangnok 669-1, Jangsan-Li, Susin-Myun, Chonan-Shi, Chungnam-Do.	☎ (41) 5609024 ✆ (41) 5609209	590		♀♀ ⑩ ® 30SE ⊟CC⊟ P
▲ **Chuncheon** - Kangchon YH 366 Kangchon-Ri, Namsan-Myun, Choonchun-Si, Kangwon-Do.	☎ (33) 2621201 ✆ (33) 2621204	196		♀♀ ⑩ ® 17W ☞ P ▣
▲ **Chung Pyung** - Chung Pyung Academy YH San 18, Duckhyun-Ri, Sang-Myun, Gapyung-kun, Kyunggi-Do.	☎ (31) 5845500 ✆ (31) 5855600	318		♀♀ ⑩ ® ☞ P
▲ **Chungju** - Chungjuho Woraksan YH 401, Tanju-Ri, Hansu-Myun, Chechun-shi, Chungbuk-Do.	☎ (43) 6517001 ✆ (43) 6517004	285		♀♀ ⑩ ® 30SE & ⊟CC⊟ ☞ P ▣
▲ **Chungju** - Suanbo Sajomaeul YH 641, Oncheon-Ri, Sangmo-Myun, Joongwon-Ku, Chungbuk, Suanbo.	☎ (43) 8460750 ✆ (43) 8461789	736		♀♀ ⑩ ® 0.8NE ☞ P
▲ **Daejon** - Yusung YH 671-4, Kyesan-Dong, Yusong-Gu, Daejon-Si.	☎ (42) 8229591 ✆ (42) 8239965	240		♀♀ ⑩ ® 7E & ☞ P
△ *Eumsung* - *Eumsung YH* *San 49-1, Saengkeuk-Myun, Eumsung-kun, Chungbuk-Do.*	☎ *(43) 8821988* ✆ *(43) 8777802*	*400*		♀♀ ⑩ ® ☞ P
▲ **Gongju** - Keryongsan Kapsa YH 136, Jungjang-Ri, Kyeryong-Myun, Kongju-Si, Chungnam-Do.	☎ (41) 8564666 ✆ (41) 8564660	530		♀♀ ⑩ ® 11NE & ☞ P
▲ **Haenam** - Haenam YH San 7-10, Kurim-Ri, Samsan-Myun, Haenam-kun, Chunnam-Do.	☎ (61) 5330170 ✆ (61) 5321730	250		♀♀ ⑩ ® ☞ P
▲ **Hongchun** - Daemyong Hongchun YH 125-1, Palbong-ri, Seo-myun, Hongchun-kun, Kangwon-Do.	☎ (33) 4348311 ✆ (33) 4358304	1307		♀♀ ⑩ ® 32W ☞ P ☕

Location/Address	Telephone No. Fax No.	Beds	Opening Dates	Facilities
▲ **Huingsung** - Dunnae YH 1140, Sapkyo-Ri, Dunnae-Myun, Heuingsung-kun, Kangwon-Do.	☎ (33) 3436488 ✆ (33) 3436487	898	🔒12	⁈↟ �㺭 Ⓡ 4NE ⚐ ☛ 🅿
▲ **Inchon** - Kanghwa YH San 177, Euipo-ri, Naega-myun, Kanghwa-kun, Inchon.	☎ (32) 9338891/ 2 ✆ (32) 9339335	354	🔒12	⁈↟ �㺭 Ⓡ 0.4S ⚐ ☛ 🅿 🗗 ☕
▲ **Inchon** - Kanghwa Namsan YH 439-16, Namsan-ri, Kanghwa-eup, Kanghwa-kun, Inchon.	☎ (32) 9347777 ✆ (32) 9347782	400	🔒12	⁈↟ �㺭 Ⓡ 2NE ⚐ -CC- ☛ 🅿 🍷
▲ **Inchon** - Kyongin YH San 253-1, Kyongseo-Dong, Seo-Gu, Inchon-City.	☎ (32) 5797195 ✆ (32) 5797198	840	🔒12	⁈↟ �㺭 Ⓡ 28.5S ⚐ ☛ 🅿
▲ **Junju** - Junju YH 712-2, Sin-Ri, Sangkwan-Hyun, Wanju-Kun, Chunbuk-Do.	☎ (63) 2320150 ✆ (63) 2320155	181	🔒12	⁈↟ Ⓡ ☛ 🅿
▲ **Kimjae** - Moaksan YH 165 Kumsan-li, Kumsan-myun, Kimje-shi, Chon Buk-do.	☎ (63) 5484401 ✆ (63) 5484403	669	🔒12	⁈↟ �㺭 Ⓡ 16SE -CC- ☛ 🅿 ☕
▲ **Kochang** - Kochanggun Sonunsan 334, Samin-Li, Asan-Myun, Kochang-Gun, Chohbuk-Do.	☎ (63) 5613333 ✆ (63) 5613448	320	🔒12	⁈↟ �㺭 Ⓡ 22NW -CC- 🅿
▲ **Kwangju** - Kwangsangu YH 38-3 Songhak-Dong, Kwangsan-Gu, Kwangju-Si.	☎ (62) 9434378 ✆ (62) 9434379	130	🔒12	⁈↟ �㺭 Ⓡ 22S ⚐ ☛ 🅿
▲ **Kyungju** - Kyungju Cheil Youth Hostel **63-63 Jinhyun-Dong, Kyungju-shi, Kyungbuk-Do.**	☎ (54) 7460086 ✆ (54) 7464215		🔒12	⁈↟ �㺭 ☛ 🅿 🗗 ☕
△ *Kyongju* - *Bulkuksa YH* *530-3, Jinhyon-Dong, Kyongju-Si,* *Kyongbuk-Do.*	☎ *(54) 7460826* ✆ *(54) 7467805*	750	🔒12	⁈↟ �㺭 Ⓡ 11SE ⚐ ☛ 🅿
▲ **Kyungju** - Kyungju Bomun San87, Sonkok-Dong, Kyungju-Shi, Kyungbuk-Do.	☎ (54) 7495000 ✆ (54) 7495022	819	🔒12	⁈↟ �㺭 Ⓡ 7E -CC- ☛ 🅿
▲ **Kyongiu** - Shilla YH 611-11, Jinhyun-dong, Kyongju-shi, Kyongbuk-Do.	☎ (54) 7487333 ✆ (54) 7487334	473	🔒12	⁈↟ �㺭 Ⓡ 10SE ☛ 🅿 🍷
▲ **Namhae** - Namhae YH 140-1 Keumsong-Ri, Samdong-Myun, Namhae-kun, Kyongnam.	☎ (55) 8674510 ✆ (55) 8674511	300	🔒12	⁈↟ �㺭 Ⓡ ☛ 🅿 🗗
▲ **Pochun** - Bears Town YH 295 Sohak-Ri, Naechon-Myun, Pochun-kun, Kyonggi-Do.	☎ (31) 5322534 ✆ (31) 5338427	600	🔒12	⁈↟ �㺭 Ⓡ ☛ 🅿 🗗
▲ **Pochun** - Kwanglim YH 456, Jikdong-ri, Soheul-eup, Pochun-kun, Kyonggi-Do.	☎ (31) 5440515 ✆ (31) 5440519	454	🔒12	⁈↟ �㺭 Ⓡ 10S ⚐ ☛ 🅿 🍷
△ *Pusan* - *Dongsung YH* *206-11 Songjeong-Dong, Haewoondae-Gu, Pusan City.*	☎ *(51) 7037564* ✆ *(51) 7450256*	*141*	🔒12	⁈↟ �㺭 Ⓡ 25NE -CC- ☛ 🅿 🗗

Location/Address	Telephone No. Fax No.	Beds	Opening Dates	Facilities
▲ **Pyongchang** - Pyongchang YH 1477, Yunkyo-li, Banlim-myun, Pyongchang-gun, Kangwon-Do.	☎ (33) 3327501 📠 (33) 3328003	742		👫 🍴 ® 17NW ♿ ☞ P ⊡ ☕
▲ **Pyongchang** - Yongpyong YH Yong Pyeong YH, Dragon Valley Resort, 130 Yongsan-Ri, Doam-Myun, Pyungchang-kun, Kangwon-Do.	☎ (33) 3355757 📠 (33) 3350160	470		👫 🍴 ® 50W -CC- ☞ P ⊡
▲ **Seoul** - International Youth Center 801, Banghwa3-Dong, Kangseo-Gu, Seoul.	☎ (2) 26670310	262		👫 🍴 ® 15W ♿ ☞ P
▲ **Seoul** - Olympic Parktel YH **88 Bangyi-Dong, Songpa-Ku, Seoul 138-050.**	☎ (2) 4102114 📠 (2) 4102100	967		👫 🍴 ® 25SE ♿ -CC- ☞ P ⊡
▲ **Sokcho** - Sulaksan YH 246-77, Sulak-Dong, Sokcho-si, Kangwon-Do.	☎ (33) 6367115 📠 (33) 6367107	844		👫 🍴 ® ☞ P
▲ **Sunchon** - Sunchonshi San160, Unpyung-Li, Seo-Myun, Sunchon-Shi, Chonnam-Do.	☎ (61) 7493521	168		👫 🍴 ® 12N ♿ ☞ P
▲ **Suwon** - Korean Folk Village YH 107, Bora-Ri, Kiheung-Eup, Yongin-shi, Kyunggi-Do.	☎ (31) 2862114 📠 (31) 2862228	313		👫 🍴 ® 10SE ♿ -CC- ☞ P ⊡
▲ **Tanyang** - Sobacksan YH San 23-6, Chundong-ri, Danyang-eup, Danyang-kun, Chungbuk-do.	☎ (43) 4215555 📠 (43) 4213860	1370		👫 🍴 ® 8E ♿ ☞ P ☕
▲ **Wonju** - Wonju Hwaseung YH San 2-4, Wolsong-Ri, Jijong-Myun, Wonju-Si, Kangwon-Do.	☎ (33) 7323700 📠 (33) 7327665	418		👫 🍴 ® 10S ♿ ☞ P
▲ **Wonju** - Hyundai Sungwoo YH 476, Duwon-Li, Dunnae-Myun, Huisung-kun, Kangwon-Do.	☎ (33) 3403000 📠 (33) 3403173	998		👫 🍴 ® 40NE ♿ P ☕
▲ **Yangju** - Ilyoung Shalom YH San 72, Ilyoung-Ri, Jangheung-Myun, Yangju-Kun, Kyonggi-Do.	☎ (31) 8428011 📠 (31) 8427085	217		👫 🍴 ® 7SE ♿ ☞ P
▲ **Yangyang** - Naksan YH 30-1, Jeonjin-Ri, Kangheun-Myun, Yangyang-Kun, Kang-wondo.	☎ (33) 6723416 📠 (33) 6723418	400		👫 🍴 ® ☞ ⊡
▲ **Yeoju** - Ipo Chonwoo 62, Janghung-Li, Kumsa-Myun, Yeju-Gun, Kyunggi-Do.	☎ (31) 8867011 📠 (31) 8867015	162		👫 🍴 ® 30SE -CC- P
▲ **Yangpyong** - Yangpyong YH San 2, Seoksan-ri, Danwol-myun, Yangpyong-kun, Kyonggi-Do.	☎ (31) 7747800 📠 (31) 7747815	1180		👫 🍴 ® 40W ☞ P ☕
▲ **Yongin** - Everland YH 310, Jeondae-ri, Pokok-myun, Yongin-shi, Kyonggi-do.	☎ (31) 3209747 📠 (31) 3209727	585		👫 🍴 ® 15N ☞ P ☕
▲ **Yongin** - Yangji Pine 34-1, Namkok-Li, Yangji-Myun, Yongin-Shi, Kyunggi-Do.	☎ (31) 3382001 📠 (31) 3387897	643		👫 🍴 ® 12SE -CC- ☞ P

**HOSTELLING
INTERNATIONAL**

Do it
the HI way!

**For HI quality
accommodation at the
best prices. Visit one
of our 4200 hostels
in over 60 countries.**

www.**iyhf.org**

Libya

LIBYE
LIBYEN
LIBIA

Libyan Youth Hostel Association,
69 Amr Ben Al-Aas Street, PO Box 10322,
Tripoli, Al-Jamahiriya, Libya.

☎ (218) (21) 4445171
✆ (218) (21) 3330118

A copy of the Hostel Directory for this Country can be obtained from:
The National Office

Capital:	Tripoli		**Population:**	4,000,000
Language:	Arabic		**Size:**	1,759,540 sq km
Currency:	LD (Libyan Dinar)		**Telephone Country Code:**	218

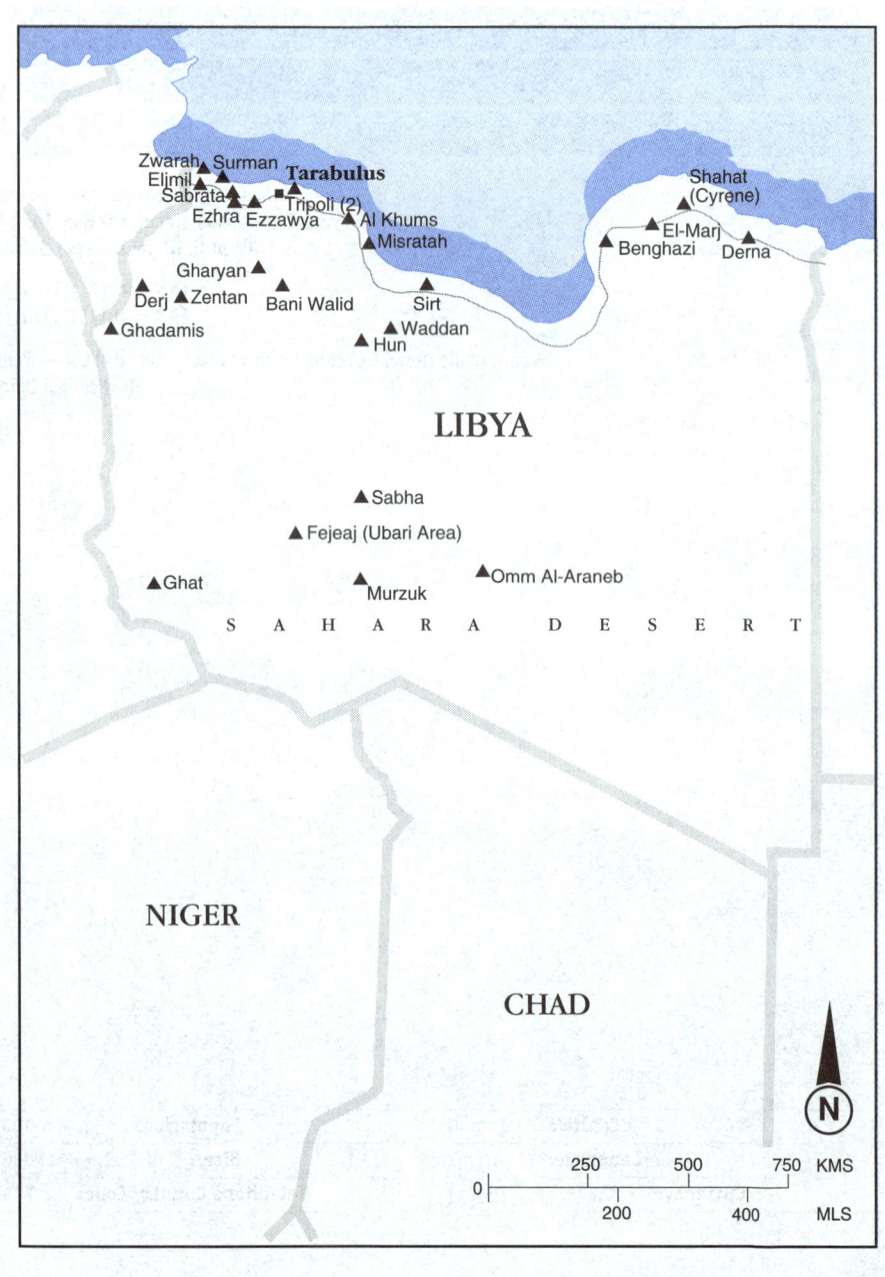

Zwarah Surman
Elimil **Tarabulus**
Sabrata Tripoli (2)
Ezhra Ezzawya Al Khums
Misratah

Shahat
(Cyrene)
El-Marj
Benghazi Derna

Gharyan
Derj Zentan Bani Walid Sirt
Ghadamis Waddan
Hun

LIBYA

Sabha

Fejeaj (Ubari Area)

Ghat Omm Al-Araneb
Murzuk

S A H A R A   D E S E R T

NIGER

CHAD

N

0
250
500
750 KMS

200
400 MLS

English

Hostels are located in cities, in the countryside, on the coast and on hills/mountains.

Price range

Price range LD 4. € 9. 🔲.

Rooms and Reservations

(R) 🔲 (1🛏 2🛏 3🛏 👪). Reservations via Hostel or National Office by ❶ ❶. All hostels are non-smoking.

Guests

Membership Card is required. The maximum stay is 3 days. Age limits may apply for children - check with hostel. 👪 welcome. Group bookings via Hostel or National Office by ❶ ❶.

Open times

Main hostels: open 🔲, 07:00-10:30hrs, 14:00-24:00hrs. Reception open: 14:00-24:00hrs. Resident manager. **Other hostels:** open 🔲, 07:00-10:30hrs, 14:00-24:00hrs. Reception open: 14:00-24:00hrs.

Meals

🍽 BLD For individuals & for 👪. 🐄.

Travelling around

For ease of travel use ✈ 🚌 Self-Drive.

Travel/Activity Packages

Tours/sightseeing and accommodation/transport packages available. Package bookings via Hostel or National Office by ❶ ❶.

Passports and Visas

Passport, Photo ID and Visa required.

Health

Vaccinations are advised - check with your medical advisor. Vaccination certificates required. Emergency medical treatment is free.

Français

Les auberges sont situées dans les villes, à la campagne, sur le littoral et à la montagne.

Tarifs des nuitées

Tarifs des nuitées 4 LD. € 9. 🔲.

Chambres et réservations

(R) 🔲 (1🛏 2🛏 3🛏 👪). Réservations via l'auberge ou le Bureau National par ❶ ❶. Toutes les auberges sont non-fumeurs.

Usagers

La carte d'adhérent est à présenter. La durée maximale du séjour est de 3 jours. Il est possible que des limites d'âge soient en vigueur pour les enfants - vérifiez auprès de l'auberge. Accueil des 👪. Réservations pour groupes via l'auberge ou le Bureau National par ❶ ❶.

Horaires d'ouverture

Grandes auberges: ouvertes 🔲, entre 7h-10h30, 14h-24h. Accueil ouvert entre 14h-24h. Gérant réside sur place. **Autres auberges:** ouvertes 🔲, entre 7h-10h30, 14h-24h. Accueil ouvert entre 14h-24h.

Repas

🍽 BLD Pour individuels & pour 👪. 🐄.

Déplacements

Modes de transport recommandés ✈ 🚌 Voiture.

Forfaits Voyages/Activités

Forfaits circuits touristiques et hébergement/
transport disponibles. Réservations des forfaits
via l'auberge ou le Bureau National par ❶ ❻.

Passeports et visas

Passeport, pièce d'identité avec photo et visa
obligatoires.

Santé

Des vaccinations sont conseillées - veuillez
vérifier auprès de votre médecin. Les certificats
de vaccination sont obligatoires. Soins
d'urgence gratuits.

Deutsch

Herbergen befinden sich in Städten, auf dem
Land, an der Küste und in Bergen/Gebirgen.

Preisspanne

Preisspanne 4 LD. € 9. 🗒.

Zimmer und Reservierungen

🆁 🗒 (¹🐄 ²🐄 ³🐄 👪). Reservierungen
über Herberge oder Landesverband per ❶ ❻.
Rauchen ist in allen Herbergen NICHT gestattet.

Gäste

Mitgliedsausweis ist erforderlich. Der maximale
Aufenthalt beträgt 3 Tage. Altersbegrenzungen
für Kinder möglich - in der Herberge
nachfragen. 👪 willkommen.
Gruppenbuchungen über Herberge oder
Landesverband per ❶ ❻.

Öffnungszeiten

Hauptherbergen: Zugang 🗒,
07:00-10:30Uhr, 14:00-24:00Uhr. Rezeption
zwischen 14:00-24:00Uhr. Herbergsmanager
wohnt im Haus. **Andere Herbergen:** Zugang
🗒, 07:00-10:30Uhr, 14:00-24:00Uhr.
Rezeption zwischen 14:00-24:00Uhr.

Mahlzeiten

🍽 BLD Für Einzelreisende & für 👪. ♂.

Reisen im Land

Reisen ist einfach mit ✈ 🚐 Selbstfahrer.

Reise-/Aktivitäten-Packages

Touren/sightseeing und Unterkunft/Transport-
Packages erhältlich. Package-Buchungen über
Herberge oder Landesverband per ❶ ❻.

Reisepässe und Visa

Reisepass, Personalausweis und Einreisevisum
erforderlich.

Gesundheit

Schutzimpfungen werden empfohlen - mit
Ihrem Arzt checken.
Schutzimpfungsbescheinigungen sind
erforderlich. Nur im Notfall sind medizinische
Behandlungen kostenlos.

Español

Los albergues están situados en las ciudades, el
campo, la costa y la montaña.

Tarifas mínima y máxima

Tarifas mínima y máxima 4 LD. € 9. 🗒.

Habitaciones y Reservas

🆁 🗒 (¹🐄 ²🐄 ³🐄 👪). Reservas a través
del albergue o la Asociación Nacional por ❶
❻. Está prohibido fumar en todos los
albergues.

Huéspedes

Los huéspedes deben presentar su Carnet de
Alberguista. La estancia máxima es de 3 días. Es
posible que exista un límite de edad para los
niños - consulte con el albergue. Se admiten
👪. Reservas de grupo a través del albergue o
la Asociación Nacional por ❶ ❻.

Horarios y fechas de apertura

Albergues principales - abiertos , 07:00-10:30h, 14:00-24:00h. Horario de recepción: 14:00-24:00h. Gerente residente.
Otros albergues - abiertos , 07:00-10:30h, 14:00-24:00h. Horario de recepción: 14:00-24:00h.

Comidas

BLD Para individuales y para .

Desplazamientos

Transportes recomendados:
Automóvil.

Viajes Combinados con Actividades

Viajes combinados con visitas turísticas y alojamiento/transporte. Reserva de viajes combinados a través del albergue o la Asociación Nacional por .

Pasaportes y Visados

Pasaporte o carnet de identidad y visado obligatorios.

Información Sanitaria

Vacunación recomendada - consulte con su centro médico. Certificados de vacunación obligatorios. Asistencia médica de urgencia gratuita.

"Own only what you can carry with you; know language, know countries, know people. Let your memory be your travel bag."

"Ne possède que ce que tu peux emporter avec toi; connais les langues, connais les pays, connais les gens. Que ta mémoire te serve de sac de voyage."

„Besitze nur, was du mitnehmen kannst; lerne Sprache, Länder, Leute kennen. Lass deine Erinnerung deine Reisetasche sein."

"Posee solamente lo que puedas llevar contigo; conoce los idiomas, conoce los países, conoce a la gente. Deja que tu memoria sea tu bolso de viaje."

Alexander Solzhenitsyn

Location/Address	Telephone No. Fax No.	Beds	Opening Dates	Facilities
▲ **Al Khums** Alkhums Sport Center SW 1.2km.	☎ (31) 20888, 21881-2	160		♂♀ ⚑ 1.2 SW ⚐ ◻
△ *Banī Walid* YH, the former Banī Walid Hotel, Banī Walid S 1km.	☎ *(322) 2415*	*30*		⚑ 1 S ⚐ P
▲ **Bengazi** Sport City Bengazi SW 1km.	☎ (61) 95961	200		♂♀ ⚑ R 1 SW ⚐ P ◻
△ *Derj* Derj YH.		20		⚑ 0.5 W P
△ *El Jmil* El Jmil City Centre.	☎ *(281) 2127*	25		♂♀ ⚑ P
△ *El-Marj* YH, El-Marg Town.	☎ *(67) 23717*	60		♂♀ ⚑ ⚐ P
△ *Elzabra YH* Elzabra City Centre.	☎ *(272) 2993*	20		⚑ ⚐ P
▲ **Ezzawya** YH, Ezzawya City: Tripoli NE 0.6km	☎ (32) 24019	80		♂♀ ⚑ ⚐ P
▲ **Fejeaj (Ubari Area)** Fejeaj YH, People's Housing Project: Village of Fejeaj.	☎ (728) 2902	40		⚑ ⚐ P
▲ **Ghadamis** YH, Ghadamis.	☎ (484) 62023	120		♂♀ ⚑ R 1 SE ⚐ P ◻
▲ **Gharyan** YH, Gharyan.	☎ (41) 31491	120		♂♀ ⚑ R 2 NE ⚐ P ◻
▲ **Misratah** YH, Misratah.	☎ (51) 642499, (51) 624419 ☏ (51) 424435	120		♂♀ ⚑ R 4 W ⚐ P ◻
▲ **Murzuk YH** Murzuk City Centre.	☎ (725) 2301	50		♂♀ ⚑ ⚐ P
▲ **Sabha** Jamal Abdel Naser ST, Sabha SW 0.8km.	☎ (71) 621178	160		♂♀ ⚑ R 0.5 NW ⚐ P ◻
▲ **Sabrata** YH, Sabrata: Tripoli NW 0.5km	☎ (24) 2821 ☏ (23) 29082	160		♂♀ ⚑ R 1 NW ⚐ P ◻
▲ **Shahat (Cyrene)** The former Cyrene (Shahat) Tourist Hotel.	☎ (851) 2102	200		♂♀ ⚑ R 2 NW ⚐ P ◻
▲ **Sirt** YH, Cost Rd, Sirt N 0.8km.	☎ (54) 61391, 61825	120		♂♀ ⚑ R 0.8 N ⚐ P ◻
▲ **Surman** YH, Surman.	☎ (273) 2581	50		♂♀ ⚑ 2 N P
▲ **Tripoli** - Gergarish YH Tripoli Gergarish YH, Gergarish Rd, Km 5.	☎ (21) 4776694 ☏ (21) 4775035	200		♂♀ ⚑ R 5 S P ◻
▲ **Tripoli** 69 Amru Ben Al-Aas St, Tripoli.	☎ (21) 4445171 ☏ (21) 3330118	120		♂♀ ⚑ ⚐ P
▲ **Waddan** YH, Waddan W 0.5km.	☎ (581) 2904	160		♂♀ ⚑ R P ◻

Location/Address	Telephone No. Fax No.	Beds	Opening Dates	Facilities
△ *Yafrin* YH, Yafrin: centre of city.	☎ *(421) 2394*	*45*	🖻	⍾◯⍾ �P
△ *Zentan* YH, Zentan: centre of city.	☎ *(451) 2826*	*30*	🖻	⍾◯⍾ �P
△ *Zwarah* Zwarah YH.	☎ *(25) 21012*	*30*	🖻	⍾◯⍾ 1NE ⬜ P

YOUTH HOSTEL ACCOMMODATION
OUTSIDE THE ASSURED STANDARDS SCHEME

Hun Hun YH.	☎ (57) 2040	50	🖻	⍾◯⍾ ☞
Omm Al-Araneb YH, Omm Al-Araneb: near Murzuq.	☎ (72) 62228	30	🖻	⍾◯⍾ ☞ P

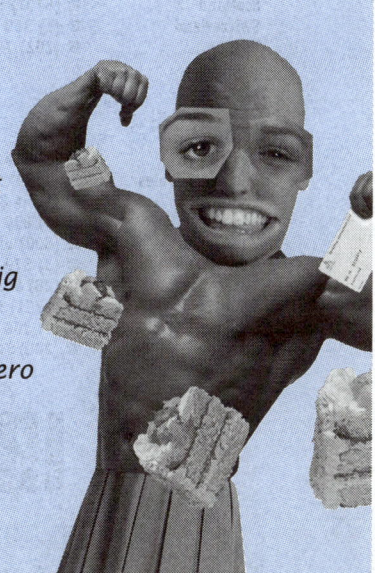

"He who would travel happily must travel light."

"Celui qui veut voyager joyeusement doit voyager légèrement."

„Wer glücklich reisen will, sollte nur wenig Gepäck mitnehmen."

"El que quiera viajar feliz debe viajar ligero de equipaje."

Antoine de Saint-Exupéry

HOSTELLING INTERNATIONAL

Make your credit card bookings at these centres
Réservez par cartes de crédit aux centres suivants
Reservieren Sie per Kreditkarte bei diesen Zentren
Reserve con tarjeta de crédito en los siguientes centros

English

Australia	☎ (2) 9261 1111
Canada	☎ (800) 663 5777
England & Wales	☎ (1629) 581 418
France	☎ (1) 44 89 87 27
Northern Ireland	☎ (28) 9032 4733
Republic of Ireland	☎ (1) 830 1766
New Zealand	☎ (3) 379 9808
Scotland	☎ (8701) 553 255
Switzerland	☎ (1) 360 1414
USA	☎ (202) 783 6161

Français

Angleterre & Pays de Galles	☎ (1692) 581 418
Australie	☎ (2) 9261 1111
Canada	☎ (800) 663 5777
Écosse	☎ (8701) 553 255
États-Unis	☎ (202) 783 6161
France	☎ (1) 44 89 87 27
Irlande du Nord	☎ (28) 9032 4733
Nouvelle-Zélande	☎ (3) 379 9808
République d'Irlande	☎ (1) 830 1766
Suisse	☎ (1) 360 1414

Deutsch

Australien	☎ (2) 9261 1111
England & Wales	☎ (1629) 581 418
Frankreich	☎ (1) 44 89 87 27
Irland	☎ (1) 830 1766
Kanada	☎ (800) 663 5777
Neuseeland	☎ (3) 379 9808
Nordirland	☎ (28) 9032 4733
Schottland	☎ (8701) 553 255
Schweiz	☎ (1) 360 1414
USA	☎ (202) 783 6161

Español

Australia	☎ (2) 9261 1111
Canadá	☎ (800) 663 5777
Escocia	☎ (8701) 553 255
Estados Unidos	☎ (202) 783 6161
Francia	☎ (1) 44 89 87 27
Inglaterra y Gales	☎ (1629) 581 418
Irlanda del Norte	☎ (28) 9032 4733
Nueva Zelanda	☎ (3) 379 9808
República de Irlanda	☎ (1) 830 1766
Suiza	☎ (1) 360 1414

IBN INTERNATIONAL BOOKING NETWORK

Malaysia

MALAISIE

MALAYSIA

MALASIA

**Malaysian Youth Hostels Association,
KL International Youth Hostel,
21, Jalan Kampung Attap, 50460 Kuala Lumpur,
Malaysia.**

**☏ (60) (3) 22736870,
(60) (3) 22736871
🖷 (60) (3) 22741115
✉ myha@pd.jaring.my**

A copy of the Hostel Directory for this Country can be obtained from:
The National Office

Capital:	Kuala Lumpur	**Population:**	18,000,000
Language:	Malay, English widely spoken	**Size:**	330,434 sq km
Currency:	RM (Malaysian Ringgit)	**Telephone Country Code:**	60

English

required. Emergency medical treatment is free. Medical insurance is recommended.

Drug trafficking is a serious offence and carries a mandatory death sentence. Hostels are located in cities, in the countryside, on the coast and on hills/mountains.

Price range

Price range RM 15.00-20.00. 🗒.

Rooms and Reservations

R 🖾. Reservations via **IBN** National Booking Centre, Hostel or National Office by **t** **f** **e**. Smoking is limited - please check.

Guests

Membership Card and Passport/Photo ID are required. **ⵜⵜⵜ** welcome. Group bookings via **IBN** National Booking Centre, Hostel or National Office by **t** **f** **e**.

Open times

Main hostels: open 🖾, 🕒. Reception open: 07:00-23:59hrs. Resident manager, **Other hostels:** open 🕒. Reception open: 07:00-23:59hrs. Resident manager.

Meals

🍽 BLD **R** For **ⵜⵜⵜ**.

Travelling around

For ease of travel use ✈ 🚌 🚐 Self-Drive.

Travel/Activity Packages

Tours/sightseeing packages available. Package bookings via National Office by **t** **f** **e**.

Passports and Visas

Passport and Visa required.

Health

Vaccinations are advised - check with your medical advisor. Vaccination certificates

Français

Le traffic de drogue est un délit très grave et passible de la peine de mort. Les auberges sont situées dans les villes, à la campagne, sur le littoral et à la montagne.

Tarifs des nuitées

Tarifs des nuitées 15.00-20.00 RM. 🗒.

Chambres et réservations

R 🖾. Réservations via **IBN** le Centre National de Réservation, l'auberge ou le Bureau National par **t** **f** **e**. Il est permis de fumer dans certaines chambres - veuillez vérifier.

Usagers

La carte d'adhérent ainsi que le passeport/pièce d'identité avec photo sont à présenter. Accueil des **ⵜⵜⵜ**. Réservations pour groupes via **IBN** le Centre National de Réservation, l'auberge ou le Bureau National par **t** **f** **e**.

Horaires d'ouverture

Grandes auberges: ouvertes 🖾, 🕒. Accueil ouvert entre 7h-23h59. Gérant réside sur place. **Autres auberges:** ouvertes 🕒. Accueil ouvert entre 7h-23h59. Gérant réside sur place.

Repas

🍽 BLD **R** Pour **ⵜⵜⵜ**.

Déplacements

Modes de transport recommandés ✈ 🚌 🚐 Voiture.

Forfaits Voyages/Activités

Forfaits circuits touristiques disponibles. Réservations des forfaits via le Bureau National par **t** **f** **e**.

Passeports et visas

Passeport et visa obligatoires.

Santé

Des vaccinations sont conseillées - veuillez
vérifier auprès de votre médecin. Les certificats
de vaccination sont obligatoires. Soins
d'urgence gratuits. Une assurance médicale de
voyage est conseillée.

Deutsch

Drogenhandel ist eine ernste Straftat, auf der
die obligatorische todesstrafe steht. Herbergen
befinden sich in Städten, auf dem Land, an der
Küste und in Bergen/Gebirgen.

Preisspanne

Preisspanne 15.00-20.00 RM. 🗐.

Zimmer und Reservierungen

R 🖾. Reservierungen über **IBN**
Nationales Buchungszentrum, Herberge oder
Landesverband per ❶ ❷ ❸. Rauchen ist
begrenzt - bitte checken.

Gäste

Mitgliedsausweis und Reisepass/
Personalausweis sind erforderlich.
♦♦♦ willkommen. Gruppenbuchungen über
IBN Nationales Buchungszentrum, Herberge
oder Landesverband per ❶ ❷ ❸.

Öffnungszeiten

Hauptherbergen: Zugang 🖾, ⊕. Rezeption
zwischen 07:00-23:59Uhr. Herbergsmanager
wohnt im Haus. **Andere Herbergen:** Zugang
⊕. Rezeption zwischen 07:00-23:59Uhr.
Herbergsmanager wohnt im Haus.

Mahlzeiten

🍽 BLD **R** Für ♦♦♦.

Reisen im Land

Reisen ist einfach mit ✈ 🚄 🚌
Selbstfahrer.

Reise-/Aktivitäten-Packages

Touren/sightseeing-Packages erhältlich.
Package-Buchungen über Landesverband per
❶ ❷ ❸.

Reisepässe und Visa

Reisepass/Einreisevisum erforderlich.

Gesundheit

Schutzimpfungen werden empfohlen - mit
Ihrem Arzt checken.
Schutzimpfungsbescheinigungen sind
erforderlich. Nur im Notfall sind medizinische
Behandlungen kostenlos.
Unfall-/Krankenversicherung wird empfohlen.

Español

El narcotráfico es un delito muy grave castigado
con la pena de muerte obligatorio. Los
albergues están situados en las ciudades, el
campo, la costa y la montaña.

Tarifas mínima y máxima

Tarifas mínima y máxima 15.00-20.00 RM. 🗐.

Habitaciones y Reservas

R 🖾. Reservas por **IBN** o a través de la
Central Nacional de Reservas, el albergue o la
Asociación Nacional por ❶ ❷ ❸. Está
permitido fumar sólo en algunas
salas/habitaciones - infórmese.

Huéspedes

Los huéspedes deben presentar su Carnet de Alberguista y su pasaporte o carnet de identidad. Se admiten ♦♦♦. Reservas de grupo por ⦗IBN⦘ o a través de la Central Nacional de Reservas, el albergue o la Asociación Nacional por ❶ ❶ ❸.

Horarios y fechas de apertura

Albergues principales - abiertos 🗓, ☾. Horario de recepción: 07:00-23:59h. Gerente residente, **Otros albergues** - abiertos: ☾. Horario de recepción: 07:00-23:59h. Gerente residente.

Comidas

🍽 BLD ⓡ Para ♦♦♦.

Desplazamientos

Transportes recomendados: ✈ 🚆 🚌 Automóvil.

Viajes Combinados con Actividades

Viajes combinados con visitas turísticas. Reserva de viajes combinados a través de la Asociación Nacional por ❶ ❶ ❸.

Pasaportes y Visados

Pasaporte y visado obligatorios.

Información Sanitaria

Vacunación recomendada - consulte con su centro médico. Certificados de vacunación obligatorios. Asistencia médica de urgencia gratuita. Seguro médico recomendado.

Kuala Lumpur -
International YH

**21 Jalan Kampung Attap,
50460 Kuala Lumpur.**
❶ (3) 22736870/71
❶ (3) 22741115
❸ myha@pd.jaring.my

Open Dates:	🗓
Open Hours:	07.00-23.59hrs
Reservations:	ⓡ ⦗IBN⦘ ⦗CC⦘
Price Range:	RM 20.00 🛏
Beds:	72 - 6x⁴🛏 3x⁶🛏 3x⁶🛏
Facilities:	6x ♦♦ 🛏 📺 🍳 🖼 🔋 ⊜ 🅿 📷

Directions: ⦗2 SE⦘ from city centre

✈	65km
🚆	1km
🚌	1km

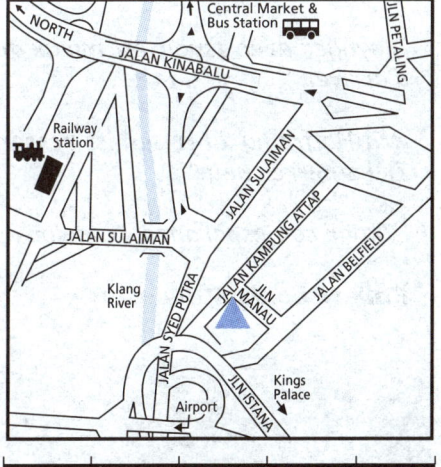

Location/Address	Telephone No. Fax No.	Beds	Opening Dates	Facilities
▲ **Kuala Lumpur** - International YH (IBN) 21 **Jalan Kampung Attap, 50460 Kuala Lumpur.** ✉ myha@pd.jaring.my	☎ (3) 22736870/ 71 📠 (3) 22741115	72	🛏12	♟ R 2SE CC P
▲ **Kuala Lumpur** - International Youth Centre Jalan Tenteram, Bandar Tun Razak, Cheras, 56000 Kuala Lumpur.	☎ (3) 9719204	210	🛏12	♟ R P
▲ **Kuala Tahan** - Taman Negara Resort National Park Kuala Tahan, 27000 Jerantut. OR: Kuala Lumpur Sales & Reservations Office, Lot G.01A, Ground Floor, Kompleks Antarabangsa, Jalan Sultan Ismail, 50250 Kuala Lumpur. . ✉ tnresort@tm.net.my	☎ (3) 2455585 📠 (3) 2455430	64	🛏12	♟ ⑂ R CC ⓢ
▲ **Melaka** (IBN) 341A, Jalan Melaka Raya 3, Taman Melaka Raya, 75000 Melaka. (next to Malacca Club).	☎ (6) 2827915	56	🛏12	♟ R P
▲ **Port Dickson** km 6, Jalan Pantai, 71000 Port Dickson.	☎ (6) 6472188	64	🛏12	♟ R P

"To travel hopefully is a better thing than to arrive."

"Voyager avec espoir est mieux que d'arriver."

„Mit Hoffnung zu reisen ist besser, als sein Ziel zu erreichen."

"Viajar con esperanza es mejor que llegar."

Robert Louis Stevenson

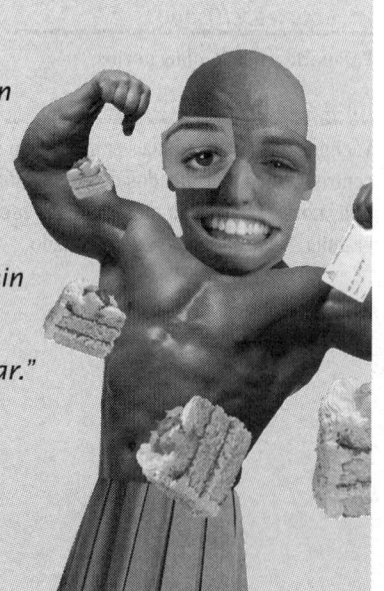

Morocco

MAROC
MAROKKO
MARRUECOS

**Fédération Royale Marocaine des Auberges de Jeunes,
Parc de la Ligue Arabe, BP No 15998, Casa-Principale,
Casablanca 21000, Morocco.**

☎ (212) (2) 470952
✆ (212) (2) 227677

Office Hours: 08.30-12.00hrs & 08.30-15.00hrs (Su)
08.30-12.00hrs & 14.00-18.00hrs (Wi)

A copy of the Hostel Directory for this Country can be obtained from:
The National Office

Capital:	Rabat		**Population:**	26,073,717
Language:	Arabic		**Size:**	710,850 sq km
Currency:	Dh (dirham)		**Telephone Country Code:**	212

SPAIN

Tanger ●▲Tanger

▲Chefchaouen

Mehdya ▲
Rabat
Rabat▲ ●   Fes

Casablanca ■   ▲Meknes
        ● Casablanca   ▲ Azrou
        ▲ El Jadida
                MOROCCO

Marrakech ●   Rissani ▲
        ● Marrakech
        ▲Asni

ALGERIA

▲ Laayoune

MAURITANIA   MALI

100   200   300   400   KMS
0
    100   200   MLS

N

English

Please be aware of the house rules of each hostel. Ask the hostel management for advice. Hostels are located in cities, in the countryside, on the coast and on hills/mountains.

Price range

Price range Dh 30-60. 🗐 🖳.

Rooms and Reservations

R during Jan, Mar, Apr, Jul, Aug, Dec. (¹🛏 ²🛏 ³🛏 ⁶⁺🛏 👬). Reservations via Hostel or National Office by ❶ ❻. (Reservation charges may apply). Smoking rooms are available.

Guests

Membership Card and Passport/Photo ID are required. 👬 welcome. Group bookings via National Office by ❶ (Reservation charges may apply).

Open times

Main hostels: open 🖾, 08:00-10:00hrs, 12:00-23:00hrs. Reception open: 08:00-10:00hrs, 12:00-23:00hrs. Resident manager. **Other hostels:** open 🖾, 08:00-10:00hrs, 12:00-16:00hrs, 18:00-23:00hrs. Resident manager. **Seasonal hostels** are generally open Jan, Mar, Apr, Jun-Aug, Dec.

Meals

🍴 B **R** For 👬. 🍴 Not all utensils provided - check with hostel. Charges may apply.

Travelling around

For ease of travel use 🚌 🚐.

Travel/Activity Packages

Tours/sightseeing, walking/trekking and accommodation/transport packages available. Package bookings via National Office by ❶ ❸.

Passports and Visas

Passport/Photo ID required.

Health

Vaccinations are advised - check with your medical advisor. Emergency medical treatment is free. Medical insurance is recommended.

Français

Prêter attention au réglement interne de chaque auberge. Demandez conseil au Père Aubergiste. Les auberges sont situées dans les villes, à la campagne, sur le littoral et à la montagne.

Tarifs des nuitées

Tarifs des nuitées 30-60 Dh. 🗐 🖳.

Chambres et réservations

R jan, mar, avril, juil, août, déc. (¹🛏 ²🛏 ³🛏 ⁶⁺🛏 👬). Réservations via l'auberge et le Bureau National par ❶ ❻. (Des frais de réservation pourront vous être facturés). Des chambres pour fumeurs sont disponibles.

Usagers

La carte d'adhérent ainsi que le passeport/pièce d'identité avec photo sont à présenter. Accueil des 👬. Réservations pour groupes via le Bureau National par ❶ (Des frais de réservation pourront vous être facturés).

Horaires d'ouverture

Grandes auberges: ouvertes 🖾, entre 8h-10h, 12h-23h. Accueil ouvert entre 8h-10h, 12h-23h. Gérant réside sur place. **Autres auberges:** ouvertes 🖾, entre 8h-10h, 12h-16h, 18h-23h. Gérant réside sur place. **Auberges saisonnières** ouvertes généralement jan, mar, avril, juin-août, déc.

Repas

🍽 B **R** Pour ♦♦♦. ☞ Pas tous les ustensils sont fournis - à vérifier auprès de l'auberge. Une contribution pourra vous être demandée.

Déplacements

Modes de transport recommandés 🚂 🚌.

Forfaits Voyages/Activités

Forfaits circuits touristiques, randonnées pédestres et hébergement/transport disponibles. Réservations des forfaits via le Bureau National par ❶ ❷.

Passeports et visas

Passeport/pièce d'identité avec photo obligatoires.

Santé

Des vaccinations sont conseillées - veuillez vérifier auprès de votre médecin. Soins d'urgence gratuits. Une assurance médicale de voyage est conseillée.

Deutsch

Beachten Sie die Regeln und Bestimmungen für jede Herberge. Fragen Sie den Herbergsleiter um Rat. Herbergen befinden sich in Städten, auf dem Land, an der Küste und in Bergen/Gebirgen.

Preisspanne

Preisspanne 30-60 Dh. 📺 📱.

Zimmer und Reservierungen

R während Jan, Mär, Apr, Jul, Aug, Dez. (🛏 🛏 🛏 🛏 ♦♦♦). Reservierungen über Herberge oder Landesverband per ❶ ❶. (Reservierungskosten könnten anfallen). Es gibt Zimmer für Raucher.

Gäste

Mitgliedsausweis und Reisepass/ Personalausweis sind erforderlich. ♦♦♦ willkommen. Gruppenbuchungen über Landesverband per ❶ (Reservierungskosten könnten anfallen).

Öffnungszeiten

Hauptherbergen: Zugang 📇, 08:00-10:00Uhr, 12:00-23:00Uhr. Rezeption zwischen 08:00-10:00Uhr, 12:00-23:00Uhr. Herbergsmanager wohnt im Haus. **Andere Herbergen:** Zugang 📇, 08:00-10:00Uhr, 12:00-16:00Uhr, 18:00-23:00Uhr. Herbergsmanager wohnt im Haus. **Saison-Herbergen** sind normalerweise Jan, Mär, Apr, Jun-Aug, Dez geöffnet.

Mahlzeiten

🍽 B **R** Für ♦♦♦. ☞ Nicht alle Utensilien werden bereitgestellt - in der Herberge nachfragen. Kosten können anfallen.

Reisen im Land

Reisen ist einfach mit 🚂 🚌.

Reise-/Aktivitäten-Packages

Touren/sightseeing, wandern/trekking und Unterkunft/Transport-Packages erhältlich. Package-Buchungen über Landesverband per ❶ ❷.

Reisepässe und Visa

Reisepass/Personalausweis erforderlich.

Gesundheit

Schutzimpfungen werden empfohlen - mit Ihrem Arzt checken. Nur im Notfall sind medizinische Behandlungen kostenlos. Unfall-/Krankenversicherung wird empfohlen.

Español

Observe las normas internas de cada albergue. Consulte al gerente. Los albergues están situados en las ciudades, el campo, la costa y la montaña.

Tarifas mínima y máxima

Tarifas mínima y máxima 30-60 Dh. .

Habitaciones y Reservas

R en ene, mar, abr, jul, ago, dic. (¹ ² ³ ⁶ ⁺⁺). Reservas a través del albergue o la Asociación Nacional por **❶ ❶**. (Es posible que se aplique un suplemento en concepto de gastos de reserva). Los albergues disponen de habitaciones para fumadores.

Huéspedes

Los huéspedes deben presentar su Carnet de Alberguista y su pasaporte o carnet de identidad. Se admiten ⁺⁺. Reservas de grupo a través de la Asociación Nacional por **❶** (Es posible que se aplique un suplemento en concepto de gastos de reserva).

Horarios y fechas de apertura

Albergues principales - abiertos 🗓, 08:00-10:00h, 12:00-23:00h. Horario de recepción: 08:00-10:00h, 12:00-23:00h.

Gerente residente. **Otros albergues** - abiertos 🗓, 08:00-10:00h, 12:00-16:00h, 18:00-23:00h. Gerente residente. **Albergues de temporada** suelen abrir: ene, mar, abr, jun-ago, dic.

Comidas

🍽 B **R** Para ⁺⁺⁺. 🗝 La cocina no dispone de todos los utensilios - consulte con el albergue. Es posible que se aplique un suplemento por el uso de la misma.

Desplazamientos

Transportes recomendados: 🚂 🚌.

Viajes Combinados con Actividades

Viajes combinados con visitas turísticas, senderismo y alojamiento/transporte. Reserva de viajes combinados a través de la Asociación Nacional por **❶ ❸**.

Pasaportes y Visados

Pasaporte o carnet de identidad obligatorio.

Información Sanitaria

Vacunación recomendada - consulte con su centro médico. Asistencia médica de urgencia gratuita. Seguro médico recomendado.

"Travel only with thy equals or thy betters; if there are none, travel alone."

"Ne voyage qu'avec tes égaux ou tes supérieurs; si tu n'en as pas, voyage tout seul."

„Reise nur mit deinesgleichen oder Höherstehenden; wenn es keine gibt, reise allein."

"Viaja solamente con tus iguales o con tus superiores; si no tienes ninguno, viaja solo."

The Dhammapada

Casablanca

6 Place Abmed Al Bidaoui,
Ville Ancienne,
Casablanca.

☎ (2) 220551
✆ (2) 295587

Open Dates:	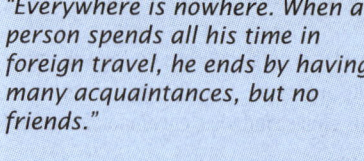
Open Hours:	08.00-10.00hrs; 12.00-23.00hrs
Reservations:	**R**
Price Range:	50.00-70.00DH
Beds:	76 - 4x² 3x³ 2x⁶ 5x⁶ᵗʰ
Facilities:	††† 2x ††† ⊙ (B) ✆ ☎ 🛵 🛌 📺 ⬛1 x 🍴 💼 🔢 ℹ
Directions:	0.35 SW from city centre
🚂	Casa Port 350m
🚌	300m

"Everywhere is nowhere. When a person spends all his time in foreign travel, he ends by having many acquaintances, but no friends."

"Partout est nulle part. Lorsque quelqu'un passe son temps à voyager à l'étranger, il finit avec beaucoup de connaissances, mais sans amis."

„Überall ist nirgendwo. Wenn jemand ständig fremde Länder bereist, hat er letztendlich viele Bekannte, aber keine Freunde."

"Todas partes es ninguna parte. Cuanda una persona dedica todo su tiempo a viajar al extranjero, acaba teniendo muchos conocidos, pero ningún amigo."

Seneca

Location/Address	Telephone No. Fax No.	Beds	Opening Dates	Facilities
△ *Asni* - *Asni Youth Hostel* Route d'Amlil par Marrakech, Asni (Grand Atlas).	☎ (04) 447713	40		
△ *Azrou* - *Azrou Youth Hostel* Route de Midelt, Ifrane, BP 147 (Moyen Atlas).	☎ (05) 563733	40		
▲ **Casablanca** 6 Place Abmed Al Bidaoui, Ville Ancienne, Casablanca.	☎ (2) 220551 ⊕ (2) 295587	76		0.35 SW
△ *Chefchaouen* - *Chaouen Youth Hostel* Pres du Camping Municipal, Chefchaouen.	☎ (09) 986031	30		
△ *El Jadida* - Hostelling International El Jadida Boulevard de la resistance - Zanket London. Près de la Gare Routiere El Jadida.	☎ (212) 01089435	25		
▲ **Fes** 18 Rue Abdeslam Seghrini, Ville Nouvelle, Fes.	☎ (05) 624085	35		
▲ **Laayoune** Laayoune Complexe Sportif, Laayoune, Sakiat Alhamra.	☎ (08) 893402	40		
▲ **Marrakech** Rue El Jahed, Quartier Industriel (near camp site), Marrakech.	☎ (04) 447713	46		
▲ **Mehdya** - Auberge Internationale Mehdya Villa No6, Lotissement Amria, Mehdya Plage.	☎ (7) 388212	35		0.7 E
▲ **Meknès** Boulvard Okba Ben Nafii, Meknès (near Transatlantique Hotel).	☎ (05) 524698	45		
△ *Rabat* 43 Rue Marassa, Bab El Had, Rabat, BP 488 RP Rabat.	☎ (07) 725769	38		
△ *Rissani* - *Rissani Youth Hostel* 107 Hay Moulay Slimane. Près De Souk Rissani.	☎ (05) 575389	25		0.1 S

YOUTH HOSTEL ACCOMMODATION
OUTSIDE THE ASSURED STANDARDS SCHEME

| Tanger 8 rue El Antaki, Av d'Espagne, Tanger. | ☎ (09) 946127 | 35 | | R |

New Zealand

NOUVELLE ZELANDE
NEUSEELAND
NUEVA ZELANDA

Youth Hostels Association of New Zealand Inc
PO Box 436,
Christchurch,
New Zealand.

☏ (64) (3) 3799970
✆ (64) (3) 3654476
e info@yha.org.nz
🖳 www.yha.org.nz

YHA New Zealand National Reservations Centre
PO Box 436,
Christchurch,
New Zealand

☏ (64) (3) 379 9808
✆ (64) (3) 379 4415
e book@yha.org.nz

A copy of the Hostel Directory for this Country can be obtained from:
The National Office

Capital:	Wellington		**Population:**	3,500,000
Language:	English		**Size:**	268,676 sq km
Currency:	NZ$		**Telephone Country Code:**	64

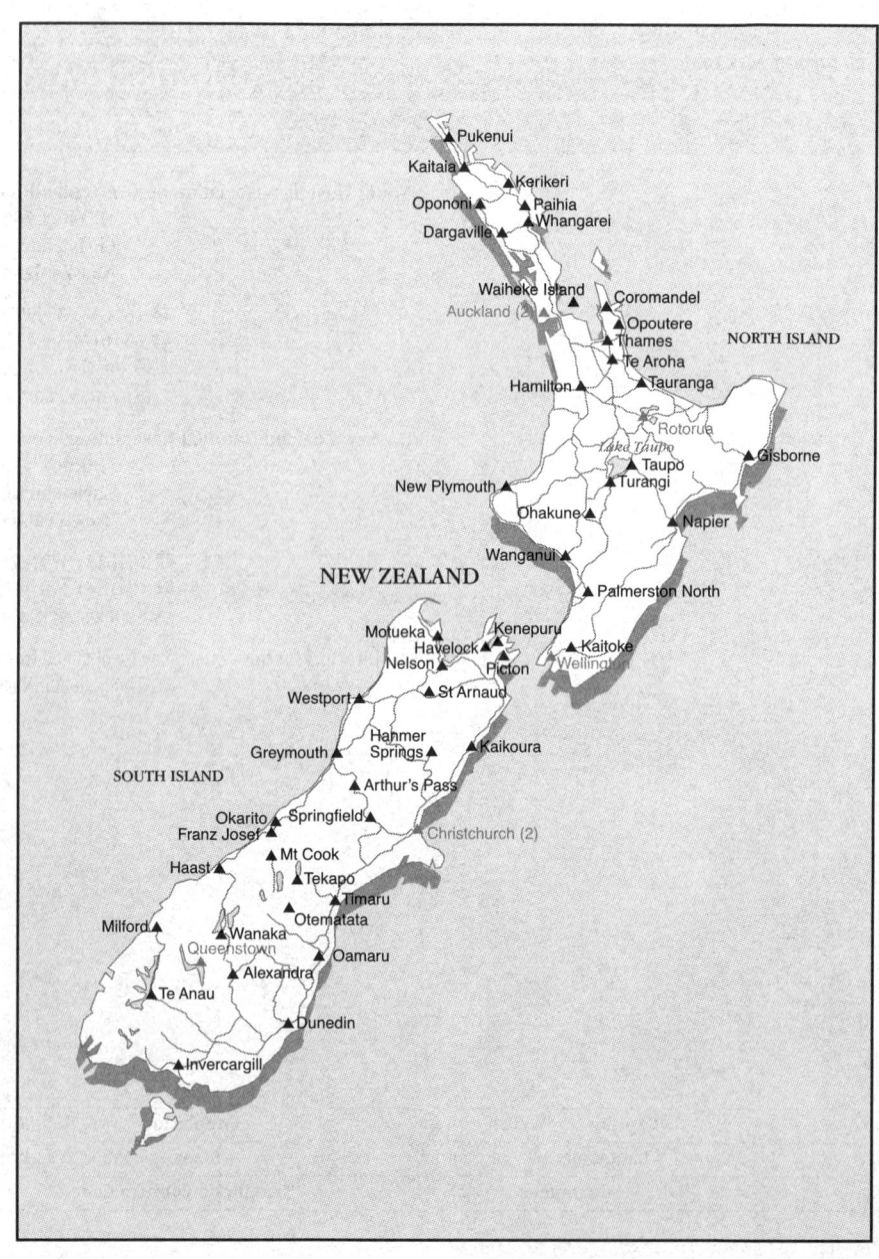

English

Hostels are located in cities, in the countryside, on the coast and on hills/mountains.

Price range

Price range NZ$ 15-25. 🗐.

Rooms and Reservations

🆁 during Jan-Apr, Oct-Dec. (🐏 🐏 🐏 👫). Reservations via 🔲IBN🔲 🖳 National Booking Centre or Hostel by ❶ ❻ ❸. (Reservation charges may apply). Smoking is limited - please check.

Guests

Membership Card is required. Age limits may apply for children - check with hostel. 👫 welcome. Group bookings via 🖳 National Booking Centre or Hostel by ❶ ❻ ❸ (Reservation charges may apply).

Open times

Main hostels: open 🗓, 🕐. Reception open: 08:00-22:00hrs. Resident manager. **Other hostels:** open 🗓, 🕐. Reception open: 08:00-10:00hrs, 17:00-20:00hrs. Resident manager. **Seasonal hostels**: summer hostels open Sep-May, winter hostels open Jun-Oct.

Meals

✆.

Discounts

HI Member Discounts available - see discounts section and www.iyhf.org.

Travelling around

For ease of travel use ✈ 🚌 🚐 Self-Drive.

Travel/Activity Packages

Tours/sightseeing and accommodation/transport packages available. Package bookings via National Booking Centre by ❶ ❻ ❸.

Passports and Visas

Passport and Visa required.

Health

Medical insurance is recommended.

Français

Les auberges sont situées dans les villes, à la campagne, sur le littoral et à la montagne.

Tarifs des nuitées

Tarifs des nuitées 15-25 NZ$. 🗐.

Chambres et réservations

🆁 jan-avril, oct-déc. (🐏 🐏 🐏 👫). Réservations via 🔲IBN🔲 🖳 le Centre National de Réservation ou l'auberge par ❶ ❻ ❸. (Des frais de réservation pourront vous être facturés). Il est permis de fumer dans certaines chambres - veuillez vérifier.

Usagers

La carte d'adhérent est à présenter. Il est possible que des limites d'âge soient en vigueur pour les enfants - vérifiez auprès de l'auberge. Accueil des 👫. Réservations pour groupes via 🖳 le Centre National de Réservation ou l'auberge par ❶ ❻ ❸ (Des frais de réservation pourront vous être facturés).

Horaires d'ouverture

Grandes auberges: ouvertes 🗓, 🕐. Accueil ouvert entre 8h-22h. Gérant réside sur place. **Autres auberges:** ouvertes 🗓, 🕐. Accueil ouvert entre 8h-10h, 17h-20h. Gérant réside sur place. **Auberges saisonnières:** auberges estivales ouvertes sep-mai, auberges hivernales ouvertes juin-oct.

Repas

✆.

Remises

Remises pour les adhérents HI - voir la section "Remises" et notre site: www.iyhf.org.

Déplacements

Modes de transport recommandés ✈ 🚆 🚐 Voiture.

Forfaits Voyages/Activités

Forfaits circuits touristiques et hébergement/ transport disponibles. Réservations des forfaits via le Centre National de Réservation par ❶ ❻ ❺.

Passeports et visas

Passeport et visa obligatoires.

Santé

Une assurance médicale de voyage est conseillée.

Deutsch

Herbergen befinden sich in Städten, auf dem Land, an der Küste und in Bergen/Gebirgen.

Preisspanne

Preisspanne 15-25 NZ$. 🛏.

Zimmer und Reservierungen

❷ während Jan-Apr, Okt-Dez. (²🛏 ³🛏 ⁴🛏 👪). Reservierungen über [IBN] 🖥 Nationales Buchungszentrum oder Herberge per ❶ ❻ ❺. (Reservierungskosten könnten anfallen). Rauchen ist begrenzt - bitte checken.

Gäste

Mitgliedsausweis ist erforderlich. Altersbegrenzungen für Kinder möglich - in der Herberge nachfragen. 👪 willkommen. Gruppenbuchungen über 🖥 Nationales

Buchungszentrum oder Herberge per ❶ ❻ ❺ (Reservierungskosten könnten anfallen).

Öffnungszeiten

Hauptherbergen: Zugang 🖥, 🕐. Rezeption zwischen 08:00-22:00Uhr. Herbergsmanager wohnt im Haus. **Andere Herbergen:** Zugang 🖥, 🕐. Rezeption zwischen 08:00-10:00Uhr, 17:00-20:00Uhr. Herbergsmanager wohnt im Haus. **Saison-Herbergen:** Sommerherbergen sind von Sept-Mai geöffnet. Winterherbergen sind von Jun-Okt geöffnet.

Mahlzeiten

🍴.

Ermäßigungen

HI-Mitgliedsrabatt ist erhältlich – siehe Teil für Rabatte und Ermäßigungen und www.iyhf.org.

Reisen im Land

Reisen ist einfach mit ✈ 🚆 🚐 Selbstfahrer.

Reise-/Aktivitäten-Packages

Touren/sightseeing und Unterkunft/Transport-Packages erhältlich. Package-Buchungen über Nationales Buchungszentrum per ❶ ❻ ❺.

Reisepässe und Visa

Reisepass/Einreisevisum erforderlich.

Gesundheit

Unfall-/Krankenversicherung wird empfohlen.

Español

Los albergues están situados en las ciudades, el campo, la costa y la montaña.

Tarifas mínima y máxima

Tarifas mínima y máxima 15-25 NZ$. 🛏.

Habitaciones y Reservas

R en ene-abr, oct-dic. (🚲 ³🚲 ⁴🚲 ♦♦♦).
Reservas por (IBN) 💻 o a través de la Central
Nacional de Reservas o el albergue por **t** **f**
e. (Es posible que se aplique un suplemento
en concepto de gastos de reserva). Está
permitido fumar sólo en algunas
salas/habitaciones - infórmese.

Huéspedes

Los huéspedes deben presentar su Carnet de
Alberguista. Es posible que exista un límite de
edad para los niños - consulte con el albergue.
Se admiten ♦♦♦. Reservas de grupo por 💻 o a
través de la Central Nacional de Reservas o el
albergue por **t** **f** **e** (Es posible que se
aplique un suplemento en concepto de gastos
de reserva).

Horarios y fechas de apertura

Albergues principales - abiertos 🗓, ⌚.
Horario de recepción: 08:00-22:00h. Gerente
residente. **Otros albergues - abiertos** 🗓, ⌚.
Horario de recepción: 08:00-10:00h,
17:00-20:00h. Gerente residente. **Albergues**

de temporada: albergues de verano abiertos
sep-may; albergues invernales abiertos jun-oct.

Comidas

🍴.

Descuentos

Se conceden descuentos a los miembros de
Hostelling International – véase la sección
sobre descuentos y nuestra página Internet en
www.iyhf.org.

Desplazamientos

Transportes recomendados: ✈ 🚅 🚌
Automóvil.

Viajes Combinados con Actividades

Viajes combinados con visitas turísticas y
alojamiento/transporte. Reserva de viajes
combinados a través de la Central Nacional de
Reservas por **t** **f** **e**.

Pasaportes y Visados

Pasaporte y visado obligatorios.

Información Sanitaria

Seguro médico recomendado.

Auckland -
City

Corner City Rd & Liverpool St,
PO Box 68-149,
Auckland.
t (9) 3092802
f (9) 3735083
e yhaauck@yha.org.nz

Open Dates: 🗓12
Open Hours: 🕐
Reservations: **R** **IBN** **CC**
Price Range: $19-24 🛏
Beds: 158 - 5x¹🛏 56x²🛏 3x³🛏 6x⁴🛏 1x⁶🛏

Facilities: ♿ ♟ 2x ♟ 🍽 (BD) 🛏 ⚙ 🛌 📺 📺 🔲 🖼 🏮 📦 🔖 📷 📧 🌲

Directions: 0.5S from city centre
✈ Auckland International 25km
🚢 Princes Wharf 1km
🚌 Link bus

There are 2 hostels in Auckland. See following pages.

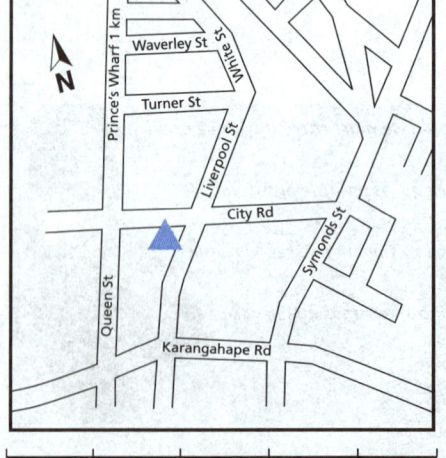

Auckland -
International

5 Turner St,
PO Box 68-149,
Auckland.
t (9) 3028200
f (9) 3028205
e yhaakint@yha.org.nz

Open Dates: 🗓12
Open Hours: 🕐
Reservations: **R** **IBN** **CC**
Price Range: $19-26 🛏
Beds: 160 - 18x²🛏 24x⁴🛏 2x⁶🛏 2x⁶🛏

Facilities: ♿ ♟ 24x ♟ 🛏 ⚙ 🛌 📺 📺 1 x🍽 🔲 🖼 🏮 📦 🔖 📷 🌲

Directions: 0.3S from city centre
✈ Auckland International 25km
🚢 Princes Wharf 1km
🚌 Link bus

Attractions:

There are 2 hostels in Auckland. See following pages.

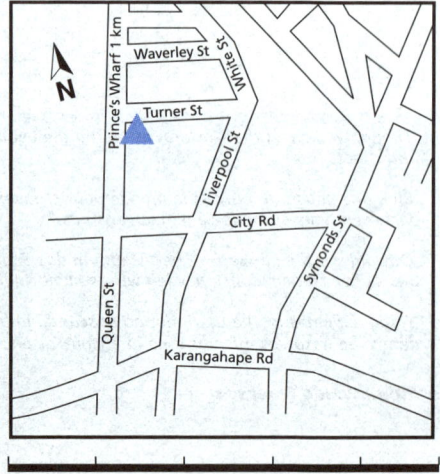

Christchurch -
City Central

273 Manchester St,
Christchurch.
- ☎ (3) 3799535
- ✆ (3) 3799537
- ✉ yhachch@yha.org.nz

Open Dates: 🔲

Open Hours: ⏱

Reservations: Ⓡ ⒾⒷⓃ ⒸⒸ

Price Range: $19-23 🛏

Beds: 131 - 24x² 2x³ 14x⁴ 4x⁵

Facilities: ♿ ⛹ 14x ⛹ ✉ ☼ ⬛ 📺 📷 📱 🗄 📦 🔟 ⬛ Ⓟ Ⓘ 🎽 🏠

Directions: 0.5NE from city centre

✈ Christchurch International 8km

A🚌 Shuttle

🚂 Addington 3km

🚌 Airport Bus 500M, Intercity Bus 300m

There are 2 hostels in Christchurch. See following pages.

Franz Josef

2-4 Cron St,
PO Box 12,
Franz Josef Village.
- ☎ (3) 7520754
- ✆ (3) 7520080
- ✉ yhafzjo@yha.org.nz

Open Dates: 🔲

Open Hours: 08.00-10.00hrs; 16.30-19.00hrs; 20.00-21.30hrs (⏱ guest access)

Reservations: Ⓡ ⒸⒸ

Price Range: $18-20 🛏

Beds: 60 - 5x² 1x³ 7x⁴ 1x⁵ 1x⁶ 1x⁶

Facilities: ⛹ 1x ⛹ ✉ ☼ ⬛ 📺 📷 📱 🔟 Ⓟ Ⓘ 🎽 🏠

Directions:

🚌 InterCity 300m ap YH

Attractions: 🏕 ⛰ 🚶 ∪6km

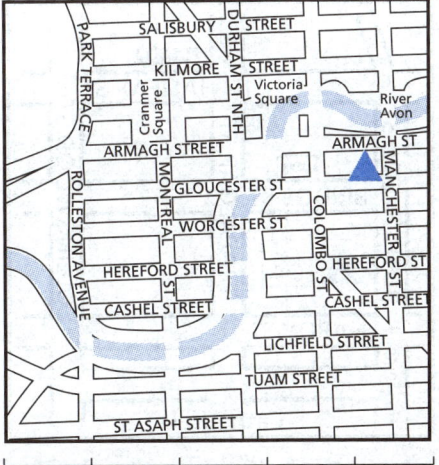

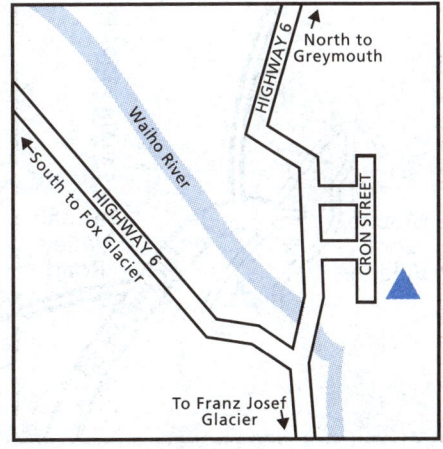

Mount Cook

Corner Bowen & Kitchener Drives,
PO Box 26,
Mount Cook National Park.
t (3) 4351820
f (3) 4351821
e yhamtck@yha.org.nz

Open Dates: 🗓️

Open Hours: 08.00-10.00hrs; 17.00-18.30hrs;
20.00-21.30hrs (🕐 guest access)

Reservations: **R** **CC**

Price Range: $21-29 🍴

Beds: 70 - 7x🛏️ 1x🛏️ 1x🛏️ 6x🛏️

Facilities: ♿ 👫 1x 👫 🚪 ⚙️ 📷 📺 🔲 🖼️
🍳 🔢 **P** ℹ️ ♻️ 🏠

Directions:

✈️ Mt Cook 5.5km

A🚌 Shuttle (drops off and picks up from hostel)

🚌 ap YHA, Newmans, Great Sights and Shuttles

Attractions: 🏌️ ⛰️ 🏊 🎣 🚶 ⛷️25km ⚓200m

Nelson - Central

59 Rutherford St,
Nelson.
t (3) 5459988
f (3) 5459989
e yhanels@yha.org.nz

Open Dates: 🗓️

Open Hours: 08.00-10.00hrs; 15.00-22.00hrs
(🕐 guest access)

Reservations: **R** **CC**

Price Range: $19-22 🍴

Beds: 90 - 1x🛏️ 19x🛏️ 3x🛏️ 5x🛏️
3x🛏️ 1x🛏️

Facilities: ♿ 👫 5x 👫 🚪 ⚙️ 📷 📺 🖼️
1 x🍴 🔲 🖼️ 🍳 🔢 ℹ️ 🖥️ ♻️
🏠

Directions: 0.2W from city centre

✈️ Nelson 7km

A🚌 Supershuttle (to door)

🚌 Central Terminal 100m

Attractions: 🏌️ ⛰️ 📷4.5km 🏊 🚶 ⛷️17km
🚣2km

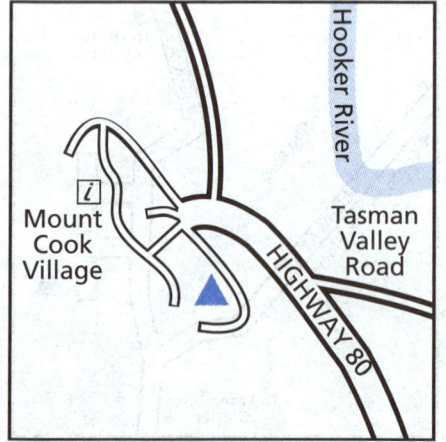

Mount Cook Village
Hooker River
Tasman Valley Road
HIGHWAY 80
0 — 3km

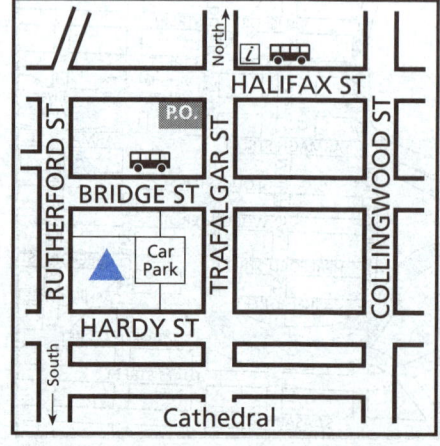

North
HALIFAX ST
P.O.
RUTHERFORD ST
BRIDGE ST
TRAFALGAR ST
COLLINGWOOD ST
Car Park
HARDY ST
South
Cathedral
0 — 500m

Queenstown

88-90 Lake Esplanade,
Queenstown.
- ☎ (3) 4428413
- 🖷 (3) 4426561
- 🅔 yhaqutn@yha.org.nz

Open Dates: 🗓

Open Hours: 06.30-22.00hrs (🕒 guest access)

Reservations: **R** **IBN** **CC**

Price Range: $19-23 🛏

Beds: 144 - 20x² 4x³ 4x⁴ 1x⁵
4x⁶ 6x⁶

Facilities: ♿ 👬 4x 👬 🛏 ⚙ 🏘 📺 🧺
🗄 🖼 🍴 🔢 🅿 📋 🏧 ⛪

Directions: 1W from city centre

✈ Queenstown 10km

A🚌 Airport Shuttle 1km

🚌 Intercity ap YH

Attractions: ⛳ ⛰ 🔍50m 🚣1620m 🎿 🏃
∪6km ≈50m

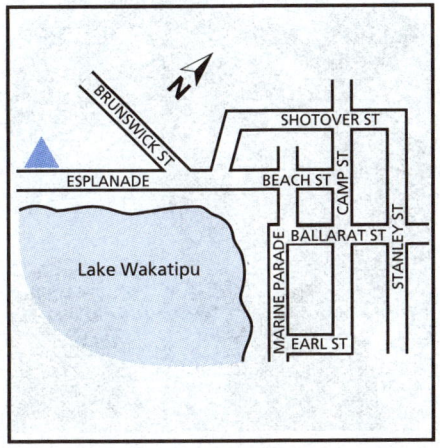

Rotorua - KiwiPaka

60 Tarewa Rd,
PO Box 905,
Rotorua.
- ☎ (7) 3470931
- 🖷 (7) 3463167
- 🅔 stay@kiwipaka-yha.co.nz

Open Dates: 🗓

Open Hours: 07.30-21.30hrs (🕒 guest access)

Reservations: **R** **IBN** **CC**

Price Range: $18-21 🛏

Beds: 120 - 27x² 6x⁴ 4x⁵

Facilities: ♿ 👬 10x 👬 🍴 (BD) 🛏 ☕
🏘 📺 🧺1 x🍷 🗄 🖼 🍴 🅿
📋 🏧 🌿 ⛪

Directions: 1N from city centre

✈ Rotorua 10km

🚌 Rotorua 750m

🚌 Courtesy Bus ap YHA

Attractions: ⛳ 🏃 ≈

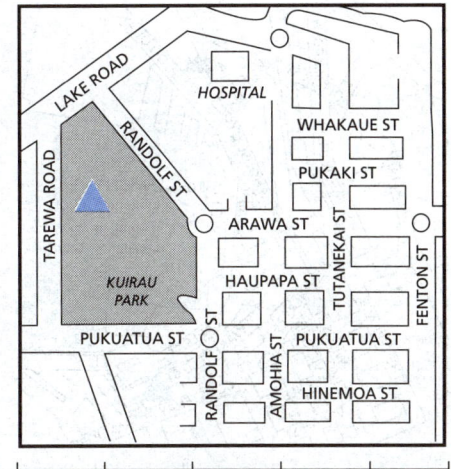

Wellington - City

292 Wakefield St (Cnr Cambridge
Terrace),
Wellington.
- ☎ (4) 8017280
- ✆ (4) 8017278
- ✉ yhawgtn@yha.org.nz

Open Dates: 🗓

Open Hours: 07.00-22.30hrs (🕐 guest access)

Reservations: **R**   IBN   CC

Price Range: $20-23 🛏

Beds: 118 - 3x^2🛏 17x^4🛏 4x^5🛏 4x^6🛏

Facilities: 👬 2x 👬 ☕ ⚙ 🏢 TV 🎮 🗑
🖼 ♿ 8 💲 ✏ 🧺 🏠

Directions: 1W from city centre

✈	Wellington 15km
A🚌	Shuttle (to door)
⛴	Inter-Islander Ferry Terminal 5km
🚃	Wellington 3km
🚌	InterCity; Newmans 3km

Attractions: ⛳ ⛰ 📷 1km 🚶 ⚲ 3km ⛵ 1km

"Certainly, travel is more than the seeing of sights; it is a change that goes on, deep and permanent, in the ideas of living."

"Il est certain que le voyage, c'est plus que la simple visite des sites touristiques; c'est un changement en continu, profond et permanent, sur l'idée que nous nous faisons de la vie."

"Gewiss ist Reisen mehr als Sehenswürdigkeiten anschauen; es findet eine tiefe und bleibende Veränderung der Lebensansichten statt."

"No cabe duda que viajar es más que hacer turismo; es un cambio continuo, profundo y permanente, en el concepto que tenemos de la vida"

Miriam Beard

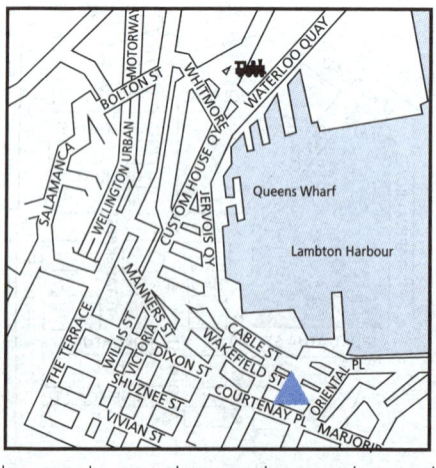

0   1.5km

Location/Address	Telephone No. Fax No.	Beds	Opening Dates	Facilities
▲ **Alexandra (Assoc)** - Two Bob Backpackers 4 Dunorling St, Alexandra. ⊖ twobobs@xtra.co.nz	☎ (3) 4488152 ✆ (3) 4488152	32	🔳12	⚲ P 🔲
▲ **Arthurs Pass** - Sir Arthur Dudley Dobson YH Main Rd, Arthurs Pass.	☎ (3) 3189230 ✆ (3) 3189230	22	🔳12	♦♦♦ ECC ⚲ P 🔲
▲ **Auckland** - City IBN **Corner City Rd & Liverpool St, PO Box 68-149, Auckland.** ⊖ yhaauck@yha.org.nz	☎ (9) 3092802 ✆ (9) 3735083	158	🔳12	♦♦♦ 🍴 R 0.5S ♿ ECC ⚲ 🔲 ☼
▲ **Auckland** - International IBN **5 Turner St, PO Box 68-149, Auckland.** ⊖ yhaakint@yha.org.nz	☎ (9) 3028200 ✆ (9) 3028205	160	🔳12	♦♦♦ R 0.3S ♿ ECC ⚲ 🔲 ☼
▲ **Christchurch** - Rolleston House YH IBN 5 Worcester Blvd (Corner Rolleston Ave), Christchurch. ⊖ yhachrl@yha.org.nz	☎ (3) 3666564 ✆ (3) 3655589	56	🔳12	♦♦♦ 0.5S ECC ⚲ P 🔲 ☼
▲ **Christchurch** - City Central IBN **273 Manchester St, Christchurch.** ⊖ yhachch@yha.org.nz	☎ (3) 3799535 ✆ (3) 3799537	131	🔳12	♦♦♦ R 0.5NE ♿ ECC ⚲ P 🔲 ☼
▲ **Coromandel (Assoc)** - Tidewater Hostel 270 Tiki Rd, Coromandel.	☎ (7) 8668888 ✆ (7) 8667231	20	🔳12	♦♦♦ ♿ ECC ⚲ P 🔲
▲ **Dargaville (Assoc)** - Greenhouse Backpackers 13 Portland St, Dargaville.	☎ (9) 4396342 ✆ (9) 4396327	22	🔳12	⚲ P 🔲
▲ **Dunedin** - Stafford Gables YH 71 Stafford St, Dunedin. ⊖ yhadndn@yha.org.nz	☎ (3) 4741919 ✆ (3) 4741919	61	🔳12	♦♦♦ 1 SW ECC ⚲ P 🔲 ☼
▲ **Franz Josef** **2-4 Cron St, PO Box 12, Franz Josef Village.** ⊖ yhafzjo@yha.org.nz	☎ (3) 7520754 ✆ (3) 7520080	60	🔳12	♦♦♦ R ECC ⚲ P 🔲 ☼
▲ **Gisborne (Assoc)** 32 Harris St, Gisborne. ⊖ yha.gisborne@clear.net.nz	☎ (6) 8673269 ✆ (6) 8673296	43	🔳12	♦♦♦ ECC ⚲ P 🔲
▲ **Greymouth** - Kainga-ra YH 15 Alexander St, Greymouth. ⊖ yhagymth@yha.org.nz	☎ (3) 7684951 ✆ (3) 7684941	41	🔳12	♦♦♦ ♿ ECC ⚲ P 🔲 ☼
▲ **Haast (Assoc)** - Haast Highway Accommodation Marks Rd, Haast.	☎ (3) 7500703 ✆ (3) 7500718	43	🔳12	♦♦♦ ECC ⚲ P 🔲
▲ **Hamilton** - Helen Heywood YH 1190 Victoria St, Hamilton.	☎ (7) 8380009 ✆ (7) 8380837	23	🔳12	♦♦♦ ECC ⚲ P 🔲
▲ **Hanmer Springs (Assoc)** - Forest Camp 300 Jollies Pass Rd, Hanmer Springs. ⊖ hanmer.forest.camp@xtra.co.nz	☎ (3) 3157202 ✆ (3) 3157202	160	🔳12	♦♦♦ 2.5NW ♿ ECC ⚲ P 🔲

Location/Address	Telephone No. Fax No.	Beds	Opening Dates	Facilities
▲ **Havelock** - Rutherford YH 46 Main Rd, Havelock.	☏ (3) 5742104 🖷 (3) 5742109	36	01.10–12.05	♠♦ ☂ 🅿 ⬚
▲ **Invercargill** 122 North Rd, Waikiwi, Invercargill.	☏ (3) 2159344 🖷 (3) 2159382	34	🗓	♠♦ ⊂CC⊃ ☂ 🅿 ⬚ ✿
▲ **Kaikoura** - Maui YH 270 Esplanade, Kaikoura. ✉ yhakaikr@yha.org.nz	☏ (3) 3195931 🖷 (3) 3196921	40	🗓	♠♦ ♿ ⊂CC⊃ ☂ 🅿 ⬚
▲ **Kaitaia (Assoc)** - Hike & Bike YH 160 Commerce St, Kaitaia.	☏ (9) 4081840 🖷 (9) 4081840	35	🗓	♠♦ ☂ 🅿 ⬚ ✿
▲ **Kerikeri** 144 Kerikeri Rd, Kerikeri, Bay of Islands.	☏ (9) 4079391 🖷 (9) 4079328	32	🗓	♠♦ ⊂CC⊃ ☂ 🅿 ⬚ ✿
△ *Kenepuru - Mary's Holiday Cottage* *RD2, Waitaria Bay, Kenepuru Sound,* *Marlborough Sounds.*	☏ (3) 5734660	*5*	🗓	Ⓡ ☂ 🅿 ⬚
▲ **Milford (Assoc)** - "Milford Wanderer" Boat Milford Harbour, Milford Sound. ✉ info@fiordlandtravel.co.nz	☏ (3) 2497416 🖷 (3) 2497022	61	🗓	♠♦ 🍽 ⊂CC⊃
▲ **Motueka (Assoc)** - Bakers Lodge 4 Poole St, Motueka. ✉ bakers@motueka.co.nz	☏ (3) 5280102 🖷 (3) 5280103	67	🗓	♠♦ ♿ ⊂CC⊃ ☂ 🅿 ⬚
▲ **Mount Cook** **Corner Bowen & Kitchener Drives,** **PO Box 26, Mount Cook National Park.** ✉ yhamtck@yha.org.nz	☏ (3) 4351820 🖷 (3) 4351821	70	🗓	♠♦ Ⓡ ♿ ⊂CC⊃ ☂ 🅿 ⬚ ✿
▲ **Napier** 277 Marine Pde, Napier. ✉ yhanapr@yha.org.nz	☏ (6) 8357039 🖷 (6) 8354641	44	🗓	♠♦ ⊂CC⊃ ☂ ⬚ ✿
▲ **Nelson** - Central **59 Rutherford St, Nelson.** ✉ yhanels@yha.org.nz	☏ (3) 5459988 🖷 (3) 5459989	90	🗓	♠♦ Ⓡ 0.2W ♿ ⊂CC⊃ ☂ ⬚ ✿
▲ **New Plymouth (Assoc)** - Egmont Lodge 12 Clawton St, New Plymouth. ✉ egmontlodge@taranaki-bakpak.co.nz	☏ (6) 7535720 🖷 (6) 7535782	30	🗓	♠♦ ☂ 🅿 ⬚
▲ **Oamaru** - Red Kettle YH Corner Reed & Cross Streets, Oamaru.	☏ (3) 4345008 🖷 (3) 4345008	19	01.10–31.05	♠♦ ⊂CC⊃ ☂ ⬚
▲ **Ohakune** 15 Clyde St, Ohakune.	☏ (6) 3858724 🖷 (6) 3858724	30	01.06–31.10	♠♦ ⊂CC⊃ ☂ 🅿 ⬚
△ *Okarito (Assoc)* *PO Box 24, Whataroa, South Westland.*	☏ *(3) 7534124*	*10*	🗓	☂ 🅿
▲ **Opononi (Assoc)** - Okopako Lodge Mountain Rd, South Hokianga.	☏ (9) 4058815 🖷 (9) 4058815	20	🗓	♠♦ ♿ ⊂CC⊃ ☂ 🅿 ⬚
▲ **Opoutere** 389 Opoutere Rd, Opoutere.	☏ (7) 8659072 🖷 (7) 8656172	36	🗓	♠♦ ⊂CC⊃ ☂ 🅿 ⬚
▲ **Otematata (Assoc)** - Country Inn 11-12 Rata Drive, Otematata.	☏ (3) 4387797 🖷 (3) 4387792	28	🗓	♠♦ 🍽 ☂ 🅿 ⬚ ●

Location/Address	Telephone No. Fax No.	Beds	Opening Dates	Facilities
▲ **Paihia (Assoc)** - Lodge Eleven Cnr Kings Rd and MacMurray Rd, Paiha, Bay of Islands.	❶ (9) 4027487 ❷ (9) 4027487	49	🔲12	⌷CC⌷ ⚐ P 🔲 ✳
▲ **Palmerston North (Assoc)** - Pepper Tree Hostel 121 Grey St, Palmerston North. ℮ peppertreehostel@clear.net.nz	❶ (6) 3554054 ❷ (6) 3554063	35	🔲12	⚑ ⚐ P 🔲
▲ **Picton (Assoc)** - Wedgwood House 10 Dublin St, Picton. ℮ wedgwoodhouse@xtra.co.nz	❶ (3) 5737797 ❷ (3) 5736426	35	🔲12	⚑ ⌷CC⌷ ⚐ P 🔲
▲ **Pukenui (Assoc)** Cnr State Hwy 1 & Wharf Rd, Houhora, RD4, Kaitaia. ℮ pukenui@igrin.co.nz	❶ (09) 4098837 ❷ (09) 4098704	16	🔲12	⚑ ⌷CC⌷ ⚐ P 🔲
▲ **Queenstown** ⌷IBN⌷ **88-90 Lake Esplanade, Queenstown.** ℮ yhaqutn@yha.org.nz	❶ (3) 4428413 ❷ (3) 4426561	144	🔲12	⚑ ⌷R⌷ ⌷1W⌷ ♿ ⌷CC⌷ ⚐ P 🔲 ✿
▲ **Rotorua** - KiwiPaka ⌷IBN⌷ **60 Tarewa Rd, PO Box 905, Rotorua.** ℮ stay@kiwipaka-yha.co.nz	❶ (7) 3470931 ❷ (7) 3463167	120	🔲12	⚑ ⌷◎⌷ ⌷R⌷ ⌷1N⌷ ♿ ⌷CC⌷ ⚐ 🔲 ☕
▲ **Springfield (Assoc)** - Smylie's Accommodation Main Rd, Springfield. ℮ stay@smylies.co.nz	❶ (3) 3184740 ❷ (3) 3184780	40	🔲12	⚑ ♿ ⌷CC⌷ ⚐ P 🔲
▲ **St Arnaud (Assoc)** - The Yellow House Main Rd, St Arnaud, Nelson Lakes National Park.	❶ (3) 5211887 ❷ (3) 5211882	42	🔲12	⚑ ⌷CC⌷ ⚐ P 🔲
▲ **Taupo (Assoc)** - Action Down Under Hostel 56 Kaimanawa St (Corner Tamamutu St), Taupo.	❶ (7) 3783311 ❷ (7) 3789612	70	🔲12	⚑ ♿ ⌷CC⌷ ⚐ P 🔲 ✿
▲ **Tauranga** 171 Elizabeth St, Tauranga. ℮ yhataur@yha.org.nz	❶ (7) 5785064 ❷ (7) 5785040	29	🔲12	⚑ ⌷CC⌷ ⚐ P 🔲 ✿
▲ **Te Anau** 29 Mokonui St, Te Anau. ℮ yhatanau@yha.org.nz	❶ (3) 2497847 ❷ (3) 2497823	74	🔲12	⚑ ⌷CC⌷ ⚐ P 🔲 ✿
△ *Te Aroha* *Miro St, Te Aroha.*	❶ *(7) 8848739*	*12*	🔲12	⚑ ⚐ P 🔲
▲ **Tekapo** 3 Simpson Lane, Lake Tekapo.	❶ (3) 6806857 ❷ (3) 6806664	30	🔲12	⚑ ⌷CC⌷ ⚐ P 🔲
▲ **Thames (Assoc)** - Dickson Holiday Park Victoria St, Thames. ℮ yha@dicksonpark.co.nz	❶ (7) 8687308 ❷ (7) 8687319	38	🔲12	⚑ ⌷CC⌷ ⚐ P 🔲
▲ **Timaru (Assoc)** - Timaru Backpackers 44 Evans St, Timaru.	❶ (3) 6845067 ❷ (3) 6845706	35	🔲12	⚑ ⌷CC⌷ ⚐ P 🔲
▲ **Turangi (Assoc)** - Club Habitat 25 Ohuanga Rd, Turangi.	❶ (7) 3867492 ❷ (7) 3860106	173	🔲12	⚑ ⌷CC⌷ ⚐ P 🔲

Location/Address	Telephone No. Fax No.	Beds	Opening Dates	Facilities
▲ **Waiheke Island (Assoc)** - Onetangi YH Seaview Rd, Onetangi, Waiheke Island. e robb.meg@bigfoot.com	t (9) 3728971 f (9) 3728971	43	12	CC P
▲ **Wanaka** 181 Upton St, Wanaka. e yhawnka@yha.org.nz	t (3) 4437405 f (3) 4437405	37	12	CC P
▲ **Wanganui (Assoc)** - Riverside Inn 2 Plymouth St, Wanganui.	t (6) 3472529 f (6) 3472529	20	12	CC P
▲ **Wellington** - City IBN **292 Wakefield St** **(Cnr Cambridge Terrace), Wellington.** e yhawgtn@yha.org.nz	t (4) 8017280 f (4) 8017278	118	12	R 1W CC
△ ***Wellington-Kaitoke*** - *The Black Stump YH* *Marchant Rd, (Cnr SH2), Kaitoke,* *Upper Hutt. (46km N Wellington).*	t *(4) 5264626*	*20*	12	P
▲ **Westport (Assoc)** - Marg's Travellers Rest 56 Russell St, Westport. e margstr@xtra.co.nz	t (3) 7898627 f (3) 7898396	52	12	CC P
▲ **Whangarei** 52 Punga Grove Ave, Whangarei. e yhawhang@yha.org.nz	t (9) 4388954 f (9) 4389525	27	12	CC P

"The true traveler is he who goes on foot, and even then, he sits down a lot of the time."

"Le vrai voyageur est celui qui va à pied, et encore, il s'assoit une grande partie du temps."

„Der wahre Reisende ist derjenige, der zu Fuß geht, und selbst dann setzt er sich sehr häufig nieder."

"El verdadero viajero es el que va a pie, y aun así pasa mucho tiempo sentado."

Colette

Pakistan

PAKISTAN

PAKISTAN

PAKISTAN

Pakistan Youth Hostels Association,
Shaheed-e-Millat Road, (Near Akhbar Market), Aabparà,
Sector G-6/4, Islamabad, Pakistan.

t (92) (51) 2826899
f (92) (51) 2826899
e pyha@comsats.net.pk

A copy of the Hostel Directory for this Country can be obtained from:
The National Office.

Capital:	Islamabad	**Population:**	131,600,000
Language:	Urdu/English	**Size:**	803,943 sq km
Currency:	Rs (rupee)	**Telephone Country Code:**	92

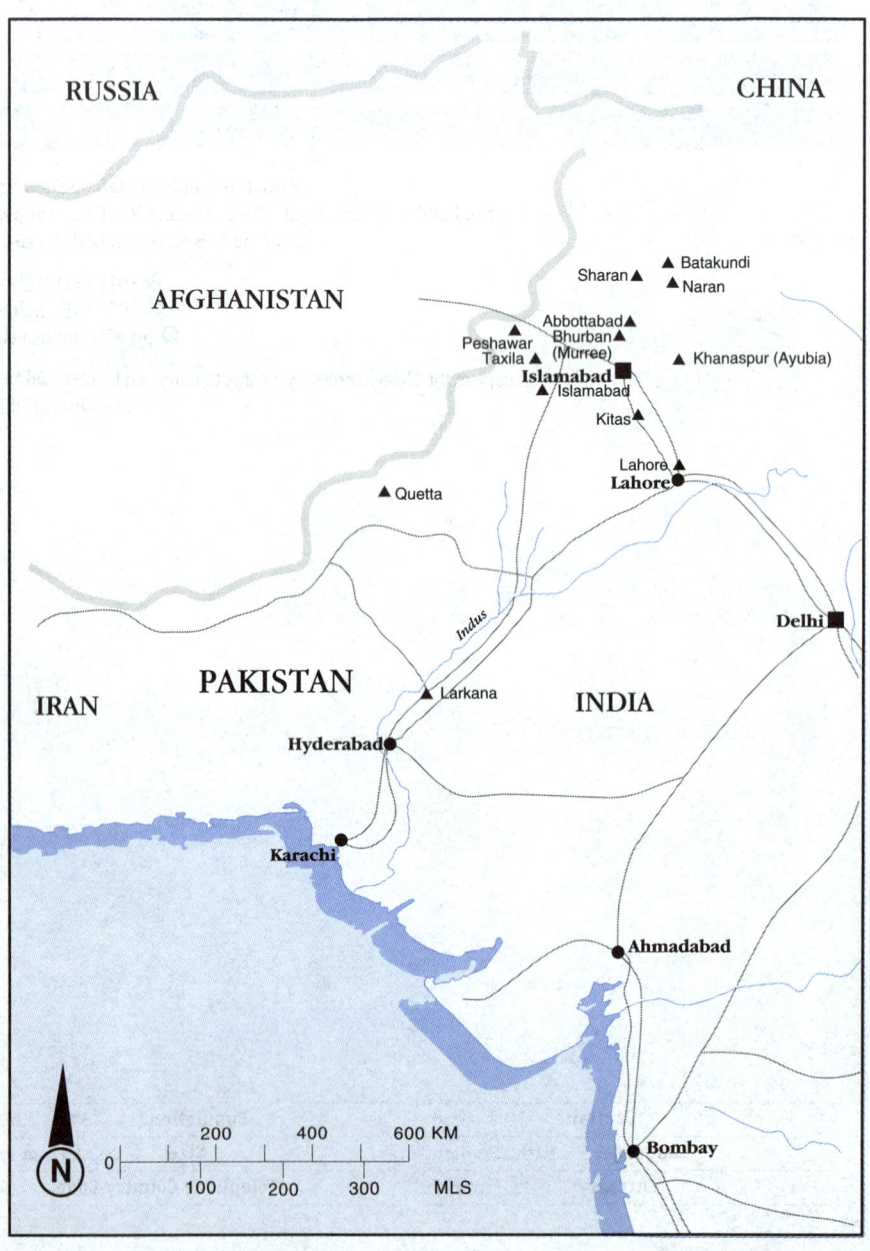

RUSSIA   CHINA

AFGHANISTAN   Sharan ▲   ▲ Batakundi
                                                       ▲ Naran

                                    Abbottabad▲
                          Peshawar   Bhurban ▲
                          Taxila ▲   (Murree)   ▲ Khanaspur (Ayubia)
                          ■ Islamabad
                          ▲ Islamabad
                             Kitas

                                              Lahore ▲
                          ▲ Quetta   Lahore ●

                                                                    Delhi ■
                                         Indus

IRAN   PAKISTAN   INDIA
                          ▲ Larkana

        Hyderabad ●

        Karachi ●

                          Ahmadabad ●

N
          200   400   600 KM
      0
          100   200   300   MLS

                          Bombay ●

English

Hostels are located in cities, in the countryside and on hills/mountains.

Price range

Price range US$ 1.35. 🛏 Sheet sleeping bag required.

Rooms and Reservations

R during May-Jul, Dec. (🚗 ⁶🚗 👬). Reservations via National Office by ☎ 🅴. Smoking is limited - please check.

Guests

Membership Card and Passport/Photo ID are required. The maximum stay is 7 days. Age limits may apply for adults and mixed age groups - check with hostel. 👬 welcome. Group bookings via National Office by ☎ 🅴.

Open times

Main hostels: open 🗓, 09:00-22:00hrs. Reception open: 09:00-12:00hrs, 15:00-20:00hrs. Resident manager. **Other hostels:** open May-Nov, 09:00-20:00hrs. Reception open: 09:00-12:00hrs, 15:00-20:00hrs. Resident manager. **Seasonal hostels** are generally open Jun-Oct.

Meals

🍽 B **R** For individuals. 🍴.

Travelling around

For ease of travel use ✈ 🚂 🚌 Self-Drive. Special jeeps may be hired in hilly areas.

Travel/Activity Packages

Tours/sightseeing, cycling/mountain biking, walking/trekking and accommodation/transport packages available. Package bookings via National Office by ☎ 🅴.

Passports and Visas

Passport and Visa required.

Health

Vaccinations are required - check with your medical advisor. Emergency medical treatment is free.

Français

Les auberges sont situées dans les villes, à la campagne et à la montagne.

Tarifs des nuitées

Tarifs des nuitées 1.35 US$. 🛏 Sac-drap obligatoire.

Chambres et réservations

R mai-juil, déc. (🚗 ⁶🚗 👬). Réservations via le Bureau National par ☎ 🅴. Il est permis de fumer dans certaines chambres - veuillez vérifier.

Usagers

La carte d'adhérent ainsi que le passeport/pièce d'identité avec photo sont à présenter. La durée maximale du séjour est de 7 jours. Il est possible que des limites d'âge soient en vigueur pour les adultes et les groupes d'âges mixtes - vérifier auprès de l'auberge. Accueil des 👬. Réservations pour groupes via le Bureau National par ☎ 🅴.

Horaires d'ouverture

Grandes auberges: ouvertes 🗓, entre 9h-22h. Accueil ouvert entre 9h-12h, 15h-20h. Gérant réside sur place. **Autres auberges:** ouvertes mai-nov, entre 9h-20h. Accueil ouvert entre 9h-12h, 15h-20h. Gérant réside sur place. **Auberges saisonnières** ouvertes généralement juin-oct.

Repas

†◎† B ⓡ Pour individuels. ☎.

Déplacements

Modes de transport recommandés ✈ 🚆
🚐 Voiture. Il est possible de louer des jeeps spéciales à la montagne.

Forfaits Voyages/Activités

Forfaits circuits touristiques, cyclotourisme/VTT, randonnées pédestres et hébergement/transport disponibles. Réservations des forfaits via le Bureau National par ☎ ✉.

Passeports et visas

Passeport et visa obligatoires.

Santé

Des vaccinations sont obligatoires - veuillez vérifier auprès de votre médecin. Soins d'urgence gratuits.

Deutsch

Herbergen befinden sich in Städten, auf dem Land und in Bergen/Gebirgen.

Preisspanne

Preisspanne 1.35 US$. ⬚ Leinenschlafsack erforderlich.

Zimmer und Reservierungen

ⓡ während Mai-Jul, Dez. (🚾 ⁶🚾 👫).
Reservierungen über Landesverband per ☎
✉. Rauchen ist begrenzt - bitte checken.

Gäste

Mitgliedsausweis und Reisepass/
Personalausweis sind erforderlich. Der maximale Aufenthalt beträgt 7 Tage.
Altersbegrenzungen für Erwachsene & Gruppen gemischten Alters möglich - in der Herberge nachfragen. 👫 willkommen.

Gruppenbuchungen über die Landesverband per ☎ ✉.

Öffnungszeiten

Hauptherbergen: Zugang 🔟,
09:00-22:00Uhr. Rezeption zwischen
09:00-12:00Uhr, 15:00-20:00Uhr.
Herbergsmanager wohnt im Haus. **Andere Herbergen:** Zugang zwischen Mai-Nov,
09:00-20:00Uhr. Rezeption zwischen
09:00-12:00Uhr, 15:00-20:00Uhr.
Herbergsmanager wohnt im Haus.
Saison-Herbergen sind normalerweise Jun-Okt geöffnet.

Mahlzeiten

†◎† B ⓡ Für Einzelreisende. ☎.

Reisen im Land

Reisen ist einfach mit ✈ 🚆 🚐
Selbstfahrer. Geländewagen können in bergigen Gegenden gemietet werden.

Reise-/Aktivitäten-Packages

Touren/sightseeing, Fahrrad/Mountainbiking, wandern/trekking und Unterkunft/Transport packages erhältlich. Package-Buchungen über Landesverband per ☎ ✉.

Reisepässe und Visa

Reisepass/Einreisevisum erforderlich.

Gesundheit

Schutzimpfungen sind erforderlich - mit Ihrem Arzt checken. Nur im Notfall sind medizinische Behandlungen kostenlos.

Español

Los albergues están situados en las ciudades, el campo y la montaña.

Tarifas mínima y máxima

Tarifas mínima y máxima 1.35 US$. 🛏 Saco sábana imprescindible.

Habitaciones y Reservas

🅡 en may-jul, dic. (🐖 🐖 ♀♀). Reservas a través de la Asociación Nacional por ❶ ❷. Está permitido fumar sólo en algunas salas/habitaciones - infórmese.

Huéspedes

Los huéspedes deben presentar su Carnet de Alberguista y su pasaporte o carnet de identidad. La estancia máxima es de 7 días. Es posible que exista un límite de edad para los adultos y los grupos de personas de diferentes edades - consulte con el albergue. Se admiten ♀♀. Reservas de grupo a través de la Asociación Nacional por ❶ ❷.

Horarios y fechas de apertura

Albergues principales - abiertos 🗓, 09:00-22:00h. Horario de recepción: 09:00-12:00h, 15:00-20:00h. Gerente residente. **Otros albergues** - abiertos may-nov, 09:00-20:00h. Horario de recepción: 09:00-12:00h, 15:00-20:00h. Gerente residente. **Albergues de temporada** suelen abrir: jun-oct.

Comidas

🍽 B 🅡 Para individuales. ☂.

Desplazamientos

Transportes recomendados: ✈ 🚃 🚐 Automóvil. Se puede alquiler jeeps especiales en las zonas de montaña.

Viajes Combinados con Actividades

Viajes combinados con visitas turísticas, cicloturismo/bicicleta de montaña, senderismo y alojamiento/transporte. Reserva de viajes combinados a través de la Asociación Nacional por ❶ ❷.

Pasaportes y Visados

Pasaporte y visado obligatorios.

Información Sanitaria

Vacunación obligatoria - consulte con su centro médico. Asistencia médica de urgencia gratuita.

"Sloth makes all things difficult, but industry, all things easy. He that rises late must trot all day, and shall scarce overtake his business at night, while laziness travels so slowly that poverty soon overtakes him."

"La paresse rend tout difficile alors que l'industrie tout facile. Celui qui se lève tard doit courir partout, et aura du mal à dépasser son travail en fin de journée, tandis que la paresse voyage si lentement que la pauvreté aura tôt fait de le dépasser."

„Trägheit macht alle Dinge schwierig, aber Fleiß alle Dinge einfach. Derjenige, der spät aufsteht, muss den ganzen Tag traben und wird selten seine Aufgaben bis zum Abend erledigt haben, wobei Faulheit sich so langsam bewegt, dass Armut ihn bald überholt."

"La indolencia lo hace todo difícil, mientras que la industria, todo fácil. El que se levanta tarde tiene que pasarse todo el día corriendo, y apenas si ha logrado adelantar su trabajo por la noche, en tanto que la pereza viaja tan lentamente que la pobreza tarda poco en adelantarle."

Benjamin Franklin

Location/Address	Telephone No. Fax No.	Beds	Opening Dates	Facilities
▲ **Abbottabad** - Viqar un Nisa Hostel 4.8km N of town on rd to Balakot (Mansehra Rd): Mandian Stop near Burn Hall School and Government Degree College.	✆ (92) 9925664	80		⑆ ☌
△ *Bhurban (Murree)* Opposite Pearl Continental Hotel, 12.8km from Murree.		32		⑆ ☌
▲ **Islamabad** Adjoining Akhbar Market, Shaheed-e-Millat Rd, Aabpara, Sector G-6/4, Islamabad. ✉ pyha@comsats.net.pk	✆ (51) 2826899 ✆ (51) 2826899	100		⑆ ☌
▲ **Khanaspur (Ayubia)** 27km from Murree on Murree-Abbottabad Rd (rd junction at Kooza Gali, 24km from Murree).	✆ (593) 355111	32	01.04–25.12	⑆ ☌
▲ **Lahore** 110-B-3, Gulberg-III, near Firdaus Market.	✆ (42) 5873612	100		⑆ ☌
▲ **Larkana** - Larkana Hostel Khorro Stadium, Larkana.	✆ (941) 440239	50		⑆ ☌ 🅿 🖸 ☃
▲ **Naran** 3km before the Naran Village; on the right side of the main rd from Balakot.		32	01.06–15.10	☌
▲ **Peshawar** Plot No 37, Block B/1, Phase V, Jamrod Rd, Hayatabad.	✆ (91) 824740	50		⑆ ☌
△ *Quetta* Inside Ayub Stadium, Chaman Phatik, Quetta.		50		⑆ ☌
△ *Sharan* Post Office, Paras, Kaghan Valley: 11km from Paras, YH on left after crossing River Kunhar.		25	01.06–15.10	☌
▲ **Taxila** Near Taxila Museum.	✆ (51) 4507	35		⑆ ☌

YOUTH HOSTEL ACCOMMODATION
OUTSIDE THE ASSURED STANDARDS SCHEME

Batakundi 17.6km from Naran.		25	01.06–15.10	☌
Kitas 1.6km from Choa Saiden Shah on Choa Saiden Shah-Kalar Kahar Rd, District Chakwal.		35		☌

Peru

PEROU
PERU
PERU

Asociación Peruana de Albergues Turísticos Juveniles,
Avda Casimiro Ulloa 328, San Antonio,
Miraflores, Lima 18,
Peru.

t (51) (1) 2423068
f (51) (1) 4448187
e hostell@terra.com.pe

A copy of the Hostel Directory for this Country can be obtained from:
The National Office

Capital:	Lima	**Population:**	23,834,000
Language:	Spanish	**Size:**	1,285,215 sq km
Currency:	S/. (Sol)	**Telephone Country Code:**	51

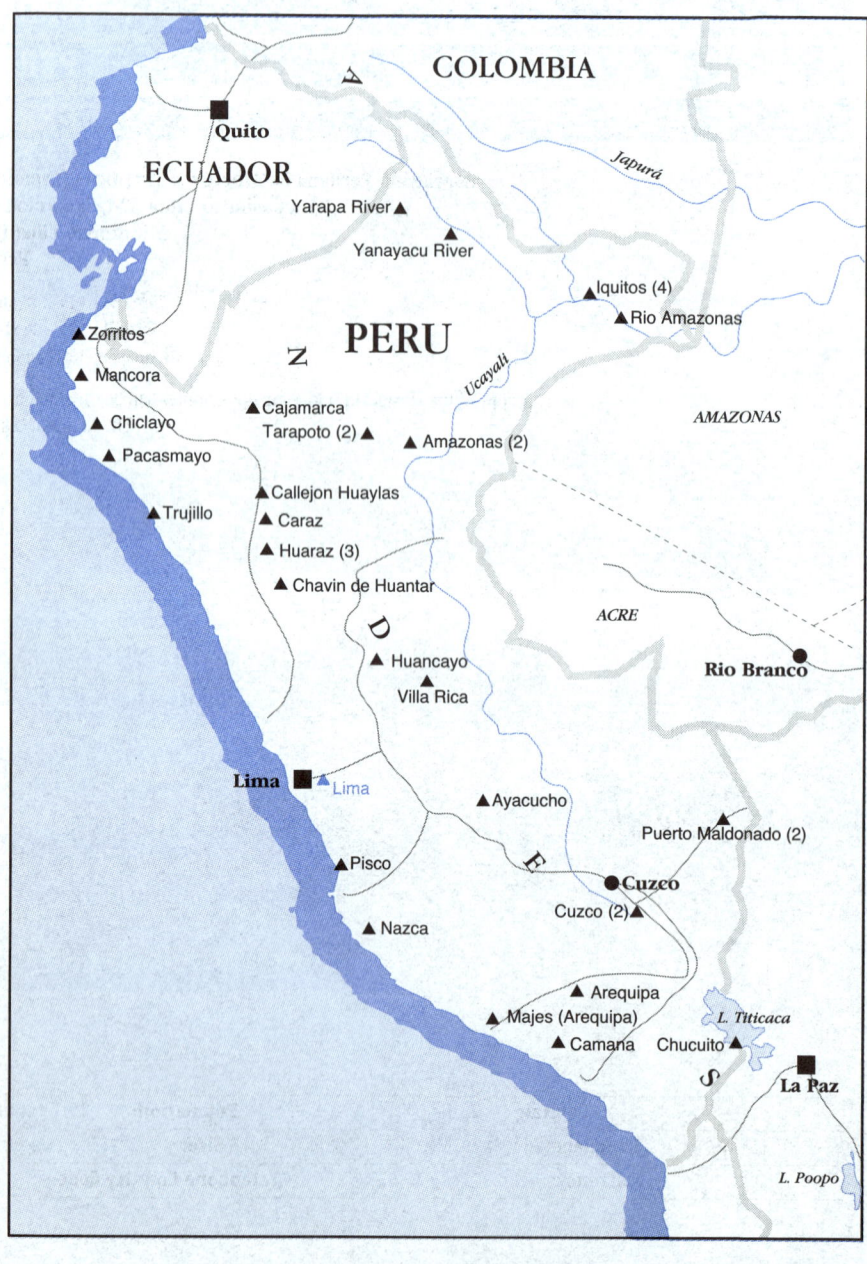

English

Hostels are located in cities, in the countryside, on the coast and on hills/mountains.

Price range

Price range US$ 9.00. 🖥.

Rooms and Reservations

R during Jan, Feb, Jul, Oct-Dec. (🛏 🛏). Reservations via ⟨IBN⟩ or Hostel by ☎ 📠 ✉. Smoking is limited - please check.

Guests

Membership Card and Passport/Photo ID are required. 👪 welcome. Group bookings via ⟨IBN⟩ or Hostel by ☎ 📠 ✉ (Reservation charges may apply).

Open times

Main hostels: open 🕐. Reception open: 🕐. Resident manager. **Other hostels:** open 🖾, 🕐. Reception open: 🕐. Resident manager.

Meals

🍽 BLD **R** For individuals & for 👪. 🍳.

Travelling around

For ease of travel use ✈ 🚆 🚐.

Travel/Activity Packages

Tours/sightseeing and accommodation/transport packages available. Package bookings via Hostel by ☎ 📠 ✉.

Passports and Visas

Passport required.

Health

Medical insurance is recommended.

Français

Les auberges sont situées dans les villes, à la campagne, sur le littoral et à la montagne.

Tarifs des nuitées

Tarifs des nuitées 9.00 US$. 🖥.

Chambres et réservations

R jan, fév, juil, oct-déc. (🛏 🛏). Réservations via ⟨IBN⟩ ou l'auberge par ☎ 📠 ✉. Il est permis de fumer dans certaines chambres - veuillez vérifier.

Usagers

La carte d'adhérent ainsi que le passeport/pièce d'identité avec photo sont à présenter. Accueil des 👪. Réservations pour groupes via ⟨IBN⟩ ou l'auberge par ☎ 📠 ✉ (Des frais de réservation pourront vous être facturés).

Horaires d'ouverture

Grandes auberges: ouvertes 🕐. Accueil ouvert 🕐. Gérant réside sur place. **Autres auberges:** ouvertes 🖾, 🕐. Accueil ouvert 🕐. Gérant réside sur place.

Repas

🍽 BLD **R** Pour individuels & pour 👪. 🍳.

Déplacements

Modes de transport recommandés ✈ 🚆 🚐.

Forfaits Voyages/Activités

Forfaits circuits touristiques et hébergement/transport disponibles. Réservations des forfaits via l'auberge par ☎ 📠 ✉.

Passeports et visas

Passeport obligatoire.

Santé

Une assurance médicale de voyage est conseillée.

Deutsch

Herbergen befinden sich in Städten, auf dem Land, an der Küste und in Bergen/Gebirgen.

Preisspanne

Preisspanne 9.00 US$. 🔲.

Zimmer und Reservierungen

🅡 während Jan, Feb, Jul, Okt-Dez. (🛏 🛏). Reservierungen über ⟨IBN⟩ oder die Herberge per 🅣 🅕 🅔. Rauchen ist begrenzt - bitte checken.

Gäste

Mitgliedsausweis und Reisepass/ Personalausweis sind erforderlich. 👪 willkommen. Gruppenbuchungen über ⟨IBN⟩ oder Herberge per 🅣 🅕 🅔 (Reservierungskosten könnten anfallen).

Öffnungszeiten

Hauptherbergen: Zugang 🕐. Rezeption 🕐. Herbergsmanager wohnt im Haus. **Andere Herbergen:** Zugang 🗓, 🕐. Rezeption 🕐. Herbergsmanager wohnt im Haus.

Mahlzeiten

🍽 BLD 🅡 Für Einzelreisende & für 👪. 🐾.

Reisen im Land

Reisen ist einfach mit ✈ 🚋 🚌.

Reise-/Aktivitäten-Packages

Touren/sightseeing und Unterkunft/Transport-Packages erhältlich. Package-Buchungen über Herberge per 🅣 🅕 🅔.

Reisepässe und Visa

Reisepass erforderlich.

Gesundheit

Unfall-/Krankenversicherung wird empfohlen.

Español

Los albergues están situados en las ciudades, el campo, la costa y la montaña.

Tarifas mínima y máxima

Tarifas mínima y máxima 9.00 US$. 🔲.

Habitaciones y Reservas

🅡 en ene, feb, jul, oct-dic. (🛏 🛏). Reservas por ⟨IBN⟩ o a través del albergue por 🅣 🅕 🅔. Está permitido fumar sólo en algunas salas/habitaciones - infórmese.

Huéspedes

Los huéspedes deben presentar su Carnet de Alberguista y su pasaporte o carnet de identidad. Se admiten 👪. Reservas de grupo por ⟨IBN⟩ o a través del albergue por 🅣 🅕 🅔 (Es posible que se aplique un suplemento en concepto de gastos de reserva).

Horarios y fechas de apertura

Albergues principales - abiertos 🕐. Horario de recepción: 🕐. Gerente residente. **Otros albergues** - abiertos 🗓, 🕐. Horario de recepción: 🕐. Gerente residente.

Comidas

🍽 BLD 🅡 Para individuales y para 👪. 🐾.

Desplazamientos

Transportes recomendados: ✈ 🚋 🚌.

Viajes Combinados con Actividades

Viajes combinados con visitas turísticas y alojamiento/transporte. Reserva de viajes combinados a través del albergue por 🅣 🅕 🅔.

Pasaportes y Visados

Pasaporte obligatorio.

Información Sanitaria

Seguro médico recomendado.

Location/Address	Telephone No. Fax No.	Beds	Opening Dates	Facilities
▲ Amazonas - Puerto Pumas Pomacochas Inn Carretera Marginal de la Selva, Olmos, Tarapoto Km. 327 La Florida, Pomacochas ℮ ctareps@puertopalmeras.com	☎ (94) 523978; (1) 2425550 ✆ (94) 523980	80	12	
▲ Amazonas River (Iquitos) - Amazonas Sinchicuy Lodge Quebrada Sinchicuysillo 30km De Iquitos. ℮ amazon@amauta.rep.net.pe	☎ (1) 2417576 ✆ (1) 4467946	80	12	30N
▲ Arequipa - Majes River Lodge Valle del Majes, Central Ongoro.	☎ (54) 280205 ✆ (54) 280205	62	12	
▲ Arequipa - Premiere Av. Quiroz 100.	☎ (54) 241091 ✆ (54) 241091	100	12	
▲ Arequipa (Camana) - San Diego Esq. Alfonso Ugarte 28 De Julio, Camana. ℮ diegoiyhf@hotmail.com	☎ (54) 572854 ✆ (54) 572854	56	12	
▲ Ayacucho - El Marquez de Valdelirios Alameda Bolognesi 720-724, Ayacucho. (Alt 2000m).	☎ (64) 813908 ✆ (64) 814014	40	12	
▲ Cajamarca - Baños del Inca Plaza de Armas, Calle Atahualpa S/N.	☎ (44) 827385; (44) 822800	100	12	
▲ Caraz - Los Pinos Parque San Martin No.103, La Merced, Caraz (Alt 3000m).	☎ (44) 791130	20	12	
▲ Chavin de Huantar - Montecarlo Jr. 17 de Enero 101 Plaza de Armas.	☎ (44) 754014	25	12	
▲ Chiclayo - Albergue Juvenil Turistico de Chiclayo Calle Manuel Arteaga 690 Urb. Los Libertadores.	☎ (74) 236628; (74) 234526	20	12	
▲ Chucuito (Puno) - Las Cabañas de Chucuito Jr. Tarapaca 153, Chucuito (Alt 3500).	☎ (54) 351276 ✆ (54) 351276	35	12	18N
▲ Cuzco - Maison de la Jeunesse Avda. El Sol Cdra, 5 Pasaje Grace (Alt 3000), Edificio San Jorge, Cusco. ℮ pazrent@latinmail.com	☎ (84) 235617; (1) 4464395 ✆ (1) 2428406	40	12	
▲ Cuzco - Municipal Del Cuzco Av. Kiskapata 240 Barrio San Cristóbal, Cuzco.	☎ (84) 252506	64	12	
▲ Huancayo - Perú Andino-Kuyai Wasi Psje San Antonio 113-115, Urb. San Carlos, Huancayo. ℮ peruandino@mixmail.com	☎ (64) 223956 ✆ (64) 223956	16	12	
▲ Huaraz - La Montanesa Av Augusto B Leguia 290 Centenario. (Alt 3000).	☎ (44) 721287	45	12	
▲ Huaraz - Eccame Km 18, Huaraz aeropeurto de Anta (Alt 3000). ℮ eccame@latinmail.com	☎ (44) 721933 ✆ (44) 721933	150	12	

Location/Address	Telephone No. Fax No.	Beds	Opening Dates	Facilities
△ **Huaraz** - Alpes Andes Casa de Guias Parque Ginebra 28G Casa de Guías. e casadeguias@hotmail.com	☏ (44) 721811 📠 (44) 722306	20	🗓12	🍴 R P 🗄 ☕
▲ **Iquitos** - Ambassador Calle Pevas 260, Iquitos. e paseosiqt@meganet.com.pe	☏ (94) 233110 📠 (94) 231618	60	🗓12	� 🍴 R CC P 🗄 ☕
▲ **Iquitos** - Muyuna Amazon Lodge & Expeditions Comunidad de San Juan de Yanayacu, Distrito de Fernando Lores Provincia de Maynas. e muyuna@waynarcp.net.pe	☏ (94) 242858; (1) 4469783	23	🗓12	� 🍴 R ☕
▲ **Iquitos** - Tambo Amazonico Lodge Yarapa River (180 km de Iquitos). e p-amazon@amautarcp.net.pe	☏ (1) 2417576 📠 (1) 4467946	20	🗓12	� 🍴 R 180 NE CC ☕
▲ **Iquitos** - Tambo Yanayacu Lodge (60km de Iquitos) Yanayacu River. e p-amazon@amautarcp.net.pe	☏ (1) 2417576 📠 (1) 4467946	30	🗓12	� 🍴 R 60 NE CC ☕
▲ **Lima** - AJ Turístico Internacional IBN Av Casimiro Ulloa 328, San Antonio, Lima 18. e hostell@terra.com.pe	☏ (1) 4465488 📠 (1) 4448187	100	🗓12	� R CC ⬖ P 🗄
▲ **Nazca** - Alegria Jr Lima No 168, Nazca. e alegriatours@hotmail.com	☏ (34) 522444; (34) 523431 📠 (34) 522444	120	🗓12	� R ⬖ 🗄 ☕
▲ **Pacasmayo** - Sol y Mar Sarmiento 112, Pacasmayo. e sertecsa@sencico.com.pe	☏ (44) 521440; (44) 235766 📠 (44) 222508	20	🗓12	� 🍴 R ⬖ P 🗄
▲ **Pisco** - Pisco Playa Jr José Balta No 639.	☏ (34) 532492 📠 (34) 532492	64	🗓12	� R ⬖ P 🗄
▲ **Piura** - La Posada de Mancora Barrio Industrial No 100, Mancora.	☏ (74) 858328 📠 (74) 858012	40	🗓12	� 🍴 R 0.2N ⬖ P 🗄
▲ **Puerto Maldonado** - & Camping Iñapari" Avda. Areopuerto Km.5 "La Joya" - Pto. Maldonado, Casilla #32 Madre de Dios. e inapari@blockbuster.com.pe	☏ (84) 572575	30	🗓12	� 🍴 R ⬖ P
▲ **Puerto Maldonado** - Ecoamazonia Lodge Bajo Rio Madre de Dios Km. 30. e ecoamazonia@terra.com.pe	☏ (84) 236159; (1) 2422708 📠 (84) 225068	90	🗓12	� 🍴 R CC ☕
▲ **Tarapoto** - Puerto. Palmeras Tarapoto Resort Marginal Sur, Km 3, Banda Shilcayo. e puertopalmeras@terra.com.pe	☏ (94) 523978; (94) 524242; (94) 524100 📠 (94) 523980	145	🗓12	� 🍴 R 0.5SE CC ⬖ P 🗄 ☕
▲ **Tarapoto** - Puerto Patos Sauce Lodge Rivera Norte-Laguna Azul Sauce, Tarapoto.	☏ (94) 523978; (1) 2425550; (1) 2425551 📠 (94) 523980	20	🗓12	� 🍴 R CC ⬖ P 🗄 ☕
▲ **Trujillo** - Centro Vacacional El Parque Autopista Huanchaco, Km 9 Poste 177.	☏ ((44) 464207	50	🗓12	� 🍴 R 0.5N ⬖ P ☕

Location/Address	Telephone No. Fax No.	Beds	Opening Dates	Facilities
▲ **Villa Rica** - Albergue Juvenil De Villa Rica Av Leopoldo Krause 451, Villa Rica, Oxapampa.	☎ (64) 530204	50	🗂	⛹ 🍽 Ⓡ 🅿
▲ **Zorritos** - Casa Grillo Los Pinos, 563 Zorritos-Tumbes: (1235km).	☎ (74) 544222 📠 (74) 544222	32	🗂	⛹ 🍽 ☞ 🅿

"A wise traveller never despises his own country."

"Le voyageur sage ne méprise jamais son propre pays."

„Ein weiser Reisender verachtet nie das eigene Land."

"El viajero sabio nunca desprecia su propio país."

Carlo Goldoni

International Booking Network

The advantages are clea[r]

www.iyhf.org

HOSTELLING INTERNATIONAL

IBN INTERNATIONAL BOOKING NETWORK

Philippines

PHILIPPINES
PHILIPPINEN
FILIPINAS

Youth & Student Hostel Foundation of the Philippines,
(YSHFP),
4227-9 Tomas Claudio St.,
Parañaque 1700, Baclaran,
Metro Manila,
Philippines.

☎ (63) (2) 8320680, 8322112
TX 41316 YSTAPHIL PM
🕿 (63) (2) 8322263
✉ yshfp@i-next.net

A copy of the Hostel Directory for this Country can be obtained from:
The National Office

Capital:	Manila		**Population:**	68,616,536
Language:	Pilipino/English		**Size:**	300,000 sq km
Currency:	Peso		**Telephone Country Code:**	63

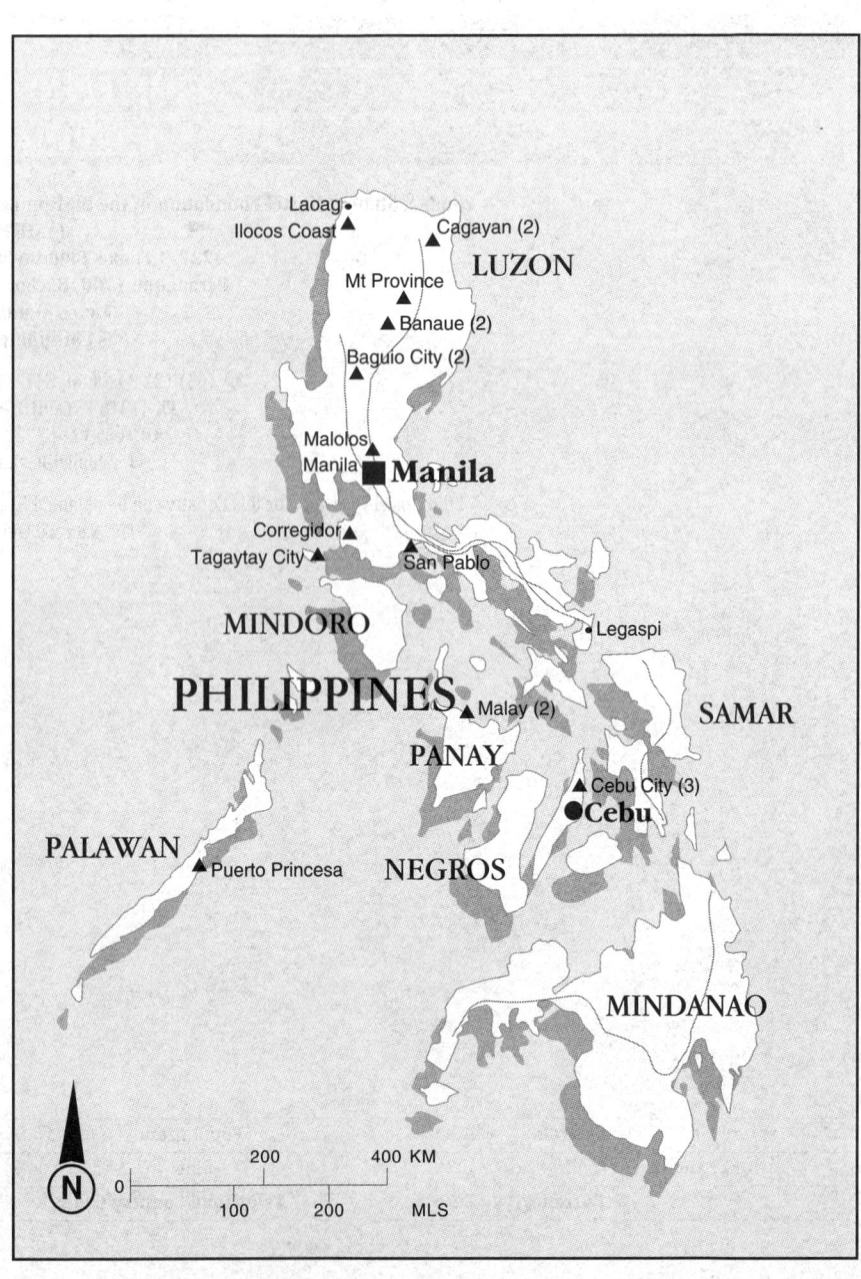

Laoag
Ilocos Coast ▲
Cagayan (2) ▲
LUZON
Mt Province ▲
▲ Banaue (2)
Baguio City (2) ▲

Malolos ▲
Manila ■ **Manila**

Corregidor ▲
Tagaytay City ▲
▲ San Pablo

MINDORO

• Legaspi

PHILIPPINES ▲ Malay (2)

SAMAR

PANAY

▲ Cebu City (3)
● **Cebu**

PALAWAN
▲ Puerto Princesa
NEGROS

MINDANAO

N

200   400 KM
0
100   200   MLS

English

Hostels are located in cities, in the countryside, on the coast and on hills/mountains.

Price range

Price range Peso 150-2000. 🗐.

Rooms and Reservations

R during Mar-May, Aug-Oct. (All Rooms). Reservations via Hostel or National Office by **t** **f** **e**. (Reservation charges may apply). Smoking is limited - please check.

Guests

Membership Card and Passport/Photo ID are required. The maximum stay is 15 days. Pets are allowed - check with hostel. **iἢi** welcome. Group bookings via Hostel or National Office by **t** **f** **e** (Reservation charges may apply).

Open times

Main hostels: open 🗓, ⌚. Reception open: ⌚. Resident manager. **Other hostels:** open 🗓, ⌚. Reception open: ⌚. Resident manager.

Meals

🍽 BD **R** For individuals & for **iἢi**. ☛ Not all utensils provided - check with hostel. Charges may apply.

Travelling around

For ease of travel use ✈ 🚢 🚌 Self-Drive. Drive on the right.

Travel/Activity Packages

Tours/sightseeing, walking/trekking and accommodation/transport packages available. Package bookings via Hostel or National Office by **t** **f** **e**.

Passports and Visas

Passport, Photo ID and Visa required.

Health

Vaccinations are required - check with your medical advisor. Vaccination certificates required. Medical insurance is recommended.

Français

Les auberges sont situées dans les villes, à la campagne, sur le littoral et à la montagne.

Tarifs des nuitées

Tarifs des nuitées 150-2000 Peso. 🗐.

Chambres et réservations

R mar-mai, août-oct. (Toutes chambres). Réservations via l'auberge et le Bureau National par **t** **f** **e**. (Des frais de réservation pourront vous être facturés). Il est permis de fumer dans certaines chambres - veuillez vérifier.

Usagers

La carte d'adhérent ainsi que le passeport/pièce d'identité avec photo sont à présenter. La durée maximale du séjour est de 15 jours. Les animaux domestiques sont autorisés mais vérifiez lesquels auprès de l'auberge. Accueil des **iἢi**. Réservations pour groupes via l'auberge ou le Bureau National par **t** **f** **e** (Des frais de réservation pourront vous être facturés).

Horaires d'ouverture

Grandes auberges: ouvertes 🗓, ⌚. Accueil ouvert ⌚. Gérant réside sur place. **Autres auberges:** ouvertes 🗓, ⌚. Accueil ouvert ⌚. Gérant réside sur place.

Repas

🍽 BD **R** Pour individuels & pour **iἢi**. ☛ Pas tous les ustensiles sont fournis - à vérifier auprès de l'auberge. Une contribution pourra vous être demandée.

Déplacements

Modes de transport recommandés ✈ ⛴ 🚌 Voiture. Conduite à droite.

Forfaits Voyages/Activités

Forfaits circuits touristiques, randonnées pédestres et hébergement/transport disponibles. Réservations des forfaits via l'auberge ou le Bureau National par 📞 📠 📧.

Passeports et visas

Passeport, pièce d'identité avec photo et visa obligatoires.

Santé

Des vaccinations sont obligatoires - veuillez vérifier auprès de votre médecin. Les certificats de vaccination sont obligatoires. Une assurance médicale de voyage est conseillée.

Deutsch

Herbergen befinden sich in Städten, auf dem Land, an der Küste und in Bergen/Gebirgen.

Preisspanne

Preisspanne 150-2000 Peso. 🗐.

Zimmer und Reservierungen

R während Mär-Mai, Aug-Okt. (Alle Zimmer). Reservierungen über Herberge oder Landesverband per 📞 📠 📧. (Reservierungskosten könnten anfallen). Rauchen ist begrenzt - bitte checken.

Gäste

Mitgliedsausweis und Reisepass/ Personalausweis sind erforderlich. Der maximale Aufenthalt beträgt 15 Tage. Haustiere sind erlaubt - in der Herberge nachfragen.

👪 willkommen. Gruppenbuchungen über Herberge oder Landesverband per 📞 📠 📧 (Reservierungskosten könnten anfallen).

Öffnungszeiten

Hauptherbergen: Zugang 🖥, 🕐. Rezeption 🕐. Herbergsmanager wohnt im Haus. **Andere Herbergen:** Zugang 🖥, 🕐. Rezeption 🕐. Herbergsmanager wohnt im Haus.

Mahlzeiten

🍽 BD **R** Für Einzelreisende & für 👪. 🍴 Nicht alle Utensilien werden bereitgestellt - in der Herberge nachfragen. Kosten können anfallen.

Reisen im Land

Reisen ist einfach mit ✈ ⛴ 🚌 Selbstfahrer. Rechts fahren.

Reise-/Aktivitäten-Packages

Touren/sightseeing, wandern/trekking und Unterkunft/Transport-Packages erhältlich. Package-Buchungen über Herberge oder Landesverband per 📞 📠 📧.

Reisepässe und Visa

Reisepass, Personalausweis und Einreisevisum erforderlich.

Gesundheit

Schutzimpfungen sind erforderlich - mit Ihrem Arzt checken. Schutzimpfungsbescheinigungen sind erforderlich. Unfall-/Krankenversicherung wird empfohlen.

Español

Los albergues están situados en las ciudades, el campo, la costa y la montaña.

Tarifas mínima y máxima

Tarifas mínima y máxima 150-2000 Peso. 🗐.

Habitaciones y Reservas

R en mar-may, ago-oct. (Todas las habitaciones). Reservas a través del albergue o la Asociación Nacional por **t** **f** **e**. (Es posible que se aplique un suplemento en concepto de gastos de reserva). Está permitido fumar sólo en algunas salas/habitaciones - infórmese.

Huéspedes

Los huéspedes deben presentar su Carnet de Alberguista y su pasaporte o carnet de identidad. La estancia máxima es de 15 días. Se admiten animales - consulte con el albergue. Se admiten **iłi**. Reservas de grupo a través del albergue o la Asociación Nacional por **t** **f** **e** (Es posible que se aplique un suplemento en concepto de gastos de reserva).

Horarios y fechas de apertura

Albergues principales - abiertos 🗓, 🕰. Horario de recepción: 🕰. Gerente residente. **Otros albergues -** abiertos 🗓, 🕰. Horario de recepción: 🕰. Gerente residente.

Comidas

🍽 BD **R** Para individuales y para **iłi**. 🍴 La cocina no dispone de todos los utensilios - consulte con el albergue. Es posible que se aplique un suplemento por el uso de la misma.

Desplazamientos

Transportes recomendados: ✈ 🚢 🚌 Automóvil. Se circula por la derecha.

Viajes Combinados con Actividades

Viajes combinados con visitas turísticas, senderismo y alojamiento/transporte. Reserva de viajes combinados a través del albergue o la Asociación Nacional por **t** **f** **e**.

Pasaportes y Visados

Pasaporte o carnet de identidad y visado obligatorios.

Información Sanitaria

Vacunación obligatoria - consulte con su centro médico. Certificados de vacunación obligatorios. Seguro médico recomendado.

"A person travels the world over in search of what he needs and returns home to find it."

"L'on parcourt le monde à la recherche de ce dont on a besoin et l'on revient chez soi pour le trouver."

„Der Mensch bereist die ganze Welt auf der Suche nach dem, was er braucht und kehrt heim, um es dort zu finden."

"Recorremos el mundo en busca de lo que necesitamos para al final encontrarlo en casa a nustro regreso"

George Moore

Manila -
International YH

4227 Tomas Claudio St,
Roxas Blvd,
Parañaque:
(behind the Excelsior Building).
☎ (2) 8320680, (2) 8322112
🖷 (2) 8322263
✉ yshfp@i-next.net

Open Dates: 🗓

Open Hours: 🕓

Price Range: Peso 150.00-250.00 💶

Beds: 122 - 3x⁴🛏 3x⁶🛏 6x⁶🛏

Facilities: 👫 👫 🍽 🚪 🏨 📺 📖 1 x 🍴 📻
📼 🛗 🔢 🌐 🅿 ℹ 🎱 🌸

Directions:

✈   Ninoy Aquino International 2km

🚃   Baclaran Lrt 1km

"Travelling is like gambling: it is always connected with winning and losing, and generally where it is least expected we receive more or less what we hoped for."

"Le voyage est pareil au jeu: il est toujours question de gagner et de perdre, et en général l'on reçoit plus ou moins ce que l'on espérait, alors que l'on s'y attend le moins."

„Reisen kommt dem Glücksspiel gleich: es ist immer mit Gewinn und Verlust verbunden, und wir bekommen allgemein dort, wo wir es am wenigsten erwarten, mehr oder weniger das, was wir erhofft hatten."

"El viajar es como un juego de azar: tiene que ver siempre con ganar y perder y, generalmente, en el momento menos pensado recibimos más o menos lo que esperábamos."

Johann Wolfgang Von Goethe

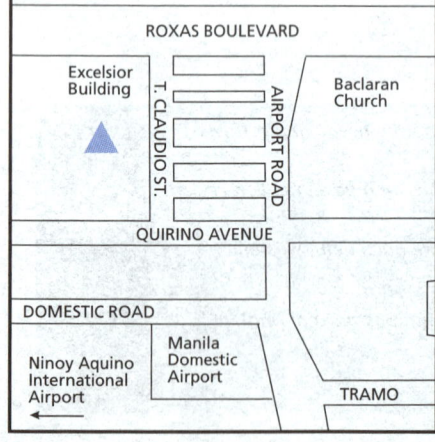

Location/Address	Telephone No. Fax No.	Beds	Opening Dates	Facilities
▲ **Baguio City** - Corfu Village 92 cor Leonard Wood cor Brent Rd and Gen Luna Sts, Baguio City.	☏ (074) 4422969	50	🗓12	♦♦♦ �🍴 P 🖨
▲ **Baguio City** - Baden Powell Hall 26 Grosvenor Park Rd.	☏ (074) 4425836	150	🗓12	♦♦♦ 🍴 P 🖨
▲ **Baguio City** - Zion Hostel 18 Palma St, Baguio City.	☏ (074) 4433146, (074) 4456970 ☏ (074) 4456997	21	🗓12	♦♦♦ 🍴 R 1.5E ♿ CC ☕ ⏚ 🚲
▲ **Banaue** - Banaue YH Banaue, Ifugao.		60	🗓12	🍴 P 🖨
▲ **Banaue** - Banaue View Inn YH Banaue, Ifugao.		30	🗓12	P 🖨
△ *Cagayan Valley* - *Callao Cave YH Peñablanca, Cagayan.*		*60*	🗓12	🍴 P 🖨
▲ **Cagayan Valley** - Villa Margarita YH Busilac, Bayombong, Nueva Vizcaya.		50	🗓12	P 🖨
▲ **Cebu City** - Ecotech Center Lahug, Cebu City.	☏ (032) 2313651, (032) 2313984 ☏ (032) 9-04-30	300	🗓12	♦♦♦ 🍴 R 25SW CC P 🖨 ☕ 🚲
▲ **Cebu City** - Four Reasons Place 3rd St, Happy Valley Subdivision V.Rama, Cebu City.	☏ (032) 2536538 (032) 2538677	14	🗓12	♦♦♦ 🍴 R 1.5S ⏚ P 🖨 🚲
▲ **Cebu City** - Myra's Pensionne 12 Escario Corner, Acacia St, Brgy. Camput Haw, Cebu City.	☏ (032) 2315557 ☏ (032) 2336625	22	🗓12	♦♦♦ 🍴 R 0.5N P 🖨 ☕ 🚲
▲ **Corregidor** - Corregidor YH Bataan.		60	🗓12	P 🖨
△ *Ilocos Coast* - *D'Coral Beach Resort Piao Sur, Currimao: (25km S of Laoag).*	☏ *(077) 7721133*	*100*	🗓12	♦♦♦ 🍴 P 🖨
▲ **Malay** - Boracay Beach Chalets Manggayad Balabag, Boracay Island, Malay, Aklan. ✉ bbchalet@boracay.i-next.net	☏ (036) 2883993 ☏ (036) 2886313	15	🗓12	♦♦♦ 🍴 R 200N CC P 🖨 🚲
▲ **Malay** - Villa De Oro Managgayad Balabag, Boracay Island, Malay, Aklan.	☏ (036) 2885456, (036) 2603070 ☏ (036) 2885456	34	🗓12	♦♦♦ 🍴 R 200N ⏚ P 🖨 ☕ 🚲
▲ **Malolos** - Hiyas NG Bulacan Convention Center Hostel Malolos, Bulacan.		300	🗓12	🍴 P 🖨
▲ **Manila** - International YH **4227 Tomas Claudio St, Roxas Blvd, Parañaque: (behind the Excelsior Building).** ✉ yshfp@i-next.net	☏ (2) 8320680, (2) 8322112 ☏ (2) 8322263	122	🗓12	♦♦♦ 🍴 ⏚ P 🖨
▲ **Mount Province** - St. Joseph's Rest House Sagada, Mountain Province.		80	🗓12	🍴 P 🖨

Location/Address	Telephone No. Fax No.	Beds	Opening Dates	Facilities
▲ **Puerto Princesa** - Casa Linda Inn Trinidad Rd, Rizal Ave, Puerto Princesa City, Palawan. @ casalind@mozcom.com	☎ (048) 4332606 📠 (048) 4332309	35	🗓	� 🍴 ℝ 2NE ⚐ 🅿 🖸 🥤 🏍
△ *San Pablo City* - *Sampaloc Lake YH Schetelig Ave, Efarca Vill., San Pablo City.*	☎ *(049) 5623376*	*40*	🗓	🍴 🅿 🖸
▲ **Tagaytay City** - 5R Youth Hostel Brgy. Sungay West, Tagaytay City.	☎ (091) 97052291	42	🗓	♛ще 🍴 ℝ 2.5W ⚐ 🅿 🖸 🥤 🏍

"They change their climate, not their soul, who rush across the sea."

"Ils changent de climat, pas d'âme, ceux qui se précipitent pour traverser les océans."

„Die, die über das Meer eilen, wechseln zwar das Klima, jedoch nicht ihre Seele."

"Cambian de clima, no de alma, quienes veloces atraviesan mares."

Horace

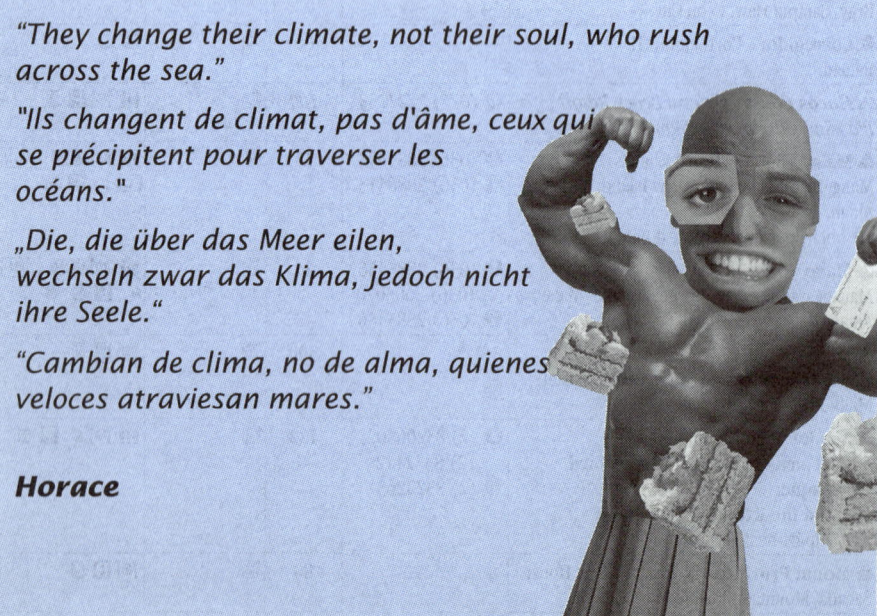

Qatar

QATAR

KATAR

QATAR

**Qatar Youth Hostels Association,
PO Box 9660, Doha, Qatar.**

☎ (974) 4867180, 4866402
🖷 (974) 4863968

A copy of the Hostel Directory for this Country can be obtained from:
Qatar Youth Hostel Association, Doha Al-Lakta, Makka Street.

Capital:	Doha	**Population:**	532,719
Language:	Arabic	**Size:**	11,427 sq km
Currency:	Qatari riyal	**Telephone Country Code:**	974

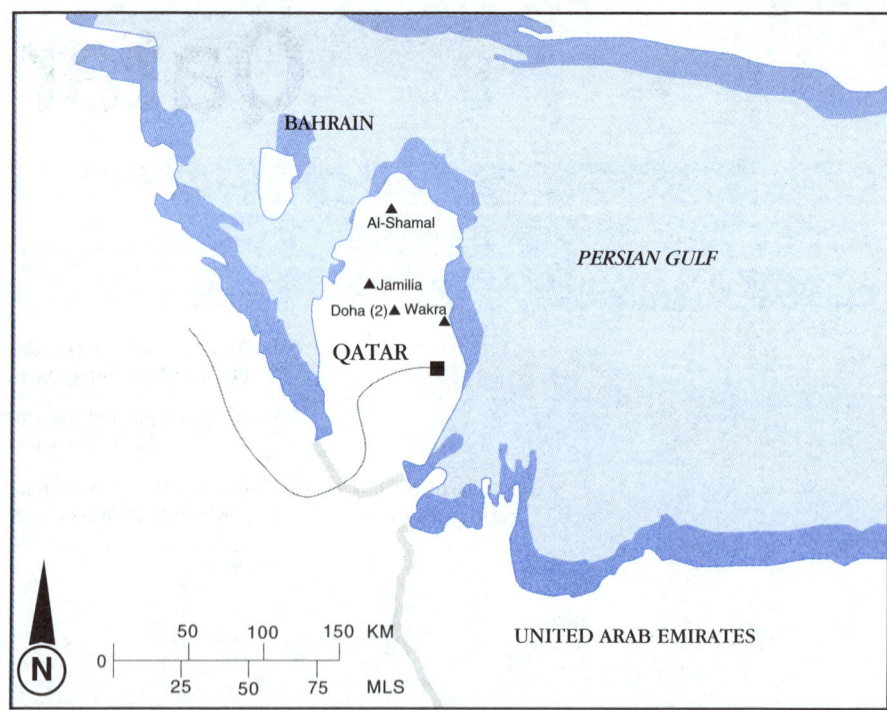

English

The best time to visit Qatar as far as weather is concerned is between November and April of each year. Hostels are located in cities.

Price range

Price range 40 Qatari Riyals. 5. .

Rooms and Reservations

 (All Rooms). Reservations via Hostel by . Hostels are single sex only. All hostels are non-smoking.

Guests

Membership Card and Passport/Photo ID are required. The maximum stay is 3 days. Age limits may apply for adults - check with hostel. welcome. Group bookings via Hostel by (Reservation charges may apply).

Open times

Main hostels: open , 08:00-12:00hrs, 16:00-21:00hrs. Reception open: . Resident manager. **Other hostels:** open , 08:00-12:00hrs, 16:00-21:00hrs. Reception open: . Resident manager.

Meals

BLD For individuals & for . .

Travelling around

For ease of travel use Self-Drive.

Travel/Activity Packages

Tours/sightseeing packages available. Package bookings via Hostel by .

Passports and Visas

Passport, Photo ID and Visa required.

Health

Emergency medical treatment is free.

Français

La meilleure période de l'année pour rendre visite a Qatar en ce qui concerne le climat est entre les mois de novembre et avril. Les auberges sont situées dans les villes.

Tarifs des nuitées

Tarifs des nuitées 40 Qatari Riyals. € 5. 🛏.

Chambres et réservations

R 🛏 (Toutes chambres). Réservations via l'auberge par ❶ ❻. Les auberges sont uniquement non-mixtes. Toutes les auberges sont non-fumeurs.

Usagers

La carte d'adhérent ainsi que le passeport/pièce d'identité avec photo sont à présenter. La durée maximale du séjour est de 3 jours. Il est possible que des limites d'âge soient en vigueur pour les adultes - vérifier auprès de l'auberge. Accueil des ♔♔♔. Réservations pour groupes via l'auberge par ❶ ❻ (Des frais de réservation pourront vous être facturés).

Horaires d'ouverture

Grandes auberges: ouvertes 🛏, entre 8h-12h, 16h-21h. Accueil ouvert ⏰. Gérant réside sur place. **Autres auberges:** ouvertes 🛏, entre 8h-12h, 16h-21h. Accueil ouvert ⏰. Gérant réside sur place.

Repas

🍽 BLD **R** Pour individuels & pour ♔♔♔. 🗡.

Déplacements

Modes de transport recommandés 🚌 Voiture.

Forfaits Voyages/Activités

Forfaits circuits touristiques disponibles. Réservations des forfaits via l'auberge par ❶ ❻.

Passeports et visas

Passeport, pièce d'identité avec photo et visa obligatoires.

Santé

Soins d'urgence gratuits.

Deutsch

Die beste Zeit Qatar zu besuchen in Hinblick auf das Wetter, sind die Monate von November bis April. Herbergen befinden sich in Städten.

Preisspanne

Preisspanne 40 Qatari Riyals. € 5. 🛏.

Zimmer und Reservierungen

R 🛏 (Alle Zimmer). Reservierungen über Herberge per ❶ ❻. Herbergen sind nur Single Sex. Rauchen ist in allen Herbergen NICHT gestattet.

Gäste

Mitgliedsausweis und Reisepass/Personalausweis sind erforderlich. Der maximale Aufenthalt beträgt 3 Tage. Altersbegrenzungen für Erwachsene möglich - in der Herberge nachfragen. ♔♔♔ willkommen. Gruppenbuchungen über Herberge per ❶ ❻ (Reservierungskosten könnten anfallen).

Öffnungszeiten

Hauptherbergen: Zugang 🛏, 08:00-12:00Uhr, 16:00-21:00Uhr. Rezeption ⏰.

Herbergsmanager wohnt im Haus. **Andere Herbergen:** Zugang 🖻, 08:00-12:00Uhr, 16:00-21:00Uhr. Rezeption ⊙. Herbergsmanager wohnt im Haus.

Mahlzeiten

🍽 BLD **ℝ** Für Einzelreisende & für ♦♦♦. ✍.

Reisen im Land

Reisen ist einfach mit 🚐 Selbstfahrer.

Reise-/Aktivitäten-Packages

Touren/sightseeing-Packages erhältlich. Package-Buchungen über Herberge per ❶ ❻.

Reisepässe und Visa

Reisepass, Personalausweis und Einreisevisum erforderlich.

Gesundheit

Nur im Notfall sind medizinische Behandlungen kostenlos.

Español

El mejor período del año para visitar a Qatar en cuanto a clima es entre noviembre y abril. Los albergues están situados en las ciudades.

Tarifas mínima y máxima

Tarifas mínima y máxima 40 Qatari Riyals. € 5. 🗐.

Habitaciones y Reservas

ℝ 🖻 (Todas las habitaciones). Reservas a través del albergue por ❶ ❻. Los albergues son sólo para hombres o mujeres. Está prohibido fumar en todos los albergues.

Huéspedes

Los huéspedes deben presentar su Carnet de Alberguista y su pasaporte o carnet de identidad. La estancia máxima es de 3 días. Es

posible que exista un límite de edad para los adultos - consulte con el albergue. Se admiten ♦♦♦. Reservas de grupo a través del albergue por ❶ ❻ (Es posible que se aplique un suplemento en concepto de gastos de reserva).

Horarios y fechas de apertura

Albergues principales - abiertos 🖻, 08:00-12:00h, 16:00-21:00h. Horario de recepción: ⊙. Gerente residente. **Otros albergues** - abiertos 🖻, 08:00-12:00h, 16:00-21:00h. Horario de recepción: ⊙. Gerente residente.

Comidas

🍽 BLD **ℝ** Para individuales y para ♦♦♦. ✍.

Desplazamientos

Transportes recomendados: 🚐 Automóvil.

Viajes Combinados con Actividades

Viajes combinados con visitas turísticas. Reserva de viajes combinados a través del albergue por ❶ ❻.

Pasaportes y Visados

Pasaporte o carnet de identidad y visado obligatorios.

Información Sanitaria

Asistencia médica de urgencia gratuita.

Doha - Al Lakta

Doha YH,
Al-Lakta Makka Street.
☎ 4867180; 4866402
✆ 4863968

Open Dates:	🗓
Open Hours:	🕐
Reservations:	**R**
Price Range:	US$ 11.00 💳
Beds:	60 - 11x¹ 🛏 22x² 🛏 33x³ 🛏 44x⁴ 🛏
Facilities:	👬 🍽 📺 📗 1 x 🍴 🔆 📷 ⛪ 🔢 ⊜ 🅿 ℹ 🧺 ⚠ 🔍 🏨 🚶

Directions:

✈	Doha International 12km
⛴	Doha 10km

Attractions: 🔍6km ∪16km ⚲4km 🏊8km

> "The tourist who moves about to see
> and hear and open himself to all the
> influences of the places which condense
> centuries of human greatness is only a
> man in search of excellence."

> "Le touriste qui voyage pour voir et
> entendre et s'ouvrir à toutes les
> influences des lieux qui condensent des
> siècles de grandeur humaine est tout
> simplement un homme à la recherche
> de l'excellence."

> „Der Tourist, der unterwegs ist, um zu
> schauen und zu hören und sich den
> Einflüssen der Orte zu eröffnen, die
> Jahrhunderte menschlicher Größe
> zusammenfassen, ist einfach ein
> Mensch auf der Suche nach
> Großartigem."

> "El turista que se desplaza para ver y
> oír y abrirse a todas las influencias de
> los lugares en que se condensan siglos
> de grandeza humana es simplemente
> un hombre en busca de excelencia."

Max Lerner

THE ARABIAN GULF

THE CORNICHE ROAD ⟶ TO DOHA INTERNATIONAL AIRPORT

POST OFFICE HEADQUARTER

TO THE EMIRI DIWAN

QATAR TV
HEADQUARTER

TO QATAR UNIVERSITY
←

TO THE TRAFFIC DEPT ➡

ALSHAMAL
ROUNDABOUT   Musqei of omar bin al-khtab

TO AL-SHAMAL TOWN
←

AL-LUQTA STREET
AL-GHARAFA AREA

MAKKAH RD

AL JAIDHA
ROUNDABOUT

△ QATAR YHA
MAIN
OFFICE

Location/Address	Telephone No. Fax No.	Beds	Opening Dates	Facilities
▲ **Al-Jamilia** Al-Ahli Sports Club Building, Al-Jamilia Town.	☎ 4672122	50	🗓	🅿 🚶
▲ **Al-Shamal** Al-Shamal Sports Club Building, Al-Shamal Town.	☎ 4731307	50	🗓	🅿 🚶
▲ **Al-Wakra** YH, Al-Wakra Sports Club Building, Al-Wakra Town.	☎ 4841010	50	🗓	🅿 🚶
▲ **Doha** - Al Lakta **Doha YH, Al-Lakta Makka Street.**	☎ 4867180; 4866402 ☏ 4863968	60	🗓	🍴 Ⓡ 🅿 📷 🚶
▲ **Doha** - Al Murabaa Doha YH, Al-Murabaa. (Behind the Traffic Department Building)	☎ 4863968	50	🗓	🅿 🚶

"Traveling is not just seeing the new; it is also leaving behind. Not just opening doors; also closing them behind you, never to return. But the place you have left forever is always there for you to see whenever you shut your eyes."

"Voyager, ce n'est pas seulement voir du nouveau; c'est aussi quitter. Non pas simplement ouvrir des portes; mais aussi en fermer derrière soi, pour ne jamais revenir. Mais le lieu que vous avez quitté pour toujours sera toujours là pour vous à chaque fois que vous fermez les yeux."

„Reisen bedeutet nicht nur, das Neue zu sehen, sondern auch Dinge zurückzulassen. Nicht nur Türen zu öffnen, sondern auch, diese hinter sich zu schließen, um niemals zurückzukehren. Aber den Ort, von dem du Abschied genommen hast, kannst du immer wieder sehen, sobald du die Augen schließt."

"Viajar no es simplemente ver cosas nuevas; es también dejar atrás. No sólo abrir puertas; sino cerralas detrás de uno, para nunca más volver; Pero el lugar que dejaste para siempre seguirá existiendo para ti y podrás verlo con sólo cerrar los ojos."

Jan Myrdal

Saudi Arabia

ARABIE SAOUDITE
SAUDI-ARABIEN
ARABIA SAUDI

Saudi Arabian Youth Hostels Association
Alshehab Alghassni St. Alnmouzajiyah District
North Almurabb'h, P.O. Box 2359, Riyadh 11451
Kingdom of Saudi Arabia.

☎ (966) (1) 4055552
(966) (1) 4051478
TX 406560 SAYHAR SJ
📠 (966) (1) 4021079

A copy of the Hostel Directory for this Country can be obtained from:
The National Office

Capital:	Riyadh	**Population:**	19,895,232
Language:	Arabic	**Size:**	2,240,000 sq km
Currency:	SR (Saudi riyal)	**Telephone Country Code:**	966

English

Adhere to the customs of Islamic way of dress. Hostels are located in cities.

Rooms and Reservations

R 🗓 (1🛏 2🛏 3🛏 4🛏 5🛏 6🛏 6+🛏).
Reservations via Hostel by ☎ 📠. Hostels are single sex only. All hostels are non-smoking.

Guests

Membership Card and Passport/Photo ID are required. The maximum stay is 10 days. Age limits may apply for adults - check with hostel. 👫 welcome. Group bookings via Hostel by ☎ 📠.

Open times

Main hostels: open 🗓, 🕐. Reception open: 🕐. Resident manager. **Other hostels:** open 🕐. Reception open: 🕐. Resident manager.

Meals

🍽 BLD R For individuals & for 👫. 🍴 Not all utensils provided - check with hostel.

Travelling around

For ease of travel use Self-Drive. Driving licence required.

Passports and Visas

Passport and Visa required.

Health

Vaccinations are advised - check with your medical advisor. Emergency medical treatment is free.

Déplacements

Modes de transport recommandés Voiture. Permis de conduire obligatoire.

Passeports et visas

Passeport et visa obligatoires.

Santé

Des vaccinations sont conseillées - veuillez vérifier auprès de votre médecin. Soins d'urgence gratuits.

Français

Il est demandé aux visiteurs de respecter les coutumes vestimentaires islamiques. Les auberges sont situées dans les villes.

Chambres et réservations

ⓡ 🖥 (1🛏 2🛏 3🛏 4🛏 5🛏 6🛏 6🛏). Réservations via l'auberge par ❶ ❻. Les auberges sont uniquement non-mixtes. Toutes les auberges sont non-fumeurs.

Usagers

La carte d'adhérent ainsi que le passeport/ pièce d'identité avec photo sont à présenter. La durée maximale du séjour est de 10 jours. Il est possible que des limites d'âge soient en vigueur pour les adultes - vérifier auprès de l'auberge. Accueil des ♔♔♔. Réservations pour groupes via l'auberge par ❶ ❻.

Horaires d'ouverture

Grandes auberges: ouvertes 🖥, 🕧. Accueil ouvert 🕧. Gérant réside sur place. **Autres auberges:** ouvertes 🕧. Accueil ouvert 🕧. Gérant réside sur place.

Repas

🍽 BLD ⓡ Pour individuels & pour ♔♔♔. ☞ Pas tous les ustensils sont fournis - à vérifier auprès de l'auberge.

Deutsch

Den Brauch islamischer Kleidungsweise befolgen. Herbergen befinden sich in Städten.

Zimmer und Reservierungen

ⓡ 🖥 (1🛏 2🛏 3🛏 4🛏 5🛏 6🛏 6🛏). Reservierungen über Herberge per ❶ ❻. Herbergen sind nur Single Sex. Rauchen ist in allen Herbergen NICHT gestattet.

Gäste

Mitgliedsausweis und Reisepass/ Personalausweis sind erforderlich. Der maximale Aufenthalt beträgt 10 Tage. Altersbegrenzungen für Erwachsene möglich - in der Herberge nachfragen. ♔♔♔ willkommen. Gruppenbuchungen über Herberge per ❶ ❻.

Öffnungszeiten

Hauptherbergen: Zugang 🖥, 🕧. Rezeption 🕧. Herbergsmanager wohnt im Haus. **Andere Herbergen:** Zugang 🕧. Rezeption 🕧. Herbergsmanager wohnt im Haus.

Mahlzeiten

🍽 BLD ⓡ Für Einzelreisende & für ♔♔♔. ☞ Nicht alle Utensilien werden bereitgestellt - in der Herberge nachfragen.

Reisen im Land

Reisen ist einfach mit Selbstfahrer. Führerschein erforderlich.

Reisepässe und Visa

Reisepass/Einreisevisum erforderlich.

Gesundheit

Schutzimpfungen werden empfohlen - mit Ihrem Arzt checken. Nur im Notfall sind medizinische Behandlungen kostenlos.

Español

Respete las costumbres islámicas en materia de indumentaria. Los albergues están situados en las ciudades.

Habitaciones y Reservas

🅡 🗒 (1🛏 2🛏 3🛏 4🛏 5🛏 6🛏 6🛏).
Reservas a través del albergue por ❶ ❶. Los albergues son sólo para hombres o mujeres. Está prohibido fumar en todos los albergues.

Huéspedes

Los huéspedes deben presentar su Carnet de Alberguista y su pasaporte o carnet de identidad. La estancia máxima es de 10 días. Es posible que exista un límite de edad para los adultos - consulte con el albergue. Se admiten

👤👤👤. Reservas de grupo a través del albergue por ❶ ❶.

Horarios y fechas de apertura

Albergues principales - abiertos 🗒, 🕒. Horario de recepción: 🕒. Gerente residente. **Otros albergues** - abiertos: 🕒. Horario de recepción: 🕒. Gerente residente.

Comidas

🍽 BLD 🅡 Para individuales y para 👤👤👤. ♂ La cocina no dispone de todos los utensilios - consulte con el albergue.

Desplazamientos

Transportes recomendados: Automóvil. Es necesario un permiso de conducir.

Pasaportes y Visados

Pasaporte y visado obligatorios.

Información Sanitaria

Vacunación recomendada - consulte con su centro médico. Asistencia médica de urgencia gratuita.

Jeddah Governorate

YH,
PO Box 8486,
Jeddah 21482,
Makkah Rd,
K7 West Stadium,
Jeddah.
☎ (2) 6886632, (2) 6886692
📠 (2) 6887112

Open Dates: 🗓

Open Hours: ⏱

Reservations: **R**

Price Range: SR6-8 💱

Beds: 200 - 35x🛏 4x⁶🛏

Facilities: ♿ 👪 🍴 🚲 🛏 📺 📖1 x🍽 🔲
🖼 🏧 ⊖ **P** 🛈 ✂ ⛰ 🌀 🔦
🏛 🎎 🚶

Directions:

✈ 14km

🚌 100m

Attractions: 🔍 🚶 ⛷ 🏊

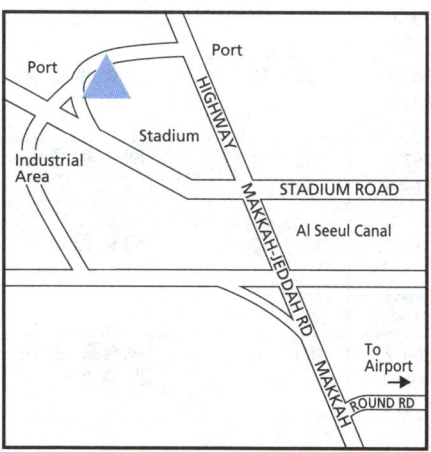

Location/Address	Telephone No. Fax No.	Beds	Opening Dates	Facilities
▲ **Albahah Area** Albahah YH, PO Box 52, Saud Bin Abdul Aziz Sports City, Albahah, Alaqeeq Rd, Albahah.	☎ (7) 7250732, (7) 7250368 🖷 (7) 7251988	120		
▲ **Algateef Governorate** Naif Bin Abdul Aziz Sports City, Eastern Area.	☎ (03) 8360897 🖷 (03) 8360897	60		
△ *Al-Jouf Area* *Al-Jouf YH, PO Box 211,* *Sakaka King Fahd St (Almwasalat), Al-Jouf.*	☎ (4) 6241884 🖷 (4) 6248341	70		
△ *Alkharj Governorate* *YH, PO Box 521, Alkharj 11942,* *King Fahd Rd, Next to* *Sporting Sho'la Club Stadium, Alkharj.*	☎ (1) 5485545 🖷 (1) 5485765	75		
▲ **Almadinah Area** YH, Prince Moh Bin Abdelaziz Sporting City, Alaziziyyah District, Almadinah.	☎ (4) 8303092 🖷 (4) 8303244	150		
▲ **Almajma'h Governorate** YH, PO Box 179, Prince Salman Bin Abdul Aziz Sports City - the Main Rd, Almajma'h.	☎ (6) 4323028 🖷 (6) 4321675	65		
▲ **Alqasseem Area** - Buraidah - Alqaseem YH, PO Box 949, Prince Abdallah Bin Abdelaziz Sporting City, Braidah, Alsafraa, Alqasseem.	☎ (6) 3812361 🖷 (6) 3813007	180		
△ *Arrass Governorate* *YH, 1986, Northern Alshifa-Riyadh Rd.*	☎ (6) 3333315 🖷 (6) 3336387	50		
▲ **Aseer Area** - Abha YH, PO Box 182, Prince Sultan Bin Abdelaziz Sporting City, Almahalah, Abha.	☎ (7) 2270495 🖷 (7) 2270503	150		
▲ **Eastern Area** - Dammam YH, PO Box 2822, Dammam 31461, Dammam - Khobar Rd, adjacent to Gymnasium.	☎ (3) 8575358, (3) 8575384 🖷 (3) 8579524	200		
▲ **Eastern Area** - Alahsa Governorate YH, Prince Abdallah Bin Galawi Sporting City, Alkhalidiyyah District, Hufuf, Alahsa.	☎ (3) 5800028 🖷 (3) 5800692	120		
▲ **Hail Area** YH, Prince Abdelaziz Bin Musaed Bin Galawi Sporting City, Hail: airport district.	☎ (6) 5325734 🖷 (6) 5331485	120		
▲ **Jazan Area** - Jazan YH, 1981, PO Box 319, Jazan King Faisal Bin Abdul Aziz Sports City, Prince Abdullah Rd, Jizan.	☎ (7) 3211639, (7) 3211637 🖷 (7) 3211653	65		
▲ **Jeddah Governorate** **YH, PO Box 8486, Jeddah 21482,** **Makkah Rd, K7 West Stadium, Jeddah.**	☎ (2) 6886632, (2) 6886692 🖷 (2) 6887112	200		

Location/Address	Telephone No. Fax No.	Beds	Opening Dates	Facilities
▲ **Makkah Area** - Makkah YH, 1979, PO Box 5403, King Abdelaziz Sporting City-Al-Sharai, Old Taif Rd, Opposite Jo'ranah Bridge, Makkah.	☏ (2) 5240414 ✆ (2) 5240966	135	📠	🍴 🚿 🅿 📷 🏃
△ *Najran Area* - *Najran* *YH, 1982, PO Box 155, Alfaisaliyyah,* *Opposite Najran Secondary School, Najran.*	☏ *(7) 5222433,* *(7) 5221668* ✆ *(7) 5225019*	*60*	📠	🍴 🚿 🅿 📷 🏃
▲ **Riyadh Area** - Prince Faisal Fahd's Youth Hostel Riyadh YH, PO Box 2359, Riyadh 11451, West King Fahd Rd, Opposite New Passport Building, Alshehab Alghassani-st.	☏ (1) 4055552, (1) 4051478 ✆ (1) 4051376	270	📠	🍴 Ⓡ ♿ 🚿 🅿 📷 🏃
△ *Shaqraa Governorate* *YH, Al Rowdah District, Alarbaeen St,* *West Alwashm Club, Shaqraa.*	☏ *(01) 6220200* ✆ *(01) 6220200*	*50*	📠	🍴 🚿 🅿 📷 🏃
▲ **Tabouk Area** - Tabouk YH, King Khalid Bin Abdul Aziz Sports City, Amman Rd, Tabouk.	☏ (4) 4276426 ✆ (4) 4276426	50	📠	🍴 🚿 🅿 📷 🏃
▲ **Taif Governorate** YH, King Fahd Sporting City, Hawiyyah, Taif.	☏ (2) 7252000, (2) 7253400 ✆ (2) 7253400	160	📠	🍴 🚿 🅿 📷 🏃

"In former days, women were unwelcome in Kyokans (Japanese-style inns) when they travelled alone. I learned from a newspaper article that such would never happen in youth hostels, and that stimulated me to stay at hostels. I was amazed to know that so many different people from all walks of life stayed together in one room, knowing each other, becoming friends and making pleasant company among themselves."

"Dans le temps, les femmes n'étaient pas les bienvenues dans les Kyokans (auberges japonaises), lorsqu'elles voyageaient seules. Lorsque j'ai lu dans un article de journal que cela n'arriverait jamais dans les Auberges de Jeunesse, j'ai eu envie d'y faire un séjour. J'ai été vraiment fascinée de voir que tant de gens d'horizons différents partageaient la même chambrée, apprenaient à se connaître, devenaient amis et passaient du bon temps tous ensemble."

"Früher waren Frauen in "Kyokans" (japanischen Gästehäusern) nicht willkommen wenn sie allein reisten. In einem Zeitungsartikel las ich, dass so etwas in Jugendherbergen niemals geschehen könnte, was mich dazu anregte, in Jugendherbergen zu übernachten. Ich war erstaunt, wieviele Menschen aus allen Berufen und Gesellschaftsschichten hier zusammenkommen, Zimmer miteinander teilen, neue Freundschaften schließen und gemeinsam viel Vergnügen haben."

"Antiguamente, las mujeres que viajaban solas no eran bienvenidas en los Kyokans (hostales japoneses). Cuando leí un día en el periódico que ésto no podría nunca suceder en un albergue juvenil, me entraron ganas de alojarme en uno de ellos. Quedé maravillada al comprobar que tantas personas diferentes, de todas las profesiones y condiciones sociales, compartían una misma habitación, se conocían, hacían amistad y lo pasaban bien juntas."

Sugako Hashida

HOSTELLING
INTERNATIONAL

Take the HI way!

For HI quality accommodation at the best prices.

Visit one of our 4200 hostels in over 60 countries.

www.iyhf.org

South Africa

AFRIQUE DU SUD
SÜDAFRIKA
SURAFRICA

Hostelling International-South Africa,
PO Box 4402, Cape Town 8001, South Africa.

Head Office Address: 3rd Floor, St. Georges House, 73 St. Georges Mall,
Cape Town 8001, South Africa.

☎ (27) (21) 424-2511
✆ (27) (21) 424-4119
e info@hisa.org.za
☖ www.hisa.org.za

A copy of the Hostel Directory for this Country can be obtained from:
The National Office

Capital:	Cape Town - Legislative	**Currency:**	Rand
	Pretoria - Administrative	**Population:**	37,859,000
	Bloemfontein - Judicial	**Size:**	1,127,200 sq km
Language:	English/Afrikaans/Zulu/Xhosa	**Telephone Country Code:**	27

ZAMBIA

ANGOLA

N

Harare ■

ZIMBABWE

Bulawayo ●

BOTSWANA

NAMIBIA

Phalaborwa ▲

Sabie ▲

Pretoria ▲
Johannesburg ■   Mlilwane ▲
Johannesburg (3) ▲   SWAZILAND

SOUTH AFRICA

Kimberley ▲

Champagne
Castle ▲
Zululand (2) ▲

LESOTHO
Durban (3) ▲

Colesburg ▲

Worcester ▲
Cape Town ■
Cape Town (7)   Stellenbosch ▲   Tsitsikamma ▲ Port Alfred ▲
Mossel ▲   ▲ ▲ Jeffreys Bay
Hermanus ▲   Bay   Plettenberg Bay

English

To ensure your stay is as pleasant and safe as possible, it is advisable to check with your hostel manager regarding local security, as well as reliable transport and tour information. Hostels are located in cities, in the countryside, on the coast and on hills/mountains.

Price range

Price range R40.00-180.00. 🖳 🖳.

Rooms and Reservations

R during Jan-Mar, Oct-Dec. (²⛱ 👬). Reservations via **IBN** National Booking Centre, Hostel or National Office by **t f e**. (Reservation charges may apply). Smoking is limited - please check.

Guests

Membership Card is required. Age limits may apply for children and mixed age groups - check with hostel. 👬 welcome. Group bookings via National Booking Centre, Hostel or National Office by **t f e** (Reservation charges may apply).

Open times

Main hostels: open 🗓, ◷. Reception open: 07:30-21:00hrs. Resident manager. **Other hostels:** open 🗓, ◷. Reception open: 08:00-19:00hrs. Resident manager.

Meals

🍽 BLD For individuals & for 👬. 🐚.

Discounts

HI Member Discounts available - see discounts section and www.iyhf.org.

Travelling around

For ease of travel use ✈ 🚌 🚐 Self-Drive. Drive on the left. International Driving Licence required. Air and rail transport exists between major cities and towns. There is a large network of bus and taxi services.

Travel/Activity Packages

Tours/sightseeing, walking/trekking and accommodation/transport packages available. Package bookings via National Booking Centre, Hostel or National Office by **t f e**.

Passports and Visas

Passport and Visa required.

Health

Vaccinations are required - check with your medical advisor. Medical insurance is recommended.

Français

Afin de rendre votre séjour aussi agréable et sûr que possible, il est conseillé de vous renseigner auprès du directeur de l'auberge sur les problèmes de sécurité qui pourraient se présenter dans la région, ainsi que sur les services de transport fiables. Les auberges sont situées dans les villes, à la campagne, sur le littoral et à la montagne.

Tarifs des nuitées

Tarifs des nuitées 40.00-180.00R. 🖳 🖳.

Chambres et réservations

R jan-mar, oct-déc. (²⛱ 👬). Réservations via **IBN** le Centre National de Réservation, l'auberge ou le Bureau National par **t f e**. (Des frais de réservation pourront vous être facturés). Il est permis de fumer dans certaines chambres - veuillez vérifier.

Usagers

La carte d'adhérent est à présenter. Il est possible que des limites d'âge soient en vigueur pour les enfants et les groupes d'âges mixtes -

vérifiez auprès de l'auberge. Accueil des ♦♦♦. Réservations pour groupes via le Centre National de Réservation, l'auberge ou le Bureau National par ☎ ❶ 🅴 (Des frais de réservation pourront vous être facturés).

Horaires d'ouverture

Grandes auberges: ouvertes 🖥, 🕐. Accueil ouvert entre 7h30-21h. Gérant réside sur place. **Autres auberges:** ouvertes 🖥, 🕐. Accueil ouvert entre 8h-19h. Gérant réside sur place.

Repas

🍽 BLD Pour individuels & pour ♦♦♦. ☎.

Remises

Remises pour les adhérents HI - voir la section "Remises" et notre site: www.iyhf.org.

Déplacements

Modes de transport recommandés ✈ 🚃 🚐 Voiture. Conduite à gauche. Permis de conduire international obligatoire. Des compagnies aériennes et un réseau ferroviaire relient les grandes villes. Il existe également un vaste réseau d'autobus et de taxis.

Forfaits Voyages/Activités

Forfaits circuits touristiques, randonnées pédestres et hébergement/transport disponibles. Réservations des forfaits via le Centre National de Réservation, l'auberge ou le Bureau National par ☎ ❶ 🅴.

Passeports et visas

Passeport et visa obligatoires.

Santé

Des vaccinations sont obligatoires - veuillez vérifier auprès de votre médecin. Une assurance médicale de voyage est conseillée.

Deutsch

Zur Gewährleistung eines angenehmen und sicheren Aufenthalts, ist es ratsam, mit Ihrem Herbergsleiter die örtliche Sicherheit sowie zuverlässige Transport- und Reiseinformationen zu überprüfen. Herbergen befinden sich in Städten, auf dem Land, an der Küste und in Bergen/Gebirgen.

Preisspanne

Preisspanne 40.00-180.00 R. 💳 💳.

Zimmer und Reservierungen

🆁 während Jan-Mär, Okt-Dez. (🛏 ♦♦♦). Reservierungen über [IBN] Nationales Buchungszentrum, Herberge oder Landesverband per ☎ ❶ 🅴. (Reservierungskosten könnten anfallen). Rauchen ist begrenzt - bitte checken.

Gäste

Mitgliedsausweis ist erforderlich. Altersbegrenzungen für Kinder und Gruppen gemischten Alters möglich - in der Herberge nachfragen. ♦♦♦ willkommen. Gruppenbuchungen über Nationales Buchungszentrum, Herberge oder Landesverband per ☎ ❶ 🅴. (Reservierungskosten könnten anfallen).

Öffnungszeiten

Hauptherbergen: Zugang 🖥, 🕐. Rezeption zwischen 07:30-21:00Uhr. Herbergsmanager wohnt im Haus. **Andere Herbergen:** Zugang 🖥, 🕐. Rezeption zwischen 08:00-19:00Uhr. Herbergsmanager wohnt im Haus.

Mahlzeiten

🍽 BLD Für Einzelreisende & für ♦♦♦. ☎.

Ermäßigungen

HI-Mitgliedsrabatt ist erhältlich – siehe Teil für Rabatte und Ermäßigungen und www.iyhf.org.

Reisen im Land

Reisen ist einfach mit ✈ 🚂 🚐 Selbstfahrer. Links fahren. Internationaler Führerschein erforderlich. Zwischen größeren Städten gibt es Flug- und Zugtransport. Außerdem besteht ein ausgiebiges Bus- und Taxinetz.

Reise-/Aktivitäten-Packages

Touren/sightseeing, wandern/trekking und Unterkunft/Transport-Packages erhältlich. Package-Buchungen über Nationales Buchungszentrum, Herberge oder Landesverband per ❶ ❶ ❷.

Reisepässe und Visa

Reisepass/Einreisevisum erforderlich.

Gesundheit

Schutzimpfungen sind erforderlich - mit Ihrem Arzt checken. Unfall-/Krankenversicherung wird empfohlen.

Español

Para asegurarse una estancia agradable y segura, es aconsejable consultar al gerente del albergue acerca de la seguridad local, los transportes recomendados y las excursiones disponibles. Los albergues están situados en las ciudades, el campo, la costa y la montaña.

Tarifas mínima y máxima

Tarifas mínima y máxima 40.00-180.00R. 🗐 🗐.

Habitaciones y Reservas

🅡 en ene-mar, oct-dic. (🛏 👫). Reservas por ⟦IBN⟧ o a través de la Central Nacional de Reservas, el albergue o la Asociación Nacional por ❶ ❶ ❷. (Es posible que se aplique un suplemento en concepto de gastos de reserva).

Está permitido fumar sólo en algunas salas/habitaciones - infórmese.

Huéspedes

Los huéspedes deben presentar su Carnet de Alberguista. Es posible que exista un límite de edad para los niños y los grupos de personas de diferentes edades - consulte con el albergue. Se admiten 👫. Reservas de grupo a través de la Central Nacional de Reservas, el albergue o la Asociación Nacional por ❶ ❶ ❷ (Es posible que se aplique un suplemento en concepto de gastos de reserva).

Horarios y fechas de apertura

Albergues principales - abiertos 🗓, 🕘. Horario de recepción: 07:30-21:00h. Gerente residente. **Otros albergues** - abiertos 🗓, 🕘. Horario de recepción: 08:00-19:00h. Gerente residente.

Comidas

🍽 BLD Para individuales y para 👫. ♂.

Descuentos

Se conceden descuentos a los miembros de Hostelling International – véase la sección sobre descuentos y nuestra página Internet en www.iyhf.org.

Desplazamientos

Transportes recomendados: ✈ 🚂 🚐 Automóvil. Se circula por la izquierda. Es necesario un permiso internacional de conducir. Existen conexiones aéreas y ferroviarias entre las grandes ciudades y poblaciones, asi como una extensa red de autobuses y taxis. Recomendamos también el automóvil.

Viajes Combinados con Actividades

Viajes combinados con visitas turísticas, senderismo y alojamiento/transporte. Reserva de viajes combinados a través de la Central

Nacional de Reservas, el albergue o la Asociación Nacional por 🅣 🅕 🅔.

Pasaportes y Visados

Pasaporte y visado obligatorios.

Información Sanitaria

Vacunación obligatoria - consulte con su centro médico. Seguro médico recomendado.

Cape Town -
Ashanti Lodge

11 Hof St Gardens,
Cape Town 8001,
Western Cape.
🅣 (21) 423 8721
🅕 (21) 423 8790
🅔 ashanti@iafrica.com

Open Dates:	🗓
Open Hours:	🕐
Reservations:	🅡 IBN CC
Price Range:	R60.00-220.00
Beds:	89 - 1x¹ 11x² 5x⁶ 4x⁶
Facilities:	👫 🍽 🛏 ☕ 🛎 TV 🧺 🗄 📷 ⑧ P ⓘ 🛄 ❄ ✆ 👥 ⛩

Directions: 1.5SW from city centre

✈ Cape Town International 20km

A🚌 To City Centre 1.5km

🚢 Cape Town 2km

🚂 Cape Town Central 1.5km

🚌 Oranjezicht bus from Adderley St 1.5km ap Mount Nelson Hotel 200m

Attractions: 🔍5km ✎10m ⚓

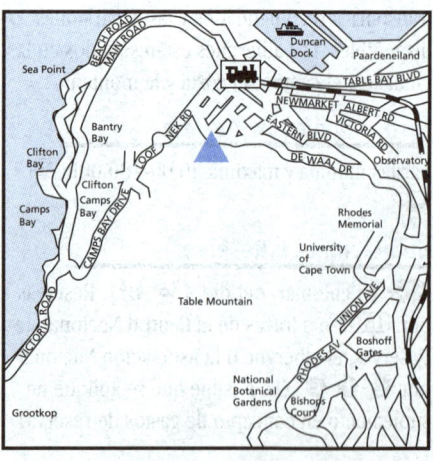

Cape Town -
Riverview Lodge

5 Anson Rd,
Observatory,
Cape Town 7925,
Western Cape.
t (21) 447 9056
f (21) 447 5192
e info@riverview.co.za

Open Dates: 🗓
Open Hours: 🕐
Reservations: IBN CC
Price Range: R50.00-70.00
Beds: 60
Facilities: 👬 👬 🍽 ⚡ ☕ 🛏 📺 🧺 1 x 🏊 🖥 💼 🅿 ℹ 🧳 ♻ 🏠
Directions: 8S from city centre
✈ Cape Town International 12km
A🚌 Central 5km
🚂 Observatory 500m
🚌 Observatory bus 5km ap Stop No. 80, 500m
Attractions: ⛳ ⛰ 🏃 ♋1km 🏊1km

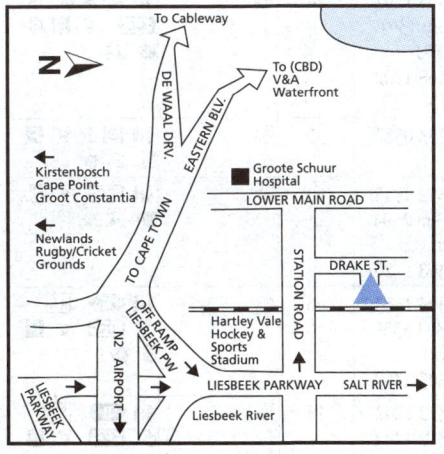

Johannesburg -
Backpackers Ritz

1A North Rd,
Dunkeld West,
Johannesburg 2196,
Gauteng.
t (11) 325 7125; (11) 325 7379 (Guests)
f (11) 325 2521
e ritz@iafrica.com

Open Dates: 🗓
Open Hours: 🕐
Reservations: R IBN CC
Price Range: R50.00-150.00 💳
Beds: 70 - 4x¹🛏 6x²🛏 1x³🛏 1x⁴🛏 4x⁶🛏
Facilities: 👬1x 👬 🍽 ⚡ ☕ 🛏 📺 💻 🧺 🖥 💼 🔢 🅿 ℹ 🧳 ♻ 🏪
Directions:
✈ Johannesburg International - phone for free pick-up 30km
A🚌 To City Centre 7.5km
🚆 Johannesburg Park 7.5km
🚌 73, 80, 80b from Eloff St - Free pick-up 7.5km ap Dunkeld West Shopping Centre 150m
Attractions: 🏊

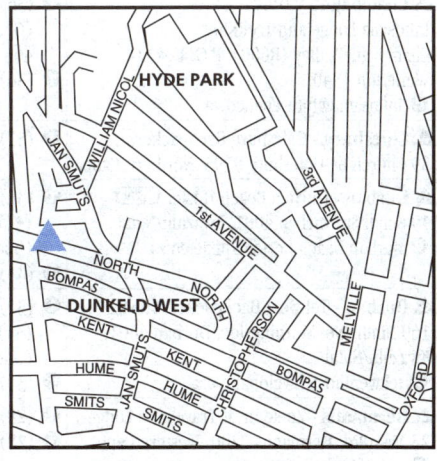

Location/Address	Telephone No. Fax No.	Beds	Opening Dates	Facilities
▲ **Botha's Hill** - The Valley Trust Zulu Reserve Rd, PO Box 33, Botha's Hill, 3660. e vtrust@wn.apc.org	☏ (31) 777 1955 🖷 (31) 777 1114	31	🖪12	††† ⟨⟩ Ⓡ 3N ♿ ⊟CC⊟ ⟨ P ⟨
▲ **Cape Town** - Aadrvark Backpackers 319 Main Rd, P.O. Box 41563, Sea Point, 8060, Cape Town. e aardbp@mweb.co.za	☏ (21) 434 4163 🖷 (21) 439 3813	40	🖪12	††† ⟨⟩ Ⓡ 5 SW ⊟CC⊟ ⟨ P ⟨ ☕ 🚲 ☼
▲ **Cape Town** - Abe Bailey 11 Maynard Rd, Muizenburg, Cape Town 7945, Western Cape. e abeb@new.co.za	☏ (21) 788 2301; (21) 788 4283 (Guests) 🖷 (21) 788 2301	47	🖪12	††† ⟨⟩ 26 S ⟨
▲ **Cape Town** - Ashanti Lodge ⟨IBN⟩ **11 Hof St Gardens, Cape Town 8001, Western Cape.** e ashanti@iafrica.com	☏ (21) 423 8721 🖷 (21) 423 8790	89	🖪12	⟨⟩ Ⓡ 1.5 SW ⊟CC⊟ ⟨ P ⟨ ☕
▲ **Cape Town** - Overseas Visitors Club 230 Upper Long St, Cape Town 8001, Western Cape. e hross@ovc.co.za	☏ (21) 424 6800; (21) 423 4477 🖷 (21) 423 4870	18	🖪12	1 SE ⊟CC⊟ ⟨ ⟨ 🚲 ☼
▲ **Cape Town** - Riverview Lodge ⟨IBN⟩ **5 Anson Rd, Observatory, Cape Town 7925, Western Cape.** e info@riverview.co.za	☏ (21) 447 9056 🖷 (21) 447 5192	60	🖪12	††† ⟨⟩ 8 S ⊟CC⊟ ⟨ P ⟨ ☕
▲ **Cape Town** - Stans Halt The Glen, Camps Bay, Cape Town 8001, Western Cape. e stanh@new.co.za	☏ (21) 438 9037; (21) 438 1405 (Guests) 🖷 (21) 4389037	30	🖪12	⟨⟩ 5 SW ⟨ P
▲ **Cape Town** - Zebra Crossing 82 New Church St, Tamboerskloof, Cape Town 8001. e zebracross@intekom.co.za	☏ (21) 422 1265 🖷 (21) 422 1265	44	🖪12	††† ⟨⟩ Ⓡ 1 SW ⟨ P ⟨ ☕ 🚲 ☼
▲ **Champagne Valley** - Inkosana Lodge and Trekking Champagne Valley (R600), P.O. Box 60, Winterton 3340. e inkosana@futurenet.co.za	☏ (36) 468 1202; (Guests) (36) 468 1851 🖷 (36) 468 1202	24	🖪12	††† ⟨⟩ Ⓡ ♿ ⊟CC⊟ ⟨ P ⟨ ☕ 🚲
▲ **Colesburg** - Colesburg Backpackers 39 Church St, Colesburg 9795, Northern Cape.	☏ (51) 753 0582	30	🖪12	††† ⟨⟩ ♿ ⟨ P ⟨ 🚲 ☼
▲ **Durban** - Durban Beach Hostel ⟨IBN⟩ 19 Smith St, Durban 4001, Kwazulu/Natal. e durban.beach.hostel@pixie.co.za	☏ (31) 332 4945; (31) 368 2594 (Guests) 🖷 (31) 368 1720	60	🖪12	††† ⊟CC⊟ ⟨ ⟨ ☕ 🚲 ☼
▲ **Durban** - Tekweni Backpackers Hostel 169 Ninth Ave, Morningside, Durban 4001, Kwazulu/Natal. e tekwenihostel@global.co.za	☏ (31) 303 1433; (31) 303 3339 (Guests) 🖷 (31) 303 4369	46	🖪12	††† Ⓡ 4N ♿ ⊟CC⊟ ⟨ P ⟨ ☕
▲ **Hermanus** - Zoete Inval Traveller's Lodge 23 Main Rd, Hermanus 7200, Western Cape. e zoetein@hermanus.co.za	☏ (28) 312 1242 🖷 (28) 312 1242	18	🖪12	††† Ⓡ 8 W ♿ ⊟CC⊟ ⟨ P ⟨ ☕ 🚲

Location/Address	Telephone No. Fax No.	Beds	Opening Dates	Facilities
▲ **Jeffreys Bay** Jeffreys Bay Backpackers, 12 Jeffrey St, Jeffreys Bay 6330, Eastern Cape. e backpac@netactive.co.za	☎ (042) 293 1379; (042) 293 1021 ✆ (042) 296 1763	30	⌂12	
△ *Johannesburg - Airport Backpackers* *3 Mohawk St, Rhodesfield, Kempton Park,* *Johannesburg 1620.* e *airbackp@mweb.co.za*	☎ *(11) 394 0485* ✆ *(11) 394 0485*	*22*	⌂12	
▲ **Johannesburg** - Backpackers Ritz [IBN] **1A North Rd, Dunkeld West,** **Johannesburg 2196, Gauteng.** e ritz@iafrica.com	☎ (11) 325 7125; (11) 325 7379 (Guests) ✆ (11) 325 2521	70	⌂12	
▲ **Johannesburg** - Inchanga Ranch Hostel Inchanga Rd, Witkoppen, Johannesburg 2021, Gauteng. e ivi@pixie.co.za	☎ (11) 708 1304; (11) 708 1310 ✆ (11) 708 1464	28	⌂12	26N
▲ **Kimberley** - Gum Tree Lodge Bloemfontein Rd, Kimberley 8301, Northern Cape. e lawrie@global.co.za	☎ (53) 832 8577 ✆ (53) 831 5409	128	⌂12	5E
△ *Kleinemonde -* *Sherwood Shack Backpackers* *(Just off the R72 along Trappe's Valley and* *Shaw Park Rd), P.O. Box 21, South Seas,* *6172, Eastern Cape.* e *src@imaginet.co.za*	☎ *(46) 675 1090* ✆ *(46) 675 1090*	*24*	⌂12	22NE
△ *Mossel Bay - Mossel Bay Backpackers* *1 Marsh St, Mossel Bay 5605, Western Cape.* e *marquette@pixie.co.za*	☎ *(44) 691 3182* ✆ *(44) 691 3182*	*17*	⌂12	
▲ **Phalaborwa** - Elephant Walk Backpackers 30 Anna Scheepers St, Phalaborwa 1390, Northern Province. e elephant.walk@nix.co.za	☎ (15) 781 2758 ✆ (15) 781 2758	13	⌂12	
▲ **Plettenberg Bay** - Nothando Backpackers 5 Wilder St, Plettenberg Bay 6600, Western Cape. e deios@global.co.za	☎ (44) 533 0220 ✆ (44) 533 0220	28	⌂12	
▲ **Pretoria** - Pretoria Backpackers 34 Bourke St, Sunnyside, Pretoria, 0002. e ptaback@netactive.co.za	☎ (12) 343 9754 ✆ (12) 343 2524	47	⌂12	2.5SE
▲ **Richards Bay** - Harbour Lights Resort P.O. Box 7099, Empangeni Rail 3910. e zebra@harbourlights.co.za	☎ (35) 796 6239 ✆ (35) 796 6753	24	⌂12	20W
△ *Sabie - Jock of the Bushveld* *Main St, Sabie 1260, Mpumalanga.* e *jocksabi@netactive.co.za*	☎ *(13) 764 2178;* *(13) 764 1097* *(Guests)* ✆ *(13) 764 3215*	*20*	⌂12	

Location/Address	Telephone No. Fax No.	Beds	Opening Dates	Facilities
△ **Stellenbosch** - *Backpackers Inn* *First Floor, De Wet Centre, Church St, Stellenbosch 7600, Western Cape.* e *bacpac1@global.co.za*	☎ *(21) 887 2020* 🖷 *(21) 887 2010*	*42*	🖷12	🛏 🖻 🝔 ☼
▲ **Swaziland** - Sondzela Backpackers Lodge Mlilwane Wildlife Sanctuary, Ezulwini Valley, P.O. Box 311, Malkerns, Swaziland. e reservations@biggame.co.sz	☎ (268) 528 3117 🖷 (268) 528 3924	26	🖷12	👫 ⊂CC⊃ 🛏 🅿 🖻
▲ **Tsitsikamma** - Bloukrantz Backpackers Tsitsikamma Khoisan Village, PO Box 93, Stormsriver, 6308. e juline@intekom.co.za	☎ (42) 281 1450 🖷 (42) 281 1457	24	🖷12	🍽 Ⓡ 🅿 🖻
▲ **Worcester** - Die Kromhout Katel Backpackers 26 Stockenström St, Worcester 6850.	☎ (023) 347 7364 🖷 (023) 347 7364	21	🖷12	👫 Ⓡ 🛏 🅿 🖻 🝔 🚲
▲ **Zululand** - Cuckoos Nest Backpackers 28 Alibizia St, PO Box 522, Kwambonambi, 3915. e cuckoos@mweb.co.za	☎ (35) 580 1001/ 1009/ 1010 🖷 (35) 580 1002	24	🖷12	👫 🍽 Ⓡ ♿ 🛏 🅿 🖻 🝔 🚲 ☼

"Own only what you can carry with you; know language, know countries, know people. Let your memory be your travel bag."

"Ne possède que ce que tu peux emporter avec toi; connais les langues, connais les pays, connais les gens. Que ta mémoire te serve de sac de voyage."

„Besitze nur, was du mitnehmen kannst; lerne Sprache, Länder, Leute kennen. Lass deine Erinnerung deine Reisetasche sein."

"Posee solamente lo que puedas llevar contigo; conoce los idiomas, conoce los países, conoce a la gente. Deja que tu memoria sea tu bolso de viaje."

Alexander Solzhenitsyn

Thailand

THAÏLANDE
THAILAND
TAILANDIA

**Thai Youth Hostels Association,
25/14 Phitsanulok Road, Si Sao Thewet,
Dusit, Bangkok 10300, Thailand.**

**☎ (66) (2) 628-7413 to 5
🅕 (66) (2) 628-7416**

A copy of the Hostel Directory for this Country can be obtained from:
The National Office

Capital:	Bangkok		**Population:**	66,000,000
Language:	Thai		**Size:**	500,000 sq km
Currency:	baht		**Telephone Country Code:**	66

Thailand

MYANMAR
(BURMA)

LAOS

▲ Chiang Mai

Vientiane ■

Mekong Riv

N

THAILAND

▲ Tak   ▲ Phitsanulok

Lop Buri ▲   ▲ Nakhon
                        Ratchasima

Kanchanaburi   ▲ Ayutthaya
▲

Bangkok
■ ▲ Bangkok (2)
▲ Chonburi

CAMBODIA

▲ Rayong

Ko Samet

Phnom Penh ■

Ko Samui

        50 100 150 200 KM
0 ├──┼──┼──┼──┤
        50   100   MLS

▲
Phuket

MALAYSIA

English

Come at any time of year to experience the most exotic and welcoming country in South East Asia. Hostels are located in cities, on the coast and on hills/mountains.

Price range

Price range Thai baht 90-350. 🖳.

Rooms and Reservations

R 🖾 (All Rooms). Reservations via IBN 🖳 Hostel or National Office by ❶ ❺ ❷. Smoking rooms are available.

Guests

Membership Card and Passport/Photo ID are required. The maximum stay is 14 days. ♟♟♟ welcome. Group bookings via IBN 🖳 Hostel or National Office by ❶ ❺ ❷.

Open times

Main hostels: open 🖾, 🕓. Reception open: 🕓. Resident manager. **Other hostels:** open 🖾, 🕓. Resident manager.

Meals

🍽 BLD For individuals & for ♟♟♟. 🍳.

Discounts

HI Member Discounts available - see discounts section and www.iyhf.org.

Travelling around

For ease of travel use ✈ 🚅 🚢 🚌 Self-Drive. Drive on the left.

Travel/Activity Packages

Tours/sightseeing, water sports, cycling/ mountain biking, walking/trekking and accommodation/transport packages available. Package bookings via 🖳 National Booking Centre, Hostel or National Office by ❶ ❺ ❷.

Passports and Visas

Passport and Visa required.

Health

Vaccinations are advised - check with your medical advisor. Medical insurance is recommended.

Français

N'importe quelle époque de l'année est idéale pour découvrir le pays le plus exotique et le plus accueillant de l'Asie du sud est. Les auberges sont situées dans les villes, sur le littoral et à la montagne.

Tarifs des nuitées

Tarifs des nuitées 90-350 Thai baht. 🖳.

Chambres et réservations

R 🖾 (Toutes chambres). Réservations via IBN 🖳 l'auberge ou le Bureau National par ❶ ❺ ❷. Des chambres pour fumeurs sont disponibles.

Usagers

La carte d'adhérent ainsi que le passeport/pièce d'identité avec photo sont à présenter. La durée maximale du séjour est de 14 jours. Accueil des ♟♟♟. Réservations pour groupes via IBN 🖳 l'auberge ou le Bureau National par ❶ ❺ ❷.

Horaires d'ouverture

Grandes auberges: ouvertes 🖾, 🕓. Accueil ouvert 🕓. Gérant réside sur place. **Autres auberges:** ouvertes 🖾, 🕓. Gérant réside sur place.

Repas

🍽 BLD Pour individuels & pour ♟♟♟. 🍳.

Remises

Remises pour les adhérents HI - voir la section "Remises" et notre site: www.iyhf.org.

Déplacements

Modes de transport recommandés ✈ 🚌 🚢 🚐 Voiture. Conduite à gauche.

Forfaits Voyages/Activités

Forfaits circuits touristiques, sports aquatiques, cyclotourisme/VTT, randonnées pédestres et hébergement/transport disponibles. Réservations des forfaits via 🖳 le Centre National de Réservation, l'auberge ou le Bureau National par ❶ ❷ ❸.

Passeports et visas

Passeport et visa obligatoires.

Santé

Des vaccinations sont conseillées - veuillez vérifier auprès de votre médecin. Une assurance médicale de voyage est conseillée.

Deutsch

Kommen Sie zu jeder Zeit des Jahres und erleben Sie das exotischste und gastfreundlichste Land in Südostasien. Herbergen befinden sich in Städten, an der Küste und in Bergen/Gebirgen.

Preisspanne

Preisspanne 90-350 Thai baht. 🖳.

Zimmer und Reservierungen

🅡 🖳 (Alle Zimmer). Reservierungen über ⌷IBN⌷ 🖳 Herberge oder Landesverband per ❶ ❷ ❸. Es gibt Zimmer für Raucher.

Gäste

Mitgliedsausweis und Reisepass/ Personalausweis sind erforderlich. Der

maximale Aufenthalt beträgt 14 Tage. 👪 willkommen. Gruppenbuchungen über ⌷IBN⌷ 🖳 Herberge oder Landesverband per ❶ ❷ ❸.

Öffnungszeiten

Hauptherbergen: Zugang 🗔, 🕓. Rezeption 🕓. Herbergsmanager wohnt im Haus. **Andere Herbergen:** Zugang 🗔, 🕓. Herbergsmanager wohnt im Haus.

Mahlzeiten

🍽 BLD Für Einzelreisende & für 👪. 🍴.

Ermäßigungen

HI-Mitgliedsrabatt ist erhältlich – siehe Teil für Rabatte und Ermäßigungen und www.iyhf.org.

Reisen im Land

Reisen ist einfach mit ✈ 🚌 🚢 🚐 Selbstfahrer. Links fahren.

Reise-/Aktivitäten-Packages

Touren/sightseeing, Wassersport, Fahrrad/ Mountainbiking, wandern/trekking und Unterkunft/Transport-Packages erhältlich. Package-Buchungen über 🖳 Nationales Buchungszentrum, Herberge oder Landesverband per ❶ ❷ ❸.

Reisepässe und Visa

Reisepass/Einreisevisum erforderlich.

Gesundheit

Schutzimpfungen werden empfohlen - mit Ihrem Arzt checken. Unfall-/Krankenversicherung wird empfohlen.

Español

Visitenos en cualquier época del año y disfrute del país más exótico y acogedor del Asia

Sudoriental. Los albergues están situados en las ciudades, la costa y la montaña.

Tarifas mínima y máxima

Tarifas mínima y máxima 90-350 Thai baht. 🛏.

Habitaciones y Reservas

R 🈺 (Todas las habitaciones). Reservas por (IBN) 🖥 o a través del albergue o la Asociación Nacional por ❶ ❷ ❸. Los albergues disponen de habitaciones para fumadores.

Huéspedes

Los huéspedes deben presentar su Carnet de Alberguista y su pasaporte o carnet de identidad. La estancia máxima es de 14 días. Se admiten 👪. Reservas de grupo por (IBN) 🖥 o a través del albergue o la Asociación Nacional por ❶ ❷ ❸.

Horarios y fechas de apertura

Albergues principales - abiertos 🈺, 🕐. Horario de recepción: 🕐. Gerente residente. **Otros albergues** - abiertos 🈺, 🕐. Gerente residente.

Comidas

🍽 BLD Para individuales y para 👪. 🍴.

Descuentos

Se conceden descuentos a los miembros de Hostelling International – véase la sección sobre descuentos y nuestra página Internet en www.iyhf.org.

Desplazamientos

Transportes recomendados: ✈ 🚌 ⛴ 🚐 Automóvil. Se circula por la izquierda.

Viajes Combinados con Actividades

Viajes combinados con visitas turísticas, deportes náuticos, cicloturismo/bicicleta de montaña, senderismo y alojamiento/transporte. Reserva de viajes combinados por 🖥 o a través de la Central Nacional de Reservas, el albergue o la Asociación Nacional por ❶ ❷ ❸.

Pasaportes y Visados

Pasaporte y visado obligatorios.

Información Sanitaria

Vacunación recomendada - consulte con su centro médico. Seguro médico recomendado.

"He who would travel happily must travel light."

"Celui qui veut voyager joyeusement doit voyager légèrement."

„Wer glücklich reisen will, sollte nur wenig Gepäck mitnehmen."

"El que quiera viajar feliz debe viajar ligero de equipaje."

Antoine de Saint-Exupéry

Bangkok - HI Bangkok

25/2 Phitsanulok Rd,
Si Sao Thewet,
Dusit,
Bangkok 10300.
📞 (2) 2810361, 2820950
📠 (2) 6287416
✉ e-bangkok@tyha.org

Open Dates: 🗓

Reservations: Ⓡ IBN

Price Range: 70-350 baht 🛏

Beds: 63

Facilities: 👨👩👧 👨👩👧 🍴 ☕ 🏨 📄 🎿 📺 💼 🔓 💲 Ⓟ 🛈 ♿

Directions:

✈	Donmuang 35km
A🚌	A2 - Sanamluang 35km
🛳	Tha Thewet Pier 1km
🚋	Samsen Station 2.5km
🚌	16, 23, 43, 72, 99 500m ap Thewet Market

Attractions: 🔍10m 🏊 400m

"Travel only with thy equals or thy betters; if there are none, travel alone."

"Ne voyage qu'avec tes égaux ou tes supérieurs; si tu n'en as pas, voyage tout seul."

„Reise nur mit deinesgleichen oder Höherstehenden; wenn es keine gibt, reise allein."

"Viaja solamente con tus iguales o con tus superiores; si no tienes ninguno, viaja solo."

The Dhammapada

[Map:]

CHAO PRAYA RIVER

7-11   Ⓜ

National Library

HI

Srlayuthaya Rd

THEWET MARKET

Phitsanulok Rd

7-11

THA THEWES PIER

CANAL

PO

Lukluang Rd

PO

7-11

BANK OF THAILAND

Krungkasem Rd

WAT INTHARAWIHAN (Standing Buddha)

Prachathipatai Rd

Samsen Rd

Wisutthikasat Rd

KEY
● Bus Stop
■ ATM
▲ Post Office
🛕 Temple

Location/Address	Telephone No. Fax No.	Beds	Opening Dates	Facilities
△ *Ayutthaya* - HI Ban-Na-Wang *T. 69/1 Tambon, Thawasukri,* *Amphor Pranakornsriayuthaya, Ayuthaya 13000.* *e-ayuthaya@tyha.org*	☎ *(35) 251806,* *252061,* *(2) 5730554* ✆ *(2) 5730554*	*10*	🗓12	♂♀ ✆ P
▲ **Bangkok** - HI Bangkok (IBN) **25/2 Phitsanulok Rd, Si Sao Thewet,** **Dusit, Bangkok 10300.** *e-bangkok@tyha.org*	☎ *(2) 2810361,* *2820950* ✆ *(2) 6287416*	*63*	🗓12	♂♀ ⑪ R P 🖬 ☕
△ *Bangkok* - HI Bansabai *8/137 Soi Sahakorn 15, Ladphrao 71,* *Bangkok 10230.* *e-bansabai.asianet.co.th,* *e-bansabai@tyha.org*	☎ *(2) 5390150,* *9329200* ✆ *(2) 5384387*	*42*	🗓12	♂♀ ⑪ R P 🖬
△ *Chiang Mai* - HI Chiang-Mai *21/8 Changklan Rd, Mooban Oon-Ruen,* *Chiang Mai 50100.* *e-chiangmai@tyha.org*	☎ *(53) 276737* ✆ *(53) 204025*	*40*	🗓12	⑪ R P 🖬
△ *Chonburi* - HI Sriracha *72/20 Soi Khongraw, Wat Wanghin Rd.,* *Sriracha, Chonburi 20110.* *sriracha@tyha.org*	☎ *(2) 3796612* ✆ *(2) 3796612*	*24*	🗓12	♂♀ ⑪ R 24S ✆ P 🖬
△ *Kanchanaburi* - HI Khum-chom-dao *850/18 Soi Thungthong, Thamuang,* *Kanchanaburi 71110.* *e-KCDIH@hotmail.com*	☎ *(34) 612122* ✆ *(34) 626325*	*20*	🗓12	♂♀ ⑪ R 0.8N CC ✆ P 🖬
△ *Lop Buri* - HI Lop-Buri *3km SE, 5/19 Moo 3. Naressuan Rd,* *Amphor Mueng, Lop Buri 15000.* *e-ruj@school.net.th,e-lopburi@tyha.org*	☎ *(36) 613390* ✆ *(36) 613390*	*32*	🗓12	♂♀ ⑪ R 3SE P 🖬
△ *Nakhorn Ratchasima* - HI Phimai *2/4 Chomsudasadet Rd, Phimai,* *Nakhorn Ratchasima 30110, 40km NE.* *e-phimai@tyha.org*	☎ *(44) 471918*	*10*	🗓12	♂♀ ⑪ R 40NE P 🖬
△ *Phitsanulok* - HI Phitsanulok *38 Sa-Nam-Bin Rd, Phitsanulok 65000.* *e-phitsanulok@tyha.org*	☎ *(55) 242060,* *210862 to 4* ✆ *(55) 210864*	*40*	🗓12	♂♀ ⑪ ✆ P 🖬
△ *Phuket* - HI Phuket *73/11 Chowfah Rd, Chalong, Muang,* *Phuket 83000.* *hostthai@ksc.th.com*	☎ *(2) 3900912,* *(2) 3916854;* *Mobile phone nos:* *(1) 8396857,* *(1) 3599820* ✆ *(2) 7111986*	*85*	🗓12	♂♀ ⑪ R 9S ✆ P ☼
△ *Rayong* - HI Ban Kon-Ao *89/4 Moo 1 Mae Ram Puang Beach Rd, Phae,* *Rayong 21160, 22km E.* *e-ban-kon-ao@tyha.org,* *e-bkayh@samart.co.th*	☎ *(38) 653374,* *(2) 5137093* ✆ *(2) 5137093*	*40*	🗓12	♂♀ ⑪ 22E ✆ P 🖬

Location/Address	Telephone No. Fax No.	Beds	Opening Dates	Facilities
△ *Tak* - *HI Ban-Tak* *9/1M10, T, Taktok A. Bantak, Tak 63120,* *Bantak village is 20km north of Tak.* ✉ *e-bantak@tyba.org*	☎ *(55) 591286* 🖷 *(55) 591286*	8	🗓	🍴 🅿 📷

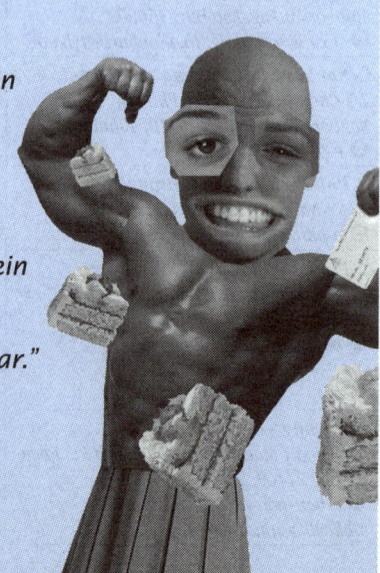

"To travel hopefully is a better thing than to arrive."

"Voyager avec espoir est mieux que d'arriver."

„Mit Hoffnung zu reisen ist besser, als sein Ziel zu erreichen."

"Viajar con esperanza es mejor que llegar."

Robert Louis Stevenson

Tunisia

TUNISIE

TUNESIEN

TUNEZ

Association Tunisienne des Auberges et Tourisme de Jeunes,
10 rue Ali Bach Hamba,
BP 320-1015 Tunis RP, Tunisia.

☎ (216) (1) 339408
❺ (216) (1) 241387
℮ ataj@planet.tn
🖳 www.cybertunisia.com/ataj

Office Hours: Monday-Friday, 08.30-18.00hrs and
Saturdays, 08.30-13.00hrs

A copy of the Hostel Directory for this Country can be obtained from:
The National Office.

Capital:	Tunis	**Population:**	8,780,000
Language:	Arabic	**Size:**	163,610 sq km
Currency:	D (dinar)	**Telephone Country Code:**	216

Tunisia

Bizerte
Rimel
Tunis-Medina
Tunis
Ain Draham
Nabeul
Hammamet
Hamman Sousse
Sousse
Kairouan

ALGERIA

Gafsa

DJerba
Gabès

TUNISIA

LIBYA

N

| | 100 | 200 | 300 | KMS |
0
| | 50 | 150 | 100 | MLS |

English

Hostels are located in cities and on the coast.

Price range

Price range U$ 5. BB^inc 🛏.

Rooms and Reservations

R during Apr, Jun-Sep, Dec. (All Rooms). Reservations via Hostel or National Office by **f** **e**. Smoking is limited - please check.

Guests

Membership Card and Passport/Photo ID are required. The maximum stay is 3 days. ♦♦♦ welcome. Group bookings via Hostel or National Office by **f** **e**.

Open times

Main hostels open Jan, Mar-Dec, 06:00-23:00hrs. Reception open: 07:00-20:00hrs. Resident manager. **Other hostels:** open 06:00-23:00hrs. Reception open: 07:00-20:00hrs. Resident manager.

Meals

🍽 BLD **R** For individuals & for ♦♦♦.

Travelling around

For ease of travel use 🚂 🚌 Self-Drive.

Travel/Activity Packages

Tours/sightseeing packages available. Package bookings via National Office by **f** **e**.

Passports and Visas

Passport, Photo ID and Visa required.

Health

Emergency medical treatment is free. Medical insurance is recommended.

Français

Les auberges sont situées dans les villes ou sur le littoral.

Tarifs des nuitées

Tarifs des nuitées 5 U$. BB^inc 🛏.

Chambres et réservations

R avril, juin-sep, déc. (Toutes chambres). Réservations via l'auberge et le Bureau National par **f** **e**. Il est permis de fumer dans certaines chambres - veuillez vérifier.

Usagers

La carte d'adhérent ainsi que le passeport/pièce d'identité avec photo sont à présenter. La durée maximale du séjour est de 3 jours. Accueil des ♦♦♦. Réservations pour groupes via l'auberge et le Bureau National par **f** **e**.

Horaires d'ouverture

Grandes auberges: ouvertes jan, mar-déc. entre 6h-23h. Accueil ouvert entre 7h-20h. Gérant réside sur place. **Autres auberges:** ouvertes entre 6h-23h. Accueil ouvert entre 7h-20h. Gérant réside sur place.

Repas

🍽 BLD **R** Pour individuels & pour ♦♦♦.

Déplacements

Modes de transport recommandés 🚂 🚌 Voiture.

Forfaits Voyages/Activités

Forfaits circuits touristiques disponibles. Réservations des forfaits via le Bureau National par **f** **e**.

Passeports et visas

Passeport, pièce d'identité avec photo et visa obligatoires.

Santé

Soins d'urgence gratuits. Une assurance médicale de voyage est conseillée.

Deutsch

Herbergen befinden sich in Städten und an der Küste.

Preisspanne

Preisspanne 5 U$. BB^inc 🛏.

Zimmer und Reservierungen

🅡 während Apr, Jun-Sept, Dez. (Alle Zimmer). Reservierungen über Herberge oder Landesverband per ❶ ❷. Rauchen ist begrenzt - bitte checken.

Gäste

Mitgliedsausweis und Reisepass/ Personalausweis sind erforderlich. Der maximale Aufenthalt beträgt 3 Tage. ♟ willkommen. Gruppenbuchungen über Herberge oder Landesverband per ❶ ❷.

Öffnungszeiten

Hauptherbergen: Zugang zwischen Jan, Mär-Dez, 06:00-23:00Uhr. Rezeption zwischen 07:00-20:00Uhr. Herbergsmanager wohnt im Haus. **Andere Herbergen:** Zugang zwischen 06:00-23:00Uhr. Rezeption zwischen 07:00-20:00Uhr. Herbergsmanager wohnt im Haus.

Mahlzeiten

🍽 BLD 🅡 Für Einzelreisende & für ♟.

Reisen im Land

Reisen ist einfach mit 🚂 🚐 Selbstfahrer.

Reise-/Aktivitäten-Packages

Touren/sightseeing-Packages erhältlich. Package-Buchungen über Landesverband per ❶ ❷.

Reisepässe und Visa

Reisepass, Personalausweis und Einreisevisum erforderlich.

Gesundheit

Nur im Notfall sind medizinische Behandlungen kostenlos. Unfall-/Krankenversicherung wird empfohlen.

Español

Los albergues están situados en las ciudades y la costa.

Tarifas mínima y máxima

Tarifas mínima y máxima 5 U$. BB^inc 🛏.

Habitaciones y Reservas

🅡 en abr, jun-sep, dic. (Todas las habitaciones). Reservas a través del albergue o la Asociación Nacional por ❶ ❷. Está permitido fumar sólo en algunas salas/ habitaciones - infórmese.

Huéspedes

Los huéspedes deben presentar su Carnet de Alberguista y su pasaporte o carnet de identidad. La estancia máxima es de 3 días. Se admiten ♟. Reservas de grupo a través del albergue o la Asociación Nacional por ❶ ❷.

Horarios y fechas de apertura

Albergues principales - abiertos ene, mar-dic, 06:00-23:00h. Horario de recepción: 07:00-20:00h. Gerente residente, **Otros albergues** - abiertos: 06:00-23:00h. Horario de recepción: 07:00-20:00h. Gerente residente.

Comidas

|O| BLD **R** Para individuales y para ⅲ.

Desplazamientos

Transportes recomendados: 🚌 🚐
Automóvil.

Viajes Combinados con Actividades

Viajes combinados con visitas turísticas.
Reserva de viajes combinados a través de la
Asociación Nacional por ❶ ❷.

Pasaportes y Visados

Pasaporte o carnet de identidad y visado
obligatorios.

Información Sanitaria

Asistencia médica de urgencia gratuita. Seguro
médico recomendado.

Tunis - Tunis Médina

**25 rue saida Ajoula,
Tunis: located in the old city of Medina,
500m from La Place du Gouvernement la
kasbah.**
❶ (1) 567.850
❶ (1) 567.850

Open Dates: 🗓

Beds: 48

Facilities: |O|

Location/Address	Telephone No. Fax No.	Beds	Opening Dates	Facilities
△ **Ain Draham** *Ave Habib Bourguiba - 8130 Ain Draham.*	☎ *(8) 655.087* 🖷 *(8) 655.087*	*150*	🖪	⦿🍴 ⛏
▲ **Bizerte** Ave Hassen Nouri - 7000 Bizerte.	☎ (2) 431.608 🖷 (2) 431.608	100	🖪	⦿🍴 1N ⛏
▲ **Hammam Sousse** - Sahloul Cite Sahloul, 4011 Hammam Sousse.	☎ (3) 362.644 🖷 (3) 362.888	65	🖪	⦿🍴 Ⓡ 1SE 🅿 🚲
▲ **Hammamet** - Centre De Sejour Ave Assad IBN El Fourat, 8050 Hammamet.	☎ (2) 280.440 🖷 (2) 278.960	65	🖪	⦿🍴 Ⓡ 2SE 🅿 🚲
▲ **Kairouan** Ave de Fez - 3100 Kairouan.	☎ (7) 228.239 🖷 (7) 226.939	70	🖪	⦿🍴 ⛏
▲ **Sousse** Ave Teïeb Mhiri Plage Boujaafar- 4000 Sousse.	☎ (3) 227.548 🖷 (3) 226.620	90	🖪	⦿🍴 ⛏
▲ **Tunis** - Tunis Médina **25 rue saida Ajoula, Tunis: located in the old city of Medina, 500m from La Place du Gouvernement la kasbah.**	☎ (1) 567.850 🖷 (1) 567.850	48	🖪	⦿🍴

YOUTH HOSTEL ACCOMMODATION
OUTSIDE THE ASSURED STANDARDS SCHEME

Djerba 11, Rue Moncef Bey, Houmt Souk - 4180 Djerba.	☎ (5) 650.619 🖷 (5) 650.619	90	🖪	⦿🍴
Gafsa Cité des Jeunes - 2119 Gafsa.	☎ (6) 220.268 🖷 (6) 225.599	60	🖪	⦿🍴 ⛏
Nabeul Ave Mongi Slim - 8000 Nabeul Plage.	☎ (2) 285.547 🖷 (2) 285.547	42	🖪	⦿🍴
Rimel 7080 (Menzel Jemil)- Bizerte.	☎ (2) 440.804	50	Youth Hostel under construction– Opening March 2001	⦿🍴

"Everywhere is nowhere. When a person spends all his time in foreign travel, he ends by having many acquaintances, but no friends."

"Partout est nulle part. Lorsque quelqu'un passe son temps à voyager à l'étranger, il finit avec beaucoup de connaissances, mais sans amis."

„Überall ist nirgendwo. Wenn jemand ständig fremde Länder bereist, hat er letztendlich viele Bekannte, aber keine Freunde."

"Todas partes es ninguna parte. Cuanda una persona dedica todo su tiempo a viajar al extranjero, acaba teniendo muchos conocidos, pero ningún amigo."

Seneca

United Arab Emirates

EMIRATS UNIS D'ARABIE

VEREINIGTE ARAB. EMIRATE

EMIRATOS ÁRABES UNIDOS

United Arab Emirates Youth Hostel Association,
PO Box 19536, Al Qusais Road,
Near Al Ahli Club, Dubai,
United Arab Emirates.

☎ (971) (4) 2988151
☎ (971) (4) 2988141

A copy of the Hostel Directory for this Country can be obtained from:
The National Office

Capital:	Abu Dhabi	**Population:**	2,200,000
Language:	Arabic	**Size:**	83,600 sq km
Currency:	Dh (dirham) (US$1 = 3.7 Dhs)	**Telephone Country Code:**	971

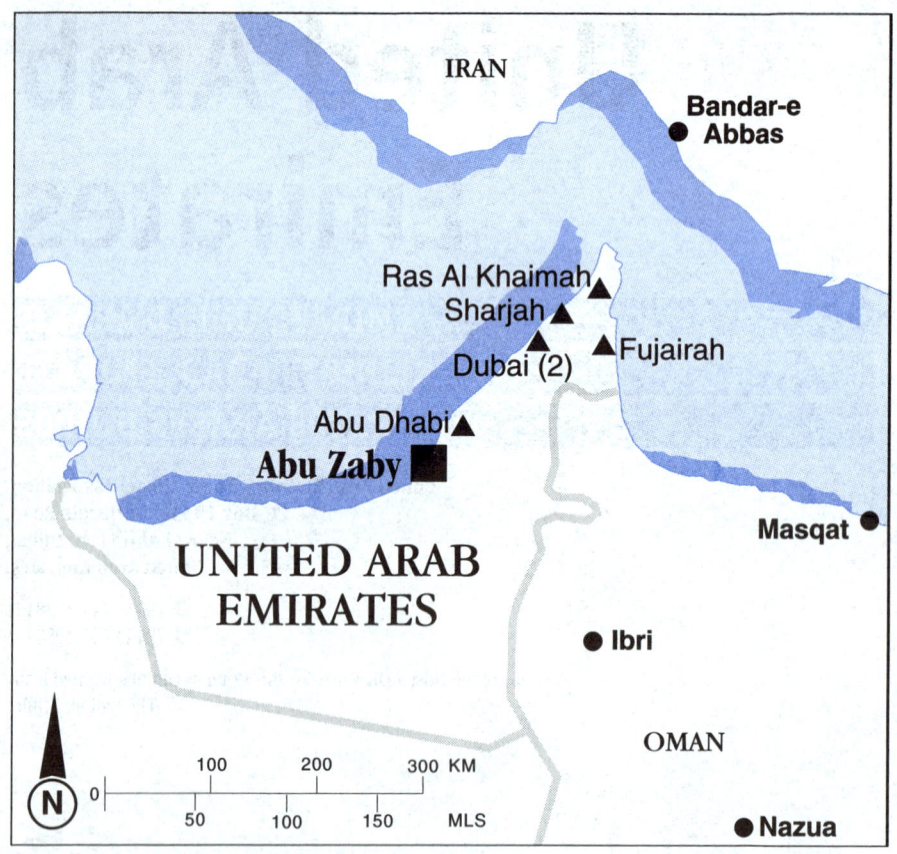

English

Visit the UAE in the months of October through to April when the climate is best. Hostels are located in cities.

Price range

Price range Dhs 35. 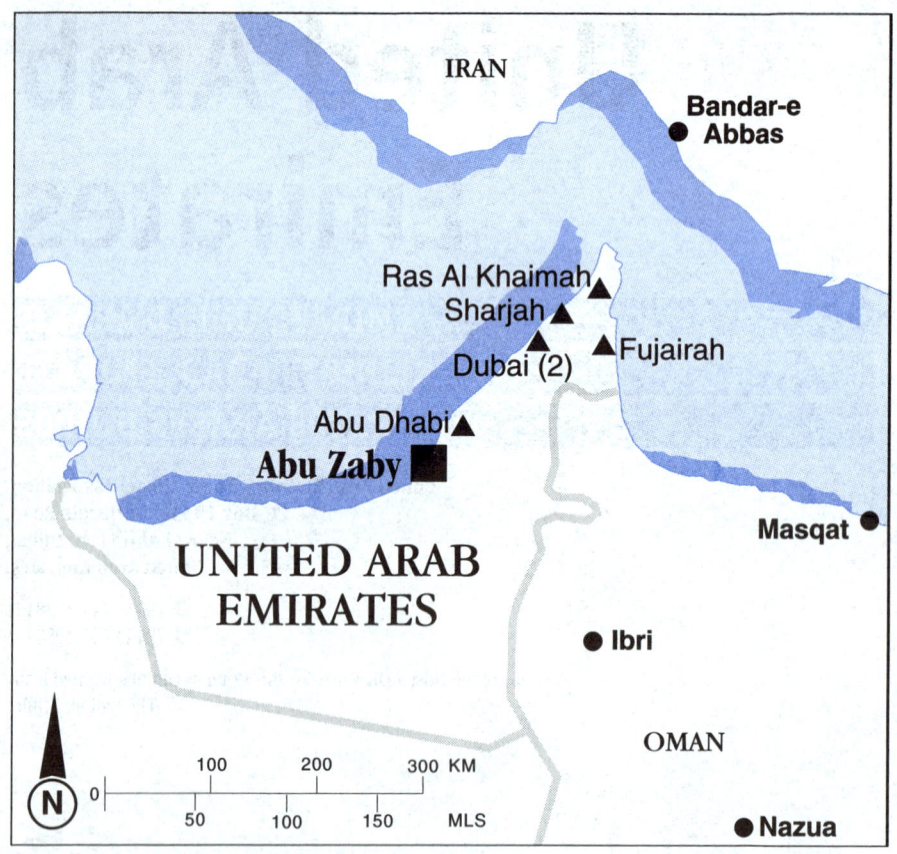.

Rooms and Reservations

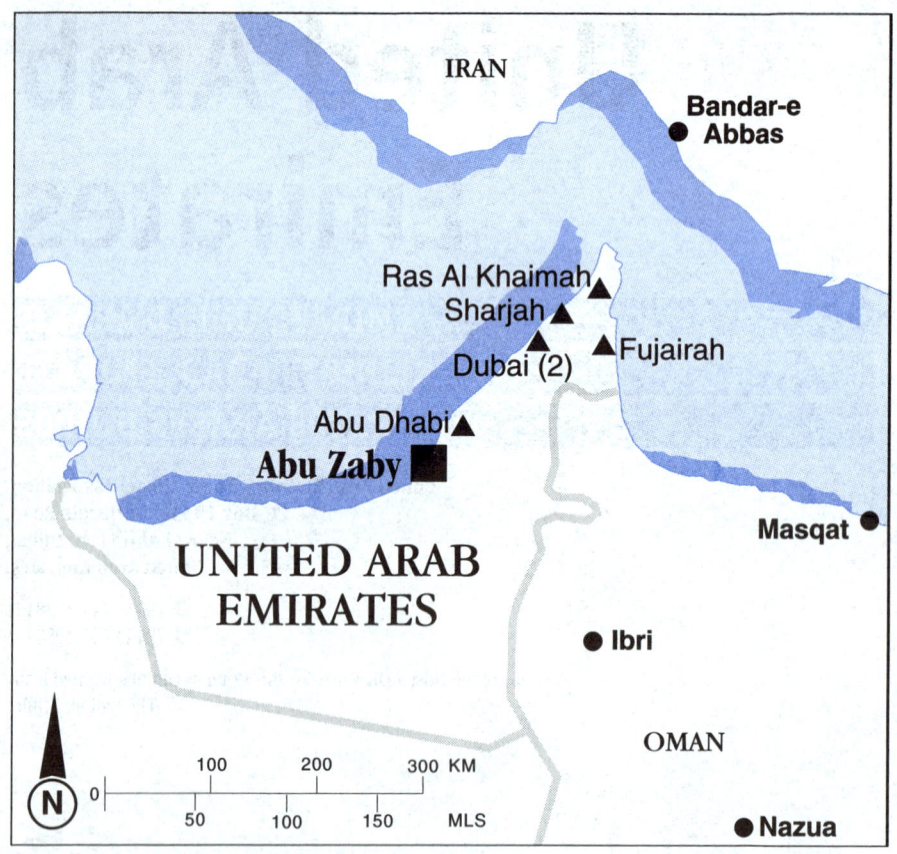   . Reservations via Hostel or National Office by . Smoking is limited - please check.

Guests

Membership Card and Passport/Photo ID are required. The maximum stay is 6 days. Age limits may apply for adults, children and mixed age groups - check with hostel. welcome. Group bookings via Hostel or National Office by .

Open times

Main hostels: open , . Reception open: . Resident manager. **Other hostels:** open , . Reception open: . Resident manager.

Meals

 BLD For individuals & for .

Travelling around

For ease of travel use 🚐 Self-Drive.
International Driving Licence required.

Travel/Activity Packages

Tours/sightseeing, water sports, walking/
trekking and accommodation/transport
packages available. Package bookings via Hostel
or National Office by ☎ ✆.

Passports and Visas

Passport, Photo ID and Visa required.

Health

Emergency medical treatment is free.

Français

Venez visiter les Etats Arabes Unis entre octobre
et avril, lorsque le climat s'y prête le plus. Les
auberges sont situées dans les villes.

Tarifs des nuitées

Tarifs des nuitées 35 Dhs. 🛏.

Chambres et réservations

R 1🛏 2🛏 3🛏 👫. Réservations via
l'auberge ou le Bureau National par ☎ ✆. Il
est permis de fumer dans certaines chambres -
veuillez vérifier.

Usagers

La carte d'adhérent ainsi que le passeport/pièce
d'identité avec photo sont à présenter. La durée
maximale du séjour est de 6 jours. Il est
possible que des limites d'âge soient en vigueur
pour les adultes, les enfants et les groupes
d'âges mixtes - vérifiez auprès de l'auberge.
Accueil des 👫. Réservations pour groupes via
l'auberge ou le Bureau National par ☎ ✆.

Horaires d'ouverture

Grandes auberges: ouvertes 📆, 🕐. Accueil
ouvert 🕐. Gérant réside sur place. **Autres
auberges:** ouvertes 📆, 🕐. Accueil ouvert 🕐.
Gérant réside sur place.

Repas

🍽 BLD R Pour individuels & pour 👫.

Déplacements

Modes de transport recommandés 🚐
Voiture. Permis de conduire international
obligatoire.

Forfaits Voyages/Activités

Forfaits circuits touristiques, sports aquatiques,
randonnées pédestres et hébergement/transport
disponibles. Réservations des forfaits via
l'auberge ou le Bureau National par ☎ ✆.

Passeports et visas

Passeport, pièce d'identité avec photo et visa
obligatoires.

Santé

Soins d'urgence gratuits.

Deutsch

Besuchen Sie die UAE in den Monaten von
Oktober bis April, weil dann das Klima am
besten ist. Herbergen befinden sich in Städten.

Preisspanne

Preisspanne 35 Dhs. 🛏.

Zimmer und Reservierungen

R 1🛏 2🛏 3🛏 👫. Reserierungen über
Herberge oder Landesverband per ☎ ✆.
Rauchen ist begrenzt - bitte checken.

Gäste

Mitgliedsausweis und Reisepass/
Personalausweis sind erforderlich. Der
maximale Aufenthalt beträgt 6 Tage.
Altersbegrenzungen für Erwachsene, Kinder,
Gruppen gemischten Alters möglich - in der
Herberge nachfragen. ††† willkommen.
Gruppenbuchungen über Herberge oder
Landesverband per ❶ ❶.

Öffnungszeiten

Hauptherbergen: Zugang 🖼, ◷. Rezeption
◷. Herbergsmanager wohnt im Haus. **Andere
Herbergen:** Zugang 🖼, ◷. Rezeption ◷.
Herbergsmanager wohnt im Haus.

Mahlzeiten

🍽 BLD ⓡ Für Einzelreisende & für †††.

Reisen im Land

Reisen ist einfach mit 🚐 Selbstfahrer.
Internationaler Führerschein erforderlich.

Reise-/Aktivitäten-Packages

Touren/sightseeing, Wassersport, wandern/
trekking und Unterkunft/Transport-Packages
erhältlich. Package-Buchungen über Herberge
oder Landesverband per ❶ ❶.

Reisepässe und Visa

Reisepass, Personalausweis und Einreisevisum
erforderlich.

Gesundheit

Nur im Notfall sind medizinische Behandlungen
kostenlos.

Español

Visite los EAU durante los meses de octubre a
abril epoca en que el clima es más agradable.
Los albergues están situados en las ciudades.

Tarifas mínima y máxima

Tarifas mínima y máxima 35 Dhs. 🗔.

Habitaciones y Reservas

ⓡ ¹🚐 ²🚐 ³🚐 †††. Reservas a través del
albergue o la Asociación Nacional por ❶ ❶.
Está permitido fumar sólo en algunas
salas/habitaciones - infórmese.

Huéspedes

Los huéspedes deben presentar su Carnet de
Alberguista y su pasaporte o carnet de
identidad. La estancia máxima es de 6 días. Es
posible que exista un límite de edad para los
adultos, los niños y los grupos de personas de
diferentes edades - consulte con el albergue. Se
admiten †††. Reservas de grupo a través del
albergue o la Asociación Nacional por ❶ ❶.

Horarios y fechas de apertura

Albergues principales - abiertos 🖼, ◷.
Horario de recepción: ◷. Gerente residente.
Otros albergues - abiertos 🖼, ◷. Horario
de recepción: ◷. Gerente residente.

Comidas

🍽 BLD ⓡ Para individuales y para †††.

Desplazamientos

Transportes recomendados: 🚐 Automóvil. Es
necesario un permiso de conducir internacional.

Viajes Combinados con Actividades

Viajes combinados con visitas turísticas,
deportes náuticos, senderismo y
alojamiento/transporte. Reserva de viajes
combinados a través del albergue o la
Asociación Nacional por ❶ ❶.

Pasaportes y Visados

Pasaporte o carnet de identidad y visado
obligatorios.

Información Sanitaria

Asistencia médica de urgencia gratuita.

Dubai

Al Qusais Rd,
Dubai (near Al Ahli Club).
☎ 2988161
✆ 2988141

Open Dates:	🗓️
Open Hours:	🕐
Reservations:	**R**
Price Range:	DHS 35 € 9.21
Beds:	91 - 8x^2 17x^3 6x^4
Facilities:	👪 11x 👪 🍽️ ☕ 🏨 📺 📖1 x 🍸 📷 🧳 ♿ 🔢 ⏰ 🅿️ ℹ️ 🧺 ☂️ ⛰️ 🎿 🏛️ 🏠

Directions:

✈️	Dubai International 5km
A🚌	#3 250m
⛴️	Rashed 10km
🚌	3, 13, 17 250m ap Dura Bus Station
Attractions:	🏛️2km 🚴 ∪500m 🏄500m 🏊2km

"Though we travel the world over to find the beautiful, we must carry it with us or we find it not."

"Bien que nous parcourons le monde pour trouver ce qui est beau, nous devons le porter en nous ou nous ne le trouvons pas."

„Obwohl wir die ganze Welt bereisen, um das Schöne zu finden, müssen wir es in uns selber tragen, sonst werden wir es nicht finden."

"Aunque demos la vuelta al mundo buscando la belleza, tenemos que llevarla dentro de nosotros mismos o no la encontraremos"

Ralph Waldo Emerson

DUBAI-SHARJAH ROAD
Emirates Bank
Institute for Australian Studies
To Sharjah, Ajmar, Umm Al Quwain & Fujeirah
Al Mulla Plaza
AL QUSAIS ROAD
AL AHIL CLUB
Emirates Motor Driving Institute

Location/Address	Telephone No. Fax No.	Beds	Opening Dates	Facilities
△ *Abu Dhabi* *Abu Dhabi.*	☎ *(2) 378400*	*50*	*Temporarily closed for reconstruction*	♙♟ ⛺ ☕
△ *Al Fujairah* - *Fujairah Youth Hostel Fujairah (near the Supreme Council of Youth and Sports Office).*	☎ *(9) 222347* 📠 *00971 4* *2988141*	*42*	📠	♙♟ ⛺ R ☕ P
▲ **Dubai** **Al Qusais Rd, Dubai (near Al Ahli Club).**	☎ 2988161 📠 2988141	91	📠	♙♟ ⛺ R ☕ P 🗄
▲ **Dubai** - Dubai Youth Hostel Alshabab Club Dubai Hostel of Al Shabab Club, Al Waheda Rd, P.O. Box 19536 Dubai.	☎ 00971 4 2967131 📠 00971 4 2988141	41	📠	♙♟ ⛺ R ♿ ☕ P 🗄 ☕
△ *Ras Al Khaimah* *Ras Al Khaimah (near the Supreme Council of Youth and Sports Office).*	☎ *(7) 663711*	*45*	📠	♙♟ ⛺ R ☕ P
▲ **Sharjah** Traffic Square, Sharkan, Sharjah. (near Sharjah Sports Club).	☎ (6) 225070	49	📠	♙♟ ⛺ R ☕ P

"Certainly, travel is more than the seeing of sights; it is a change that goes on, deep and permanent, in the ideas of living."

"Il est certain que le voyage, c'est plus que la simple visite des sites touristiques; c'est un changement en continu, profond et permanent, sur l'idée que nous nous faisons de la vie."

„Gewiss ist Reisen mehr als Sehenswürdigkeiten anschauen; es findet eine tiefe und bleibende Veränderung der Lebensansichten statt."

"No cabe duda que viajar es más que hacer turismo; es un cambio continuo, profundo y permanente, en el concepto que tenemos de la vida"

Miriam Beard

United States of America

ETATS UNIS
VEREINIGTE STAATEN
ESTADOS UNIDOS

Hostelling International-American Youth Hostels (HI-AYH),
733 15th Street NW, Suite 840,
Washington, DC 20005,
United States of America.

☎ (1) (202) 783-6161
🖷 (1) (202) 783-6171
📧 General enquiries & information :
hiayhserv@hiayh.org
🖳 www.hiayh.org

A copy of the Hostel Directory for this Country can be obtained from:
The National Office

Capital:	Washington, DC		**Population:**	234,000,000
Language:	English		**Size:**	9,363,123 sq km
Currency:	US$ (100 cents = 1 dollar)		**Telephone Country Code:**	1

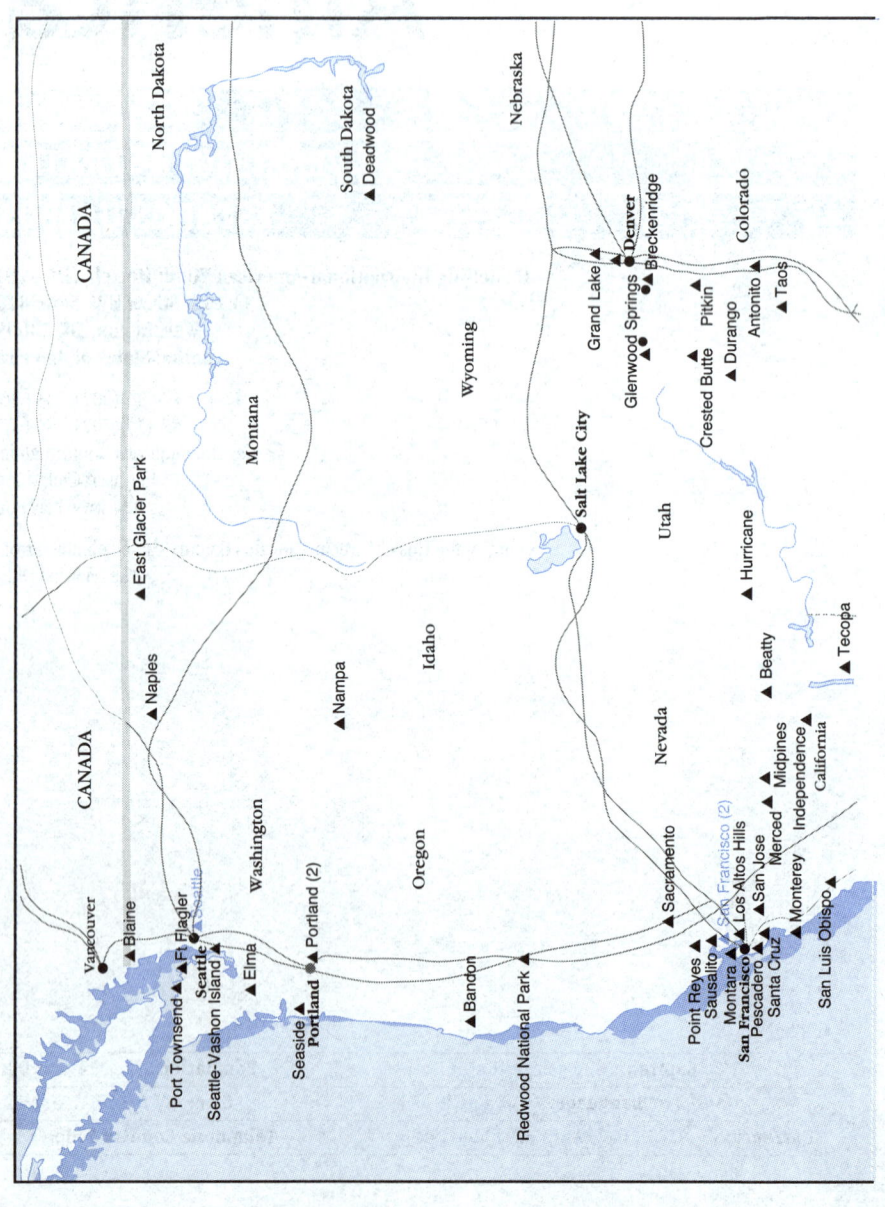

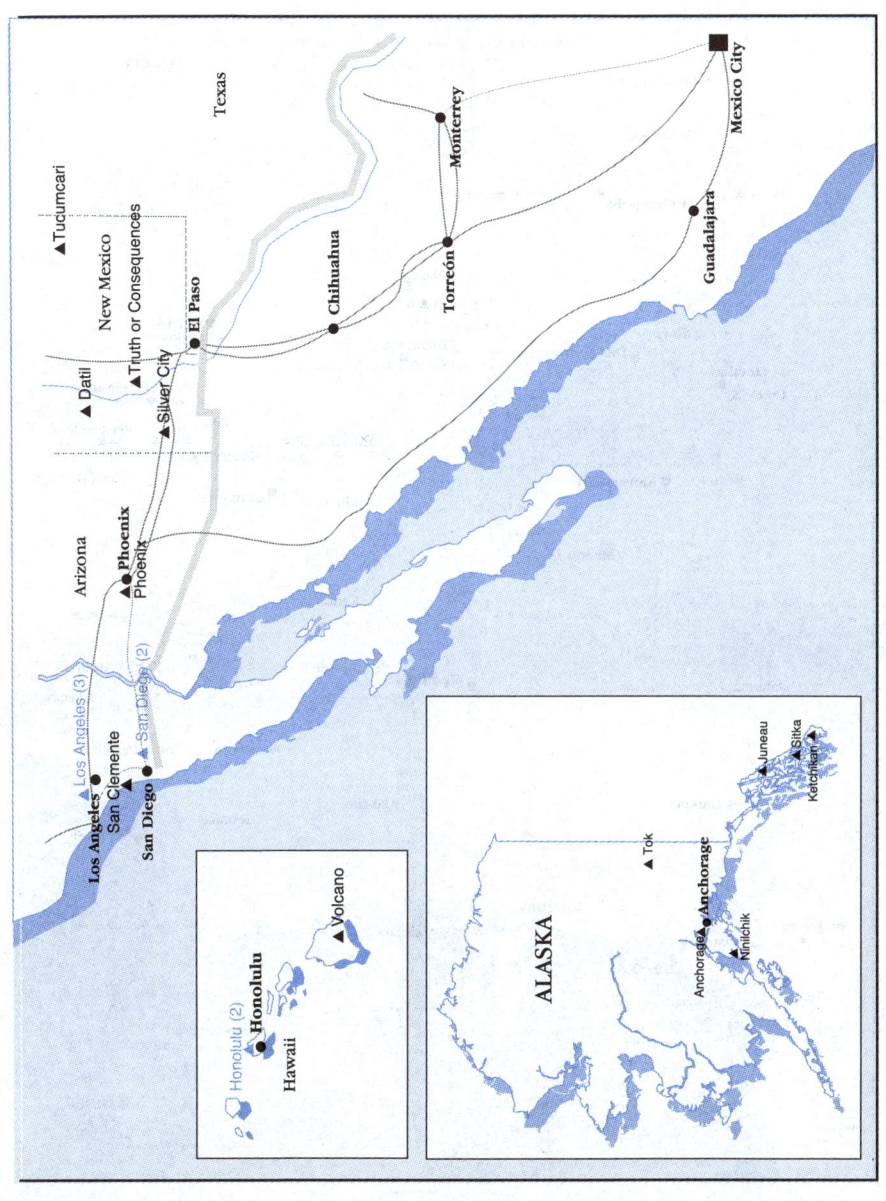

Texas

▲ Tucumcari

New Mexico

Monterrey

▲ Truth or Consequences

Chihuahua

Torreón

Mexico City

▲ Datil

El Paso

Guadalajara

Silver City

Arizona

Phoenix
▲ Phoenix

Los Angeles (3)

San Diego (2)

Los Angeles
San Clemente ▲

San Diego

ALASKA

▲ Tok

Juneau ▲

▲ Sitka

Ketchikan ▲

Anchorage

Anchorage ▲

Ninilchik ▲

Honolulu (2)

Honolulu

Hawaii

▲ Volcano

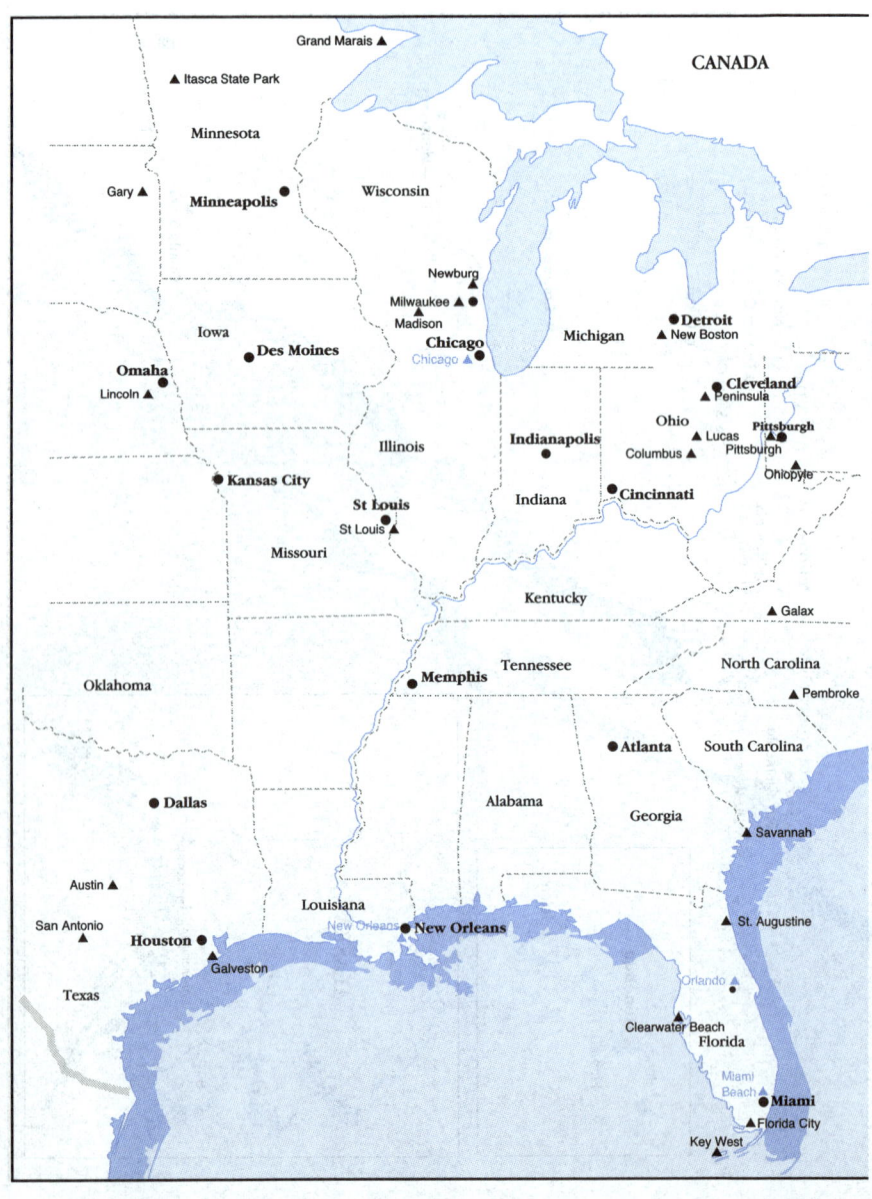

Grand Marais ▲

CANADA

▲ Itasca State Park

Minnesota

Gary ▲

Minneapolis ●

Wisconsin

Newburg
▲
Milwaukee ▲ ●
Madison
Chicago
Chicago ▲ ●

Michigan

● **Detroit**
▲ New Boston

Iowa

Des Moines ●

Omaha ●
Lincoln ▲

● **Cleveland**
▲ Peninsula

Ohio

Pittsburgh
▲ Lucas ▲ ●
Columbus ▲ Pittsburgh

Illinois

Indianapolis ●

● Ohiopyle ▲

Kansas City ●

St Louis ●
St Louis ▲

Indiana

● **Cincinnati**

Missouri

Kentucky

▲ Galax

Oklahoma

Tennessee

Memphis ●

North Carolina

▲ Pembroke

● **Atlanta**

South Carolina

Dallas ●

Alabama

Georgia

▲ Savannah

Austin ▲

Louisiana

San Antonio
▲

Houston ●
Galveston ▲

New Orleans ● **New Orleans**

▲ St. Augustine

Texas

Orlando ▲

Clearwater Beach
Florida

Miami
Beach

● **Miami**
▲ Florida City

Key West
▲

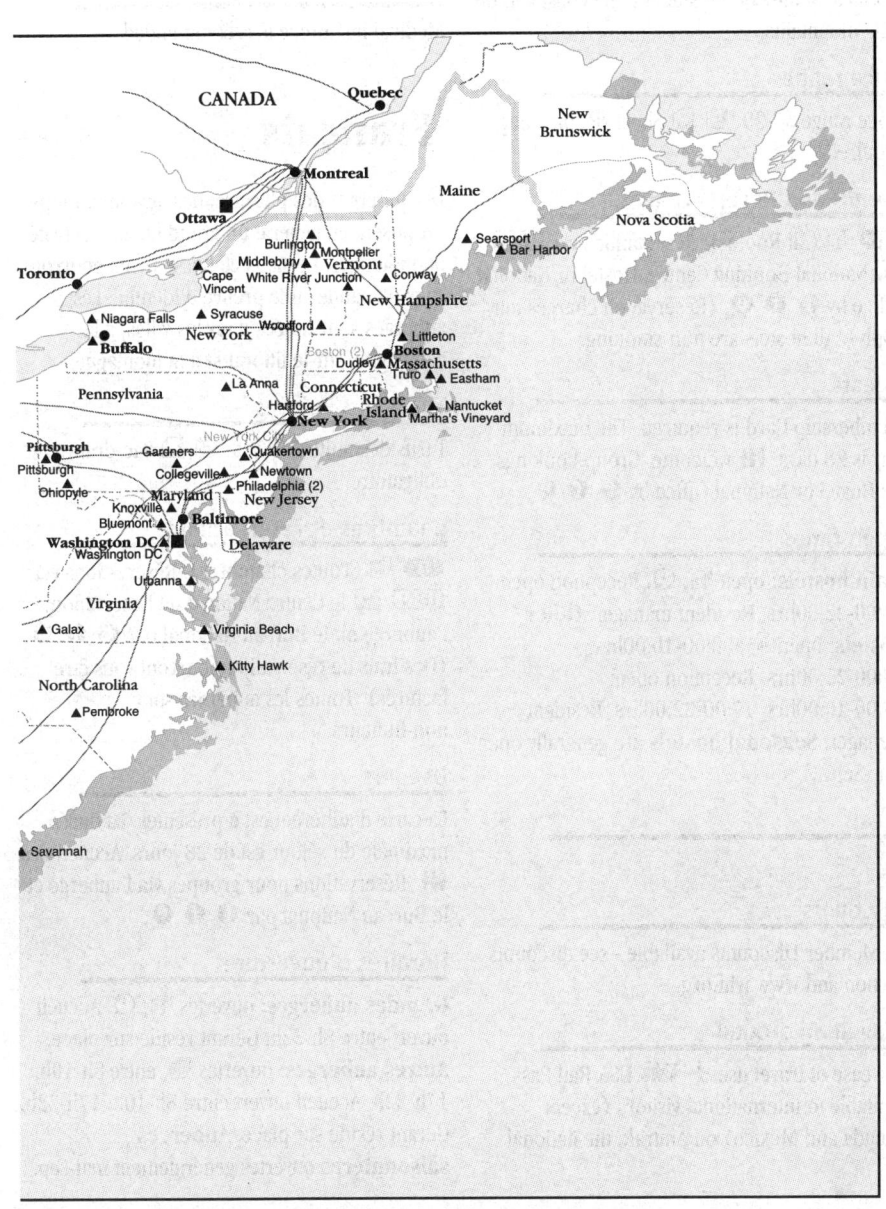

English

Hostels in major cities usually offer a wide range of daily activities. Some hostels may require a form of photo ID. Hostels are located in cities, in the countryside, on the coast and on hills/mountains.

Price range

Price range $7-29. Sheet sleeping bag required.

Rooms and Reservations

R (All Rooms). Reservations via **IBN** National Booking Centre, Hostel or National Office by **t** **f** **e**. (Reservation charges may apply). All hostels are non-smoking.

Guests

Membership Card is required. The maximum stay is 28 days. welcome. Group bookings via Hostel or National Office by **t** **f** **e**.

Open times

Main hostels: open , . Reception open: 08:00-22:00hrs. Resident manager. **Other hostels:** open , 08:00-10:00hrs, 17:00-22:00hrs. Reception open: 08:00-10:00hrs, 17:00-22:00hrs. Resident manager. **Seasonal hostels** are generally open May-Sep.

Meals

.

Discounts

HI Member Discounts available - see discounts section and www.iyhf.org.

Travelling around

For ease of travel use USA Rail Pass available to international visitors (except Canada and Mexico) on Amtrak, the national railroad. Self-Drive. Drive on the right. Do not drink & drive.

Passports and Visas

Passport, Photo ID and Visa required.

Health

Medical insurance is recommended.

Français

Les auberges des plus grandes agglomérations proposent en général un grand choix d'activités quotidiennes. Certains établissements pourront vous demander une preuve d'identité. Les auberges sont situées dans les villes, à la campagne, sur le littoral et à la montagne.

Tarifs des nuitées

Tarifs des nuitées 7-29$. Sac-drap obligatoire.

Chambres et réservations

R (Toutes chambres). Réservations via **IBN** le Centre National de Réservation, l'auberge ou le Bureau National par **t** **f** **e**. (Des frais de réservation pourront vous être facturés). Toutes les auberges sont non-fumeurs.

Usagers

La carte d'adhérent est à présenter. La durée maximale du séjour est de 28 jours. Accueil des . Réservations pour groupes via l'auberge et le Bureau National par **t** **f** **e**.

Horaires d'ouverture

Grandes auberges: ouvertes , . Accueil ouvert entre 8h-22h. Gérant réside sur place. **Autres auberges:** ouvertes , entre 8h-10h, 17h-22h. Accueil ouvert entre 8h-10h, 17h-22h. Gérant réside sur place. **Auberges saisonnières** ouvertes généralement mai-sep.

Repas

☞.

Remises

Remises pour les adhérents HI - voir la section "Remises" et notre site: www.iyhf.org.

Déplacements

Modes de transport recommandés ✈ 🚂 Les visiteurs étrangers (sauf les ressortissants du Canada et du Mexique) peuvent se munir d'une carte passe-partout "USA Rail Pass" pour leurs déplacements sur le réseau national de chemin de fer, Amtrak. 🚐 Voiture. Conduite à droite. Ne conduisez pas sous l'influence de l'alcool.

Passeports et visas

Passeport, pièce d'identité avec photo et visa obligatoires.

Santé

Une assurance médicale de voyage est conseillée.

Deutsch

Herbergen in den größeren Städten bieten gewöhnlich ein breites Programm täglicher Aktivitäten. Einige Herbergen verlangen u. U. eine Art von Ausweis mit Foto. Herbergen befinden sich in Städten, auf dem Land, an der Küste und in Bergen/Gebirgen.

Preisspanne

Preisspanne 7-29 $. 🈺 🛏 Leinenschlafsack erforderlich.

Zimmer und Reservierungen

🅁 🈺 (Alle Zimmer). Reservierungen über IBN 🐾 Nationales Buchungszentrum, Herberge oder Landesverband per ❶ ❷ ❸. (Reservierungskosten könnten anfallen). Rauchen ist in allen Herbergen NICHT gestattet.

Gäste

Mitgliedsausweis ist erforderlich. Der maximale Aufenthalt beträgt 28 Tage. 👫 willkommen. Gruppenbuchungen über Herberge oder Landesverband per ❶ ❷ ❸.

Öffnungszeiten

Hauptherbergen: Zugang 🈺, 🕐. Rezeption zwischen 08:00-22:00Uhr. Herbergsmanager wohnt im Haus. **Andere Herbergen:** Zugang 🈺, 08:00-10:00Uhr, 17:00-22:00Uhr. Rezeption zwischen 08:00-10:00Uhr, 17:00-22:00Uhr. Herbergsmanager wohnt im Haus. **Saison-Herbergen** sind normalerweise Mai-Sept geöffnet.

Mahlzeiten

☞.

Ermäßigungen

HI-Mitgliedsrabatt ist erhältlich – siehe Teil für Rabatte und Ermäßigungen und www.iyhf.org.

Reisen im Land

Reisen ist einfach mit ✈ 🚂 Internationalen Besuchern (Kanada und Mexiko ausgenommen)steht ein USA Rail Pass für Amtrak, der nationalen Eisenbahn, zur Verfügung. 🚐 Selbstfahrer. Rechts fahren. Kein Alkohol, wenn Sie fahren.

Reisepässe und Visa

Reisepass, Personalausweis und Einreisevisum erforderlich.

Gesundheit

Unfall-/Krankenversicherung wird empfohlen.

Español

Los albergues de las grandes ciudades suelen ofrecer diariamente una gama de actividades. En algunos albergues es posible que le pidan un documento de identidad. Los albergues están situados en las ciudades, el campo, la costa y la montaña.

Tarifas mínima y máxima

Tarifas mínima y máxima 7-29$. 🔌 🛏 Saco sábana imprescindible.

Habitaciones y Reservas

R 🖻 (Todas las habitaciones). Reservas por **IBN** 🖵 o a través de la Central Nacional de Reservas, el albergue o la Asociación Nacional por ❶ ❶ ❸. (Es posible que se aplique un suplemento en concepto de gastos de reserva). Está prohibido fumar en todos los albergues.

Huéspedes

Los huéspedes deben presentar su Carnet de Alberguista. La estancia máxima es de 28 días. Se admiten 👬. Reservas de grupo a través del albergue o la Asociación Nacional por ❶ ❶ ❸.

Horarios y fechas de apertura

Albergues principales - abiertos 🖻, ☺. Horario de recepción: 08:00-22:00h. Gerente residente. **Otros albergues** - abiertos 🖻, 08:00-10:00h, 17:00-22:00h. Horario de recepción: 08:00-10:00h, 17:00-22:00h. Gerente residente. **Albergues de temporada** suelen abrir: may-sep.

Comidas

🍴.

Descuentos

Se conceden descuentos a los miembros de Hostelling International – véase la sección sobre descuentos y nuestra página Internet en www.iyhf.org.

Desplazamientos

Transportes recomendados: ✈ 🚌 La compania ferroviaria nacional Amtrak ofrece un abono llamado USA Rail Pass a los visitantes extranjeros (excepto a los procedentes del Canada y Mexico). 🚐 Automóvil. Se circula por la derecha. No conduzca bajo la influencia del alcohol.

Pasaportes y Visados

Pasaporte o carnet de identidad y visado obligatorios.

Información Sanitaria

Seguro médico recomendado.

"The true traveler is he who goes on foot, and even then, he sits down a lot of the time."

"Le vrai voyageur est celui qui va à pied, et encore, il s'assoit une grande partie du temps."

„Der wahre Reisende ist derjenige, der zu Fuß geht, und selbst dann setzt er sich sehr häufig nieder."

"El verdadero viajero es el que va a pie, y aun así pasa mucho tiempo sentado."

Colette

Anchorage

700 'H' St,
Anchorage AK 99501.
📞 (907) 2763635
📠 (907) 2767772
✉ hianch@alaska.net

Open Dates:	🗓12
Open Hours:	08.00-23.00hrs
Reservations:	R ⊂CC⊃
Price Range:	$16.00 💷
Beds:	95 - 4x³🛏 7x⁴🛏 11x⁵🛏
Facilities:	♿ � 5x � 🍴 🖥 📺 📖 1 x 🍷 🖥 🖼 🕗 ℹ 🛁 ♻

Directions:

✈	Anchorage International 10km
A🚌	Rt 6, 4 times daily to Transit Centre
🚋	Alaska RR 500m
Attractions:	🚲 🏊 1800 🏃 🎿 ⚲250m

Austin

2200 S Lakeshore Blvd,
Austin TX 78741.
📞 (512) 4442294
📠 (512) 4442309
✉ hiaustin@swbell.net

Open Dates:	🗓12
Open Hours:	08.00-11.00hrs; 17.00-22.00hrs
Reservations:	⊂CC⊃
Price Range:	$15.50 💷
Beds:	39 - 1x⁵🛏 3x⁶🛏
Facilities:	� 🍴 🖥 📖 🗟 1 x 🍷 🖥 🖼 🚻 🍴 🅿 ℹ 🛁 ♻ 🖼 🏠

Directions:

✈	Austin-Bergstrom 8km
A🚌	350 to Austin Community College; 26 to Burton and Riverside 100m
🚋	Amtrak 5km
🚌	Greyhound #7 to Burton and Riverside 100m
Attractions:	🌳 ⛰ 🚲 🎿 ⚲3.5km 🏊2.5km

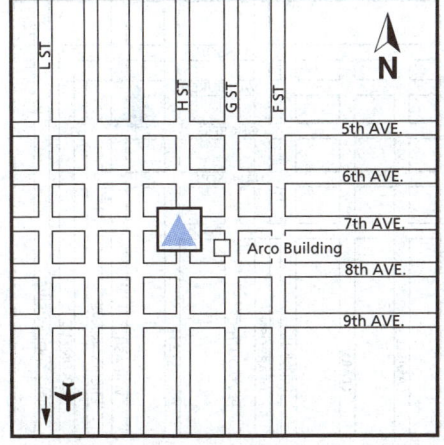

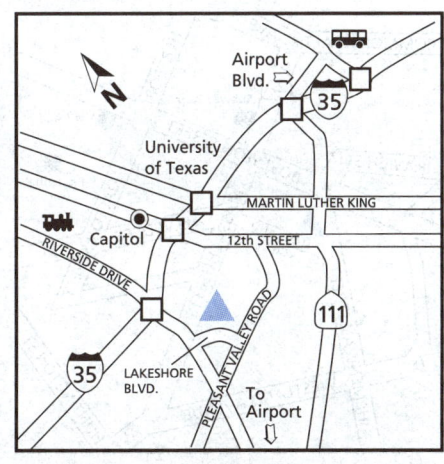

Boston

12 Hemenway St,
Boston MA 02115.
- ☏ (617) 5369455
- 🖷 (617) 4246558
- ✉ bostonhostel@bostonhostel.org

Open Dates:	🗓
Open Hours:	⏱
Reservations:	Ⓡ IBN CC
Price Range:	$24.00-26.00 💬
Beds:	205 - 10x² 7x⁴ 23x⁵ 7x⁶
Facilities:	♿ ⚦ 9x ⚦ 👕 🛏 🍳 1 x 🍸 🔲 💼 🍺 🔒 ✉ 🖥 🌳
Directions:	3SW from city centre
✈	Logan International 6km
A🚌	Blue/Green "T" bus to Hynes 600m
🚂	South Station to Red/Green "T" 200m
Ⓤ	Green Line "T" Hynes - Convention Center 200m

There are 2 hostels in Boston. See following pages.

Chicago

24 East Congress Parkway,
Chicago,
IL 60605.
- ☏ (312) 3600300
- 🖷 (312) 3600313
- ✉ reserve@hichicago.org

Open Dates:	🗓
Open Hours:	⏱
Reservations:	Ⓡ IBN CC
Price Range:	$19.00-23.00 (+Tax)
Beds:	500 - 56x² 44x⁴ 26x⁵ 8x⁶
Facilities:	♿ ⚦ ⚦ 🍽 👕 ☕ 🚲 ⚙ 🛏 📺 🔲 🍳 3 x 🍸 🔲 📷 🍺 🔒 ⊜ 💱 ✉ 🖥 🌳 🎿
Directions:	0.5S from city centre
✈	O'Hare International 29 km, Midway National 15km
A🚌	Use metro
🚂	Union/Amtrak Station 600m
🚌	Intercity Bus Terminal - Greyhound 600m
Ⓤ	Library/Van Buren

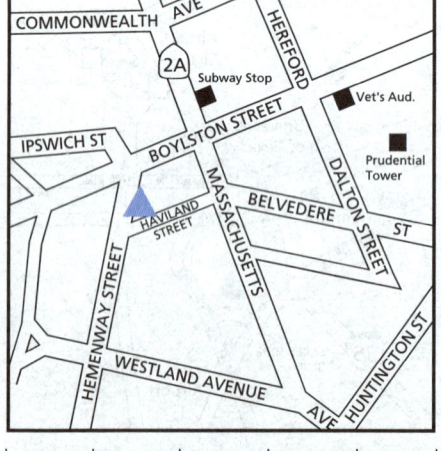

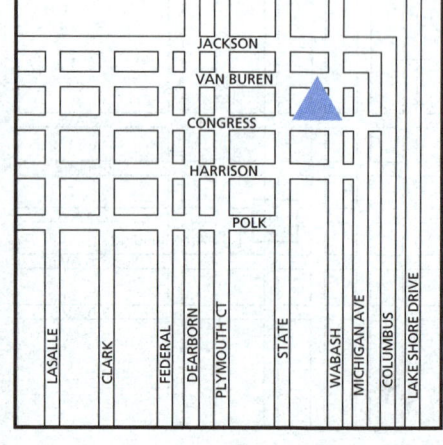

0   1km

Denver - Hostel of the Rocky Mountains

1530 Downing St,
Denver,
Co 80218.
☎ (303) 861 7777
🖷 (303) 861 1448
✉ innkeeperdenver@aol.com

Open Dates: 🗓
Open Hours: 07.00-23.00hrs
Reservations: Ⓡ ⳽CC⳽
Price Range: $15.00 BB inc
Beds: 48
Facilities: 👬 👬 🛏 💻 📺 📺 📀 📷 👤 🅿 ♿

Directions:

✈	Denver International 24km
A🚌	AF to Market St, the #15 to Downing 200m
🚂	Amtrak (☎ for pick-up) 3.2km
🚌	Greyhound (☎ for pick-up) 2km

Honolulu - University

2323A Seaview Ave,
Honolulu HI 96822.
☎ (808) 9460591
🖷 (808) 9465904

Open Dates: 🗓

Open Hours: 08.00-12.00hrs; 16.00-24.00hrs
Reservations: Ⓡ ⟮IBN⟯ ⳽CC⳽
Price Range: $14.00
Beds: 43 - 1x² 🛏 1x³ 🛏 1x⁴ 🛏 3x⁶ 🛏 2x⁶⁺ 🛏
Facilities: 👬 2x 👬 🛏 💻 📺 📀 📷 👤 🅿 ℹ 🌸 ⛪

Directions: ⟮5W⟯ from city centre

✈	Honolulu 10km
A🚌	19 or 20 then 4 or 6
🚌	19 or 20, then 4 or 6

Attractions: ⛺ ⛰ 🚶 ⚓1km 🏊4km

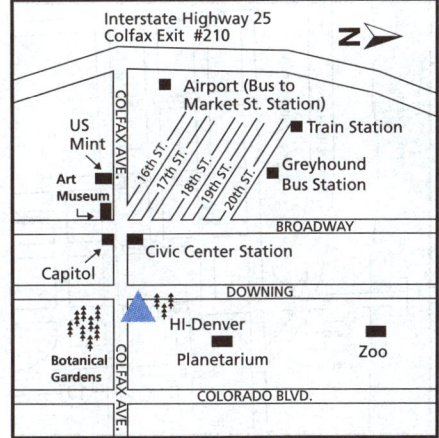

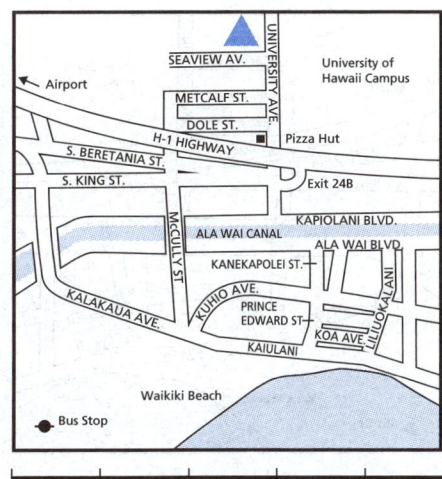

Honolulu -
Waikiki

2417 Prince Edward St,
Honolulu HI 96815.
📞 (808) 9268313
📠 (808) 9223798
✉ halealoha@webtv.net

Open Dates:	🗓
Open Hours:	07.00-03.00hrs
Reservations:	Ⓡ (IBN) CC
Price Range:	$17.00 💷
Beds:	60 - 4x🛏 8x🛏 4x🛏 1x🛏
Facilities:	👪 2x 👪 🚿 🍴 📺 🖊 🧺 ⊙ 🖼 🎫 🅿 📋 ♿ ♻

Directions:	5W from city centre
✈	Honolulu International 10km
A🚌	#20 to Kings Village 100m
Attractions:	📷150m 🎿 ⚓500m ⛴150m

Los Angeles -
Santa Monica

1436 2nd St,
Santa Monica CA 90401.
📞 (310) 3939913
📠 (310) 3931769
✉ reserve@HILosAngeles.org

Open Dates:	🗓
Open Hours:	🕐
Reservations:	Ⓡ (IBN) CC
Price Range:	$21.00-23.00 (+Tax) 💷
Beds:	200 - 9x🛏 4x🛏 15x🛏 16x🛏
Facilities:	♿ 👪 4x 👪 🍴 (B) 🚿 🍴 📺 🖊 🧺 1 x 🔑 ⊙ 🖼 🎫 🅿 📋 🛗 💲 🅿 📋 ♻ 🏧

Directions:	
✈	Los Angeles International (LAX) 11km
A🚌	Call hostel upon arrival for discount shuttle
🚃	Union (Amtrak) 30km
🚌	Greyhound Depot 26km
Attractions:	📷500m ⛴1km

There are 3 hostels in Los Angeles. See
following pages.

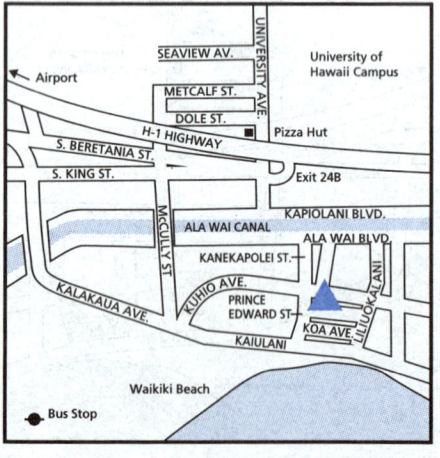

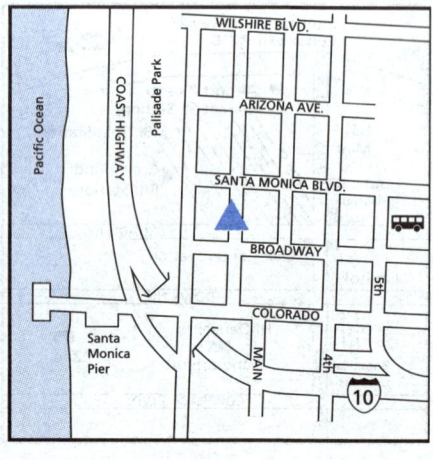

Los Angeles - South Bay

3601 South Gaffey St,
Building 613,
San Pedro CA 90731-6969.
☎ (310) 8318109
🖷 (310) 8314635
🖳 hisanpedro@aol.com

Open Dates:	🗓
Open Hours:	07.00-24.00hrs June-Sept; 08.00-23.00hrs Oct-May
Reservations:	R CC
Price Range:	$13.00-15.00 🛏
Beds:	60 - 5x1🛏 5x2🛏 4x3🛏 3x5🛏 1x6🛏
Facilities:	ᵗᵗᵗ 4x ᵗᵗᵗ 🖳 🛋 TV 🖳 🖳 1x 🍴 🖳 📷 8 P i ♻ 🏛 🖳
Directions:	32S from city centre
✈	LAX 24km
A🚐	Super Shuttle to Hostel
⛴	LA Harbour 3km
🚂	Amtrak; Metrolink 40km
🚌	446 ap Korean Bell
U	Long Beach Transit Centre 16km
Attractions:	🔍 🚴 🏃 🏊 1km

There are 3 hostels in Los Angeles. See
following pages.

Miami Beach

1438 Washington Ave,
Miami Beach FL 33139.
☎ (305) 5342988,
 (800) 3792529 (R only)
🖷 (305) 6730346
🖳 info@clayhotel.com

Open Dates:	🗓
Open Hours:	🕐
Reservations:	R IBN CC
Price Range:	$15.00-16.00 🛏
Beds:	200 - 10x2🛏 30x4🛏 10x6🛏
Facilities:	ᵗᵗᵗ 10x ᵗᵗᵗ 🍴 🖳 🍵 🛋 TV 🖳 1 x 🍴 📷 📷 8 ⊜ i 🖳 ♻ 🏛
Directions:	
✈	Miami International 16km
A🚐	Super Shuttle to YH; "J" bus to 41st Street, then "C" bus to alighting point 200m
⛴	Miami 4km
🚂	Amtrak 10km
🚌	Greyhound bus to "C" bus 8km ap Washington and 15th Street 200m
Attractions:	🔍 500m 🐟 50m 🏊 50m

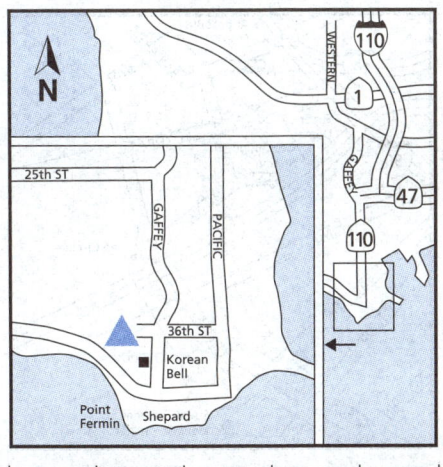

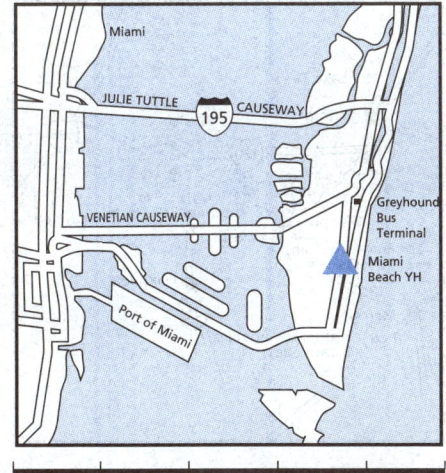

Midpines -
The Yosemite Bug Hostel

6979 Hwy 140,
PO Box 81,
Midpines CA 95345.
t (209) 9666666
f (209) 9666667
e bughost@sierratel.com

Open Dates: 🗓12

Open Hours: 06.30-23.00hrs

Reservations: **R** ⊂CC⊃

Price Range: $14.00-16.00

Beds: 52

Facilities: ♿ ♛♛♛ ♛♛ 🍴 🛢 ☕ ▤ ⌸3 x ⚓
🔲 🖼 🔋 🅿 ℹ

Directions:

✈ Yosemite/Mariposa 24km

🚆 Merced 72km

🚌 Amtrak Bus, Greyhound, via
Yosemite Area Regional Transit
System ap Midpines

Attractions: ⛵ ⛰ 🚴 ⚓ ⛷ 90m

New Orleans -
Marquette House

2253 Carondelet St,
New Orleans LA 70130.
t (504) 5233014
f (504) 5295933
e HINewOrlns@aol.com

Open Dates: 🗓12

Open Hours: 07.00-24.00hrs (Later by
arrangement)

Reservations: **R** ⟦IBN⟧ ⊂CC⊃

Price Range: $15.09 ($20.00 27.04-06.05;
29.12-02.01; $25.00 23.02-27.02)
⟦H⟧

Beds: 166 - 10x⁴⚓ 11x⁶⚓

Facilities: ♛♛♛ 8x ♛♛♛ 🍴 (B) 🛢 🛏 ▤ 🔲 🖼
♿ 🔋 ☕ 🅿 ℹ 🛋

Directions: ⟦3SW⟧ from city centre

✈ New Orleans 18km

A🚌 Elk Place and Tulane Avenue 3km

⛴ New Orleans 4km

🚆 Amtrak/Greyhound 2.5km

🚌 Greyhound 2.5km

🚋 St. Charles Ave. Streetcar
ap Jackson Ave and St. Charles
Avenue 100m

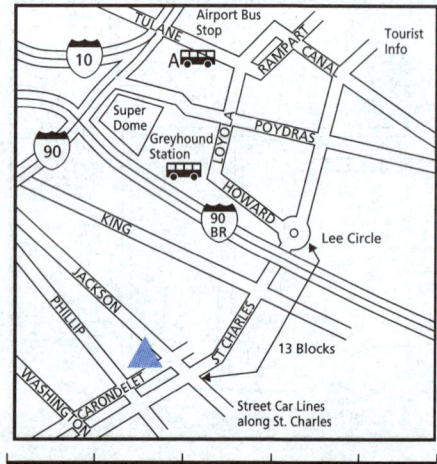

New York -
International

891 Amsterdam Ave at West 103rd St,
New York NY 10025.
📞 (212) 9322300
📠 (212) 9322574
✉ reserve@hinewyork.org

Open Dates:	🗓
Open Hours:	🕐
Reservations:	Ⓡ (IBN) (CC)
Price Range:	$27.00-29.00 📖
Beds:	624 - 16x⁴🛏 22x⁶🛏 38x⁶🛏
Facilities:	♿ 👫 7x 👫 🍽 ☞ ☕ 🏨 📺 📖 🗎4 x🍷 🗄 🧳 ⌨ ⑧ 🚻 🛗 ℹ 🍴 🌿 🔨 🎪

Directions:

✈	Kennedy 20km; LaGuardia 8km; Newark 25km
🚌 A	Grayline to YH
🚂	Penn 4.5km
🚌	Port Authority 3.5km
Ⓤ	#1 or #9 to 103rd St Station 200m
Attractions:	⤵1.5km ⚲1.5km ⚓1km

Orlando -
Kissimmee Resort

4840 W Irlo Bronson Hwy,
Kissimmee FL 34746.
(Route 192 at Route 535).
📞 (407) 3968282
📠 (407) 3969311
✉ hi_orlandoresort@compuserve.com

Open Dates:	🗓
Open Hours:	🕐
Reservations:	Ⓡ (IBN) (CC)
Price Range:	$16.00-18.00 (+Tax) 📖
Beds:	192 - 7x¹🛏 3x²🛏 10x³🛏 21x⁶🛏
Facilities:	♿ 👫 13x 👫 ☞ 🏨 📺 📖 🗎 1 x🍷 🗄 🧳 ⑧ 🚻 Ⓟ ℹ 🍴 🌿 🛗

Directions:

✈	Orlando International 27km
🚌 A	Mears to Hostel
🚂	Amtrak - Kissimmee 16km
🚌	Lynx #56 4km ap Bamboo Lane
Attractions:	⚓

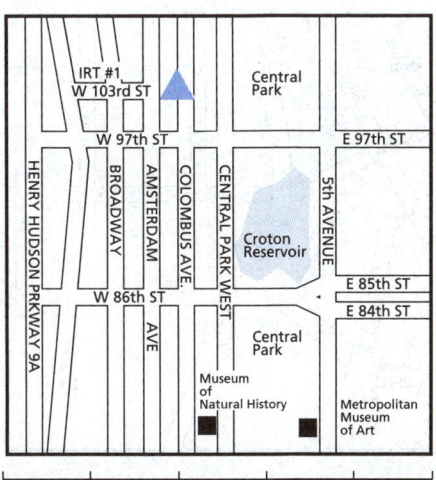

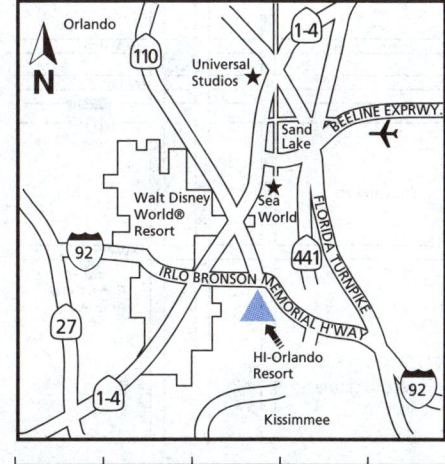

Portland (Oregon) -
Northwest Neighborhood

1818 NW Glisan,
Portland,
OR 97209.
t (503) 2412783
f (503) 5255910
e hinwp@transport.com

Open Dates: 🔲

Reservations: **R** **-CC-**

Beds: 33

Facilities: 👭👭 🍴 🍷 🚲 ⚙ 🛏 🧺 💻 ▢
            💼 🏢 ⑧ ♿

Attractions: 🏞 🏃 🏊

Portland (Oregon) -
Hawthorn District

3031 Hawthorne Blvd SE,
Portland OR 97214.
t (503) 2363380
f (503) 2367940
e hip@teleport.com

Open Dates: 🔲

Reservations: **R** **-CC-**

Beds: 33

Facilities: 👭 🍽 (B) 🍷 🚲 ⚙ 🛏 📺 💻
            ▢ 💼 ⑧ 🍺 🅿 ♿ 🌷

Directions:

✈   30km

A🚌   12 to 14 Hawthorne

🚂   Amtrak 6km

🚌   14 Hawthorne

Attractions: 🚴

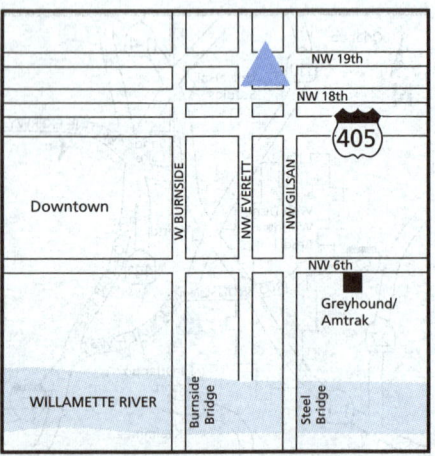

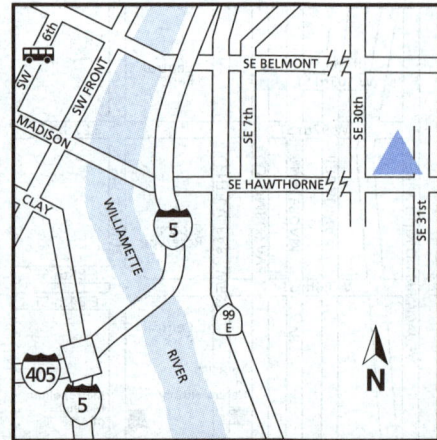

San Diego - Downtown

521 Market St,
San Diego CA 92101.
📞 **(619) 5251531**
📠 **(619) 3380129**
✉ **hisddowntown@aol.com**

Open Dates:	🗓
Open Hours:	07.00-24.00hrs
Reservations:	Ⓡ IBN CC
Price Range:	$18.00-19.00 🍽
Beds:	134 - 7x² 20x⁴ 2x⁶ 3x⁶

Facilities: ♿ 🚻 2x 🚻 ♂ 🛏 📺 🧺 1 x 🍴
🔒 💼 8 ⤵ 🚷 💱 🏕

Directions:

✈	San Diego International 5km
A🚌	#992 to 5th & Broadway 500m
🚆	Santa Fe Depot (Amtrak) 1km
🚌	Greyhound 500m
🚋	ap 5th Avenue 500m

Attractions: 🔍 4km 🚴

San Diego - Point Loma

3790 Udall St,
San Diego CA 92107-2414.
📞 **(619) 2234778**
📠 **(619) 2231883**
✉ **HISDPTLOMA@aol.com**

Open Dates:	🗓
Open Hours:	08.00-22.00hrs
Reservations:	Ⓡ IBN CC
Price Range:	$15.00-16.00 🍽
Beds:	61 - 4x¹ 2x² 2x³ 4x⁴ 1x⁶ 2x⁶

Facilities: 🚻 2x 🚻 ♂ 🛏 📺 🧺 🔒 🏢 8
P 💱 ♻ 🔍

Directions:	10W from city centre
✈	Lindbergh Field 5km
⛴	Broadway Pier/Embarcadero 9km
🚆	Santa Fe Depot/Amtrak 9km
🚌	#35 ap Voltaire and Poinsetta 500m
🚋	Oldtown Transit Center 5km ap to 🚌 #35

Attractions: 🔍 1.5km 🚴 🎿 500m 🏊 2km

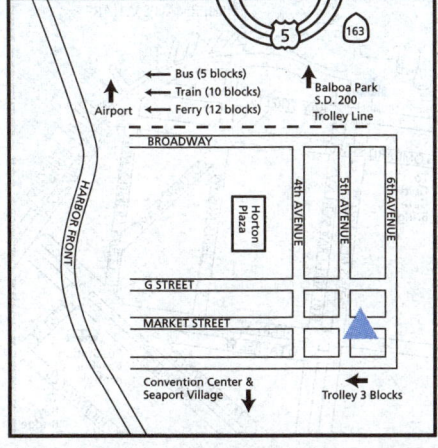

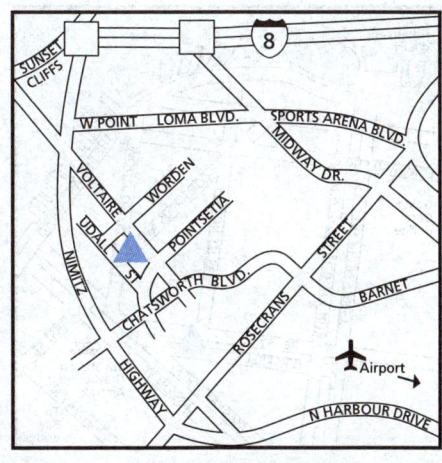

San Francisco -
Downtown

Union Square,
312 Mason St,
San Francisco CA 94102.
☎ (415) 7885604
f (415) 7883023
e sfdowntown@norcalhostels.org

Open Dates:	🗓12
Open Hours:	🕐
Reservations:	**R** IBN CC
Price Range:	$19.00-21.00 (+Tax) 💬
Beds:	260 - 36x² 20x³ 28x⁴ 2x⁵ 1x
Facilities:	�980x92x ♟ 🍴 🏠 📺 ⬛ 🖥 1 x 🍽 💼 ♨ 8 ⬆ P i 🌺

Directions:

✈	San Francisco International 8.7km
A🚌	#7F to Mission and 5th 200m
🚂	Amtrak 1.5km
🚌	Greyhound - Transbay Terminal to #38 ap Mason and Geary St Station 100m
🚋	100m
U	Muni/Bart to Powell St Station 100m

Attractions: 🏛 ⛰ 🔍4km 🚶 ⛵4km

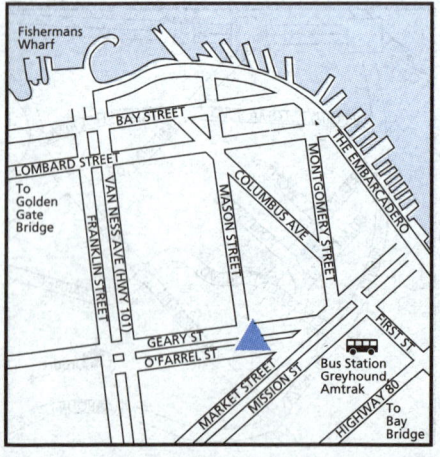

San Francisco -
Fisherman's Wharf

Fort Mason,
Building 240,
San Francisco,
CA 94123.
☎ (415) 7717277
f (415) 7711468
e sfhostel@norcalhostels.org

Open Dates:	🗓12
Open Hours:	🕐
Reservations:	**R** IBN CC
Price Range:	$19.00-21.00 (+Tax) BBinc 💬
Beds:	170 - 2x³ 7x⁴ 1x⁶ 10x⁶
Facilities:	♿ ♟ 4x ♟ 🍴 (B) 🍴 🍽 🏠 📺 ⬛ 🖥 🖥 💼 ♨ 8 P i 🌺 🏠 🏡 🎱

Directions:

✈	San Francisco International 22km
A🚌	Lorrie's to Hostel
⛴	San Francisco Ferry Building 4km
🚂	Amtrak/Ferry Building to 🚌 #42 4km
🚌	30, 32, 42, 47, 49 ap North Point 200m

Attractions: 🏛 ⛰ 🔍4km 🚴 🚶 ⛵4km

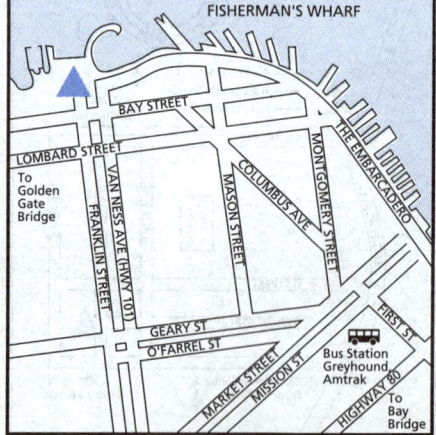

Seattle - Downtown

84 Union St,
Seattle WA 98101.
☎ (206) 6225443
🖷 (206) 6822179
✉ reserve@hiseattle.org

Open Dates: 🗓
Open Hours: 🕐
Reservations: ℝ IBN CC
Price Range: $16.00-19.00 (+Tax) 📖
Beds: 199 - 4x³🛏 10x⁴🛏 5x⁶🛏 13x⁶🛏
Facilities: ♿ 👪 4x 👪 ☞ 🛏 📺 📖 🏷
2 x 🍽 🔲 🖼 🔢 ℹ 🚲 🏠 🎁

Directions:

✈	Seattle - Tacoma 24km
A🚌	#194 to University or #174 to 4th and Union 200m
🚢	Victoria Clipper 1km
🚂	Amtrak 1.5km
🚌	#15 or #18 ap 1st and Union 100m

There are 2 hostels in Seattle. See following pages.

Washington, DC

1009 11th St NW,
Washington DC 20001.
☎ (202) 7372333
🖷 (202) 7371508
✉ reservations@hiwashingtondc.org

Open Dates: 🗓
Open Hours: 🕐
Reservations: ℝ CC
Price Range: $19.00-24.00 📖
Beds: 270 - 24x⁶🛏
Facilities: ♿ 👪 ☞ 🛏 📺 🏷 1 x 🍽 🔲 🖼
🏢 🔢 ♿ ⬍ ℹ

Directions:

✈	Washington National 8.1km; Dulles International 43.4km
A🚌	Orange or Blue line to Ⓤ 200m
🚂	Union to Ⓤ 3km
🚌	1km
Ⓤ	Metro Center 200m

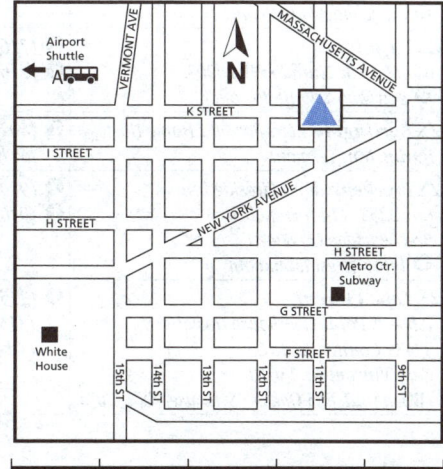

Location/Address	Telephone No. Fax No.	Beds	Opening Dates	Facilities
Akron ☞**Peninsula**				
▲ **Anchorage** **700 'H' St, Anchorage AK 99501.** ✉ hianch@alaska.net	☎ (907) 2763635 🖷 (907) 2767772	95	🔒12	ᴉᵗᵢ Ⓡ ♿ ⊟CC⊟ ☞ 🔲
△ *Antonito - Conejos River Hostel* *3038 County Rd D.5, Antonito CO 81120.*	☎ *(719) 3762518*	10	20.05–20.10	☞ 🅿
▲ **Austin** **2200 S Lakeshore Blvd, Austin TX 78741.** ✉ hiaustin@swbell.net	☎ (512) 4442294 🖷 (512) 4442309	39	🔒12	⊟CC⊟ ☞ 🅿 🔲
▲ **Bandon** - Sea Star 375 2nd St, Bandon OR 97411. ✉ seastar@iname.com	☎ (541) 3479632 🖷 (541) 3479533	35	🔒12	ᴉᵗᵢ ⊟CC⊟ ☞ 🔲
△ *Bar Harbor - Mount Desert Island* *27 Kennebec St, PO Box 32,* *Bar Harbor ME 04609.*	☎ *ahead (207)* *2885587*	20	16.06–31.08	Ⓡ ☞ 🅿
△ *Beatty* *100 Main St, Beatty, NV 89003.*	☎ *(775) 5539130*	18	🔒12	ᴉᵗᵢ 🅿 ☞
△ *Blaine - Birch Bay* *7467 Gemini St., Blaine WA 98230.* ✉ *bbhostel@az.com*	☎ *(360) 3712180*	45	01.05–30.09	⊟CC⊟ ☞ 🅿 🔲
△ *Bluemont - Bear's Den Lodge* *18393 Blueridge Mountain Rd (Hwy 601).* *Bluemont, VA 20135.* ✉ *bearden@crosslink.net*	☎ *(540) 5548708* 🖷 *(540) 5548708*	20	01.02–24.12; 26–31.12	ᴉᵗᵢ ⊟CC⊟ ☞ 🅿 🔲
▲ **Boston** ⟨IBN⟩ **12 Hemenway St, Boston MA 02115.** ✉ bostonhostel@bostonhostel.org	☎ (617) 5369455 🖷 (617) 4246558	205	🔒12	ᴉᵗᵢ Ⓡ ⟨3SW⟩ ♿ ⊟CC⊟ ☞ 🔲
△ *Boston - Back Bay Summer Hostel* *512 Beacon St, Boston MA.* *(All mail to: ENEC Reservations, 12* *Hemenway St, Boston, MA 02115).* ✉ *hibackbay@juno.com*	☎ *(617) 3533294;* *(617) 5310459* *(When shut)*	100	09.06–13.08	ᴉᵗᵢ Ⓡ ⊟CC⊟ ☞ 🔲
△ *Buffalo* *667 Main St, Buffalo, NY 14203.* ✉ *stay@hostelbuffalo.com*	☎ (716) 8525222 🖷 (716) 8521642	48	🔒12	ᴉᵗᵢ Ⓡ ♿ ⊟CC⊟ ☞ 🔲
△ *Burlington - Mrs Farrell's Home Hostel* *Burlington, Vermont.*	☎ (802) 8653730 *for information*	6	01.04–31.10	ᴉᵗᵢ Ⓡ ☞ 🅿
△ *Breckenridge - Fireside Inn* *Box 2252, 114 N French St,* *Breckenridge CO 80424.* ✉ *info@firesideinn.com*	☎ (970) 4536456 🖷 (970) 4539577	12	01.01–07.05; 26.05–31.12	Ⓡ ⊟CC⊟ ☞ 🅿
△ *Cape Vincent -* *Tibbetts Point Lighthouse Hostel* *33439 County Route 6,* *Cape Vincent NY 13618.* *(When shut: 535 Oak St., Syracuse, NY 13203).*	☎ (315) 6543450; (315) 4725788 *(When shut)*	26	15.05–24.10	ᴉᵗᵢ Ⓡ ☞ 🅿

Location/Address	Telephone No. Fax No.	Beds	Opening Dates	Facilities
▲ Chicago [IBN] 24 East Congress Parkway, Chicago, IL 60605. **e** reserve@hichicago.org	**☎** (312) 3600300 **✆** (312) 3600313	500	🖪	♯♯ 🍴 Ⓡ 0SS ⓖ 🏧 ⚿ 🄰 🍺 🚲 ✿
▲ Clearwater Beach 606 Bay Esplanade, Clearwater Beach, FL 33767. **e** magillr1@juno.com	**☎** (727) 4431211 **✆** (727) 4431211	33	🖪	♯♯ 🏧 ⚿ P 🄰
Cleveland ☞Peninsula				
△ *Collegeville - Evansburg State Park* *837 Mayhall Rd, Collegeville, PA 19426.* **e** *hievansburg@hi-dvc.org*	**☎** *(610) 4090113*	*18*	🖪	♯♯ Ⓡ ⚿ P
△ *Columbus* *95 East 12th Ave, Columbus OH 43201.*	**☎** *(614) 2947157* **✆** *(614) 2947157*	*22*	*26–23.12*	♯♯ Ⓡ ⚿ P 🄰
△ *Conway - Albert B. Lester Memorial Hostel* *White Mountains, 36 Washington St, Conway NH 03818.* **e** *hiconway@nxi.com*	**☎** *(603) 4471001* **✆** *(603) 4473346*	*43*	*01.12–31.10*	♯♯ Ⓡ ⚿ 🏧 ⚿ P 🄰
▲ Crested Butte - International Hostel 615 Teocalli Ave, P.O. Box 1332, Crested Butte, CO 81224. **e** hostel@crestedbutte.net	**☎** (970) 3490588, (888) 3890588 **✆** (970) 3490586	52	01.01–19.04; 27.04–31.12	♯♯ 🍴 Ⓡ ⚿ 🏧 ⚿ P 🄰 🍺
▲ Datil 201 Main St, Datil, NM 87821.	**☎** (505) 7725954	8	01.02–30.09	Ⓡ ⚿ P
▲ Deadwood - Black Hills at the Penny Motel 818 Upper Main St, Deadwood, SD 57732. **e** pennymot@mato.com	**☎** (605) 5781842 (877) 5658140 toll free (US only) **✆** (605) 5781842	20	01.01–02.08; 15.08–31.12	Ⓡ 🏧 ⚿ P 🄰
▲ Denver - Hostel of the Rocky Mountains **1530 Downing St, Denver, Co 80218.** **e** innkeeperdenver@aol.com	**☎** (303) 861 7777 **✆** (303) 861 1448	48	🖪	♯♯ Ⓡ 🏧 ⚿ P 🄰
△ *Dudley - Dudley Home Hostel* *75 Marsh Rd, Dudley, MA 01571.*	**☎** *(508) 9436520* *for information.*	*7*	*01.04–30.11*	Ⓡ ⚿ P 🄰
△ *Durango* *543 1/2 E 2nd Ave, Durango, CO 81301.*	**☎** *(970) 2479905* **✆** *(970) 3829150*	*18*	🖪	♯♯ 🏧 ⚿ P
▲ East Glacier Park - Brownie's 1020 Montana Hwy 49, PO Box 229, East Glacier Park MT 59434.	**☎** (406) 2264426	25	01.05–14.10 (**☎** for exact dates)	♯♯ Ⓡ 🏧 ⚿ P 🄰
△ *Eastham* *Mid-Cape, 75 Goody Hallet Drive, Eastham MA 02642. (When shut: ENEC Reservations, 12 Hemenway St, Boston, MA 02115).* **e** *eastham@cape.com*	**☎** *(508) 2552785;* *(617) 5310459* *(When shut)*	*50*	*07.05–12.09*	Ⓡ 🏧 ⚿ P
△ *Elma - Grays Harbor Hostel* *6 Ginny Lane, Elma, WA 98541.* **e** *ghhostel@techline.com*	**☎** *(360) 4823119*	*14*	🖪	♯♯ Ⓡ ⚿ P

Location/Address	Telephone No. Fax No.	Beds	Opening Dates	Facilities
▲ **Florida City** - Everglades 20 S.W. Second Ave, Florida City, FL 33034. 🄴 gladeshostel@hotmail.com	🕿 (305) 2481122; (800) 3723874 (in US only) 🖷 (305) 2457622	47	🄵12	♟ Ⓡ ☞ 🅿 🗗
△ *Fort Flagler* *Fort Flagler State Park, 10621 Flagler Rd,* *Nordland WA 98358. (Marrowstone Island).* 🄴 *ffhostel@olypen.com*	🕿 *(360) 3851288*	*14*	*16.03–30.09*	♟ Ⓡ ⧼CC⧽ ☞ 🅿
Fullerton ☞**Los Angeles**				
△ *Galax* - *Blue Ridge Mountains Hostel* *Blue Ridge Pkwy at milepost 214.5,* *Eastern Side MAIL, 214507 Blue Ridge Pkwy,* *Galax VA 24333.*	🕿 *(540) 2364962*	*22*	*01.04–31.10*	☞ 🅿
▲ **Galveston** 201 Seawall Boulevard, Galveston, TX 77550. 🄴 sndpipr325@aol.com	🕿 (409) 7659431	24	🄵12	♟ Ⓡ ☞ 🅿
△ *Gardners* - *Ironmaster's Mansion* *Pine Grove Furnace State Park,* *1212 Pine Grove Rd, Gardners PA 17324.* 🄴 *hiironmasters@hi-dvc.org*	🕿 *(717) 4867575* 🖷 *(717) 4865115*	*46*	🄵12	♟ ⧼CC⧽ ☞ 🅿 🗗
△ *Gary* - *Pleasant Valley Hostel* *South Dakota Hwy 22, Box 256,* *Gary SD 57237.*	🕿 *(605) 2725614*	*18*	🄵12	♟ ⧼CC⧽ ☞ 🅿
△ *Glenwood Springs* - *Glenwood Springs Hostel* *1021 Grand Ave, Glenwood Springs CO 81601.* 🄴 *gshostel@rof.net*	🕿 *(970) 9458545;* *(800) 9467835* *(toll free in US* *only)*	*42*	🄵12	♟ Ⓡ ⧼CC⧽ ☞ 🅿 🗗
▲ **Grand Lake** - Shadowcliff Hostel 405 Summerland Park Rd, PO Box 658, Grand Lake CO 80447.	🕿 (970) 6279220 🖷 (970) 6279220	14	27.05–23.09	♟ Ⓡ ☞ 🅿
△ *Grand Marais* - *Spirit of the Land IslandHostel* *Wilderness Canoe Base, 12477 Gunflint Trail,* *Grand Marias MN 55604.*	🕿 *(218) 3882241* 🖷 *(218) 3882241* *(call first)*	*12*	*01.01–31.03;* *01.05–31.10;* *29–31.12*	Ⓡ ⧼CC⧽ ☞ 🅿 🗗
△ *Hartford* - *The Mark Twain Hostel* *131 Tremont St, Hartford, CT 06105.*	🕿 *(860) 5237255* 🖷 *(860) 2331767*	*42*	🄵12	♟ Ⓡ ⧼CC⧽ ☞ 🅿 🗗
▲ **Honolulu** - University ⧼IBN⧽ **2323A Seaview Ave, Honolulu HI 96822.**	🕿 (808) 9460591 🖷 (808) 9465904	43	🄵12	♟ Ⓡ 5W ⧼CC⧽ ☞ 🅿 🗗
▲ **Honolulu** - Waikiki ⧼IBN⧽ **2417 Prince Edward St,** **Honolulu HI 96815.** 🄴 halealoha@webtv.net	🕿 (808) 9268313 🖷 (808) 9223798	60	🄵12	♟ Ⓡ 5W ⧼CC⧽ ☞ 🅿 🗗
▲ **Hurricane** - The Dixie Hostel 73 S.Main St, Hurricane, UT 84737.	🕿 (435) 6358202	32	🄵12	♟ ☞ 🅿 🗗
▲ **Independence** - The Winnedumah Hotel 211 N. Edwards St, PO Box 147, Independence, CA 93526. 🄴 winnedumah@qnet.com	🕿 (760) 8782040 🖷 (760) 8782833	12	13.10–09.10	♟ 🍽 Ⓡ ⧼CC⧽ ☞ 🅿

Location/Address	Telephone No. Fax No.	Beds	Opening Dates	Facilities
△ *Itasca State Park* - Mississippi Headwaters Itasca State Park, HC 05, Box 5A, Park Rapids, MN 56470.	☏ (218) 2663415 🖷 (218) 2663451	31	01.01–17.03; 27.04–27.10; 13–31.12	�02 🔴 ⟨ -CC- ☞ 🅿 ⬚
△ *Juneau* 614 Harris St, Juneau AK 99801. ✉ juneauhostel@gci.net	☏ (907) 5869559	47	🗓12	�02 🔴 ☞ ⬚
△ *Ketchikan* Grant and Main St, PO Box 8515, Ketchikan AK 99901.	☏ (907) 2253319	23	01.06–31.08	🔴 ☞ 🅿
△ *Key West* 718 South St, Key West FL 33040. ✉ keyshostel@aol.com	☏ (305) 2965719 🖷 (305) 2960672	92	🗓12	�02 🔴 -CC- ☞ 🅿 ⬚
▲ *Kitty Hawk* Outer Banks, 1004 West Kitty Hawk Rd, Kitty Hawk, NC 27949. ✉ outerbankshostel@msn.com	☏ (252) 2612294 🖷 (252) 2612294	40	🗓12	�02 🔴 -CC- ☞ 🅿 ⬚
△ *Knoxville* - Harpers Ferry Lodge 19123 Sandy Hook Rd, Knoxville MD 21758. ✉ ferrylodge@aol.com	☏ (301) 8347652 🖷 (301) 8347652	39	16.03–14.11	�02 🔴 ☞ 🅿 ⬚
△ *La Anna* - Poconos La Anna Rd, RR 2-Box 1026, Cresco, PA 18326. ✉ hipoconos@hi-dvc.org	☏ (570) 6769076 🖷 (570) 6769076	40	🗓12	�02 🔴 128N ☞ 🅿
▲ *Lincoln* - Cornerstone 640 North 16th St, Lincoln NE 68508.	☏ (402) 4760926	9	08.01–17.12	🔴 ☞ 🅿 ⬚
△ *Littleton* - Friendly Crossways PO Box 2266, Littleton MA 01460. ✉ friendly@ma.ultranet.com	☏ (978) 4569386	50	🗓12	�02 ⟨ ☞ 🅿
Los Altos Hills ☞Palo Alto				
▲ *Los Angeles* - Santa Monica **IBN** **1436 2nd St, Santa Monica CA 90401.** ✉ reserve@HILosAngeles.org	☏ (310) 3939913 🖷 (310) 3931769	200	🗓12	�02 🍽 🔴 ⟨ -CC- ☞ 🅿 ⬚
▲ *Los Angeles* - South Bay **3601 South Gaffey St, Building 613, San Pedro CA 90731-6969.** ✉ hisanpedro@aol.com	☏ (310) 8318109 🖷 (310) 8314635	60	🗓12	�02 🔴 32S -CC- ☞ 🅿 ⬚
△ *Los Angeles* - Fullerton 1700 N Harbor Blvd, Fullerton CA 92835. (Disneyland area). ✉ hifull@aol.com	☏ (714) 7383721 🖷 (714) 7380925	20	🗓12	🔴 ⟨ -CC- ☞ 🅿 ⬚
△ *Lucas* - Malabar Farm Hostel 3954 Bromfield Rd, Lucas OH 44843.	☏ (419) 8922055 🖷 (419) 8922055	19	15.01–15.12	�02 🔴 ☞ 🅿 ⬚
△ *Madison* - Hi-Madison 141 South Butler St, Madison, WI 53703. ✉ madisonhostel@yahoo.com	☏ (608) 2829013	23	🗓12	�02 🔴 -CC- ⬚

Location/Address	Telephone No. Fax No.	Beds	Opening Dates	Facilities
△ *Martha's Vineyard* Edgartown Rd, PO Box 3158, West Tisbury MA 02575. (When shut: ENEC Reservations, 12 Hemenway St, Boston, MA 02115). e marthasvineyardhostel@juno.com	t (508) 6932665; (617) 5310459 (When shut) f (508) 6932699	78	01.04–06.11	R ♿ CC ✶ P
△ *Merced* - Merced Home Hostel PO Box 3755, Merced CA 95344. e merced-bostel@juno.com	t (209) 7250407 for information	8	🔲	R ✶ P
▲ Miami Beach (IBN) 1438 Washington Ave, Miami Beach FL 33139. e info@clayhotel.com	t (305) 5342988 (800) 3792529 (R only) f (305) 6730346	200	🔲	♂♀ �🍴 R CC ✶ ▣ ☕
△ *Middlebury* - Covered Bridge Home Hostel Middlebury, VT.	t (802) 3880401 Call for information	8	🔲	R ✶ P
▲ Midpines - The Yosemite Bug Hostel 6979 Hwy 140, PO Box 81, Midpines CA 95345. e bughost@sierratel.com	t (209) 9666666 f (209) 9666667	52	🔲	♂♀ �🍴 R ♿ CC ✶ P ▣ ☕
△ *Milwaukee* - Red Barn 6750 W Loomis Rd, Greendale WI 53129. e redbarn@hostellingwisconsin.org	t (414) 5293299	20	15.05–15.09	R ✶ P
△ *Montara* - Point Montara Lighthouse PO Box 737, 16th St at California Hwy 1, Montara CA 94037.	t (650) 7287177 f (650) 7287177	45	🔲	♂♀ R ♿ CC ✶ P ▣
▲ Monterey 778 Hawthorne St, Monterey, CA 93940. e info@montereyhostel.com	t (831) 6490375	45	🔲	♂♀ R ♿ CC ✶ P
△ *Montpelier* - Capitol Home Hostel RD1, Box 2750, Montpelier, VT 05602.	t (802) 2232104 for information	3	🔲	♂♀ R ✶ P
▲ Nampa 17322 Canada Rd, Nampa, ID 83687. e mail@hostelboise.com	t (208) 4676858	12	🔲	♂♀ R ✶ P
△ *Nantucket* - Surfside 31 Western Ave, Nantucket MA 02554. (When shut: ENEC Reservations, 12 Hemenway St, Boston, MA 02115). e nantuckethostel@juno.com	t (508) 2280433; (617) 5310459 (When shut) f (508) 2285672	49	21.04–15.10	R CC ✶ P
△ *Naples* Hwy 2, Naples ID 83847.	t (208) 2672947 f (208) 2674118	18	02.01–06.04; 08.04–24.12; 26–31.12	♂♀ ✶ P ▣
△ *New Boston* - Country Grandma's Home Hostel RR3, New Boston, MI 48164.	t (734) 7534901 for information	6	01.04–31.10	♂♀ R ✶ P
▲ New Orleans - Marquette House (IBN) 2253 Carondelet St, New Orleans LA 70130. e HINewOrlns@aol.com	t (504) 5233014 f (504) 5295933	166	🔲	♂♀ �🍴 R 3SW CC ✶ P ▣

Location/Address	Telephone No. Fax No.	Beds	Opening Dates	Facilities
▲ New York - International IBN 891 Amsterdam Ave at West 103rd St, New York NY 10025. ❸ reserve@hinewyork.org	☎ (212) 9322300 ✆ (212) 9322574	624	🏢	ᴴᴵ ♨ R ♿ ECC ♂ ⊡ ☕
△ Newburg - Wellspring 4382 Hickory Rd, PO Box 72, Newburg WI 53060-0072.	☎ (262) 6756755	15	01.01–03.04; 05.04–24.11; 26.11–24.12; 26–31.12	ᴴᴵ R ECC ♂ P
△ Newtown - Tyler Hostel PO Box 94, Newtown, PA 18940. ❸ hityler@hi-dvc.org	☎ (215) 9680927 ✆ (215) 5572100	25	01.01–24.11; 29.11–23.12; 27–31.12	ᴴᴵ R ♂ P
△ Niagara Falls 1101 Ferry Ave, Niagara Falls NY 14301.	☎ (716) 2823700	46	31.01–19.12	R ♂ P ⊡
△ Ninilchik - The Eagle Watch Mile 3, Oil Well Rd, Box 39083, Ninilchik, AK 99639.	☎ (907) 5673905	20	15.05–15.09	ᴴᴵ R ♂ P
△ Ohiopyle State Park Ferncliff Peninsula, PO Box 99, Ohiopyle PA 15470.	☎ (724) 3294476 ✆ (724) 3294476	24	01.01–22.12; 30–31.12	ᴴᴵ R ♂ P ⊡
▲ Orlando - Kissimmee Resort IBN 4840 W Irlo Bronson Hwy, Kissimmee FL 34746. (Route 192 at Route 535). ❸ hi_orlandoresort@compuserve.com	☎ (407) 3968282 ✆ (407) 3969311	192	🏢	ᴴᴵ R ♿ ECC ♂ P ⊡
△ Palo Alto - Hidden Villa 26870 Moody Rd, Los Altos Hills CA 94022.	☎ (650) 9498648 ✆ (650) 9484159	35	07.09–31.12	ᴴᴵ R ♂ P
△ Pembroke - Pembroke House Baptist Student Center, 300N Odom St, UNC Pembroke, Pembroke NC 28372. ❸ sanders@carolina.com	☎ (910) 5218777 ✆ (910) 5217166	8	🏢	ᴴᴵ R ♿ ♂ P ⊡
△ Peninsula - Stanford House 6093 Stanford Rd, Peninsula OH 44264. ❸ hi-stanfordhostel@juno.com	☎ (330) 4678711 ✆ (330) 4678711	30	🏢	ᴴᴵ R ♂ P ⊡
△ Pescadero - Pigeon Point Lighthouse 210 Pigeon Point Rd, Pescadero CA 94060.	☎ (650) 8790633 ✆ (650) 8799120	52	🏢	ᴴᴵ R ♿ ECC ♂ P
△ Philadelphia - Bank Street Hostel 32 S.Bank St, Philadelphia, PA 19106. ❸ manager@bankstreethostel.com	☎ (215) 9220222 ✆ (215) 9224082	70	🏢	R ♂ ⊡
△ Philadelphia - Chamounix Mansion Chamounix Drive, W Fairmount Park, Philadelphia PA 19131. ❸ chamounix@philahostel.org	☎ (215) 8783676 (800) 3790017 (in US only) ✆ (215) 8714313	80	16.01–14.12	ᴴᴵ ECC ♂ P ⊡
△ Phoenix - The Metcalf House 1026 N 9th St, Phoenix AZ 85006.	☎ (602) 2549803	20	🏢	♂ ⊡
△ Pitkin - Pitkin Hostel 4th & Main Sts, PO Box 164, Pitkin CO 81241.	☎ (970) 6412757 (888) 5412013 (toll free in US)	6	🏢	ᴴᴵ R ♂ P ⊡

Location/Address	Telephone No. Fax No.	Beds	Opening Dates	Facilities
△ *Pittsburgh* 830 E. Warrington Ave, Pittsburgh, PA 15210. e hipgh@sgi.net	☎ (412) 4311267 ✆ (412) 4312625	54	01.01–22.12; 27–31.12	ᵗᵗᵗ R ♿ CC ♂ P ◫
△ *Point Reyes National Seashore* (off Limantour Rd), Box 247, Point Reyes Station CA 94956.	☎ (415) 6638811 ✆ (415) 6638811	44	▦₁₂	R ♿ CC ♂ P
△ *Port Townsend* - Olympic Hostel #272 Battery Way, Port Townsend WA 98368. e olyhost@olympus.net	☎ (360) 3850655	24	02.01–24.12	ᵗᵗᵗ R CC ♂
▲ *Portland (Oregon)* - Northwest Neighborhood **1818 NW Glisan, Portland, OR 97209.** e hinwp@transport.com	☎ (503) 2412783 ✆ (503) 5255910	33	▦₁₂	ᵗᵗᵗ R CC ♂ ◫ ☕ ☎ ⚙
▲ *Portland (Oregon)* - Hawthorn District **3031 Hawthorne Blvd SE,** **Portland OR 97214.** e hip@teleport.com	☎ (503) 2363380 ✆ (503) 2367940	33	▦₁₂	¹⁰¹ R CC ♂ P ◫ ☎ ⚙
△ *Quakertown* Weisel, 7347 Richlandtown Rd, Quakertown PA 18951.	☎ (215) 5368749	20	01.01–24.12; 26–31.12	ᵗᵗᵗ R ♂ P
△ *Redwood National Park* 14480 Hwy 101 at Wilson Creek Rd, Klamath CA 95548. e theredwoodhostel@earthlink.net	☎ (707) 4828265 ✆ (707) 4828265	30	▦₁₂	R ♿ CC ♂ P ◫
△ *Sacramento* 900 H St, Sacramento CA 95814. e hisac@norcalhostels.org	☎ (916) 4431691 ✆ (916) 4434763	70	▦₁₂	ᵗᵗᵗ R ♿ CC ♂ P ◫
▲ *San Antonio* 621 Pierce St, PO Box 8059, San Antonio TX 78208. e hisananton@aol.com	☎ (210) 2239426 ✆ (210) 2991479	42	▦₁₂	ᵗᵗᵗ 3NE CC ♂ P
▲ *San Clemente* - San Clemente Beach 233 Avenida Granada, San Clemente CA 92672-4029. e hiayhsc@aol.com	☎ (949) 4922848 ✆ (949) 3619018	40	01.05–31.10	ᵗᵗᵗ R ♿ CC ♂ P ◫
▲ *San Diego* - Downtown IBN **521 Market St, San Diego CA 92101.** e hisddowntown@aol.com	☎ (619) 5251531 ✆ (619) 3380129	134	▦₁₂	ᵗᵗᵗ R ♿ CC ♂ ◫
▲ *San Diego* - Point Loma IBN **3790 Udall St, San Diego CA 92107-2414.** e HISDPTLOMA@aol.com	☎ (619) 2234778 ✆ (619) 2231883	61	▦₁₂	ᵗᵗᵗ R 10W CC ♂ P ◫
▲ *San Francisco* - Downtown IBN **Union Square, 312 Mason St,** **San Francisco CA 94102.** e sfdowntown@norcalhostels.org	☎ (415) 7885604 ✆ (415) 7883023	260	▦₁₂	ᵗᵗᵗ R CC ♂ P
▲ *San Francisco* - Fisherman's Wharf IBN **Fort Mason, Building 240, San Francisco,** **CA 94123.** e sfhostel@norcalhostels.org	☎ (415) 7717277 ✆ (415) 7711468	170	▦₁₂	ᵗᵗᵗ R ♿ CC ♂ P ◫ ☕

Location/Address	Telephone No. Fax No.	Beds	Opening Dates	Facilities
△ *San Jose (Saratoga)* - *Sanborn Park Hostel* *15808 Sanborn Rd, Saratoga CA 95070.*	☎ *(408) 7410166*	*39*	🗓12	♔♔ ⅙ ☛ 🅿 ⬛
△ *San Luis Obispo* - *Hostel Obispo* *1617 Santa Rosa St., San Luis Obispo,* *CA 93401.* ✉ *esimer@slonet.org*	☎ *(805) 5444678*	*22*	🗓12	♔♔ **R** ⅙ ☛ 🅿 ⬛
△ *Santa Cruz* *321 Main St, PO Box 1241,* *Santa Cruz CA 95061.* ✉ *info@hi-santacruz.org*	☎ *(831) 4238304* 🖷 *(831) 4298541*	*40*	🗓12	♔♔ **R** ⅙ ᴄᴄ ☛ 🅿
Saratoga ☞San Jose (Saratoga)				
▲ Sausalito - Marin Headlands Fort Barry, Building 941, Sausalito CA 94965.	☎ *(415) 3312777* 🖷 *(415) 3316943*	104	🗓12	♔♔ **R** ⅙ ᴄᴄ ☛ 🅿 ⬛
△ *Savannah* *304 E Hall St, Savannah GA 31401.*	☎ *(912) 2367744* 🖷 *(912) 2367744*	*18*	*01.03–30.11*	♔♔ ☛ 🅿
△ *Searsport* - *The Penobscot Bay Hostel* *132 W. Main St (Rt 1), P.O. Box 306,* *Searsport, ME 04974.* ✉ *info@newenglandhostel.com*	☎ *(877) 3346783* *- toll free in US;* *(207) 5482506*	*10*	*15.04–31.10*	**R** ⅙ ☛ 🅿
▲ Seaside 930 N Holladay, Seaside, OR 97138. ✉ hiseaside@transport.com	☎ *(503) 7387911* 🖷 *(503) 7170163*	56	🗓12	♔♔ ⁑◎ **R** ⅙ ᴄᴄ ☛ 🅿 ⬛ 🍴
▲ Seattle - Downtown ⟦IBN⟧ **84 Union St, Seattle WA 98101.** ✉ reserve@hiseattle.org	☎ *(206) 6225443* 🖷 *(206) 6822179*	199	🗓12	♔♔ **R** ⅙ ᴄᴄ ☛ ⬛
▲ Seattle - Vashon Island AYH Ranch Hostel 12119 Cove Rd SW, Vashon Island WA 98070. ✉ dirk@vashonhostel.com	☎ *(206) 4632592* 🖷 *(206) 4636157*	70	*01.05–31.10*	♔♔ **R** ᴄᴄ ☛ 🅿
▲ Silver City The Carter House (Silver City), 101 North Cooper St, Silver City NM 88061.	☎ *(505) 3885485*	22	🗓12	♔♔ ᴄᴄ ☛ ⬛
△ *Sitka* *303 Kimsham St, PO Box 2645,* *Sitka AK 99835.*	☎ *(907) 7478661*	*18*	*01.06–31.08*	**R** ☛ 🅿
▲ St. Augustine - Hi-St. Augustine 32 Treasury St, St. Augustine, FL 32084. ✉ reserve@internationalhaus.com	☎ *(904) 8081999*	35	🗓12	♔♔ **R** ᴄᴄ ☛ ⬛
△ *St. Louis* - *The Huckleberry Finn Hostel* *1904-1908 S 12th St, Tucker Blvd,* *St. Louis MO 63104.* ✉ *huckfinn@mindspring.com*	☎ *(314) 2410076*	*44*	🗓12	♔♔ **R** ⟦1 SW⟧ ᴄᴄ ☛ 🅿
△ *Syracuse* - *Downing International Hostel* *535 Oak St, Syracuse NY 13203-1609.*	☎ *(315) 4725788* 🖷 *(315) 4260662*	*34*	🗓12	♔♔ ⟦2 NE⟧ ☛ ⬛
△ *Taos (Arroyo Seco)* *Taos Ski Valley Rd, PO Box 3271,* *Taos NM 87571.* ✉ *snowman@newmex.com*	☎ *(505) 7768298* 🖷 *(505) 7762107*	*38*	🗓12	♔♔ **R** ᴄᴄ ☛ 🅿

Location/Address	Telephone No. Fax No.	Beds	Opening Dates	Facilities
△ *Tecopa/Death Valley* - *Desertaire Hostel* *2000 Old Spanish Trail Hwy, PO Box 306,* *Tecopa CA 92389.*	☎ *(760) 8524580*	*10*	🄲	♦♦ Ⓡ ☞ Ⓟ
△ *Tok* *PO Box 532, Tok AK 99780.*	☎ *(907) 8833745*	*10*	*15.05–15.09*	Ⓡ ☞ Ⓟ
△ *Truro* *North Pamet Rd, PO Box 402, Truro,* *MA 02666. (When shut: ENEC Reservations,* *12 Hemenway St, Boston, MA 02115).* ⓔ *trurohostel@juno.com*	☎ *(508) 3493889;* *(617) 5310459* *(When shut)*	*42*	*18.06–07.09*	Ⓡ ⊂CC⊃ ☞ Ⓟ
▲ **Truth or Consequences** Riverbend Hot Springs, 100 Austin, Truth or Consequences NM 87901. ⓔ truthorconsequences@hotmail.com	☎ (505) 8946183	16	🄲	♦♦ Ⓡ ⊂CC⊃ ☞ Ⓟ 🄾
▲ **Tucumcari** - Redwood Lodge 1502 W. Tucumcari Blvd, Tucumcari, NM 88401.	☎ (505) 4613635 🄵 (505) 4613635	20	🄲	Ⓡ ☞ Ⓟ
△ *Urbanna* *Sangraal by-the-Sea, Carlton Rd, Rt 626,* *Wake, VA 23175.*	☎ *(804) 7766500*	*20*	🄲	🍴 Ⓡ ☞ Ⓟ 🄾
Vashon Island 🖙Seattle				
△ *Virginia Beach* - *Angie's Guest Cottage* *302 24th St, Virginia Beach VA 23451.* ⓔ *angiesinvb@cs.com*	☎ *(757) 4284690*	*34*	*01.04–30.09*	♦♦ Ⓡ ☞
△ *Volcano* - *Holo Holo In* *19-4036 Kalani Honua Rd, P.O. Box 784,* *Volcano, HI 96785.* ⓔ *holoholo@interpac.net*	☎ *(808) 9677950* 🄵 *(808) 9678025*	*10*	🄲	♦♦ Ⓡ ☞ Ⓟ 🄾
▲ **Washington, DC** **1009 11th St NW, Washington DC 20001.** ⓔ reservations@hiwashingtondc.org	☎ (202) 7372333 🄵 (202) 7371508	270	🄲	Ⓡ ♿ ⊂CC⊃ ☞ 🄾
△ *White River Junction* *The Hotel Coolidge, PO Box 515, 17 S. Main St,* *White River Junction, VT 05001.* ⓔ *hotel.coolidge@valley.net*	☎ *(802) 2953118,* *(800) 6221124* *(in US only)* 🄵 *(802) 2915100*	*26*	🄲	♦♦ ⊂CC⊃ ☞ Ⓟ 🄾 ☕
▲ **Woodford** - Greenwood Lodge Prospect Ski Mountain, RT 9, Woodford, PO Box 246, Bennington VT 05201. ⓔ grnwd@compuserve.com	☎ (802) 4422547 🄵 (802) 4422547	20	20.05–22.10	♦♦ Ⓡ ♿ ☞ Ⓟ

Uruguay

URUGUAY

URUGUAY

URUGUAY

Asociación de Alberguistas del Uruguay,
Pablo de Maria 1583/008,
PC 11200 PO Box 10680, Montevideo, Uruguay.

☏ (598) (2) 4004245, 4000581
🖷 (598) (2) 4001326
✉ aau@adinet.com.uy
🖳 www.internet.com.uy/aau

A copy of the Hostel Directory for this Country can be obtained from:
The National Office

Capital:	Montevideo	**Population:**	3,061,000
Language:	Spanish	**Size:**	176,215 sq km
Currency:	$ (Peso Uruguayo)	**Telephone Country Code:**	598

English

Uruguay is one of the safest countries in the continent. The months of June to August are generally cold. Hostels are located in cities, in the countryside and on the coast.

Price range

Price range $5-7. 🛏 Sheet sleeping bag required.

Rooms and Reservations

R 🛏 (All Rooms). Reservations via **IBN** Hostel or National Office by ❶ ❻ ❷. Smoking is limited - please check.

Guests

Membership Card and Passport/Photo ID are required. The maximum stay is 15 days. Age limits may apply for children - check with hostel. ♦♦♦ welcome. Group bookings via **IBN** or National Office by ❶ ❻ ❷.

Open times

Main hostels: open 🛏, 🕐. Reception open: 08:00-22:00hrs. Resident manager. **Other hostels:** open 🛏, 🕐. Reception open: 08:00-22:00hrs. Resident manager. **Seasonal hostels** are generally open Jan-Apr, Nov, Dec.

Meals

🍽 BLD **R** For individuals & for ▥. ☞.

Discounts

HI Member Discounts available - see discounts section and www.iyhf.org.

Travelling around

For ease of travel use 🚐 Self-Drive.

Travel/Activity Packages

Tours/sightseeing and accommodation/ transport packages available. Package bookings via National Office by ❶ ❷ ❸.

Passports and Visas

Passport/Photo ID required.

Health

Emergency medical treatment is free. Medical insurance is recommended.

Français

L'Uruguay est l'un des pays du continent sud-américain les plus sûrs. Les mois de juin à août sont en général froids. Les auberges sont situées dans les villes, à la campagne et sur le littoral.

Tarifs des nuitées

Tarifs des nuitées 5-7$. 🛏 Sac-drap obligatoire.

Chambres et réservations

R 🖼 (Toutes chambres). Réservations via **IBN** l'auberge ou le Bureau National par ❶ ❷ ❸. Il est permis de fumer dans certaines chambres - veuillez vérifier.

Usagers

La carte d'adhérent ainsi que le passeport/pièce d'identité avec photo sont à présenter. La durée

maximale du séjour est de 15 jours. Il est possible que des limites d'âge soient en vigueur pour les enfants - vérifiez auprès de l'auberge. Accueil des ▥. Réservations pour groupes via **IBN** ou le Bureau National par ❶ ❷ ❸.

Horaires d'ouverture

Grandes auberges: ouvertes 🖼, 🕐. Accueil ouvert entre 8h-22h. Gérant réside sur place. **Autres auberges:** ouvertes 🖼, 🕐. Accueil ouvert entre 8h-22h. Gérant réside sur place. **Auberges saisonnières** ouvertes généralement jan-avril, nov, déc.

Repas

🍽 BLD **R** Pour individuels & pour ▥. ☞.

Remises

Remises pour les adhérents HI - voir la section "Remises" et notre site: www.iyhf.org.

Déplacements

Modes de transport recommandés 🚐 Voiture.

Forfaits Voyages/Activités

Forfaits circuits touristiques et hébergement/ transport disponibles. Réservations des forfaits via le Bureau National par ❶ ❷ ❸.

Passeports et visas

Passeport/pièce d'identité avec photo obligatoires.

Santé

Soins d'urgence gratuits. Une assurance médicale de voyage est conseillée.

Deutsch

Uruguay ist eines der sichersten Länder auf dem Kontinent. Die Monate von Juni bis August sind

generell kalt. Herbergen befinden sich in
Städten, auf dem Land und an der Küste.

Preisspanne

Preisspanne 5-7 $. 🛏 Leinenschlafsack
erforderlich.

Zimmer und Reservierungen

🅡 🛏 (Alle Zimmer). Reservierungen über
[IBN] Herberge oder Landesverband per ➊
❸ ❹. Rauchen ist begrenzt - bitte checken.

Gäste

Mitgliedsausweis und Reisepass/
Personalausweis sind erforderlich. Der
maximale Aufenthalt beträgt 15 Tage.
Altersbegrenzungen für Kinder möglich - in der
Herberge nachfragen. ❖ willkommen.
Gruppenbuchungen über [IBN] oder die
Landesverband per ➊ ❸ ❹.

Öffnungszeiten

Hauptherbergen: Zugang 🛏, 🕐. Rezeption
zwischen 08:00-22:00Uhr. Herbergsmanager
wohnt im Haus. **Andere Herbergen:** Zugang
🛏, 🕐. Rezeption zwischen 08:00-22:00Uhr.
Herbergsmanager wohnt im Haus.
Saison-Herbergen sind normalerweise
Jan-Apr, Nov, Dez geöffnet.

Mahlzeiten

🍽 BLD 🅡 Für Einzelreisende & für ❖. ☞.

Ermäßigungen

HI-Mitgliedsrabatt ist erhältlich – siehe Teil für
Rabatte und Ermäßigungen und www.iyhf.org.

Reisen im Land

Reisen ist einfach mit 🚐 Selbstfahrer.

Reise-/Aktivitäten-Packages

Touren/sightseeing und Unterkunft/Transport-
Packages erhältlich. Package-Buchungen über
Landesverband per ➊ ❸ ❹.

Reisepässe und Visa

Reisepass/Personalausweis erforderlich.

Gesundheit

Nur im Notfall sind medizinische Behandlungen
kostenlos. Unfall-/Krankenversicherung wird
empfohlen.

Español

Uruguay es uno de los países más seguros del
continente. Los meses de junio a agosto son,
por lo general, fríos. Los albergues están
situados en las ciudades, el campo y la costa.

Tarifas mínima y máxima

Tarifas mínima y máxima 5-7$. 🛏 Saco sábana
imprescindible.

Habitaciones y Reservas

🅡 🛏 (Todas las habitaciones). Reservas
por [IBN] o a través del albergue o la
Asociación Nacional por ➊ ❸ ❹. Está
permitido fumar sólo en algunas
salas/habitaciones - infórmese.

Huéspedes

Los huéspedes deben presentar su Carnet de
Alberguista y su pasaporte o carnet de
identidad. La estancia máxima es de 15 días. Es
posible que exista un límite de edad para los
niños - consulte con el albergue. Se admiten
❖. Reservas de grupo por [IBN] o a través de
la Asociación Nacional por ➊ ❸ ❹.

Horarios y fechas de apertura

Albergues principales - abiertos 🛏, 🕐.
Horario de recepción: 08:00-22:00h. Gerente
residente. **Otros albergues** - abiertos 🛏, 🕐.
Horario de recepción: 08:00-22:00h. Gerente
residente. **Albergues de temporada** suelen
abrir: ene-abr, nov, dic.

Comidas

¶◎¶ BLD ® Para individuales y para ▮▮▮. ✿.

Descuentos

Se conceden descuentos a los miembros de Hostelling International – véase la sección sobre descuentos y nuestra página Internet en www.iyhf.org.

Desplazamientos

Transportes recomendados: 🚌 Automóvil.

Viajes Combinados con Actividades

Viajes combinados con visitas turísticas y alojamiento/transporte. Reserva de viajes combinados a través de la Asociación Nacional por ❶ ❷ ❸.

Pasaportes y Visados

Pasaporte o carnet de identidad obligatorio.

Información Sanitaria

Asistencia médica de urgencia gratuita. Seguro médico recomendado.

Montevideo - Schirrmann-Münker

Canelones 935, Montevideo.
❶ (2) 9081324
❶ (2) 9081324
❸ almont@adinet.com.uy

Open Dates:	📅
Open Hours:	🕐
Reservations:	® IBN
Price Range:	01.04-30.11 US$9.00 01.12-31.03 US$10.50 BB inc 🍴
Beds:	50 - 1x² 1x⁴ 6x⁶ 1x⁶
Facilities:	▮▮▮ ¶◎¶ ✿ ⚙ 🏠 📺 📄 🧺 🔲 📷 ℹ 🔍

Directions:

✈	Montevideo 16km
A🚌	209, 214 + Copsa Lines 700m
⛴	Montevideo 2km
🚌	116, 117, 118, 164, 165, 409, 411 100m

Attractions: 🚲

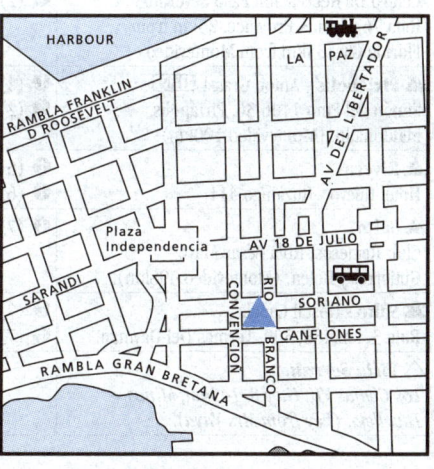

Location/Address	Telephone No. Fax No.	Beds	Opening Dates	Facilities
△ *Artigas* *Club Deportivo Artigas,* *Pte Berreta s/n. (Montevideo 627km).*	☎ *(77) 23860* ☏ *(77) 22532*	*24*	🗓	⑂ Ⓡ
△ *Barra Valizas* *Artigas YH, Barra Valizas,* *Rocha. (Montevideo 265km, Rocha 60km).*	☎ *(470) 5273*	*56*	*01.11–30.04*	Ⓡ ☞ ⃞
△ *Colonia Suiza* *Hotel del Prado YH, Ruta 1, Colonia Suiza.* *(Montevideo 129km, Colonia 58km).*	☎ *(55) 44169*	*15*	🗓	⑆ ⑂ Ⓡ
△ *Durazno - "Hostal El Nazareno"* *Ruta 5, Km 180 (Rural).*	☎ *(36) 23564*	*16*	🗓	0.3S ☞ ⃞
△ *Flores* *Albergue Estancia "El Silencio", Ruta 14-km166,* *Departmento de Flores. (Rural Farm).*	☎ *(36) 22014*	*15*	🗓	⑆ ⑂ Ⓡ ☞ ⃞
△ *La Coronilla* *Hotel Las Maravillas,* *L. Fernandez Y La Linea.*	☎ *(476) 2892;* *(476) 2786* ☏ *(476) 2892*	*60*	🗓	⑆ ⑂ ☞ Ⓟ ⃞
△ *La Paloma* *'Altena 5000' YH, Parque Municipal* *'Andresito', Parada 12, La Paloma, Rocha.* *(Montevideo 240km, Rocha 28km).*	☎ *(473) 6396*	*50*	🗓	⑂ Ⓡ ☞ ⃞
△ *Manantiales* *Puebla Nueva YH, Km 164, Hwy 10,* *Manantiales, Maldonado.*	☎ *(42) 774427*	*30*	*01.11–30.04*	⑂ Ⓡ ☞ ⃞
▲ **Montevideo** - Schirrmann-Münker ⟨IBN⟩ **Canelones 935, Montevideo.** ⓔ almont@adinet.com.uy	☎ *(2) 9081324* ☏ *(2) 9081324*	*50*	🗓	⑂ Ⓡ ☞ ⃞ ☼
▲ **Paysandu** 'La Posada', JP Varela Y Solis, CP 60000 Paysandu.	☎ *(72) 27879* ☏ *(72) 27879*	*35*	🗓	⑆ ⑂ ⒸⒸ Ⓟ ⃞
▲ **Paso Severino** - Centro De Recreacion Paso Severino Ruta 76, Florida Province. 25km from Florida City. 83km from Montevideo.	☎ *(2) 4004245* ☏ *(2) 4001326*	*90*	*01.01–23.02;* *05.03–06.04;* *16.04–31.12*	⑆ ⑂ Ⓡ ⃞ Ⓟ ⃞ ☞ 🏍
▲ **Piriápolis** - Anton Grassl ⟨IBN⟩ Simón del Pino 1106-36, Piriápolis, Maldonado. (Montevideo 100km).	☎ *(43) 20394* ☏ *(2) 4001326*	*322*	🗓	⑆ ⑂ Ⓡ ☞
▲ **Rivera** Hotel Nuevo - Ituzaingo 411.	☎ *(62) 23039* ☏ *(62) 23147*	*40*	🗓	⑆ ⑂ ⃞
▲ **Salto** Club Remeros, Rbla César Mayo Gutierrez y Belén. (Montevideo 498km).	☎ *(73) 23418*	*40*	🗓	⑂ Ⓡ
▲ **Salto** - Hostal Canela Ruta 3, km.488, 300, Termas Del Dayman.	☎ *(73) 32121* ☏ *(73) 32121*	*15*	🗓	⑆ ⑂ Ⓡ 9S ☞ Ⓟ ⃞ ☞
△ *Villa Serrana* *Los Chafas YH, Hwy 8, 145km, Minas,* *Lavalleja. (key from Mrs Yaya).*		*15*	🗓	Ⓡ ☞

Location/Address	Telephone No. Fax No.	Beds	Opening Dates	Facilities

YOUTH HOSTEL ACCOMMODATION
OUTSIDE THE ASSURED STANDARDS SCHEME

Location/Address	Telephone No. Fax No.	Beds	Opening Dates	Facilities
Durazno Campus Municipal de Durazno, Saravia y Dr Pensa, Durazno. (Montevideo 182km).	✆ (362) 2835	56	🏠	ⓡ

"Sloth makes all things difficult, but industry, all things easy. He that rises late must trot all day, and shall scarce overtake his business at night, while laziness travels so slowly that poverty soon overtakes him."

"La paresse rend tout difficile alors que l'industrie tout facile. Celui qui se lève tard doit courir partout, et aura du mal à dépasser son travail en fin de journée, tandis que la paresse voyage si lentement que la pauvreté aura tôt fait de le dépasser."

„Trägheit macht alle Dinge schwierig, aber Fleiß alle Dinge einfach. Derjenige, der spät aufsteht, muss den ganzen Tag traben und wird selten seine Aufgaben bis zum Abend erledigt haben, wobei Faulheit sich so langsam bewegt, dass Armut ihn bald überholt."

"La indolencia lo hace todo difícil, mientras que la industria, todo fácil. El que se levanta tarde tiene que pasarse todo el día corriendo, y apenas si ha logrado adelantar su trabajo por la noche, en tanto que la pereza viaja tan lentamente que la pobreza tarda poco en adelantarle."

Benjamin Franklin

ADDITIONAL HOSTEL INFORMATION

At the time of printing, no information has been received from the countries listed below for this 2001 Edition. We have, therefore, reprinted the information available from the 2000 edition for reference purposes only.

BAHRAIN

Bahrain Youth Hostels Society,
P.O. Box 2455, H No.1105, R No.4225,
Block 342, Manama, Bahrain.

☎ (973) 727170 ✆ (973) 729919

Location/Address	Telephone No. Fax No.	Beds	Opening Dates	Facilities
▲ **Manama** Al-Juffair YH, Building 1105, Rd 4225, Block 342, PO Box 2455, Manama.	☎ 727170 ✆ 729919	168	🗓	
▲ **Muharraq** Al-Muharraq YH, Building 116, Rd 375, Block 450, PO Box 2455, Muharraq.	☎ 320015 ✆ 729919	56	🗓	

SUDAN

Sudanese Youth Hostels Association,
House No 66, Street No 47, Khartoum East
PO Box 1705, Khartoum, Sudan.

☎ (249) (11) 722087 ✆ (249) (11) 780308

Location/Address	Telephone No. Fax No.	Beds	Opening Dates	Facilities
△ *Kassala* *c/o Ministry of Youth & Sports Kassala,* *Kassala State: near centre of town.*	☎ *2251-2550*	*60*	🗓	Ⓡ ♿ 🅿 🗓
▲ **Khartoum** House No 66, St 47, Khartoum East (Souk Two), PO Box No 1705 Khartoum.	☎ (11) 722087 ✆ (11) 460475	80	🗓	♙ Ⓡ ♿ ☞ 🅿 🗓
▲ **Port Sudan** Salabona, Port Sudan YH, Red Sea State, PO Box No 829, Port Sudan.	☎ 23478-22362	80	🗓	Ⓡ ♿ 🅿 🗓
△ *Wad Medani* *c/o Ministry of Youth & Sports, Wad Medani,* *Gazeira State: town centre 3km.*		*60*	🗓	Ⓡ ♿ 🅿 🗓
YOUTH HOSTEL ACCOMMODATION **OUTSIDE THE ASSURED STANDARDS SCHEME**				
Elobied PO Box 338, Elobied, North Kordofan State.	☎ 2843-2732	40	🗓	
Elrosaris Elnile St, Blue Nile Province: c/o Ministry of Youth & Sports, Youth Office.		60	🗓	Ⓡ ♿ 🅿 🗓

AFFILIATED ORGANIZATIONS

The International Youth Hostel Federation also has Affiliated Organizations in a number of countries. These are not listed in the main body of the Guide, as they do not fulfil the minimum requirements for full membership, and hostel standards may be outside the assured standards scheme. In some instances, approval has been given for the inclusion of details on their hostel network and/or other relevant information.

Those organizations which are in the African, American, Asian and the Pacific regions are as follows:-

ORGANISATIONS AFFILIEES

La Fédération Internationale des Auberges de Jeunesse a également des organisations affiliées dans un certain nombre d'autres pays. Celles-ci ne figurent pas sur la liste des pays dans la partie principale du Guide, car elles ne répondent pas aux exigences minimales régissant l'adhésion de membre à part entière et la conformité de leurs établissements aux Normes Minimales n'est pas garantie. Dans certains cas, la publication de renseignements concernant leurs auberges de jeunesse et/ou d'autres informations utiles a été approuvée.

Les organisations en question en Afrique, Amérique, Asie et dans le Pacifique sont les suivantes:-

ANGESCHLOSSENE ORGANISATIONEN

Der Internationale Jugendherbergsverband steht ebenso in Verbindung mit angeschlossenen Organisationen in verschiedenen anderen Ländern. Diese sind jedoch nicht im Hauptverzeichnis angegeben, weil sie zum einen keine vollberechtigten Mitgliedsverbände sind und zum anderen der Standard dieser Herbergen nicht den zugesicherten Normen entspricht. In einigen Fällen konnten jedoch Angaben über JH solcher Verbände sowie andere wesentliche Angaben ins Verzeichnis aufgenommen werden.

Es handelt sich dabei um folgende Organisationen in Afrika, Amerika, Asien und dem Pazifik:-

ORGANIZACIONES AFILIADAS

La Federación Internacional de Albergues Juveniles (IYHF) también posee Organizaciones Afiliadas en otros países. Estas no han sido incluidas en la parte principal de la Guía, ya que no cumplen con los requisitos mínimos necesarios para ser miembros de pleno derecho y es posible que el nivel de calidad de sus albergues no corresponda al garantizado por nuestras normas. En algunos casos, se ha aprobado la publicación de información sobre su red de albergues y/u otros datos pertinentes.

En Africa, América, Asia y en el Pacífico, estas organizaciones son las siguientes:

ARGENTINA:

Red Argentina de Alojamiento para Jóvenes (RAAJ),
Florida 835 3rd Floor, Of 319, C1005AAQ, Buenos
Aires.
- ☎ (54) (11) 4 511 8712
- ✆ (54) (11) 4 312 0089
- ✉ raaj@hostels.org.ar
- 🖳 www.hostels.org.ar

BANGLADESH:

Bangladesh Youth Hostel Association,
18 Elephant Rd, Dhaka 1205.
- ☎ (880) (2) 8626119, 8625651, 8124479
- ✆ (880) (2) 866915
- ✉ afeef@bdoline.com

COLOMBIA:

Federación Colombiana de Albergues Juveniles,
Carrera 7, N.6-10, PO Box 240167,
Santafé de Bogotá DC.
- ☎ (57) (1) 280 3202/3041/3318
- ✆ (57) (1) 280 3460
- ✉ hostelling@fcaj.org.co, hostels@fcaj.org.co

ECUADOR:

Idiomas Grupo,
Junin 203 y Panama, Piso 2 - Of. 4, Guayaquil.
- ☎ (593) (4) 564488
- ✆ (593) (4) 566939
- ✉ hostelling@idiomas.com.ec

GUATEMALA:

Intercambios Culturales y Academicos,
2 calle 5-28 Zona 1, 01001 Ciudad, Guatemala C.A.
- ☎ (502) 221 0944/221 1044
- ✆ (502) 232 8919
- ✉ intercas@starnet.net.gt

Representaciones OTEC S.A. Guatemala,
Avenida la Reforma 12-01, Zona 10, Edificio Reforma
Montufar local 103-104.
- ☎ (502) 3322184, 3602791
- ✆ (502) 3603808, 3319474
- ✉ turisjoven@guaweb.net

INDONESIA:

Indonesian Youth Hostels Association,
Jl. Jenderal Sudirman, Direktorat Binmud,
Gedung E Lantai 6 Depdikbud, Senayan, Jakarta 10270.
- ☎ (62) (21) 5725 503/504
- ✆ (62) (21) 5725 041

LEBANON

Campus Travel
Ras Beirut, Makhould Street, Maktabi Bld (Khoury
Hospital), PO Box 13-6109, 1102-2100 Beirut.
- ☎ (961) (1) 744588
- ✆ (961) (1) 744583
- ✉ hala-liban@destination.com.ib

MEXICO:

Red Mexicana de Alojamiento para Jóvenes,
Republica de Guatemala #4, Colonia Centro, 06020,
Mexico DF.
- ☎ (52) (5) 668244
- ✆ (52) (5) 5103442
- ✉ hostellingmexico@remaj.com
- 🖳 www.remaj.com, www.hostellingmexico.com

Associacion Mexicana de Albergues Juveniles,
A.C. AMAJ,
Insurgentes Sur 421 109B, Col. Hipodromo Condesa,
CP. 06170, Mexico, D.F.
- ☎ (52) (5) 5640333
- ✆ (52) (5) 5743521
- ✉ info@hostels.com.mx
- 🖳 www.hostels.com.mx

NEPAL

Nepal Youth Hostels Association,
Mahendra Youth Hostel, Jawalakhel, Lalitpur.
- ☎ (977) (1) 521003
- ✆ (977) (1) 220161

NEW CALEDONIA:

*Association des Auberges de Jeunesse de Nouvelle
Calédonie*,
51 Bis Rue Olry, BP 767, Nouméa.
- ☎ (687) 275879
- ✆ (687) 254817

NICARAGUA

Turismo Joven Nicaragua,
Calle 27 de Mayo, Antiguo Cine Cabrera, 3 Cuadras al
Este, Managua.
- **t** (505) 2222619
- **f** (505) 2222143
- **e** turjoven@munditel.com.ni

PANAMA

OTEC Turismo Joven S.A.,
Edificio Romanei, Calle Del Cangrejo, Local l, Panamá.
- **t** (507) 264 8789
- **f** (507) 264 2842
- **e** turjovpa@sinfo.net

SINGAPORE:

Youth Hostels Association (Singapore),
20 Kramat Lane, #04-12 United House,
Singapore 228773
- **t** (65) 7336753
- **f** (65) 7336754

STA Travel Pte Ltd,
33A Cuppage Rd, Cuppage Terrace,
Singapore 229458
- **t** (65) 7377188
- **f** (65) 7372591
- **e** sales@statravel.com.sg
- **w** www.statravel.com.sg

TAIWAN:

Chinese Taipei Youth Hostel Association,
12F-12, 50 Chung Hsiao West Rd, Sec 1, Taipei
- **t** (886) (2) 23317272
- **f** (886) (2) 23317272
- **e** iysosc@ms28.hinet.net
- **w** www.yh.org.tw

Federal Vacation Co Ltd,
7F, 41 Tung-Hsin Rd, Taipei
- **t** (886) (2) 87681600
- **f** (886) (2) 87681515
- **e** service@gofederal.com.tw
- **w** www.gofederal.com.tw

Kang Wen Culture & Education Foundation,
Suite 1208, No 142 Chung Hsiao East Rd,
Sec 4, Taipei
- **t** (886) (2) 27751138
- **f** (886) (2) 87732450
- **e** sta@statravel.org.tw
- **w** www.statravel.org.tw

Kaohsiung International Youth Hostel,
120 Wen wu First St, Kaohsiung.
- **t** (886) (7) 2012477
- **f** (886) (7) 2156322
- **e** kokiyh@ms57.hinet.net

VENEZUELA:

IVI Idiomas Vivos s.r.l.,
Res. La Hacienda, Local 1-4-T Final Av., Ppal de Las
Mercedes, Aptdo. 80160, Caracas 1080.
- **t** (58) (2) 9933930/9936082
- **f** (58) (2) 9929626
- **e** ivi@etheron.net
- **w** www.ividiomas.com

HI - Venezuela,
Av Lecuna, Parque Central, Edificio Tajamar,
Nivel Oficinas 1, Of 107, Caracas.
- **t** (58) (2) 5764493
- **f** (58) (2) 5774915
- **e** hostellingven@cantv.net

ARGENTINA

Red Argentina de Alojamiento para Jóvenes,
Florida 835 Piso 3 Of 319, C1005AAQ, Buenos Aires.
☎ (54) (11) 45118712 🖷 (54) (11) 43120089
✉ raaj@hostels.org.ar 🖳 www.hostels.org.ar

YOUTH HOSTEL ACCOMMODATION
OUTSIDE THE ASSURED STANDARDS SCHEME

Location/Address	Telephone No. Fax No.	Beds	Opening Dates	Facilities
Bariloche - Alaska Hostel Calle Lilinquen 328, km. 7.5, de Avenida Bustillo. ✉ alaska@bariloche.com.ar	☎ (02944) 461564 🖷 (02944) 461564	62	🖾	♦♦♦ 🍴 ℝ 7W 🛏 🄿 🗑 ❄
Buenos Aires - Hostel Internacional Buenos Aires Moreno 1273, Ciudad de Buenos Aires. ✉ bahostel@hostels.org.ar	☎ (011) 43819760 🖷 (011) 43819760	100	Future Opening information at National Association	♦♦♦ 🍴 ℝ ♿ CC 🛏 🗑 ☕ ❄
Calafate - Del Glaciar Hostel Los Pioneros 251, Provincia de Santa Cruz. ✉ alberguedelglaciar@cotecal.com.ar	☎ (02902) 491243 🖷 (02902) 491243	150	01.09–15.04	♦♦♦ 🍴 ℝ CC 🛏 🄿 🗑 ☕ ❄
El Bolson - El Pueblito Hostel Barrio Lujan A 1km Ruta Nac No 258, Provincia de Rio Negro. ✉ elbolson@hostels.org.ar	☎ (02944) 493560 🖷 (02944) 493560	40	🖾	🍴 4N 🛏 🄿 ❄
El Chalten - Patagonia Hostel Av. San Martin 493, Provincia de Santa Cruz. ✉ alpatagonia@infovia.com.ar	☎ (02962) 493019 🖷 (02962) 493019	32	🖾	♦♦♦ 🍴 ℝ 🛏 🗑
El Chalten - Rancho Grande Hostel Av. San Martin, s/n, Provincia de Santa Cruz. ✉ rancho@cotecal.com.ar	☎ (02962) 493005 🖷 (02962) 493005	44	🖾	♦♦♦ 🍴 ℝ 🛏 🄿 🗑 ☕
Esquel - Lago Verde Hostel Volta 1081, Provincia de Chubut. ✉ patagverde@teletel.com.ar	☎ (02945) 454396 🖷 (02945) 452251	15	🖾	♦♦♦ 🍴 05N 🄿 🗑
Las Cuevas - Las Cuevas Hostel Ruta Internacional No 7, Provincia de Mendoza. ✉ info@campo-base.com.ar	☎ (0261) 4290707 🖷 (0261) 4290707	40	🖾	♦♦♦ ℝ ♿ 🛏 🄿 🗑
Mendoza - Hostel Internacional Campo Base Mitre 946, Provincia de Mendoza. ✉ info@campo-base.com.ar	☎ (0261) 4290707 🖷 (0261) 4290707	37	🖾	🍴 ℝ ♿ 🛏 🗑
Mendoza - Hotel Internacional Mendoza. España 343, Provincia de Mendoza. ✉ info@hostelmendoza.net	☎ (0261) 4240018 🖷 (0261) 4240018	76	🖾	♦♦♦ 🍴 ℝ ♿ 🛏 🄿 🗑 ☕
Puerto Iguazu - La Cabaña Hostel Av. Tres Fronteras 434, Provincia de Misiones. ✉ iguazu@hostels.org.ar	☎ (03757) 420564 🖷 (03757) 420564	36	🖾	♦♦♦ 🍴 ℝ ♿ 🛏 🄿 🗑 ☕

Location/Address	Telephone No. Fax No.	Beds	Opening Dates	Facilities
Puerto Madryn - Hostel Internacional Puerto Madryn 25 de Mayo 1136, Provincia de Chubut. ✉ hi-pm@satlink.com.ar	☎ (02965) 474426 📠 (02965) 474426	25	01.09–31.03	♂♀ 🍴 ☞ 🅿 🔒 ✿
Salta - Backpacker's Hostel Buenos Aires 930, Provincia de Salta. ✉ hostelsalta@impsat1.com.ar	☎ (0387) 4235910 📠 (0387) 4235910	40		♂♀ 🍴 Ⓡ ☞ 🔒
San Martin De Los Andes - Puma Hostel A. Fosbery 535, Provincia de Neuquen. ✉ puma@smandes.com.ar	☎ (02972) 422443 📠 (02972) 428544, (02972) 428545	30		♂♀ Ⓡ 04 SE ♿ ☞ 🅿 🔒
San Rafael - Puesta del Sol Hostel Dean Funes 998, Provincia de Mendoza. ✉ puestadelsol@infovia.com.ar	☎ (02627) 434881 📠 (02627) 434881	200		♂♀ 🍴 Ⓡ ♿ 🅿 🔒 ✿
Tilcara - Malka Hostel Calle San Martin s/n Barrio Malka, Provincia de Jujuy. ✉ tilcara@hostels.org.ar	☎ (0388) 4955197 📠 (0388) 4955197	30		♂♀ 🍴 Ⓡ ☞ 🅿 🔒 🛏 ✿
Trevelin - Casaverde Hostel Los Alerces S/N, Provincia de Rio Negro. ✉ trevelin@hostels.org.ar	☎ (02945) 480091 📠 (02945) 480091	22		♂♀ Ⓡ 04 E ☞ 🅿 🔒 ✿
Ushuaia - Torre al Sur Hostel Gobernador paz 1437, Provincia de Tierra del Fuego. ✉ torrealsur@impsat1.com.ar	☎ (02901) 430745, (02901) 437291	50		♂♀ 🍴 Ⓡ ☞ 🅿 🔒 ✿
Villa Gral Belgrano - El Rincon Hostel Calle Fleming s/n, Valle de Calamuchita, Provincia de Cordoba. ✉ rincon@calamuchitanet.com.ar	☎ (03546) 461323 📠 (03546) 461761	56		♂♀ 🍴 Ⓡ ☞ 🅿 🔒 ✿
Villa Paranacito - Top Malo Hostel Ruta Prov No46 km 18200, Provincia de Entre Rios. ✉ topmalo@infovia.com.ar	☎ (03446) 495255 📠 (03446) 495255	32		♂♀ 🍴 Ⓡ 2 W ☞ 🅿 🔒 ✿

"A wise traveller never despises his own country."

"Le voyageur sage ne méprise jamais son propre pays."

„Ein weiser Reisender verachtet nie das eigene Land."

"El viajero sabio nunca desprecia su propio país."

Carlo Goldoni

COLOMBIA

Federación Colombiana de Albergues Juveniles,
Carrera 7 No.6-10, PO Box 240167,
Santafé de Bogotá DC.
☎ (57) (1) 280 3202/3041/3318 ❼ (57) (1) 280 3460
📧 hostelling@fcaj.org.co, hostels@fcaj.org.co

YOUTH HOSTEL ACCOMMODATION
OUTSIDE THE ASSURED STANDARDS SCHEME

Location/Address	Telephone No. Fax No.	Beds	Opening Dates	Facilities
Bogotá D.C. - Hostelling International deBogotá Carrera 7 No.6-10, Bogotá D.C. 📧 hostelling@fcaj.org.co, hostells@fcaj.org.co	☎ (91) 2803318, (91) 2803202, (91) 2803041 ❼ (91) 2803460	105		⁞⁞⁞ ⦿ R 2S P ⏚ ☕
Cartagena - H.Costa del sol Avenida la. calle 9, Esquina- Bocagrande- Cartagena.	☎ (95) 6650844, (95) 6653776 ❼ (95) 6653755	280		⁞⁞⁞ ⦿ R 1N ŀCCŀ P ⏚ ☕
Cartagena - Hostal Santodomingo Calle Santodomingo No. 33-46, Cartagena.	☎ (95) 6642268 ❼ (95) 6642268	23		⁞⁞⁞ ⦿ R 1SW P ⏚ ☕
Medellin - Hotel Casa Dorada Calle 50, No 47-25, Medellín, Antioquia.	☎ (94) 5125300 ❼ (94) 5719032	155		⁞⁞⁞ ⦿ R 1NE ŀCCŀ P ⏚
Pasto - Hotel Concorde Calle 19, No. 29A-09, Pasto, Nariño.	☎ (927) 310658 ❼ (927) 233232, (927) 222357	33		⁞⁞⁞ R 0.5N P ⏚
Paipa - H.Cabañas El Portón Avenida Piscinas termales, Paipa, Boyacá.	☎ (0987) 850168, (0987) 850864 ❼ (0987) 851391	95		⁞⁞⁞ ⦿ R 1SE ŀCCŀ P ⏚ ☕
San Agustin - H. El Jardín Carrera 11 No. 4-10, San Agustín-Huila.	☎ (988) 373455, (988) 379581	36		⁞⁞⁞ ⦿ R 0.2N P ⏚ ☕
Santa Marta Hostel Tima-Uraka, Calle 18 No.2-59 El Rodadero.	☎ (954) 228433 ❼ (954) 228433	25		⁞⁞⁞ ⦿ 1SW P ⏚
Santa Marta - H. Medellín Calle 22 No. 2A-62, Santa Marta.	☎ (954) 212380 ❼ (954) 212654	37		⁞⁞⁞ ⦿ R 0.5N ŀCCŀ P ⏚ ☕
Santa Marta - H. Medellín Calle 19 No.1c-30, El Rodadero.	☎ (954) 220220, (954) 220202 ❼ (954) 228250	110		⁞⁞⁞ ⦿ R 13S ŀCCŀ ⏚ ☕
Villa de Leyva - Hostel Los Aceitunos Transversal 10 # 9-41 (Salida al Fósil), Villa de leyva, Boyacá.	☎ (987) 320282, (987) 320822 ❼ (91) 2859854	150		⁞⁞⁞ ⦿ R 1NE ŀCCŀ P ⏚ ☕
Villavicencio Los Girasoles - Granja Turistica Vacacional A continuación, Barrios la Campiña y Chapinerito, Villavicencio, Meta.	☎ (986) 642712, (986) 645322	160		⁞⁞⁞ ⦿ R 2N P ⏚

MEXICO

Red Mexicana de Alojamiento para Jóvenes,
Republica de Guatemala #4, Colonia Centro, 06020, Mexico DF.
☎ (52) (5) 668244 ✆ (52) (5) 5103442
✉ hostellingmexico@remaj.com 🖳 www.remaj.com, www.hostellingmexico.com

YOUTH HOSTEL ACCOMMODATION
OUTSIDE THE ASSURED STANDARDS SCHEME

Location/Address	Telephone No. Fax No.	Beds	Opening Dates	Facilities
Cuernavaca Villa Calmecac, Zacatecas #114 Col. Buenavista, Cuernavaca Morelos C.P. 62130. ✉ hostellingmexico@remaj.com	☎ (5) 5181772 ✆ (5) 5103442	32	🔒	♨ 🍴 R 3N CC P 🗄
Mexico DF - Catedral Guatemala #4, Centro, Mexico DF. ✉ hostellingmexico@remaj.com	☎ (5) 5181772 ✆ (5) 5103442	209	🔒	♨ 🍴 R ♿ CC 🍴 🗄 ☕
Mexico DF - Home Tabasco #303, Colonia Roma, Mexico DF. ✉ hostellingmexico@remaj.com	☎ (5) 5181772 ✆ (5) 5103442	20	🔒	R 3NE CC P
Morelos - Fuerte Bambú Kilometro #6, Carretera, Foo De Morelos. ✉ hostellingmexico@remaj.com	☎ (5) 5181772 ✆ (5) 5103442	191	🔒	♨ 🍴 R 37S ♿ CC P ☕
Xalapa - Ecologica del Cofre 'ValleAlegre' Insurgentes #138 1er. Piso. Xalapa Veracruz. ✉ hostellingmexico@remaj.com	☎ (5) 5181772 ✆ (5) 5103442	40	🔒	♨ 🍴 🍴 P

MEXICO

Associacion Mexicana de Albergues Juveniles, A.C. AMAJ
Insurgentes sur 421-109B, Col. Hipodromo Condesa,
C.P. 06170 Mexico, D.F.
☎ (52) (5) 5640333 ✆ (52) (5) 5743521
✉ info@hostels.com.mx 🖳 www.hostels.com.mx

Location/Address	Telephone No. Fax No.	Beds	Opening Dates	Facilities
▲ **Guanajuato** - Parador del Convento Calzada Guadalupe 17, Guanajuato. ✉ info@hostels.com.mx	☎ (473) 22524		🔒	♨ 🍴 CC 🍴 P 🗄
▲ **Merida** - Nomadas Calle 62 Numero 433 x 51, Centro Historico, Merida, Yucatan. ✉ info@hostels.com.mx	☎ (99) 245223 ✆ (99) 245223	25	🔒	♨ 🍴 CC 🍴 🗄 ☼
▲ **Mexico City** - Moneda Moneda 8 Centro Historico, Mexico, D.F. ✉ info@hostels.com.mx	☎ (5) 5225821 ✆ (5) 5225803	97	🔒	♨ 🍴 R 0.1E CC 🍴 🗄 ☕ ☼

Location/Address	Telephone No. Fax No.	Beds	Opening Dates	Facilities

YOUTH HOSTEL ACCOMMODATION
OUTSIDE THE ASSURED STANDARDS SCHEME

Location/Address	Telephone No. Fax No.	Beds	Opening Dates	Facilities
Can Cun - Mexico Hostel Palmera 30, Centro, Can Cun. info@hostels.com.mx		60		⦿ R 02N CC
Contepec - Instituto JFK Adolfo Lopez Mateos 4, Contepec, Michoacan. info@hostels.com.mx	(5) 3894764	40		⦿ 2N P
Frontera Corozal - Escudo Jaguar Frontera Corozal, Zona La Candona, Chiapas. info@hostels.com.mx	(5) 1479300 Ext 52016441 (5) 1479300 Ext 52016440	20		⦿ 0.5N P
Guanajuato - Guanajuato Carretera Dolores Hidalgo km. 2.5. info@hostels.com.mx	(473) 20689 (473) 20633			⦿ CC
Oaxaca - Guadalupe Av. Juarez 409, Centro Historico, Oaxaca. info@hostels.com.mx	(9) 5166365	30		⦿ 0.5N
Ocuitulco - La Joya Carretera a Jumiltepec Sin Numero, Ocuitulco, Morelos. info@hostels.com.mx	(5) 5443193	25		⦿ 1E P
Palenque - Maya Bell Carretera Palenque Las Ruinas km. 5. info@hostels.com.mx	934842	40		⦿ 5NW P
Playa del Carmen - Posada Marina Quinta Avenida Calle 24, Playa del Carmen. info@hostels.com.mx		45		⦿ 0.5N P
Puerto Escondido - Mayflower Andador Libertad Sin Mumero, Puerto Escondido Oaxaca. info@hostels.com.mx	(958) 21755 (958) 20422	20		⦿
San Miguel de Allende - Hostal Alcatraz Relox 54. info@hostels.com.mx	(4) 1528543 (4) 1528543	35		⦿
San Miguel de Allende - Hostal Internacional, Jaime Nuño 28. info@hostels.com.mx	(4) 1523175 (4) 1523175	35		
Tulum - Cabañas Copal Carretera Tulum Las Ruinas Km. 5. info@hostels.com.mx	(987) 12000 (987) 12001	40		⦿ P
Tulum - Copal Hostel Carretera Playa Del Carmen Y, Avenida Ruinas. info@hostels.com.mx	(987) 12000 (987) 12001	30		⦿ 0.3N P
Valladolid - La Candelaria Parque La Candelaria, Calle 35 Con 44. info@hostels.com.mx	(985) 62267	40		⦿ P

NEW CALEDONIA

Fédération Unie des Auberges de Jeunesse (France),
Association des Auberges de Jeunesse de Nouvelle Calédonie,
51 Bis Rue Olry, BP 767, Nouméa, Nouvelle Calédonie
t (687) 275879 f (687) 254817

Expect to pay in the region of 1200-3000 CFP per night. Sheet sleeping bags are available, free of charge.

YOUTH HOSTEL ACCOMMODATION OUTSIDE THE ASSURED STANDARDS SCHEME

Location/Address	Telephone No. Fax No.	Beds	Opening Dates	Facilities
Nouméa City Hostel 51 bis rue Olry, BP 767, 98845 Nouméa Cedex, New Caledonia, South Pacific.	t (687) 275879 f (687) 254817	94	12	R 0.3NE CC P

TAIWAN

Chinese Taipei Youth Hostel Association,
12F-12, 50 Chung Hsiao West Rd, Sec 1, Taipei
t (2) 23317272 f (2) 23317272
e iysosc@ms28.hinet.net www.yh.org.tw

Expect to pay in the region of US$15.00-US$20.00 per night. Travelling information office. It is essential to book in advance during peak periods.

N.B. For Chinese address in detail, please contact head office in Taipei.

YOUTH HOSTEL ACCOMMODATION OUTSIDE THE ASSURED STANDARDS SCHEME

Location/Address	Telephone No. Fax No.	Beds	Opening Dates	Facilities
Datong - Shangrila Noble Hanging Garden & Country Club 8 Rongguang Lane, Datong Village, Ren'ai Xiang, Nantou County. e wgloria@ms9.hinet.net	t (4) 29802166 f (4) 29802169	110	12	R P
Hualian - Hualian YH 95-7 Zhongmei Rd, Hualian.	t (38) 223307 f (38) 223820	44	12	R P
Kaohsiung Modern Plaza Hotel, 332 Chiuju 2nd Rd, Kaohsiung City.	t (7) 3122151 f (7) 3218282	40	12	R 0.2S CC P
Kenting Wu Fong YH, 12 Foukuang Lane, Kenting Li, Hengchun, Pintong County.	t (8) 8861061, (8) 8861661 f (8) 8861661	26	12	CC P

Location/Address	Telephone No. Fax No.	Beds	Opening Dates	Facilities
Lugu - Chingku Village Restaurant 127, Sec 3, Zhongzheng Rd, Lugu Xiang, Nantou County.	☎ (4) 29750178 ✆ (4) 29750141	26	🏠	♀♂ 🍴 Ⓡ 0.5N ♿ 🛏 🅿 📷 🍺 ⚕
Tainan Guang Haw Hotel, No. 155 Beimen Rd, Section 1, Tainan.	☎ (6) 2263171 ✆ (6) 2263175	63	🏠	♀♂ 🍴 🅿 📷
Taipei Asiaworld YH, 12F-14 No 50 Chunghsiao W Rd, Sec 1 Taipei. @ iysosc@ms35.hinet.net	☎ (2) 23756625, (2) 23318366 ✆ (2) 23316427	25	🏠	🍴 Ⓡ

TAIWAN

Kaohsiung International Youth Hostel,
120 Wen wu First Street, Kaohsiung City.
☎ (886) (7) 2012477 ✆ (886) (7) 2156322

YOUTH HOSTEL ACCOMMODATION
OUTSIDE THE ASSURED STANDARDS SCHEME

Location/Address	Telephone No. Fax No.	Beds	Opening Dates	Facilities
Kaohsiung - International Wen Wu YH #120 Wen wu First St, Kaohsiung.	☎ (7) 2012477 ✆ (7) 2156322	28	🏠	♀♂ Ⓡ 🛏 🅿 📷
Kaohsiung - Kaohsiung International Youth Hostel #7, Wu Chian St, Kaohsiung, Taiwan ROC.	☎ (7) 2159177 ✆ (7) 2156322	12	🏠	♀♂ Ⓡ 🛏 🅿 📷 ⚕

"A person travels the world over in search of what he needs and returns home to find it."

"L'on parcourt le monde à la recherche de ce dont on a besoin et l'on revient chez soi pour le trouver."

„Der Mensch bereist die ganze Welt auf der Suche nach dem, was er braucht und kehrt heim, um es dort zu finden."

"Recorremos el mundo en busca de lo que necesitamos para al final encontrarlo en casa a nustro regreso"

George Moore

WHAT IS FIYTO ?

FIYTO

Ever since its inception in 1951, the aim of FIYTO (Federation of International Youth Travel Organisations) has been to promote educational, cultural and social travel among young people.

In its fifty year history, FIYTO has become the largest and most influential organisation in the youth travel industry. Towards the mainstream travel and tourism community, international, governmental and non-governmental organisations, FIYTO advocates the special identity of young travellers and their right to affordable travel and travel-related services.

FIYTO is today the premier trade association for youth travel and tourism, a rapidly growing segment of the travel industry. Today we represent the unique interests of an estimated 20% of the tourism population. Our nearly 400 Members account for a turn-over of more than 8 billion US Dollars, serve some 16 million young travellers annually and sell over 9 million air- and surface tickets. FIYTO Members can be found in over 70 countries on all continents.

FIYTO is an open, world-wide, non-political and non-sectarian organisation. Non-profit and for-profit companies, public and private, retailers, wholesalers, buyers, sellers and suppliers are all represented in the FIYTO membership.

FIYTO is an affiliate member of the World Tourism Organisation (WTO) and a member of the Pacific Asia Travel Association (PATA). FIYTO enjoys operational relations with UNESCO, the United Nations Educational, Scientific and Cultural Organisation.

For qualified companies, actively engaged in incoming or outgoing youth travel, FIYTO provides the pre-eminent professional forum to trade, exchange information and advance the interests of the young traveller.

For more information on FIYTO please contact:

FIYTO, Bredgade 25H
1260 Copenhagen K, Denmark
E-mail: mailbox@fiyto.org
www.fiyto.org

International Student Travel Confederation (ISTC)

ISTC

THE WORLD OF
STUDENT TRAVEL
SINCE 1949

In 1949 a group of emerging student travel organisations formed the International Student Travel Confederation (ISTC). They shared a common goal - "to increase international understanding through travel and exchange opportunities for students, young people and the academic community".

Today, ISTC members continue to lead in the development of specialised products and services for the student travel community. Students recognise these organisations as "the source" for reliable products and sound advice. Through a network of 17,000 locations in more than 90 countries, ISTC members provide a truly global network for student and youth travellers.

To better develop products and services for today's student and youth travellers, and negotiate benefits on their behalf, the ISTC is a confederation of five associations active in specialised areas of student and youth travel services - surface travel, international identity cards, student flights, insurance and work exchange programs. The Associations include:

IAEWEP International Association for Educational and Work Exchange Programmes
IASIS International Association for Student Insurance Services
ISIC International Student Identity Card Association
ISSA International Student Surface Travel Association
SATA Student Air Travel Association

As the world-wide administrator of the International Student Identity Card (ISIC), the ISTC oversees the distribution and promotion of over 4 million cards annually. UNESCO endorses the ISIC and recognises it as the unique document for student mobility.

The ISTC maintains relationships with UNESCO, the IYHF, the World Tourism Organisation and other international organisations.

For more information contact:

ISTC
PO Box 15857
1001 NJ Amsterdam
The Netherlands
E-mail: istcinfo@istc.org
www.istc.org

... help us to implement our assurance of standards at hostels by writing to us or by using the reply slip in this Guide to tell us what you think of our hostels.

Just tick the boxes to indicate how well the hostel did in the five areas, and remember to let us have your comments on how you found your stay.

Simply put your reply in an envelope and post to us at the address shown on the slip.

NOUS AIMERIONS CONNAITRE VOTRE OPINION...

... aidez-nous à mettre en place les normes garanties dans nos auberges en nous faisant part de ce que vous pensez d'elles, soit en nous écrivant, soit en remplissant la fiche prévue à cet effet que vous trouverez dans ce guide.

Il vous suffira de cocher les cases pour évaluer la performance de l'auberge dans les cinq domaines indiqués, sans oublier d'ajouter vos observations sur votre séjour.

Envoyez-nous votre fiche sous enveloppe, à l'adresse indiquée dessus.

WIR MÖCHTEN IHRE MEINUNG HÖREN...

... helfen Sie uns, unsere zugesicherten Standards zu gewährleisten, indem Sie uns wissen lassen, was Sie von unseren Herbergen halten. Bitte schreiben Sie uns oder benutzen Sie dazu die am Ende dieses Führers beigefügte Antwortkarte.

Kreuzen Sie bitte Ihre Beurteilung für die jeweilige Kategorie in dem entsprechenden Kästchen an, und vergessen Sie nicht, uns Ihren Kommentar über Ihren Aufenthalt mitzuteilen.

Ihre Antwort ganz einfach in einen Umschlag stecken und an die auf der Antwortkarte angegebene Adresse schicken.

QUEREMOS SABER LO QUE USTED OPINA...

... ayúdenos a implementar nuestras normas garantizadas en los albergues. Escríbanos, o haga uso de las hojas provistas en la Guía, para comunicarnos lo que piensa de nuestros albergues.

Sólo tiene que marcar las casillas según la opinión que le merezca el albergue en lo que respecta a los cinco apartados de consulta. No olvide añadir comentarios sobre su estancia en el recuadro de las observaciones.

Envíe su comunicación en un sobre dirigido a la dirección indicada.

We want to hear from YOU ....

TELL US WHAT YOU THINK!

DITES-NOUS CE QUE VOUS EN PENSEZ!
SAGEN SIE UNS IHRE MEINUNG!
¡DIGANOS LO QUE OPINA!

Hostel Name-Address/
Nom de l'Auberge-Adresse/
Name der Jugendherberge
Anschrift/
Nombre y Dirección del Albergue

City/Ville/Stadt/Ciudad

Country/*Pays*/Land/*País*

Date(s) stayed/*Dates du séjour/*
Daten des Aufenthaltes/
Fechas de la Estancia

Please return to:
INTERNATIONAL YOUTH HOSTEL FEDERATION,
1st Floor, Fountain House, Parkway, Welwyn Garden City,
Hertfordshire AL8 6JH. ENGLAND

Welcome/*Accueil/*
Aufnahme/*Recibimiento*

Comfort/*Confort/*
Komfort/*Comodidad*

Cleanliness/*Propreté/*
Sauberkeit/*Limpieza*

Security/*Sécurité/*
Sicherheit/*Seguridad*

Privacy/*Intimité*,
Privatsphäre/*Intimidad*

COMMENTS/*COMMENTAIRES*/BEMERKUNGEN/*OBSERVACIONES*

Name/*Nom/*
Name/*Nombre*

Address/*Adresse/*
Anschrift/*Dirección*

... help us to implement our assurance of standards at hostels by writing to us or by using the reply slip in this Guide to tell us what you think of our hostels.

Just tick the boxes to indicate how well the hostel did in the five areas, and remember to let us have your comments on how you found your stay.

Simply put your reply in an envelope and post to us at the address shown on the slip.

NOUS AIMERIONS CONNAITRE VOTRE OPINION...

... aidez-nous à mettre en place les normes garanties dans nos auberges en nous faisant part de ce que vous pensez d'elles, soit en nous écrivant, soit en remplissant la fiche prévue à cet effet que vous trouverez dans ce guide.

Il vous suffira de cocher les cases pour évaluer la performance de l'auberge dans les cinq domaines indiqués, sans oublier d'ajouter vos observations sur votre séjour.

Envoyez-nous votre fiche sous enveloppe, à l'adresse indiquée dessus.

WIR MÖCHTEN IHRE MEINUNG HÖREN...

... helfen Sie uns, unsere zugesicherten Standards zu gewährleisten, indem Sie uns wissen lassen, was Sie von unseren Herbergen halten. Bitte schreiben Sie uns oder benutzen Sie dazu die am Ende dieses Führers beigefügte Antwortkarte.

Kreuzen Sie bitte Ihre Beurteilung für die jeweilige Kategorie in dem entsprechenden Kästchen an, und vergessen Sie nicht, uns Ihren Kommentar über Ihren Aufenthalt mitzuteilen.

Ihre Antwort ganz einfach in einen Umschlag stecken und an die auf der Antwortkarte angegebene Adresse schicken.

QUEREMOS SABER LO QUE USTED OPINA...

... ayúdenos a implementar nuestras normas garantizadas en los albergues. Escríbanos, o haga uso de las hojas provistas en la Guía, para comunicarnos lo que piensa de nuestros albergues.

Sólo tiene que marcar las casillas según la opinión que le merezca el albergue en lo que respecta a los cinco apartados de consulta. No olvide añadir comentarios sobre su estancia en el recuadro de las observaciones.

Envíe su comunicación en un sobre dirigido a la dirección indicada.

We want to hear from YOU....

TELL US WHAT YOU THINK!

DITES-NOUS CE QUE VOUS EN PENSEZ!
SAGEN SIE UNS IHRE MEINUNG!
¡DIGANOS LO QUE OPINA!

Hostel Name-Address/
Nom de l'Auberge-Adresse/
Name der Jugendherberge
Anschrift/
Nombre y Dirección del Albergue

City/Ville/Stadt/Ciudad

Country/*Pays*/Land/*País*

Date(s) stayed/*Dates du séjour/*
Daten des Aufenthaltes/
Fechas de la Estancia

Please return to:
INTERNATIONAL YOUTH HOSTEL FEDERATION,
1st Floor, Fountain House, Parkway, Welwyn Garden City,
Hertfordshire AL8 6JH. ENGLAND

Welcome/*Accueil/*
Aufnahme/*Recibimiento*

Comfort/*Confort/*
Komfort/*Comodidad*

Cleanliness/*Propreté/*
Sauberkeit/*Limpieza*

Security/*Sécurité/*
Sicherheit/*Seguridad*

Privacy/*Intimité,*
Privatsphäre/*Intimidad*

COMMENTS/*COMMENTAIRES*/BEMERKUNGEN/*OBSERVACIONES*

Name/*Nom/*
Name/*Nombre*

Address/*Adresse/*
Anschrift/*Dirección*

DISCOUNTS & CONCESSIONS

Hostelling International Membership enables you to claim discounts and concessions on everything from travel and museums, to eating and entertainment! The top discounts are included here – for the full story check out the Global Discounts Database at **www.iyhf.org.** Simply present your Hostelling International Membership Card to claim a discount – and begin recovering the cost of Membership!

Discounts are sorted by **Country**. Within each country, discounts are listed alphabetically by **City** – national discounts are listed first. Within each city, discounts are listed by **Discount Category** – Entertainment 𝍫, General ⊖, Museums and Culture 🏛 , Retail 🏢, or Travel ✚. For each discount, we list: discount provider's name, address and telephone number, along with a brief description of the discount available.

Please note: The information about discounts has been supplied by the Youth Hostel Association of each country represented. Every effort has been made to ensure that this information is correct, and Hostelling International can accept no responsibility for any inaccuracies or for changes subsequent to publication.

REMISES ET RÉDUCTIONS

Votre adhésion à Hostelling International vous permet de profiter de nombreuses remises et réductions sur presque tout, des transports aux entrées de musées en passant par la restauration et les spectacles! Seuls les avantages les plus importants sont cités ci-après – pour la liste complète, faites donc un tour sur notre site Internet, **www.iyhf.org**, où vous trouverez notre base de données mondiale des remises. Présentez votre carte d'adhérent Hostelling International pour bénéficier d'une réduction et commencez à amortir le coût de votre adhésion!

Les différents avantages que l'on vous propose sont d'abord répertoriés par **Pays** puis en ordre alphabétique par **Ville** – les offres qui sont valables à l'échelle nationale sont en tête de liste. Elles sont ensuite classées par **Catégorie** – Voyages ✚ *(Travel)*, Magasins et Restaurants 🏢 *(Retail)*, Spectacles et Activités 𝍫 *(Entertainment)*, Musées et Culture 🏛 *(Museums and Culture)* ou Général ⊖. Pour chaque remise, nous fournissons le nom de l'entité qui la propose, son adresse et numéro de téléphone, ainsi qu'un bref descriptif de l'offre en question.

Remarque: Les renseignements sur ces remises nous sont communiqués par l'Association d'Auberges de Jeunesse de chaque pays représenté. Tout a été mis en oeuvre pour s'assurer que ces données sont correctes mais Hostelling International ne peut accepter aucune responsabilité pour toute inexactitude ou tout changement intervenant ultérieurement à la publication du présent ouvrage.

RABATTE & ERMÄßIGUNGEN

Die Mitgliedschaft bei Hostelling International sichert Ihnen Anspruch auf Rabatte und Ermäßigungen bei Reisen und Museen, in der Gastronomie und Unterhaltung! Die Top-Preisnachlässe sind hier enthalten – für einen kompletten Überblick schauen Sie in die Datenbank für internationale Rabatte *(Global Discounts Database)* unter **www.iyhf.org**. Legen Sie einfach Ihre Hostelling International Mitgliedskarte vor, um einen Nachlaß in Anspruch zu nehmen – und fangen Sie an, den Mitgliedsbeitrag wieder einzuholen!

Die Rabatte sind nach **Ländern** *(Country)* und innerhalb jedes Landes nach **Städten** *(City)* in alphabetischer Reihenfolge geordnet. Die nationalen Preisnachlässe *(National)* sind zuerst aufgeführt. Sie sind für jede Stadt nach **Rabattkategorien** *(Discount Category)* – Unterhaltung ☰ *(Entertainment)*, Allgemeines ☻ *(General)*, Museen und Kultur ☰ *(Museum and Culture)*, Einzelhandel ☰ *(Retail)* sowie Reisen ✦ *(Travel)* – systematisiert. Für jeden Nachlaß ist, neben dem Namen des Anbieters, dessen Adresse und Telefonnummer, eine kurze Beschreibung des verfügbaren Rabattes *(Discount Discription)* aufgeführt.

Bitte beachten Sie: Die Informationen über die Rabatte wurden von den Jugendherbergsverbänden jedes aufgeführten Landes zur Verfügung gestellt. Wir haben alles unternommen, um sicherzugehen, daß diese Informationen korrekt sind. Hostelling International kann keine Verantwortung für jegliche Ungenauigkeiten oder Änderungen im Anschluß an die Veröffentlichung übernehmen.

OFERTAS Y DESCUENTOS

Su afiliación a Hostelling International le permite disfrutar de ofertas y descuentos de todo tipo: en los transportes y entradas de museo, restaurantes y espectáculos – ¡la lista es interminable! A continuación se relacionan los descuentos más importantes solamente. Si desea verlos todos, consulte nuestra Base de Datos Mundial de Descuentos *(Global Discounts Database)* en Internet en **www.iyhf.org**. Para conseguir un descuento, no tiene más que presentar su tarjeta de socio de Hostelling International – y así ir amortizando el coste de la misma.

Los descuentos están clasificados en primer lugar por **país** y en segundo lugar por **ciudad o población**, ambos en orden alfabético. Los que son válidos a nivel nacional aparecen primero y todos están ordenados por **categoría**, a saber: Viajes ✦*(Travel)*, Tiendas y Restaurantes ☰ *(Retail)*, Actividades Recreativas ☰ *(Entertainment)*, Museos y Cultura ☰ *(Museums and Culture)*, y General ☻. Para cada uno de ellos, se indica el nombre de la organización o compañía que concede el descuento, su dirección y número de teléfono, y una breve descripción del mismo.

Importante: La información sobre estos descuentos nos ha sido suministrada por la Asociación de Albergues Juveniles de cada país representado. Hemos hecho todo lo posible por asegurarnos de que los datos son correctos y Hostelling International no se responsabiliza de ninguna inexactitud ni de ningún cambio que se produzca en fecha posterior a la publicación de la presente guía.

Explanation of Symbols

☻ General	☻ Général	☻ Allgemeines	☻ General
☰ Entertainment	☰ Spectacles et Activités	☰ Unterhaltung	☰ Actividades Recreativas
☰ Retail	☰ Magasins et Restaurants	☰ Einzelhandel	☰ Tiendas y Restaurantes
☰ Museums and Culture	☰ Musées et Culture	☰ Museen und Kultur	☰ Museos y Cultura
✦ Travel	✦ Voyages	✦ Reisen	✦ Viajes

GLOBAL

GLOBAL

✝ **Budget Rent a Car**
🖰 www.budget.com

15% OFF STANDARD CAR RENTAL RATES - A SPECIAL OFFER FOR HOSTELLING INTERNATIONAL MEMBERS. Budget Rent a Car - The world's third largest car and truck rental company, offers Hostelling International Members 15% off standard rental rates. To claim your discount simply quote BCD G514400 when making a reservation. See www.iyhf.org for a full list of countries. Conditions apply

Ⓖ **Travelex**
🖰 www.travelexgrp.com

COMMISSION FREE CURRENCY EXCHANGE - A SPECIAL OFFER FOR HOSTELLING INTERNATIONAL MEMBERS. TRAVELEX - the world's largest airport and passenger terminal bureau de change - has offered Hostelling International members a very special service to reduce the cost of international travel. By showing your membership card and quoting "Hostelling International" or "IYHF" you can enjoy Commission Free Currency exchange at any of the 300 Travelex offices world-wide. The list of their offices can be found on the Travelex website at www.travelexgrp.com. Conditions apply

✝ **Greyhound International**
🖰 www.greyhound-uk.co.uk

10% discount on the purchase of any Ameripass or Canada Coach Pass purchased before you travel to North America. To see the list of agents in your area please visit www.greyhound-uk.co.uk. Please note that this offer only applies to pass products. It does not apply to single/return journey tickets (point to point)

✝ **Greyhound Pioneer Australia**
❶ 13 20 30 (Australia)

15% discount on passes when purchased outside Australia. 10% discount on passes and point to point tickets purchased in Australia

Ⓖ **Lonely Planet Guide Books**
🖰 www.lonelyplanet.com

Lonely Planet, the world's leading publisher of independent travel information, offer various discounts to Hostelling International members around the world. Please check the global discount database at www.iyhf.org for further details.

EUROPEAN

EUROPE

✝ **Hertz**
❶ **Call one of the following Reservation Hotlines or contact your local reservation office:** Belgium: 02 717 3200, France: 0803 861 861, Germany: 01 805 000 768, Italy: 199 11 77 11, The Netherlands: 020 504 0584, Spain: 902 303 230, UK: 0870 844 4 844. **General reservations: Switzerland: 0848 822020, Austria: 0800 20 1111.**
🖰 www.hertz.com

Hertz are offering Hostelling International members a discount of between 10-25% (sometimes more) on standard car rental rates depending on the make and model of the car and length of time. The discount is available on both business and leisure rentals in Europe and when travelling from Europe to North America, Australia, Asia and South Africa. Simply quote CDP number 532239 when making your booking. You may be asked to show your membership card upon collection of vehicle. Normal restrictions apply.

ARGENTINA

BARILOCHE - PROVINCE OF RIO NEERO

✈ **Cumbres Patagonia**
Villeas 222
5% and 10% discount on local adventures and car rental

BUENOS AIRES

▦ **Casi Grill & Restaurant**
Avellaneoa 1254, Mar del Plata
☎ 54 223 4510912
At Sport Bar 2 beers for the price of one. At restaurant 10% discount and a free coffee.

▦ **Farmacia Rios**
Avenida Corrientes 3650
☎ 4862-6424
15-20% Off

▦ **Hard Rock Café-Buenos Aires**
Av. Pueyrredon 2501, Piso 2
☎ +54 11 4807 7625
✆ +54 11 4807 7625
15% discount on food & beverages except special offers

▦ **Lansky Bar**
Juncal 2019, ZC 1116
☎ 54 11 5806 9664
25% Off, except during happy hour (Monday - Friday 7-10pm)

▦ **Lave-Rap**
Marcelo T. de Alvear 2018
☎ 4961-6241
10% on valet, ironing & dry-cleaning services: 20% on washing machine

▦ **Marroquineria Rossi**
Avenida Cabildo 4420
☎ 4702-7676
10% Off

▦ **Ofiura**
Reconquista 1046-408
☎ 4311 8473
20% Discount

▦ **Optica Quind - Laboratorio Optico**
Peru 76, Acassuso
☎ 54 11 4742 9917
10% Discount on sunglasses. 30% discount with medical receipt and HI card on all types of glasses and contact lenses.

✈ **Remises Travel Car**
Av Santa Fe 2502, Martinez
☎ Tel: 4798 5266
10% discount. Special price on journey to the International Airport

▦ **Rix Café**
Av Pueyrredon 2501, Local 82
20% off all drinks

▦ **World Sport Café**
Junin 1745
☎ 4807-3800
50% every day from 17.00 to 21.00; 20% from Sunday to Thursday after 21.00hr, (except happy hour menu and promotions).

CHALTEN

▦ **Ranchito' Grocery**
Av San Martin s/n. Santa Cruz
10% Off

CORDOBA

✈ **AI Rent a Car**
Entre Rios 70
☎ 54 351 422 4867
10% on the daily rate and on the week rental only pay for 5 days

ESQUEL

▦ **"Don Pipo Pieea"**
Av Fontana Esquel, Province of Chubut
10% Discount

▦ **"Dos 22" Pizzeria**
Sarmiento y Av Ameghino, Chubut
☎ 54 2945 454995
10% Discount on food and beverages

▦ **Dulzuras Esquel Chocolateria Store**
Sarmiento 580, Chubut
10% Off chocolates, sweets

Ⓖ **Esquel Patagonia Aventura**
Rivadavia 873, Chubut
10% Off

MENDOZA

Ⓖ **Buscando America Tour Operator**
Patricias Mendocinas 1959
☎ 0261 4294131
10% off local excursions

✝ **Turismo Uspallata**
Las Heras 699
☎ 0261 458206
20% Off

EL BOLSON - PROVINCE OF RIO NEGRO

✝ **"Transitando Lo Natural"**
Dorreeo 416
☎ +54 11 2944 49295
✉ transitando@elbolson.com
🖥 www.elbolson.net
10% discount on local activities

PROVINCE OF SANTA CRUZ

✝ **Del Glaciar Hostel**
Los Pioneros 251
☎ +54 11 2902 491243
☎ +54 11 2902 491243
✉ alberguedelglaciar@cotecal.com.ar
🖥 www.glaciar.com
10% discount on the alternative tour to the glacier

TILCARA - PROVINCE OF SALTA

✝ **"Oscar" Archaeological Tours**
Plaza Tilcara
☎ +54 11 388 4955117
10% discount on archaeological tours

TRAVELIN - PROVINCE OF CHUBUT

✝ **"Gales Al Sur" Local Tourism**
Av. Patagonia 186
✉ info@galesalsur.com.ar
10% discount on local activities

VILLA GRAL BELGRANO - PROVINCE OF CORDOBA

✝ **Guillermo Friedrich Excursions**
Av. Julio Roca 224
10% discount on local activities

VILLA PARANACITO

🏢 **Autoservicio LA JUVENIL**
5% Discount

🏢 **Prooveduria TOP MALO**
Ruta Prov No 46km 18200
☎ 03446 495255
5% Discount

AUSTRALIA

National

🎭 **Dendy Cinemas**
🖥 www.dendy.com.au
$10 entry at all Dendy locations in Sydney, Melbourne and Brisbane

✝ **Great Southern Rail**
5% discount on Great Southern rail products in all classes of travel on the Ghan, Indian Pacific and Overland.

🎭 **Entertainment IMAX**
Free popcorn and soft drink.

Ⓖ **YHA Travel Insurance**
5-10% nationwide discount on all Australian and overseas travel insurance policies at all YHA Membership and Travel Centres

Ⓖ **Travelex Money Exchange**
Commission free transactions of foreign currency to all HI members at any Travelex location

Ⓖ **Australian Council of National Trusts**
☎ 1800 246 766
$20 off national membership rates. Membership gives you free entry into hundreds of heritage properties in Australia and 17 other countries around the world - over 700 properties in the UK

Ⓖ **Lonely Planet Guides**
10% off when purchased at YHA Membership and Travel Centres

Ⓖ **The Travel Clinic**
☎ 1300 369 359
10% off travel health care products and a free pocket guide and vaccination certificate (value $6.95) with first consultation

© **Travel Health Service - HSA**
➊ 1300 361 046
10% discount on travel vaccines. Conveniently located in every Australian capital city

© **Travellers Medical & Vaccination Centre (TMVC)**
➊ 1300 658 844
10% discount on TMVC vaccines, products and medical kits. Free copy of Travelling Well, essential travel health handbook valued at $14.95 with travel health consultation. Clinics all over Australia

Paddy Pallin
➊ 1800 805 398
10% discount for cash, 7% for credit card purchases over $50 for all outdoor and travel equipment (does not apply to sales items). Stores all over Australia. Mail order available

Snowgum
10% off normal price of all outdoor and travel equipment

Mountain Designs
➊ 07 3252 8894
💻 www.mountaindesigns.com
10% off all outdoor and travel equipment (already discounted items excluded)

Kathmandu
➊ 1800 333 484
25% off Kathmandu packs, tents and Goosedown sleeping bags, plus 10% off all full-priced stock (outdoor and travel equipment). Stores in Victoria, New South Wales and Queensland. Mail order available

✈ **McCafferty's Coaches**
10% discount on all McCafferty's passes and point-to-point tickets. 15% discount on passes and point-to-point tickets when purchased outside Australia

✈ **AAT King's Tours**
10% discount on one day sightseeing tours

✈ **Oz Experience**
5% discount on selected passes in Australia and New Zealand (Kiwi Experience)

✈ **Countrylink Rail**
10% off New South Wales Discovery Pass

✈ **Hertz Australia**
➊ 13 30 39
Hertz is pleased to offer YHA members up to 35% off standard car hire rates. To access these rates quote Customer Discount Program (CDP) number 317961. Drive safely

✈ **Budget Rent a Car**
➊ 1300 362 848
Special rates with an average discount of 30%. Rent a small manual car for 7 days for $55 per day with unlimited kilometres. Please quote BCD (Budget Customer Discount) number E013609

✈ **Network Rentals**
➊ 1800 2077
Nationwide discount from Network car and truck rentals - corporate rate (approximately 20% off). Contact YHA Membership and Travel Centres or Network offices nationally

✈ **Avis Australia**
➊ 1800 255 533
A minimum of 30% off standard rates, and if applicable, a further 5% off promotional rates (excludes commercial vehicles). Conditions apply. To ensure members receive discounts, quote discount number P081600 when making a reservation

✈ **Delta**
➊ 1300 362 848
15% discount if this ad is mentioned. Quote YHA Delta corporate discount number DC161200

ADELAIDE

✈ **Kangaroo Island Ferry Connections**
➊ 08 8231 5583
5% off all tours

ALICE SPRINGS

✈ **Sahara Outback Tours**
➊ 08 8952 8855
5% discount on all tours

✈ **Ballooning Downunder**
➊ 08 8952 8855
20% discount on all flights

BLUE MOUNTAINS
✝ **Blue Mountains Adventure Co.**
☎ **02 4782 1271**
10% off various abseiling tours

BRISBANE
✝ **Far Horizons Discovery Tours**
☎ **07 3236 1004**
10% off day tours

CAIRNS
✝ **Sunlover Cruises**
☎ **07 4051 1368**
10% off

✝ **Raging Thunder Adventures**
☎ **07 4051 1368**
5% off rafting, ballooning, sea/river kayaking

CANBERRA
🍴 **Dirt Track Adventures**
☎ **02 6231 1377**
25% off

DARWIN, KAKADU & LITCHFIELD
✝ **Crocodylus Park**
☎ **08 8981 2561**
15% off entry

✝ **The Blue Banana**
☎ **08 8981 2560**
10% off all tours

GOLD COAST
🍴 **Kirra Dive**
☎ **07 5536 6622**
2 persons for the price of one

HOBART
✝ **Tasmania Tours and Travel**
☎ **1300 653 633**
10% off day and half-day sightseeing tours

MELBOURNE
🍴 **A B Ocean Divers**
☎ **03 9579 2600**
10% Discount

✝ **Adventurama**
☎ **03 9670 9611**
10% Off rafting packages

✝ **Backpacker Winery Tours**
☎ **03 9670 9611**
Free beer, wine or soft-drink (1p.p)

🍴 **Bungy Vic**
☎ **03 9670 9611**
20% off jump

🏢 **Camera Action Camera House**
☎ **03 9670 6901**
Bring in 2 rolls of film for processing, get a free roll of 200 ASA film (35mm of APS) or 10% off processing

🏢 **Dental Car Rental**
☎ **03 9670 9611**
Special member rate

🍴 **Diamond Valley Mountaineering**
☎ **03 9670 9611**
10% Discount

✝ **Eco Adventure Tours**
☎ **03 9670 9611**
10% off Yarra Valley Tours

🏢 **Melbourne Central Internet Café**
☎ **03 9663 8410**
10% off internet rates

🍴 **Melbourne IMAX Theatre**
☎ **03 9663 5454**
20% Off admission

✝ **Ozzie Bush Tours**
☎ **03 9670 9611**
10% Off

🍴 **Rialto Tower's Observation Deck**
☎ **03 9629 8222**
15% off adult entry

🏢 **Surf Dive 'N' Ski**
☎ **03 9650 1039**
5-10% Discount

🍴 **The Dude Ranch-Kinglake**
☎ **03 9670 9611**
20% Off horse-riding

✝ **Victorian Harley Tours**
   ☎ 03 9489 7524
   Up to 20% off tours

✝ **Way to Go Travel Needs**
   ☎ 03 9591 0991
   Free "Travel Checklist" and free guidebook with every travel pack purchased

PERTH

🛖 **The Stables Yanchep**
   ☎ 08 9561 1606
   20% off selected horse rides

✝ **Oceanic Cruises**
   ☎ 08 9325 1616
   15% discount on Rottnest Island Ferry and Swan River Cruises

✝ **West Australia Travel and Dive**
   ☎ 08 9421 1883
   5% discount

✝ **Top Deck Tours**
   ☎ 08 9227 5122
   5% discount

PORT CAMPBELL

✝ **Port Campbell Boat Charters**
   ☎ 03 5598 6411
   33% off scenic tours

PORT MACQUARIE

✝ **Beach to Bush Eco Tours**
   ☎ 0428 667 913
   6% off Sydney-Byron Bay Eco Tours

QUEENSLAND

✝ **Queensland Rail**
   ☎ 07 3236 1680
   10% off adult economy seat, economy and first class booths

SUNSHINE COAST

🛖 **Underwater World**
   ☎ 07 5444 8488
   20% off admission

SYDNEY

🏛 **Australian Museum**
   ☎ 02 9320 6000
   $4 adult entry (conditions apply)

🛖 **Australian Reptile Park**
   ☎ 02 4340 1102
   25% off entry - conditions apply

✝ **Captain Cook Cruises**
   ☎ 02 9261 1111
   Concession rates on most tours

✝ **Gray Line**
   ☎ 02 9261 1111
   20% off Sydney day tours

🏢 **Planet Hollywood**
   ☎ 02 9267 7827
   10% off food and merchandise

✝ **Premier Motor Service**
   ☎ 02 9261 1111
   20% off bus tickets

🛖 **Sega World Sydney**
   ☎ 02 9273 9273
   20% off, unlimited fun pass

🛖 **The Rocks Walking Tours**
   ☎ 02 9261 1111
   20% discount

TASMANIA

✝ **Tasmanian Redline Tours**
   ☎ 1300 360 000
   20% off main road route services

WAGGA WAGGA

🛖 **Tilly's Camping and Outdoors**
   ☎ 02 6921 7779
   10% Discount on selected items

WHITSUNDAYS

✝ **Southern Cross Sailing Adventures**
   ☎ 07 4946 6312
   $10 off 3 day sailing adventures

AUSTRIA

INNSBRUCK

🏛 **Tiroler Volkskunstmuseum**
Universitätsstraß2 2

📞 0512 58 43 02
📠 0512 58 43 70

Admission at student's discount for ATS 35 instead of 60

SALZBURG

🏛 **Mozart's Geburtshaus**
Getreidegasse 9

📞 0662 84 43 13
📠 0662 84 06 93

Membership card holder gets group discount

✝ **Salzburg VELOactive**
Willibald Hauthaler Straße 10

📞 0662 43 55 95-0
📠 0662 43 55 95-22

10% discount on bike hire

WIEN

🏛 **Beethoven Gedenkstätte**
Probusgasse 6

📞 01 402 12 60
📠 01 408 80 83

Admission ATS 10 instead of 25

🏛 **Schubert Geburtshaus**
Nußdorferstraße 54
ATS 10 instead of 25

✝ **DDSG Blue Danube Schiffahrt GmbH**
Friedrichstraße 7

📞 01 588 80-0
📠 01 588 80-440

10% discount on round trips within Vienna and Wachau

BELGIUM

National

✝ **Eurolines**
10% discount

🏛 **Grote Routepaden**
15% discount on maps and guidebooks for long distance walking and cycling

CANADA

✝ **Greyhound lines of Canada**
📞 403 265 9111 (Calgary) 403 413 8747 (Edmonton)
10% off all regular fares

✝ **Rent-a-Wreck**
📞 1800 327 0116
$25.00 off weekly rental

REGIONAL

Ⓖ **Canadian Rockies Hot Springs**
📞 403 762 1515
15% Discount on single hot pool admission at Banff, Radium and Miette Hot Springs. SUMMERS ONLY.

BANFF

✝ **Avis Rent-a-Car**
📞 403 762 3222
Extra 50 free km on regular daily rates (Rate code G3 and GA)

✝ **Banff Adventures Unlimited**
📞 403 762 4554
20% discount on daily rental rates for mountain bikes ranging from $24-$40

✝ **Hydra River Guides**
📞 403 762 4554
20% discount on white-water rafting day trips includes transportation and gear

CALGARY

Ⓖ **Big Rock Rafting**
📞 403 823 0456
15% off one day white-water rafting on the upper Red Deer River - includes hot lunch. Need a minimum of 8 persons/group. Individuals on 'has room' basis.

Ⓖ **Bow Valley Massage Clinic**
103, 803 -1 Avenue NE
📞 403 264 7151
20% Discount on 30 minute and 1 hour massages

✝ **Cactus Coulee Float Tours**
15% discount on all camp-hike treks, fossil safaris and river float tours of Alberta's Badlands

Calgary Canoe Club
6449 Crowchild Trail SW
☎ 403 246 5757
15% discount on reservoir canoe rentals

Calgary Tower
101-9 Avenue SW
☎ 403 266 7171
Group rate admission for individuals

Fitness on 5th
320-5 Avenue SE
☎ 403 232 1575
$5 day rate for non Calgary area members only, or Corporate rate for annual memberships.

Glenbow Museum
130-9 Avenue SE
☎ 403 268 4100
15% Off regular adult admission for cardholder

Globe Cinema
617-8 Avenue
☎ 403 262 3308
$4.50 admission on all non-discount screenings (Wed-Mon Evenings)

Hammerhead Scenic Tours
☎ 403 260 0940
15% off one-day guided tours to the Drumheffer badlands and Head-Smashed-In-Buffalo Jump

Sports Rent
22 2950 Macleod Trail SE
☎ 403 292 0077
15% Off rentals (excludes motorized products)

CANMORE

Trailmasters Mountain Bike Guides Ltd
☎ 403 678 0384
15% discount on half day and full day bike trips

EDMONTON

Out An' About Tours Travel Adventures
☎ 780 909 8687
15% discount for groups of more than 6 people

JASPER

Alpine Art (Eco-Tours)
☎ 403 852 3709
15% discount on 1/2 day or full day wildlife viewing, snoeshoe or cross country ski shows

Sekani Mountain Tours
☎ 403 852 4337 (winter)
15% discount on raft tours and cross country skiing and snowshoeing trips

KANANASKIS

Mirage adventure Tours Ltd
☎ 403 678 4919
15% off the "Whitewater Thriller" raft trip

MONTRÉAL

Via Route inc
1255 Mackay Street
☎ 514 271 1166
5-10% discount on car rental

NIAGARA FALLS

Explorer Passport
Discount (must be purchased from hostel)

Ride Niagara
Discounts available

Whirlpool Jetboat
$1.00 off with coupon

NORDEGG

Baldy Mountain Trail Rides
☎ 403 721 2030
15% off all rides (minimum 4 riders, Mine Tour excluded)

OTTAWA

Capital Trolley Tours
Elgin at Sparks Street
$1.00 off Ottawa trolley tour

Enterprise Rent-A-Car
☎ 1800 736 8222
Corporate rate. Fli # T20786

PROCTER
✝ **Lodestar Adventures**
PO Box 84, V0G 1V0
☏ **250 299 5354**
10% off llama treks

REGINA
✝ **Saskatchewan Transportation Company**
2014-14th Avenue
One way ticket to any Saskatchewan destination for $24. Tickets to be purchased at HI-Saskatchewan

SALTSPRING ISLAND
✝ **Sea Otter Kayaking**
149 Lower Granges Road, V8K 2T2
☏ **250 537 5678**
15% off rentals, lessons, tours, sunset/full moon paddles, and multiday trips in the Gulf Islands

TORONTO
🍽 **2-4-1 Pizza**
122 Dundas St E
15% off on all purchases

🍽 **Currency Exchange**
N.E. Corner of Dundas/Yonge
Best Rates

🍽 **Hard Rock Café**
279 Yonge St & Sky Dome
Complementary souvenir with a purchase of any meal or merchandise

🍽 **Hungary Eyes Café**
50a King St E
10% Off

🍸 **Nightclub Passes**
Free - Upon availability

🍸 **Voyageur Quest**
Discount

VANCOUVER
🍽 **Abruzzo Cappuccino Bar**
1321 Commercial Drive, V5L 3X5
☏ **604 254 2641**
10% Off

✝ **Aquabus Ferries Ltd**
1617 Foreshore Walk
☏ **604 689 5858**
Hostelling International members receive $.25 off regular one-way fare and/or $1 off the regular price of a mini-cruise

🍽 **European Delicatessen**
1220 Davie Street, V6E 1N3
☏ **604 688 3442**
10% Off all products (EXCLUDING cigarettes).

🍸 **The Lookout**
555 West Hastings Street
☏ **604 689 0421**
50% off regular admission to viewing deck. Not valid with any other offer.

🍸 **The Side Door Cabaret Ltd**
2291 West Broadway V6K 2E4
☏ **604 733 2821**
Special Hostelling International night weekly on Mondays. (Evening includes prizes, a complimentary beverage, and International Trivia Quiz contest).

WHISTLER
✝ **Whistler River Adventures**
Box 202
☏ **604 932 3532**
10% off all rafting and jet boat trips

CZECH REPUBLIC
PRAGUE
🏛 **Národni Museum/National Museum & Branch offices**
35% discount for members under 26 years especially groups booked via KMC

CHILE
SANTIAGO
✝ **Ansa Rent A Car**
Av. Eliodoro Yañez 1198
☏ **+56-2 251 0256**
🖷 **+56-2 2510425**
15% discount on car rental

✝ **Cascada Expediciones**
Orrego Luco 054 20 Piso
- ☎ +56-2 2327214
- ✆ +56-2 2339768
- ✉ info@cascada-expediciones.com
- 🖥 www.cascada-expediciones.com
10% discount on all services

COSTA RICA
SAN JOSÉ
Ⓖ **Academia Latinoamericana de Español**
Ave. 8 Calles 31-33, #3113
- ☎ +506 2249917
- ✆ +506 2258125
- ✉ espalesa@sol.racsa.co.cr
15% discount on all Spanish courses

DENMARK
AALBORG
✝ **Eurolines**
J.F Kennedys plads 1, 9000 Aalborg
- ☎ +45 9934 4488
10% discount on all tickets

🏰 **Nordjyllands Kuntsmuseum**
Kong Christians Allé 50, 9000 Aalborg
- ☎ +45 9813 8088
50% discount

ESBJERG
🏰 **Esbjerg Museum**
Torvegade 45, 6700 Esbjerg
- ☎ +45 7512 7811
20% discount

FREDERIKSVÆRK
🏰 **Frederiksværk Bymuseum**
Torvet 18-20, 3300 Frederiksværk
- ☎ +45 4772 0605
50% discount

HERNING
🏰 **Danmarks Fotomuseum**
Museumsgade 28, 7400 Herning
- ☎ +45 9722 5322
Two for the price of one

KOPENHAVN K
🏰 **Guiness World of Records museum**
Ostergade 16, 1100 Kobenhavn K
- ☎ +45 3332 3183
DKK5.00 discount

ODENSE
🏰 **Jernbanemuseet**
Dannebrogsgade 24, 5000 Odense
- ☎ +45 6612 3265
25% discount

ENGLAND & WALES
ASHBOURNE
🏭 **Carsington Sports and Leisure Ltd**
Carsington Water, Ashbourne, Derbyshire DE6 1ST
- ☎ +44 1629 540478
- ✆ +44 1629 540666
- ✉ carsington@ryh-online.net
10% off watersports and cycle hire including tuition

BATH
🏰 **The Jane Austen Centre**
40 Gay Street, Bath, BA1 2NT
- ☎ +44 1225 443000
- ✆ +44 1225 443000
- ✉ info@janeausten.co.uk
- 🖥 www.janeausten.co.uk
20% discount

BRIGHTON
🏰 **Newhaven Fort**
Fort Road, Newhaven, East Sussex BN9 9DL
- ☎ +44 1273 517622
- ✆ +44 1273 512059
- ✉ enquiries@newhavenfort.org.uk
- 🖥 www.newhavenfort.org.uk
2 for the price of 1

BRISTOL
🏟 **John Nike Leisure Sport- Bristol Ice Rink**
Frogmore Street, Bristol, BS1 5NA
- ☎ +44 117 9292148
- ✆ +44 117 9259736
- 🖥 www.nikegroup.co.uk
£3.30 admission including skate hire

CAMBRIDGE

Geoff's Bike Hire

65 Devonshire Road, Cambridge, Cambridgeshire

☏ +44 1223 365629

10% off cycle hire and guided cycle tours

CANTERBURY

Dickens House Museum

Victoria Parade, Broadstairs, Kent CT10 1QS

☏ +44 1843 862853

30% discount

CAPEL - Y -FFIN

Black Mountain Holidays

Castle Farm, Capel-y-Ffin, Abergavenny, Wales

☏ +44 1873 890961

☏ +44 1497 821058

e bmholidays@cma-int.demon.co.uk

☖ www.hay-on-wye.co.uk/bmholidays

15% discount

CARDIFF

Rhondda Heritage Park

Lewis Merthyr Colliery, Coed Cae Road, Trehafod, Rhondda Cynon Taff, CF37 7NP

☏ +44 1443 682036

☏ +44 1443 687420

e rhonpark@netwales.co.uk

☖ www.netwales.co.uk/rhondda-heritage

20% off admissions (not special event days)

Techniquest

Stuart Street, Cardiff CF10 5BW

☏ +44 29 2047 5475

☏ +44 29 2048 2517

e gen@techniquest.org

☖ www.techniquest.org

10% discount on adult, child and family admission

CHESTER

Chester Gateway Theatre

Hamilton Place, Chester, Cheshire CH1 2BH

☏ +44 1244 344238

☏ +44 1244 341296

☖ www.gateway-theatre.org

£2 off all seat prices

Sygun Copper Mine

Beddgelert, Caernarfon, Gwynedd LL55 4NE

☏ +44 1766 510100

☏ +44 1766 510100

e sygunmine@cs.com

☖ http://ourworld.compuserve.com/homepages/snowdoniamine

10% discount

EXETER

BikeTrail Cycle Hire

Unit 6, Estuary Business Park, Yelland, Barnstaple EX31 3EZ

☏ +44 1271 861424

e info@biketrail.co.uk

☖ www.biketrail.co.uk

10% discount on cycle hire

LAKE DISTRICT

Windermere Steamboat Museum

Rayrigg Road, Windermere, Cumbria LA23 1BN

☏ +44 15394 45565

☏ +44 15394 48769

☖ www.steamboat.co.uk

2 for the price of 1

The Climbers Shop

Compston Corner, Ambleside, Cumbria LA22 9DS

☏ +44 15394 32297

☏ +44 15394 34165

e info@climbersshop.demon.co.uk

10% off full price items except publications and electricals

Windermere Lake Cruises

Waterhead Pier, Ambleside, Cumbria LA22 0EY

☏ +44 15395 31188

☏ 15395 31947

e w.lakes@virgin.net

10% off sailings between Ambleside Bowness, Lakeside & Brockhole

LIVERPOOL

The Boat Museum

South Pier Head, Ellesmere Port, CH65 4FW

☏ +44 151 955 5017

☏ +44 151 355 4079

20% discount

Blue Planet
Cheshire Oaks, Ellesmere Port, Cheshire CH65 9LF
☎ +44 151 357 8800
🖷 +44 151 356 7288
✉ info@blueplanetaquarium.co.uk
🖳 www.blueplanetaquarium.co.uk
10% discount

LONDON

Florence Nightingale Museum
2 Lambeth Palace Road, London SE1 7EW
☎ +44 20 7620 0374
🖷 +44 20 7928 1760
🖳 www.florence-nightingale.co.uk
£1 off all admission prices for individuals

BBC Experience
Rm 319 Egton House, 8 Langham Street, London
W1A 1AA
☎ +44 20 77651109
🖷 +44 20 7765 0540
🖳 www.bbc.co.uk/experience
£1 off admission price for adults; 50p off admission
price for children

MANCHESTER

Museum of Science and Industry
Liverpool Road, Castlefield, Manchester M3 4FP
☎ +44 161 832 2244
🖷 +44 161 833 1471
🖳 www.msim.org.uk
Group rate for individuals

NEWCASTLE

Outdoor World
49 Ilfracombe Gardens, Whitley Bay, Tyne and Wear
NE26 3LZ
☎ +44 191 2514388
🖷 +44 191 2514388
10% discount

OXFORD

Oxford Campus Stores
various addresses in Oxford
☎ +44 1865 727517
🖷 +44 1865 248160
10% discount on all purchases

Upton House
Near Banbury, Oxfordshire
☎ +44 1295 670266
🖷 1295 670266
🖳 www.ntrustsevern.org.uk
2 non members of National Trust get in for the price
of 1

**Wycombe Summit Ski and Snowboard
Centre**
Abbey Barn Lane, High Wycombe, Buckinghamshire
HP10 9QQ
☎ +44 1494 474711
🖷 1494 443757
✉ wycombesummit@skico.uk
🖳 www.ski.co.uk/wycombesummit
20% discount on open practice and group lessons

PEAK DISTRICT

The Bass Museum
Box 220, Horninnglow Street, Burton upon Trent,
Staffordshire
☎ +44 1283 511000
🖷 +44 1283 516316
🖳 www.bass-museum.com
2 for the price of 1

Peak Rail PLC
Matlock Station, Matlock, Derbyshire DE4 3NA
☎ +44 1629 580381
🖷 +44 1629 760645
10% discount on adult and childrens tickets

PENZANCE

Harry Safari
Tamarisk, Fore Street, Penzance TR20 9LL
☎ +44 1736 711427
🖷 +44 1736 711427
✉ harrysafari@compuserve.com
£2.50 discount on normal prices

ROCHESTER

Royal Engineers Museum
Prince Arthur Road, Gillingham, Kent ME4 4UG
☎ +44 1634 406397
🖷 1634 822371
✉ remuseum.rhqre@gtnet.gov.uk
🖳 www.army.mod.uk/museums
£1 off adults; 50p off children

World Naval Base - The Historic Dockyard
Chatham, Kent ME4 4TZ
- +44 1634 823800
- 1634 823801
- info@worldnavalbase.org.uk

£1 off entry

STRATFORD UPON AVON
National Waterways Museum
Llanthony Warehouse, Gloucester Docks, Gloucester GL1 2BH
- +44 1452 318054
- +44 1452 318066
- infor@nwm.deom.co.uk
- www.nwm.org.uk

20% discount for adults on museum entry

Winchcombe Railway Museum & Gardens
23 Gloucester Street, Winchcombe, Gloucestershire Gl54 5LX
- +44 1242 602257

20% off admissions

TREFDRAETH (NEWPORT)
Cenarth Paintball Games
Swiss Cottage, Pentrecagal, Newcastle Emlyn, Carmathenshire SA38 9HT
- +44 1559 371621
- fun@cenarthpaintball.fsnet.co.uk
- www.cenarthpaintball.fsnet.co.uk

10% off game fee for each player

TREYARNON BAY
Harlyn Surf School
16 Boyd Avenue, Padstow, Cornwall PL28 8ER
- +44 1841 533076
- +44 1841 533076
- www.harlynsurf.co.uk

10% discount on all surfing courses and beach hire

YORK
Royal Armouries Museum
Armouries Drive, Leeds, Yorkshire LS10 1LT
- +44 113 2201895
- +44 113 2201955
- enquiries@armouries.org.uk
- www.armouries.org.uk

2 for the price of 1

National Railway Museum
Leeman Road, York, Yorkshire YO26 4XJ
- +44 1904 621261
- +44 1904 611112
- nrm@nmsi.ac.uk
- www.nrm.org.uk

£1 off full adult price; children 16 and under and over 60's free

ESTONIA
TALLINN
Balti Puhkemajad
Tatari 39-310
- 372 6461 457
- 372 6461 595
- puhkemajad@online.ee
- www.bmp.jg.ee

5% discount on travel services. 5-10% discount on airfare tickets

Inges Kindlustus
- 372 6410 436
- www.inges.ee

5% discount on travel insurance

FINLAND
National
Cruises to the Coast
- 400 840 591

10-20% discount on normal rates on most cruises off the coast and on most lake routes and cruises. Season in summertime. Tickets usually on board

Transvell Car Rental
- 9 350 5590 (Helsinki)

15% discount on car hire

FRANCE

✚ **Eurolines**
3% discount

BOURGES

🏰 **Bourge's museums**
All museums in Bourges - Free entrance

MONTPELLIER

💿 **Le Comptoir du disque (CD, Music)**
20% discount

PARIS

✚ **Tour Montparnasse**
5% discount

✚ **Vedettes de Pont Neuf (Cruises on La Seine)**
5% discount

VERDUN

🏰 **World Peace Center (museum)**
30% discount

INDIA

NEW DELHI

✚ **Travel Corporation (India) Ltd**
C-35, Connaught Place, New Delhi 110 001
🕿 91 11 3319992
📠 91 11 3328363
🖳 www.tcindia.com
10% discount on Eurail, Eurostar and Greyhound and 5% discount on Amtrak (American Railway system)

🍴 **Lazeez Affaire**
Malcha Marg Shopping Centre, Chanakyapuri, New Delhi 110 021
🕿 6114380
10% discount on food

IRELAND, NORTHERN

BELFAST

✚ **Carriageway Cars**
92 Bloomfield Road
10% discount on car hire

✚ **TIC Walking Tours**
N.I.T.B, St Annes Court, 59 North Street
£1.00 off

IRELAND, REP OF

IRELAND, REP OF

There are discounts available on Transport, Tours, Tourism and Cultural activities for Hostelling International members on production of a current membership card. For details check the National or IYHF web pages under discounts or enquire to the National Office.

ISRAEL

EILAT

🍴 **Eilat Youth Hostel**
Ha'atava St.
🕿 972 7 6370088
📠 972 7 6375835
✉ eilat@iyha.org.il
🖳 www.youth-hostels.org.il
Sea Jeeps. 10% discount. Tickets available for Youth Hostel guests

EIN GEDI

🍴 **Ein Gedi Youth Hostel**
🕿 972 7 6584165
📠 972 7 6584445
Ein Gedi Spa - 10% discount. Purchase tickets at the Youth Hostel

🍴 **Ein Gedi Youth Hostel**
🕿 972 7 6584165
📠 972 7 6584445
Mineral Beach - 10% discount. Purchase tickets at the Youth Hostel

JERUSALEM

🍴 **Yitzhak Rabin Youth Hostel**
1 Nahman Avigad St.
🕿 972 2 6780101
📠 972 2 6796566
✉ rabin@iyha.org.il
🖳 www.youth-hostels.org.il
Givat Ram Swimming Pool. 10% discount. Purchase tickets at Youth Hostel

ITALY

National

✝ **Italian Railways**
 ☏ +39 06 4871152
 🖥 www.hostels-aig.org
 HI Members aged under 26 can obtain a 50% discount on the Carta Verde (Green Card) which entitles them to 20% discount on 2nd class, and 30% discount on 1st class travel.

✝ **Sixt Agency (Rent a Car)**
 ☏ 800 900686 (toll free)
 Special rates for HI members. Contact the AIG National Office for the code to access the concession

ⓖ **Didattica e Metodo**
 ☏ +39 06 5781141
 Special price for the Italian Language course on CD "The Italian Treasure".

🏢 **Mondadori and Mel Bookstores**
 10% off all books

✝ **Bike and Moto rental**
 🖥 www.hostels-aig.org
 Various discounts on bike and moto rental in Rome and other towns in Italy.

🎭 **Italian Theatres**
 🖥 www.hostels-aig.org
 Discounted entrance tickets in several Italian Theatres. See www.hostels-aig.org for full list

🏢 **Calderini and Edagricole Bookshops**
 20% off all books

🏢 **Modi e Moda Visa Gina Lebole Department stores**
 🖥 www.hostels-aig.org
 Free admission to stores that are not normally open to the public. See www.hostels-aig.org for full list of the stores

🏢 **Cisalfa Sportswear Network**
 Various discounts on purchasing

🎭 **Amusement Parks**
 🖥 www.hostels-aig.org
 Discounted entrance tickets to the best amusement parks in Italy such as Genoa Aquarium, Safari park, Fantasy World and much more

MILAN, ROME & TURIN

ⓖ **Vacupan Dental Care**
 ☏ 800 861104
 Special rates for Dental Care

ROME

🏢 **Planet Hollywood**
 Via Del Tritone 118
 ☏ +39 06 42818909
 🖥 www.hostels-aig.org
 Various discounts. See www.hostels-aig.org for further details

🎭 **Rome Biopark**
 P.L.E. del Giardino Zoologie 1
 ☏ +39 06 3608211
 20% discount on the entrance fee

JAPAN

National

✝ **Japan Rent-a-Car**
 ☏ 03 3580-3410 (head office)
 20% discount off the basic rate (except for "joyful JSS, JS" class car)

✝ **Nissan Rent-a-Car**
 ☏ 03 5424-4123 (Tokyo)
 5% discount off the basic rate (except for at Station Rent-a-Car & Service cars)

🏢 **Sanyo-do**
 ☏ 03 3580-3410 (head office)
 Suitcases 20% off, Backpacks 15% off, Small travel goods 5% off

🏢 **Sogo department stores**
 ☏ 03 3284-6711 (Tokyo - Yurakuo-cho)
 5% discount for over ¥1,000 purchase. "Shopping ticket" should be purchased in advance at GAISHO-salon. (As for Osaka & Kobe Sogo, they are available at YH information center)

FUKUSHIMA, NIHONMATSU

🏢 **Tohoku Safari Park**
 ☏ 0243 24 2336
 10% discount off the entrance fee

HOKKAIDO, BIEI-CHO

Ⓖ **Bibaushi guide no Yamagoya**
☎ 0166 95 2277
10-50% discount off outdoor experience, 10% discount off bicycle rental

NAGASAKI

✛ **Mazda Rent-a-Car**
☎ 095 828 2231
30-50% dependent on car type

✛ **Mazda rent-a-car**
☎ 095-828-2231
30-50% discount dependent on car type

NARA

▦ **Nara Bank (headquarters & all 23 branches)**
☎ 0120 39 3800 (Nara headquarters - free dial)
50% discount off travellers check issue commission

TOKYO, ASAKUSA

♒ **Asakusa Hana-yashiki amusement park**
☎ 03 3842 8780
30% discount off amusement ticket (¥1,000)

TOKYO, HINO

♒ **Tama Tech amusement park**
☎ 0425-91-0820
entrance fee (+all-you-can-take ticket) ¥3,900 - ¥3,400 (adult), ¥3,100 - ¥2,800 (children)

SOUTH KOREA

SEOUL

♒ **Lotte World**
40-1, Zamsil-dong, Songpa-ku
☎ +82 2 411 2000
🖷 +82 2 419 1767
💻 www.lotteworld.com
20% off entrance ticket. Free ticket, BIG 5 ticket (Possible for HI member to buy 5 tickets at one time)

YONGIN-SI

♒ **Samsung Everland**
310, Jeondae-ri, Pokok-myun, Yongin-shi, Kyonggi-do
☎ +82 31 320 9747
🖷 +82 31 320 9727
💻 www.everland.co.kr
15-30% off entrance ticket. (possible for HI member to buy 5 tickets at one time)

LUXEMBOURG

BEAUFORT

🏰 **Castle Beaufort "Amis de l'Ancien Château"**
L-6313 Beaufort
☎ +352 83 60 02
Normal price: LUF80-, Reduced price LUF30.50-

LAROCHETTE

🏰 **Castle Larochette "Amis de la Ville Larochette"**
33 Chemin J.A. Zinnen, L-7626 Larochette
☎ +352 83 74 97
Normal price: LUF60-, Reduced price LUF40-

LUXEMBOURG

🏰 **Bock Casemates "City Tourist Office"**
BP 181, L-2011 Luxembourg
☎ +352 22 67 52
🖷 +352 47 48 18
Normal price LUF70-, Reduced price LUF40-

♒ **Casino Luxembourg**
41 Rue Notre-Dame, L-2013 Luxembourg
☎ +352 22 50 45
🖷 +352 22 95 95
Normal price LUF150-, Reduced price LUF100-

🏰 **Castle Vianden "Amis du Château"**
Montée du Château, L-9408 Vianden
☎ +352 84 9291
🖷 +352 849284
Normal price LUF 180-, Reduced price LUF130-

KOCKELSCHEUER

🍴 **CK Sport Center Kockelscheuer**
20, route de Bettembourg, L-1899 Kockelscheuer
☎ **+352 47 22 85**
20% discount

MACEDONIA

SKOPJE

🍴 **Olimpiski Bazen**
bul. Koco Racin bb
☎ **+389 91 114 143**
30% discount

🏰 **Muzej na Makedonija**
Kurliska bb
☎ **+389 91 221 973**
60% discount

THE NETHERLANDS

National

✈ **Budget Rent a Car**
☎ **0800 0537 (toll free in The Netherlands)**
🖥 **www.budget.nl**
10% discount on car rental. Ask for Budget traveller (1 or 2 days) or Budget World Travel Plan (from 3 days)

Eurolines
☎ **See below**
10% discount by showing your membership card at the following Eurolines offices: Amsterdam Rokin: +31 20 560 87 88, Amsterdam Julianaplein 5: +31 20 560 87 88, Rotterdam Conradstraat 20: +31 10 412 44 44

Ⓖ **GWK**
🖥 **www.gwk.nl**
25% discount on transaction costs for cash currency exchange at any of the 65 GWK outlets, situated at main railway stations and border crossings

NEW ZEALAND

✈ **Air New Zealand**
☎ **0800 737 000**
50% off full economy fare when flying standby on domestic flights. Available only to international visitors to New Zealand. Conditions apply

✈ **All NZ Rental Cars (Scotties)**
Nationwide
☎ **0800 RENTAL 09 630 2625**
Free upgrades to YHA members, nationwide guarantee, cars and campers

Ⓖ **YHA Travel**
Nationwide
☎ **09 379 4224**
5% - 30% off. Specialists for all your travel needs. Ask for details about the wide range of discounts on your domestic or international travel plans.

📖 **Wildwood Books**
RD 9 Masterton
☎ **06 378 7458**
10% Off retail prices, specialists in natural history, track guides, etc. Free catalogue available.

🍴 **Federated Mountain Clubs of NZ (Inc)**
PO Box 1604, Wellington
☎ **04 233 8244**
33% off first year membership.

✈ **Ansett NZ**
☎ **0800 267 388**
50% off full domestic economy fare when flying standby. Available to international visitors. Conditions apply

✈ **Trans Scenic Unique Train Journeys**
☎ **0800 802 802**
30% off standard adult fares. Cannot be used in conjunction with any other offer

✈ **Mt Cook Landline**
30% off standard adult fares exceeding NZ$20 one way. Cannot be used in conjunction with any other offer

✈ **Intercity Coachlines**
☎ **09 913 6100 (Auckland)**
20% off standard adult fares. Cannot be used in conjunction with any other offer

✝ **Kiwi Experience**
  ☎ 09 366 9830
  5% off NZ adventure transport network. Cannot be used in conjunction with any other offer

✝ **Magic Travellers Network**
  ☎ 09 358 5600
  ℮ info@magicbus.co.nz
  5% off NZ's transport network for the independent traveller. Cannot be used in conjunction with any other offer

✝ **Newmans Coachlines**
  ☎ 09 913 6200 (Auckland)
  20% off standard adult fares exceeding NZ$20 one way. Cannot be used in conjunction with any other offer

✝ **Shoestring Rentals**
  ☎ 03 385 3647
  10% off car hire. Conditions apply

✝ **Pegasus Rental Cars**
  ☎ 0800 803 580
  Free day when booking a vehicle for 10 days or more. Cannot be used in conjunction with any other offer

🎦 **Hoyts Cinemas**
  Student rates for HI members. Cannot be used in conjunction with any other offer

AUCKLAND

✝ **Airbus**
  ☎ 09 303 0309
  Special fares. Airport to Auckland City and Auckland International YHA and return.

🎦 **Auckland Canoe Centre**
  Special rates for kayak sales and hire, guided tours, instruction. Whitewater, seakayaking, multisport.

Ⓖ **Auckland Metro Doctors Travel Care**
  ☎ 09 373 4621
  10% Off consultation fees.

🏬 **Bivouac Outdoor**
  109 Queen Street or 326 Broadway, Newmarket
  ☎ 09 366 1966
  Various Discounts

✝ **Bush and Beach**
  ☎ 0800 4230224
  10% Off. Explore the remote wilderness areas of Auckland. See the true New Zealand, waterfalls, beaches, rainforest and much more. Half and full day trips.

🎦 **Fergs Kayaks**
  ☎ 09 529 2230
  10% discount on all services on presentation of the YHA card

🎦 **IMAX Auckland**
  Village Force Entertainment Centre, Level 4, Queen Street
  ☎ 64 9 303 3345
  $10.95 adult entry all sessions (normal admission $14.95)

🏬 **Scout Shop**
  Motu Moana Scout Camp, Connaught St. Blockhouse Bay
  ☎ 09 827 9180
  10% Off all outdoor gear

🎦 **Sky Tower**
  ☎ 09 912 6000
  $5 off entry to main observation deck. Cannot be used in conjunction with any other offer

🎦 **Volcanoes Geo Tours**
  ☎ 09 525 3991
  10% off discovery one (normally $59pp) 2 people minimum.

CHRISTCHURCH

✝ **Akaroa Harbour "Nature" Cruises**
  ☎ 03 304 7641
  10% Off all scenic cruises

🏬 **Bivouac Outdoor**
  76 Cashel Mall (by the bridge)
  ☎ 03 366 3197
  Various Discounts.

🏬 **Boulevard Bakehouse Café**
  Arts Centre, Worcester Boulevard
  Free 15 minutes voucher for e-mail to use upstairs at the e-caf, when you buy a Supreme Coffee. Open 8am to midnight 7 days.

Kiwi Bone Carving Studio
☎ 03 377 8942
$5 Off any product or any service. Come in and carve your own bone carving.

Mainland Great Outdoors Centre
54 Lichfield Street
☎ 03 365 2178
Various discounts.

Michael Shand Dentist
☎ 03 366 1614
10% Off. Prompt emergency care. All forms of treatment available including hygienist care and after hours.

New Regent Medical Centre
161 - 167 Gloucester Street
☎ 03 366 3581
10% Off consultation fees for travellers. Excellent medical and accident care, and travel medicine. No appointment necessary.

Pro-Fitness
Level 2, Harvey Norman Centre, Moorhouse Ave
☎ 03 366 2221
Special offer. Casual visits $10 to all YHA Members.

MILFORD

Milford Wanderer Daytime Cruises
☎ 0800 656 501 (freephone)
10% off. Enjoy Milford Sound in a more leisurely casual way. Friendly crew includes specialist nature guide. Cruises depart 10:45am and 1:30pm daily (Oct-April).

NELSON

Tandem Skydiving Nelson Ltd
☎ 0800 422 899 (freephone)
$10 off. Share the adventure of a skydive from 9000ft or 12000ft over sunny Nelson with our owner operator professional Tandem Masters

NORTH ISLAND

Northliner Express Coachlines
Auckland, Whangarei, Bay of Islands
☎ Auckland 09 307 5873
30% off travel in Northland or enquire about our Backpacker Passes for YHA members. Luxury video-equipped, air conditioned coaches. Whangarei tel: 09438 3206 Bay of Islands tel: 09 402 7857

QUEENSTOWN

Shotover Jet
☎ 03 442 8570
10% off this exciting jet boat ride. Cannot be used in conjunction with any other offer

NORWAY

National

Hertz Car rental
☎ +47 671680 00
Call for special rates. Remember to give the agreement number CDP 85 83 59. You must be aged 25 or more to qualify

BERGEN

Bergen
Floeybanen - (The Funicular Railway). 10% discount when you buy a ticket at the Montana hostel or the YMCA Hostel

Bergen
Fjord sightseeing on MS Bruvik: 20% discount, 8-9 hours fjord sightseeing around Osterøy Island between 1st July and 31st August

DOMBÅS

Dovrefjell Aktivitetssenter
15% on canoeing, rafting, musk ox tours, elk safaris, mountain-climbing etc

EVJE

Troll Mountain AS
10% discount on rafting and safaris

LAKSELV

☗ **Lakselv Youth Hostel**
P.B. 74, N-9700 Lakselv
☎ +47 78 46 14 76
🖷 +47 78 46 19 96
Free hire of canoe, boat and fishing rod. Free use of sauna and Sami barbeque hut

LILLEHAMMER

☗ **Lillehammer Youth Hostel**
Jernbanetorget 2, N-2609 Lillehammer
☎ +47 61 24 87 00
🖷 +47 61 26 25 66
✉ lillehammer.vandrerhjem@c2i.net
Free rental of cross country skis for guests of the hostel

MO I RANA

☖ **Mo Youth Hostel Fageråsen**
Postboks 1227, N-8602, Mo
☎ +47 75 15 09 63
🖷 +47 90 16 21 35
✉ mo.vandrerhjem@c2i.net
Arctic Circle Centre - 15% discount

MJOELFJELL

☗ **Mjoelfjell Youth Hostel**
Mjoelfjell, N-5700, Voss
☎ +47 56 52 31 50
🖷 +47 56 52 31 51
✉ muhas@online.no
🖳 www.bgif.no/netcon/mjfjell
Heated outdoor swimming pool from 23 June to Mid September

OSLO

☺ **Oslo Youth Hostel Haraldsheim**
Haraldsheimveien 4, P.B. 41 Grefsen, N-0409 Oslo
☎ +47 22 22 29 65
🖷 +47 22 22 10 25
✉ booking@haraldsheim.oslo.no
🖳 www.haraldsheim.oslo.no
Oslo Promotion card. Oslo card can be purchased here. The card gives you discounts and benefits all over Oslo city

SJOA

☗ **Heidal Rafting AS**
10% discount on rafting, glaciering, canyoning etc.

STAMSUND

☗ **Stamsund Youth Hostel**
Justad Rorbuer Og Vandrerhjem, P.B. 110, N-8378 Stamsund
☎ +47 76 08 93 34
🖷 +47 76 08 97 39
Free loan of boat and fishing tackle (deposit required)

STRYN

☗ **Stryn Sommerski (summer skiing centre)**
10-15% discount on ski pass for downhill, snowboarding and cross country skiing

SCOTLAND

National

✚ **Arnold Clarke Car Rental**
10% off basic tariffs (except economy class)

☺ **National Trust for Scotland**
30% off site entrance fees

✚ **Stena Sealink Services**
10% off (except Friday and Saturday sailings during July and August). Tickets only available from port sailing office

☺ **Wildfowl Trust**
Reduction on entry fees

AYR

☖ **Burns Cottage**
Two for the price of one. One free child admission per paying adult

INVERNESS

☗ **Inverness Traction**
☎ +44 1463 239292
Student rate for members. Loch Ness Tours, Inverness-Durness and Inverness-Gairloch

SOUTH AFRICA
National
✈ **Intercape Mainliner Buses/Coaches**
 ✉ info@intercape.co.za
 🖥 www.intercape.co.za
 15% discount to all HI card holders on all Southern African Routes. Discount available when booked at any location nationally

CAPE TOWN
🍴 **Two Oceans Aquarium**
 🖥 www.aquarium.co.za
 All HI card holders receive student rates on admission and adventure diving

DURBAN, KWAZULU-NATAL
🍴 **Gibela Safaris**
 ✉ gibela@gibela.co.za
 🖥 www.gibela.co.za
 10% discount on all products when booked directly with Gibela

PRETORIA
✈ **Packer Tours**
 ✉ ptaback@hotmail.com
 10% discount when booking any of 7 day tours. These bookings can be nationally. The choice of tours: Pretoria City Tour, Soweto Tour, Suncity Tour, Pilansberg Tour, Ndebele Village Tour, Cullinan Diamond mine Tour, De Wildt Cheetah Centre Tour

SWITZERLAND
BASEL
✈ **Youth Hostel Basel**
 St. Alban—Kirchrain 10, CH-4052 Basel
 ☎ +41 61 272 05 72
 📠 +41 61 272 08 33
 ✉ basel@youthhostel.ch
 🖥 www.youthhostel.ch/basel
 Checked in guests receive a "Mobility Ticket" for free transportation in Basel

BÖNIGEN
🍴 **Youth Hostel Bönigen-Interlaken**
 Aareweg 21, Am See, 3806 Bönigen
 ☎ +41 33 822 43 53
 📠 +41 33 823 20 58
 ✉ boenigen@youthhostel.ch
 🖥 www.youthhostel.ch/boenigen
 50% discount on cow craving

THAILAND
BANGKOK
🏨 **Bangkok International Youth Hostel**
 25/2 Phitsanulok Road, Thaywej Market, Dusit, Bangkok 10300
 ☎ 2 2810361
 Free guided tours by local university students for checked in guests. A look into the Thai lifestyle and cultural sights of Bangkok

UNITED STATES OF AMERICA
National
✈ **Alamo Rental Cars**
 5-15% off the daily rate for rental cars from all U.S. domestic locations

✈ **Hertz Car Rental**
 5-15% off the daily rate for rental cars from all U.S. domestic locations

For a more complete listing of local discounts in U.S.A., visit our website at www.hiayh.org

HOSTELLING
INTERNATIONAL

Make your credit card bookings at these centres
Réservez par cartes de crédit aux centres suivants
Reservieren Sie per Kreditkarte bei diesen Zentren
Reserve con tarjeta de crédito en los siguientes centros

English

Australia	☎ (2) 9261 1111
Canada	☎ (800) 663 5777
England & Wales	☎ (1629) 581 418
France	☎ (1) 44 89 87 27
Northern Ireland	☎ (28) 9032 4733
Republic of Ireland	☎ (1) 830 1766
New Zealand	☎ (3) 379 9808
Scotland	☎ (8701) 553 255
Switzerland	☎ (1) 360 1414
USA	☎ (202) 783 6161

Français

Angleterre & Pays de Galles	☎ (1692) 581 418
Australie	☎ (2) 9261 1111
Canada	☎ (800) 663 5777
Écosse	☎ (8701) 553 255
États-Unis	☎ (202) 783 6161
France	☎ (1) 44 89 87 27
Irlande du Nord	☎ (28) 9032 4733
Nouvelle-Zélande	☎ (3) 379 9808
République d'Irlande	☎ (1) 830 1766
Suisse	☎ (1) 360 1414

Deutsch

Australien	☎ (2) 9261 1111
England & Wales	☎ (1629) 581 418
Frankreich	☎ (1) 44 89 87 27
Irland	☎ (1) 830 1766
Kanada	☎ (800) 663 5777
Neuseeland	☎ (3) 379 9808
Nordirland	☎ (28) 9032 4733
Schottland	☎ (8701) 553 255
Schweiz	☎ (1) 360 1414
USA	☎ (202) 783 6161

Español

Australia	☎ (2) 9261 1111
Canadá	☎ (800) 663 5777
Escocia	☎ (8701) 553 255
Estados Unidos	☎ (202) 783 6161
Francia	☎ (1) 44 89 87 27
Inglaterra y Gales	☎ (1629) 581 418
Irlanda del Norte	☎ (28) 9032 4733
Nueva Zelanda	☎ (3) 379 9808
República de Irlanda	☎ (1) 830 1766
Suiza	☎ (1) 360 1414

IBN INTERNATIONAL BOOKING NETWORK